The
Organic
Directory
2006

The Organic Directory 2006

Edited by Clive Litchfield

Foreword by Sophie Grigson

PUBLISHED BY GREEN BOOKS
WITH THE SOIL ASSOCIATION

Acknowledgements

Ever since I started work on the first edition of this Directory in 1991, I have had enormous amounts of help and encouragement from a variety of people and organisations: thanks especially to my wife Annie, our daughters Sophie, Lydia and Ella, Mark Redman, Paul Adams, Tom de Pass, Martin Trowell, Sam Platt, everyone at the Soil Association, Basil Caplan, Alan and Jackie Gear, Robert Sculthorpe, James Anderson at the BDAA, Dr. Mae-Wan Ho, G.P. Lawson for Mac and website help, Jan Hurst for introducing me to organics twenty-odd years ago, and John Elford at Green Books for taking on this project.

This edition published in October 2005
by Green Books Ltd, Foxhole, Dartington, Totnes, Devon TQ9 6EB
sales@greenbooks.co.uk www.greenbooks.co.uk
www.theorganicdirectory.co.uk

with the Soil Association
Bristol House, 40–56 Victoria Street, Bristol BS1 6BY
info@soilassociation.org www.soilassociation.org

Copyright © Clive Litchfield 2005
Design by Julie Martin
Cover by Rick Lawrence
Typeset at Green Books

Printed and bound by MPG Books, Bodmin, Cornwall, UK. Text printed on Corona Natural 100% recycled paper; colour plates on Evolution Satin 75% recycled paper, and cover on GreenCoat Velvet 80% recycled board.

First edition published October 1992; Second edition October 1996
Third edition October 1998; Fourth edition May 2000
Fifth edition June 2002; Sixth edition June 2004

A CIP record for this book is available from the British Library.

ISBN 1 903998 64 6 (10–copy counterpack for retailers: ISBN 1 903998 71 9)

Contents

ENGLAND, CHANNEL ISLANDS & NORTHERN IRELAND

SCOTLAND

WALES

ASSOCIATIONS & ORGANISATIONS

INDEXES

Foreword

by Sophie Grigson

In picking up this book you've shown that you're part of a growing movement of people looking for more honest, healthier and more enticing food, and, I hope, a revival in the best of our traditional food culture and practices, harnessed to the best of modern agricultural knowledge.

I wonder what made you select it? Perhaps you're a seasoned organic shopper like me, who has already embraced the pleasures of cooking and eating meals made with good organic produce. If so, then like me, you will find *The Organic Directory* an invaluable aid, guiding you to new discoveries in your area, and when you travel further afield. Organic producers are on the increase, and you may be missing out on newcomers, or new lines from familiar sources. And even when you know where to head for everyday organic supplies, having opening times and phone numbers at your fingertips is brilliant if you are after something special.

Maybe you've heard about the benefits of organic and local food more recently, and you're just setting out on the path that will lead you to better meals and a healthier outlook. Perhaps you've read about Food for Life, the Soil Association initiative, which inspired Jamie Oliver's television series on school meals and is helping to improve the health and concentration of children in dozens of schools through the use of more fresh, organic and local ingredients.

Or maybe you've visited your local farmers' market and realised how much more fun it can be to buy food directly from farmers, getting a chance to talk to the actual people who produce what you eat. That's something I just love, even if I only have time to exchange a few words, or to ask how best to cook or store what I'm buying. More and more of us are reaping the benefits of a renaissance of food culture in which we can discover the origins of what we eat, celebrate traditional varieties and recipes, and rebuild a sense of community with the farmers who put so much into producing the foods we eat.

Projects such as Food for Life, as well as supporting healthier eating in schools and hospitals, are helping local organic producers to find more markets for their food and switch more of our countryside to organic methods. This is where we all benefit again—organic farming methods enrich our wildlife, reduce pollution and strengthen local economies.

For way too long, control over food production and consumption has been taken out of the hands of the very people who should be the main players—the farmer and the shopper. At last the tide is turning, and in 2004 direct sales of organic food and drink—through farmers' markets, farm shops, home-delivery box schemes and the like—increased by a healthy 16 per cent to £108 million. Farmers' markets increased from 450 to nearly 500, and the number of box schemes also topped 500. The media are showing more and more interest in organic products—it's no longer an area they can ignore or dismiss as cranky— and supermarkets continue to expand their organic ranges. And that means that we keen organic customers have an increasingly easy time of it, with ever widening access to organic produce. Yippee! And long may it continue.

The one major criticism made of organic food is that it costs more, but that's not necessarily so. A number of price surveys have shown that buying organic food produced locally need be no more expensive than buying non-organic food at a supermarket, and naturally what you take home will be considerably superior and more satisfying. And if you really want to reduce prices even further, then you should consider setting up a local organic food-buying co-operative with friends and neighbours.

Having said that, there's no doubt in my mind that you do get what you pay for. It's a cliché, but an undeniable one. An organic free-range chicken will always cost more than a miserable, pallid battery-raised chicken, and none of us should begrudge the extra expense. Not only will that Sunday roast taste so much more delicious—there's no comparison between the rich, deeply chickeny taste of an organic bird and the pappy, cotton wool blandness of the confined animal—but we can eat with a clear conscience, knowing that this creature has led a decent life.

At this point it's worth trotting out another old adage, too often forgotten: quality not quantity. In other words, choose the best meats but eat a little less and make up any shortfall (as far as your stomach's concerned) with extra vegetables and potatoes, organic of course. Once again, you'll find that the difference in price need not be prohibitive. When you get down to it, the real question is: are you willing to put up with the inferior flavour, potentially harmful additives, poor animal welfare standards and residues of pesticides and antibiotics that characterise so much of the cheapest foods on the shelves?

When the Soil Association carried out a survey of over a thousand people recently, they found that 95 per cent of respondents said 'the taste and quality of the food' were important to them when buying food for a meal for family or friends. That compared with only 57 per cent who said that low prices were important. So you're joining a growing number of people who want real food at honest prices, rather than cheap food at a price we can't afford.

Now that you've taken this first step towards the enjoyment of the best food, I hope you will be as keen as I am to spread the word. You can't beat locally grown organic food, and we shouldn't be keeping that a secret—everyone deserves to enjoy food to the full. How about investing in a second copy of this Directory and passing it on to a friend? I bet you'll soon be thanked royally, and with any luck they will cook up a fantastic meal for you from the excellent organic produce to be found wherever you live.

It is a real pleasure to introduce this book and so to introduce more people to the pleasures of local organic shopping. You will find more to tempt your palate online at www.whyorganic.org—a new Soil Association website, which also offers nutritional advice, offers, competitions and recipes—including some from me!

Sophie Grigson

Introduction

What does organic mean?

Organic agriculture is a safe, sustainable farming system, producing healthy crops and livestock without damage to the environment. It avoids the use of artificial chemical fertilisers and pesticides on the land, relying instead on developing a healthy, fertile soil and growing a mixture of crops. In this way, the farm remains biologically balanced, with a wide variety of beneficial insects and other wildlife to act as natural predators for crop pests and a soil full of micro-organisms and earthworms to maintain its vitality. Animals are reared without the routine use of the array of drugs, antibiotics and wormers which form the foundation of most non-organic livestock farming.

How do I know if a product is organic?

'Organic' is a term defined by law, and all organic food production and processing is governed by strict standards. Producers, manufacturers and processors of organic foods have to be registered with one of the approved certification bodies and are required to keep detailed records ensuring a full trail of traceability from farm, through any processing operations, to table. Any major infringement of this results in the suspension of their licence and withdrawal of products from the market. All organic farmers, food manufacturers and processors are inspected annually, as well as being subject to random inspections.

The standards are stringent and cover every aspect of registration and certification, organic food production, permitted and non-permitted ingredients, the environment and conservation, processing, packaging and distribution. The standards are regularly updated and are then enforced by certification bodies.

To avoid any confusion with non-organic produce, most organic food is sold pre-packaged. Always check for the symbol and/or number of recognised certification bodies. Where produce is sold loose, proof of certification must be available to consumers. If the retailer cannot prove certification of the produce being sold, then find out who their supplier is and contact them to find out about their certification. All manufacturers must be registered with a certification body. Some shops pay a certification fee to register as organic in their own right. This gives an added assurance to customers. Any shop that repackages goods out of sight of customers, or cooks its own food and labels it 'organic', must also have its own licence to do so.

Is organic food healthier for me?

"Many research publications have shown that organically produced foods have higher amounts of beneficial minerals, essential amino acids, vitamins and lower potential risks from food pathogens and mycotoxins"—Carlo Leifert, Professor of Ecological Agriculture, Director of the Tesco Centre for Organic Agriculture.

Over 400 chemical pesticides are routinely used in intensive farming, and residues are often present in non-organic food. So-called 'acceptable levels' are calculated for each of these chemicals, and their risks to human health evaluated. However, surveys consistently show high and multiple residues occurring in a proportion of food samples such as baby food, spinach, dried fruit, bread, apples, celery, and chips. There is also little knowledge of the long-term effects of these compounds or of the 'cocktail' effect (the way in which their toxicity may be increased by mixing them together). The routine use of synthetic pesticides is not allowed under organic standards. Only four chemicals are allowed in restricted circumstances under Soil Association regulations.

Research has also shown that on average, organic food contains higher levels of vitamin C and essential minerals such as calcium, magnesium, iron and chromium, as well as cancer-fighting antioxidants. Even organic processed food is different—hydrogenated fat and artificial flavourings and sweeteners are banned, along with other food additives that can cause health problems.

Why should I buy local?

Buying locally produced food helps to support the producers in your region, maintaining a well established rural way of life. It gives the local economy a boost by keeping money within the community, sustaining local businesses and creating jobs for people who live in the area. Food that is grown closer to us has travelled less distance to reach us—this means less environmental pollution. Locally produced food can also be fresher, healthier and more nutritious, having been spared lengthy periods of storage, chilling and travel. And culturally, local organic food has its own 'story', bringing a shared meaning at mealtimes and a deeper connection to the land.

Introduction

What is a box scheme?

A box scheme is a box (bag, sack or net), containing freshly picked, locally grown produce, delivered weekly to your door or to a local drop-off point. Box scheme operators usually offer small, medium and family size boxes with prices ranging from £5 to £15. The operator decides what vegetables go into the box, and this will vary each week depending on the seasonal vegetables available. Healthy, tasty vegetables just as you would want to grow them your-self—but without the digging!

Organic box schemes are now one of the fastest growing forms of direct marketing in the UK: that is, getting food straight from the farmer to the consumer. The original concept was developed by vegetable growers to shortcut the extended food supply chain in order to sell their fresh produce direct to local consumers. Not surprisingly, a number of variations on the basic model have evolved, and there are an increasing number of home delivery business-es that buy their produce from farms and wholesalers. They may also supply fruit, dairy produce, meat, wines and wholefoods. Most schemes operate locally or on a regional basis, but some also deliver nationally. Box schemes usually source produce locally, keeping unnecessary packaging, storage and transportation to a minimum, which ensures it arrives fresh to your home.

What is a farmers' market?

Farmers' markets help local producers and processors to sell their goods direct to the public, near the source of origin, creating benefits to them and the local community. Usually held on a weekly basis, farmers' markets place an emphasis on added value, quality and freshness. They aim for an atmos-phere that is vibrant, upbeat and fun, helping to revitalise urban centres and to make shopping an enjoyable experience. Although the concept is not a new one, farmers' markets are becoming increasingly popular—more and more people are demanding quality, locally produced food, sold at a fair price to both consumer and producer.

Is organic farming better for the environment?

Extensive research has shown that organic farming can be better for the environment than conventional agriculture. Surveys by, among others, the Ministry of Agriculture and the British Trust for Ornithology, have shown the beneficial effects of organic farming on wildlife. It's not difficult to see why: the pesticides used in intensive agriculture kill many soil organisms, insects and other larger species. They also kill plants considered to be weeds. This means fewer food sources available for other animals, birds and beneficial insects, and the destruction of many of their habitats.

In contrast, organic farming provides a much wider range of habitats: more hedges, wider field margins, herb and clover-rich grassland and a mixed range of crops. Wildlife is not a luxury for the organic farmer, but an essential part of the farming system, and conservation is an integral part of the Soil Association's standards.

The avoidance of artificial chemicals means organic farmers minimise health and pollution problems. They also reduce the use of non-renewable resources such as the fossil fuels which are used to produce fertilisers and other agrochemicals.

What are biodynamic farming standards?

You will notice that some of the producers listed in this directory are certified as biodynamic. Biodynamic farmers apply organic standards, but in addition use special preparations for field sprays, and compost and manure treatments. Close attention is also paid to practical rhythms in husbandry, concentrating on closed systems. Biodynamics is a contemporary organic philosophy, following the ideas of Rudolf Steiner; it sees the whole earth as a living organism interrelating with the universe. Biodynamic produce is certified by the Demeter Standards Committee and carries their symbol, which is their trademark.

What about farm animals—how well are they looked after?

"Organic farming has the potential to offer the very highest standards of animal welfare. The Soil Association's welfare standards are leaders in the field" —Joyce de Silva, Chief executive, Compassion in World Farming, 2003

Organic standards place a strong emphasis on animal welfare. Animals have access to fields and are allowed to express their natural behaviour patterns. They always have comfortable bedding and plenty of space when they are housed. Organic livestock farmers can manage their animals without the routine use of antibiotics and other drugs because they run a healthy, balanced system: not keeping too many animals on a given area, keeping a mixture of species wherever possible, and using natural organic feedstuffs. Grazing animals like cows and sheep are fed mainly on herb and clover-rich grass. Homoeopathy and herbal remedies are used widely in organic livestock management. In a case of acute illness, where the animal might otherwise suffer, a conventional drug treatment would be used.

The Soil Association is one certification body that has chosen to set higher standards for animal welfare in certain key areas, to ensure that the highest possible standards are being met. These standards are constantly under review by a group of experienced organic farmers, vets and scientists, to ensure that all the farm animals are reared in optimal conditions on organic farms.

What are genetically modified organisms (GMOs)?

Genetic modification involves the artificial insertion of a foreign gene into the genetic material of an organism in an essentially random way. There are currently two main types of genetically modified crops: those engineered to be resistant to herbicides in order to kill weeds, and those engineered to produce toxins to kill pests.

Though GMOs have been marketed for several years, scientific knowledge of the processes involved is actually at a very early stage. Very little is known about the side effects of the inserted genes' random location, how gene location is controlled, and gene transfer into other micro-organisms such as bacteria in the human gut. In addition, evidence set out in the Soil Association's *Seeds of Doubt* report illustrates that GM crops have no economic benefits and can actually harm the environment.

Organic standards prohibit the use of GMOs and GM derivatives in organic food production and in animal feed.

What about organic imports—just how 'organic' are they?

Each EU member state has its own national organic certifying authority that applies the EU regulation in that country. These approve private certification bodies, or in some cases take on the role of certification themselves. As in the UK, each certification body may apply additional specifications on top of the EU standards.

Food imported from outside Europe into the EU is subject to similar rigorous checks and standards. Imported produce must come either from countries recognised as applying equivalent standards and inspection procedures, or from identified supply chains where it can be verified that equivalent standards and certification criteria have been permanently and effectively applied at all stages. Importers and their storage facilities are also inspected and certified to ensure all their importing activities comply with the above.

Is it possible to visit an organic farm?

Yes! The Soil Association's Organic Farms Network was set up in 1998 to help the public and schools connect with organic food and farming. The project supports organic farmers who want to welcome the public and schools on to their farms. These farms play a key role in forging a bridge of knowledge and understanding between rural and urban communities, inspiring visitors through the 'seeing is believing' principle to inform them about farming practices and their relationship with the countryside. This will help to encourage a life-long commitment to supporting organic food, local farms and the environment.

The farm network promotes 'green tourism', developing a national network of working farms with informal access to way-marked farm trails; opportunities to buy fresh food from farm shops and box schemes; and the potential for longer stays through camping or bed and breakfast accommodation.

Open days and special events recreate the link between the consumer, the land and the cultural aspects of farming that have for centuries been at the heart of rural life. During Organic Week in September each year, we encourage farms to open their gates as part of the special Organic Experience weekend.

The farms also provide a platform for more structured education, both for groups seeking guided tours, and schools wishing to enthuse their pupils with a visit to a working organic farm.

The Soil Association aims to give every child of primary school age the opportunity to visit an organic farm to discover where their food really comes from. They believe the development of demonstration farms will enhance the education of the public and farmers, but more importantly will reach thousands of children in their formative years, providing them with interesting and stimulating first hand experiences of food, farming, wildlife and the countryside.

The Soil Association aims to ensure that membership of the Organic Farms Network fits in with the farming enterprise concerned. There are three types of farm:

∑ • those which are open to groups 'by arrangement' or with a farm trail
∑ • local centres where the farm may, for example, have a farm shop and staffing to enable them to be open all the time, and
∑ • regional centres that provide dedicated visitor centres, conference facilities and sometimes an education officer

All members of the Soil Association Organic Farms Network are highlighted in *The Organic Directory*. For more information about the network, visit the Soil Association website www.soilassociation.org/farmvisits or call 0117 914 2422.

How easily can I find organic food and drink in restaurants and cafés?

The market for food eaten outside the home grew to over 30% of food spend in 2004 and now stands at £36 billion. Yet there's been an even more noticeable shift in what people are buying.

There has never been such an interest in organic food, slow food, local produce, seasonal menus and traditional recipes. People are rediscovering food culture and demanding good quality food, and this has a positive effect on the number of restaurants, hotels and cafes serving local, organic and seasonal food.

Applications from restaurants for Soil Association certification have doubled in the past year, and our new 'catering code of practice' helps restaurants that do not have full organic certification to back up their claims when using organic ingredients. It also supports them in finding suitable organic producers and suppliers. Fully certified organic eateries in this Directory carry the

Soil Association symbol next to their entry.

You'll find many organic eateries in this Directory and we expect many more in 2007. Newly certified venues include the first wholly organic restaurant in Cornwall, based at the first Soil Association certified B&B establishment, Bangor's House.

Local, fresh organic produce used to be a bonus—now it's an expectation, so remember to ask for it!

What about other products like health, beauty and textiles?

So you are convinced of the benefits of eating organic food—no nasty pesticides, benefits for the environment and high animal welfare standards—but what about the health and beauty products you use and the clothes you wear? Maybe it is time to consider going organic in other areas of your life.

Are all 'organic' beauty products really organic?

It is estimated that our skin absorbs over half of what we put on it: a worrying fact, when you consider that most of today's skin care products contain a toxic cocktail of parabens, petro-chemicals and hydrogenated fat. In addition, non-organic beauty products can contain harsh surfactants that literally strip oils away from skin and hair, leaving them dry, dull and flaky. Extra care needs to be taken with babies and children as their bodies are still developing so they are a lot more susceptible to chemicals and fragrances present in cosmetics.

Many people are turning to 'organic' cosmetics to avoid the risks associated with these chemicals. But how can you be sure that what you are buying really is organic? There is currently no national legislation governing organic beauty products—a product labelled 'organic' may only contain a tiny amount of an organic ingredient and could still contain ingredients that are linked with health risks.

However, a product bearing the Soil Association symbol means that it has been independently audited and checked under rigorous organic standards, which aim to provide you with cosmetics that are as natural as possible. This means eliminating chemicals and replacing them with natural preservatives and antibacterial agents such as honey, sugar and alcohol. The standards work on a precautionary principle and do not permit ingredients or processes that have been linked to health risks, such as parabens and phthalates, or do not have enough evidence to support them yet, such as nanoparticles. Plant extracts can also be used, such as rose, cinnamon, cloves, calendula and vanilla. So to feel beautiful on the outside as well as the inside, check the product label for organic certification as well as the word 'organic'.

Why would I buy organic textiles?

Sales of organic cotton have reached an estimated £20 million in the UK. The environmental and ethical benefits of organic textiles are being increasingly recognised by consumers—even a leading supermarket has introduced an organic baby wear range—and who can blame them? Take a look at the harmful effects of producing non-organic T-shirts:

- Non-organic cotton production is the biggest user of insecticides in the world—over 20 per cent of the world's insecticides are sprayed on cotton crops
- Around 30 teaspoons of pesticides are used to grow the cotton for each T-shirt
- The World Health Organisation estimates that at least 20,000 people die each year in developing countries as a result of sprays used on non-organic cotton
- Large-scale non-organic production uses irrigation, which can put pressure on scant water resources

The Soil Association has licensed manufacturers to produce textiles to its standards, covering every aspect of production including the way in which animals are reared, the growing of natural fibres and the processing and manufacture of the end product. They are also working with suppliers to develop more certified organic clothing, bedding and cotton-based products—so watch this space, and wear it with pride!

The Soil Association's Organic Food Awards 2006

The Organic Food Awards are held very year and aim to celebrate the very best of organic fare. In 2006 the judging of the Awards will take place in the spring, moving them from their previous autumn date. This means that winners will be able to showcase their winning products to the public at the annual Organic Food Festival in September 2006.

The product categories and closing dates will be available early in 2006 and full information will be published on the Soil Association's website (www.soilassociation.org).

The awards regularly attract over 1,000 entries, and involve a team of 90 judges, including well-known chefs and food writers, to ensure that the exceptional quality of winning products is maintained.

Categories in previous years have ranged from 'food to go' and 'local food initiative of the year' to the best organic sausages! Businesses that win an award can then go on to use the Organic Food Awards logo on their winning products. So if there's an Organic Food Awards logo on a product, you know it comes well recommended!

In 2006 Organic Restaurant of the Year will become part of the Organic Industry Awards to be judged in March 2006 and announced at the Organic and Natural Products Show in April 2006.

Businesses in this Directory that have won an Organic Food Award for one of their products are marked with the Organic Food Awards logo.

What do the UK organic certification codes mean?

Each certification body within the UK is given a UK code—the Soil Association is UK5. The number awarded has nothing to do with stringency standards but rather the order in which DEFRA received applications from the certification bodies. Legally, a company does not need to show a certification symbol on pack, but if the product has been produced and/or processed in the UK they must show the UK code. The Soil Association standards are among the highest in the world.

The UK certification bodies and their codes are listed on the next page.

The UK Organic Certification bodies

The organic food sector in the UK is expanding rapidly. Although over 70% of all organic products in the UK carry the Soil Association symbol, there are a number of other certifiers who, unlike the Soil Association and Demeter, operate on a profit-making basis. The certification bodies are:

 Soil Association Certification (SA Cert)—UK5

 Organic Farmers and Growers Ltd (OF&G)—UK2

 The Scottish Organic Producers Association (SOPA)—UK3

 The Organic Food Federation (OFF)—UK4

 Demeter (BDAA)—UK 6

 The Irish Organic Farmers and Growers Association (IOFGA)—UK7

 Organic Trust Ltd—UK9

 CMi Certification—UK10

 Quality Welsh Food Certification—UK13

Ascisco Limited—UK15

The Labelling of Organic Food

Strict EC regulations cover the labelling of organic foods, with the aim of ensuring that consumers are not misled. Natural products such as potatoes and lettuce may only be described as 'Organic' if they have been grown by a registered organic producer; they will probably be labelled 'Organically Grown Lettuce' or just 'Organic Lettuce'. The inspection system for organic producers is covered in the Introduction to this book. Manufactured goods such as bread are covered by the same regulations and will probably be labelled, e.g., 'Bread baked from Organic Flour'. Where it is not possible to manufacture goods from wholly organic ingredients, the manufacturer can use up to 5% non-organic minor ingredients—these are specified in the regulations and are recognised as not being available in sufficient quantities in organic form. So products labelled 'Organic' will be between 95% and 100% organic.

Products containing between 70% and 95% organic ingredients cannot be labelled 'Organic'. These products may use the term 'Organic' only in their ingredients list in descending weight order, e.g. Organically grown wheat (55%), Organically grown barley (15%), Organically grown oats (7%).

Products containing less than 70% organic ingredients may not use the term 'Organic' or any derivative of the term anywhere on the label. Percentages refer to agricultural ingredients; non-agricultural ingredients (e.g. water and salt) are not included in the calculations. No genetically modified or irradiated organisms are allowed in organic food products.

The UK registration body, UKROFS, also recognises all other EC certification bodies and a limited number of non-EC certification bodies that have an equivalent standard and inspection system. For all other countries, importers must demonstrate, either to UKROFS or an equivalent body in another EC country, that the food has been produced to equivalent standards and inspection systems in order for them to be allowed to use the term 'Organic' or its derivatives. A list of worldwide organic logos is available from the International Federation of Organic Agricultural Movements (IFOAM)—see under Associations listing.

How to Use this Directory

The heart of this Directory (pages 2–488) comprises the entries for suppliers of organic goods and services: producers, wholesalers, retailers, bed & breakfast, restaurants & cafés, and garden and farm sundries. This is followed by (pages 489–527) a listing of a wide range of associations working in the field. Finally there are several indexes by name of the companies and organisations listed.

The symbols for the various kind of entries are shown before each company name. Sets of symbols with their meaning are scattered throughout the Directory, depending on the space available.

Please telephone suppliers before making a special journey to visit them! Inevitably, some companies in the Directory will move premises, or even go out of business. The world of organics is changing fast.

There have been changes in recent years as regards the naming of Welsh and Scottish counties. We have used the current county and unitary authority names in this book.

Disclaimer

The information in this Directory regarding the producers, retailers etc. and the products they grow and sell has been gathered primarily from the entrants themselves. We have not verified any claims as to whether any produce described as such is 100% organic. Please note therefore that we cannot be held responsible for any claims made as to the quality of the produce or goods offered. There has recently been a proliferation of 'Green' labelling schemes, and we advise you to satisfy yourself as to the validity of any such claims.

What the symbols mean

The symbols of the organic certifying bodies are given on page xx.

 Accommodation: this can be anything from a field for camping to a hotel with full board.

 Box Schemes/Local Deliveries: local box schemes and/or delivery services. Boxes may be delivered to the door or to a central pick-up point.

 Day Visits: generally farms open to visitors. Some may require prior booking.

 Eco Products: non-food items, cleaning materials, toiletries etc.

 Farm Gate Sales: sales of produce from the farm (may need prior notification).

 Garden and Farm Sundries: composts, seeds, tools, etc.

 Farmers' Market Stall: sales of produce from local farmers' market stall.

 Manufacturers/Processors: mainly food manufacturers and/or processors, but can be any manufacturing process.

 Importers and/or exporters.

 Mail Order Suppliers including internet suppliers.

 Producers: farmers, growers etc.

 Restaurants/Cafés/Caterers. All claim to serve some organic produce.

 Retail shops.

 Textiles: clothes, nappies, mattresses, bed linen etc.

 Wholesalers and distributors.

CATLIN, DAVID
CHURCH FARM, CHURCH LANE, FLITTON MK45 5EL
Tel: 01525 860277 Fax: 01525 861452 Contact: David Catlin
farmercatlin@aol.com
Organic vegetable and asparagus grower and wholesaler supplying local and
national box schemes.

JORDANS (CEREALS) LTD, W
HOLME MILLS, BIGGLESWADE SG18 9JY
Tel: 01767 318222 Fax: 01767 600695 Contact: Emily Turner
www.jordanscereals.co.uk
Jordans have been producing natural cereals for 30 years, and their organic
range combines superior quality, exceptional taste and support for British
farming. Organic Food Awards 2004: Breakfast Cereals Highly Commended.

PRATT, SH & CO (BANANAS) LTD
LAPORTE WAY, LUTON LU4 8EN
Tel: 01582 436503 Fax: 01582 436570 Contact: Brice Lamarque
bricelamarque@shpratt.com
Soil Association P2512. S.H. Pratt & Co (Bananas) Ltd import and ripen organic
bananas for the UK market.

RIVER NENE HOME DELIVERY CAMBRIDGE
20 MEADOW ROAD, GREAT GRANSDEN, SANDY SG19 3BD
Tel: 01767 677852 Fax: 01767 677852 Contact: Martin Chenery
martinandjulie@rivernene.co.uk www.rivernene.co.uk
Box scheme delivery service.

RIVER NENE ORGANIC VEGETABLES—BEDFORDSHIRE

1 NIGHTINGALE MEWS, SHEFFORD SG17 5YX
Tel: 0845 078 6868 Fax: 01462 811811 Contact: Jackie Cooper
markandjackie@rivernene.co.uk www.rivernene.co.uk
River Nene Organic Vegetables: home delivery box scheme for Bedfordshire.

SHERRY'S HEALTH FOODS

58 HIGH ST., BIGGLESWADE SG18 0LJ
Tel: 01767 220020 Fax: 01767 782663 Contact: Christine Soulsby
sheradbrit@aol.com
Health food shop with wide range of organic foods, vitamins and mineral
supplements, herbs, homoeopathy and aromatherapy.

WHOLEFOODS & HEALTH

1 THURLOW ST., BUS STATION SQUARE, BEDFORD MK40 1LR
Tel: 01234 219618 Fax: 01234 312929 Contact: Paul Martin
Extensive range of natural food products, vitamins, minerals, herbal
supplements special dietary and organic foods.

	Accommodation		Garden and Farm Sundries		Producers
	Box Schemes/ Local Deliveries		Farmers' market Stall		Restaurants/ Cafés/Caterers
	Day Visits		Manufacturers/ Processors		Retail shops
	Eco Products		Importers/ exporters		Textiles
	Farm Gate Sales		Mail order suppliers		Wholesalers

A LOT OF CHOCOLATE

33 DOUGLAS ROAD, CAVERSHAM, READING RG4 5BH
Tel: 0118 375 9375 Contact: Andrea Clifford
info@alotofchocolate.co.uk www.alotofchocolate.co.uk
A great selection of organic and Fairtrade chocolates. Including Green & Blacks
and Booja Booja. From single bars to fancy gift boxes.

A LOT OF COFFEE

DOUGLAS HOUSE, 33 DOUGLAS RD., CAVERSHAM, READING RG4 5BH
Tel: 0118 901 2210 Fax: 0118 901 2210 Contact: The Directors
info@alotofcoffee.co.uk www.alotofcoffee.co.uk
Quality freshly roasted organic and Fairtrade superior-tasting coffees. For coffee
drinkers who appreciate a first rate cup of coffee and have concerns about the
environment.

BONDUELLE LTD

5 RICHFIELD PLACE, 12 RICHFIELD AVENUE, READING RG1 8EQ
Tel: 0118 957 6020 Fax: 0118 957 6030 Contact: Vanessa Nagy
info@bonduelle.co.uk
Production and wholesaling of vegetables from the field to finished production
in cans and jars.

BROCKHILL FARM ORGANIC SHOP

BROCKHILL FARM, BROCK HILL, WARFIELD, BRACKNELL RG42 6JU
Tel: 01344 882643 Fax: 01344 882643 Contact: Silvana Keen
A complete range of organic food under one roof; fresh fruit and vegetables,
meat, poultry, fish, dairy produce, groceries, wine, beer, spirits, confectionery, eco-
products, etc..

CHURCH FARM

BEALE PARK, LOWER BASILDON, READING RG8 9 NH
Tel: 0118 984 5172 Contact: Clive Hill
farmnet@soilassociation.org

The farm has chosen rare breeds of sheep and cattle (such as Portland sheep and British white cows)—their grazing habits create the right conditions in the meadows to sustain the wild flowers. Farmer Clive Hill manages the livestock according to organic standards, and care is taken that they do not overgraze the pastures and upset its delicate ecology. The farm trail is open to visitors all year round. Please always contact the farm to check opening times before you set off. Member of the Soil Association Organic Farms Network.

DOVES FARM FOODS LTD

SALISBURY RD., HUNGERFORD RG17 0RF
Tel: 01488 684880 Fax: 01488 685235 Contact: Clare Marriage
mail@dovesfarm.co.uk www.dovesfarm.co.uk

Soil Association PD03. Growers and manufacturers of a large range of organic cereal based foods including home-baking flour, breakfast cereal, biscuits, cookies, cereal bars and flapjacks, several of which are ethical trade or Fairtrade certified. Also produce a separate range of special diet and gluten-free foods. Organic Food Awards 2004 Breakfast Cereals Winner; Cakes, Pastries, Biscuits Commended.

ELM FARM RESEARCH CENTRE

HAMSTEAD MARSHALL, NEWBURY RG20 0HR
Tel: 01488 658298 Fax: 01488 658503 Contact: Pat Walters
elmfarm@efrc.com www.efrc.com

EFRC provides agricultural and policy research, education and training courses, a farm trail, organic, OCIS and in conversion advisory service, organic demonstration farm network, soil analysis, publications, consultancy and producer groups. Member of the Soil Association Organic Farms Network.

GARLANDS ORGANIC

6 READING ROAD, PANGBOURNE RG8 7RS
Tel: 0118 984 4770 Fax: 0118 984 4220 Contact: Denise Ingrem

Soil Association G1619. A fantastic organic emporium, home-grown vegetables, groceries, fine cheeses, local and British meat, supplements, etc. Special diets, regional breads, consulting room, lovely shop, great staff. Parking behind.

THE KINDERSLEY CENTRE AT SHEEPDROVE ORGANIC FARM

THE KINDERSLEY CENTRE, SHEEPDROVE ORGANIC FARM, WARREN FARM, LAMBOURN RG17 7UU
Tel: 01488 674737 Fax: 01488 72285 Contact: Pippa Regan
pippa.regan@thekindersleycentre.com www.thekindersleycentre.com
Sustainable, organic and environmentally sound, The Kindersley Centre combines exceptional surroundings with the most advanced technology and attentive service. Set at the heart of award-winning Sheepdrove Organic Farm, the centre is housed within a beautiful, eco-friendly building, surrounded by fields and woodlands. A range of meeting places and adaptable seating for up to 200 people.

MONTEZUMA'S CHOCOLATES

12 PEASCOD ST., WINDSOR SL4 1DU
Tel: 0845 450 6304 Fax: 0845 450 6305 Contact: Claire Beech
claire.beech@montezumas.co.uk www.montezumas.co.uk
Soil Association P6067. Manufacturer and retailer of award-winning British organic chocolate. Highly acclaimed innovative and exciting products.

ORGANIC BUFFET

2 COLLIS ST., READING RG2 OAE
Tel: 0118 987 3740 Contact: Vincent Charles
vincecharles@onetel.com www.organicbuffet.co.uk
We specialise in buffets served at corporate events, meetings, training-days, networking lunches, private parties, weddings . . . any occasion, any numbers, where good food is required. Based in Berkshire, we cover the Thames Valley area. Alternative tel no 07876 236412.

ORGANICO

60–62 KINGS RD, READING RG1 3AA
Tel: 0118 951 0518 Fax: 0118 951 0519 Contact: Charles Redfern
info@organico.co.uk www.organico.co.uk
Import and distribution of authentic high-quality produce supplying the specialist organic and wholefood trade as well as fine food stores. Winner of 10 Great Taste Awards 2003. Wide range of quality organic brands and food products: juices, pasta, sauces, babyfoods, tinned fish, dairy- and gluten-free products, veggie spreads, cordials, jams, fruit purées, oils, vinegars, soups.

PRODUCT CHAIN LTD

TWYFORD MILL, 55 HIGH ST., TWYFORD RG10 9AJ
Tel: 0118 934 4944 Fax: 0118 934 1399 Contact: The Manager
info@productchain.com www.productchain.com
Soil Association P5339; Organic Food Federation 00424/01. Product Chain is the
foremost broker/agent in the UK, having been personally involved in the movement
since 1974. Associated with most of the key brands and players, including Martlet,
Grove Fresh, Tim's Dairy, Amy's Kitchen and more to come.

RANGER ORGANICS LTD

HOLMES OAK FARM, COLLINS END, GORING HEATH, READING RG8 7RJ
Tel: 01491 682568 Fax: 01491 681694 Contact: Theresa Whittle
ranger.organics@virgin.net
Soil Association R07M. Traditional range of English and Continental cuts of home-
produced organic beef sold at local and London Farmers' Markets. Beef Highly
Commended at the Organic Food Awards 2002; poultry Winner 1999 and
Highly Commended 2000. Rare breed poultry and laying geese.

RIVERFORD HOME DELIVERY

28 MATTHEWS GREEN RD., WOKINGHAM RG41 1JU
Tel: 0118 989 0053 Contact: Ruth Oakman
ruth@riverfordhomedelivery.co.uk www.riverford.co.uk
Organic vegetable box scheme operating in Berkshire; varied box sizes to suit
different households. Can order online at www.riverford.co.uk.

ROCKS ORGANICS

LODDON PARK FARM, NEW BATH RD., TWYFORD RG10 9RY
Tel: 0118 9342344 Fax: 0118 934 4539 Contact: Melanie Ketch
hugh@rocksorganic.com www.rocksorganic.com
Soil Association P2150. Specialist producer of organic dilutable drinks, we are
a dedicated organic producer only.

RUSHALL FARM

SCRATCHFACE LANE, BRADFIELD RG7 6DL
Tel: 0118 974 4547 Contact: The Manager
jst@rushallfarm.org.uk www.rushallfarm.org.uk
Rushall Farm is a mixed organic farm situated in the heart of the beautiful Pang valley. It has cattle, sheep, and woodland, and grows a range of cereal crops. It is also home to the John Simonds Trust, an educational charity that promotes a love and understanding of farming and the countryside.

SHEEPDROVE ORGANIC FARM

WARREN FARM, SHEEPDROVE, LAMBOURN, HUNGERFORD RG17 7UU
Tel: 01488 674721 Fax: 01488 73335 Contact: Hayley Smith
manager@sheepdrove.com www.sheepdrove.com
Driven by a passionate concern for animal welfare, wildlife preservation and a sustainable rural economy we produce our own organic beef, lamb, mutton, chicken and pork. We hang and cut all our meat on the farm and offer a bespoke service with nationwide delivery. Organic and environmentally sound, The Kindersley Centre combines exceptional surroundings with state of the art technology for meeting, conferences and events for between 8 and 200 delegates. Member of the Soil Association Organic Farms Network. Organic Food Awards 2004 Special Award for Innovation. See display ad.

THE ORGANIC BEEF COMPANY

THE OLD CRAVEN ARMS, INKPEN, HUNGERFORD RG17 9DY
Tel: 01488 668326 Fax: 01488 668429 Contact: Bernard Harris
enquiries@theswaninn-organics.co.uk www.theswaninn-organics.co.uk
Organic beef farm and butchery managed with The Swan Inn: organic restaurant, bar food and organic farm shop specialising in all organic meats and ready meals. An integrated organic business.

THE SWAN INN ORGANIC FARM SHOP

CRAVEN RD., INKPEN, HUNGERFORD RG17 9DX
Tel: 01488 668326 Fax: 01488 668306 Contact: Mary Harris
enquiries@theswaninn-organics.co.uk www.theswaninn-organics.co.uk
Organic beef, lamb, pork, chicken and turkey, all matured and butchered on the
premises. Bacon, gammons, sausages, burgers and ready to eat organic meals all
manufactured on the premises, and sliced cold roast beef and ham. Special orders
available. Over 1,000 items of veg, dairy, dry goods in stock. 10 luxurious
bedrooms and gourmet restaurant. Public House, organic bar meals.

THERE MUST BE A BETTER WAY

9 THETFORD MEWS, CAVERSHAM PARK VILLAGE, READING RG4 6SN
sales@theremustbeabetterway.co.uk http://www.theremustbeabetterway.co.uk
We sell natural, organic skincare & cosmetics, free from all harsh synthetic
chemicals for a healthy, balanced lifestyle.

VINTAGE ROOTS LTD

FARLEY FARMS, BRIDGE FARM, READING ROAD, ARBORFIELD RG2 9HT
Tel: 0118 976 1999 Fax: 0118 976 1998 Contact: Neil Palmer
info@vintageroots.co.uk www.vintageroots.co.uk
Specialist shippers of the finest organic wines, beers, ciders, spirits, and other
products from around the world. Call for free brochure (Freephone 0800 980
4992) or visit our website. The organic wine specialists: trade@vintageroots.co.uk.
Organic Food Awards 2004 Wines Commended. See display ad.

WALTHAM PLACE FARM

WALTHAM PLACE FARM, CHURCH HILL, WHITE WALTHAM, MAIDENHEAD SL6 3JH
Tel: 01628 825517 Fax: 01628 825045 Contact: Steve Castle
estateoffice@walthamplace.com www.walthamplace.com
Soil Association No G557 since 1989. Mixed organic farm and gardens open to
the public Wed (NGS) and Fri only (bookings please) 10am–4pm to September.
Produce available at farmers' markets and farm shop include seasonal vegetables,
preserves, meat, eggs and bread. Tea room serves light organic lunches and teas.
Member of the Soil Association Organic Farms Network. See display ad.

WILTON HOUSE

33 HIGH STREET, HUNGERFORD RG17 0NF
Tel: 01488 684228 Fax: 01488 685037 Contact: D Welfare
welfares@hotmail.com www.wiltonhouse.freeserve.co.uk
Although not totally organic, Wilton House offers mainly organic or locally
produced wholesome food in its classic English town house. Elegant, high standard
accommodation with 2 beautiful en-suite bedrooms from £30pp per night.

WISTBRAY TEAS LTD

P.O. BOX 125, NEWBURY RG20 9LY
Tel: 01635 278648 Fax: 01635 278672 Contact: Lynn Painter
info@wistbray.com www.elevenoclocktea.com
Wistbray Teas is an exciting and innovative family business with over 100 years
of passionate tea experience. Eleven O'Clock Rooibosch Tea is the original
caffeine-free tea, and the Dragonfly Organic speciality range offers high
quality teas for every taste. Alternative website: www.dragonfly-teas.com.

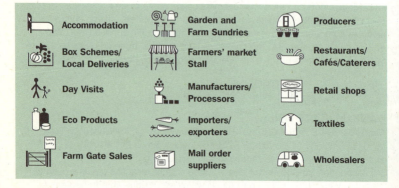

Accommodation

Garden and Farm Sundries

Producers

Box Schemes/ Local Deliveries

Farmers' market Stall

Restaurants/ Cafés/Caterers

Day Visits

Manufacturers/ Processors

Retail shops

Eco Products

Importers/ exporters

Textiles

Farm Gate Sales

Mail order suppliers

Wholesalers

BARLEY WOOD WALLED GARDEN

THE BETTER FOOD COMPANY, THE BRISTOL PROVING HOUSE,
SERVIER STREET, BRISTOL BS2 9QS
Tel: 0117 935 1725 Fax: 0117 941 4520 Contact: Phil Haughton
admin@betterfood.co.uk www.walledgarden.co.uk
Restored Victorian kitchen garden open to the public, with weekly box scheme
using seasonal produce from the garden. The produce is sold in the Better Food
Company in Bristol, and also direct to the public, other shops and restaurants. A
wonderful piece of our heritage for all to enjoy, set on a gentle southern slope overlooking the Mendips. Ideal for a family visit—learn about the garden's history, buy
the plants and produce, and visit the tea rooms and craft workshops.

BART SPICES LTD

YORK ROAD, BRISTOL BS3 4AD
Tel: 0117 977 3474 Fax: 0117 972 0216 Contact: Matthew Shaw
bartspices@bartspices.com www.bartspices.com
Bart Spices produces a range of organic herbs and spices destined for multiple
retailers. We also sell bulk organic herbs and spices to other food manufacturers.
Bart Spices is registered by the Soil Association.

THE BETTER FOOD COMPANY

THE BRISTOL PROVING HOUSE, SERVIER ST., ST. WERBURGHS BS2 9QS
Tel: 0117 935 1725 Fax: 0117 941 4520 Contact: Phil Haughton
admin@betterfood.co.uk www.betterfood.co.uk
Organic grocery store, based in the Centre for Ethical Trade and Creative Play,
specialising in fresh vegetables, salads and fruit from their Walled Garden in
Wrington, near Bristol. The huge range of other produce includes a delicatessen
counter and butcher's counter, dairy, all basics such as rice, pasta and cereals,
chocolate, wine & spirits and cleaning materials. Opening times are
Monday–Wednesday 9am–6pm, Thursday–Friday 9am–7pm and Saturday
9am–5pm. Organic Food Awards 2004: Local Food Initiative Joint Winner.

BOCM PAULS LTD

1ST AVENUE, ROYAL PORTBURY DOCK, BRISTOL BS20 7XS
Tel: 01275 378384 Fax: 01275 373828 Contact: Mike Thompson
mike.thompson@bocmpauls.co.uk www.bocmpauls.co.uk
Soil Association P2091. BOCM Pauls manufacture approved feeds for dairy cows, youngstock, beef, sheep, pigs and poultry. The products are supported by specialist management services for organic producers in England and Wales.

BORN

64 GLOUCESTER RD, BRISTOL BS7 8BH
Tel: 0117 924 5080 Fax: 0117 924 9040 Contact: Eva Fernandes
info@borndirect.com www.borndirect.com
Retail and internet shop specialising in organic, natural and practical products for parents and their babies. We're the experts on washable cotton nappies! Organic range includes organic cotton and wool babywear (underwear, nightwear, outerwear and bedding), organic herbal teas for pregnancy and afterwards, toiletries made with organic ingredients (Weleda, Green People, Urtekram), organic massage oils. We are open Monday–Saturday 9.30–5.30.

BRITISH SEED HOUSES LTD

PORTVIEW RD., AVONMOUTH, BRISTOL BS11 9JH
Tel: 0117 982 3691 Fax: 0117 982 2198 Contact: Paul Billings
seeds@bshavon.co.uk www.britishseedhouses.com
Soil Association P5945. Wholesale seed merchants producing and supplying both agricultural and amenity seed trade with conventional and organic seeds of grass, clover and cereal varieties.

CAFE MAITREYA

89 ST MARK'S ROAD, EASTON, BRISTOL BS5 6HY
Tel: 0117 951 0100 Fax: 0117 951 0200 Contact: Rob Booth
thesnug@cafemaitreya.co.uk www.cafemaitreya.co.uk
The UK's top gourmet vegetarian restaurant (Vegetarian Society Awards 2004). Café Maitreya is a café-restaurant serving modern vegetarian food prepared with love and care and using quality seasonal ingredients, many of which are organic. Daytimes: Fri–Sun, Evenings: Tue–Sat.

EARTHBOUND

8 ABBOTSFORD RD., COTHAM, BRISTOL BS6 6HB
Tel: 0117 904 2260 Contact: Pat & Martin Clark
Friendly, local shop selling a wide range of organic foods including fruit and
vegetables, a wide selection of organic and natural groceries, organic chocolate,
jams, juices and bread from the South-west.

EQUOP

UNIT 4, OLD MALTHOUSE, LITTLE ANN STREET, BRISTOL BS2 9EB
lynn@equop.com www.equop.com
equop is a modern, design-led, Fairtrade organic (Skal, Agrocel) clothing company
and a promoter of public talent. Based online (www.equop.com) it offers a truly
unique collection of exciting products, services and communities. It works in partnership with a variety of Fairtrade and ethical organisations to promote responsible
trade and living to everyone. equop promotes public talent through the production
of 'limited edition' garments, allowing the public to send in designs which are voted
for by site users and may become limited edition clothing, earning the designer
25% of the profits. The 'illustrated' section of the equop site is a free platform for
designers, artists, musicians and writers to show off their work.

ESSENTIAL TRADING CO-OPERATIVE LTD

UNIT 3 & 4, LODGE CAUSEWAY TRADING ESTATE, FISHPONDS BS16 3JB
Tel: 0117 958 3550 Fax: 0117 958 3551 Contact: Frances Barnsley
sales@essential-trading.coop www.essential-trading.coop
Trade only. Essential trading is a natural foods wholesaler supplying the independent retail sector. Our product range is entirely vegetarian and we carry only GMO-
free products. Aiming for totally organic product range. Registered with OF&G and
BDAA. Customer careline 0845 458 1459.

FIRST QUALITY FOODS

UNIT 29, THE BEECHES, LAVENHAM ROAD, YATE BS37 5QX
Tel: 01454 880044 Fax: 01454 853355 Contact: Steve Fisher
fqf@mail.com www.firstqualityfoods.co.uk
Sammy's Organic couscous in 3 varieties: Mediterranean Tomato, French
Provencale, Italian Pesto. Ma Baker Organic cereal bars in 4 varieties: Date &
Walnut, Almond, Apricot, Apple & Sultana.

FRESH & WILD

85 QUEENS ROAD, CLIFTON, BRISTOL BS8 1QS
Tel: 0117 910 5930 Contact: Carl Farrell
Fresh & Wild are the leading specialist retailer of organic foods and natural remedies.

HARVEST NATURAL FOODS

11 GLOUCESTER ROAD, BRISTOL BS7 8AA
Tel: 0117 942 5997 Fax: 0117 924 9073 Contact: Ruth Alderman
harvest@bristol-trading.coop
We are a wholefood retailer specialising in organic and Fairtraded goods, including fresh produce, chocolate, ice cream, tea, coffee, wine, beer. Also bodycare and eco-cleaning products.

HEART OF DEVON ORGANICS

ALBERT CRESCENT, BRISTOL BS2 0XM
Tel: 01647 24894 Fax: 01647 24894 Contact: Geoff Jones
Soil Association P6946. The largest sole wholesaler of quality organic fresh fruit and vegetables in the South-west. Working closely with local and near continent growers (visit website). Deliveries from M4 to Lands End.

JEKKA'S HERB FARM

ROSE COTTAGE, SHELLARDS LANE, ALVESTON, BRISTOL BS35 3SY
Tel: 01454 418878 Fax: 01454 411988 Contact: Jekka McVicar
farm@jekkasherbfarm.com www.jekkasherbfarm.com
Soil Association G5869. This farm grows over 500 different varieties of herb and native wild flowers. The transplants are grown to Soil Association Standards. The herb displays have won RHS Gold Medals at the Chelsea Flower Show in 1995–7 and 1999–2003. The farm also has Open Days throughout the year and runs herb workshops.

MURRAY, T & PA
153 GLOUCESTER RD., BISHOPSTON, BRISTOL BS7 8BA
Tel: 0117 942 4025 Contact: Tom Murray
Butcher and delicatessen. Purveyors of organic meats and delicatessen foods.

THE NATURAL NURSERY
185 NORTH ST., SOUTHVILLE, BRISTOL BS3 1JQ
Tel: 0117 966 8483 Contact: Arabella Greatorex
info@naturalnursery.co.uk www.naturalnursery.co.uk
Organic and fairly traded products for families including organic clothes for
newborns to 7 years, cloth nappies, natural toiletries, slings, fair toys. Secure
online ordering or visit our Bristol shop.

NEAL'S YARD REMEDIES
126 WHITELADIES RD., CLIFTON, BRISTOL BS8 2RP
Tel: 0117 946 6034 Fax: 0117 946 6034 Contact: Clare Proctor
mail@nealsyardremedies.com www.nealsyardremedies.com
Stockists of a wide variety of natural remedies and cosmetics. Many certified
organic, including herbs and tinctures, homoeopathic and flower remedies, e.g.
essential oils, bath and body products, massage oils and books.

NEWBABYBASKETS.CO.UK
Tel: 01275 818275 Contact: Tim Berry
sales@newbabybaskets.co.uk www.newbabybaskets.co.uk/
We are an online baby goods and gift shop specialising in organic baby gift
baskets, organic baby clothes, and eco-friendly nappies and toiletries.

ONE PLANET

39–41 PICTON ST., BRISTOL BS6 5PZ
Tel: 0117 942 6644 Contact: Roger Cole
roger@oneplanetwholefoods.co.uk
Vegetarian and vegan community wholefoods store selling organic, Fairtraded
and local produce, fruit and veg, dairy, breads, with 100% organic juice bar.

PERFECTA LTD

ASHMEAD ENTERPRISE CENTRE, ASHMEAD RD., KEYNSHAM BS31 1SX
Tel: 0117 986 8800 Fax: 0117986 1687 Contact: Mark Garrett
sales@perfecta.ltd.uk www.perfecta.ltd.uk
Suppliers of organic herbs, spices and other ingredients. Manufacturers of
organic seasonings and blends including sausage, burger, bakery and vegetarian
products. Kosher production available.

PRIMROSE CAFE ICE CREAM

BOYCES AVENUE, CLIFTON, BRISTOL BS8 4AA
Tel: 0117 946 6577 Contact: Patrick Glennie-Smith
primrosecafe@talk21.com
Soil Association P7528. Producer of small quantities of pure natural ice creams,
sorbets and frozen yoghurts. All handmade on our own premises. Organic Food
Awards 2004 Ice Cream Highly Commended.

PUKKA HERBS LTD

THE OLD SAWMILL, THE HOME FARM, BARROW COURT LANE,
BARROW GURNEY, BRISTOL BS48 3RW
Tel: 01275 461950 Fax: 01275 464165 Contact: Bolyn Moeun
bolyn@pukkaherbs.com www.pukkaherbs.com
Providers of delicious award-winning organic herbal teas and ayurvedic remedies
that have proven traditional usage over thousands of years. Pukka Herbs is
committed to Fairtrade, organic farming and personal wellbeing.

R & B (BRISTOL) LTD
UNIT 4, BRISTOL DISTRIBUTION PARK, HAWKLEY DRIVE, BRADLEY STOKE BS32 9BF
Tel: 01454 456700 Fax: 01454 456710
We are a Soil Association certified site (P2492) and produce organic pasta
sauces for retail.

SHEEPDROVE ORGANIC FARM FAMILY BUTCHER
3 LOWER REDLAND RD., BRISTOL BS6 6T
Tel: 0117 973 4643 Fax: 0117 946 7957 Contact: Graham Symes
graham.symes@sheepdrove.com www.sheepdrove.com
Family butcher selling the Sheepdrove Farm range of meats including beef, lamb,
mutton, pork, bacon, gammon, sausages, burgers and poultry. Alternative tel no.
0117 973 1153.

SOUTHVILLE DELI
262 NORTH ST, SOUTHVILLE, BRISTOL BS3 1JA
Tel: 0117 966 4507 Contact: Paul Wick
pgw-awe@dircon.co.uk
We are a retail store selling organic wholefoods including bread, dairy products &
eggs. In addition, we have a small delicatessen carrying as wide a range of organic
luxury goods as possible, including fresh olives, cheeses & chocolates. We also
grind organic & Fairtrade coffees to order.

STONEGROUND
5 THE MALL, CLIFTON, BRISTOL BS8 4DP
Tel: 0117 974 1260 Contact: Jackie Budd
Veggie, GM-free shop stuffed with pulses, cereals and soya plus 200 organic
delights and award-winning fresh bread. Excellent organic, veggie wines and
beers. Also vits/supplements and herbal remedies. Local where possible.

WILD OATS WHOLEFOODS
9–11 LOWER REDLAND ROAD, REDLAND, BRISTOL BS6 6TB
Tel: 0117 973 1967 Fax: 0117 923 7871 Contact: Mike Abrahams
info@woats.co.uk www.woats.co.uk
Organic natural foods grocery specialising in chilled, frozen and ambient
foods, wines, beers, toiletries, natural medicines, household products, organic
and natural paints, books. Mail order service available.

WINDMILL HILL CITY FARM SHOP
PHILIP STREET, BEDMINSTER, BRISTOL BS3 4EA
Tel: 0117 963 3233 Fax: 0117 963 3252 Contact: Keith Ladbrooke
Info@windmillhillcityfarm.org.uk www.windmillhillcityfarm.org.uk
We sell locally produced food including organic meat, free-range eggs, goats milk
and vegetables grown by organic methods on our inner-city farm. Open Tuesday to
Saturday, 10am to 5pm.

Nature is self-sustaining
The view of Nature as self-organizing, self-sustaining, self-regenerating and self-
regulating, is at the heart of the organic and sustainable approach to agriculture. It means that the farmer has faith in natural processes to nurture plants
and animals in the same way that it has been doing for millions of years. Of
course the organic farmer sows the crops and keeps the animals he or she
finds most useful for food production, but it is done in a co-operative and
respectful frame of mind. It is a recognition that no gardener has ever 'grown' a
plant, no farmer has ever 'produced' an animal. The best we can do is create
the right conditions for them to grow themselves.
**From *Organic Futures: The Case for Organic Farming* by Adrian Myers,
Green Books, £12.95.**

Buckinghamshire

CHURCH FARM

CHURCH FARM, 4 WINSLOW RD, SWANBOURNE, MILTON KEYNES MK17 0SW
Tel: 01296 720219 Contact: Nicole Alderman
We produce and sell bottled raw organic milk at the farm gate, from our herd of
organic British Friesian cows. We also sell beef store cattle.

CUMFYBUMFY

10 JOULES COURT, SHENLEY LODGE, MILTON KEYNES MK5 7BA
Tel: 01908 660096 Contact: Christine Cooper
info@cumfybumfy.co.uk
Organic washable nappies and baby clothes to order.

DUDLEY, JC & CO LTD

CHEYNEY HOUSE, FRANCIS YARD, EAST STREET, CHESHAM HP5 1DG
Tel: 01494 792839 Fax: 01494 792875 Contact: Mark Dudley
sales@jcdudley.co.uk www.jcdudley.co.uk
Soil Association P4449. Importers/agents dealing in organic fruit juice
concentrates, NFC fruit juices and purées, along with frozen elderflowers and
frozen and dehydrated cranberries, blueberries and lingonberries.

THE ETHICAL FOOD COMPANY

VERNEY JUNCTION BUSINESS PARK, UNITS 4–5, VERNEY JUNCTION,
BUCKINGHAM MK18 2LB
Tel: 01296 713332 Contact: Ian Nutt
ian.nutt@ethicalfoods.co.uk www.ethicalfoods.co.uk
The Ethical Food Company is an online grocery store that sells food and drink
produced to high standards, including organics, animal welfare, Fairtrade and
local/sustainable production. We guarantee excellent quality products,
outstanding customer service and peace of mind for our customers. Orders can be
taken by internet, phone, email and fax and delivered to your door. We
currently deliver locally with our own vehicles and nationally by courier.

FIELDFARE ORGANIC AND NATURAL LTD

THE BARNS, NASH LEE LANE, WENDOVER HP22 6BG
Tel: 0845 601 3240 Fax: 01296 622245 Contact: Sandie Calow
office@fieldfare-organics.com www.fieldfare-organics.com
Soil Association P1870. Organic Retail Guild. Home delivery of all your organic
requirements: fruit and vegetables, bakery and dairy, meat, poultry and fish,
wholefoods, wines, beers, aromatherapy and baby care.

FULLER'S ORGANIC FARM SHOP

MANOR FARM, BEACHAMPTON, MILTON KEYNES MK19 6DT
Tel: 01908 269868 Fax: 01908 262285 Contact: Sally Barwell
fullers.organics@farmline.com
Superb quality home-produced rare breed organic meat and poultry. Resident
Master Butcher, own cured ham and bacon, also eggs, vegetables, dairy and wide
range of artisan products.

GILES FOODS LTD

6 TANNERS DRIVE, BLAKELANDS, MILTON KEYNES MK14 5BU
Tel: 01908 217824 Fax: 01908 217825 Contact: David Marx
info@gilesfoods.com www.gilesfoods.com
Soil Association P5044. Chilled bakery products: primarily quiche, Danish pastries,
garlic slices (frozen), party foods (fresh and frozen). Speciality breads, garlic bread
and dough balls (all chilled).

GREAT HUNDRIDGE MANOR FARM

THE ESTATE OFFICE, GREAT HUNDRIDGE MANOR, GREAT MISSENDEN HP16 0RN
Tel: 01494 794551 Fax: 01494 794552 Contact: Charles Mullins
Soil Association G2520. Farm: mainly arable.

HEALTHRIGHT

48C FRIARS SQUARE, AYLESBURY HP20 2SP
Tel: 01296 397022 Contact: Anne Redstone www.healthright.co.uk
We are a health store stocking a range of organic wholefoods and grocery
products, also a growing range of bodycare products with organic ingredients.

HEALTHRIGHT
27 HIGH ST., CHESHAM HP5 1BG
Tel: 01494 771267 Contact: Roger Oliver
Health food store selling a full range of foods, supplements, herbal and homoeo-pathic remedies, aromatherapy oils, filters, cleaning products, books, cassettes, CDs plus Bach care products.

ONLY NATURAL
41 ST. PETERS COURT, CHALFONT ST. PETER SL9 9QQ
Tel: 01753 889441 Fax: 01753 889441 Contact: Sachdev
Small volume of pre-packed organic products including frozen organic ready meals.

ONLY ORGANIC
NOTLEY FARM, LONG CRENDON HP18 9ER
Tel: 01844 238064 Contact: Dominic Shadbolt
talktous@onlyorganic.org www.onlyorganic.org
We are an organic produce home delivery company that is Soil Association certi-fied. We cover Bucks, Berks, Oxon & Northants. We primarily deliver fresh fruit and veg, and deliver free to your home or office.

THE ORGANIC WINE COMPANY
PO BOX 81, HIGH WYCOMBE HP13 5QN
Tel: 01494 446557 Fax: 01494 446557 Contact: Tony Mason
afm@lineone.net
Importers and wholesalers, including mail order (by the case) of organic wines, beers, spirits, juices, and olive oils. Established over 18 years, with a range of over 300 lines.

ORIGO HOME

2 COLDGROVE COTTAGES, TAPLOW SL6 0HD
Tel: 020 7386 0856 Fax: 020 7385 8056 Contact: Alan Sharp
alan@origohome.co.uk www.origohome.co.uk
We've been making beautiful natural goods for more than 15 years in Europe. We believe in classic designs but we also really like our planet, so we make our products from organic and natural materials. We strive to ensure that our products are produced with the best interests of the environment in mind, and also the people living in it. Because we use certified organic cottons and wools, and woods from sustainable forestry, you can enjoy our products knowing that you've made a positive difference to the world and its environment. What's more, our products aren't that expensive, which just goes to show that products don't have to cost the earth for you to help look after it.

PIZZA ORGANIC LTD

54 LONDON END, OLD BEACONSFIELD HP9 2JH
Tel: 01494 677758 Contact: Mike Traszko
info@pizzapiazza.co.uk www.pizza-organic.co.uk
A great menu packed full of organic options, featuring stonebaked pizza, sautéed pasta, gourmet burgers, grilled fish and fabulous desserts. Pizza Organic is certified by the Soil Association and was Highly Commended in the 2003 Organic Food Awards. All restaurants open 7 days a week but opening times may vary, call 020 8397 3330 for further details.

REDFIELD COMMUNITY

BUCKINGHAM RD., WINSLOW MK18 3LZ
Tel: 01296 713661 Fax: 01296 714983 Contact: Chrissy Schmidt
info@redfieldcommunity.org.uk www.redfieldcommunity.org.uk
Redfield is an intentional community. We grow and raise our own organic produce as well as running courses, and offer accommodation for groups.

REVITAL HEALTH AND BEAUTY

12 THE HIGHWAY, STATION RD, BEACONSFIELD HP9 1QQ
Tel: 01494 678787 Contact: The Manager
www.revital.com
Health shop.

RIVER NENE ORGANIC VEGETABLES—HOME DELIVERY (MILTON KEYNES)

14 ENTERPRISE LANE, CAMPBELL PARK, MILTON KEYNES MK9 4AP
Tel: 0845 078 6868 Contact: Russell Cook
russell@rivernene.co.uk www.rivernene.co.uk
Award-winning organic vegetable box scheme delivering in Milton Keynes and
Buckinghamshire. Offering differing box sizes to suit all households, from a single
occupant to a large family. A selection of fruit, dairy products, wine, fruit juices etc.
also available. Order weekly, fortnightly or whenever you like. Can order online at
www.rivernene.co.uk or by telephone on 0845 078 6868.

RIVERFORD HOME DELIVERY

24 BADGERS WAY, MARLOW SL7 3QU
Tel: 01628 440227 Contact: Jill Dowling
jillandsteve@riverfordhomedelivery.co.uk www.riverford.co.uk
Organic vegetable boxes delivered to your door in the Maidenhead, High Wycombe
and Slough areas. Order online at www.riverford.co.uk

THE SUSTAINABLE LIFESTYLES RESEARCH CO-OP LTD

THE OFFICE, POND COTTAGE EAST, CUDDINGTON RD., DINTON,
AYLESBURY HP18 0AD
Tel: 01296 747737 Contact: Mike George
mikegeorge.lara@btinternet.com
Organic Food Federation 0071/01/981. Free range eggs, seasonal vegetables and
fruit, especially Victoria Plums. Occasional lamb, mutton (Jacobs sheep).
Selling at Tring Farmers' market and from farm stall. Full public access to 70 acres.
Farm Walks through woodland to the riverside. Run by volunteers.

SYNERGY

SYNERGY HOUSE, HILLBOTTOM ROAD, SANDS INDUSTRIAL ESTATE,
HIGH WYCOMBE HP12 4HJ
Tel: 01494 492222 Contact: Crispin Gell
info@synergyflavours.com www.synergyflavours.com
Organic flavours and extracts.

Cambridgeshire

BELSOS (UK) CEREALS LTD

38–40 STAPLEDON RD., ORTON SOUTHGATE, PETERBOROUGH PE2 6TD
Tel: 01733 362900 Fax: 01733 394111 Contact: Terry Black
terry@belso.co.uk www.belsos.co.uk
Manufacture and packing of breakfast cereals including traditional blended mueslis and baked crunchy products. Able to supply in bulk or in retail units, cartons or bags, especially own-label.

BRITISH SUGAR PLC

OUNDLE ROAD, PETERBOROUGH PE2 9QU
Tel: 08000 688022 Fax: 01733 422916 Contact: Daniel Johnson
sales@britishsugar.co.uk www.britishsugar.co.uk
British Sugar's organic range includes granulated, cane, icing and liquid sugars. The range is supplied to meet all your product requirements, and provides all the functionality expected from quality sugars.

BRITISH SUGAR PLC

OUNDLE RD., PETERBOROUGH PE2 9QU
Tel: 0870 240 2314 Fax: 0870 240 2729 Contact: Richard Cogman
rcogman@britishsugar.co.uk www.britishsugar.co.uk
British Sugar Plc manufactures LimeX products which are ideal for rapid, persistent correction of acidity. LimeX contains useful nutrients and may be used in organic systems. Flexible service options meet the needs of individual customers. Email: coproducts@britishsugar.co.uk.

DAILY BREAD CO-OPERATIVE (CAMBRIDGE) LIMITED

UNIT 3, KILMAINE CLOSE, CAMBRIDGE CB4 2PH
Tel: 01223 423177 Fax: 01223 425858 Contact: Nick Williams
cambridge@dailybread.co.uk www.dailybread.co.uk
Soil Association P4448. We retail and wholesale wholefoods with a good and increasing range of organic flours, grains, cereals, pulses, fruit and vegetables.

DELFLAND NURSERIES LTD
BENWICK ROAD, DODDINGTON, MARCH PE15 0TU
Tel: 01354 740553 Fax: 01354 741200 Contact: Jill Vaughan
jill@delfland.co.uk www.organicplants.co.uk
Vegetable, salad, herb, strawberries and ornamental plants for outdoor and
greenhouse/polytunnel production. Wholesale deliveries made all over the UK.
Retail shop and mail order for gardeners and allotment holders: online catalogue at
www.organicplants.co.uk. See display ad.

DISCOVER ORGANICS
51 SEARLE ST, CAMBRIDGE CB4 3DB
Tel: 01223 355984 Contact: James Knight-Smith
jknightsmith@gmail.com www.discoverorganics.com
Certified organic by the USDA, BFA and JAS. The first internationally certified
cosmetic and personal care range in the world.

EDGEBANK ORGANICS
KELVINSIDE, EDGE BANK, EMNETH HUNGATE, WISBECH PE14 8EJ
Tel: 01945 430971 Contact: Lucio Salas & Anna Wardman
enquiries@edgebankorganics.co.uk www.edgebankorganics.co.uk
Edgebank Organics produces and sells soft and top fruit including strawberries,
raspberries, gooseberries, blackcurrants, blackberries, rhubarb, apples, pears,
cherries and plums from May through to October. Fresh fruit and home-made jam
are available at the farm gate and local farmers' markets. Mobile: 07798 641202.

FRESH NETWORK, THE
THE FRESH NETWORK LTD., PO BOX 71, ELY CB6 3ZQ
Tel: 0870 800 7070 Fax: 0870 800 7071 Contact: Karen Knowler
info@fresh-network.com www.fresh-network.com
The Fresh Network—trying to eat more healthily? We are here to help. We
specialise in promoting and supplying organic raw and living foods and publish
Get Fresh! magazine, hold an annual Fresh Festival featuring many of the world's
leading authorities on natural healthy living and offer an extensive range of specialist books, foods and kitchen equipment by mail order including juicers, sprouting
equipment, dehydrators and much more.

G'S MARKETING LTD

HASSE RD., SOHAM, ELY CB7 5UN
Tel: 01353 727513 Fax: 01353 624388 Contact: Paul Heaton
paul.heaton@gs-marketing.com www.gs-marketing.com
Soil Association P4445. Growers and packers of organic salads and vegetables.
Growing in Cambridgeshire and the West Midlands producing the finest quality
organic produce. Sourcing product worldwide when out of the UK season.

GREENVALE AP

FLOODS FERRY ROAD, DODDINGTON, MARCH PE15 0UW
Tel: 01354 672059 Fax: 01354 677561 Contact: Phil Britton
phil.britton@greenvale.co.uk www.greenvale.co.uk
Greenvale AP is the UK's largest handlers of organic potatoes, supplying fresh
organic potatoes and organic dehydrated potato flake across the UK and Europe.

GREENVALE FOODS LTD

BOLENESS RD., WISBECH PE13 2RB
Tel: 01945 469840 Fax: 01945 581414 Contact: K Smith
www.greenvale.co.uk
Soil Association P2334. Manufacturer and supplier of dehydrated drum-dried potato
flake for use in snacks, potato mash and other food preparations and dishes.

GUILDEN GATE SMALLHOLDING

86 NORTH END, BASSINGBOURN, ROYSTON SG8 5PD
Tel: 01763 243960 Contact: Simon Saggers
simon.saggers@home.pipex.com www.guildengate.co.uk
Soil Association G5970. Mixed organic smallholding offering local 'veggie box'
scheme and guided tours. Wildflower meadow, Veg & Herb fields, Woodland, Pond
and Orchards. Interesting on-site water and energy resource cycles. A practical
design for living and working in a more ecologically sound and sustainable way.
Member of the Soil Association Organic Farms Network.

HERON FARM

HERON FARM, LONG DROVE, WATERBEACH, CAMBRIDGE CB5 9LR
Tel: 01223 441823 Contact: Chris McBride
enquiries@heronfarm.co.uk www.heronfarm.co.uk
Small farm situated between Cambridge and Ely, producing pork, bacon, gammon
and sausages, mostly from rare breed Saddleback sows crossed to a large white
boar. We retail direct to the public, either from the farm, or on Ely Farmers' Market.

JDM INGREDIENTS LTD

BROAD END RD., WALSOKEN, WISBECH PE14 7BQ
Tel: 01945 465556 Fax: 01945 465796 Contact: William Cook
jdmuk@dialstart.net
Soil Association P6068. Producers of garlic purée, ginger purée, roasted vegetables.

LANDAUER HONEY LTD

TOP BARN, FOWLEMERE RD., NEWTON, CAMBRIDGE CB2 5PG
Tel: 01223 872444 Fax: 01223 872512 Contact: Mr Steen
landauerhoney@compuserve.com www.landauergroup.co.uk
Honey refiner supplying the food manufacturing industry.

MASTEROAST COFFEE COMPANY LTD

50–54 IVATT WAY BUSINESS PARK, WESTWOOD, PETERBOROUGH PE3 7PN
Tel: 01733 842000 Fax: 01733 266934 Contact: D Baxter
info@masteroast.co.uk www.masteroast.co.uk
Soil Association P2995. Roasting, grinding and packing of fresh coffee beans to
customers' requirements.

NATURALLY YOURS

HORSE AND GATE, WITCHAM TOLL, ELY CB6 2AB
Tel: 01353 778723 Contact: Jo & Bob Horton
orders@naturally-yours.demon.co.uk www.naturally-yours.co.uk
Suppliers of organic and additive-free foods including meat, fish, fruit and
vegetables and groceries. Full traditional butchery service. Fruit and vegetable box
scheme. Free delivery within defined area.

NEAL'S YARD REMEDIES

1 ROSE CRESCENT, CAMBRIDGE CB2 3LL
Tel: 01223 321074 Contact: Ali Hunte
cambridge@nealsyardremedies.com www.nealsyardremedies.com
Neal's Yard Remedies manufactures and retails natural cosmetics in addition to
stocking an extensive range of herbs, essential oils, homoeopathic remedies and
reference material.

NORGROW INTERNATIONAL LTD

GRANGE FARM LODGE, LEVERINGTON COMMON, WISBECH PE13 5JG
Tel: 01945 410810 Fax: 01945 410850 Contact: Henri Rosenthal
sales@norgrow.com www.norgrow.com
Food ingredients: wide range of soya products, sugar and natural sweeteners,
beans, peas, pulses, seeds, nuts, fruit, vegetables, culinary and medicinal herbs
and spices, essential oils, oleoresins, plant extracts and powders. Bulk and
Wholesale only. See our website for full range of products.

OAKLEY FARMS

HALL RD., OUTWELL, WISBECH PE14 8PE
Tel: 01945 773387 Fax: 01945 774101 Contact: David Murfit
technical@oakleyfarms.co.uk www.oakleyfarms.co.uk
Growers and packers of organic vegetables, specialising in courgettes, pumpkins
and broccoli.

ORGANIC CONNECTIONS INTERNATIONAL LTD

RIVERDALE, TOWN ST., UPWELL, WISBECH PE14 9AF
Tel: 01945 773374 Fax: 01945 773033 Contact: Edwin Broad
sales@organic-connections.co.uk www.organic-connections.co.uk
Soil Association IP1653 & G1885. Fruit and vegetable suppliers to all aspects
of the organic market. We grow, market and pre-pack, and make nationwide
deliveries of our award-winning box scheme. Suppliers to pre-packers.

ORGANIC HEALTH (CAMBRIDGE)

87 CHURCH ROAD, HAUXTON, CAMBRIDGE CB2 5HS
Tel: 01223 870101 Contact: Jackie Garfit
www.organichealth.biz
Specialist retailer of organic, biodynamic and special diet foods. Thousands of
lines including organic fruit and veg, meat and fish, breads, dairy, vegetarian
and vegan foods, and lots more. Phone for details. Opening times Tues–Sat
9–5pm, Thurs 9–6.30.

PETERBOROUGH HEALTH FOOD CENTRE

25 THE ARCADE, WESTGATE, PETERBOROUGH PE1 1PZ
Tel: 01733 566807 Fax: 01733 566807 Contact: H Walji
We stock organic beans and pulses, dried fruit, teas, honey, cooking oils, juices,
cereals, flour, chocolate and soya milk.

PRO-VEG SEEDS LTD

6 SHINGAY LANE, SAWSTON, CAMBRIDGE CB2 4SS
Tel: 01293 833001 Fax: 01293 833006 Contact: John Burrows/ Julie Jones
johnburrows@provegseeds.com www.provegseeds.com
Wholesaler and retail vegetable seed suppliers, supplying other seed companies,
including packet seed companies, and professional growers.

PROSPECTS TRUST

SNAKEHILL FARM, REACH, CAMBRIDGE CB5 0HZ
Tel: 01638 741551 Fax: 01638 741873 Contact: Phil Creme
prospect@farming.co.uk www.prospectstrust.org.uk
Soil Association registered. Charitable trust, working together with people with
learning disabilities. Provision of training, work experience and work opportunities in
organic market gardening and horticulture for people with learning disabilities.

RIVER NENE ORGANIC VEGETABLES

STAN'S FARM, YAXLEY PE7 3TW
Tel: 0845 078 6868 Contact: Rob Haward
boxscheme@rivernene.co.uk www.rivernene.co.uk
Home delivery of fresh organic vegetable boxes, direct to the door. Growing over
60 varieties throughout the seasons, with five vegetables boxes. Prices start at £7
including delivery.

RUSSELL SMITH FARMS

COLLEGE FARM, GRANGE ROAD, DUXFORD, CAMBRIDGE CB2 4QF
Tel: 01223 839002 Fax: 01223 837874 Contact: Andrew Nottage
rsmithfarms@fwi.co.uk
Arable and field scale vegetables—producer. Soil Association membership no.
G2440.

THE TRADITIONAL GARDENING COMPANY

ASHVIEW, 48D BLACKHORSE DRIVE, LITTLEPORT, ELY CB6 1EG
Tel: 01353 861133 Contact: Sam Johnson
Landscape and gardening services. Providing landscaping design and the supply of
materials. Offering gardening and groundskeeping services. Promoting the use of
traditional and organic methods and principles in garden maintenance.

UNWINS SEEDS LTD
HISTON, CAMBRIDGE CB4 9LE
Tel: 01223 236236 Contact: Colin Hambidge
colin.hambidge@unwins-seeds.co.uk www.unwins-mailorder.co.uk
Soil Association P4413. Seedsman. Supplier of vegetable and flower seeds to gardeners.

WATERLAND ORGANICS
WILLOW FARM, LODE, CAMBRIDGE CB5 9HF
Tel: 01223 812912 Fax: 01223 812912 Contact: Paul Robinson
www.waterlandorganics.co.uk
Soil Association G1709. Run local box scheme around Cambridge. Supply local shops and restaurants with fruit and vegetables. Mail order strawberry and soft fruit bushes.

WILDCOUNTRY ORGANICS
11 CHALKY RD., GREAT ABINGTON, CAMBRIDGE CB1 6AT
Tel: 07787 552515 Fax: 01223 891804 Contact: Adrian Izzard
adrian@wildcountryorganics.co.uk www.wildcountryorganics.co.uk
We grow a wide variety of organic vegetables and salads all year round to supply box schemes, wholesalers and our own box scheme delivering in and around Cambridge. Alternative telephone: 01223 560038

Roasted Beetroot with Thyme
Fresh thyme combines brilliantly with the sweetness of baby beetroots, and gentle roasting enhances the flavour of both.

Wash 16 baby beetroots and dry. Toss them in a roasting tray with 4 tbsps of olive oil, sea salt, black pepper and a tsp of thyme leaves. Cook at 200°C for 10 minutes, then lower the temperature to 180°C for 30 minutes. Eat hot or cold with crusty French bread.

From *Allotment Gardening: An Organic Guide for Beginners* by Susan Berger, Green Books, £9.95.

FARM FRESH ORGANICS

LA BIENVENUE FARM, LA GRANDE ROUTE DE ST. LAURENT, ST. LAWRENCE,
JERSEY JE3 1GZ
Tel: 01534 861773 Fax: 01534 861772 Contact: Steven & Linda Carter
We grow a wide range of organic vegetables and import fruit which we supply island-wide through our box scheme. We supply pre-packed produce to supermarkets.

GUERNSEY ORGANIC GROWERS

LA MARCHERIE, RUETTE RABEY, ST MARTIN'S, GUERNSEY GY4 6DU
Tel: 01481 237547 Fax: 01481 233045 Contact: Anne Sandwith
guernseyorganics@cwgsy.net www.cwgsy.net/business/guernseyorganics
We operate a box delivery scheme in Guernsey, using as much of our own produce
as possible, supplemented with vegetables from Jersey organic farmers and occa-sionally topped up from the UK. We also offer organic fruit and Jersey organic eggs.

HANSA WHOLEFOOD

SOUTHSIDE, ST. SAMPSONS, GUERNSEY GY
Tel: 01481 249135 Contact: Ruby Farrell
hansa@cwgsy.net
Established 27 years; over 5,000 lines of quality vitamins, minerals, herbal products
(Solgar, FSC, etc). Natural toiletries, sports nutrition, wholefoods, organic products.
Mail order specialists. VAT-free. Friendly, reliable service.

HANSA WHOLEFOOD

20 FOUNTAIN ST., ST. PETER PORT, GUERNSEY GY1 1DA
Tel: 01481 723412 Fax: 01481 716388 Contact: Jane Molloy
hansa@cwgsy.net
Established 27 years; over 5,000 lines of quality vitamins, minerals, herbal products
(Solgar, FSC, etc). Natural toiletries, sports nutrition, wholefoods, organic products.
Mail order specialists. VAT-free. Friendly reliable service.

JERSEY DAIRY

FIVE OAKS DAIRY, ST. SAVIOUR, JERSEY JE2 7UD
Tel: 01534 818500 Fax: 01534 818535 Contact: Janet Wyatt
www.jerseydairy.je
Soil Association P4608. Dairy product range. Manufacture, supply and marketing.

THE ORGANIC SHOP

68 STOPFORD RD., ST. HELIER, JERSEY JE2 4LZ
Tel: 01534 789322 Contact: Celina Sochaczewska
Fresh fruit, vegetables, dairy, meat and poultry, wine and beer. Full range of
household cleaning materials and toiletries. Comprehensive delivery service
including box scheme.

VERMONT FARM

ROUTE DU COIN, ST. BRELADE, JERSEY JE3 8BT
Tel: 01534 742383 Fax: 01534 498500 Contact: John Hannon
We produce a large range of fresh seasonal organic vegetables, home-grown
strawberries and organic eggs. Organic pork, home-made sausages, organic whole
chickens, chicken joints and Christmas turkeys are all prepared in our butchery
room on the farm. In our farm shop we also sell a wide range of imported
organic fruit.

VERS LES MONTS ORGANIC FARM

LA RUE DE LA PRESSE, ST. PETER, JERSEY JE2 3FE
Tel: 01534 481573 Contact: Stephen Jones
Soil Association G2465 P5325. A small mixed farm producing a wide range of
mixed vegetables, potatoes and eggs, sold from the farm stall and box scheme.

ABBEY LEYS FARM

ABBEY LEYS FARM, PEACOCK LANE, HIGH LEGH, NR. KNUTSFORD WA16 6NS
Tel: 01925 753465 Fax: 01925 753465 Contact: Tim Harrison
tim.abbeyleys@virgin.net www.abbeyleys.co.uk
Soil Association G4985. Organic free range hens including Speckledy and Hebden
Black breeds. Free range duck eggs, home-grown Cheshire potatoes, fresh
vegetables, fruit, farmhouse ice cream, home-made cakes, cheese and Abbey Leys
honey. Local delivery available, not a box scheme.

ALLWOOD, MICHAEL & SANDRA

BURLAND FARM, WREXHAM ROAD, BURLAND, NANTWICH CW5 8ND
Tel: 01270 524210 Fax: 01270 524501 Contact: Sandra Allwood
info@ravensoakdairy.co.uk www.ravensoakdairy.co.uk
Wholesaling milk mainly to Ravens Oak Dairy.

AROMART

28 STOCKPORT RD., ROMILEY, STOCKPORT SK6 4BN
Tel: 0161 406 7176 Fax: 0161 494 1129 Contact: Susan Goto
aromart@tiscali.co.uk www.aromart.co.uk
We are a retail shop selling natural and organic products including herbs, spices
and herbal teas.

BARBER, JB & SON

BENTLEY FARM, WHITLEY, WARRINGTON WA4 4QA
Tel: 01925 730784 Contact: Philip Barber
barber@foxbent.freeserve.co.uk
Soil Association G4565. Dairy production and beef.

BOOTHS SUPERMARKETS
STANLEY ROAD, KNUTSFORD WA16 0BS
Tel: 01565 652522 Fax: 01565 652504 Contact: J Roskell
Supermarket with broad range of organic food, clearly labelled in store. Fresh produce, meat, dairy, Village Bakery products, many other groceries.

THE CHEESE SHOP
116 NORTHGATE STREET, CHESTER CH1 2HT
Tel: 01244 346240 Fax: 01244 314659 Contact: Carole Faulkner
carole@faulkner73.fsnet.co.uk www.chestercheeseshop.com
Specialist cheese shop with local delivery (not a box scheme). We promote local, organic and British cheeses, particularly cheeses sourced direct from the farm, mature and cared for in our cellars below the shop. Also organic wine, chutneys and biscuits.

CHESHIRE ORGANICS
5 BOOTHS HILL ROAD, LYMM WA13 0DJ
Tel: 01925 758575 Fax: 01925 758043 Contact: Jackie Lees
jackie@cheshireorganics.co.uk
Soil Association R2955. Over 1,000 product lines, fruit, vegetables, bread, dairy, grocery, gluten/dairy/sugar-free products, meat and poultry, homecare, wine and beer. All delivered direct to your home or office.

DEER PARK FARM
FORTY ACRE LANE, KERMINCHAM, HOLMES CHAPEL, CREWE CW4 8DX
Tel: 01477 532188 Fax: 01477 544638 Contact: Martin & Sue Steer
martin.steer@lineone.net
Organic lamb (whole and half) available to order. Steer Ethelston Rural Ltd. Rural Chartered Surveyors specialists in environmental and organic land management. Member of the Soil Association Organic Farms Network.

DEMETER WHOLEFOODS LTD
12 WELLES ST., SANDBACH CW11 1GT
Tel: 01270 760445 Contact: Phillip Shallcross
demeter@gynger.co.uk www.allaboutginger.co.uk
Retail outlet in Cheshire supplying the following organic merchandise: basic foodstuffs, drinks, culinary & medicinal herbs, nutritional supplements, environmentally sound cleaning products, recycled products. Trading in Sandbach since 1980, we have developed supply lines for a large number of obscure items which we increasingly despatch by post. The shop is widely described as 'fascinating'.

DUCKWORTH FLAVOURS
ASTMOOR ROAD, RUNCORN WA7 1PJ
Tel: 0161 886 0226 Fax: 0161 848 7331 Contact: Mike Gilligan
www.duckworth.co.uk
Manufacturer of organic fruit juice compounds. Supplier of organic fruit juices. Manufacturer of food flavourings suitable for use in organic products.

GOODLIFE FOODS LTD
34 TATTON COURT, KINGSLAND GRANGE, WARRINGTON WA1 4FF
Tel: 01925 837810 Fax: 01925 838648 Contact: Fran Sawyer
enquiry@goodlife.co.uk www.goodlife.co.uk
Manufacturer of frozen vegetarian foods. Soil Association P2241.

MARTON VILLA FARM
WHITE GATE, NR. WINSFORD CW7 2QG
Tel: 01829 760289 Contact: Robert Bates
Marton Villa is a 80-hectare mixed farm set in the heart of the Cheshire countryside. The farm converted to organic farming in 2001 with a long-term aim of being a mixed farm with laying hens and chickens, dairy cows, beef, sheep and bees. Marton Villa aims to sell much of its produce direct to the public, and welcomes visitors to the farm. Member of the Soil Association Organic Farms Network.

NATURE'S REMEDIES
10 TIME SQUARE, WARRINGTON WA1 2AR
Tel: 01925 444885 Fax: 01925 654821 Contact: Janet Hignett
Health food shop stocking wide range of organic foods.

NORTHERN HARVEST
KENYON HALL FARM, CROFT, WARRINGTON WA3 7ED
Tel: 01942 608299 Fax: 01942 608329 Contact: Ed Woolley
enquiry@northernharvest.co.uk www.northernharvest.co.uk
Award-winning home delivery service with over 3,000 products including fresh
produce, dairy, meat, bakery and eco-friendly goods. We deliver to Cheshire,
Greater Manchester, south Lancashire and Merseyside. Shop online at our website.

OAKCROFT ORGANIC GARDENS
OAK CROFT, CROSS 'O' THE HILL, MALPAS SY14 8DH
Tel: 01948 860213 Contact: M.S. Fardoonji
Organic since 1962. Grow large variety of veg and soft fruit, but offer fruit not
grown here, bread by order and eggs. All 100% organic. Delivery to CW5, SY14,
CW8, CW4, CH3, WA1. Nantwich, Crewe, Chester, Northwich, Knutsford areas.

ORGANIC ON THE HILL, BUTTERLANDS FARM
BUTTERLANDS FARM, WINCLE, MACCLESFIELD SK11 0QL
Tel: 01260 227672 Fax: 01260 227672 Contact: Jane & Brian Clarkson
jane@organiconthehill.com www.organiconthehill.com
Home-reared organic beef, lamb and pork. Grazed on clover-rich meadows, giving
an excellent taste and quality to the meat. Own processing facilities on the
farm allowing us to give individual and personal attention at all times. All
cuts available, including our own-recipe sausages and burgers. Local market in
Macclesfield attended every Friday, plus other local Farmers' Markets on monthly
basis. Please ring or email for further details and price list.

ORGANICFAIR

43 ST. JAMES ST., CHESTER CH1 3EY
Tel: 01244 400158 Fax: 01244 342228 Contact: Mark Holme
mark@organicfair.co.uk www.organicfair.co.uk
Organicfair is the award-winning store specialising in organic, Fairtrade and local products. We stock around 1500 lines and run a highly popular veg box delivery service for Chester, Cheshire and North Wales. We are open 6 days a week from 10am to 7pm.

THE ORGANIC VEG. COMPANY LTD.

131 WALTON RD, STOCKTON HEATH, WARRINGTON WA4 6NT
Tel: 01925 480895 Contact: Simon Howell
theorganicvegcompany@hotmail.co.uk
The Organic Veg. Company is a local firm committed to offering you, the consumer, fresh, quality organic, salad, fruit and vegetables. We offer this produce through our organic home delivery box scheme. Each week we select the best seasonal pro-duce available, then deliver fresh to your door in a choice of three box sizes. Of course there will always be staple foods such as potatoes, carrots, onions and apples; however, the rest of the box's content will vary depending on the season. Regardless of the time of year, you will always receive the best service and finest quality produce. We also offer eggs and supply to the trade as well as to our domestic customers.

RAVENS OAK DAIRY

BURLAND FARM, WREXHAM ROAD, BURLAND, NANTWICH CW5 8ND
Tel: 01270 524624 Fax: 01270 524724 Contact: Patrick Brunt
info@ravensoakdairy.com www.butlerscheeses.co.uk
Soft cow Brie and fresh cow cheese.

THE SALT COMPANY

WORLESTON, NANTWICH CW5 6DN
Tel: 01270 611112 Fax: 01270 611113 Contact: Dawn Storey
dawn@thesaltcompany.co.uk www.thesaltcompany.co.uk
Importer of Red Sea salt for use in the organic industry. Packer of salt for manufacturing and retail use.

STOCKLEY FARM ORGANICS

SMITHY FARMHOUSE, ARLEY, NORTHWICH CW9 6LZ
Tel: 01565 777492 Fax: 01565 777501 Contact: John Walton
organics@stockleyfarm.co.uk www.stockleyfarm.co.uk
Stockley Farm is open to the public and schools from March to October. Stockley
Farm Organics operates a box scheme, hand-delivered throughout Cheshire and
south Manchester.

SUGARBROOK FARM

MOBBERLEY RD., ASHLEY, NR. ALTRINCHAM WA14 3QB
Tel: 0161 928 0879 Contact: JF Erlam
mail@sugarbrookfarm.co.uk www.sugarbrookfarm.co.uk
Soil Association G4603. Bed and breakfast with en-suite facilities from £25 per
person, close to Manchester airport and Tatton Park. Sheep and arable farm
welcoming educational access under Countryside Stewardship i.e. free visits.

URENBIO

WOODPARK, NESTON, SOUTH WIRRAL CH64 7TB
Tel: 0151 353 0330 Fax: 0151 353 0251 Contact: Jamie Uren
james.uren@uren.co.uk www.uren.com/organic
Soil Association P1723. Urenbio imports, distributes and stocks a wide range of
organic ingredients for food manufacturing: fruits, vegetables, beans, seeds, nuts,
honey, oils, etc.. We also re-clean and pack in our store in Whitchurch, Shropshire.

	Accommodation		Garden and Farm Sundries		Producers
	Box Schemes/ Local Deliveries		Farmers' market Stall		Restaurants/ Cafés/Caterers
	Day Visits		Manufacturers/ Processors		Retail shops
	Eco Products		Importers/ exporters		Textiles
	Farm Gate Sales		Mail order suppliers		Wholesalers

A & N HEALTH FOODS

62 FORE ST., SALTASH PL12 6JW
Tel: 01752 844926 Contact: Janice Clegg
Small health food shop selling organic and non-organic produce. We have a veg box scheme, large selection of vitamins and minerals, gluten-free, dairy-free etc.

ALDERMAN, CG

MENABURLE FARM, BOCONNOC, LOSTWITHIEL PL22 0RT
Tel: 01208 873703 Contact: Chris Alderman cgalderman@hotmail.com
A mixed farm of cereals, vegetables, sheep and beef, which also offers self-catering accommodation.

ARCHIE BROWNS HEALTHFOODS

OLD BREWERY YARD, BREAD ST., PENZANCE TR18 2EQ
Tel: 01736 362828 Contact: Helen Swift
Retail shop and vegetarian/vegan restaurant selling organic and/or vegan dairy, goats milk, cheeses, yoghurts, soya products, jams, chocolates, pasta, flour, cereals, nuts, grains, fruits, pulses, biscuits, artisan bread, preserves, honey, drinks, gluten-free products, natural beauty products, natural cleaning products. Deli counter and oriental section.

BANGORS ORGANIC TEA ROOM, RESTAURANT AND B&B

BANGORS HOUSE, POUNDSTOCK, BUDE EX23 0DP
Tel: 01288 361297 Fax: 01288 361508 Contact: Gill Faiers
info@bangorsorganic.co.uk www.bangorsorganic.co.uk
The first certified, totally organic tea room in the UK. We are open throughout the summer, serving traditional cream teas and home-made cakes, splits and bread. The lunchtime restaurant (from 12 to 2.30pm) serves delicious freshly prepared lunches, using seasonal ingredients from our own organic gardens as well as locally sourced produce, complemented by a good selection of organic wines beer and cider. Luxury bed & organic breakfast accommodation available all year round. Superb location one mile from the sea on the North Cornish coast.

BARWICK FARM

TREGONY, TRURO TR2 5SG
Tel: 01872 530208 Contact: Nick & Barbara Michell
nick@michell.fsbusiness.co.uk www.theorganicfarmersmarket.co.uk
Soil Association G7204. Producing Cornish Jersey dairy products: milk, butter,
clotted cream and liquid creams from our own cows. Good, healthy, natural products.

BODINNICK FARM

ST STEPHENS, ST AUSTELL TR2 4EH
Tel: 01726 882421 Contact: Charles & Rose Barnecut
rose.barnecut@virgin.net
Cornish family-run farm producing prime organic beef and lamb for top local and
London outlets. Box scheme direct from farm for local customers.

BOSAVERN FARM

ST. JUST, PENZANCE TR19 7RD
Tel: 01736 786739 Fax: 01736 786739 Contact: Guy & Joanna Clegg
joandguy@bosavern.fsnet.co.uk
Farm Gate shop, open Saturdays 10am–2pm. Selling freshly picked organic
vegetables, organic beef, naturally reared pork and free-range eggs, all produced at
Bosavern Farm.

BOSWEDNACK MANOR

ZENNOR, ST IVES TR26 3DD
Tel: 01736 794183 Contact: E Gynn
boswednack@ravenfield.co.uk
Peaceful vegetarian B&B on 3-acre wildlife reserve and smallholding. Five rooms
and self-catering cottage. Sea, sunsets, superb walks, non-smoking. St. Ives,
Tate Gallery and beaches 5 miles.

BROWDA FARM

LINKINHORNE, CALLINGTON PL17 7NB
Tel: 01579 362235 Contact: Lavinia Halliday
Soil Association G4671. East Cornwall: Bed and breakfast accommodation in our large comfortable 17th-century farmhouse on lovely 250-acre organic farm near Bodmin Moor. Informal and friendly. Wonderfully peaceful and gloriously unspoilt. B&B £32pp pn. No smoking, no pets.

CALLESTICK VEAN FARM

CALLESTICK VEAN, TRURO TR4 9NF
Tel: 01872 561442 Contact: P Hilton
peter@vean73.freeserve.co.uk
Soil Association G3072. Producers of organic North Devon cattle.

CAMEL VALLEY FARM SHOP

ST. KEW SERVICES, BODMIN, NR. WADEBRIDGE PL30 3ED
Tel: 01208 841343 Fax: 01208 841343 Contact: Alan Vague
info@camelvalleyfarms.co.uk
Meat, cheeses, yoghurt, vegetables, ice cream, pickles, chutneys, eggs, bread.

CAMEL VALLEY FARMS

LOWER TREDORE, ST. ISSEY, WADEBRIDGE PL27 7QS
Tel: 01841 540767 Fax: 01841 540767 Contact: Alan & Margaret Vague
alan@camelvalleyfarms.freeserve.com www.camelvalleyfarms.co.uk
We produce and sell our own beef, pork, lamb and vegetables. We also have a farm shop at St. Kew Highway, nr. Wadebridge, where we sell other local produce. Alternative phone/fax: 01208 841343.

CARLEYS OF CORNWALL LTD

34–36 ST. AUSTELL STREET, TRURO TR1 1SE
Tel: 01872 277686 Fax: 01872 277686 Contact: John & Rachel Carley
sales@carleys.co.uk www.carleys.co.uk
Soil Association P1584. We are an organic supermarket specialising in locally
produced fresh fruit and vegetables, meat and dairy foods. We also import
fruit and veg directly from suppliers, manufacture our own 'Carleys' brand
products, and have a rapidly expanding home delivery service.

CARLEYS ORGANIC FOODS LTD

THE PARADE, TRURO TR1 1UJ
Tel: 01872 270091 Fax: 01872 270092 Contact: John Carley
sales@carleys.co.uk www.carleys.co.uk
We manufacture our own 'Carleys' brand products.

THE CHEESE SHOP

29 FERRIS TOWN, TRURO TR1 3JH
Tel: 01872 270742 Contact: The Manager
Farmhouse cheeses handmade and unpasteurised, including organic cheeses from
Cornwall and across the UK.

CHURCHTOWN FARM

CHURCHTOWN FARM, LANTEGLOS BY FOWEY PL23 1NH
Tel: 01726 870375 Fax: 01726 870376 Contact: M & C Russell
National Trust coastal farm selling organic beef and lamb. Extensive range available
in any quantity including delicious barbecue products. Phone first. Soil Association
no. G 1784. Organic Food Awards 2004: Fresh Meat, Highly Commended.

COOMBE MILL FARM

PILLATON MILL, NR. SALTASH PL12 5AN
Tel: 01579 350315 Contact: Giles and Angela Greenhough
Organic lamb and eggs.

CORNISH ORGANICS

FOUR LANES, REDRUTH TR16 6LZ
Tel: 01209 215789 Fax: 01209 202579 Contact: Kim Thomas
cornishorganics@hotmail.com
Totally organic farm shop. Our own Aberdeen Angus beef, Large Black pork and bacon, eggs, veg and fruit. Bread baked daily in the farmhouse kitchen, milk and cream from our own cows, ice cream, fish and lots more.

COSWINASAWSIN

THE DUCHY COLLEGE, ROSEWARNE, CAMBOURNE TR14 0AB
Tel: 01209 722100 Fax: 01209 722159 Contact: Steve Roderick
Coswinsawsin grows a variety of crops including field vegetables, sugar beet, potatoes, and cereals. Farm trail, educational visits, open days and farm walks are all available by arrangement with the office. Coswinsawsin Farm is an important resource for the newly created Organic Studies Centre at the Duchy College, Rosewarne, and is the most westerly of the Elm Farm Research Centre demonstration farms network. Member of the Soil Association Organic Farms Network.

COTNA ORGANICS

COTNA BARTON, COTNA LANE, GORRAN, ST. AUSTELL PL26 6LG
Tel: 01726 844827 Fax: 01726 844827 Contact: Mike Nicholson
mikenich@gn.apc.org www.cotnaorganics.co.uk
Renewable energy demos. Wide variety of exotic and culinary vegetables, herbs and fruits. Free range eggs. Visitors welcome any time—come and see our ecobarn along with wind turbine and solar panels.

COUNTRYSTORE HEALTHFOODS

3–5 BOND STREET, REDRUTH TR15 2QA
Tel: 01209 215012 Contact: The Manager
2 shops, one completely organic, selling a whole range of organic foods, eco-products, bodycare, babycare, toiletries, etc.

CUSGARNE ORGANIC FARM

CUSGARNE WOLLAS, CUSGARNE, NR. TRURO TR4 8RL

Tel: 01872 865922 Contact: Teresa & Greg Pascoe

organicbox@btconnect.com

Box scheme serving from Helston to Fowey and in between. Grow more than 70 varieties of organic vegetables and fruit, organic free range eggs, organic Angus x suckler herd for beef.

CUT4CLOTH

4 FORE ST., CONSTANTINE, FALMOUTH TR11 5AB

Tel: 01326 340956 Fax: 01326 340956 Contact: Kurt Jewson

kurt@cut4cloth.co.uk www.cut4cloth.co.uk

Cut4Cloth offer an extensive range of bright and funky organic cotton baby and children's clothing. Retailing via www.cut4cloth.co.uk, and wholesale by request.

EAST PENREST FARM

LEZANT, LAUNCESTON PL15 9NR

Tel: 01579 370186 Contact: J Rider

jrider@lineone.net www.eastpenrest.freeserve.co.uk

Lamb sold from the farm gate as available; please telephone first. Beef sold wholesale.

GEAR FARM SHOP

ST. MARTIN, HELSTON TR12 6DE

Tel: 01326 221150 Fax: 01326 221150 Contact: David Webb

gearfarmshop.hotmail.com

Farm shop selling organic vegetables, fruit, bakery, wholefoods, dairy, fish.

GOONGILLINGS FARM

GOONGILLINGS FARM, CONSTANTINE, FALMOUTH TR11 5RP
Tel: 01326 340630 Contact: CL Pugh
enquiries@goongillings.co.uk www.goongillings.co.uk
Soil Association G4621. Four attractive holiday cottages and a restored antique
gypsy caravan on a beautiful waterside organic farm, on the renowned Helford
River in West Cornwall. Quay, boats, tennis court. Pets welcome.

THE GRANARY

NEWHAM ROAD, TRURO TR1 2ST
Tel: 01872 274343 Fax: 01872 223477 Contact: Jill Thomas
sales@granarywholefoods.co.uk www.granarywholefoods.co.uk
Wholesale distributors of health foods, natural foods and delicatessen products
throughout Cornwall, Devon, Somerset, parts of Wiltshire and Dorset.

GREAT GARGUS FARM

TREGONY, TRURO TR2 5SQ
Tel: 01872 530274 Fax: 01872 530274 Contact: Rachel Heywood
gargonauts@farming.co.uk
Lamb, grown on Cornish grass, from our long-standing Dorset x Texel flock. Whole
or half, jointed and packed to choice, ready for freezer or oven, available to order.
Simply delicious.

THE GREENHOUSE

6 HIGH ST., ST. KEVERNE, HELSTON TR12 6NN
Tel: 01326 280800 Contact: Neil & Leonie Woodward
thegreenhouse-stkeverne@hotmail.co.uk www.thegreenhouse-stkeverne.co.uk
We are not certified organic as yet. All our wines, beers and spirits are organic on
top of meat, vegetables, dairy, and dry store goods.

HEART OF DEVON ORGANICS

C/O 37 JUBILEE STREET, NEWQUAY TR7 1LA
Tel: 01647 24894 Fax: 01647 24894 Contact: Geoff Jones
The largest sole wholesaler of quality organic fresh fruit and vegetables in the
South-west. Working closely with local and near continent growers (visit website).
Deliveries from M4 to Lands End.

HELSETT FARM CORNISH ICE CREAM

HELSETT FARM, LESNEWTH, BOSCASTLE PL35 0HP
Tel: 01840 261207 Contact: Sarah Talbot-Ponsonby
helsett.icccream@lineone.net
Manufacturer of real Cornish ice cream made in small batches. No stabilisers or
emulsifiers, all added ingredients e.g. butterscotch, fruit purée, prepared in the dairy.

HELSETT LAMB

HELSETT FARM, THE BUNGALOW, LESNEWTH, BOSCASTLE PL35 0HP
Tel: 01840 261713 Contact: Nina Talbot-Ponsonby
ntalbotponsonby@aol.com
Seasonal lamb, hoggets, mutton. Will sell privately by arrangement; telephone
first for availability.

HENDRA FARM ORGANICS

HENDRA FARM, ROSE, TRURO TR4 9PS
Tel: 01872 572301 Fax: 01872 572301 Contact: Janet Symons
josymons@bushinternet.com
A wide range of vegetables grown for box scheme. Salads and leafy greens
usually picked the morning of delivery. Beef available to order.

KEIGWIN FARMHOUSE

NR. MORVAH, PENZANCE TR19 7TS
Tel: 01736 786425 Fax: 01736 786425 Contact: Gilly Wyatt-Smith
g.wyatt-smith@virgin.net www.yewtreegallery.com
Member of the Soil Association, registered with the Wholesome Food Association.
Vegetarian B&B in a 300 year old farmhouse on Penwith peninsula. Organic and
home-grown and home-made produce; extensive gardens and beach nearby. Packs
of herbs and saladings for sale.

KENIDJACK FARM

ST. JUST IN PENWITH TR19 7QW
Tel: 01736 788675 Contact: Mike Bratt
Soil Association symbol holder. Dexter cattle.

KEVERAL FARMERS LTD

KEVERAL FARM, NR SEATON, LOOE PL13 1PA
Tel: 01503 250135 Contact: Gina Cooper
www.keveral.org
Soil Association PK02W. Workers' co-op, organic veg and fruit sold through local
box scheme. Also available: apple juice and cider, preserves, Shiitake/oyster
mushrooms and fruiting logs, wild magic liquid feed, organic herb plants, willow
cuttings, camping.

LANSALLOS BARTON FARM

LANSALLOS, LOOE PL13 2PU
Tel: 01503 272293 Contact: Mark Russell
Soil Association Demonstration Farm. Cream teas and organic meat for sale in
tearoom. Open at Easter and June to September. Member of the Soil Association
Organic Farms Network.

LESQUITE FARM

LANSALLOS, LOOE PL13 2QE
Tel: 01503 220315 Fax: 01503 220137 Contact: Richard & Annette Tolputt
tolputt@lesquite-polperro.fsnet.co.uk www.lesquite-polperro.fsnet.co.uk
Bed and breakfast, self-catering, organic potatoes, Aberdeen Angus vacuum-
packed beef, all found on delightful secluded farm, easily accessible to all
parts of Cornwall: 3 miles to the coast, between Fowey and Polperro.

LITTLE CALLESTOCK FARM

ZELAH, TRURO TR4 9HB
Tel: 01872 540445 Fax: 01872 540445 Contact: Liz & Nick Down
liznick@littlecallestockfarm.co.uk www.littlecallestockfarm.co.uk
Organic Farmers and Growers UKF090940. Delightful spacious barn conversions,
ETC 4 and 5 stars, luxuriously equipped. Whirlpool baths, four-poster beds,
woodburners, on organic dairy farm with Jersey herd. Peaceful location,
countryside, coastal walks. Centrally positioned. Brochure available. Organic
eggs from farm gate.

LOWER POLGRAIN

ST. WENN, BODMIN PL30 5PS
Tel: 01637 880082 Contact: Jenni Thomson
Organic beef by arrangement, telephone first.

MAKING WAVES VEGAN GUEST HOUSE

3 RICHMOND PLACE, ST IVES TR26 1JN
Tel: 01736 793895 Contact: Simon Money
simon@making-waves.co.uk www.making-waves.co.uk
Beautiful eco-renovated 19th-century house. Ocean views, peaceful, minutes from
shop, beaches and harbour. Delicious organic food. Special diets catered for.
Children welcome. Voted Best Vegan Guest House (*Vegan* magazine).

MALCHRIS
GRAVESEND GARDENS, TORPOINT PL11 2HN
Tel: 01752 815508 Contact: M. Whitworth
Top fruit, soft fruit and vegetables.

MANN, J & P
PENWARNE, FALMOUTH TR11 5PH
Tel: 01326 250136 Contact: J & P Mann
Organic beef.

MARSHLAND MANOR
MORWENSTOW, BUDE EX23 9ST
Tel: 01288 331349 Contact: Jane Marsh
Herd of pedigree Aberdeen Angus suckler cows sold to producers. Traditional
organic Cornish apple orchard suitable for cider making and cooking.

MASSINGALE, STEPHEN CW
HIGH MEADOWS, MORWENSTOW, BUDE EX23 9PH
Tel: 01420 520888 Fax: 01420 22348 Contact: Stephen Massingale
Soil Association G5021. Organic Southdown lamb produced.

MEWTON, PG
NANCARROW FARM, MARANZANVOSE, TRURO TR4 9DQ
Tel: 01872 540343 Contact: PG Mewton
pgmewton@talk21.com
Great beef and great lamb, organic, wholesome and delicious. Meat as it should
be! Tastes just right.

MICROTECH PRODUCTION HOLDINGS PLC

MICROTECH PRODUCTION HOLDINGS PLC, 13D CARDREW INDUSTRIAL ESTATE, REDRUTH TR15 1PS
Tel: 01209 314734 Fax: 01209 314694 Contact: Chris Gates
cgates@microtechph.com www.microtechph.com
Manufacturer of seaweed based plant feeds and fertilisers for horticultural/ agricultural/ gardening markets sold under the ShoreGrow logo. Microtech also manufacture non-toxic, non-chemical insect traps including indoor and outdoor fly traps, a wasp trap and a cockroach trap.

THE NATURAL STORE

TRENGROUSE WAY, HELSTON TR13 8RT
Tel: 01326 564226 Fax: 01326 564226 Contact: Paul Johnson
A comprehensive range of organic foods, wholefoods and natural remedies including organic fruit and vegetables and organic meat. Natural foods and products of all sorts, including babycare and eco-friendly cleaning products in our newly extended premises.

THE NATURAL STORE

16 HIGH ST., FALMOUTH TR11 2AB
Tel: 01326 311507 Fax: 01326 311507 Contact: Paul Johnson
A comprehensive range of organic foods, wholefoods and natural remedies including organic fruit and vegetables, organic meat. Natural foods and products of all sorts. Eco friendly babycare and cleaning products.

OIL IN THE RAW

DILLETTS COTTAGE, ST. DOMINICK PL12 6TE
Tel: 01579 351178 Contact: Dina Iwanski
dina@oilintheraw.co.uk www.oilintheraw.co.uk
Direct supplies to restaurants and private households. Import and distribution of organic olive oil, table olives and olive paté direct from Greek organic farms—mostly single estates. Greek organic inspection body: DIO 21301930156; 23301980033; 26301980575; 21301940085 and Greek organic inspection body: SOYE 013061.

OLDS, VIVIAN LTD
2 CHAPEL ROAD, ST. JUST, PENZANCE TR19 7HS
Tel: 01736 788520 Fax: 01736 788520 Contact: Randall Olds
mail@vivianolds.co.uk www.vivianolds.co.uk
Soil Association P2997. Butchers with own slaughterhouse offering local and
nationwide delivery of locally reared and purchased organic beef, pork and lamb
including meat boxes. Why not try our special sausages?

THE ORGANIC BREWHOUSE
UNIT 1, HIGHER BOCHYM RURAL WORKSHOPS, CURY CROSS LANES,
HELSTON TR12 7AZ
Tel: 01326 241555 Contact: Andy Hamer
a.hamer@btclick.com
Soil Association registered. Brewery producing solely organic real ales in cask-
and bottle-conditioned form.

ORIGIN COFFEE
MILL HOUSE, TREWARDREVA MILL, CONSTANTINE, FALMOUTH TR11 5QD
Tel: 01326 340320 Fax: 01326 340660 Contact: Tom Sobey
tom@origincoffee.co.uk www.origincoffee.co.uk
Origin Coffee trade in outstanding environmentally and ethically sound coffees
in volumes suitable for catering and retail. Origin organic coffee is shade-grown in
Papua New Guinea. It has an intense, well rounded, fruit flavour, with lush nutty
chocolate overtones. Available in espresso bean, espresso grind and cafetière grind.

OUGHS UNICORN GROCERS
10 MARKET ST., LISKEARD PL14 3JJ
Tel: 01579 343253 Contact: The Manager
www.oughs.co.uk
Delicatessen stocking some organic goods.

PENHEALE ORGANICS LTD

1 RUNDLE COURT, STATION ROAD, LISKEARD PL14 4DA
Tel: 01579 345777 Fax: 01579 346886 Contact: Ray Boyd
rayboyd@btconnect.com www.cornishlegend.co.uk
Manufacturers of the Cornish Legend range of luxury organic ice creams; a wide and interesting range of Cornish products, all made at our creamery in Liskeard, using milk from our own organic dairy farm. Winners of the 2004 Soil Association Organic Food Awards Ice Cream section, plus Highly Commended in the same category.

PLANTS FOR A FUTURE

THE FIELD, HIGHER PENPOL, ST. VEEP, LOSTWITHIEL PL22 0NG
Tel: 01208 873554
www.pfaf.org
Day visits and tours, courses on woodland gardening, permaculture, nutrition, research, information, demonstration and supply of edible and otherwise useful plants. Plants for a Future is a registered charity researching and demonstrating ecologically sustainable vegan organic horticulture in the form of woodland gardening and other permacultural practices.

PURE NUFF STUFF

THE EGYPTIAN HOUSE, 6 CHAPEL ST., PENZANCE TR18 6AJ
Tel: 01736 366008 Fax: 01736 366008 Contact: Helen Prudames
helen@purenuffstuff.co.uk www.purenuffstuff.co.uk
100% natural skincare, toiletries and cosmetics with pure essential oils and organic ingredients. Free of SLS, paraben, synthetic fragrance, synthetic colours.

RENAS-NATURALS

PO BOX 140, PENZANCE TR18 4YW
Tel: 01736 732399 Fax: 01736 732399 Contact: Rena Hine
info@renas-naturals.com www.renas-naturals.com
Very special gifts! Handmade cosmetics including our own big range of over 70 unusual, handmade designer soaps filled with organic ingredients. Website also sells organic & fair-traded teas and links to other interesting sites. Wholesale to Europe & New Zealand.

RIDER, J & J
EAST PENREST, LEZANT, LAUNCESTON PL15 9NR
Tel: 01579 370186 Fax: 01579 370477 Contact: Jo Rider
jrider@lineone.net www.eastpenrest.freeserve.co.uk
Soil Association G1897. Organic beef and sheep farm of 120 acres with 5 star
self-catering accommodation in converted barn. Children especially welcome.
Beautiful countryside. Home cooked meals available. Lamb sold from the farm
gate as available; please telephone first.

RIVERFORD HOME DELIVERY
6 CAMELOT VIEW, CAMELFORD PL32 9TU
Tel: 01840 211470 Contact: Sharon Managou
sharon@riverfordhomedelivery.co.uk www.riverford.co.uk
Licensed distributor for Riverford Organic Vegetables. Organic vegetable box
scheme operating in north & mid-Cornwall, varied box sizes delivered to your
door. Can order online at www.riverford.co.uk.

RIVERFORD HOME DELIVERY WEST CORNWALL
VEYN BARN, BENOAK, ST.KEYNE, LISKEARD PL14 4RR
Tel: 01579 346134 Fax: 01579 346134 Contact: Joyce Bennallick
tonyandjoyce@riverfordhomedelivery.co.uk
West Cornwall's independent local licensed distributor from Riverford Organic
Vegetables award-winning vegetable box scheme. Weekly home delivery to most
areas of west Cornwall.

ROSEVINNICK ORGANIC FARM
BOFARNEL, LOSTWITHIEL PL22 0LP
Tel: 01208 871122 Contact: Doreen Hassell
Organic beef, pork, ham, bacon, pork sausages and hogs pudding from traditional
Large Black pigs, chives, parsley and sage. Telephone first.

ROSKILLY'S ORGANIC FARM

ROSKILLY'S, TREGELLAST BARTON FARM, ST KEVERNE, HELSTON TR12 6NX
Tel: 01326 280479 Contact: Vicky Rogers
vicky@roskillys.co.uk www.roskillys.co.uk
A family-run organic Jersey farm on the Lizard Peninsula in Cornwall.
Producing various products using their organic Jersey milk including an award-winning organic clotted cream fudge.

ROSUICK ORGANIC FARM & CORNISH CAMELS

ROSUICK ORGANIC FARM, ST.MARTIN, HELSTON TR12 6DZ
Tel: 01326 231302 Fax: 01326 231302 Contact: Chris Oates
oates@rosuick.co.uk www.oatesorganic.co.uk
Family-run organic farm and shop specialising in home-produced beef, lamb, pork, sausages, burgers, eggs, veg and organic wool along with other local gifts. Great for a day visit to see the camels, farm and shop. Beautiful farmhouses, sleep 10/11; cottages, sleep 6, available for holidays. All with modern facilities and access to tennis court. Well worth a visit. Also available: camel trekking with 'Cornish Camels' operating from the farm. Most of the self-catering cottages are less than 20 metres from the camel pen and are surrounded by a multitude of free range barn yard animals. See website for more details, also www.cornishcamels.co.uk.

SCILLY ORGANICS

MIDDLE TOWN, ST. MARTINS, ISLES OF SCILLY TR25 0QN
Tel: 01720 423663 Contact: Jonathan Smith
enquiries@scillyorganics.co.uk www.scillyorganics.co.uk
Scilly Organics is a small-scale market garden producing a wide range of vegetables, fruit and herbs for local sale. Run on permaculture principles, diversity is paramount. Visitors welcome—by appointment please.

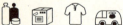

SMILECHILD

UNITS 3 & 10, CALLINGTON BUSINESS PARK, TINNERS WAY, MOSS SIDE
INDUSTRIAL ESTATE, CALLINGTON PL17 7SH
Tel: 0800 1956 982 Fax: 01579 383050 Contact: Rebecca Cambridge
customerservices@smilechild.co.uk www.smilechild.co.uk
Online shopping for the planet-conscious parent. Smilechild offers a full range
of fair-trade and organic clothes, wooden toys, natural toiletries, eco-nappies
and more. Founded in 2000, this family-run business has dedicated itself to
bringing the best for mother, baby and the environment to your door. Backed by
the Prince's Youth Business Trust and finalists in the Gloucestershire
Environmental Business Awards. Visit Smilechild for shopping, information and discussion or request a catalogue.

SOUTH PENQUITE FARM

SOUTH PENQUITE, BLISLAND, BODMIN PL30 4LH
Tel: 01208 850491 Fax: 0870 136 7926 Contact: Dominic & Cathy Fairman
thefarm@bodminmoor.co.uk www.southpenquite.co.uk
Soil Association G4771. Camping and field studies on a working organic hill
farm high on Bodmin Moor. Interesting farm walk, including diverse wildlife
habitats, a bronze age hut settlement, a mile of beautiful river bank and an
imposing standing stone. Mongolian Yurt available for that 'back to nature'
holiday! Member of the Soil Association Organic Farms Network.

SOUTH TORFREY FARM LTD/ORGANIC FARM HOLIDAYS

GOLLANT, FOWEY PL23 1LA
Tel: 01726 833126 Fax: 01726 832625 Contact: Debbie Andrews
www.southtorfreyfarm.com
Soil Association G2019. A small family farm growing poultry for meat, Longhorn
cattle and mixed arable crops. We offer peaceful breaks in our award-winning
barn conversions—children and pets very welcome.

SPIEZIA ORGANICS LTD

DOVE HOUSE, TREGONIGGIE, FALMOUTH TR11 4SN
Tel: 0870 850 8851 Fax: 01326 377712 Contact: Marianne Tregoning
info@spieziaorganics.com www.spieziaorganics.com
Skincare: 100% organic skin care, body care and healing ointments, handmade in
Cornwall by Dr Mariano Spiezia. Infusions of herbs and flowers in oils to make
highly concentrated, water-free ointments. For all skin types, especially sensitive
and delicate. Also soaps and home fragrances. See display ad.

STAMPAS FARM

TREAMBLE, ROSE, TRURO TR4 9PR
Tel: 01872 572837 Contact: Michael R Payne
Soil Association GCS081/G2322. Organic market garden growing vegetables and
soft fruits for sale at local country markets (Truro and Perranporth). Some
produce sold through local box schemes and direct from the farm.

STEPHEN GELLY FARM

LANIVET, BODMIN PL30 5AX
Tel: 01208 831213/832557 Contact: Martin Collinge
mhcollinge@aol.com
Organic poultry, lamb and beef.

STERLING, P & V

GLUVIAN FARM, MAWGAN PORTH, NEWQUAY TR8 4BG
Tel: 01637 860635 Fax: 01637 860635 Contact: Mr Sterling
Organic beef and lamb producers.

STONEYBRIDGE ORGANYKS

TYWARDREATH, PAR PL24 2TY
Tel: 01726 813858 Contact: David Pascoe
Vegetables, soft fruit and herbs. Also retail SA certified organic meat. Farm
shop open Tuesdays to Saturday noon, from Easter to the end of October.

SUNFLOWER WHOLEFOODS
16A CROSS ST., CAMBORNE TR14 8EX
Tel: 01209 715970 Contact: M. Webb
Organic wholefoods.

TREE OF LIFE ORGANICS
SCALA NIJ, MITHIAN, ST AGNES, TRURO TR5 0QE
Tel: 01872 552661 Contact: Marie Welsh
treeoflife@eurobell.co.uk
Soil Association registered nos. P2068, G2068. We are a small company that is committed to the sustainable organic way of life. We can supply top quality fresh fruit and vegetables and eggs produced locally. Delivery area: Perranporth, St. Agnes, Redruth, Truro and St. Austell.

TRELEASE FARM
ST. KEVERNE TR12 6RT
Tel: 01326 280379 Contact: John Pascoe
john@trelease.biz
Poultry and eggs, beef cattle, sheep, pigs and vegetables. Attends variety of farmer's markets. Holiday cottages to let.

TRENBERTH, WD & BD
TREVALLARD FARM, MOUNT HAWKE, TRURO TR4 8DL
Tel: 01209 890253 Contact: D Trenberth
Soil Association G2763. Producing beef and winter vegetables.

TRETHINNICK FARM
ST. CLEER, LISKEARD PL14 6RR
Tel: 01579 346868 Contact: CM & PT Gregory
Organic lamb and beef supplied to own local client base.

TREVARNO ORGANIC SKINCARE

TREVARNO MANOR, HELSTON TR13 0AB
Tel: 01326 555977 Fax: 01326 574282 Contact: Brenda Clark
enquiry@trevarno.co.uk www.trevarno.co.uk
We produce a wide range of natural skin care products including facial cleansing, toning and moisturising. Hand care, body care and a dedicated baby care range. A full range of natural organic soaps are also available.

TREVAYLOR ORGANIC EGGS

TREVAYLOR, KILLIOW, REA, TRURO TR3 6AG
Tel: 01872 864 949 Contact: Jayne Spenceley
Organic eggs.

TREVELYAN FARM

ROSUDGEON, PENZANCE TR20 9PP
Tel: 01736 710410 Contact: Tim Jones
Organic seasonal vegetables, meat and other local produce.

WAINGATES FARM

STRATTON, BUDE EX23 9DL
Tel: 01288 356828 Contact: Barbara Mills
barbara.mills2@btopenworld.com
Soil Association G4152. Holiday accommodation: Bed and Breakfast plus self-catering on organic holding one and a half miles from sandy beach.

WETHERDEN, BEN & CATHY

DOWNACAREY BRIDGE, ST GILES ON THE HEATH, LAUNCESTON PL15 9RT
Tel: 01566 775732 Contact: Ben & Cathy Wetherden
info@organicpullets.co.uk www.organicpullets.co.uk
Organic pullets available all year, Black Rock, Speckeldy, Utility Light Sussex, Lohmann Tradition, Silver Link, Bluebell and Magpie, any age, any quantity. Delivery possible others reared to order.

WIDDICOMBE FARE
4 WEST ST., MILLBROOK, TORPOINT PL10 1AA
Tel: 01752 822335 Contact: Jo Widdicombe
jowidd@beeb.net
Retail fruit and vegetables, wholefoods etc including large range of organic produce.

WOODA FARM
CRACKINGTON HAVEN EX23 0LF
Tel: 01840 230140 Contact: Max Burrows
max@woodafarm.co.uk www.woodafarm.co.uk
Producer of organic lamb, eggs, apples, juice and vegetables. Self-catering
cottage or catered accommodation with large barn workspace.

Using Less Washing Powder
I experimented by cutting the dosage in half. The clothes got clean. I cut it in half again—the water still felt "slippery", and the laundry got clean. I continued in this way, and found that a heaped teaspoon, or even less, was enough for my laundry. I also discovered that cuffs and collars did not get really clean no matter how much detergent I used—they had to be scrubbed by hand. Using so little detergent I needed only one rinse cycle, not the four rinses that are standard on my machine. So I could use less rinse water and be finished in half the time. One kilogram of detergent powder now lasts me 2 years!
From *Ecology Begins at Home* by Archie Duncanson, Green Books, £4.95.

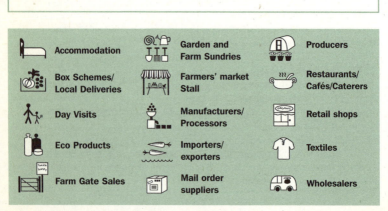

Accommodation

Box Schemes/Local Deliveries

Day Visits

Eco Products

Farm Gate Sales

Garden and Farm Sundries

Farmers' market Stall

Manufacturers/Processors

Importers/exporters

Mail order suppliers

Producers

Restaurants/Cafés/Caterers

Retail shops

Textiles

Wholesalers

ALADDIN AROMAS
NENTHEAD, ALSTON CA9 3NP
Tel: 01434 382820 Fax: 01434 382820 Contact: Adam Herdman
alaromas@aol.com www.aladdinaromas.co.uk
Aromatherapy products—essential oils. Available by mail order only.

ALLEGARTH ORGANICS
ALLEGARTH, ROWELTOWN, CARLISLE CA6 6JU
Tel: 01697 748065 Contact: Stuart Boyd & Julia Cobby
Soil Association G797. A 12-acre smallholding offering unique holiday
accommodation for up to 8 persons in a secluded and unspoilt part of North
Cumbria. A member of Hadrian Organics.

ALSTON WHOLEFOODS LIMITED
FRONT STREET, ALSTON CA9 3HU
Tel: 01434 381588 Contact: Carol Sutton
Workers co-operative shop with range of wholefoods and organic products.
Speciality cheeses, dietary needs, local eggs, bread, cakes, mustards. Walkers'
and cyclists' snacks, delicious ice creams. Mon–Sat, 9am–5pm.

THE ANIMAL HEALING CENTRE
HEGGERSCALES COTT, KABER, KIRKBY STEPHEN CA17 4HZ
Tel: 01768 372691 Contact: Joy Barrett
joy@animalhealing.org.uk www.animalhealing.org.uk
We educate about natural healing methods for pets, equines and farm animals and
sell 100% organic product remedies. We sell 100% organic wormers, probiotics
and a variety of supplements.

ASKERTON CASTLE ESTATE

ASKERTON CASTLE, BRAMPTON CA8 2BD
Tel: 01697 73332 Contact: Jane Eden & Chris Evans
askerton.castle@btinternet.com www.askertoncastle.co.uk
Quality meat producer—our pedigree Belted Galloway cattle, Scottish Blackface
and Kerry Hill sheep, traditional purebred laying hens and hybrid table birds are all
born and bred on the farm. We also breed alpacas. Visit our website. See display ad.

BOCM PAULS LTD

PENRITH INDUSTRIAL ESTATE, PENRITH CA11 9EH
Tel: 01275 378384 Fax: 01275 373828 Contact: Mike Thompson
mike.thompson@bocmpauls.co.uk www.bocmpauls.co.uk
Soil Association P4688. BOCM Pauls manufacture approved feeds for dairy cows,
youngstock, beef, sheep, pigs and poultry. The products are supported by
specialist management services for organic producers in England and Wales.

BOOTHS SUPERMARKETS

THE OLD STATION, VICTORIA STREET, WINDERMERE LA23 1QA
Tel: 015394 46114 Fax: 015394 88918 Contact: M. Boothman
www.booths-supermarkets.co.uk
Organic fruit and veg, fresh meat, dairy, frozen burgers, frozen veg, wines, preserves,
flour, bread, cakes.

CASTLETOWN FARM SHOP

FLORISTON RIGG, ROCKLIFFE, CARLISLE CA
Tel: 01228 674400 Fax: 01228 674400 Contact: Hilary Bliss
info@castletownfarmshop.co.uk www.castletownfarmshop.co.uk
Soil Association registered. Retail specialists in locally sourced organic fine foods,
including meat, dairy, jams, pickles, fruit and vegetables and a range of ready meals.

CHILTERN SEEDS

BORTREE STILE, ULVERSTON LA12 7PB
Tel: 01229 581137 Fax: 01229 584549 Contact: D Taylor
info@chilternseeds.co.uk www.chilternseeds.co.uk
Chiltern Seeds catalogue lists over 4,600 items including an organic vegetable
section. There are also flowers, trees, shrubs, annuals, houseplants, exotics for
your greenhouse, unusual vegetables and herbs.

ECOS PAINTS

UNIT 34, HEYSHAM BUSINESS PARK, MIDDLETON RD., HEYSHAM LA3 3PP
Tel: 01524 852371 Fax: 01524 858978 Contact: Ian West
mail@ecospaints.com www.ecospaints.com
Organic odourless solvent-free paints, varnishes and other related products.

EVA'S ORGANICS

EVA BOTANICALS LTD., MEDBURN, MILTON, BRAMPTON CA8 1HS
Tel: 01697 741906 Fax: 01697 741205 Contact: Debbie Simpson
debbie.simpson@evabotanicals.co.uk www.evabotanicals.co.uk
We offer a wide range of fruit and vegetables in a box scheme with big savings for
drop off points. We also grow organic vegetables, culinary and medicinal herbs.

GARDENS & PETS DIRECT

SEAVIEW NURSERIES, NETHERTOWN, EGREMONT CA22 2UQ
Tel: 01946 820412 Fax: 01946 824091 Contact: Keith Singleton
enquiries@cumbriagardensandpetsdirect.co.uk
www.cumbriagardensandpetsdirect.co.uk
Browse through our vast range of products, all available online. Organic tomato,
plant and lawn food, poultry pellets, organic soil improvers and peat-free composts.

HALLSFORD (AN & HS TOMKINS)

HALLSFORD FARM, HETHERSGILL, CARLISLE CA6 6JD
Tel: 01228 577329 Fax: 01228 577148 Contact: Andrew
thefarm@hallsford.co.uk www.hallsford.co.uk
Soil Association G7042. Beef and lamb producer in North Cumbria. Pedigree beef
Shorthorn cattle and one of the largest flocks of rare breed Llanwenog sheep.
Top quality marbled Shorthorn beef and rare breed lamb via local farmers' markets,
regional food fairs and nationally by mail order. Rare breed pork to be introduced
in 2004. Visit the website.

HARLEY FOODS LTD

BLINDCRAKE HALL, BLINDCRAKE, COCKERMOUTH CA13 0QP
Tel: 01900 823037 Fax: 01900 828276 Contact: M Watson
Importer of organic dried fruits, nuts, beans, pulses, herbs, spices, plus a large
variety of ingredients for the wholesaler and manufacturer. We also source products
on demand.

HOWBARROW ORGANIC FARM

CARTMEL, GRANGE-OVER-SANDS LA11 7SS
Tel: 015395 36330 Fax: 015395 36330 Contact: Paul Hughes
enquiries@howbarroworganic.demon.co.uk www.howbarroworganic.demon.co.uk
Grow and process medicinal herbs into tinctures and oils. 13-acre small holding
producing meat (lamb, beef, turkeys), eggs, vegetables and medicinal herbs.
Supply local box scheme, farmers' markets and our award-winning Organic Farm
Shop of the year, 2002. Demonstration farm, walks and displays. Soil Association
licensed organic B&B and dinner. Member of the Soil Association Organic Farms
Network.

KAN FOODS

9 NEW SHAMBLES, OFF MARKET PLACE, KENDAL LA9 4TS
Tel: 01539 721190 Contact: Elizabeth Kan
lizkan@inthelight.info
A wholefood shop with high-grade vitamins, herb, oils, organic make-up, juices,
water filters, harmonisers, help and advice.

LADY JANE'S TEA ROOM
CUMBRIAN ANTIQUE CENTRE, ST. MARTIN'S HALL, BRAMPTON CA18 1NT
Tel: 07941 731255 Contact: Victoria Holt
Delicious home-made food prepared with locally grown organic and Fairtrade produce where possible. Outside catering a speciality. We are also a drop-off point for an organic produce box scheme.

LOW SIZERGH BARN FARM SHOP, TEA ROOM & CRAFT GALLERY
LOW SIZERGH FARM, SIZERGH, KENDAL LA8 8AE
Tel: 01539 560426 Fax: 01539 561475 Contact: Alison Park
apark@lowsizerghbarn.co.uk www.low-sizergh-barn.co.uk
Soil Association G5843. Large farm shop with full range of fine locally produced food; cheese & ice cream made with the farm's milk; tea room (watch the cows being milked at 3.45pm); also crafts. Farm trail. Member of the Soil Association Organic Farms Network.

MOTHER EARTH
BIRKROW COTTAGE, BLAWITH, ULVERSTON LA12 8EG
Tel: 01229 885266 Contact: Jane Holroyd
enquiries@motherearth.co.uk www.motherearth.co.uk
The Mother Earth Holistic skin care collection is a range of 100% natural cleansers, toners and moisturisers made with organic herbs and essential oils, hand-made in small batches and formulated by professional therapists.

MOTHER EARTH
CHURCH BRIDGE, GRASMERE LA22 9SN
Tel: 01539 435166 Fax: 01229 885266 Contact: Jane Holroyd
enquiries@motherearth.co.uk www.motherearth.co.uk
Natural skin care hand-made on the premises, organic baby clothes and textiles, eco-health care products.

SUNDANCE WHOLEFOODS
33 MAIN STREET, KESWICK CA12 5BL
Tel: 01768 774712 Contact: Julian Holdsworth
Soil Association member. A wholefood shop with many organic lines.

THE VILLAGE BAKERY
MELMERBY, PENRITH CA10 1HE
Tel: 01768 881811 Fax: 01768 881848 Contact: Chris Curry
info@village-bakery.com www.village-bakery.com
Organic speciality breads, cakes, savoury biscuits, flapjacks, slices, Christmas
goods. Special diet products. Mail order. Nationwide stockists. Baking courses.
Organic Food Awards 2004: Cakes, Pastries, Biscuits, Highly Commended.

THE WATERMILL
LITTLE SALKELD, PENRITH CA10 1NN
Tel: 01768 881523 Fax: 01768 881047 Contact: Ana Jones
organicflour@aol.com www.organicmill.co.uk
Soil Association (P632) and Biodynamic Agriculture Association registered.
Specialist organic flours, milled by water power in our 18th-century watermill
to SA and BDAA standards. Mill shop, tea room, mill tours and baking courses.

WHITEHOLME FARM
WHITEHOLME, ROWELTOWN, CARLISLE CA6 6LJ
Tel: 016977 48058 Contact: Jon and Lynne Perkin
whiteholmefarm@hotmail.com www.whiteholmefarm.co.uk
Whiteholme Farm is an organic livestock farm situated in the north-east of
Cumbria. Home-reared organic beef, lamb and pork are prepared at our on-farm
butchery from traditional breeds and sold to local customers through direct
sales and farmers' markets. Accommodation, education and farm walks are all
available. Member of the Soil Association Organic Farms Network.

ALLSOP, D
BROOKFIELDS, BRASSINGTON, MATLOCK DE4 4HL
Tel: 01629 540370 Fax: 01629 540370 Contact: Dorothy Allsop
We can offer winter grazing for 200 sheep and summer grazing for 150 yearling heifers for beef.

AMBROSIAN VEGETARIAN FOODS
HIGHFIELDS LODGE, 69 OCCUPATION RD., ALBERT VILLAGE, SWADLINCOTE DE11 8HA
Tel: 01283 225055 Fax: 01283 550536 Contact: Alan Beck
ambrosian@btopenworld.com ambrosianvegetarianfoods.co.uk
Soil Association P6694. Manufacturer of high quality home-made vegan organic food. The range includes pies, pasties, sos rollo, burgers, sosages and sosage and burger mixes. All products are registered with the Vegan Society and produced under organic standards.

ASHBOURNE BISCUITS
BLENHEIM RD., AIRFIELD IND. ESTATE, ASHBOURNE DE6 1HA
Tel: 01335 342373 Fax: 01335 346394 Contact: Roy Johnson
enquiries@ashbournebiscuits.co.uk www.ashbournebiscuits.co.uk
Soil Association registered. An award-winning independent family-run biscuit baker specialising in production of traditional hand-baked biscuits using only the purest natural ingredients, including a developing range of organic sweet and savoury biscuits. Organic Food Awards 2004: Cakes, Pastries, Biscuits Winner.

BEANO'S WHOLEFOODS
HOLME ROAD, MATLOCK BATH DE4 3NU
Tel: 01629 57130 Fax: 01629 57143 Contact: Anne Thorne
john@beanos.go-plus.net
Box scheme delivering selection of organic fruit & vegetables.

DERBYSHIRE DALES ORGANICS

COMMON END FARM, BRADLEY, NR. ASHBOURNE DE6 3BQ
Tel: 01335 370356 Fax: 01355 370356 Contact: James Howson
jwhowson@wildmail.com
Small family-run mixed organic farm nestled in the Derbyshire dales specialising in
poultry, lamb, pork and related products.

DOVEDALE CONFECTIONERY LTD

VERNON STREET INDUSTRIAL ESTATE, SHIREBROOK NG20 8SL
Tel: 01623 742277 Fax: 01623 743020 Contact: George Robinson
dovedale@o2.co.uk
Soil Association P3084. We are a private label manufacturer of novelty chocolate
items and biscuits. All our production is own label, therefore all work is confidential.

ENGLISH ORGANIC FOODS PLC

THE OLD VICARAGE, 226 ASHBOURNE RD., TURNDITCH DE56 2LH
Tel: 01773 550173 Fax: 01773 550855 Contact: Brian Ashby
Organic matching agency.

FRANK WRIGHT LTD

BLENHEIM HOUSE, BLENHEIM RD., ASHBOURNE DE6 1HA
Tel: 01335 341155 Fax: 01335 341171 Contact: Cara Freeston-Smith
cara.freeston-smith@basf-a-n.co.uk
Soil Association P6918. The manufacturers of Soil Association-approved mineral
supplements for organic ruminant livestock, which are essential to maintain
performance, health and welfare. Also available as bespoke formulations for
specific farm needs.

THE GREEN BOX COMPANY

23 PYEGROVE RD., GLOSSOP SK13 8QS
Tel: 01457 856843 Contact: Jo Farrar & Steve Mellor
info@greenboxco.fsnet.co.uk www.thegreenboxcompany.co.uk
Fruit and vegetable box scheme delivering in Glossop, Derbyshire and surrounding area. Also eggs, cheese, jams and marmalades. Mobile number 07906 494065.

HEARTHSTONE FARM

RIBER, MATLOCK DE4 5JW
Tel: 01629 534304 Fax: 01629 534372 Contact: Ian & Joy Gilman
enquiries@hearthstonefarm.co.uk www.hearthstonefarm.co.uk
B&B in the farmhouse three en-suite double rooms. We produce beef, pork, and lamb and make our own sausages, bacon and burgers. We grow and sell organic potatoes and buy in organic chicken, all for sale in the farm shop. Open every day except Wed afternoons, Sundays open 10am–12pm.

HI PEAK FEEDS LTD

HI PEAK FEEDS MILL, SHEFFIELD RD., KILLAMARSH S21 1ED
Tel: 0114 248 0608 Fax: 0114 247 5189 Contact: P Whitfield
info@hipeak.co.uk www.hipeak.co.uk
Manufacturers and distributors of organic and UKROFS-permitted animal feeds for all farm livestock, horses and dogs. Nationwide delivery and mail order. Soil Association licence no. P2486, OF&G licence no. 11UKP090258. We supply farmers and smallholders.

HUNTER, MANDY & ADRIAN

TURLOW FIELDS FARM, HOGNASTON, NR. ASHBOURNE DE6 1PW
Tel: 01335 370884 Fax: 01335 370884 Contact: Mandy & Adrian Hunter
Small farm shop selling our own produce only: Angus beef, rare breed pork, lamb, chicken, eggs. From September 2005 we will have self-catering accommodation on the farm to sleep 5.

JEFFERY, H & SON

ASTON HOUSE FARM, SUDBURY, NR. ASHBOURNE DE6 5AG
Tel: 01283 585410 Contact: Robert Jeffery
r.jeffery@farmline.com www.newlandowner.co.uk
Beef from longhorn cattle born and reared on this organic farm is available fresh or
frozen by appointment from the farmhouse, mobile: 07971 566907. The farm is
conveniently situated just off the A50 on Lichfield Rd, Sudbury.

LOWER HURST FARM

LOWER HURST FARM, HARTINGTON, NR. BUXTON SK17 0HJ
Tel: 01298 84900 Fax: 01298 84732 Contact: Catherine Pyne
sales@lowerhurstfarm.co.uk www.lowerhurstfarm.co.uk
Soil Association G7616, P7654. A small farm in Derbyshire producing exclusive
organic beef from its own herd of pure bred Hereford cattle. Awarded 'Best
Beef/Sheep Farm' in the 2003 Organic Food Awards and also the winner of the
Waitrose Small Producer Awards 2002. Full range of products are available including award-winning Steak & Cider Pies. Available through mail order or secure online
shop. A monthly shop is held at the farm on the 1st Friday in every month and the
farm also holds Open Days where visitors can walk the farm trail, take a tractor
tour around the Herefords or simply relax in the stunning surroundings whilst enjoy-
ing a delicious steak and a glass of wine. Member of the Soil Association Organic
Farms Network. Organic Food Awards 2004 Highly Commended; Fresh Meat
Commended.

MEYNELL LANGLEY ORGANIC FARM SHOP

MEYNELL LANGLEY, KIRK LANGLEY, ASHBORNE DE6 4NT
Tel: 01332 824815 Contact: Helen & Godfrey Meynell
Home produced/locally sourced beef, lamb, chicken, turkey, pork, eggs and
vegetables. Christmas turkeys and geese. Additional local or organic products.
Open Fridays 1pm to 6.30pm, Saturdays 10am to 2pm and by telephone
arrangement Monday to Thursday.

MIMMO'S
1 ST. MARY'S GATE, WIRKSWORTH, MATLOCK DE4 4DQ
Tel: 01629 826724 Contact: Melanie Glendinning
Soil Association member (personal, not business). Home-made Sicilian dishes using seasonal organic meat and vegetables, pasta, rice and herbs.

NATURAL CHOICE
24 ST. JOHN ST., ASHBOURNE DE6 1GH
Tel: 01335 346096 Fax: 01335 346096 Contact: Steve Parker
naturalchoice@tiscali.co.uk www.naturalchoicehealth.co.uk
Health foods, wholefoods, natural supplements. Natural therapy centre.

NEW HOUSE ORGANIC FARM
KNIVETON, ASHBOURNE DE6 1JL
Tel: 01335 342429 Contact: RA Smail
bob@newhousefarm.co.uk
OF&G 11UK F030109. Hill farm producing beef, lamb, eggs, veg and fruit. Farm shop. School visits. Waymarked archaeological farm trail. Accommodation in converted barn with solar panel and wind turbine, plus large organised camping.

NIXORGANIX
CRYSTAL SPRINGS FARM, BRAILSFORD, ASHBOURNE DE6 3BG
Tel: 01335 360996 Contact: Nick Adams
nick@adams4.wanadoo.co.uk www.nixorganix.org
Soil Association G5056. Lowland livestock farm in the Derbyshire dales.
Aberdeen Angus cattle and Polled Dorset sheep are kept for the quality of their meat and suitability for natural methods. Beef and lamb always available. Educational visits and informal circular walks to view farm and conservation activities.

NORTHERN TEA MERCHANTS

CROWN HOUSE, 193 CHATSWORTH ROAD, CHESTERFIELD S40 2BA
Tel: 01246 232600 Fax: 01246 555991 Contact: James Pogson
enquiries@northern-tea.com www.northern-tea.com
We are organic coffee roasters and packers of organic cocoas. We can also offer
organic tea packing and organic tea bag manufacture.

ORGANIC PUMPKIN

KINGFISHER COTTAGE, KING ST., DUFFIELD, DERBY DE56 4EU
Tel: 01332 370254 Fax: 01332 370254 Contact: David Yolshina-Cash
www.organicpumpkin.co.uk
Organic Food Federation 00461. Fresh seasonal organic vegetables picked and
delivered the same day. Evening delivery Wednesdays and Thursdays.

THE ORGANIC SHOP

3 SETT CLOSE, NEW MILLS SK22 4AQ
Tel: 01663 747550 Fax: 01663 747550 Contact: D Carroll
theorganicshop@aol.com
Complete range of organic products.

SUNFLOWER HEALTH STORE

20 MARKET PLACE, ILKESTON DE7 5QA
Tel: 0115 930 4750 Contact: P Leach
We sell a wide range of groceries, supplements and cosmetics, stocking as many
organic and ethically produced goods as possible. We are pleased to order items
not stocked if available.

UNSTONE GRANGE ORGANIC GARDENING FOR HEALTH

CROW LANE, UNSTONE, NR. CHESTERFIELD S18 4AL
Tel: 01246 411666 Fax: 01246 412344 Contact: Jennie Street
garden@unstonegrange.co.uk www.unstonegrange.co.uk
We provide gardening opportunities for volunteers from all over Derbyshire:
people with learning disabilities, mental health issues, single parents,
retired, people changing careers or down-shifting. Others are well and want to
stay well, or want to learn about organic horticulture. We run an OCN-approved
organic horticulture course.

WELEDA (UK) LTD

HEANOR ROAD, ILKESTON DE7 8DR
Tel: 0115 944 8200 Fax: 0115 944 8210 Contact: Roger Barsby
info@weleda.co.uk www.weleda.co.uk
Demeter certified. Weleda produces natural medicines and body care products,
using ingredients from our Demeter-certified gardens.

WILD CARROT

5 BRIDGE ST., BUXTON SK17 6BS
Tel: 01298 22843 Contact: Julian Grant
shop@wildcarrot.freeserve.co.uk www.wildcarrot.freeserve.co.uk
Soil Association GC5018, R7228. We are a wholefood workers co-op specialising
in organic foods and alcohol, fair-traded goods and environmentally friendly
products. We support local and UK growers and prepare organic veg boxes. We are
a member of Organic 2000.

Natural Fertility

The decline in natural fertility caused by conventional farming methods is exem-
plified most powerfully by a phenomenon that occurs when farmers convert
their farms to organic methods. There is a drop in crop yields during the first
few years, then a gradual recovery as the soil life recovers. This phenomenon
indicates how denuded the soil life becomes when chemical fertilizers and pesticides are used whilst good humus levels are not maintained in the soil.
**From *Organic Futures: The Case for Organic Farming* by Adrian Myers,
Green Books, £12.95.**

ACLAND ORGANIC MEATS

EAST ACLAND FARM, LANDKEY, BARNSTAPLE EX32 0LD
Tel: 01271 830216 Contact: Charles Morrish
Soil Association M12W. Beef and lamb.

AGROFORESTRY RESEARCH TRUST

46 HUNTERS MOON, DARTINGTON, TOTNES TQ9 6JT
Tel: 01803 840776 Contact: M Crawford
mail@agroforestry.co.uk www.agroforestry.co.uk
Research charity producing books and information on fruits, nuts and agroforestry;
also plants, seeds and rootrainers.

ALAN'S APPLE

26 FORE STREET, KINGSBRIDGE TQ7 1NY
Tel: 01548 852308 Contact: Alan Knight
Traditional greengrocer, stocking organic vegetables, organic dairy produce, organic
ice cream and organic meat and poultry.

THE ARK WHOLEFOODS SHOP

38 EAST STREET, ASHBURTON TQ13 7AX
Tel: 01364 653020 Contact: M. Kennedy
the-ark@clara.co.uk
Small is beautiful: this shop is crammed full of a huge variety of lines including
many organic ones. Vegetables are sourced from Heart of Devon and Woodlands
Organics. Baked goods are home-made or come from a local vegetarian bakery.
Organic lines are represented in most dry goods and dairy sectors too.

ATLANTIC ORGANICS

BOWDEN FARM, MUDDIFORD, BARNSTAPLE EX31 4HR
Tel: 01271 850502 Fax: 01271 850502 Contact: Sue Watson & Jon Perkins
c@spyjamas.fsnet.co.uk
Traditional 17th-century farm with sea views offering superb Bed & Breakfast.
Shetland sheep and beef Shorthorn cattle for lamb, mutton and beef with
outstanding flavour. Beautiful naturally coloured woollen products and sheepskins.

THE BARTON

THE BARTON, POUGHILL, CREDITON EX17 4LE
Tel: 01363 866349 Contact: Anne Wander a.wander@btinternet.com
Luxury on-farm self-catering holiday accommodation with indoor pool.

BEAMING BABY

UNIT 1, PLACE BARTON FARM, MORELEIGH, TOTNES TQ9 7JN
Tel: 0800 0345 672 Fax: 01548 821 589 Contact: Charlie Wynne
charlie@beamingbaby.com www.beamingbaby.com
Beautiful organic baby clothes, the best choice of washable nappies, eco-disposable
nappies, natural wipes, organic and natural baby toiletries. Eco-friendly toys, natural
bedding. Essentials for mother, and many treats too.

BEDPORT FARM

BEDPORT FARM, BURRINGTON, UMBERLEIGH EX37 9LE
Tel: 01769 560592 Fax: 01769 560592 Contact: S Tyler-Upfield
12,000 organic laying hens producing eggs.

BEE ORGANIC

56 HIGHWEEK VILLAGE, NEWTON ABBOT TQ12 1QQ
Tel: 07817 467936 Contact: Paul Hutchings & Marcus Clay
Soil Association G6389. A small-scale operation growing a huge range of vegetables and herbs and fruit. We particularly specialise in heritage varieties to conserve
genetic diversity, and grow for flavour. Alternative telephone: 07789 741339.

BEST OF THE WEST

4B LAPFORD CROSS IND. ESTATE, LAPFORD, CREDITON EX17 6YQ
Tel: 01363 83626 Fax: 01363 83624 Contact: Nigel Schofield
nschofield@talk21.com
Soil Association P2050. Supply a huge range of local, national and imported
organic foods, both chilled and ambient. An environmentally friendly distribution
and delivery service for small producers.

BISHOPS FARM

STAPLEDON, ANVIL CORNER, HOLSWORTHY EX22 6NR
Tel: 07812 756430 Contact: Tom & Sue Barnes
Soil Association G7841. Producing free range organic eggs for supermarket outlets.

BLACKLAKE FARM

EAST HILL, OTTERY ST. MARY EX11 1QA
Tel: 01404 812122 Contact: Catherine & Nick Broomfield
catherine@blacklakefarm.com www.blacklakefarm.com
The Ruby Red Devon cattle and Dorset sheep thrive on the old pasture of Blacklake
Farm. The Gloucester Old Spot pigs are free-range. Blacklake Farm sells fine quality
meats from traditional breeds of cattle, sheep and pigs—all born, bred, reared and
finished on the farm. The meat is butchered locally and hung for the correct times
to give optimum flavour and tenderness. Shepherds Flock wool throws and scarves
are made from the wool of Blacklake Farm's pedigree flock of Dorset Down sheep.
The Hay House is a beautifully restored and furnished self-catering holiday house.
Educational visits. Member of the Soil Association Organic Farms Network.

BOWDEN FARM

BOWDEN FARM, MUDDIFORD, BARNSTAPLE EX31 4HR
Tel: 01271 850502 Fax: 01271 850502 Contact: Sue Watson & Jon Perkins
c@spyjamas.fsnet.co.uk
Revive your senses at our wonderful organic farm: breathe fresh sea air, feast
on a delicious breakfast, hear the amazing birdsong, touch new born lambs and
take in the panorama, with Dartmoor to the south and the Atlantic in the West.
Luxury B&B in 17th-century farmhouse, rare breeds and wildlife galore!

BRAGG, MC

THE GATEHOUSE, SHILLINGFORD ABBOTT, EXETER EX2 9QU
Tel: 01392 833040 Contact: Martyn Bragg
martyn.bragg@virgin.net
Soil Association G2572. We grow fresh vegetables and herbs for our box scheme, delivering to the Exeter area. We also grow cereals: wheat, barley, triticale and protein crops.

BRAMLEY WOOD & BUCKLAND FILLEIGH ORGANIC

BRAMLEY WOOD, BUCKLAND FILLEIGH, BEAWORTHY EX21 5JD
Tel: 01409 281693 Contact: Jane & Peter Bartlett
Sustainable woodland organic enterprise deriving main income from organic free range eggs, horticulture, plant raising and forests fruits. Forestry products include charcoal, logs, timber, mushrooms, new log cabin built from our own timber. Sustainable planning permission advice, alternative energy.

BUCKFAST ORGANIC BAKERY

HAMLYN HOUSE, MARDLE WAY, BUCKFASTLEIGH TQ11 0NR
Tel: 01364 642279 Fax: 01364 642279 Contact: Sally Carson
sallycarson@clivespies.co.uk
Soil Association P2974. Producers of 'Clive's' pies and cakes, delicious organic vegetarian pies in wholemeal pastry and gluten-free pastry, also luxury gluten-free cakes, plus organic flapjacks.

CERIDWEN HERBS

CERIDWEN, OLD RECTORY LANE, PYWORTHY EX22 6SW
Tel: 01409 254450 Contact: Rob Meredith
cdt-dlee@supanet.com
Soil Association G2255/P7995. Organic veg, fruit, herbs, plants, jams, chutneys, eggs. Part of Holsworthy Organics veg box scheme. Farmers' markets and Tavistock pannier market (Fridays).

CHIMAN'S
CLEAVE FARM, EAST DOWN, BARNSTAPLE EX31 4NX
Tel: 01271 883864 Fax: 01271 882843 Contact: Sally Agarwal
sallyagarwal@chimans.co.uk www.chimans.co.uk
Soil Association P5692. A unique range of 16 spice blends from authentic Indian recipes, ready to cook at home.

COTONS CONTINENTAL CHOCOLATES
UNIT 1 ISLAND SQUARE, ISLAND STREET, SALCOMBE TQ8 8DP
Tel: 01584 844004 Fax: 01458 844345 Contact: Robin Coton
robin@cotonschocolates.co.uk www.cotonschocolates.co.uk
Hand-made chocolates using Belgian organic chocolate. Cotons brands include award-winning plain and milk chocolate 100g bars. We also make truffles, Easter egg and Christmas models.

THE COURTYARD CAFE AND SHOP
THE SQUARE, CHAGFORD TQ13 8AE
Tel: 01647 432571 Fax: 01647 432985 Contact: Ruth Olley
compost@properjob.eclipse.co.uk www.properjob.ik.com
Café, wholefood and greengrocery shop, all goods are either organic, Fairtraded, local or all three.

COWLING, MR & MRS NR
DOCKWELL FARM, WIDECOMBE IN THE MOOR, NEWTON ABBOT TQ
Tel: 01364 621268 Contact: NR Cowling
vennorm@btinternet.com
Soil Association P5549. Organic beef, single suckler herd raised on Dartmoor. Simmental cross calves for sale in the autumn.

DARTMOOR DIRECT CO-OPERATIVE LTD
MITCHELCOMBE FARM, HOLNE, NEWTON ABBOT TQ13 7SP
Tel: 01364 631528 Contact: Roger Mitchell
Home delivery service: bottled water, local produce and organic foods.

DEVON FOODS LTD

KNIGHTSWOOD FARM, BLUEBELL LANE, CULLOMPTON EX15 1RW
Tel: 01884 32816 Fax: 01884 32806 Contact: Graham Frankpitt
sales@devonfood.co.uk www.devonfood.co.uk
Specialise in production of Soil Association certified organic day old chicks, table
birds, duck, guinea fowl, hatching eggs and point of lay pullets.

DITTISHAM FARM

CAPTON, DARTMOUTH TQ6 0JE
Tel: 01803 712452 Contact: Sue Fildes
sue@self-cater.co.uk www.self-cater.co.uk/dff
Organic beef—Red Ruby Devon breed. Organic rare-breed pork Berkshire breed.
See our pigs at the Devon, Cornwall, Bath & West & Royal Shows—ring me for con-
firmation. Organic hen & duck eggs. Self-catering accommodation in rural bungalow
for 2 adults (+ cot).

DRAGONFLY FOODS

2A MARDLE WAY, BUCKFASTLEIGH TQ11 0NR
Tel: 01364 642700 Fax: 01364 642700 Contact: Simon Boreham
info@beany.co.uk www.beany.co.uk
Manufacturer of organic chilled soya bean products, including tofu, Beanys,
Soysage and Tatty, an organic chilled potato product. Sold to independent health
food shops in the UK. Organic Food Awards 2004 Soya Foods Winner.

DROUGHTWELL FARM

SHELDON, HONITON EX14 4QW
Tel: 01404 841349 Contact: Ian & Sue Cochrane
droughtwellfarm@aol.com
Organic sheep and beef. Self-catering for 2 plus a cot in one end of the farmhouse, dog welcome.

EARTHSTAR, LITTLE EAST LAKE FARM

EAST CHILLA, BEAWORTHY EX21 5XF '
Tel: 01409 221417 Contact: M Robley
morobley549@hotmail.com
Producers and sellers direct to the consumer of Soil Association symbol standard eggs, vegetables, preserves and soft fruit. Produce delivered locally. Members of Holsworthy Organics veg box scheme.

ECO SCI—WEST COUNTRY COMPOST

·WOLFSON LABORATORIES, HIGHER HOOPERN LANE, EXETER EX4 4SG
Tel: 01392 424846 Fax: 01392 425302 Contact: Steve Bullock
mail@ecosci.co.uk www.ecosci.co.uk
Soil Association I1848. Eco Sci compost over 40,000 tons of recycled green waste to produce West Country Compost, quality compost that both nourishes and conditions the soil. Available in bags, on pallets and in bulk, throughout the South-west.

EDWIN TUCKER & SONS LTD

BREWERY MEADOW, STONEPARK, ASHBURTON, NEWTON ABBOT TQ13 7DG
Tel: 01364 652233 Fax: 01364 654211 Contact: Chrissie Gregory
seeds@edwintucker.com www.edwintucker.com
Mail order and retail shop selling seeds, organic seeds and potatoes. We have retail outlets which carry stocks of feed, saddlery, gardening equipment and agricultural fertilisers. Our mail order department sells seeds, organic seeds and potatoes including some unusual varieties.

ELDER, D

LOWER CHITTERLEY FARM, SILVERTON, EXETER EX5 4BP
Tel: 01392 860856 Fax: 01392 860856 Contact: D Elder
darren1963landie@aol.com
Direct sales to the public of beef, lamb, poultry and eggs produced to Soil Association standards.

ENDACOTT, WA LTD
21 EAST ST., OKEHAMPTON EX20 1AT
Tel: 01837 52888 Fax: 01837 54381 Contact: Michael Finucane
Soil Association P4830. Wholesale and retail bakers and confectioners—organic bread and rolls.

EVERSFIELD MANOR
BRATTON CLOVELLY, OKEHAMPTON EX20 4JF
Tel: 01837 871400 Fax: 01837 871114 Contact: Mark Stewart
shop@eversfieldmanor.co.uk www.eversfieldmanor.co.uk
Organic meat box scheme. Local and national coverage. Regular at local farmers' markets. Organic Food Awards 2004 Fresh Meat Commended.

FERRYMAN POLYTUNNELS
BRIDGE RD., LAPFORD, CREDITON, DEVON, EX17 6AE
Contact: Hugh Briant-Evans Tel: 01363 83444   Fax: 01363 83050
info@ferryman.uk.com www.ferryman.uk.com
Manufacturers of polytunnel greenhouse kits for private and commercial growers.

FISHLEIGH ESTATE
FISHLEIGH HOUSE, OKEHAMPTON EX20 3QA
Tel: 01837 810124 Fax: 01837 810124 Contact: Victoria Sargent
enquiries@fishleighestate.com www.fishleighestate.com
We sell fully traceable, well hung organic beef and lamb, we have won many prestigious conservation awards including the Bronze Otter Award. We are members of CLA & NFU. Member of the Soil Association Organic Farms Network.

FORD BARTON
FORD BARTON, STOODLEIGH, TIVERTON EX16 9PP
Tel: 01398 351139 Fax: 01398 351157 Contact: Sally
sales@fordbarton.co.uk www.fordbarton.co.uk
Soil Association G5659. Naturally dyed, organic Wensleydale wool from our own sheep, using mainly dyes from the farm. Producing an exclusive range of knitted and woven household goods and garments.

FOUNTAIN VIOLET FARM

MOUNT RIDLEY RD., KINGSWEAR, DEVON, TQ6 0DU
Tel: 01803 752363 Fax: 01803 752885 Contact: Emma Jones
ed@fvfarm.freeserve.co.uk
Soil Association G4744. Organic beef from pure breed South Devon herd available
via convenient mail order, box scheme.

GREAT CUMMINS FARM

TEDBURN ST. MARY, EXETER, DEVON, EX6 6BJ
Tel: 01647 61278 Fax: 01647 61278 Contact: David Garaway
davidgaraway@yahoo.co.uk
Production and sale of organic vegetables, soft fruit, lamb and eggs.

THE GREEN HOUSE

2A LOWER PANNIER MARKET, CREDITON EX17 2BL
Tel: 01363 775580 Contact: Loo Brown
Comprehensively stocked, mostly organic wholefood shop, including dried, chilled,
frozen goods, fresh local fruit and veg, environmentally friendly cleaning products, Ecover
refills, cosmetics, natural remedies, Fairtrade, gifts and cards. Friendly, helpful staff.

GREENACRES ORGANIC PRODUCE

COOMBE BANK, TIPTON ST. JOHN, SIDMOUTH EX10 0AX
Tel: 01404 815829 Fax: 01404 815829 Contact: Roger Cozens
roger@greenacres-consultancy.co.uk
Herbs (culinary and medicinal), vegetables, lamb and eggs. Consultancy in arable
and horticulture, overseas aid and relief consultancy.

GREENFIBRES

99 HIGH ST., TOTNES TQ9 5PF
Tel: 01803 868001 Fax: 01803 868002 Contact: William Lana
mail@greenfibres.com www.greenfibres.com
Organic clothing, bedding, fabrics, household linen and mattresses made from
organic raw materials (organic cotton, organic linen, organic wool) under fair
and safe working conditions. Feel and look good while supporting organic
agriculture and ethical work practices. See display ad.

GREENLIFE DIRECT
11 THE PADDOCKS, TOTNES IND. PARK, TOTNES TQ9 5XT
Tel: 01803 868733 Fax: 01803 864948 Contact: Liz and Penny
enquiries@greenlife.co.uk www.greenlife.co.uk
Greenlife Direct retail a wide range of nutritional supplements including competitively
priced own label and hard-to-find products. Practitioner discounts. Established
1989. Now the largest independent health/wholefood shop in the West Country.

GREENLIFE SHOP
11–13 FORE ST., TOTNES TQ9 5DA
Tel: 01803 866738 Fax: 01803 866538 Contact: Wendy Stevens
shop@greenlife.co.uk www.greenlife.co.uk
Although Greenlife is not entirely organic, all fresh fruit and vegetables are certified
organic, plus we have a huge selection of organic foods and other products including
personal care products.

GRIFFIN'S YARD
NORTH RD., SOUTH MOLTON EX36 3AZ
Tel: 01769 572372 Fax: 01769 572372 Contact: Graeme & Jenny Wilkinson
Natural and organic foods retailer, plus café and crafts gallery. Local and organic
fresh produce wherever possible. Car parking.

GROWERS ORGANIC PLANT CENTRE
MILIZAC CLOSE, YEALMPTON PL8 2JS
Tel: 01752 881180 Contact: Joa Grower & Charlie Wakeham
joa@growersorganics.com www.growersorganics.com
Vegetable, herb, fruit and ornamental plants suitable for outside or inside production.
Retail plant centre and mail order. Stalls at local Devon markets. Wholesale available
in south Devon area. Mail order catalogue and directions available on website.

THE HEALTH FOOD STORE
GAMMON WALK, BARNSTAPLE EX31 1DJ
Tel: 01271 345624 Contact: Pat Jackman
Organic spreads, oats, flakes, oils and much more, with a friendly information service.

HEALTHWISE

81 FORE STREET, KINGSBRIDGE TQ7 1AB
Tel: 01548 857707 Contact: Irene Jeeninga
Health shop stocking organic nuts, seeds, breakfast cereals, pies, Beany burgers, dairy products, juices, soya milk and yoghurts, teas, coffee, artisan bread, bodycare products and Ecover household products.

HEART OF DEVON ORGANICS

LANGRIDGE FARM, CREDITON EX17 5HH
Tel: 01647 24894 Fax: 01647 24894 Contact: Geoff Jones
The largest sole wholesaler of organic fresh fruit and vegetables in the South-west. Working closely with local and near continent growers (visit website). Deliveries from M4 to Lands End.

HEAVEN SCENT HERBS

UNIT 9, GIDLEYS MEADOW, CHRISTOW, EXETER EX6 7QB
Tel: 01647 252847 Fax: 01647 252847 Contact: Anne Tarrant
enquiries@heavenscentherbs.co.uk www.heavenscentherbs.co.uk
Handmade herb and spice mustards—12 distinctively flavoured organic varieties available in a selection of sizes. Contact for nearest stockists. Starter packs available for retail outlets. Mail order service.

HERBIE'S WHOLE FOOD VEGETARIAN RESTAURANT

15 NORTH ST., EXETER EX4 6Q
Tel: 01392 258473 Contact: Tony Mudge
Vegetarian restaurant using organic ingredients where available and local produce in season.

HERON VALLEY CIDER AND ORGANIC JUICE

CRANNACOMBE FARM, HAZELWOOD, LODDISWELL, KINGSBRIDGE TQ7 4DX
Tel: 01548 550256 Fax: 01548 550256 Contact: Shirley & Stephen Bradley
National award-winning producers of organic apple-based fruit juices and sparkling and traditional still organic ciders, pressed from hand-selected fruit at our farm based in stunning river Avon valley. Organic Food Awards 2004: Non Alcoholic Drinks Highly Commended.

HIGHDOWN ORGANIC FARM

HIGHDOWN FARM, BRADNINCH, EXETER EX5 4LJ
Tel: 01392 881028 Fax: 01392 881272 Contact: Sandra Vallis
svallis@highdownfarm.co.uk www.highdownfarm.co.uk
Soil Association G2121. We offer quality self-catering accommodation on our
organic dairy farm. Peacefully situated in the heart of Devon with breathtaking
views of the surrounding countryside.

HIGHER CROP

'PYNES', BRIDFORD, NR. EXETER EX6 7JA
Tel: 01647 252470 Contact: Chris Towell
Soil Association G6688. To grow products that are unavailable in supermarkets
and maintain the availability of rare and old vegetable forms from around the
world, we have started a seed bank for ourselves.

HIGHER HACKNELL ORGANIC MEAT

HIGHER HACKNELL FARM, BURRINGTON, UMBERLEIGH EX37 9LX
Tel: 01769 560909 Fax: 01769 560909 Contact: Jo Budden
enquiries@higherhacknell.co.uk www.higherhacknell.co.uk
Producer and retailer of quality tasty organic meat. Our 350-acre family farm
in Devon has been organic since 1988 and won numerous awards for conservation
and for our produce. Nationwide weekly deliveries and local delivery. Also available
from Exeter and Exmouth farmers' markets. Member of the Soil Association Organic
Farms Network. Organic Food Awards 2004 Highly Commended: Fresh Meat
Commended.

HIGHER SHARPHAM BARTON FARM,

COACHYARD COTTAGE, SHARPHAM, ASHPRINGTON, TOTNES TQ9 7UT
Tel: 01803 732324 Contact: Richard Smith
Annual on-farm family camp, 1st week in August.

HIGHFIELD HARVEST

HIGHFIELD FARM, CLYST RD., TOPSHAM EX3 0BY
Tel: 01392 876388 Fax: 01392 876388 Contact: Ian Shears
www.devonorganics.co.uk
Highfield Harvest organic farm shop, award-winning organic vegetables from our
118-acre family farm plus organic meat, dairy, wines, groceries. Open Tues to
Sat 9 to 6, Sun 10 to 1, closed Mondays. Soil Association certified (no. S41M).
Member of the Soil Association Organic Farms Network.

HILL COTTAGE & SOUTH BEER

BEER MILL FARM, CLAWTON, NR. HOLSWORTHY EX22 6PF
Tel: 01409 253093 Contact: Elaine Green
lgsg@supanet.com www.selfcateringcottagesdevon.co.uk
Self-catering cottages, we grow our own organic veg and eggs (not certified)
and supply guests from local certified sources (veg box scheme and Providence
Farm). Soil Association members as individuals.

HILLHEAD FARM

UGBOROUGH, IVYBRIDGE PL21 0HQ
Tel: 01752 892674 Fax: 01752 690111 Contact: Jane Johns
info@hillhead-farm.co.uk www.hillhead-farm.co.uk
Accommodation in comfortably appointed Victorian farmhouse with lovely views
over the rolling south Devon countryside. Delicious breakfasts with organic,
home-baked bread and home-made preserves, local bacon and sausages.

HOLSWORTHY ORGANICS

C/O LITTLE EAST LAKE FARM, EAST CHILLA, BEAWORTHY EX21 5XF
Tel: 01409 221417 Contact: Mo Robley
morobley549@hotmail.com
Marketing co-op selling organic veg, fruit, herbs, eggs, preserves and other
produce. Producer member of Soil Association (no. PR30W).

HORWOOD ORGANICS

HORWOOD HOUSE, HORWOOD, BIDEFORD EX39 4PD
Tel: 01271 858231 Fax: 01271 858413 Contact: Gill Barriball
gill@horwoodhouse.co.uk www.horwoodhouse.co.uk
Beautiful Grade 2 listed Georgian house surrounded by own organic farmland with
far reaching views across landscaped gardens and rolling Devon countryside. Two
large bedrooms, en-suite, south facing, from £35pp pn.

HURFORD, T & J

WIXON FARM, CHULMLEIGH EX18 7DS
Tel: 01769 580438 Contact: T & J Hurford
Soil Association G1747. Organic Aberdeen Angus beef and chicken produced to
Soil Association standards, sold from farm or from Bristol Farmers' market
every Wednesday 9am–2pm, Corn Street, Bristol.

KEENOR, CJ & ME

MOUNTICOMBE FARM, CHULMLEIGH EX18 7EQ
Tel: 01769 580305 Contact: Colin Keenor
ckeenor@uks.net
Organic milk production.

KILWORTHY KAPERS

11 KING ST., TAVISTOCK PL19 0DS
Tel: 01822 615039 Contact: Mr & Mrs Kiely
We stock a wide range of organically grown foods including fruit, vegetables and
eggs. Also supplements, herbal remedies etc.

KINGDOM, RUTH

GIBBETT MOOR FARM, RACKENFORD, TIVERTON EX16 8DJ
Tel: 01884 881457 Contact: Ruth Kingdom
Soil Association G2438. Small suckler herd of Devon cattle on rare Culm
grassland. Their meat is well hung, of excellent flavour.

KITTOW, JD & SE
ELBURY FARM, BROADCLYST, EXETER EX5 3BH
Tel: 01392 462817 Fax: 01392 462817 Contact: Jon Kittow
Soil Association G7302. Traditional Devon mixed farm: farm trail and the
opportunity to see how the dairy, beef, sheep and arable enterprises integrate
into a sustainable farming system. Visitors by appointment, occasional open days.

LEAFCYCLE
COOMBE FARM, COVE, TIVERTON EX16 7RU
Tel: 01398 331808 Fax: 01398 331808 Contact: Michael Cole
www.leafcycle.co.uk
Soil Association C37W. Leafu—a highly nutritious vegan organic food ingredient
made from leaves. Leafcycle camps—a green space for green camps. The
Occasional Café, an outdoor organic experience.

LINSCOMBE FARM
NEWBUILDINGS, SANDFORD, CREDITON EX17 4PS
Tel: 01363 84291 Contact: Phil Thomas
farmers@linscombe.fsnet.co.uk
Soil Association G2047. Box scheme within 10-mile radius of farm. 300 varieties
of vegetable grown. Joint Box Scheme of the Year Award winner 2001. Crediton
farmers' market 1st Sat of month, Exmouth farmers' market 2nd Wed, Plymouth
farmers' market 2nd Sat, Exeter farmers' market every Thursday. Member of the
Soil Association Organic Farms Network.

LITTLE COMFORT FARM
LITTLE COMFORT FARM, BRAUNTON EX33 2NJ
Tel: 01271 812414 Fax: 01271 817975 Contact: Jackie Milsom
jackie.milsom@btclick.com www.littlecomfortfarm.co.uk
Soil Association G7089. Organic mixed farm of 70 acres producing Devon cattle,
Lleyn x Texel sheep, poultry and pigs, farm gate and mail order sales. Self-catering
holidays in four barn conversions. School visits for farm and wildlife. Coarse fishing.

LOWER TURLEY FARM

LOWER TURLEY FARM, CULLOMPTON EX15 1NA
Tel: 01884 32234 Contact: Peter & Maggie Whiteman
Soil Association registered no. W32/W. Small farm with occasional sale of lamb.
Organic fleece, carded wool and hand-made felted products (mainly hats) for
sale. Traditional woodcrafts, chairs, yew longbows and trugs made to order.

LUGG SMALLHOLDING, SUE

ORSWELL COTTAGE ORGANIC GARDEN, STOKE RIVERS, BARNSTAPLE EX32 7LW
Tel: 01598 710558 Contact: Sue & John Lugg
Soil Association G7413; Henry Doubleday Organic Research Association. Small
organic holding: sheep, goats and poultry are part of the ecosystem of vegetable
production. Eggs from free range roaming hens, ducks. Guinea fowl, lamb, vegetables and herb plants. Barnstaple Pannier market on Fridays.

LUSCOMBE ORGANIC DRINKS

LUSCOMBE FARM, COLSTON ROAD, BUCKFASTLEIGH TQ11 0LP
Tel: 01364 643036 Fax: 01364 644498 Contact: Gabriel David
g@luscombe.co.uk www.luscombe.co.uk
Soil Association P2222. Produce and bottle the most genuine soft drinks using
all organic ingredients and great attention to detail. From apple juice through
ginger beer, elderflower to Sicilian lemonade.

MARSHFORD ORGANIC PRODUCE

11 BUTCHERS ROW, BARNSTAPLE EX31 1BW
Tel: 01271 322855 Contact: Vanessa Ebdon
enquiries@marshford.co.uk www.marshford.co.uk
Soil Association E19W, PE19W. Award-winning growers and retailers, 100%
organic. Our own vegetables, salads and herbs. Other local Devon meat, poultry,
eggs, dairy etc. Selection of groceries. Best Small Organic Shop 2001/2002.
Customer service 01237 477160.

MARSHFORD ORGANIC PRODUCE
CHURCHILL WAY, NORTHAM, NR. BIDEFORD EX39 1NG
Tel: 01237 477160 Contact: Vanessa Ebdon
enquiries@marshford.co.uk www.marshford.co.uk
Soil Association E19W, PE19W. Award-winning growers and retailers, 100%
organic. Our own vegetables, salads and herbs. Other local Devon meat, poultry,
eggs, dairy etc. Selection of groceries. Best Small Organic Shop 2001/2002.

MAUNDER LTD, LLOYD
WILLAND, CULLOMPTON EX15 2PJ
Tel: 01884 820534 Fax: 01884 821404 Contact: Adrian Blyth
adrian.blyth@lloydmaunder.co.uk www.lloydmaunder.co.uk
Lloyd Maunder supply organic lamb and organic chicken to the major multiples to
Soil Association standards.

THE MEAT JOINT
HILLSBOROUGH HOUSE, LOXHORE, BARNSTAPLE EX31 4SU
Tel: 01271 850335 Fax: 01271 850335 Contact: Kim Seggons
themeat.joint@care4free.net
Soil Association G4331. From our small farm in Loxhore, North Devon, we supply
beef, pork, lamb, chicken, bacon, sausages and Christmas turkeys. Contact Kim
Seggons for price list and delivery arrangements.

MIDDLE CAMPSCOTT FARM
MIDDLE CAMPSCOTT FARM, LEE, ILFRACOMBE EX34 8LS
Tel: 01271 864621 Contact: Karen Wright
middle.campscott@farmersweekly.net www.middlecampscott.co.uk
Soil Association G1923, P1923. We produce hard pressed ewe's and goat's milk
cheeses using milk from our own farm; wool and woollen products from our
naturally coloured Shetland sheep and milking flock; lamb; Ruby Devon beef.

MILK LINK LTD
PLYM HOUSE, 3 LONGBRIDGE RD, PLYMOUTH PL6 8LT
Tel: 01752 331805 Fax: 01752 331812 Contact: Lee Richards
lee.richards@milklink.com www.milklink.co.uk
Milk Link is the UK's third largest integrated dairy business with the capacity to process and add value to up to 80 per cent of our members' milk; allowing them to benefit from a long-term secure outlet for their milk, together with the additional margins available from processing it into added-value products.

NATURAL WAY
28 HYDE RD., PAIGNTON TQ4 5BY
Tel: 01803 665529 Fax: 01803 665529 Contact: Michael Jull
info@naturalwayhealth.co.uk www.naturalwayhealth.co.uk
Organic drinks, fruits, nuts, pulses and cereals. Range of organic herbal supplements and body care products. Mail order service available.

NATURE'S PLATE—ORGANIC VEGETARIAN CATERERS
8 TADDIFORD RD., EXETER EX4 4AY
Tel: 01392 413578 Fax: naturesplate@yahoo.com Contact: Rob Barker
www.naturesplate.co.uk
Nature's Plate—organic vegetarian wholefood experience. Event and private function caterers. Locally sourced, freshly prepared, delicious and nutritious cuisine. Soil Association, Vegetarian and Vegan Society certified and also carbon balanced.

NATURE'S ROUND
DART MILLS, OLD TOTNES RD, BUCKFASTLEIGH, NEWTON ABBOT TQ11 0NF
Tel: 07810 127376 Contact: Brent Tebbutt
naturesround@beeb.net
Bulk fruit and vegetable enquiries. Year round home delivery: vegetables, fruit, eggs, Dartmoor water (still & sparkling), fruit juices, tofu, wholefoods. Three sizes of vegetable boxes; can modify or you choose from a weekly price list. Wholesome Food Association.

NATUREMADE OASIS

EAST JOHNSTONE, BISH MILL, SOUTH MOLTON EX36 3QE
Tel: 01769 573571 Fax: 01769 573571 Contact: Esme Brown
sales@naturemade.co.uk www.naturemade.co.uk
Soil Association P1741. Vegetarian food manufacturers. Small family business
manufacturing and distributing vegetarian foods. Mail order available. Also producing Cows milk yoghurts, drinking yoghurts and cream. Goats milk and products.

NICHOLSONS WHOLEFOOD & HEALTH SHOP LTD

12 FORE ST., KINGSBRIDGE TQ7 1DQ
Tel: 01548 854347 Fax: 01548 854335 Contact: Frances Stathers
An Aladin's cave packed with a vast selection of wholefoods including gluten-free
and eco-friendly products, wide choice of supplements and toiletries.

NORWEGIAN WOOD ORGANIC BED & BREAKFAST

NORWEGIAN WOOD, BERRY POMEROY, TOTNES TQ9 6LE
Tel: 01803 867462 Contact: Heather Nicholson
heather@norwegianwood.eclipse.co.uk www.organicbedandbreakfast.info
Generous organic breakfasts. In-house nutritional therapist/iridologist. No
microwaves, no smoking. Ecologically sensitive household. Meat eaters, vegan,
lacto-vegetarian, wheat-free or raw food catered for with confidence. One mile
from Totnes.

OLD CUMMING ORGANIC FARM

OLD CUMMING ORGANIC FARM, COLSTON ROAD, BUCKFASTLEIGH TQ11 0LP
Tel: 01364 642672 Contact: The Manager
Soil Association G2495. Family-run organic farm producing high quality fresh
pre-packed organic produce. Salad packs, leaf vegetables and fruit juice.
Highly commended fruit juice in 2003 Soil Association awards. Organic Food
Awards 2004: Fresh Fruit and Veg Highly Commended.

ORCHARD WHOLEFOODS
16 HIGH ST., BUDLEIGH SALTERTON EX9 6LQ
Tel: 01395 442508 Contact: Jane Long
janelong@gmx.net
We are a well-stocked health shop with an ever-growing organic section, including almost all vegetarian foods except for fresh fruit and vegetables.

THE ORGANIC FARMERS MARKET LTD
THE BARN, HITCHCOCKS FARM, UFFCULME, CULLOMPTON EX15 3BZ
Tel: 01884 840160 Fax: 01884 840160 Contact: Fennella Reeves
mail@theorganicfarmersmarket.co.uk www.theorganicfarmersmarket.co.uk
Online home delivery service offering nationwide home delivery of organic products from the finest west country farms. The online market is packed with a variety of wonderful seasonal products including vegetables, meat, dairy, textiles and much more. See display ad.

ORGANIC POULTRY EQUIPMENT LTD
PETERHALES HOUSE, TRINITY, CULLOMPTON EX15 1PE
Tel: 07974 353073 Fax: 01884 35004 Contact: Peter Crowe
organicpoultryequipment@yahoo.co.uk www.organicpoultryequipment.co.uk
Suppliers of well insulated, low cost, modular poultry housing, developed by organic table bird producers. Features include a highly efficient feeding system, excellent welfare standards and a very durable structure. Secondary telephone number: 01884 33218.

ORIGINAL ORGANICS LTD
UNIT 9 LANGLANDS BUSINESS PARK, UFFCULME EX15 3DA
Tel: 01884 841515 Fax: 01884 841717 Contact: Clive Roberts
Manufacturer of the world famous Original Wormery and Rotol Composter.

OTTER VALLEY POULTRY

SPURTHAM FARM, UPOTTERY, HONITON EX14 9QD
Tel: 01404 861209 Fax: 01404 861715 Contact: RG Gardner
Soil Association P5599. Family-run poultry abattoir, offering a personal service to customers, specialising in the processing of all aspects of organic poultry.

OTTERY HEALTH STORE

14 BROAD ST., OTTERY ST. MARY, EX11 1BZ
Tel: 01404 812109 Fax: 01404 815020 Contact: Vanessa Coxon
ottery.wholefoods@virgin.net
We sell an extensive selection of fresh, local, organic produce: dried fruit, cereals, grains, pasta, flour, toiletries, complementary medicines, and ecological cleaning and sanitary products.

PALMER, MS KATE

WEST YEO FARM, WITHERIDGE, TIVERTON EX16 8PY
Tel: 01884 861269 Contact: Kate Palmer
Soil Association G7284. Historic farm with Red Devon beef, rare breed coloured sheep and arable production. Culm grassland borders the Little Dart River, featuring otters and kingfishers. Old orchard restoration.

THE PANTRY

13 STATION RD, SOUTH BRENT TQ10 9BE
Tel: 01364 73308 Contact: Jill Cruz thepantry@btinternet.com
Local sausages & bacon (some organic), organic vegetables, bread, milk, yoghurt.

PERCY'S COUNTRY HOTEL & RESTAURANT

COOMBESHEAD ESTATE, VIRGINSTOW, NR. OKEHAMPTON EX21 5EA
Tel: 01409 211236 Fax: 01409 211460 Contact: Ross Hayward
info@percys.co.uk www.percys.co.uk
Percy's were the 2003 Organic Restaurant of the Year, and is a showcase for the Westcountry's expansive larder of superlative organic produce. A tremendous amount of the menu including a bespoke breed of lamb, vegetables, herbs and dazzling eggs, is home-grown. Exmoor duck and chicken, too, set on a stunning 130-acre estate. Eight deluxe bedrooms with jacuzzis and king size beds, relaxation and rejuvenation.

PROPER JOB

CRANNAFORDS IND PARK, CHAGFORD TQ13 8DJ
Tel: 01647 432985 Fax: 01647 432985 Contact: Jo Hodges
compost@properjob.eclipse.co.uk www.properjob.ik.com
Community business. Holistic co-op. Working on waste and resource issues, especially composting, collecting compostables, education/consciousness raising.
Organic veg production and sale in our community shop/café. Setting up training in
related issues. Organic collection round.

PROVIDENCE FARM ORGANIC MEATS

PROVIDENCE FARM, CROSSPARK CROSS, HOLSWORTHY EX22 6JW
Tel: 01409 254421 Fax: 01409 254421 Contact: Pammy Riggs
info@providencefarm.co.uk www.providencefarm.co.uk
Winners of Organic Food Awards 2000–2003. Producing quality chicken, duck,
guinea fowl, goose, pork, bacon, sausages, lamb, beef and eggs. Farm shop selling
whole range of local organic fayre.

REAPERS

18 BAMPTON ST., TIVERTON EX16 6AA
Tel: 01884 255310 Contact: Carole Peard
Reapers is a wholefood health food store, featuring a wide range of organic
goods, including fresh fruit and vegetables.

REGIONAL CENTRE FOR ORGANIC HORTICULTRE

RCOH, SCHOOL FARM, DARTINGTON, NR. TOTNES TQ9 6EB
Tel: 01803 400999 Fax: 01803 408168 Contact: Mike Blakeley
mblakeley@dartingtontech.co.uk www.dartingtontech.co.uk
The Regional Centre for Organic Horticultre is based on the Dartington Hall Estate
near Totnes in South Devon. Established as a training centre under the guide of its
parent company Dartington Tech, to promote horticultural training throughout South
Devon. It is a thriving commercial operation with 6.5 acres of Soil Association cer-
tificated land producing a variety of fruits and vegetables both in the field and
under glass. We supply a range of products throughout the year and welcome
enquiries in relation to both training and sales.

RICHARD'S

64 FORE ST., TOPSHAM, EXETER EX3 0HL
Tel: 01392 873116 Fax: 01392 873116 Contact: Richard Tucker
r4richard@aol.com
Fruit and vegetables, eggs and fruit juices.

RIVERFORD—BRISTOL

RIVERFORD, BUCKFASTLEIGH TQ11 0LD
Tel: 01803 762720 Fax: 01803 762718 Contact: Sales Team
sales@riverford.co.uk riverford.co.uk
Independent local licensed distributor of Riverford Organic Vegetables.

RIVERFORD FARM FOOD SHOP AT KITLEY

KITLEY, YEALMPTON, PLYMOUTH PL8 2LT
Tel: 01752 880925 Fax: 01752 880263 Contact: Peter Marr
office@riverfordfarmshop.co.uk www.riverford.co.uk
Organic Farmers and Growers registered. Farm shop and café offering a wide
range of organic food (vegetables, meat, dairy, wine, dry goods and plant seeds
etc.). Emphasis on quality food from local producers.

RIVERFORD FARM SHOP

RIVERFORD, STAVERTON, TOTNES TQ9 6AF
Tel: 01803 762523 Fax: 01803 762571 Contact: Deborah Nash
office@riverford.co.uk www.riverford.co.uk
Organic Farmers and Growers, cert no. UKP100357. Organic and locally produced
beef, lamb, chicken, pork, free range eggs, cheese, wine, bread and pies, dry
goods and Riverford Organic Milk.

RIVERFORD FARM SHOP TOTNES
HIGH ST., TOTNES TQ9
Tel: 01803 863959 Fax: 01803 868380 Contact: Lynda
office@riverford.co.uk www.riverfordfarmshop.co.uk
Carrying an excellent selection of meat, poultry, dairy, fruit, vegetables and
delicatessen, you can be always sure of finding something for supper! (and the
perfect bottle of wine to go with it). If the shop doesn't have something you
want, we can order it for you.

RIVERFORD HOME DELIVERY EXETER & EAST DEVON
Tel: 01803 865015 Contact: Jon Ripley
jonripley@riverfordhomedelivery.co.uk www.riverford.co.uk
Independent local licensed distributor of Riverford Organic Vegetables.

RIVERFORD HOME DELIVERY SOUTH GLOUCESTERSHIRE & STROUD
WASH BARN, BUCKFASTLEIGH TQ11 0LD
Tel: 01803 762720 Contact: Neal Whitehouse Piper
neal@riverfordhomedelivery.co.uk www.riverford.co.uk
Independent local licensed distributor of Riverford Organic Vegetables.

RIVERFORD ORGANIC VEGETABLES
WASH BARN, BUCKFASTLEIGH TQ11 0LD
Tel: 01803 762720 Contact: Tieneka Drew
boxscheme@riverford.co.uk www.riverford.co.uk
Soil Association W24W. Award-winning organic vegetable box scheme, delivering
to houses across the South and South-west of England. One of the founding
members of the South Devon Organic Producers, a producer group of 13 family-run
farms who grow 85 different varieties for the box scheme, making Riverford one
of the largest producer's of organic vegetables in the UK. Member of the Soil
Association Organic Farms Network. Organic Food Awards 2004: Box Scheme
Commended; Fresh Fruit and Veg Highly Commended.

ROBERT OWEN COMMUNITIES

LOWER SHARPHAM BARTON FARM, ASHPRINGTON, TOTNES TQ9 7DX
Tel: 01803 732502 Fax: 01803 732502 Contact: B Roodenburg-Vermaat
sharphamfarm@roc-uk.org
Day centre for people with learning disabilities. Dairy, beef, sheep, laying
birds and vegetables. Produce milk, meats, eggs and veg.

ROCOMBE FARM FRESH ICE CREAM LTD

OLD NEWTON RD., HEATHFIELD, NEWTON ABBOT TQ12 6RA
Tel: 01626 834545 Fax: 01626 835777 Contact: Peter Redstone (M.D.)
info@rocombefarm.co.uk www.rocombefarm.co.uk
Luxury organic dairy ice cream, organic frozen yoghurt and organic fruit sorbet. Soil
Association P1006.

RODANDBENS

BICKHAM FARM, KENN, EXETER EX6 7XL
Tel: 01392 833833 Fax: 01392 833832 Contact: Rodney Hall
rod@rodandbens.com www.rodandbens.com
Mixed farm supplying vegetables locally and nationwide using mail order. Highly
commended Organic Food Awards 2002 and 2003. Rick Steins food superheroes.
Organic Food Awards 2004: Highly Commended Box Scheme; Winner Eggs.

ROSE COTTAGE ORGANICS

RUMLEIGH, BERE ALSTON PL20 7HN
Tel: 01822 840297 Contact: Pete Mayston pmayston@fish.co.uk
Soil Association G5300. Seasonal vegetables, apples, soft fruit and herbs, grown in
Tamar Valley. Produce sold via local farmers' markets.

SACKS

80 HIGH ST., TOTNES TQ9 5SN
Tel: 01803 863263 Contact: Dave Lacey
Soil Association R1907. We sell a comprehensive range of organic vegetarian
food. A wide range of fresh organic fruit and vegetables always in stock.

SEASONS

8 WELL ST., EXETER EX4 6QR
Tel: 01392 201282 Contact: Parviz Kargar
Organic vegetables, grains, beans, pulses, dried fruit and natural groceries.

SEEDS BAKERY & HEALTH STORE

35 HIGH ST, TOTNES TQ9 5NP
Tel: 01803 862526 Contact: Barry Pope
Bakery, baking organic bread and non-organic cakes and savouries.

SEEDS BAKERY & HEALTH STORE

22 DUKE ST., DARTMOUTH TQ6 9TZ
Tel: 01803 833200 Contact: Barry Pope
Bakery, baking organic bread and non-organic cakes and savouries.

SEEDS BAKERY & HEALTH STORE

19 HIGH ST, EXMOUTH EX8
Tel: 01395 265741 Contact: Barry Pope
Bakery, baking organic bread and non-organic cakes and savouries.

SHARPHAM PARTNERSHIP LTD

SHARPHAM ESTATE, ASHPRINGTON, TOTNES TQ9 7UT
Tel: 01803 732203 Fax: 01803 732122 Contact: M Sharman
info@sharpham.com www.sharpham.com
Soil Association G2483. A 200-acre tenancy on a 500-acre estate that is almost all organic (and biodynamic). Producing organic milk, organic cheeses. Non-organic estate grown and bottled wines.

SHILLINGFORD ORGANICS

THE BARNS, BARTON LANE, SHILLINGFORD ABBOT, EXETER EX2 9QQ
Tel: 01392 832729 Fax: 01392 832729 Contact: Martyn Bragg
info@shillingfordorganics.co.uk www.shillingfordorganics.co.uk
Family-run farm producing fresh organic vegetables, herbs and eggs for box
deliveries to Teign Valley and Exeter area. Plans to develop fresh salad products,
bread and ready made meals from Autumn 2005. We pride ourselves on
producing top quality boxes with plenty of variety and unbeatable freshness.

SKYSPROUTS

GOSWORTHY COTTAGE, HARBERTON, TOTNES TQ9 7LP
Tel: 01364 72404 Fax: 01364 72404 Contact: Brett Kellett
skysprouts@ic24.net
Growers of organic beansprouts, alfalfa sprouts, alfalfa and broccoli sprouts, alfalfa
and fenugreek sprouts, mung, aduki, lentil, chickpea, sunflower and sunflower salads.
Supplying wholesalers, shops and veg box schemes throughout the UK.

SMALE, PM & ME

THE BARTON, BURRINGTON, UMBERLEIGH EX37 9JQ
Tel: 01769 520216 Contact: Peter & Marilyn Smale
bartonfarm@yahoo.com www.burrington-barton.co.uk
Soil Association G4554. An organic farm with an abundance of wildlife, raising
cattle and sheep. Also providing quality B&B accommodation using organic or
local produce where ever possible. En-suite rooms. Prices from £25pp pn.

SOUTH DEVON ORGANIC PRODUCERS LTD

C/O WASH BARN, BUCKFASTLEIGH TQ11 0LD
Tel: 01803 762100 Fax: 01803 762100 Contact: Ian Noble
sdop@farmersweekly.net www.sdopltd.co.uk
Co-operative of growers producing organic vegetables.

TAMAR ORGANICS

THE ORGANIC GARDEN CENTRE, GULWORTHY, TAVISTOCK PL19 8JE
Tel: 01822 834887 Fax: 01822 834284 Contact: Cathy or Neil Guilfoy
sales@tamarorganics.co.uk www.tamarorganics.co.uk
Soil Association G1823, P1823. Seed and organic mail order company specialising
in organic seeds for gardeners and growers. Organic garden centre, seeds, plants
and soft fruit, open Tuesday–Friday 9.30am to 5pm, Saturday 10.30am to 3pm;
Closed Sundays and Bank Holidays.

TIDEFORD ORGANIC FOODS LIMITED

UNIT 5, THE ALPHA CENTRE, BABBAGE ROAD, TOTNES TQ9 5JA
Tel: 01803 840555 Fax: 01803 840551 Contact: Sue Mappin
tideford@btconnect.com www.tidefordorganics.com
Soil Association P2178. Tideford produces award-winning soups, sauces, pestos
and puddings.

TOMS, R & M

PARKHILL FARM, SHIRWELL, BARNSTAPLE EX31 4JN
Tel: 01271 850323 Fax: 01271 850323 Contact: The Manager
Soil Association G2959. Organic beef and sheep. Non-organic free range chicken.
Camping. Residential caravan for holiday let.

TOPRACK

THROWCOMBE, STOODLEIGH NR, TIVERTON EX16 9QQ
Tel: 01884 881 471 Contact: Carol Lynne Ellis-Jones
cej@toprack.co.uk www.toprack.co.uk
Prime tender organic park venison, cutting and packing information, cooking
instructions and recipes. Selling points: e.g. lowest in fat, high in iron, contains
Omega 3 fatty acids, etc.

URSELL, DJ & SJ

ALLER FARM, DOLTON, WINKLEIGH EX19 8PP
Tel: 01805 804414 Fax: 01805 804737 Contact: David Ursell
ursell@farmersweekly.net
Soil Association G791.Supply traditional beef which has hung for four weeks.
Also supply lupins and cereals, all organic.

WARD, GR & RJ

PARSONAGE FARM, IDDESLEIGH, WINKLEIGH EX19 8SN
Tel: 01837 810318 Contact: The Manager
Soil Association G6241. Organic dairy.

WATERGATE MUSHROOM FARM

UMBERLEIGH EX37 9AG
Tel: 01769 540502 Fax: 01769 540502 Contact: Marie Flanagan
Soil Association P5255. Situated in North Devon, we only produce organic
mushrooms.

WELL HUNG MEAT CO

TORDEAN FARM, DEAN PRIOR, BUCKFASTLEIGH TQ11 0LY
Tel: 0845 230 3131 Contact: Graeme Roy
sales@wellhungmeat.com www.wellhungmeat.com
Soil Association Organic Food Awards Winners (2001, 2002, 2004) and Rick Stein
'Food Hero', we deliver the very best organic meat to your door. Our range includes
organic lamb, beef, poultry and pork including turkeys for Christmas. All of our
meat is hung in the traditional manner, this makes it taste 'how meat used to
taste'. The meat has a succulence and tenderness that is second to none, something for you, your family and friends to enjoy. Orders can be placed via the website, by email or phone We will be very happy to help. Organic Food Awards 2004
Fresh Meat Winner & Highly Commended.

WEST CHILLA FARM

WEST CHILLA, BEAWORTHY EX21 5XQ
Tel: 01409 221256 Contact: Tim Ramsay
ramsay@westchilla.fsnet.co.uk www.westchillafarm.co.uk
Soil Association G5225. We are a small beef and sheep enterprise with Devon
cattle and Poll Dorset sheep. We run a self-catering holiday cottage that sleeps 5.
The farm is abundant with wildlife.

WEST EMLETT FARM

BLACK DOG, CREDITON EX17 4QB
Tel: 01363 877689 Fax: 01363 877468 Contact: Olly Curtis
Soil Association G4950. On our 240-acre farm we grow cereals and keep cattle
and sheep. We also produce Soil Association standard eggs which we distribute
to retailers and wholesalers throughout southern England. Organic Food Awards
2004: Eggs Commended.

WEST FORDE ORGANICS

THE BARTON, POUGHILL, CREDITON EX17 4LE
Tel: 01363 866349 Contact: Anne Wander
westfordeorganics@btopenworld.com
Direct sales of top quality home-produced organic lamb.

WEST HILL FARM

WEST HILL FARM, WEST DOWN, ILFRACOMBE EX34 8NF
Tel: 01271 815477 Fax: 01271 813316 Contact: Susi Batstone
info@westhillfarm.org www.westhillfarm.org
High on the north Devon coast, our dairy herd graze organic pastures in sight of the
sea and have views for 50 miles. Their milk is processed in our modern dairy into a
wide range of products, and distributed within 25 mile radius in our chiller vans. We
welcome school visits and are a demonstration farm for the Soil Association. Our full
range and new products are available to sample in our farm shop, which is open 24
hours, 7 days a week. Member of the Soil Association Organic Farms Network.

WEST ILKERTON FARM

WEST ILKERTON FARM, LYNTON EX35 6QA
Tel: 01598 752310 Fax: 01598 752310 Contact: Victoria Eveleigh
eveleigh@westilkerton.co.uk www.westilkerton.co.uk
Hill livestock farm: store and breeding stock for sale at certain times of the year.
Organic Devon cattle and Exmoor Horn and Exmoor Horn x sheep (breeding stock
and young stock) will be for sale in autumn—see our website. Self-catering holiday
cottage, ETC 4 star, to let. Horse drawn tours over Exmoor using Shire horses.

WEST LAKE FARM

CHILLA, BEAWORTHY EX21 5XF
Tel: 01409 221991 Fax: 01409 221991 Contact: George Travis
westlakefarm@lineone.net
West Lake press and produce a range of award-winning organic single variety and
blended apple juices, slowly fermented ciders, cider vinegar and organic fruit
vinegars. Hand-crafted from west country apples.

THE WESTCOUNTRY CURRY CO LTD

UNITS 8/9, KNIGHTON BUSINESS CENTRE, WEMBURY PL9 0ED
Tel: 01752 863123 Fax: 01752 863123 Contact: David Lea & Chris Carnegie
enquiries@westcountrycurry.com www.westcountrycurry.com
Hand-made curry pastes, marinades and dipping sauces. All created using authentic
recipes, following traditional methods, with no additives or flavourings. All made with
care in our south Devon kitchen.

WESTCOUNTRY ORGANICS

NATSON FARM, TEDBURN ST. MARY, EXETER EX6 6ET
Tel: 0164 724724 Fax: 0164 724031 Contact: Bruce Burton
enquiries@westcountryorganics.co.uk www.westcountryorganics.co.uk
National mail order of organic foods including a range of vegetables and fruit,
dairy products, drinks and vegetarian products.

WILLOW VEGETARIAN GARDEN RESTAURANT

87 HIGH STREET, TOTNES TQ9 5PB
Tel: 01803 862605 Contact: Maha Roberts
Tasty vegetarian and vegan meals hand-prepared using masses of organic ingredients.
Drinks are all organic. Prices are very reasonable. Sunny secluded walled garden.
Special nights every week. Children welcome.

WINSLADE, LB

BEECH GROVE FARM, KNOWSTONE, SOUTH MOLTON EX36 4RS
Tel: 01398 341551 Contact: LB Winslade
Organic beef producer.

WOODLAND ORGANICS

MOORFOOT CROSS, WOODLAND, NR. DENBURY, NEWTON ABBOT TQ12 6EQ
Tel: 01803 813760 Contact: Mike Jones
Wholesome Food Association member. 7-acre holding ethically producing over 80
varieties of fruit and vegetables plus free range eggs. Operating direct delivery veg
boxes plus supplying trade locally.

YARNER

BOVEY TRACEY TQ13 9LN
Tel: 01364 661503 Fax: 01364 661504 Contact: Patrick & Maja Holman
mail@yarner.com
Soil Association G7555. Organic farm and function venue. High quality bulk
spring water supplied to Yeo Valley as an ingredient for Rocombe Farm and Marks
& Spencer organic sorbet product ranges.

BARTON MEADOWS

BARTON MEADOWS FARM, DORCHESTER RD., CERNE ABBAS DT2 7JS
Tel: 01300 341336 Fax: 01300 341336 Contact: DG Gourley
bartonmeadows@tiscali.co.uk
Soil Association G956. We sell prime Angus beef, pork, lamb and mutton, both
fresh and frozen, plus honey and Romney fleece for spinners. Also available are
organic watercolours and prints by Elizabeth Bairstow.

BECKLANDS FARM

BECKLANDS FARM, WHITCHURCH CANONICORUM, BRIDPORT DT6 6RG
Tel: 01297 560298 Contact: Hilary & Francis Joyce
becklandsorganicfarm@btopenworld.com www.becklandsorganicfarm.com
Small farm shop with farm produce, organic groceries and Ecover cleaning products,
eco-environmental information and crafts. Sells own Red Ruby Devon x beef,
geese, eggs, cheese and vegetables in season, home-made preserves using farm
fruit. Sometimes en-suite B&B with full organic breakfast. From 14th July—8th
September, organic lunches and teas outside from 12.30 on Thursdays plus guided
farm walks at 2pm. Groups any time by arrangement. Member of the Soil
Association Organic Farms Network.

BIBBY, R & E

WHITE SHEET FARM, BEAMINSTER DT8 3SF
Tel: 01308 862066 Contact: Elaine Bibby
Soil Association G4325. We produce organic, suckled 12 months store cattle from
a small suckler herd fed only grass or hay.

BOTHEN HILL PRODUCE

7 GREEN LANE, BOTHENHAMPTON, BRIDPORT DT6 4ED
Tel: 01308 424271 Fax: 01308 424271 Contact: ML De Greeff
sales@bothenhillproduce.co.uk www.bothenhillproduce.co.uk
Family-run smallholding producing wide range of quality vegetables throughout
the year, also lamb from our closed flock of pedigree Hampshire Down sheep.
Local box delivery scheme. Wholesale available.

BOURNE ORGANIC

39 ST. CLEMENTS RD., BOURNEMOUTH BH1 4DX
Tel: 01202 778516 Contact: Lisa Northover
mail@bourneorganic.co.uk www.bourneorganic.co.uk
Bourne Organic delivers organic fresh produce, grocery products, Ecover products
and natural toiletries to homes and businesses throughout the Bournemouth area.

CAKE, JE, M & R

WALLIS FARM, CATTISTOCK, DORCHESTER DT2 0JL
Tel: 01300 320653 Contact: Rupert Cake
rupert@wallisfarm.com www.wallisfarm.com
Organic hay.

CANNINGS COURT ORGANIC FARM SHOP AND BOX SCHEME

CANNINGS COURT, PULHAM, NR. STURMINSTER NEWTON DT2 7EA
Tel: 01258 818035 Contact: John Dennison
john.cannings-court@care4free.net
We have a farm shop and local delivery box scheme, supplying fresh vegetables,
eggs and salads from our own fields and polytunnels. We also sell local organic
bread, milk, cream, cheese and yoghurt and a range of organic fruit from near and
far. Our produce is better, fresher and on average cheaper than anything supermarkets sell. Visit us and find out.

CHILDHAY MANOR ORGANICS

CHILDHAY MANOR, BLACKDOWN, BEAMINSTER DT8 3LQ
Tel: 01308 868709 Fax: 01308 868119 Contact: Lucy Blackburn
lucy@childhaymanor.com www.childhaymanor.com
We produce our own organic pork, bacon and beef, which we supply, as well as
organic lamb and chickens from other local farmers. We deliver to butchers
throughout the south of England, and operate an overnight hamper delivery
scheme to the general public, nationwide.

CLIPPER

BEAMINSTER BUSINESS PARK, BEAMINSTER DT8 3PR

Tel: 01308 863344 Contact: Paul Machin

enquiries@clipper-teas.com www.clipper-teas.com

Clipper is one of Britain's favourite organic brands, with a huge range of great tasting organic Fairtrade tea, coffee, hot chocolate and infusions. Check out the full range on our website www.clipper-teas.com. Organic Food Awards 2004: Coffee Highly Commended.

COVENT GARDEN FRUIT MARKET

COVENT GARDEN FRUIT MARKET, 38A, SOUTHBOURNE GROVE, BOURNEMOUTH BH6 3RA

Tel: 01202 425493 Contact: Mark & Lisa Pierson

mark@displayer.co.uk www.coventgardenfruit.co.uk

Bournemouth's longest established greengrocers, providing a wide range of fresh fruit and vegetables, locally sourced, including an extensive organic range of fresh vegetables, fruit and eggs. Delivery service includes home delivery organic box scheme. Fabulous fruit baskets are created using fresh produce and wicker baskets as an ideal gift. Locally made jams, chutneys, preserves and honey available. Seasonal plants flowers bulbs and organic compost are also available. Visitors wanting to visit the Dorset area and attend farmers markets can stay over night in B&B nearby at Hengistbury Head. To arrange Accommodation call 01202 425493; organic breakfast available by prior request. Order on the website, or by phone.

COWDEN HOUSE

FRYS LANE, GODMANSTONE, DORCHESTER DT2 7AG

Tel: 01300 341377 Contact: Tim Mills

www.cowdenhouse.co.uk

Vegetarian bed and breakfast located in beautiful downland. Wonderful views and walking/cycling country. Warm hospitality, peace and quiet, local organic produce used to create delicious breakfasts and optional dinners.

DORSET FARMS

LITTLEWINDSOR, BEAMINSTER DT8 3QU
Tel: 01308 868822 Fax: 01308 868973 Contact: Sarah Chaffey
admin@dorset farms.co.uk www.dorsetfarms.co.uk
Soil Association P2595. Producers of quality organic ham and bacon. Ham
available on or off the bone and pre-packed. Bacon sliced in packs of 2.27kg or
pre-packed.

DORSET PASTRY

UNIT 8D HYBRIS BUSINESS PARK, WARMWELL RD., CROSSWAYS, DORCHESTER
DT2 8BF
Tel: 01305 854860 Fax: 01305 854870 Contact: Moira Blake
enquiries@dorsetpastry.com www.dorsetpastry.com
Small Producer of the Year 2003/4. Produces fine organic pure butter frozen,
ready rolled puff, sweet and flavoured pastry. Local ingredients hand-folded and
rested in the traditional manner.

DORSET WILDLIFE TRUST

45 HIGH ST., TOLLER PORCORUM, DORCHESTER DT2 0DN
Tel: 01300 320573 Contact: Paul Comer
paul@paulcomer1.f9.co.uk
Soil Association G898. We run as a farmed nature reserve, producing fat and
store lambs and suckled calves/store cattle.

DOWN TO EARTH

18 PRINCES ST., DORCHESTER DT1 1TW
Tel: 01305 268325 Contact: A Bowley
Retailers of a wide range of organic produce including butter, cheese, eggs, fruits
and vegetables, bread, dried foods, frozen and chilled produce. Specialists in
British cheeses.

EWELEAZE FARM

THE CARTSHED, CHURCH LANE, OSMINGTON, WEYMOUTH DT3 6EW
Tel: 01305 833690 Contact: Peter Broatch
peter@eweleaze.co.uk www.eweleaze.co.uk
Soil Association G6652. Small organic farm producing Aberdeen Angus beef, lamb and eggs. Direct sales of eggs and meat from the door. Camping is available during August, with access to a private beach. A holiday cottage is available for weekly lets, in nearby Osmington village (see website).

FOOTS EGGS

STONEY FARM, BISHOPS CAUNDLE, SHERBORNE DT9 5ND
Tel: 01963 23033 Fax: 01963 23093 Contact: Bill Foot emmafoot@hotmail.com
Wholesale other producers' eggs to hotels, shops etc..

FORD FARM, ASHLEY CHASE ESTATES

PARKS FARM, LITTON CHENEY, DORCHESTER DT2 9AZ
Tel: 01308 482580 Fax: 01308 482608 Contact: Claire Pike
cheese@fordfarm.com www.fordfarm.com
Soil Association P4414. Traditional West Country farmhouse cheese producers. Organic, kosher and flavoured cheeses are our speciality, including traditional cloth-wrapped cheddar.

FOX, JH

WEST CLIFF FARM, WEST BAY, BRIDPORT DT6 4HS
Tel: 01308 425316 Contact: Shaun Fox
shaunfox@farmersweekly.net or shaun.fox@fwi.co.uk
We specialise in fruit and veg together with lamb and potatoes, supply some box schemes but sell through local farm shop or Sunday markets. Orders by phone welcome.

FRUITS OF THE EARTH

2A VICTORIA GROVE, BRIDPORT DT6 3AA
Tel: 01308 425827 Contact: The Manager
Organic vegetables, milk, cereals, wine, teas, rice, coffees, pulses, bread, chocolate, yoghurts, dried fruit, herbs, spices, and lots more.

GOLD HILL ORGANIC FARM

CHILD OKEFORD, NR. BLANDFORD FORUM DT11 8HB
Tel: 01258 861413 Fax: 01258 861413 Contact: Sara Cross
From May until March sell up to 35 varieties of vegetables, fruit, organic beef, milk
and bread through our farm shop, at weekends only: Fri & Sat 9–1, 2–5.30 Sun
9–1. Veg box scheme. Also at Castle Cary Market (Tuesdays). Deliver to Blandford
and Shaftesbury.

GREEN VALLEY FARM SHOP

LONGMEADOW, GODMANSTONE, DORCHESTER DT2 7AE
Tel: 01300 342164 Fax: 01300 342164 Contact: David Nesling
We are a farm shop selling principally organic products, including organic
vegetables, local organic meat, eggs, milk, bread, cheese, wines, wholefoods,
groceries, Ecover products and refill systems.

THE HEALTH MINISTRY

16 HIGH ST., CHRISTCHURCH BH23 1AY
Tel: 01202 471152 Fax: 01202 471152 Contact: Hilary Bateman
Wide range of organic dried goods e.g. nuts, pulses, flour, drinks, ice cream,
spreads, etc.

HERITAGE PRIME—EARNESTLY BRITISH MEATS OF RARE QUALITY

SHEDBUSH FARM, MUDDY FORD LANE, STANTON ST. GABRIEL, BRIDPORT DT6 6DR
Tel: 01297 489304 Fax: 01297 489304 Contact: Denise Bell
sales@heritageprime.co.uk or heritageprime@aol.com www.heritageprime.co.uk
Biodynamic farming—food more carefully produced than the highest organic
standard. All produce to Demeter biodynamic standards: lamb, beef, pork and
occasional poultry. Domestic boxes, all joints and cuts butchered, with Slow Food
recipes. Mail order only. Nationwide. Favourite of the finest chefs in England, where
Nigella buys her meat! Organic Food Awards 2004: Commended.

JUICE CAFE LTD
9 BURLINGTON ARCADE, OLD CHRISTCHURCH RD., BOURNEMOUTH BH1 2HZ
Tel: 01202 314143 Contact: M De Wal'esch
Café using some organic ingredients.

THE KINGCOMBE CENTRE
LOWER KINGCOMBE, TOLLER PORCORUM, DORCHESTER DT2 0EQ
Tel: 01300 320684 Fax: 01300 321409 Contact: Nigel Spring
nspring@kingcombe-centre.demon.co.uk www.kingcombe-centre.demon.co.uk
Residential study centre in converted farm buildings beside the river Hooke; offers
courses and holidays in a wide range of subjects for adults and children, fit and disabled. Day visits for schools and guided walks. Organically reared pork and lamb.

LEAKERS BAKERY
29 EAST ST, BRIDPORT DT6 3JX
Tel: 01308 423296 Contact: The Manager
Organic milk, eggs, cream and we use many organic ingredients in our products.

LONG CRICHEL BAKERY
LONG CRICHEL, WIMBORNE BH21 5JU
Tel: 01258 830852 Fax: 01258 830855 Contact: Jamie Campbell & Kathy Davies
info@longcrichelbakery.co.uk www.longcrichelbakery.co.uk
Soil Association P6534. Organic bakery including hand-crafted bread and cakes
baked in a wood-fired brick oven. Open Thurs, Friday afternoons, Saturday all day,
phone first as times vary. Fresh organic vegetables in season from walled garden.

LONG CRICHEL ORGANIC GARDEN
LONG CRICHEL GARDEN, (OPPOSITE LONG CRICHEL BAKERY), LONG CRICHEL,
WIMBORNE BH21 5LF
Tel: 01258 830295 Contact: Anni Sax longcrichelgarden@cooptel.net
Soil Association G7461. We grow organic vegetables and fruit in 2.5 acres
including a delightful walled garden using permaculture/forest garden methods.
Our speciality is oriental salad and herb production. Local veg box scheme.
Registered for WWOOFers.

LONGMEADOW ORGANIC VEGETABLES

GODMANSTONE, DORCHESTER DT2 7AE
Tel: 01300 341779 Fax: 01300 341779 Contact: Patsy Chapman
chapmans.longmeadow@virgin.com
Soil Association C60W. We ar an organic market garden, established 1987,
growing a variety of vegetables and some fruit, available through our own box
scheme and Green Valley Farm Shop.

MANOR FARM

GODMANSTONE, DORCHESTER DT2 7AH
Tel: 01300 341415 Fax: 01300 341170 Contact: Will Best
will@manor-farm-organic.co.uk www.manor-farm-organic.co.uk
Mixed farm, organic since 1986. Pasteurised whole and semi-skimmed milk and
cream. Lamb and mince prepared for the freezer. Also wheat, combed wheat reed
and rearing calves. Day visits for schools, etc. Accommodation—self-catering
or partially catered, economic. Occasional open days.

MANOR FARM ORGANIC MILK LTD

MANOR FARM, GODMANSTONE, DORCHESTER DT2 7AH
Tel: 01300 341415 Fax: 01300 341170 Contact: Pam Best
pam@manor-farm-organic.co.uk www.manor-farm-organic.co.uk
Producers of organic cartonned, pasteurised whole milk, semi-skimmed milk and
cream. Distribution over the South of England. Member of the Soil Association
Organic Farms Network. Organic Food Awards 2004 Fresh Meat Commended.

MODBURY FARM

BURTON BRADSTOCK, BRIDPORT DT6 4NE
Tel: 01308 897193 Fax: 01308 897193 Contact: Tim & Julie Garry
timgarry@btinternet.com
Soil Association P7552, G7551. Organic Jersey herd with farm shop selling our
own milk, cream and summer vegetables. Also locally sourced organic and
non-organic produce (meat, eggs, cheese, ice cream, preserves, etc).

NATURAL DYE COMPANY

STANBRIDGE, WIMBORNE BH21 4JD
Tel: 01258 840549 Fax: 01258 840958 Contact: Sarah Burnett
naturaldyecompany@boltblue.com www.naturaldyecompany.com
The Natural Dye Company offers hand-knitted jackets, coats and cardigans in
silk, wool and cashmere, coloured with our famous natural, organic dyes.

NEAL'S YARD (NATURAL) REMEDIES LTD

PEACEMARSH, GILLINGHAM SP8 4EU
Tel: 01747 834634 Fax: 01747 834601 Contact: Stephanie MacLean
cservice@nealsyardremedies.com www.nealsyardremedies.com
Manufacturer and seller of natural skincare products, herbal remedies,
homoeopathic remedies and aromatherapy products.

ORGANIX BRANDS LTD

KNAPP MILL, MILL ROAD, CHRISTCHURCH, DORSET BH9 2SD
Tel: 01202 479701 Fax: 01202 479712 Contact: Marie Van-Hagen
marie.vanhagen@organix.com www.organix.com
Organix Brands are manufacturers of organic baby and children's foods. Its range
for babies includes, infant cereals, fruit purées for weaning and developing babies,
rice cakes, fruity wheels and jumbo breadsticks to encourage self-feeding. Its
'Goodies' range for children from 12 months, includes: savoury snacks, chewy fruit
& cereal bars, fruit purées, fruit dippers, animal biscuits and gingerbread men. All
Organix Goodies snacks for children are made without any adulteration. They do
not contain any added processed sugars, additives, colourings, preservatives or
flavourings. They taste great—go on, give them a try!

REAL MEALS

64 ARNEWOOD RD., BOURNEMOUTH BH6 5DL
Tel: 01202 418381 Contact: J De Comyn
Caterer, delivery of hot organic lunches. Nice, friendly people, will do gluten-free,
dairy-free, wheat-free.

RECTORY FARM

EAST CHALDON ROAD, WINFRITH NEWBURGH, NR. DORCHESTER DT2 8DJ
Tel: 01305 852835 Contact: Annette Evans
Organic eggs. Soil Association G2057. The farm lies approx 2.5 miles from
Lulworth Cove. Open, free of charge to visitors.

RESPECT ORGANICS

31 BELL ST., SHAFTESBURY SP7 8AR
Tel: 01747 851561 Fax: 01747 851715 Contact: Vince Adams
info@respectorganics.com www.respectorganics.com
Owner of the Respect brand, specialising in the ambient cake market. We license
other manufacturers to produce our cakes for us.

SLEPE FARM LTD

SLEPE FARM, SLEPE, NR. POOLE BH16 6HS
Tel: 01202 622737 Fax: 01202 620844 Contact: James Selby Bennett
j.selbybennett@virgin.net
Soil Association G7085. Beef and corn farm with wild heath grazed beef and wild
game, wildlife and large barn available for exhibitions and craftsmen's workshops
(furniture design and restoration).

SPETCH, LEONARD

THORNCOMBE FARM, HIGHER BOCKHAMPTON, DORCHESTER DT2 8QH
Tel: 01305 251695 Contact: Leonard Spetch
Small family farm specialising in high quality beef reared on well managed
grassland. Some cereals also grown.

STOATE, NR AND SONS

CANN MILLS, SHAFTESBURY SP7 0BL
Tel: 01747 852475 Fax: 01747 851936 Contact: Michael Stoate
michaelstoate@lineone.net
Traditional stoneground flour millers since 1832 producing a full range of organic
flour for all your baking requirements.

STURTS FARM COMMUNITY

SHEILING TRUST, THREE CROSS ROAD, WEST MOORS, FERNDOWN BH22 0NF
Tel: 01202 870572 (farm) Fax: 01202 854763 Contact: Markus Konig (Farmer)
office@sturtsfarm.com www.sturtsfarm.com
Fully biodynamic certified large market garden, farm includes dairy, beef, poultry, pigs, 90 acres. Farm shop includes full range of fruit and veg, dry goods, health products. Shop tel: 01202 894292. Garden tel: 01202 875275.

SUNNYSIDE ORGANIC FARM

SUNNYSIDE FARM, LOWER KINGCOMBE, TOLLER PORCORUM, DORCHESTER DT2 0EQ
Tel: 01300 321537 Fax: 01300 321537 Contact: Mandie Fletcher
mandiefletcher@sunnyside95.fsnet.co.uk www.sunnysideorganicfarm.co.uk
Soil Association G875, P7913. Mixed organic farm with luxury holiday cottage, farm shop for seasonal vegetables, lamb, beef, eggs and local artist exhibiting in the middle of the Dorset Wildlife Trust Reserve.

SYDLING BROOK ORGANIC FARM SHOP

SYDLING ESTATE, UP SYDLING, DORCHESTER DT2 9PQ
Tel: 01300 341991 Fax: 01300 341166 Contact: Sarah Lindley
info@sydling.co.uk www.sydling.co.uk
Home-reared, traditional and rare breed meats, direct from the estate. Game and poultry, award-winning hand-made cheeses. Smoked products, fruit and vegetables. Alternative telephone number: 01300 341133.

TAMARISK FARM

WEST BEXINGTON, DORCHESTER DT2 9DF
Tel: 01308 897781/897784 Contact: Adam Simon
farm@tamariskfarm.co.uk www.tamariskfarm.co.uk
All home-grown on family farm by the sea. Order direct from the farm: beef, lamb, mutton, sausages, wholemeal wheat and rye flours and vegetables all year round (Soil Association no. P07W). Deliver to DT6. Farm shop open every Friday morning between 8.30 and 10.30 for meat and flour or at any other time by arrangement.

THE WATERCRESS COMPANY

MAEN, CULLIFORD RD., DORCHESTER DT1 1QQ
Tel: 01929 401400 Fax: 01929 462693 Contact: Tom Amery
tom.amery@thewatercresscompany.com
Soil Association G4732. Growers of organic watercress from our farms in UK,
Spain and Florida.

WEST HEMBURY FARM

WEST HEMBURY FARM, ASKERSWELL, DORCHESTER DT2 9EN
Tel: 01308 485289 Fax: 01308 485041 Contact: Andy & Chris Hunt
farm@westhembury.com www.westhembury.com
Soil Association G2097. A mixed organic farm with self-catering accommodation
for 2 to 6 people in converted stone barns (4 star). Farm gate sales of organic
beef. Rare breed White Park cattle and Sussex chickens.

WOODLANDS PARK DAIRY LTD

WOODLANDS, WIMBORNE BH21 8LX
Tel: 01202 822687 Fax: 01202 826051 Contact: Richard Murray
sales@woodlands-park.co.uk www.woodlands-park.co.uk
Soil Association P5037. Producers of live sheep and goats milk yoghurts and
fromage frais in natural and four fruit flavours; goats milk butter and organic
sheeps milk yoghurts. No GMOs. Organic Food Awards 2004 Sheeps Milk Yoghurt
Winner.

 **Accommodation**

 Garden and Farm Sundries

 Producers

 Box Schemes/ Local Deliveries

 Farmers' market Stall

 Restaurants/ Cafés/Caterers

Day Visits

 Manufacturers/ Processors

 Retail shops

Eco Products

 Importers/ exporters

 Textiles

 Farm Gate Sales

 Mail order suppliers

 Wholesalers

ACORN DAIRY

ARCHDEACON NEWTON, DARLINGTON DL22YB
Tel: 01325 466999 Fax: 464567 Contact: Graham Tweddle
organic@acorndairy.co.uk www.
Process organic milk from own farm, delivering to doorsteps in and around the
Darlington area with organic bread, eggs, cheeses, yoghurts, butter, fruit juices and
clotted cream. Poultry once a month.

BUTTERBY

LOW BUTTERBY FARM, CROXDALE, DURHAM DH6 5JN
Tel: 0191 378 9193 Contact: Edward Richardson
edward.richardson@tesco.net www.butterby.co.uk
We run a box scheme in Durham city and its surrounding areas (and in north-west
Durham from June 2005 onwards). The walled garden at Croxdale Hall is in its first
year of organic conversion, we grow our own salad crops, summer vegetables,
apples, pears, and plums. During the summer also offer our cut flowers and honey.

ECOBOO LTD

ALEXANDER COTTAGE, STATION ROAD, HEIGHINGTON, NEWTON AYCLIFFE DL5 6PU
Tel: 01325 316202 Fax: 01325 316202 Contact: Clare Adamson
contact@ecoboo.co.uk www.ecoboo.co.uk
An organic, eco, Fairtrade collection of clothing, toiletries, gifts and a re-usable
nappy system and accessories for 0–4 years and for pregnancy. The organic lavender products are certified by Ecocert, the French certifier, the nappies are oeko-tex
certified, many of the toiletries contain organic ingredients and do not contain synthetic additives/ paraben preservatives and SLS.

HARBOUR HOUSE FARMS

PLAWSWORTH, CHESTER-LE-STREET DH3 4EJ
Tel: 0191 388 3184 Contact: Mark Nicholson hhf@hhfarms.fsnet.co.uk
Soil Association G5832. Cereals, lamb, beef and top fruit.

THE HEALTH WAREHOUSE

15 POST HOUSE WYND, DARLINGTON DL3 7LU

Tel: 01325 468570 Contact: Michael Barker mjbarker2@hotmail.com

Large independent health store specialising in home-baked products and organic chilled and ambient foods. Also herbal and natural remedies and supplements.

THE LAND OF ROOTS LTD

17 KINGSTON AVENUE, BEARPARK, DURHAM DH7 7DJ

Tel: 0191 373 5109 Contact: Wilf Richards

15-acre permaculture smallholding, 2 miles from Durham City, using sustainable methods to grow veg, salad and fruit. Also rare breed lamb produced on our wild flower pasture and wood products from our coppiced woodland.

PIERCEBRIDGE FARM

PIERCEBRIDGE, DARLINGTON DL2 3SE

Tel: 01325 374251 Contact: Chris Hodgson

piercebridgefarm@zoom.co.uk

A 280-acre organic farm by the river Tees built on a Roman site producing dried plucked chickens, eggs, potatoes, meat. Retailing a vast range of 100% organic products, including bread and fruit juices from Botton Village, and special dietary products. Coffee shop.

POLEMONIUM PLANTERY

28 SUNNYSIDE, TRIMDON GRANGE, TRIMDON STATION TS29 6HF

Tel: 01429 881529 Contact: David Nichol-Brown

organic@polemonium.co.uk www.polemonium.co.uk

Specialist organic peat-free plant nursery selling flower plants and seeds, also organic bed and breakfast with local produce, garden visits, talks and garden plans. See website for full details.

ADM MILLING

KINGSGATE, 1 KING EDWARD RD., BRENTWOOD CM14 4HG
Tel: 01277 262525 Fax: 200320 Contact: Jason Hall
jason-hall@admworld.com www.admmilling.co.uk
Manufacturer of high quality flours, improvers, premixes and concentrates,
including organic flours.

ALLAN, PP & PARTNERS

LANGFORD BRIDGE FARM, KELVEDON HATCH, BRENTWOOD CM15 0LB
Tel: 01277 362012 Contact: Juliet Moore
Producer of combinable crops: milling wheat, feed wheat, barley, beans, oats, rye.

ASHLYNS ORGANIC FARM

HIGH LAVER HALL, HIGH LAVER, ONGAR CM5 0DU
Tel: 01277 890188/9 Fax: 01277 890188 Contact: Jim Collins
info@ashlyns.co.uk www.ashlyns.co.uk
Soil Association G2401, P5815. Home grown produce delivered direct to your door
through our box scheme or available in our new Organic Farm Shop, offering
home-grown vegetables, fruit, meat and home-made delicatessen. Member of the
Soil Association Organic Farms Network.

AURO ORGANIC PAINT SUPPLIES

UNIT 2, PAMPHILLIONS FARM, DEBDEN, SAFFRON WALDON CB11 3JT
Tel: 01799 543077 Fax: 01799 542187 Contact: Richard Hadfield
sales@auroorganic.co.uk www.auroorganic.co.uk
Importers of natural organic paints 100% free from petrochemicals and their
derivatives. The range includes emulsions, glosses, eggshells, woodstains, floor finishes, waxes, varnishes and adhesives all of which are uncompromising in their use
of natural ingredients.

AVENANCE

TERLINGS PARK, EASTWICK ROAD, HARLOW CM2 0QR
Tel: 01279 440116 Fax: 01279 440390 Contact: Gary Bray
gary.bray@avenance.co.uk
Avenance is a contract caterer working in the following areas: B&I, schools, concession catering, stadium catering & healthcare.

BROWNING, ROBERT & SON

TEY BROOK FARM, GREAT TEY, COLCHESTER CO6 1JE
Tel: 01206 210320 Fax: 01206 212597 Contact: Richard Browning
teybrook@aol.com www.cleanearth.co.uk
Organic producer of vegetables for sale through local retail outlet, restaurant and box scheme.

BUNTINGS

89 HIGH STREET, MALDON CM9 5EP
Tel: 01621 853271 Fax: 01376 561233 Contact: Stephen Bunting
www.buntingfoods.co.uk
Retail fine food shop specialising in butchery, delicatessen, home-made pies, cooked meats, patés. Delivery areas CM8, CM9, CO6.

DALGETY

MORETON MILL, ONGAR CM5 0DP
Tel: 01277 899700 Fax: 01277 898206 Contact: Organic Seed Department
seed.marketing@dalgety.co.uk www.dalgety.co.uk
Organic seed producers.

DOUBLE DRAGON CO

4 TRING CLOSE, BARKINGSIDE, ILFORD IG2 7LQ
Tel: 020 8554 3838 Fax: 020 8554 3883 Contact: Alice Chiu
info@doubledragon.co.uk www.doubledragon.co.uk
Soil Association P6143. Importer of organic teas: Green, China Green, Pure Ginseng, Pure Ginkgo Biloba, Jasmine, Green with Ginkgo Biloba. We are a wholesaler of Ginseng, Royal Jelly, essential balm etc. Beautiful packaging, reasonable prices.

ETHICAL JUICERS
3 CORONATION HILL, EPPING CM16 5DT
Tel: 0845 330 6781 Fax: 0870 706 2744 Contact: James Summers
info@livingearth.co.uk www.ethicaljuicers.co.uk
We supply juicers, blenders, soya milk-making machines, tofu-making kits, UK
grown organic soya beans, uk grown organic soya beans, sprouters and a wide
selection of organic sprouting seeds.

FARMER KIT ORGANICS
LITTLE BOWSERS FARM, BOWSERS LANE, LITTLE WALDEN, SAFFRON WALDEN
CB10 1XQ
Tel: 01799 527315 Fax: 01799 527315 Contact: The Manager
sales@farmerkit.co.uk www.farmerkit.co.uk
Soil Association G2143. Little Bowsers Farm produces organic free range eggs and
organic top fruit, apples, pears, plums. Also organic soft fruits. We deliver regularly
to London wholesalers.

FUERST DAY LAWSON LTD
UNIT 4, FOURTH AVENUE, BLUEBRIDGE IND. ESTATE, HALSTEAD CO9 2SY
Tel: 01787 473826 Fax: 01787 475029 Contact: Mark Clarke
mclarke.halstead@fdl.co.uk www.fdl.co.uk
We are a processor of dried cereals, fruit and seeds.

HALSTEAD FOOD SERVICES LTD
UNIT 1, 1ST AVENUE, BLUEBRIDGE, HALSTEAD CO9 2EX
Tel: 01787 473222 Fax: 01787 479026 Contact: Nick Galley
halsteadfoods@hotmail.com
Soil Association registered. We clean, dice and pack organic nuts, dried
fruits, seeds and cereals.

HART WORLDWIDE LTD
MILL HOUSE, RIVERWAY, HARLOW CM20 2DW
Tel: 01279 639669 Fax: 01279 635257 Contact: Andrew Howe
ahowe@hartww.com
Soil Association P6778. Importer of organic top fruit.

HDRA, HENRY DOUBLEDAY RESEARCH ASSOCIATION, THE ORGANIC KITCHEN GARDEN
AUDLEY END HOUSE, SAFFRON WALDEN CB11 4JF
Tel: 024 7630 3517 Fax: 024 7663 9229 Contact: Susan Kay-Williams
enquiry@hdra.org.uk www.hdra.org.uk
HDRA, the organic organisation, runs the walled kitchen garden at Audley End House, an English Heritage property. The 2-acre walled gardens include heritage vegetables, vinery and fruit house. For opening hours, please contact English Heritage: 01799 522399.

HEPBURNS OF MOUNTNESSING
269 ROMAN ROAD, MOUNTNESSING, BRENTWOOD CM15 0UH
Tel: 01277 353289 Fax: 01277 355589 Contact: Gordon Hepburn
Traditional butcher and grazier with a reputation for quality and service. Established 1932. Highgrove organic beef, lamb and pork when available. Deliver locally and to London (over £50 free).

ILFORD FARMERS' MARKET
PEDESTRIANISED ILFORD HIGH RD., NR. TOWN HALL, ILFORD
Tel: 020 7704 9659 Contact: Cheryl Cohen
info@lfm.org.uk www.lfm.org.uk
First and third Saturdays of the month 9am to 2pm. Here farmers sell home-grown foods grown or made within 100 miles of the M25, including fruit, veg, meat, dairy, eggs, honey, juice, bread, preserves, plants. Note: some, but not all, producers are organic. Run by London Farmers' Markets, PO Box 37363, London N1.

KINGS SEEDS

MONKS FARM, COGGESHALL RD., KELVEDON CO5 0PG
Tel: 01376 570000 Fax: 01376 571189 Contact: A Ward
sales@kingsseeds.com www.kingsseeds.com
Soil Association P5847. Leading supplier of organic seed suitable for UK
climatic conditions.

LEGG, ROGER

HEARDS FARM, HEARDS LANE, SHENFIELD, BRENTWOOD CM15 0SF
Tel: 01277 211883 Contact: Roger Legg
Local grower and producer of vegetables, fruit, herbs, plants, cut flowers &
eggs, marketing through Blackmore and Stock farmers' markets, Shenfield Country
Market and seasonal local box scheme in Brentwood/Shenfield area.

MANNINGTREE ORGANIC GROWERS

83 HUNGERDOWN LANE, LAWFORD, MANNINGTREE CO11 2LY
Tel: 01206 231399 Contact: Marina O'Connell
marina_oconnell@onetel.com
We are a group of 4 growers producing top fruit and soft fruit, salads and eggs,
lavender oils and associated cosmetic products in the Stour valley. Wholesale and
Stoke Newington farmers' market.

ONLYFINEBEER

37 BROOMFIELD ROAD, CHELMSFORD CM1 1SY
Tel: 01245 255579 Contact: Gavin Preston
chelmsford@onlyfinebeer.co.uk www.onlyfinebeer.co.uk
A retailer of 39 different organic beers, ciders and perrys. This range will continue
to increase as more and more brewers are turning to using organic ingredients. You
can use www.onlyfinebeer.co.uk to search for the word 'Organic' in the brand title,
or use the advanced search facility to find the word 'Organic' when it is used in the
description.

ORGANIC CHOICE

60 HIGH ST., HALSTEAD CO9 2JG
Tel: 01787 478471 Fax: 01787 478457 Contact: Peter & Nathalie Coleby
info@organicchoice.net www.organicchoice.net
Organic delicatessen offering fresh fruit & vegetables, traditional & speciality
cheeses, paté, hand-carved ham, award-winning breads, wine, groceries, dairy,
chilled & frozen foods, environmentally friendly products. Free home delivery
throughout Essex and Suffolk borders. Price list available. Credit cards accepted.

OXLEY HILL FARM

LAYER RD., ABBERTON, COLCHESTER CO5 7NH
Tel: 01206 735522 Fax: 01206 561622 Contact: Steve Miller
Soil Association G7658. Farm producer of cattle and sheep, timber, sloes and
blackberries.

PILGRIM'S NATURAL

4 KING GEORGES PLACE, HIGH ST., MALDON CM9 5BZ
Tel: 01621 858605 Contact: Mary Chimba
Retailer and packer of a wide range of organic food including butter and yoghurts,
ice cream, bread and cakes.

RIVERFORD HOME DELIVERY

NO 11, THE OAKLEIGHS, 630 HIGH ROAD, WOODFORD GREEN IG8 0PU
Tel: 0845 600 2311 Fax: 01803 762718 Contact: David Fisher
boxscheme@riverford.co.uk www.riverford.co.uk
Award-winning organic vegetable box scheme operating in Enfield and surrounding
areas of north London. Various box sizes to suit all households from a single
occupant upwards. A wide selection of fruit, dairy products, wine, eggs, chocolate,
fruit juices etc are also available. Order weekly, fortnightly or whenever you like.
Can order online at www.riverford.co.uk or by telephone on 0845 600 2311. BBC
Radio 4 Farmer of the Year 2005.

SALLY GREEN'S
74 HIGH ST., MALDON CM9 5ET
Tel: 01621 854727 Contact: Sally Green
greens@tillinghamfarm.fsnet.co.uk
Retail shop selling Sarah Green's locally grown seasonal organic vegetables.

SARAH GREEN'S ORGANICS
TILLINGHAM HALL FARM, NORTH STREET, TILLINGHAM, SOUTHMINSTER CM0 7ST
Tel: 01621 779500 Fax: 01621 779500 Contact: Sarah & Steven Green
sarahgreen@farming.co.uk
A family-run farm growing a variety of fresh seasonal vegetables all year round.
There is a farm shop in North Street, Tillingham, open Thurs, Fri and Sat
9am–4pm. We also supply Sally Green's, 74 High Street, Maldon (01621
854727) with fresh seasonal organic vegetables. As well as attending Burnham-on-
Crouch Farmers Market. In summer 2005 we plan to have started producing a
range of home-grown fruit. All our produce is organically grown in Tillingham and
sold fresh from the field.

SAWDON, J M
PELDON HALL, PELDON, NR. COLCHESTER CO5 7PU
Tel: 07973 750367 Fax: 01206 735791 Contact: J Sawdon
j.sawdon@farmline.com www.peldonhall.com
Store/bag/dress/clean/dry/blend wheat, barley, triticale, oats, beans, peas, maize,
lucerne and bran.

SUFFOLK HERBS
MONKS FARM, COGGESHILL RD., KELVEDON CO5 9PG
Tel: 01376 572456 Fax: 01376 571189 Contact: A F Ward
sales@suffolkherbs.com www.suffolkherbs.com
Leading supplier of organic produced seed for the home gardener and professional
user.

SUNRISE HEALTHFOODS LTD
31 SPA RD., HOCKLEY SS5 4AZ
Tel: 01702 207017 Contact: Richard
Modern health food shop offering 2,000 products including many organic lines,
frozen and chilled foods, special diet foods and supplements. Friendly service
and competent advice always available.

UNILEVER BESTFOODS
LONDON RD., PURFLEET RM19 1SD
Tel: 01708 684533 Fax: 01708 684544 Contact: RM Livingston
bob.livingston@unilcvcr.com
Soil Association P7592. Food manufacturers: principally vegetables, fruit, spreads
and savoury products.

USHER, JENNY
GREEN OAKS, THRESHERS BUSH, NR. HARLOW CM17 0NS
Tel: 01279 444663 Contact: Jenny Usher
Soil Association U02E. Organic fruit, veg, herbs and plants. Direct marketing
consultant, especially practical advice.

WATER LANE NURSERIES
NAYLAND, COLCHESTER CO6 4JS
Tel: 01206 262880 Fax: 01206 262880 Contact: Simon Faithfull
Soil Association G3059. Soil Association licensed mixed vegetable and fruit growers.

THE WHOLEFOOD STORE
26 HIGH ST., MANNINGTREE CO11 1AJ
Tel: 01206 391200 Contact: Jon or Sarah
jondyvig@hotmail.com
We are an independent and friendly wholefood store selling an extensive range
of organic dried foods, fresh fruit and vegetables, dairy products, drinks, bread and
pastries.

ADEYS FARM ORGANIC MEATS

ADEYS FARM, BREADSTONE, BERKELEY GL13 9HF
Tel: 01453 511218 Fax: 01453 511218 Contact: Caroline Wilson
cwilson@adeysfarm.fsnet.co.uk
Organic beef, lamb, pork, bacon, burgers, speciality sausages. Traditional breeds
including Aberdeen Angus, Gloucester Old Spot, well hung and traditionally
butchered.

ALDERTON NURSERIES

STOW RD., ALDERTON, NR. TEWKESBURY GL20 8NH
Tel: 01242 620394 Fax: 01242 620261 Contact: Stephen Haslum
Soil Association G5705. Small family business growing protected glasshouse
crops: tomatoes, cucumbers, beans, courgettes, peppers.

ALLIED GRAIN LTD

103 CIRENCESTER BUSINESS PARK, LOVE LANE, CIRENCESTER GL7 1XD
Tel: 01285 6491430 Contact: David Whyte
david.whyte@alliedgrain.co.uk www.alliedgrain.co.uk
Organic and in conversion, wheat, barley, oats and brans.

THE AUTHENTIC BREAD CO

UNIT 2, STRAWBERRY HILL BUSINESS PARK, STRAWBERRY HILL, NEWENT GL18 1LH
Tel: 01531 828181 Fax: 01531 828151 Contact: Jane & Alan Davis
breadbaron@authenticbread.co.uk www.authenticbread.co.uk
Established producer of high quality organic bakery and Christmas products.
Everything from bread to pasties are lovingly hand-made in our Gloucestershire
bakery. Winners of 6 Soil Association Good Food awards. Soil Association symbol
no. P1912. Organic Food Awards 2004: Puddings Winner. See display ad.

BETTER FOR ORGANICS
22 PARSONAGE STREET, DURSLEY GL11 4AA
Tel: 01453 545090 Fax: 01453 548895 Contact: Kathryn Francis
info@betterfororganics.co.uk www.betterfororganics.co.uk
High quality organic food store stocking fresh fruit and vegetables, fresh meat and
poultry, eggs, milk, freshly baked craft bread and much more. Delivery service available.

BOWLDOWN FARMS LTD
BOWLDOWN FARMS LTD, TETBURY GL8 8UD
Tel: 01666 890224 Fax: 01666 890433 Contact: GEM or JFG Vernon
admin@bowldownfarmsltd.co.uk
Soil Association G4157. We seek to retain the traditional Cotswold farm, specialising in organic North Devon beef, lamb and arable products. Conservation and
amenity issues are uppermost in our priorities. Box scheme for lamb in autumn
and developing box scheme for beef from March to May.

BUTTERCUP ORGANIC DAIRY AND FARM SHOP
BROOKTHORPE, GLOUCESTER GL4 0UN
Tel: 01452 812322 Contact: Amanda Dyer
Fresh organic milk, yoghurt, cream and butter produced from the Buttercup herd.
Organic fruit and vegetables grown on the farm and in the walled garden are sold in
the farm shop, as well as home-produced beef and lamb. Shop also stocks organic
bread, free range eggs, traditional cheeses, ice cream and a range of organic gro-
ceries. Ample parking. Open: Tues–Fri 11am to 4.30pm, Sat 10am to 1pm.

CAMPHILL OAKLANDS PARK
HORTICULTURE, OAKLANDS PARK, NEWNHAM ON SEVERN GL14 1EF
Tel: 01594 516550 Fax: 01594 516550 Contact: Kai Lange
kaigarden@onetel.com www.oaklandspark.org.uk
Biodynamic Agricultural Association (Demeter) 101, Soil Association V01M.
Working community with people with special needs. Involved with regional
biodynamic land training (2 years), vegetables, herbs and fruit for wholesaling
and box scheme. Some meat available for box scheme customers. Above contacts
are for wholesale; box scheme contacts are: 01594 516344/510365,
anna@bergamot.basil.freeuk.com and www.bergamot.basil.freeuk.com.

COTSWOLD HEALTH PRODUCTS LTD
UNIT 5/8 TABERNACLE RD., WOTTON-UNDER-EDGE GL12 7EF
Tel: 01453 843694 Fax: 01453 521375 Contact: Keidrich Davies
sales@cotsherb.co.uk www.cotsherb.co.uk
Soil Association no. P1926. Importers of herbs and spices.

COTSWOLD SEEDS LTD
THE COTSWOLD BUSINESS VILLAGE, LONDON RD., MORETON IN MARSH GL56 0JQ
Tel: 01608 652552 Fax: 01608 652256 Contact: Ian Wilkinson
info@cotswoldseeds.com www.cotswoldseeds.com
Soil Association P5985. Seed merchants: Cotswold Seeds is a supplier of seeds:
grass, clover, wild flowers and green manures. Next day delivery service to most
parts of the UK.

CROOKED END FARM ORGANICS
RUARDEAN, FOREST OF DEAN GL17 9XF
Tel: 01594 544482 Contact: Morag Norman
crooked.end@talk21.com
Soil Association (G2393) and HDRA. Small mixed organic farm, close to forest
and Wye Valley, producing free range eggs, fruit & vegetables in season, lamb,
beef, pork, cider, perry. Self-catering holiday cottage. Stunning views to Welsh
mountains.

DAIRY CREST LTD
OLDENDS LANE, STONEHOUSE GL10 2DG
Tel: 01453 435543 Fax: 01453 435812 Contact: John Middleton
john.middleton@dairycrest.co.uk www.dairycrest.co.uk
Dairy Crest process organic dairy products, produced from raw milk, to suit
market requirements, including organic cream and butter.

DAYLESFORD CREAMERY

DAYLESFORD CREAMERY, DAYLESFORD, NR. KINGHAM GL56 0YG
Tel: 01608 658005 Fax: 01608 658009 Contact: Joe Schneider
j.schneider@daylesfordcreamery.com www.daylesfordorganic.com
Celebrated for craftsmanship and taste: we make award-winning organic cheeses
the traditional way, aged for full flavour and using milk from our own organically
raised Friesians. Organic Food Awards 2004: Cheese Commended.

DAYLESFORD ORGANIC FARMSHOP

DAYLESFORD ORGANIC FARMSHOP, DAYLESFORD, NR. KINGHAM GL56 0YG
Tel: 01608 731700 Fax: 01608 658009 Contact: Stuart Gates
enquries@daylesfordfarmshop.com www.daylesfordorganic.com
At Daylesford we offer the freshest food in season, from our fully organic
estates; we have a passionate commitment to quality. We practise compassionate
farming and sustainability: organic beef, lamb, venison and poultry; heritage
variety vegetables and fruits; award-winning hand-made organic cheeses; organic
breads, pastries, and much more. Discover the authentic taste of the best
organic food from Daylesford—to take home or to enjoy in our café which was
awarded Organic Restaurant of the Year in the Organic Food Awards 2004;
Prepared Dishes Highly Commended; Soups and Sauces Winner; Sweet Preserves
and Spreads Winner. See display ad.

EASTLEACH DOWNS ORGANIC FARM

TALLET BARN, EASTLEACH DOWNS FARM, EASTLEACH, CIRENCESTER GL7 3PX
Tel: 01367 850315 Fax: 01367 850315 Contact: Helen and Sam Wade
helen@eastleachdowns.co.uk www.eastleachdowns.co.uk
Home delivery of locally produced free-range organic pork direct from the farmer.

FUTURA FOODS UK LTD

WYNCHFIELD HOUSE, CALCOT, NR. TETBURY GL8 8YJ
Tel: 01666 890500 Fax: 01666 890522 Contact: Ellen Svensson
info@futura-foods.com www.futura-foods.com
Soil Association P1642. Danish manufacturing and dairy trading organisation. Selling and developing organic dairy products for UK retail/wholesale sectors. Marketed under Futura Organic label. Organic Food Awards 2004: Cheese Commended.

GLOBAL ORGANIC MARKETS

UNIT 5, CANAL IRONWORKS, HOPE MILL LANE, LONDON ROAD, BRIMSCOMBE, STROUD GL5 2SH
Tel: 01453 884123 Fax: 01453 884123 Contact: Andie Soutar
globalorganicmarkets@fsmail.net
Fresh fruit, vegetables and eggs: wholesale delivery and collection for box schemes, shops, restaurants and growers. Retail sales from our stalls in Stroud (Gloucestershire) Shambles Market (Friday 8.30–5pm) and Old Spitalfields, London (Sunday 9.30–6pm).

THE GOURMET MUSHROOM COMPANY

HAYMES FARM, NEW RD., SOUTHAM, CHELTENHAM GL52 3NX
Tel: 01242 238021 Fax: 01242 237614 Contact: Garrett O'Connor
sales@haymesfarm.co.uk www.haymesfarm.co.uk
18-acre organic farm supplying organic brown or chestnut and white mushrooms, portabello, oyster, enoki and shiitake mushrooms. We supply box schemes, multiples and local retailers. Organic spent mushroom compost is available in large commercial quantities to other organic farmers.

GRAINFARMERS PLC

UNIT 3, COMPTON BUSINESS CENRE, COMPTON ABDALE, CHELTENHAM GL54 4LD
Tel: 01242 890003 Fax: 01242 890516 Contact: Andrew Trump
andrew.trump@grainfarmers.co.uk www.grainfarmers.co.uk
Trading arable produce we will help you sell your produce or source the feed ingredients you need.

THE GREEN SHOP

BISLEY GL6 7BX
Tel: 01452 770629 Fax: 01452 770104 Contact: Jane Powell
enquiries@greenshop.co.uk www.greenshop.co.uk
Huge selection of books, one of the largest selections of natural paints & finishes, organic bodycare, environmentally friendly cleaning products, solar radios and torches, Fairtrade tea and coffee plus hundreds of other environmental products.

HEALTH-WISE

27 NORTH WALK, YATE BS37 4AP
Tel: 01454 322168 Fax: 01454 322168 Contact: W Round
Open 9–5.30 Mon–Sat supplying organic cereal, nuts, seeds, jam, flour, vegetarian food, margarines, sheep and goats milk products.

HIGHLEADON HOLIDAY COTTAGES

NEW HOUSE FARM, HIGHLEADON, NEWENT GL18 1HQ
Tel: 01452 790209 Fax: 01452 790209 Contact: Janet Corbett
cjojan@aol.com
Four star self-catering cottages, one cottage suitable for the disabled. Excellent tourist base for the Royal Forest of Dean, farm walk, no children, short breaks.

HOBBS HOUSE BAKERY

UNIT 6, CHIPPING EDGE ESTATE, HATTERS LANE, CHIPPING SODBURY BS37 6AA
Tel: 01454 321629 Fax: 01454 329757 Contact: Clive Wells
trevor@hobbshousebakery.co.uk www.hobbshousebakery.co.uk
Soil Association P1632. A traditional craft bakery producing award-winning breads. Three retail outlets, and supplies to outlets within 50-mile radius.

HOBBS HOUSE BAKERY

39 HIGH ST, CHIPPING SODBURY BS37 6BA
Tel: 01454 317525 Fax: 01454 329757 Contact: Clive Wells & Trevor Herbert
admin@hobbshousebakery.co.uk www.hobbshousebakery.co.uk
We are licensed by the Soil Association (P1632), producing organic white and wholemeal bread for our own shops and wholesale outlets.

JUST WHOLEFOODS

UNIT 16 CIRENCESTER BUSINESS EST., ELLIOTT ROAD, LOVE LANE,
CIRENCESTER GL7 1YS
Tel: 01285 651910 Fax: 01285 650266 Contact: James White
info@justwholefoods.co.uk www.justwholefoods.co.uk
Manufacturers of award-winning vegetarian organic products, including confectionery (VegeBears), instant soup mixes, stuffing mixes, etc. We also manufacture
for other companies under contract, providing the products are vegetarian.

KITCHEN GARDEN PRESERVES

UNIT 15, SALMON SPRINGS TRADING ESTATE, CHELTENHAM ROAD,
STROUD GL6 6NU
Tel: 01453 759612 Fax: 01453 755899 Contact: Barbara Moinet
info@kitchengardenpreserves.co.uk www.kitchengardenpreserves.co.uk
We produce a range of hand-made jams, chutneys, marmalades and condiments.
We have been category winners in the Organic Food Awards three times in the last
five years. We supply independent delicatessens, farm shops, box schemes and
hamper companies. Organic Food Awards 2004: Savoury Preserves and Spreads
Winner.

LA BODEGA

TAURUS CRAFTS, THE OLD PARK, LYDNEY GL15 6BU
Tel: 01594 844841 Fax: 01594 845636 Contact: Dirk Rohwedder
bodega@tauruscrafts.co.uk www.tauruscrafts.co.uk
La Bodega stocks local produce and organic foods, specialising in organic wines,
chocolates, coffees and deli foods. We are part of the Taurus Crafts Centre, cele-
brating healthy living and creative design by bringing together wholesome food, fine
arts and handmade crafts. The centre is open to the public from 10am to 5.30pm
every day.

LIVING EARTH PRODUCE

RUSKIN MILL, OLD BRISTOL RD, NAILSWORTH GL6 0LA
Tel: 01453 837510 Fax: 01453 835029 Contact: Andy Horton
Organic and biodynamic food store. Vegetables, fruit, frozen meat, milk,
cheese, yoghurts, herbs and spices, eggs and a wide range of groceries.

MAD HATTERS ORGANIC RESTAURANT
3 COSSACK SQUARE, NAILSWORTH GL6 0DB
Tel: 01453 832615 Fax: 01453 832615 Contact: Carolyn Findlay
mafindlay@waitrose.com
Since there are GMOs in animal feeds we use totally organic meat, milk, butter,
cream and cheese. Non-smoking. Wheelchair access. Local seasonal organic
produce cooked classically without additives or cheap substitutes by four
enthusiastic and idealistic chefs. Organic wines, beers and soft drinks. Bright
informal décor.

MELCOURT INDUSTRIES LTD
BOLDRIDGE BRAKE, LONG NEWTON, TETBURY GL8 8RT
Tel: 01666 502711 Fax: 01666 504398 Contact: Catherine Dawson
mail@melcourt.co.uk www.melcourt.co.uk
Soil Association I1222. Melcourt are specialist manufacturers of growing media
products derived from sustainable forest residues. We supply professional
growers and the landscape industry with bark and wood-derived mulches, soil
ameliorants and play surfaces.

MOTHER NATURE
2 BEDFORD ST., STROUD GL5 1AY
Tel: 01453 758202 Fax: 01453 752595 Contact: Kurt Hilder
mnstroud@aol.com
Food on three floors. Organic wine, meat, bread, dairy products, champagne and
perry. Specialist in water filtration filters, purifiers and systems.

MULADULA
9 UNION ST., STROUD GL5 2HE
Tel: 01453 768549 Fax: 01453 768549 Contact: Oly Duane
email@muladula.com www.muladula.com
Finest baby and children's products including organic clothes and wooden toys.
100% of net profit is re-invested into the promotion of the finest ethical
eco-products.

THE NATURAL GROCERY STORE LTD

150–156, BATH ROAD, CHELTENHAM GL53 7NG
Tel: 01242 243737 Fax: 01242 238872 Contact: Paul Lewis
triple8.trading@virgin.net
Organic Fresh fruit and vegetables, dairy, meat, poultry, fish, bread, cakes,
wine, beer, spirits, cider, canned, dried and bottled groceries and provisions.
All under one roof of 2,000 square feet. Open daily 8am–10pm.

NEAL'S YARD REMEDIES

9 ROTUNDA TERRACE, MONTPELLIER ST., CHELTENHAM GL50 1SW
Tel: 01242 522136 Fax: 01242 522136 Contact: Sally Lorman
nyr@chelt.net www.nealsyardremedies.com
Neal's Yard Remedies manufacture and sell natural skincare products, and stock
an extensive range of herbs, essential oils, homoeopathic remedies and books.
We also have therapy rooms.

NEWARK FARM

OZLEWORTH, WOOTON-UNDER-EDGE GL12 7PZ
Tel: 01453 842144 Fax: 01453 521432 Contact: Steve Redman
We produce beef, lamb, multicoloured free range hens' eggs, Ministry approved
seed potatoes, ware potatoes and vegetables.

NUTRITION CENTRE

98 HIGH ST., TEWKESBURY GL20 5JZ
Tel: 01684 299620 Fax: 01684 274462 Contact: V BALE
sales @nutritioncentre.co.uk www.nutritioncentre.co.uk
Retail and mail order health food store with large range of organic foods and
related products. Experienced, friendly, trained staff. New internet shop.

NUTRITION CENTRE
133 BATH RD., CHELTENHAM GL53 7LT
Tel: 01242 514150 Fax: 01242 580509 Contact: Anne Mitchell
sales @nutritioncentre.co.uk www.nutritioncentre.co.uk
Retail and mail order health food store with large range of organic foods and
related products. Experienced and friendly trained staff. New internet shop.

NUTRITION CENTRE
28 WINCHCOMBE ST., CHELTENHAM GL52 1LX
Tel: 01242 529934 Fax: 01242 528700 Contact: Vicky Calderone
sales@nutrition centre.co.uk www.nutritioncentre.co.uk
Retail and mail order health food store with large range of organic foods and
related products. Experienced and friendly trained staff. New internet shop.

THE ORANGE TREE
317 HIGH STREET, CHELTENHAM GL50 3HW
Tel: 01242 234232 Contact: M. Khan
Vegetarian/vegan restaurant offering world cuisine in relaxed atmosphere.
Special diets catered for. Small courtyard patio open in summer.

THE ORGANIC FARM SHOP
ABBEY HOME FARM, BURFORD ROAD, CIRENCESTER GL7 5HF
Tel: 01285 640441 Fax: 01285 644827 Contact: Hilary Chester-Master
info@theorganicfarmshop.co.uk www.theorganicfarmshop.co.uk
Soil Association G1715, R5253. 100% organic, award-winning farm, shop and
vegetarian café with garden. Cookery courses, educational visits, woodland walk.
Our own vegetables, meat, eggs and soft fruit, a vast range of organic food, textiles
and environmentally friendly skin care, bodycare, books and magazines. Large
meeting room, yurt and hut for hire, greenfield camping. Member of the Soil
Association Organic Farms Network.

THE ORGANIC SHOP
THE SQUARE, STOW-ON-THE-WOLD GL54 1AB
Tel: 01451 831004 Contact: Sheila Wye
The first independently owned retail shop in the UK specialising in the sale of
Soil Association symbol produce, including meat. Open 9.00am to 5.30pm every
day except Christmas and Boxing Day.

PARK CORNER FARMS
PARK CORNER, CIRENCESTER GL7 6LS
Tel: 01285 760850 Fax: 01285 760850 Contact: J Hoskins
jeremy.hoskins@ukonline.co.uk
Soil Association G5440, OLMC. We breed and feed top beef (Shorthorn & Angus
cows) by a Charolais. We also sell high index Charolais bulls, selected for
calving and natural fleshing. Weight pays.

PHILLIPS, CG & JF
MACARONI FARM, EASTLEACH, CIRENCESTER GL7 3NG
Tel: 01367 850237 Fax: 01367 850526 Contact: Charles Phillips
cphillips@macaroni-farm.co.uk
Soil Association G6372. Pedigree South Devon beef herd, Aberdeen Angus beef
herd, Lleyn x Texel lambs, wheat, barley, peas, beans, forage crops.

PIE AND MASH
10 BENNINGTON STREET, CHELTENHAM GL50 4ED
Tel: 01242 702785 Fax: 07092 169006 Contact: Kat McLeod
kat@pienmash.com www.pienmash.com
Healthy home-cooked comfort food for meat eaters, vegans, vegetarians, coeliacs
diabetics. Low fat & low salt policy. All ingredients organic & locally sourced.
Families & well behaved dogs welcome. Fully licensed. Now open: 3rd certified
organic & non-smoking bar in the country!

PINETUM PRODUCTS

PINETUM LODGE, CHURCHAM GL2 8AD
Tel: 01452 750402 Fax: 01452 750402 Contact: David Wilkin
Associated with Good Gardeners Association. We run a B&B with excellent
accommodation. Natural products and food used and a lecture on organics if
required. Organic products for sale via mail order.

RUSKIN MILL COLLEGE

THE FISHERIES, HORSLEY GL6 1PL
Tel: 01453 837500 Fax: 01453 837506 Contact: Julian Pyzer
www.ruskin-mill.org.uk
Biodynamic Agricultural Association 245. Part of special needs further education
college with biodynamic market garden and mixed farm, and fish farm. Café and
shop, crafts, exhibitions, workshops, concerts, storytelling and talks.

SEVERN BANK ORGANICS

CAMAROY FARM, BROADOAK, NEWNHAM-ON-SEVERN GL14 1JB
Tel: 01594 516367 Contact: Joanna Babij
We are an organic small-holding producing fresh seasonal vegetables and mixed
salad bags all year round. We also produce organic eggs and limited amounts of
pork. Our farm shop is open all year, Tuesday–Friday 2pm–6pm, Saturdays
9am–5pm and Sunday mornings. Please phone before visiting if you wish to check
produce availability or place an order especially during winter.

SHIPTON MILL LTD

LONG NEWNTON, TETBURY GL8 8RP
Tel: 01666 505050 Fax: 01666 504666 Contact: John Lister
enquiries@shipton-mill.com www.shipton-mill.com
We are a small flour mill in the heart of the Cotswolds producing stoneground
organic flours for the craft baker as well as supplying the home baker through
our friendly mail order service. Members of the Soil Association.

SLIPSTREAM ORGANICS

34A LANGDON RD., CHELTENHAM GL53 7NZ
Tel: 01242 227273 Fax: 01242 227798 Contact: Nick McCordall
info@slipstream-organics.co.uk www.slipstream-organics.co.uk
Soil Association R1732. Award-winning box scheme, established June 1994,
supplying locally grown organic food to over 500 households in Cheltenham,
Gloucester and Stroud. Good local supplier links.

STROUD COMMUNITY AGRICULTURE LTD

48C HIGH ST., STROUD GL5 1AN
Tel: 0845 458 0814 Contact: Carole Vaughan
info@stroudcommunityagriculture.org www.stroudcommunityagriculture.org
A community co-operative which runs a farm business. The farm grows vegetables
and has pigs and cattle. Anyone can become a member and a weekly veg bag with
an option to buy meat also. Membership Tel: 01453 840037.

ST. AUGUSTINES FARM

ARLINGHAM, GLOUCESTER GL2 7JN
Tel: 01452 740277 Fax: 01452 740277 Contact: Rob & Elaine Jewell
staugustines@btconnect.com
Visit a friendly family working organic dairy farm in the beautiful Severn Vale. Feed
the many different farm animals, watch the milking, discover the wildlife and enjoy
the real countryside. Member of the Soil Association Organic Farms Network.

SUNSHINE CRAFT BAKERY

THE BRITISH SCHOOL, SLAD ROAD, STROUD GL5 1QW
Tel: 01453 752592 Contact: Michael Hill
Bake and supply organic bread, cakes and savouries (vegetarian) for our own
shop (see below) and Cheltenham Nutrition Centres.

SUNSHINE HEALTH SHOP & ORGANIC BAKERY

25 CHURCH ST., STROUD GL5 1JL

Tel: 01453 763923 Contact: Ray Hill

Over 3,000 organic and health food products including dietary supplements, herbal and homoeopathic medicines, cosmetics and toiletries. Hand-crafted bread using nature's organic ingredients. Manufacturers of Thompson's Slippery Elm foods.

THORNBURY ORGANIC CO-OP

9 CROSSWAYS RD., THORNBURY BS35 2YL

Tel: 01454 415345 Contact: Judith Dale

judithdale@blueyonder.co.uk

Local buying co-op. We provide a wide range of organic groceries, fruit, vegetables, dairy, bread, wines, beers, fish and meat, which are locally sourced where possible. Local delivery only.

WHITFIELD FARM ORGANICS

WHITFIELD FARM ORGANICS, WHITFIELD FARM, FALFIELD, WOTTON UNDER EDGE GL12 8DR

Tel: 0845 283 0232 Fax: 0845 283 0232 Contact: James Blair

jfb@whitfieldfarmorganics.co.uk www.whitfieldfarmorganics.co.uk

We produce beef that is grass fed and organic beef, sold on farm and at local farmers' markets, and organic soft fruit. We grow strawberries, raspberries, tayberries, gooseberries, redcurrants & blackcurrants.

WYEDEAN WHOLEFOODS

13 MARKET STREET, CINDERFORD GL14 2RT

Tel: 01594 825455 Contact: Barry Cocker

Hundreds of organic lines. Wholefoods, gluten and dairy-free, cruelty-free cosmetics; SLS-free toiletries. Excellent range of vitamins, minerals and herbals. Wide range of chilled and frozen products.

WYEDEAN WHOLEFOODS
15 MARKET PLACE, COLEFORD GL16 8AW
Tel: 01594 810303 Contact: Barry Cocker
Hundreds of organic lines. Wholefoods, gluten and dairy-free, cruelty-free cosmetics; SLS-free toiletries. Excellent range of vitamins, minerals and herbals. Wide range of chilled and frozen products.

WYEDEAN WHOLEFOODS
2 HARE LANE, GLOUCESTER GL1 2BB
Tel: 01452 423577 Contact: Barry Cocker
Hundreds of organic lines. Wholefoods, gluten and dairy-free, cruelty-free cosmetics; SLS-free toiletries. Excellent range of vitamins, minerals and herbals. Wide range of chilled and frozen products.

WYEDEAN WHOLEFOODS
18 NEWERNE STREET, LYDNEY GL15 5RF
Tel: 01594 841907 Contact: Barry Crocker
Hundreds of organic lines. Wholefoods, gluten and dairy-free, cruelty-free cosmetics; SLS-free toiletries. Excellent range of vitamins, minerals and herbals. Wide range of chilled and frozen products.

WYEDEAN WHOLEFOODS
MARKET SQUARE, NEWENT GL18 1PS
Tel: 01531 821922 Contact: Barry Cocker
Hundreds of organic lines. Wholefoods, gluten and dairy-free, cruelty-free cosmetics; SLS-free toiletries. Excellent range of vitamins, minerals and herbals. Wide range of chilled and frozen products.

ABSOLUTE AROMAS LTD

2 GROVE PARK, MILL LANE, ALTON GU34 2QC
Tel: 01420 540400 Fax: 01420 540401 Contact: David Tomlinson
relax@absolute-aromas.com
Aromatherapy products. Available by mail order and from health food stores.

BRIDGEGUILD LTD

BUDBRIDGE MANOR NURSERY, MERSTONE, NEWPORT PO30 3DH
Tel: 01983 840623 Fax: 01983 840225 Contact: JPH Verey
piers.verey@wightsalads.com
Organic glasshouse-grown cherry and beef tomatoes, sold through our marketing
company 'Wight Salads Ltd' to UK supermarkets.

BROUGHTON ORGANICS

THE ANCHORAGE, SALISBURY RD., BROUGHTON, NR. STOCKBRIDGE SO20 8BX
Tel: 01794 301234 Contact: SL Tidy
Soil Association T07S and ECEAT (European Centre for Eco-Agro Tourism).
Broughton Organics grow and supply organic produce (specialising in vegetables,
eggs and poultry meat). We aim to provide an alternative to globalisation by
supplying local food to local people. Camping available.

CHEEKY RASCALS

STONE BARN, 1 BROWS FARM, FARNHAM RD, LISS GU33 6JG
Tel: 0870 873 2600 Fax: 0870 873 2800 Contact: Selina Russell
sales@cheekyrascals.co.uk www.cheekyrascals.co.uk
Importers of baby and toddler nursery equipment, in particular washable nappies
and kiddy and buggy boards. Member of the Real Nappy Association. National
delivery.

COLLINS, MJ&LK

PARK FARM, HECKFIELD, HOOK RG27 0LD
Tel: 0118 932 6535 Fax: 0870 167 4860 Contact: Martin Collins
martin@parkfarm.fsnet.co.uk
Organic beef, pork and lamb produced with traditional breeds, also fresh fruit and
veg and dairy products. Visitors to the shop are welcome to walk around the
farm—bring your wellies. Open Tuesday, Wednesday a.m., Thursday, Friday &
Saturday. Shop tel: 0118 932 6650.

COMPLETE ORGANICS

LILACS, MOUNT PLEASANT, LYMINGTON SO41 9LS
Tel: 01590 678409 Contact: Hella Clark
info@completeorganics.org www.completeorganics.org
Certified by USDA, ACO, and JAS and BFA (United States, Australia and Japan).The
world's first certified organic complete range of body care, skincare, toiletries,
shampoos, toothpastes, probiotics and cosmetics. Miessence and MiVitality,
manufactured in Australia, newly available in the U.K.

FUNDAMENTALLY FUNGUS

MYCOMARKETING LTD, MEON HILL FARM, STOCKBRIDGE SO23 0QD
Tel: 01264 811170 Fax: 01264 811170 Contact: Jane Dick
jdfungus@mycomarketing.fsnet.co.uk www.fundamentallyfungus.co.uk
Soil Association P5809. Speciality mushrooms. Growers and sellers of fresh
speciality mushrooms to catering and restaurant trade. Retail packs of mixed
and single variety speciality mushrooms for shops.

GODSHILL ORGANICS

NEWPORT RD., GODSHILL, ISLE OF WIGHT PO38 3LY
Tel: 01983 840723 Fax: 01983 840723 Contact: R Illman (Partner)
godshill.organics@virgin.net www.godshillorganics.com
Soil Association G1724, P5015. Wide range of fresh produce grown on-site.
Weekly deliveries and seasonal box scheme. On-site shop selling very wide range
of groceries and fresh veg. Local farmers' market each Friday.

HARROWAY ORGANIC GARDENS

KINGSCLERE RD., WHITCHURCH RG28 7QB
Tel: 01256 895346 Fax: 01256 895346 Contact: Steve Forster
hogveg@hotmail.com
Soil Association G971, P971. Organic farm and farm shop, selling organic
vegetables, fruit, eggs and cheese.

LAVERSTOKE PARK PRODUCE

HOME FARM, LAVERSTOKE PARK, WHITCHURCH RG28 7NT
Tel: 01256 890900 Fax: 01256 890900 Contact: Robert McAlpine
lin@laverstokepark.co.uk
Soil Association G2740. Box scheme delivering vegetables, fruit and eggs in
Basingstoke and Winchester areas. Wholesale supplies to local independent retailers.

LYME REGIS FINE FOODS LTD

STATION IND. ESTATE, LIPHOOK GU30 7DR
Tel: 01428 722900 Fax: 01428 727222 Contact: The Manager
info@lymeregisfoods.com www.lymeregisfoods.com
Soil Association P4348. Manufacturers of natural and organic healthy snack bars, particularly fruit, cereal and marzipan bars. Found in health food shops and major supermarkets. Organic Food Awards 2004: Sweets Commended, Snack Foods Winner.

MATSOFRESH LTD

FENWICK HARRISON BUILDING, 16–20 CAMP RD., FARNBOROUGH GU14 6EW
Tel: 08702 405420 Fax: 01252 669009 Contact: Matt Rogers
sales@matsofresh.co.uk www.matsofresh.co.uk
Soil Association P6392. Growers, importers and distributors to processors,
catering, retail and packers.

MILL FARM ORGANIC SHOP

MILL FARM, ISINGTON, NR. ALTON GU34 4PN
Tel: 01420 22331 Fax: 01420 22331 Contact: James Mayhew
info@millfarmorganic.co.uk www.millfarmorganic.co.uk
Soil Association G6840. Fully organic farm, status achieved Dec 2002. Producer
of pedigree beef and lamb. Farm Open Days at certain times of the year. Shop
open Thursday, Friday & Saturday 9am to 5pm. Shop stocks own as well as other
organic and local produce. Farm trails open all year with maps available in the
shop. Member of the Soil Association Organic Farms Network.

MYRIAD NATURAL TOYS & CRAFTS

THE BUCKMAN BUILDING, 43 SOUTHAMPTON ROAD, RINGWOOD BH24 1HE
Tel: 01725 517085 Fax: 01725 517152 Contact: Richard Parks
veronica@myriadonline.co.uk www.myriadonline.co.uk
Natural toys made from wood, wool and cotton. Dolls made from organic cotton
and wool. Plant-dyed organic wool craft products. Plant dye paints, crayons and
colouring pencils. Environmentally aware products for children and families.
Wide range available by mail order. Free catalogue.

NATURAL COLLECTION

PO BOX 135, SOUTHAMPTON SO14 0AF
Tel: 0870 331 3333 Fax: 0870 331 3334
info@naturalcollection.com www.naturalcollection.com
Natural Collection is a large showcase of unusual and beautiful lifestyle products
chosen with a fairer planet in mind, including certified organic, natural, eco, fairly
traded and hand-crafted products.

NATURALLY HEALTH FOODS

5 WATERLOO COURT, ANDOVER SP10 1QJ
Tel: 01264 332375 Contact: Karen Harmer
naturally.andover@btopenworld.com www.naturallyhealthfoods.co.uk
Independent health store supplying a wide selection of organic foods, an extensive
range of VMS, herbal and homoeopathic remedies, local veggie box scheme, eco
household products and much more.

NATURALLY ORGANIC

ELM COTTAGE, POND LANE, CLANFIELD PO8 0RG

Tel: 023 9236 0196 Fax: 023 9236 0196 Contact: Alex Handford

Wholesale distribution of certified organic fruit and vegetables. Also organic fruit and vegetable box home delivery service.

NORTHDOWN ORCHARD

SOUTH LITCHFIELD, BASINGSTOKE RG25 3BP

Tel: 01256 771168 Contact: Mike Fisher

northdownorchard@ukonline.co.uk

Organic growers established for 15 years, marketing produce through our local box scheme delivering to Overton and Basingstoke. We also sell seasonal produce at Basingstoke farmers' market.

ORGANIC BOX DELIVERY

5 FATHOMS REACH, HAYLING ISLAND PO11 0RA

Tel: 023 9235 9933 Contact: Hugh Keogh

info@organicboxdeliveries.com www.organicboxdeliveries.com

I am a retail outlet utilising Soil Association accredited supplier Sunnyfields Organics for all of my produce. I serve all of Portsmouth, Havant, Hayling Island areas.

ORGANICALLY SPEAKING

2 HARTLEY MEWS, HIGH STREET, HARTLEY WINTNEY RG27 8NX

Tel: 01252 845577 Contact: Jessica Hughes

organic-speaking@btclick.com www.organically-speaking.co.uk

Our shop in Hartley Wintney sells a large range of organic products including fruit, veg, bread, groceries, meat, fish, dairy, household products, skincare and hampers. Our delivery service operates in Surrey, Hampshire and Berkshire.

PARK FARM ORGANICS

HECKFIELD, HOOK RG27 0LD
Tel: 0118 932 6650 Contact: Roger David & Mandy Tarrant
mandy@parkfarmorganics.co.uk www.parkfarmorganics.co.uk
Organic beef, pork and lamb produced with traditional breeds, also fresh fruit and
veg and dairy products. Open Tuesday, Wednesday, Thursday, Friday and Saturday.
Local box scheme.

PETTY, WOOD & CO

P.O. BOX 66, LIVINGSTONE RD., ANDOVER SP10 5LA
Tel: 01264 345500 Fax: 01264 332025
info@pettywood.co.uk www.pettywood.co.uk
Petty Wood sells, distributes and markets speciality ambient food products to
the retail and wholesale sectors. Portfolio includes Duchy Originals, Yarrah Pet
Food, Sacla, Baxters and our own Epicure Organics.

POLLEN ORGANICS LIMITED

THREE FIRS HOUSE, BRAMSHOTT CHASE GU26 6DG
Tel: 01428 608870 Fax: 01428 608890 Contact: Richard Pollen
organics@pollenorganics.com www.pollenorganics.com
Soil Association registered. Organic sauces, relishes, dressings, nuts and nibbles.
Pollen Organics has established a strong brand identity in organic grocery foods
such as Soil Association award-winning pesto sauces, mayonnaise and hollandaise
sauces, pasta sauce, red onion marmalade and Seville orange marmalade with
exceptional taste, dressings, nuts and nibbles. Organic Food Awards 2004:
Condiments Commended.

PURE WINE

OCEAN HOUSE, 51 ALCANTARA CRESCENT, OCEAN VILLAGE, SOUTHAMPTON
SO14 3HR
Tel: 023 8023 8214 Fax: 023 8023 8186 Contact: Barry Martin
service@purewine.co.uk www.purewine.co.uk
Organic wine merchant supplying organic wines from around the world by mail
order, via printed catalogue or web. To contact, either Freephone 0808 100 3123
or visit our website. The Pure Wine company also runs wine clubs for third party
organisations with organic or environmentally minded customers/supporters.

RASANCO LTD

THE ESTATE OFFICE, SUTTON SCOTNEY SO21 3JW
Tel: 01962 761935 Fax: 01962 761860 Contact: Russell Smart
ras@rasanco.com www.rasanco.com
Soil Association P2960. Rasanco is a specialist organic ingredients supplier
offering the food and drink manufacturer a one-stop shop for their organic raw
materials. We subscribe to a 'from field to finished foods' ethic.

RE LTD

207 CHRISTCHURCH ROAD, RINGWOOD BH24 3AN
Tel: 08700 419 432 Contact: Ben Grigg
feelgood@be-re.com www.be-re.com
Retailer of a wide and stylish range of eco-ethically sourced home furnishings,
bed and bath-linens, clothing, baby-wear and accessories. Re pursues Fairtrade
and fair play principles when choosing its products.

RHIMES ORGANIC GROWERS, G&S

HILL VIEW, CHURCH LANE, WEST MEON, PETERSFIELD GU32 1JB
Tel: 01730 829208 Contact: G Rhimes
Soil Association Licence no. G2039. Vegetables, potatoes and soft fruit in season
(summer and autumn).

RIVERFORD HOME DELIVERY

208 GAINSBOROUGH RD, BASINGSTOKE RG21 3EQ
Tel: 0845 600 2311 Fax: 01803 762718 Contact: David Morgan
boxscheme@riverford.co.uk www.riverford.co.uk
Independent Local Licensed Distributor from Riverford Organic Vegetables,
delivering vegetable boxes to parts of Hampshire, Surrey and Berkshire.

RIVERFORD HOME DELIVERY—PORTSMOUTH AND CHICHESTER

5 THE VALE, LOCKS HEATH, FAREHAM SO31 6NL
Tel: 0800 600 2311 Contact: Sue Bushnell
paulandsue@riverfordhomedelivery.co.uk www.riverford.co.uk
Award-winning Riverford organic vegetable box scheme. A range of different
boxes to suit most households and needs. Visit the web site www.riverford.co.uk or
telephone 0800 600 2311 to see if we deliver in your area, to check predicted
box contents, and to place orders. Alternative tel no. 01489 557208.

SCOLTOCKS HEALTH FOODS

1 MARKET PLACE, RINGWOOD BH24 1AN
Tel: 01425 473787 Contact: Yvonne Tilley
Member of National Association of Health Stores, member of Institute of Health
Food Retailing. Jams, pulses etc. Dietary foods, vegetarian specialist.

SPIRIT OF NATURE

UNIT 7, HANNAH WAY, GORDLETON INDUSTRIAL PARK, LYMINGTON SO41 8JD
Tel: 0870 725 9885 Fax: 0870 725 9886 Contact: Liz Fletcher
marketing@spiritofnature.co.uk http://spiritofnature.co.uk
Spirit of Nature offers an extensive range of natural and environmentally
friendly products including baby clothing made from organic raw materials,
clothing for adults, environmentally friendly disposable nappies, wooden toys,
natural cosmetics and skin care, household products without harmful substances
and 600 more natural products . . . order a free mail order catalogue!

SUNNYFIELDS ORGANIC

JACOBS GUTTER LANE, TOTTON, SOUTHAMPTON SO40 9FX
Tel: 023 8087 1408 Fax: 023 8087 1146 Contact: Louise
info@sunnyfields.co.uk www.sunnyfields.co.uk
Sunnyfields grows a large range of organic vegetables and sells a full range of
organic products through our shop (open 7 days) and home delivery service to
Hampshire and London.

TIMBER!
5 STAR LANE, RINGWOOD BH24 1AL
Tel: 01425 483505 Contact: Sana Stephens
sanastephens@yahoo.co.uk www.loveorganic.com
Organic clothing from well established organic companies such as People Tree,
Bishopston trading and many more. All the companies we use have their own
certified cotton. We also sell Green Baby clothing and other organic products
such as bedding.

TURF CROFT ORGANIC HERBS
TURF CROFT COTTAGE, BURLEY, RINGWOOD BH24 4DF
Tel: 01425 403502 Fax: 01425 403502 Contact: Simon Weir
Soil Association W165 and BDAA member. Wholesale specialists in fresh culinary
herbs all year round. Extensive range, home-produced in season, imported out of
season. A range of packet sizes and styles available.

UPTON HOUSE FARM
UPTON HOUSE FARM, WONSTON, WINCHESTER SO21 3LR
Tel: 01962 760219 Fax: 01962 761419 Contact: Robin Readhead
Producing British chickens that taste like those that granny produced before
chemicals intruded. Supplier of organic poultry compost.

WARBORNE ORGANIC FARM
WARBORNE FARM, WARBORNE LANE, BOLDRE, LYMINGTON SO41 5QD
Tel: 01590 688488 Fax: 01590 688096 Contact: George Heathcote
Soil Association G2404. We deliver boxes of organic vegetables, grown on our
farm, to local households. Free range eggs and organic meat also available.
Farm shop. 'Buy local—eat organic.' Organic Food Awards 2004: Best Mixed Farm.

WEEK FARM/AVON ORGANICS

WATTONS LANE, MATCHAM, RINGWOOD BH24 2DG
Tel: 01202 484628 Contact: CJ Snow
csnow-weekfarm@btinternet.com
Organic beef/sheep farmer/producer, together with vegetable box scheme,
supplying Bournemouth to Ringwood and surrounding areas.

THE WINCHESTER BAKERY

51 HATHERLEY RD., WINCHESTER SO22 6RR
Tel: 01962 861477 Contact: Alison Reid
Soil Association P5584. Organic home-made bread, available through local shops
and farmers' markets.

WWW.STIRRUPHOES.CO.UK

UNIT 4 EMSWORH HOUSE CLOSE, EMSWORTH PO10 7JR
stirruphoe@tiscali.co.uk www.stirruphoes.co.uk
Specialist supplier of Stirrup Hoes for professional growers.

Accommodation	Garden and Farm Sundries	Producers
Box Schemes/ Local Deliveries	Farmers' market Stall	Restaurants/ Cafés/Caterers
Day Visits	Manufacturers/ Processors	Retail shops
Eco Products	Importers/ exporters	Textiles
Farm Gate Sales	Mail order suppliers	Wholesalers

ABUNDANCE PRODUCE

GLENTHORPE MARKET GARDEN, LITTLE BIRCH, HEREFORD HR2 8BD
Tel: 01981 540181 Fax: 01981 540181 Contact: Tim Headley
Biodynamic Agricultural Association (Demeter) no. 260. Box scheme and local
delivery in Herefordshire.

ACONBURY SPROUTS

UNIT 4, WESTWOOD INDUSTRIAL ESTATE, PONTRILAS, HEREFORD HR2 0EL
Tel: 01981 241155 Fax: 01981 241386 Contact: Jim Hardy & Philippa Swattridge
info@aconbury.co.uk www.aconbury.co.uk
A speciality food business, growing and supplying high quality fresh organic
sprouted seeds, pulses and organic wheatgrass, sold throughout the UK and
Ireland in organic and health food retailers. Alternative email and website:
philippa@aconbury.co.uk and www.wheatgrass-uk.com

ARKSTONE MILL PRODUCE

ARKSTONE MILL, KINGSTONE, HEREFORD HR2 9HU
Tel: 01981 251135 Contact: Paul Izod
arkstone@arkstonemill.ndirect.co.uk
Organic vegetable box scheme serving Hereford and the Golden Valley area.

BATCHLEY MILL ORGANIC FEEDS

GRENDON BISHOP, BROMYARD HR7 4TH
Tel: 01885 483377 Fax: 01885 483321 Contact: Mary Wakefield-Jones
Soil Association P628. The first animal feed business to have SA standard.
Organic feeds for most classes of farm livestock.

BIOSPHERE ORGANICS

2 WYNNS GREEN COTTAGES, BURLEY GATE, HEREFORD HR1 3QT
Tel: 01432 820082 Fax: 01432 820088 Contact: Paul Burgess
biosphere-organics@supanet.com www.biosphere-organics.supanet.com
Growers, importers and wholesalers of fresh fruit, vegetables, herbs and spices. We
can supply frozen products in bulk. Suppliers to packers, processors, box schemes,
restaurants, shops, caterers throughout the UK.

BUTFORD ORGANICS

BUTFORD FARM, BOWLEY LANE, BODENHAM HR1 3LG
Tel: 01568 797195 Fax: 01568 797885 Contact: Janet & Martin Harris
tuolomne@aol.com www.butfordorganics.co.uk
We are certified with the Soil Association (no. G5368). We are small-scale
producers of award-winning cider and perry, organic pork, geese, eggs, seasonal
vegetables, soft and top fruit.

CAVES FOLLY NURSERIES

EVENDINE LANE, COLWALL, MALVERN WR13 6DU
Tel: 01684 540631 Contact: Bridget Evans
bridget@cavesfolly.com www.cavesfolly.com
Specialist growers of perennials, grasses and alpines, all peat-free. Wonderful
display gardens, wild flower meadow, etc.. Garden design and advisory service
specialising in organics and using environmentally sound products.

DUNKERTONS CIDER CO LTD & SHOP

LUNTLEY, PEMBRIDGE, NR. LEOMINSTER HR6 9ED
Tel: 01544 388653 Fax: 01544 388654 Contact: Ivor Dunkerton
dunkertons@pembridge.kc3.co.uk www.dunkertons.co.uk
Ciders and Perry, still and sparkling. Draught and bottled. Traditional local varieties
of cider apples pressed, fermented and bottled at the mill. Retail shop open
Monday to Saturday 10am to 6pm (5pm in winter) for sales of ciders and perry.
Organic Food Awards 2004: Cider Commended.

EPIKOUROU UK

2 WYNNS GREEN COTTAGES, BURLEY GATE, HEREFORD HR1 3AT
Tel: 01432 820082 Fax: 01432 820088 Contact: Paul Burgess
biosphere-organics@supanet.com www.epikouros.gr
Greek certified (DIO Greece No. 411-5/481-3/04) grower and processor of organic olives, olive oil, feta cheese and wines from Greece. Wholesale quantities only.

FIELD FAYRE

18–19 BROAD STREET, ROSS-ON-WYE HR9 7EA
Tel: 01989 566683 Fax: 01989 566924 Contact: Denise Meek
denise@field-fayre.co.uk www.field-fayre.co.uk
Friendly shop in the town centre specialising in organic produce including local fruit and vegetables, bread, dairy products, meat and fish, chocolate, wine, beer, local cider and much more! Ecover products also available.

FLIGHTS ORCHARD ORGANICS

UNITS 3 & 4, LOWER ROAD TRADING ESTATE, LEDBURY HR8 2DJ
Tel: 0845 658 9808 Fax: 0845 658 9809 Contact: Mike Hamilton
sales@flightsorchardorganics.co.uk www.flightsorchardorganics.co.uk
Marketing group of growers based in Herefordshire. Home delivery throughout the Midlands, wholesale delivery nationwide. Over 85 different sorts of fruit and vegetables grown throughout the year.

FODDER THE HEALTH STORE

26–27 CHURCH ST., HEREFORD HR1 2LR
Tel: 01432 358171 Fax: 01432 277861 Contact: Sue Jordan
The largest range of organic wholefood, veg, bread, yoghurts, wines, cider in the area, plus herbal and homoeopathic remedies. Also Ecover products, essential oils.

GEIMA UK

2 WYNNS GREEN COTTAGES, BURLEY GATE, HEREFORD HR1 3QT
Tel: 01432 820082 Fax: 01432 820088 Contact: Paul Burgess
paulburgess@geima.it www.geima.it
Italian certified growers (Ecocert Italia CDD.OP.C728) of organic citrus (oranges, blood oranges, mandarins, clementines, lemons) and melons. Selling whole or mixed pallets into the UK.

GEORGE'S DELICATESSEN

25 HIGH ST., KINGTON HR5 3AX
Tel: 01544 231400 Contact: Clive & Kathryn Genders
A busy delicatessen selling a large range of cheeses, tea, coffee, loose spices, home-made cakes, wines and local ciders.

GREEN ACRES ORGANIC GROWERS

GREEN ACRES FARM SHOP, DINMORE, HEREFORD HR4 8ED
Tel: 01568 797045 Contact: Sheila Jenkins
Soil Association J14M. Organic market garden and farm shop established 1982.
Sunday and Monday open by arrangement, Tuesday–Saturday 9am–5.30pm.
Produce includes meat, vegetables, fruit, ice cream, cider, wine, preserves etc..
Local delivery service.

GREEN CUISINE LTD

PENRHOS COURT, KINGTON HR5 3LH
Tel: 01544 230720 Fax: 01544 230754 Contact: Daphne Lambert
info@greencuisine.org www.greencuisine.org
Soil Association E2051. Green Cuisine runs courses on food and health and offers consultations and natural therapies. The company also produces books and educational material. See also Penrhos Ltd and The Penrhos Trust.

HANDLEY ORGANICS

HARDWICKE ORGANICS FARM, UPPER HARDWICKE LANE, WINSLOW, BROMYARD
HR7 4SX
Tel: 01885 483364 Contact: Horace Handley
Soil Association G2141. Organic growers for wholesalers.

HAY WHOLEFOODS AND DELICATESSEN

41 LION ST., HAY-ON-WYE HR3 5AA
Tel: 01497 820708 Contact: Mandy
Large and comprehensive wholefood shop with wide range of organic goods including
wine, cheese, vegetables and groceries. Good delicatessen with organic choice where
possible.

HAYGROVE FRUIT

REDBANK, LEDBURY HR8 2JL
Tel: 01531 631797 Fax: 01531 634069 Contact: Alan Hale
packhouse@haygrove.co.uk www.haygrove.co.uk
Soil Association Grower code G6412, Producer code P5435. Fresh fruit and
frozen bulk juice sales from Organic fruits. Haygrove Organic production in UK,
South Africa and Hungary.

HELME, EBM AND SONS

POOL HULLOCK, LLANDINABO HR
Tel: 01989 730632 Fax: 01989 730632 Contact: Jeremy Helme
Soil Association G613. General veg and Pool Hullock extra delicious organic chickens.

HENCLOSE ORGANIC FARM PRODUCE

LITTLE DEWCHURCH, HEREFORD HR2 6PP
Tel: 01432 840826 Contact: Karen Tibbetts
Demeter organic certification No. 394. Home-produced lamb, pork, kid, bacon,
sausages and goats milk from old and semi-rare breeds. 25 years organic status.
Phone for availability and collection. Self-catering converted barn for holidays or
long lets. Gloucester Old Spot registered organic weaners for sale.

HOPES OF LONGTOWN
THE FARMERS BARN, LONGTOWN HR2 0LT
Tel: 01873 860444 Contact: Christine Hope
info@hopesoflongtown.co.uk www.hopesoflongtown.co.uk
An independent village shop and post office retailing local products, Fairtrade teas and coffees, organic and vegan supplies, fresh fruit and veg and home-made cakes.

JAMES' GOURMET COFFEE CO LTD
UNIT 7, CROPPER ROW, HAIGH IND. EST., ALTON RD., ROSS ON WYE HR9 5LA
Tel: 0870 787 0233 Fax: 01989 566244 Contact: Peter James
enquiries@jamesgourmetcoffee.com www.jamesgourmetcoffee.com
Discerning, ethical, passionate coffee specialists. Great coffee! Traditional service.

LEDBURY WHOLEFOODS
82 THE HOMEND, LEDBURY HR8 1BX
Tel: 01531 632889 Contact: Nelson & Alice Shield
ledbury.wholefoods@virgin.net
Natural food and medicine store. Speciality and diet foods, gluten-free, organic and Fairtrade products. Vitamins and remedies, therapists, allergy testing, homoeopathy, therapy rooms.

MEE, J R
SPRINGFIELD FARM, STEENSBRIDGE, LEOMINSTER HR6 0LU
Tel: 01568 760270 Fax: 01568 760418 Contact: R. Mee
Farmers and packers of high grade table birds (chickens and turkeys) for sale to wholesalers and retailers—also at our farm gate.

Broad Bean Purée
Add 1kg of fresh podded broad beans to a pan of unsalted water, bring to the boil and cook for 6 minutes. Drain and put into a food processor with a clove of garlic, squeeze of lemon, 3 tbsps of olive oil and a small bunch of chopped dill. Whizz until smooth, and season with sea salt and black pepper. This Middle Eastern starter is sumptuous served with warm pitta bread.
From *Allotment Gardening: An Organic Guide for Beginners* by Susan Berger, Green Books, £9.95.

NATURE'S CHOICE RESTAURANT & GUESTHOUSE
RAGLAN HOUSE, 17 BROAD STREET, ROSS-ON-WYE HR9 7EA
Tel: 01989 763454 Fax: 01989 763064 Contact: Kathryn Roberts
nature@roberts9535.freeserve.co.uk www.natures-choice.biz
Licensed organic restaurant and guesthouse specializing in varied dietary
needs, gluten-free, vegan, vegetarian, meat, non-dairy etc. Delicious American
and Mexican influenced foods in a smoke-free, eco-friendly environment.
Centrally located in downtown Ross-on-Wye. Summers, Monday–Saturday
10am–5pm. Tuesday–Saturday year round 10am–5pm. Evenings,
Thursday–Saturday. Menus available on the website: www.natures-choice.biz.

NITTY GRITTY WHOLEFOODS
24 WEST ST., LEOMINSTER HR6 8ES
Tel: 01568 611600 Contact: Pamela Horsley
Traditional wholefood shop. Free range eggs and dairy produce, trees and
herbaceous.

OLD KING STREET FARM
EWYAS HAROLD, HEREFORD HR2 0HB
Tel: 01981 240208 Contact: Amanda Huntley
info@oldkingstreetfarm.co.uk www.oldkingstreetfarm.co.uk
llama trekking and holiday cottages on our organic farm. Pomona cottage sleeps
4 and the Cider House sleeps 2. Day trekking with our gentle llamas, local
organic picnic included.

ORGANIC OPTIONS
15A BROAD ST., LEOMINSTER HR6 8BT
Tel: 01568 612154 Fax: 01568 617510 Contact: Richard Sharpham
Specialist organic shop. Everything you need: meat and fish, dairy, bakery, fruit &
vegetables, frozen meals, dairy and dairy-free ices, wine and beer. Living Nature
and Green People bodycare range. Ecover with refills, organic clothing. Fresh juice
bar using organic produce.

PAUL RICHARDS HERBAL SUPPLIES

THE FIELD, EARDISLEY HR3 6NB
Tel: 01544 327360 Fax: 01544 327360 Contact: Paul Richards
paul.herbs@ntlworld.com
Soil Association PR10M. Fresh herbal tinctures (echinacea and many others), herbal oils and ointments (comfrey, calendula/hypericum, chickweed, horse chestnut). Wholesale, retail, mail order, own label. Contract herb grower and herbal product supplier.

PENRHOS

PENRHOS COURT, KINGTON HR5 3LH
Tel: 01544 230720 Fax: 01544 230754 Contact: Martin Griffiths
info@penrhos.co.uk www.penrhos.co.uk
700-year-old farmstead-now the most delightful hotel anywhere. Millennium Marque award for environmental excellence. Voted Best Organic Restaurant of the Year 2002. See also Green Cuisine Ltd and The Penrhos Trust.

POSTLETHWAITE'S HERBAL PRODUCTS

THE FIELD, EARDISLEY HR3 6NB
Tel: 0870 240 3379 Fax: 0870 240 3379 Contact: Paul Richards
paul.herbs@ntlworld.com
Soil Association PR10M. We supply a wide range of tinctures and other herbal products in retail sizes with the familiar gold label. Most are fresh tinctures made using home-grown herbs and we offer an own label service for large and small runs. Mail order also available.

RAPUNZEL UK

2 WYNNS GREEN COTTAGES, BURLEY GATE, HEREFORD HR1 3QT
Tel: 01432 820082 Fax: 01432 820088 Contact: Paul Burgess
rapunzelorganic@supanet.com www.rapunzel.com.tr
Swiss certified (IMO No. TR7116) Turkish processor of dried fruits, nuts, olives, seeds, dried legumes, dried vegetables, alll available diced, sliced, powdered. Rapunzel is 100% organic processing factory. Whole or mixed containers.

THE RICE CAKE

THE HOMEND MEWS, THE HOMEND, LEDBURY HR8 1BN
Tel: 01531 635860 Fax: 01531 631892 Contact: Clio Lever
help@thericecake.co.uk www.thericecake.co.uk
Top-quality organic and wholefood groceries, natural products and homoeopathic remedies at discount prices. Resource website. Helping you in some way.

THE SEPTEMBER ORGANIC DAIRY

WHITEHILL PARK, WEOBLEY HR4 8QE
Tel: 01544 312910 Fax: 01544 312911 Contact: Adam Glyn-Jones
sales@september-organic.co.uk www.september-organic.co.uk
Soil Association P4691. Manufacturers of award-winning organic ice cream in a range of unusual flavours available for home, retail, catering and wholesale. Member of the Soil Association Organic Farms Network.

SNELL, AJ & CI

PENCOYD COURT FARM, ST. OWENS CROSS, HEREFORD HR2 8JY
Tel: 01989 730229 Fax: 01989 730603 Contact: A Snell
a.snell@pcf.u-net.com
Soft fruit farm producing amongst other crops, organic blackcurrants. Available fresh, frozen or processed.

STEPHENS, TP

NEWTON COURT, NEWTON, LEOMINSTER HR6 0PF
Tel: 01568 611721 Contact: T Stephens
tps1@dialstart.net
Soil Association G7479. Organic cider makers.

STEVENSON, PEGGYANNE

WINDLE PARK, CLIFFORD, HAY-ON-WYE HR3 5HA
Tel: 01497 831666 Contact: Peggyanne Stevenson
Small organic farm in an idyllic setting with traditional Hereford cattle and a flock of Portland sheep. Accommodation for riders and their horses, caravan site.

SUNNYBANK VINE NURSERY

JOURNEY'S END, KING STREET, EWYAS HAROLD, HEREFORD HR2 0EE
Tel: 01981 240256 Contact: BR Edwards
vinenursery@hotmail.com www.vinenursery.netfirms.com
Specialist producer of vines for both eating and wine. Plants grown without sprays
or artificial fertilisers. Growing collection of seedless and disease-resistant varieties.

SURVIVAL WHOLEFOODS

UNIT 1, PRINCE OF WALES BUSINESS PARK, BRIDGE ST., LEOMINSTER HR6 8EA
Tel: 01568 614147 Fax: 01568 612678 Contact: Mark & Mary Hatt
'A unique wholefoods experience'. Shop with delivery service to the Midlands,
Wales, Herefordshire, Shropshire, Worcestershire, Gloucestershire. Run by Mark
and Mary Hatt.

WELSH FRUIT STOCKS

LLANERCHIR, BRYNGWYN, VIA KINGTON HR5 3QZ
Tel: 01497 851209 Fax: 01497 851209 Contact: Sian Fromant
sian@welshfruitstocks.co.uk www.welshfruitstocks.co.uk
Propagators of top quality soft fruit plants, including organic strawberry plants,
raspberry canes, black/red/white currant bushes, gooseberry bushes, jostaberry
bushes. Mail order gardeners list and growers list available.

WESTON'S CIDER

THE BOUNDS, MUCH MARCLE, LEDBURY HR8 2NQ
Tel: 01531 660233 Fax: 01531 660619 Contact: Jules Schad
marketing@westons-cider.co.uk www.westons-cider.co.uk
Soil Association P1776. Westons have been producing cider since 1880. The
organic cider was winner at the Organic Food Awards in 1998 and 2003.
Producers of Organic Vintage Cider and Organize, the non-alcoholic nutrient drink.
Organic Food Awards 2004 Cider Winners. See display ad.

WIGGLY WIGGLERS

LOWER BLAKEMERE FARM, BLAKEMERE HR2 9PX
Tel: 01981 500391 Fax: 01981 500108 Contact: David Pitman
david@wigglywigglers.co.uk www.wigglywigglers.co.uk
Wiggly Wigglers supply natural gardening products including worm and conventional composters, garden bird food and feeders including live feed, insect and mammal habitats and wild flowers.

WILLEY WINKLE PURE WOOL BEDDING MANUFACTURERS

OFFA HOUSE, OFFA ST., HEREFORD HR1 2LH
Tel: 01432 268018 Fax: 01432 268018 Contact: Jeff Wilkes
www.willeywinkle.co.uk
Traditional mattress makers using organic wool filling and organic outer cover ticking. Also suppliers of organic bedding sheets, duvets, pillows, towelling etc.

WYEDEAN WHOLEFOODS

4 GLOUCESTER ROAD, ROSS-ON-WYE HR9 5BU
Tel: 01989 562340 Contact: Barry Crocker
Hundreds of organic lines. Wholefoods, gluten and dairy-free, cruelty-free cosmetics; SLS-free toiletries. Excellent range of vitamins, minerals and herbals. Wide range of chilled and frozen products.

Transportation

The long-distance transportation of food means lorries criss-crossing our cities and motorways filled with all that we eat every day. Very few foods come from the area in which we live: most come from more like 300 miles away, and some are transported 3,000 miles or more. Look at the labels, and you will see what I mean!

I realized that what I do when I purchase these items is pay for their shipping—and for the pollution from the lorries.

Worst of all are bulky items such as bread, cornflakes, pasta, biscuits and potato crisps. They take up lots of space in a lorry—the box contains mostly air!

A bag of rice is another matter—it takes up little space, and many meals can be prepared from it. Dried beans, nuts, seeds and straight spaghetti are also compact.

From *Ecology Begins at Home* by Archie Duncanson, Green Books, £4.95.

ALCOHOLS LTD

CHARRINGTONS HOUSE, THE CAUSEWAY, BISHOP'S STORTFORD CM23 2EW
Tel: 01279 658464 Fax: 01279 757613 Contact: Peter McKay
peter.mckay@alcohols.co.uk www.alcohols.co.uk
Alcohols Ltd. produce organic gin and vodka and market organic alcohol, supplying
in bulk and packed.

BROUGHTON PASTURES ORGANIC FRUIT WINE CO

THE SILK MILL, BROOK STREET., TRING HP23 5EF
Tel: 01442 823993 Fax: 01442 823993 Contact: Brian Reid
organicfruitwine@aol.com www.broughtonpastures.co.uk
The UK's foremost producer of organic fruit wines. Available in several delicious
flavours including mead, ginger wine and a sparkling elderflower wine made in the
traditional 'Methode Champenoise'. Look out for our new range of Fairtrade organic
wines and our delicious Fairtrade organic liqueurs. Phone or email for local outlets.
Soil Association no. P1652. See display ad.

CEREAL PARTNERS

2 ALBANY PLACE, 28 BRIDGE ROAD EAST, WELWYN GARDEN CITY AL7 1RR
Tel: 01707 824400 Fax: 01707 824569 Contact: Aline Spittal
aline.spittal@uk.nestle.com www.cerealpartners.co.uk
Cereal Partners UK manufacture a wide range of ready-to-eat breakfast cereals
and include organic within the portfolio.

CLARE JAMES HEALTH FOODS

13A HEMPSTEAD RD., KINGS LANGLEY WD4 8BJ
Tel: 01923 263195 Contact: Bridget & Lewis Johnstone
Health food shop selling an extensive range of organics: flour, dried fruit, nuts,
pasta, grains, yoghurts, eggs, bread, sugar, honey, jams, cereals, juices, tea,
toiletries and much more besides. Sorry, no fresh vegetables.

COOKS DELIGHT

360–364 HIGH STREET, BERKHAMSTED HP4 1HU
Tel: 01442 863584 Fax: 01442 863702 Contact: Rex Tyler
cooksd@globalnet.co.uk www.organiccooksdelight.co.uk
Queens Award 2001/Business in the Community. National Training Award
Champion. Certified organic and biodynamic shop buying ethically from UK where
available, otherwise trading in an environmentally and socially responsible way,
recycling. Fresh fruit and vegetables, grains, flours, 4,500 organic foods.

EASTWOODS OF BERKHAMSTED

15 GRAVEL PATH, BERKHAMSTED HP4 2EF
Tel: 01442 865012 Fax: 01442 877212 Contact: Joe Collier
joe.collier@btinternet.com www.eastwoodsofberkhamsted.co.uk
Organic meat specialist, national winners of 8 Soil Association Awards. Order
on line, mail order, fax, phone. 'Highgrove' meats, many products.

EQ WASTE MANAGEMENT

APPSPOND LANE, POTTERS CROUCH, ST. ALBANS AL2 3NL
Tel: 0870 560 2060 Fax: 01727 867866 Contact: Jo Fitzpatrick
jo.fitzpatrick@eqwaste.com www.organeq.co.uk
OrganEQ's peat-free range of composts and soil blends are produced from a
sustainable botanical source providing a high quality supplement for the
horticultural and agricultural markets. Delivery available nationwide.

FAIRHAVEN WHOLEFOODS

27 JUBILEE TRADE CENTRE, OFF JUBILEE ROAD, OFF BALDOCK ROAD,
LETCHWORTH SG6 1SP
Tel: 01462 675300 Fax: 01462 483008 Contact: Robin Sternberg
sales@fairhaven.co.uk www.fairhaven.co.uk
Large store, easy parking, personal service. Ring for directions. Deliveries
throughout N. Herts & S. Beds. Huge range of organics, diet foods, supplements,
bodycare and more.

FARM2DOOR.ORG

PO BOX 2067, WATFORD WD17 4ZH
Tel: 01923 490526 Fax: 01923 490526 Contact: Barry Couldridge
mail@farm2door.org www.farm2door.org
Check the website or ring for details—delivery to local collection points (within approximately 30 mile radius north of Watford). Fruit & vegetables—seasonal boxed selection. All produce sourced from Soil Association Licensed suppliers.

GOOSE FAT AND GARLIC

52 BELL STREET, SAWBRIDGEWORTH CM21 9AN
Tel: 01279 722554 Contact: Lyndon Wootton
info@goosefatandgarlic www.goosefatandgarlic.co.uk
Located in the picturesque town of Sawbridgeworth, Goose Fat and Garlic is one of Hertfordshire's most popular restaurants, using only quality fresh ingredients. They have recently introduced a selection of dishes, using organic meat from Soil Association certified Childhay Manor Farm, to their new Summer 05 menus, such as slow-roasted shoulder of pork with sauté potatoes, apple and red wine jus; chicken breast stuffed with pesto butter and served with spaghetti; leg of lamb steak simply chargrilled with rosemary and garlic served with buttered spinach and mash; organic spaghetti tossed with seafood, chilli, garlic and olive oil. As time goes on they expect to increase the presence of organic ingredients on their menus.

HARMONY

53 HIGH STREET, TRING HP23 5AG
Tel: 01442 822311 Contact: Susan Gould
Dried goods, tinned goods and other foodstuffs. No fresh vegetables or meat produce. Environmentally friendly household cleaners, organic shampoos, body care ranges.

MILL GREEN MUSEUM & MILL

MILL GREEN, HATFIELD AL9 5PD
Tel: 01707 271362 Fax: 01707 272511 Contact: Carol Rigby
museum@welhat.gov.uk
Soil Association P1470. Working water mill producing organic stoneground wholemeal flour.

ORGANIC HARVEST

4 MIDDLE ROW, OLD STEVENAGE SG1 3AN
Tel: 01438 225222 Fax: 01438 225111 Contact: Penny Hope
Family-run organic supermarket. Complete range of organic foods, eco-products, allergy foods. Box scheme, range of fairly traded gifts and jewellery.

PLANT HEALTH CARE

121 HIGH ST., BERKHAMSTED HP4 2DJ
Tel: 01442 864431 Fax: 01442 870148 Contact: Jason Holohan
info@planthealthcare.co.uk www.planthealthcare.co.uk
Manufacturers and suppliers of Soil Association approved liquid organic fertilizers, based on all-plant extracts. We supply 5 different analyses; 9:2:2, 9:2:7, 8:3:3, 6:5:6 and 4:2:8. We also supply bacterial and fungal products.

REDBOURNBURY WATERMILL

REDBOURNBURY LANE, REDBOURN ROAD, ST. ALBANS AL3 6RS
Tel: 01582 792874 Fax: 01582 792874 Contact: Justin James
RedbryMill@aol.com www.RedbournMill.co.uk
18th-century working watermill producing a range of stoneground organic flours, including 100% wholemeal, unbleached white, brown, malted wheatflake, rye and spelt. Available in 500g to 32kg sizes. Mill open to public every Sunday afternoon from March to October—see website for more details.

SUNRISE ORGANICS

4 GOLDS NURSERIES BUSINESS PARK, JENKINS DRIVE, ELSENHAM, NR. BISHOPS STORTFORD CM22 6JX
Contact: Kiran Shaw
info@sunriseorganics.co.uk www.sunriseorganics.co.uk
Soil Association Certification DA16695. Soil Association certified organic veg box home delivery service. We provide tasty, seasonal, locally grown produce, sourced from local organic farms. We cover Herts & Essex and provide a great range of boxes to choose from. You can order weekly, fortnightly, or just when you want.

BARKER LTD, JJ

HOOK PLACE FARM, SOUTHFLEET, GRAVESEND DA13 9NH
Tel: 01474 833555 Fax: 01474 834364 Contact: Lawrence Frohn
sales@jjbarker.co.uk
UK based grower and importer, packer and distributor of organic produce—mainly salads and legumes primarily for the UK multiples. Soil Association no. P2380.

BROCKMAN, AG & CO

PERRY COURT FARM, GARLINGE GREEN, CANTERBURY CT4 5RU
Tel: 01227 732001 Fax: 01227 732001 Contact: Patrick Brockman
agbrockmanco@farmersweekly.net
Producers of Demeter certified organic foods since 1953. Beef, milling wheat, oats, wheat flour, vegetables, salads and herbs. Sales through farm shop, box scheme, farmers' markets, local shops and wholesalers.

BURSCOMBE CLIFF FARM

EGERTON, ASHFORD TN77 5RB
Tel: 01233 756468 Fax: 01233 756468 Contact: Ben Garratt & Hilary Jones
Soil Association symbol no. G683. Organic livestock farm offering beef, lamb, pork, bacon, sausages. Occasionally fleece, top fruit, eggs. WWOOF host open farm—telephone us. Most produce sold via local farmers' markets.

CANON GARTH LTD

ALEXANDER HOUSE, 31–39 LONDON RD., SEVENOAKS TN13 1AR
Tel: 01732 228500 Fax: 01732 743444 Contact: David Kelman
david.kelman@ctcs-ltd.co.uk
Bulk trader and importer/exporter of groundnuts, treenuts and dried fruit. Peanuts, almonds, cashews, hazelnuts, sultanas and walnuts.

CANTERBURY WHOLEFOODS

1 & 2 JEWRY LANE, CANTERBURY CT1 2RP
Tel: 01227 464623 Fax: 01227 764838 Contact: Jason Robbins
info@canterbury-wholefoods.co.uk www.
Soil Association R1676. We are a large, traditional wholefood store specialising in
organics, fresh fruit and vegetables, bulk sales and discounts, county-wide delivery
service.

CHEGWORTH VALLEY JUICES

WATER LANE FARM, CHEGWORTH, HARRIETSHAM ME17 1DE
Tel: 01622 859272 Fax: 01622 850918 Contact: David Deme
info@chegworthvalley.com www.chegworthvalley.com
A range of award-winning drinks including apple juice and pear juice and blended
juices with strawberries, raspberries, rhubarb, blackcurrants, blackberries and cranberries grown and pressed on our family farm in Kent. All are full of natural goodness and free from added sugars, sweeteners, concentrates, artificial colourings,
flavourings or preservatives and presented in 250ml and 1litre wine shaped glass
bottles featuring stunning photography from the farm. We supply direct to private
customers through numerous farmers markets and by mail order service and also to
quality independent retailers nationwide. Please visit our website to find out more.

CHUN FARM

CHURN LANE, HORSMONDEN, TONBRIDGE TN12 8HL
Tel: 01892 722577 Contact: Roger Couchman
Soil Association G4567. Seven-acre smallholding producing salads, vegetables,
fruit and nuts sold through local farmers' markets.

CHURCH VIEW FARM

IGHTHAM BY-PASS, SEVENOAKS TN15 9AZ
Tel: 01732 886680 Contact: Karl & Julie Weller
churchvieworganicfarm@hotmail.com
Soil Association G6051. Local organic box delivery scheme including vegetables,
fruit, eggs and juice supplying Tonbridge and Sevenoaks.

COMMONWORK

BORE PLACE, CHIDDINGSTONE, EDENBRIDGE TN8 7AR
Tel: 01732 463255 Fax: 01732 740264 Contact: Lyn Kelly
info@commonwork.org www.commonwork.org
Conference and study centre with organic, wildlife and permaculture gardens on commercial organic farm. Residential accommodation for groups undertaking their own training and development work. Environmental/arts education programme and organic farm/food study days offered to schools and community groups by Commonwork, plus hands-on vocational training in organic farming for people of all abilities, and seasonal open days for the public. Commonwork also runs a development education centre (global education) from Maidstone, going out to schools, youth and community groups.

COMMONWORK ORGANIC FARMS LTD

BORE PLACE, CHIDDINGSTONE, EDENBRIDGE TN8 7AR
Tel: 01732 463255 Fax: 01732 740264 Contact: Michael Cottrell
www.commonwork.org
Approved milk producer selling to OMSCo.

CUCKOO'S PIT ORGANIC FARM

KIPPINGTON, REDBROOK STREET, WOODCHURCH, ASHFORD TN26 3QU
Tel: 01233 860199 Contact: Maria Bugden
thebugdengang@aol.com
We are an expanding organic farm in heart of the Kent countryside. We produce and sell all our own home-reared livestock. We sell organic beef, lamb, pork, sausages, ham and bacon. Several of our livestock breeds are rare breeds, e.g. Gloucester Old Spot pigs and White Park cattle. We sell at our gate or can deliver locally.

DABBS PLACE ORGANIC FARM

COBHAM, GRAVESEND DA13 9BL
Tel: 07712 439304 Contact: J Fermor
mail@organicveg.net www.organicveg.net
Soil Association F165. Local box scheme, vegetables, arable farm.

DAVIES & DAVIES, JEFFREY LTD
ARCTIC HOUSE, RYE LANE, DUNTON GREEN, SEVENOAKS TN24 5HL
Tel: 01732 450948 Fax: 01732 452012 Contact: Dominic Wright
info@ www.davies-davies.co.uk
Jeffrey Davies & Davies Ltd are a pork processing and export company. Trading
in a wide variety of meats throughout Great Britain, Europe and the Far East.

DEFENDERS LTD
OCCUPATION RD., WYE, ASHFORD TN25 5EN
Tel: 01233 813121 Fax: 01233 813633 Contact: The Manager
help@defenders.co.uk www.defenders.co.uk
Defenders supplies a comprehensive range of biological controls and integrated
control products to gardeners by mail order.

EAST MALLING RESEARCH
NEW RD, EAST, MALLING ME19 6BJ
Tel: 01732 843833 Fax: 01732 849067 Contact: Jean Fitzgerald
jean.fitzgerald@emr.ac.uk www.eastmallingresearch.com
We carry out research projects on organic apples and strawberries and plan to
include more top and soft fruits in our organic demonstration area.

ESPECIALLY HEALTH
119 HIGH STREET, SEVENOAKS TN13 1UP
Tel: 01732 741181 Fax: 01732 740719 Contact: Wendy Kent
wendy.kent@totalise.co.uk www.especiallyhealth.co.uk
Wholefoods and health foods including sprouted wheat (essene), spelt and other
non-wheat breads. Dietary consultations, blood group advice, allergy testing,
vitamin and mineral testing, massage, flower therapy and medical herbalism.

FOOD FOR LIVING
MARKET PLACE, DARTFORD DA1 1EX
Tel: 01322 278790 Fax: 01322 278790 Contact: John Frisby
john@foodforliving.co.uk www.foodforliving.co.uk
Health food shop with a wide range of organic foods. Vitamins and supplements also supplied.

GALA COFFEE & TEA LIMITED
MILL HOUSE, RIVERSIDE WAY, DARTFORD DA1 5BS
Tel: 01322 272411 Fax: 01322 278600 Contact: Louise Lloyd-Rossi
gala@gala-coffee-tea.co.uk www.gala-coffee-tea.co.uk
Gala is a unique company focused on the special requirements of both retailers and food service companies producing coffee and tea under private label.

GOOD FOOD WINES LTD
NO. 3 WAREHOUSE, WHITEWALL RD., STROOD ME2 4EW
Tel: 01634 290592 Fax: 01634 716617 Contact: Heather Bennett
info@goodfoodwines.com www.goodfoodwines.com
Suppliers of ingredients to the food industry for wines, beers, spirits and vinegars: organic and non-organic.

THE GOODS SHED
STATION RD WEST, CANTERBURY CT2 8AN
Tel: 01227 459153 Contact: Susannah Atkins
A permanent farmers' market, open six days a week and including a restaurant which sources seasonal ingredients from the local and regional producers who run the stalls. Converted from an industrial coal store, it opened in 2002 and now has its own on-site bakery, and an on-site retail butchery selling well-matured meats from 5 local and organic producers. Organic Food Awards 2004: Local Food Initiative Joint Winner.

GRANARY HERBS

THE GRANARY, MILGATE PARK, ASHFORD ROAD, BEARSTED ME14 4NN
Tel: 01622 737314 Fax: 01622 739781 Contact: Christine Brown
Mail order only (no callers). Tinctures, fluid extracts and creams made from fresh organic home-grown herbs. Swedish bitters.

GREENCELL LTD

ST. JOHNS HOUSE, 37–41 SPITAL ST., DARTFORD DA1 2DR
Tel: 01322 425555 Fax: 01322 425500 Contact: Jeff Geary
info@greencell.com www.greencell.com
Fresh imported organic fruit sourced to give 12 month continuity. We store, condition, pack and distribute to retailers, wholesalers, food service providers and processors through the UK.

HDRA, HENRY DOUBLEDAY RESEARCH ASSOCIATION, YALDING ORGANIC GARDENS

BENOVER RD., YALDING, NR. MAIDSTONE ME18 6EX
Tel: 01622 814650 Fax: 01622 814650 Contact: Tania Neumann
enquiry@hdra.org.uk www.hdra.org.uk
Yalding Organic Gardens trace the course of garden history through 16 landscaped displays, illustrating the organic techniques used to maintain them. Shop for browsing and organic café for refreshments.

HEALTH MATTERS

28 ROYAL STAR ARCADE, MAIDSTONE ME14 1SL
Tel: 01622 691179 Fax: 01622 691179 Contact: Marion Allen
www.maidstonehealthfoods.co.uk
We offer a wide range of organic wholefoods and also offer food intolerance testing.

HERBAL HEALTH LTD
PO BOX 114, SISSINGHURST, CRANBROOK TN17 2XQ
Tel: 01580 713613 Fax: 01580 712714 Contact: Jo d'Armenia
joe.d@qi-teas.com www.qi-teas.com
Supplier of top quality organic China tea under the Qi (chee) label, including
traditional loose leaf teas and green tea blends with abundant organic fruit and
herbs.

HERBS, GARDENS & HEALTH
27 NORTHDOWN RD., ST. PETER'S, BROADSTAIRS CT10 2UW
Tel: 01843 600201 Fax: 01843 863134 Contact: Juliet Seeley
juliet@herbsgardenshealth.com www.herbsgardenshealth.com
Mostly organic health foods, special diet foods, natural and organic toiletries,
Ecover, herbal remedies, vitamins, minerals and supplements, organic veg-in-a-box
from Wingham, etc..

HIGHFIELD FARM
BETSHAM RD., SOUTHFLEET DA13 9PD
Tel: 01474 832850 Fax: 01474 832850 Contact: The Manager
Beef and hay producer.

HORTON PARK FARM
THE PENT, POSTLING, HYTHE CT21 4EY
Tel: 01303 862436 Fax: 01303 863723 Contact: Chris Reynolds
cr.reynolds@farmline.com
Soil Association G4082. 900-acre mixed farm, 100 sucklers, 160+ ewes. Angus x
South Devon beef freezer packs available by prior booking, also whole or half
lambs during the summer months. Arable crops grown for seed.

INTERNATIONAL PRODUCE LTD
SHEERNESS PRODUCE TERMINAL, SPADE LANE, SITTINGBOURNE ME9 7TT
Tel: 01634 269200 Fax: 01634 269269 Contact: Bruce Bell
info@internationalproduce.com www.internationalproduce.com
International importers of organic and non-organic produce.

IVY HOUSE FARM

IVY HOUSE, SANDHILLS, ASH, NR. CANTERBURY CT3 2NG
Tel: 01304 812437 Fax: 01304 812437 Contact: Andrew Ward
Our farm, registered with the Soil Association, produces a range of organically
grown vegetables for wholesale and retail. Our farm shop also sells organically
grown produce from other certified producers.

JUBILEE FARM

RHODES MINNIS, NR. CANTERBURY CT4 6YA
Tel: 01303 862317 Fax: 01303 864257 Contact: Wilf Missing
jubilee@farmline.com
Soil Association G7668. Mixed farm, livestock including Aberdeen Angus herd,
sheep, poultry, free range eggs, vegetables, cereals, top fruit and soft fruit.

LOWER THORNE FARM

LOWER THORNE, SMARDEN RD, PLUCKLEY TN27 0RF
Tel: 01233 840493 Contact: Elizabeth Harrison
info@lowerthorne.com www.lowerthorne.com
Lower Thorne is an organic holding in Pluckley, Kent, certified with the Soil
Association. The farm has a long history of traditional, non-intensive management
and was acquired by the current owners in 1995. The farm specializes in rearing
traditional English breeds & produces organically reared free-range chicken and
Devon Dimple turkeys for Christmas, organic beef, lamb and pork. Our meat is for
sale direct from the farm or by mail order.

LUDDESDOWN ORGANIC FARMS LTD

COURT LODGE, LUDDESDOWN, NR. COBHAM DA13 0XE
Tel: 01474 813376 Fax: 01474 815044 Contact: Gerry Minister
organic@luddesdown.u-net.com www.luddesdownorganicfarms.co.uk
Soil Association S38S. 950 acres producing cereals, beans, red clover for seed,
forage, beef and vegetables. All grown to Soil Association standards. Wholesaler
and retailer, including vegetable box scheme delivery scheme and home-produced
beef. Member of the Soil Association Organic Farms Network.

MACK BANANAS

MACK MULTIPLES DIVISION, TRANSFESA ROAD, PADDOCK WOOD TN12 6UT
Tel: 01892 831224 Fax: 01892 837670 Contact: Elliot Mantle
elliot.mantle@mackmultiples.com www.mwmack.co.uk
Importers & ripeners of bananas—organic and Fairtrade organic.

MICHAELS WHOLEFOODS

UNITS 1, 5 & 7, NORTHDOWN IND. PARK, ST. PETERS, BROADSTAIRS CT10 3JP
Tel: 08451 306307 Fax: 01843 604603 Contact: Michael Pile
enquiries@michael-wholefoods.co.uk
Dried foods hand-packed to order. Own label available.

MURCH LTD, C E, AMERY COURT FARM

AMERY COURT FARM, CHAPEL LANE, BLEAN, CANTERBURY CT2 9HF
c.e.murch@btopenworld.com
We have been growing organic apples and pears since 1997 main varieties are
Conference Pears and Red Falstaff Apples. The farm is situated just north of
Canterbury and we would be interested in supplying box schemes with fruit to
supplement their range.

NASH NURSERY LTD

NASH, NR. ASH, CANTERBURY CT3 2JU
Tel: 01304 812250 Contact: Paul Dovey
paul@nashnursery.co.uk www.nashnursery.co.uk
Soil Association G2528. Organic farm producing chicken, turkey, ducks and geese,
fruit and vegetables. Abattoir and processing room on-site.

NEAL'S YARD REMEDIES

8 EAST ST., BROMLEY BR1 1QX
Tel: 020 8313 9898 Fax: 020 8313 9898 Contact: Anja Lange
mail@nealsyardremedies.com www.nealsyardremedies.com
Retail store specialising in natural remedies and cosmetics including herbs,
homoeopathy, aromatherapy, nutrition and flower remedies.

THE ORGANIC HEALTH SHOP
10 HIGH ST., TUNBRIDGE WELLS TN1 1UX
Tel: 01892 538155 Fax: 01892 538155 Contact: Richard Keates
A wide range of organic food and drink including vegetable and fruit boxes,
vitamins, minerals, supplements, skin and hair care products, cosmetics, books,
cleaning products, natural paint, organic pet food and supplements.

PIZZA ORGANIC LTD
3C DORSET ST., SEVENOAKS TN13 1LL
Tel: 01732 454664 Contact: Mike Traszko
info@pizzapiazza.co.uk www.pizza-organic.co.uk
A great menu packed full of organic options, featuring stonebaked pizza, sautéed
pasta, gourmet burgers, grilled fish and fabulous desserts. Pizza Organic is certified
by the Soil Association and was Highly Commended in the 2003 Organic Food
Awards. All restaurants open 7 days a week but opening times may vary, call 020
8397 3330 for further details.

PIZZA ORGANIC LTD
76 MOUNT PLEASANT RD., TUNBRIDGE WELLS TN1 1RJ
Tel: 01892 547124 Contact: Mike Traszko
info@pizzapiazza.co.uk www.pizza-organic.co.uk
A great menu packed full of organic options, featuring stonebaked pizza, sautéed
pasta, gourmet burgers, grilled fish and fabulous desserts. Pizza Organic is certified
by the Soil Association and was Highly Commended in the 2003 Organic Food
Awards. All restaurants open 7 days a week but opening times may vary, call 020
8397 3330 for further details.

THE REAL ICE COMPANY
LODGE RD., STAPLEHURST TN12 0QY
Tel: 01580 892200 Fax: 01580 893414 Contact: Carl Whitewood
carl@realiceco.co.uk
Manufacturer of private label organic ice cream for major retailers and food service.

REGENT HEALTH
12 ALBERT ROAD, BELVEDERE DA17 5LJ
Tel: 01322 446244 Contact: Derek Rogers (Owner)
Large range organic gluten-free, dairy-free, diabetic, chilled and frozen foods available. Local deliveries (minimum order). Friendly advice, mail service. If we haven't got it, we will get it!

RIPPLE FARM ORGANICS
CRUNDALE, CANTERBURY CT4 7EB
Tel: 01227 730898 Contact: Martin Mackey
martin@ripplefarmorganics.co.uk www.ripplefarmorganics.co.uk
Soil Association G737. Growers of organic vegetables, salad and soft fruit to supply own local, year-round, box scheme, farmers' markets and London organic shops.

RIVERFORD ORGANIC VEGETABLES—HOME DELIVERY (KENT)
63 OAKLANDS, SOUTH GODSTONE RH9 8HX
Tel: 0845 009 3564 Fax: 0845 009 3564 Contact: Andrew Garnham
andrewg@riverfordhomedelivery.co.uk www.riverford.co.uk
Award-winning (BBC Radio 4 Farmer of the Year 2005) organic vegetable box scheme operating in various parts of West Kent. Various box sizes to suit all households from a single occupant to a large family. A selection of fruit, dairy products, wine, fruit juices etc. also available. Order weekly, fortnightly or whenever you like. Can order online at www.riverford.co.uk or by telephone on 0845 600 2311.

RIVERFORD ORGANIC VEGETABLES—NORTH WEST KENT
67 BYRON DRIVE, ERITH DA8 1YD
Tel: 0845 600 2311 Fax: 01322 434 286 Contact: Patrick Murphy
pat@riverfordhomedelivery.co.uk www.riverford.co.uk
Award-winning (BBC Radio 4 Farmer of the Year 2005) organic vegetable box scheme operating in Bexley, Dartford, Orpington and surrounding areas. Box sizes to suit all households from a single person to a large family. A selection of fruit, dairy products, wine, juices and chocolate are also available. Order weekly, fortnightly or whenever you like. Can order and pay online at www.riverford.co.uk or by phone: 0845 600 2311.

ROMSHED FARM
UNDERRIVER, SEVENOAKS TN15 0SD
Tel: 01732 463372 Fax: 01732 454136 Contact: Fidelity Weston
romshed@weald.co.uk
Organic eggs, chicken meat, duck, lamb and beef. Monthly deliveries and local sales outlets including farm gate.

ROWCLIFFE, ANTHONY & SON LTD
UNIT B, PADDOCK WOOD DISTRIBUTION CENTRE, PADDOCK WOOD TN12 6UU
Tel: 01892 838999 Fax: 01892 836585 Contact: Steve Smith
arowcliffeinfo@aol.com www.rowcliffe.com
Nationwide distributors of dairy products.

SIMPLY WILD FOOD COMPANY
84–86 GROSVENOR RD., TUNBRIDGE WELLS TN
Tel: 08456 586140 Fax: 08456 586148 Contact: Ian Nuttall
enquiries@simplywildorganics.co.uk www.simplywild.biz
Simply Wild is a retail outlet for organic fruit, vegetables, eggs, home-produced meat and freshly baked bread. A large selection of other organic products and a café are also available.

SIMPLY WILD FOOD COMPANY
BOURNES STORES, HIGH ST., BRENCHLEY TN12 7NQ
Tel: 01892 722066 Contact: Ian Nuttall
enquiries@simplywildorganics.co.uk www.simplywild.biz
Simply Wild at Bournes Stores is a retail outlet for organic fruit, vegetables, eggs, home-produced meat and freshly baked bread. A large selection of other organic products is also available.

SIMPLY WILD FOOD COMPANY

PULLENS FARM, LAMBERHURST RD., HORSMONDEN TN12 8ED
Tel: 08456 586141 Fax: 08456 586141 Contact: Emily Reiss
enquiries@simplywildorganics.co.uk www.simplywild.biz
Simply Wild is a family-run business which offers a range of home-delivery boxes,
each containing fresh locally produced organic vegetables, fruit, eggs, bread and
meat to your doorstep.

TATTY BUMPKIN LTD

ALLENS FARM, ALLENS LANE, PLAXTOL, SEVENOAKS TN15 0QZ
Tel: 01732 812212 Fax: 01732 812219 Contact: Samantha Petter
info@tattybumpkin.com www.tattybumpkin.com
SKAL certified fun, practical clothes and accessories for kids—inspired by yoga and
an organic lifestyle. Range includes long and short sleeve t-shirts, trousers, skirts,
sweatshirts, first aid in a bag kit; quilted cotton yoga mat; toys and a unique bendy
yoga doll.

TERRA MIA

37E CAMBRIDGE RD., BROMLEY BR1 4EB
Tel: 07816 419055 Contact: Guido Traverso
info@terramiaorganic.net www.terramiaorganic.net
Terra Mia is a small business dedicated to importing organic Italian food directly
from Italy to the London area. Our products are made by small hand-craft
companies producing typical regional organic delicatessen goods.

TINY SPROUT

LITTLE BOURNE, FURZEFIELD AVE., SPELDHURST TN3 0LD
Tel: 01892 863646 Contact: Sian van Zyl
sian.vanzyl@tinysprout.co.uk www.tinysprout.co.uk
Organic baby gift hampers mail order and web delivery service, featuring award
winning ethically produced, eco-friendly products and organic cotton clothing
to welcome new baby and pamper new parents.

WILLOW FARM B&B
STONE CROSS, BILSINGTON, ASHFORD TN25 7JJ
Tel: 01233 721700 Fax: 01233 720484 Contact: Renee Kemp Hopper
renee@willow-farm.freeserve.co.uk www.willowfarmenterprises.co.uk
B&B on an organic smallholding in peaceful rural area. Close to Yalding Gardens.
Easy access M20, Channel ports and Tunnel. From £25 per person per night.

WINGHAM COUNTRY MARKET
SHATTERLING, CANTERBURY CT3 1JW
Tel: 01227 720567 Fax: 01227 720567 Contact: Andrew Ward
We sell an extensive range of organic produce at our farm shop, including fresh
vegetables grown on our Soil Association registered (G977) farm.

WINTERWOOD FARMS
CHARTWAY ST., EAST SUTTON, MAIDSTONE ME17 3DN
Tel: 01622 844286 Fax: 01622 844274 Contact: Stephen Taylor
organics@winterwood.co.uk www.winterwood.co.uk
Soft fruit grower & packer. Main customers are UK multiples. Also actively growing
in Poland, France, Spain and South Africa.

School Lunches
Producing a waste-free lunch each day can make considerable savings. The
table below gives you an idea of what you can save:

Lunch with disposable packaging	Waste-free lunch
Pre-packed sausage roll or pasty £1.50	Home-made sandwich (cheese and salad) 30p
Crisps 40p	Crisps (decanted from a larger bag) (in re-useable container) 20p
Pre-packed cake bar 40p	Slice of cake (home-made), (wrapped in foil or greaseproof paper) 20p
Apple 20p	Apple 20p
Drink pouch/can/bottle £1.00	Drink made from larger bottle of squash 5p
Total per day £3.50	Total per day 95p

From *Reduce, Reuse, Recycle* by Nicky Scott, Green Books, £3.95.

BLAIRS ORGANIC NURSERY

LOW CARR NURSERY, HEAD DYKE LANE, PILLING, PRESTON PR3 6SJ
Tel: 01253 790471 Fax: 01253 790099 Contact: David Purple
Growing organically for over 30 years, Blairs Organic Nursery is an organic grower of salad tomatoes, plum tomatoes, vine tomatoes and red and green peppers.

BOOTHS SUPERMARKETS

4–6 FISHERGATE, PRESTON PR1 3LJ
Tel: 01772 251701 Fax: 01772 204316 Contact: The Manager
admin@booths-supermarkets.co.uk www.booths-supermarkets.co.uk
Regional supermarket chain.

CHORLEY HEALTH FOOD STORE LTD

18 NEW MARKET ST., CHORLEY PR7 1DB
Tel: 01257 276146 Fax: 01257 276146 Contact: John Clark
sales@yourhealthfoodstore.co.uk www.yourhealthfoodstore.co.uk
Town centre shop adjacent to main car park, taxi rank and bus station. We offer a wide variety of organic foods, drinks and supplements, special orders welcome. Open 6 days Monday–Saturday 8.15 to 5.16. Discount on full case orders.

COMMERCIAL FREEZE DRY LTD

45 ROMAN WAY, LONGRIDGE RD., RIBBLETON, PRESTON PR2 5BD
Tel: 01772 654441 Fax: 01772 655004 Contact: Garry Hincks
gh@commercialfreezedry.co.uk www.commercialfreezedry.co.uk
Soil Association P2697. Freeze drying on a commission dry or product sourced basis of any organic products. Meat, dairy, fruit, vegetables—all handled.

FLINTOFF, LIBBY

BROOK HOUSE FARM, TARNACRE LANE, ST MICHAEL'S ON WYRE,
PRESTON PR3 0TB
Tel: 01995 679728 Fax: 01995 679728 Contact: Libby Flintoff
lib@theflintoffs.fsnet.co.uk
Soil Association G1898. Grower-mainly protected cropping including cucumbers,
aubergines, French beans, celery and onions. Also some field vegetables.

FOLD HOUSE FARM

HEAD DYKE LANE, PILLING, PRESTON PR3 6SJ
Tel: 01253 790541 Fax: 01253 790541 Contact: R Harrison
Soil Association G2176. Growers of field vegetables for sale to box schemes,
market stalls, shops, supermarkets and wholesalers plus organic beef suckler
herd with store cattle available for sale.

FREE RANGE KIDS

GARSTANG RD. EAST, POULTON-LE-FYLDE FY6 8HJ
Tel: 01253 896290 Contact: Lynda Howard
info@freerangekids.co.uk www.freerangekids.co.uk
One stop shop for baby slings, carriers, real washable nappies, organic and
Fairtrade clothing and toys from around the world. Family-run business. Carefully
researched products, thoroughly tested, beautiful and practical.

GIELTY, A&D

LYNCROFT FARM, BUTCHERS LANE, AUGHTON GREEN, ORMSKIRK L39 6SY
Tel: 01695 421712 Fax: 01695 422117 Contact: Alf Gielty
Organic Farmers and Growers. Organic vegetables grown for wholesale. Also farm
shop open Thursdays 10am–3pm and local box delivery scheme on Thursday and
Friday evenings.

GREEN MAN DELIVERIES
HAWTHORNE COTTAGE, 24 GREENGATE LANE, CRAG BANK, CARNFORTH LA5 9JJ
Tel: 01524 730175 Fax: 01524 730175 Contact: Lynne Rees
greenmandeliveries@btopenworld.com
Delivering organic fruit, vegetables and eggs in the Lancaster, Kendal, north and
south lakes area, with a high percentage of locally grown produce.

GREMBO ORGANICS UK
BANKS FARM COTTAGE, STAYNALL LANE, HAMBLETON,
POULTON-LE-FYLDE FY6 9DT
Tel: 01253 701518 Fax: 01253 700523 Contact: Suzanne Thompson
info@grembo.co.uk www.grembo.co.uk
Producers of beautiful organic cotton sleeping bags from birth to 4 years of age.
Made in the USA from the highest quality organic cotton, they are excellent in
design and are must for all children. Choose from winter, spring and summer
bags, six different designs.

GROWING WITH NATURE
BRADSHAW LANE NURSERY, PILLING, NR. PRESTON PR3 6AX
Tel: 01253 790046 Fax: 01253 790046 Contact: Alan Schofield
Soil Association S44N, RS44N. Growers box scheme with seasonal vegetables and
salads. Organic Food Awards 2004: Organic Trophy Winners.

JIGSAW ENVIRONMENTAL
MAIN STREET, GISBURN, CLITHEROE BB7 4HN
Tel: 01200 415979 Contact: Ellen Pope
gisburnproject@hotmail.com
We aim to support the long term development of people with disabilities and those
disadvantaged through economic or social exclusion. Organic horticulture is the
platform from which we deliver accredited horticultural training. Best environmental practice is also a key component of the site and the project as a whole.

KEER FALLS FOREST FARM
ARKHOLME, CARNFORTH LA6 1AP
Tel: 015242 21019 Fax: 015242 21730 Contact: PJ Onions
philip@keerfalls.co.uk www.keerfalls.co.uk
Soil Association G7569. Producers of delicious organic lamb and beef, rare
breed lamb, forest ducklings, herbs, hardwood timber and firewood. See our web
site for more details.

LEHMANN SFI LTD, GUY
ALSTON HOUSE, WHITE CROSS, SOUTH ROAD, LANCASTER LA1 4QX
Tel: 01524 581560 Fax: 01524 581562 Contact: Mark Lehmann
sales@guylehmann.com www.guylehmann.com
Specialists in supply of organic bulk dry mustard ingredients. Bulk organic wine,
spirit and speciality vinegar. Organic sunflower, millet, linseed, caraway, pumpkin.
All UK and Europe—minimum delivery: dry goods 25kg, liquids 1,000ltrs.

McKINSEY HEALTHY HERBS
ORRELL RD., ORRELL, WIGAN WN5 8QZ
Tel: 01695 632825 Fax: 01942 736286 Contact: Mandy Welland-Bray
Organic herb nursery. We specialise in pot-grown and fresh-cut culinary and
medicinal herbs. Browse our extensive stock, talk to our knowledgeable staff or
relax in our tea room. Open Monday, Wednesday, Friday & Saturday 10 till 4.

OLVERSON LTD, NORMAN
KERSHAW'S FARM, SMITHY LANE, SCARISBRICK, ORMSKIRK L40 8HL
Tel: 01704 840392 Fax: 01704 841096 Contact: Brian Olverson
sales@redvelvet.co.uk www.redvelvet.co.uk
Farming. Prepacking and beetroot processing. Soil Association P2631.
Vegetables.

ONLY NATURAL
64 STANDISHGATE, WIGAN WN1 1UW
Tel: 01942 236239 Contact: B Arrowsmith
Health food shop selling a wide range of vitamins, body building, food supplements, cosmetics, wholefoods including organic ranges. Allergy testing once a month. Friendly and helpful staff.

THE ORGANIC GIFT HAMPER COMPANY
BANKS FARM COTTAGE, STAYNALL LANE, HAMBLETON, POULTON-LE-FYLDE FY6 9DT
Tel: 01253 701518 Contact: Suzanne Thompson
info@theorganicgifthampercompany.co.uk www.theorganicgifthampercompany.co.uk
Exclusive luxury and everyday hampers. Gifts for every occasion, beautifully packaged and delivered straight to your door or that of a loved one. Products include Japanese, Italian, Greek, Chocolate, Champagne and Christmas hampers. Also specialises in organic new baby hampers.

PENNINE ORGANICS LTD
THE POULTRY FARM, SQUARE LANE, CATFORTH, PRESTON PR4 0HQ
Tel: 01772 690261 Fax: 01772 690985 Contact: Martin Tomlinson
martin@pennineorganics.co.uk www.pennineorganics.co.uk
Pelleted, crumbled, micro poultry manure. Liquid feeds—plant 6:2:4, tomato 4:2:6. Liquids mixed to your own specification.

PORTER, ROY
9 BRIDGE RD., CHATBURN, CLITHEROE BB7 4AW
Tel: 01200 441392 Fax: 01200 441096 Contact: Roy Porter
Soil Association R4342. A very traditional butchers shop, whose products include organic meat and poultry. All meat is hung for 7–10 days depending on species and butchered to customers' individual requirements.

ROYAL OAK FARM ORGANICS
ROYAL OAK FARM, BICKERSTAFFE, NR. ORMSKIRK L39 0EE
Tel: 01695 423259 Fax: 01695 423259 Contact: Peter Lydiate
Soil Association G5301. Potatoes, vegetables and other horticultural produce.

SAKER VEGETARIAN FOODS LTD
CANTEEN MILL, BURNLEY ROAD, TODMORDEN OL14 7DR
Tel: 01706 818189 Fax: 01706 818189 Contact: Karl Badger
bdb1205691@hotmail.co.uk
Small, long established wholesale bakers, supplying the north of England. We specialise in organic breads and sugar-free cakes. We also produce vegan and vegetarian savouries, flapjacks and crumbles.

SINGLE STEP CO-OPERATIVE LTD
78A PENNY ST, LANCASTER LA1 1NN
Tel: 01524 63021 Contact: David Tizard
Wholefood co-op selling a wide range of organic and Fairtrade products, including fresh fruit and vegetables. Vegetarian and sugar-free policies.

STAVELEY'S EGGS LTD
COPPULL MOOR FARM, PRESTON ROAD, COPPULL, NR. CHORLEY PR7 5EB
Tel: 01257 791595 Fax: 01257 794700 Contact: KT Staveley
eggs@staveleys.sagehost.co.uk www.staveleyseggs.co.uk
Organic egg production and distribution, Lion quality standards and RSPCA Freedom Food standards, wholesale deliveries, most places to shops etc. Eggs in pre-packs to Organic Food Federation standards.

TASTE CONNECTION
76 BRIDGE ST., RAMSBOTTOM, BURY BL0 9AG
Tel: 01706 822175 Fax: 01706 822941 Contact: Iseult or Adrian Richards
tasteconnection@aol.com www.tasteconnection.com
Speciality and organic food shop (two storey). First floor is almost entirely organic: veg, meats, dairy, general grocery. Basement has deli counter with huge cheese selection. Speciality: olive oils from around the world.

WARD & THOMPSON

THE MARKET GARDEN, GREEN LANE, PREESALL, POULTON-LE-FYLDE FY6 0NS
Tel: 01253 811644 Fax: 01253 811644 Contact: Y Thompson
Soil Association W15N. Salad and vegetable crops.

WHALE TAIL CAFE

78A PENNY ST, LANCASTER LA1 1XN
Tel: 01524 845133 Contact: Tricia Rawlinson
Spacious and friendly café offering home-made veggie and vegan food, and on
Fridays an organic main meal option.

Support Buy Nothing Day

Instead of rushing to the shops to buy something—why don't you *not* buy something instead? Buy Nothing Day is organised to challenge the consumer culture
and switch off from shopping for a day. It normally takes place at the end of
November. For information and tips on what to do instead of shopping on that
day, visit www.buynothingday.co.uk.

**From *Go MAD! Go Make A Difference 2: Over 500 daily ways to save the
planet* by The Ecologist, Think Books, £6.99.**

AROMA INTERNATIONAL LTD

THE PADDOCKS FARM, LEICESTER RD., KIBWORTH LE8 0NP
Tel: 0116 279 2211 Fax: 0116 279 6922 Contact: John Brebner
chantal@sdaroma.com www.sdaroma.com
Producers of organic essential oils that promote the welfare and structure of
villages in Nepal, India, Ghana, Malawi and South Africa.

BAMBURY ORGANIC FARM

BAMBURY FARM, BAMBURY LANE, PEATLING MAGNA LE8 5UE
Tel: 0116 247 8907 Fax: 0116 247 8907 Contact: Nick, Sue, Anthony Staines
bamburyfarm@btinternet.com
Soil Association G1104. Bambury Organic Farm is a small family-run farm
providing fresh organic vegetables to the local community. There are a range of
box sizes, plus a wide selection of fruit and free range eggs. Free delivery is
included in the service.

BROCKLEBY FARM SHOP

ASFORDBY HILL, MELTON MOWBRAY LE14 3QU
Tel: 01664 813200 Contact: Ian Jalland
www.brocklebys.co.uk
We are farmers of rare breed sheep and pigs and we have a farm shop that
retails a good range of organic products.

CHEVELSWARDE ORGANIC GROWERS

THE BELT, SOUTH KILWORTH, LUTTERWORTH LE17 6DX
Tel: 01858 575309 Contact: Ruth Daltry
john@chevelswardeorganics.co.uk www.chevelswardeorganics.co.uk
Soil Association D03M (organic status awarded 1975), HDRA. Off licence. Growers
to Soil Association standards: vines for white and red wine, vegetables for local box
scheme and farm shop supplies. Shop open daily for veg, fruit, wines and organic
groceries.

CLAYBROOKE MILL

FROLESWORTH LANE, CLAYBROOKE MAGNA LE17 5DB
Tel: 01455 202443 Contact: Sally Craven
claybrookemill@yahoo.co.uk
Soil Association P1578. We are a 300-year-old working watermill producing high
quality flours and mueslis. Over 40 different varieties of flour and mueslis.

CORNER PLOT VEGETABLES

THE BOATYARD, MILL LANE, THURMASTON, LEICESTER LE4 8AF
Tel: 0116 269 7920 Contact: Matthew Beamish
cesca@cornerplotvegetables.co.uk www.cornerplotvegetables.co.uk
Bag scheme—with total customer choice from a weekly emailed list. Produce
from 3/4-acre organic smallholding and other organic producers. Requests
encouraged. Free delivery in Leicester.

CURRANT AFFAIRS

9A LOSEBY LANE, LEICESTER LE1 5DR
Tel: 0116 251 0887 Contact: Kevin Taylor
www.currantaffairs.co.uk
Currant Affairs is a natural food store selling a wide range of organic produce. We
also have an on-site bakery producing freshly prepared takeaway.

EVERARDS BREWERY

CASTLE ACRES, NARBOROUGH LE19 1BY
Tel: 0116 201 4100 Fax: 0116 282 7164 Contact: Graham Giblett
mail@everards.co.uk www.everards.co.uk
Public house. Beer production, wholesaling and public house retailing.

FARMCARE

OADBY LODGE FARM, GARTREET RD., LEICESTER LE2 2FG
Tel: 0116 259 2342 Fax: 0116 259 2352 Contact: Nick Padwick
nick.padwick@letsco-operate.com
Organic dairy and arable producer based on Farmcare's Stoughton Estate.

GLOBALKIDS.CO.UK
24 HOLLY HAYES RD., WHITWICK COALVILLE, LEICESTER LE67 5GG
Tel: 01530 457146 Contact: Michelle Smith
sales@globalkids.co.uk www.globalkids.co.uk
Organic baby clothes and bedding, natural and organic baby skincare, Fairtrade toys, natural wood personalised products.

GNC
18 SILVER ST., LEICESTER LE1 5ET
Tel: 0116 262 4859 Contact: L Baker
www.gnc.co.uk
Organic dried fruits, nuts, pastas etc.

GRIFFITHS, DT & PM
PIPER FARM, LONG WHATTON, LOUGHBOROUGH LE12 5BE
Tel: 01509 650291 Contact: DT & PM Griffiths
davidgriffiths1@amserve.com
7.4 hectare holding running 60 breeding ewes. Contract hedging and stone walling. Lamb producers.

GROWING CONCERN
HOME FARM, WOODHOUSE LANE, NANPANTAN, LOUGHBOROUGH LE11 3YG
Tel: 01509 239228 Fax: 01509 239228 Contact: M Bell
Redevelopment since winning Organic Food Award includes visitors' rare breed centre, on-farm bakery-restaurant, ready-made meals. Mail order.

HOME FARM ORGANICS, BETH'S KITCHEN & RURAL ROASTERS
HOME FARM, WOODHOUSE LANE, NANPANTON, LOUGHBOROUGH LE11 3YG
Tel: 01509 237064 Fax: 01509 239228 Contact: The Manager
Combined award-winning rare breed farm, restaurant, outside caterers and spit roasters set in national forest. Our speciality sausages were voted some of the UK's finest, October 2004. Organic Food Awards 2004: Prepared Dishes Highly Commended.

LONG CLAWSON DAIRY LTD

WEST END, LONG CLAWSON, MELTON MOWBRAY LE14 4PJ
Tel: 01664 821732 Fax: 01664 823236 Contact: John Burdett
enquiries@clawson.co.uk www.clawson.co.uk
Stilton-blended cheese manufacturers (dairy). Organic Food Awards 2004: Cheese
Winners.

MANOR FARM

LONG WHATTON, LOUGHBOROUGH LE12 5DF
Tel: 01509 646413 Fax: 01509 843344 Contact: V Matravers
vw@manororganicfarm.co.uk www.manororganicfarm.co.uk
Soil Association G1778, Shop Licence P4948, Elm Farm Research Centre
Demonstration Farm. Award-winning mixed organic family farm producing cereals,
vegetables, potatoes, meat and eggs. All sold through our farm shop and at
local farmers' markets, including home-made sausages and burgers. Farm trail
open. Farm shop open Thursday, Friday & Saturday. Member of the Soil
Association Organic Farms Network.

NATURALLY GOOD FOOD LTD

THE STABLE YARD, COTESBACH HALL, MAIN STREET, COTESBACH,
LUTTERWORTH LE17 4HX
Tel: 01455 556878 Fax: 01455 550855 Contact: Sue McGrath
orders@goodfooddelivery.co.uk www.goodfooddelivery.co.uk
Soil Association P6641. Shop Home delivery and mail order for huge range of
organic wholefoods, fruit & veg, plus gluten-free and dairy-free foods, toiletries and
household cleaners. Hard to find foods found! Also the Keeper, an alternative to
tampons.

Saving Electricity

I pondered how I could save electricity. Switching off lights, electronics and
appliances is simple; the only difficulty being that they seem so insignificant! I
used to think, "One little light doesn't matter", until I realized that turning off
one of the two lamps lit in a room meant halving the energy. Gradually I got in
the habit of turning off all the lights when I left the room, and my computer or
stereo when I was done for the day or evening.

From *Ecology Begins at Home* by Archie Duncanson, Green Books, £4.95.

NEWCOMBE, PC & KJ

LUBCLOUD FARM, OAKS IN CHARNWOOD, LOUGHBOROUGH LE12 9YA
Tel: 01509 503204 Fax: 01509 651267 Contact: Phil & Kay Newcombe
Soil Association G2934. Organic dairy farm with 120 milking cows. Bed and
breakfast accommodation in the beautiful Charnwood Forest within the National
Forest area.

OSBASTON KITCHEN GARDEN

OSBASTON HALL, OSBASTON, NR. NUNEATON CV13 0DR
Tel: 01455 440811 Contact: Flick Rohde
Soil Association G1523. Walled kitchen garden (1 acre) growing organic fruit,
vegetables and herbs.

PAUL'S TOFU

66–68 SNOW HILL, MELTON MOWBRAY LE13 1PD
Tel: 01664 560572 Fax: 01664 410345 Contact: I Brammer
paul@soyfoods.co.uk
Wholesale supplier of organic fruit and vegetables and baked goods.

PICKS ORGANIC FARM SHOP

THE COTTAGE, HAMILTON GROUNDS, KING ST., BARKBY THORPE LE4 3QF
Tel: 0116 269 3548 Fax: 0116 269 3548 Contact: Nicola Chambers
Home produced organic pork, beef, lamb, chicken, turkey, guinea fowl, duck and
eggs. Seasonal fruit and vegetables, free local delivery and box scheme available.
Farm shop selling organic meats, vegetables, wines, beers, ales, breads, ice
creams, dairy produce, jams, chutneys, etc..

QUENBY HALL ORGANIC FOODS

QUENBY HALL, HUNGARTON LE7 9JF
Tel: 0116 259 5224 Fax: 0116 259 5224 Contact: Aubyn de Lisle
enquiries@quenbyhall.co.uk www.quenbybeef.co.uk
Soil Association G2914. Organic English Longhorn beef, born and raised on the
ancient natural grassland, sold to order, free local delivery; mail order throughout
UK mainland.

RIVER NENE HOME DELIVERY

47 CARTER CLOSE, ENDERBY, LEICESTER LE19 4BZ
Tel: 0116 286 9713 Contact: Gev Jones
gev@rivernene.co.uk www.rivernene.co.uk
Independent local licensed distributor for River Nene organic vegetables. Award
winning organic vegetable box scheme delivering in West Leicestershire, Nuneaton,
Hinckley and the surrounding area. Offering differing box sizes to suit all households from a single occupant to a large family. A selection of fruit & vegetables,
dairy products,wine and juices are also available. Order weekly,fortnightly or whenever you like. Can order online at www.rivernene.co.uk or by telephone on 0845
078 6868.

RUTLAND ORGANIC POULTRY

CUCKOO FARM, KETTON, NR. STAMFORD PE9 3UU
Tel: 01780 722009 Fax: 01780 722488 Contact: Pat Taylor
cuckoofarm@farmersweekly.net www.rutlandorganicpoultry.co.uk
Soil Association G5618, P7892. Chickens, Chicken portions, Guinea Fowl, year
round Norfolk Black turkeys, Barbary Ducks and Christmas Geese.

SEEDS OF CHANGE

FREEBY LANE, WALTHAM ON THE WOLDS LE14 4RS
Tel: 0800 952 0000
www.seedsofchange.co.uk
Seeds of Change offer accessible day-to-day products, all 100% certified organic.
The range includes dried pasta, pasta sauces, ethnic sauces, stir-in sauces, soups
and cereal bars.

SWEET EARTH

BEAUMONT ENTERPRISE CENTRE, 72 BOSTON ROAD, LEICESTER LE4 1HB
Tel: 0845 233 5599 Contact: Vimal Morjaria
inquiry@sweetearth.co.uk www.sweetearth.co.uk
Sweet Earth deals in organic and eco-friendly products from fruit and vegetable
boxes to baby products and hampers. It's an online supermarket providing a
delivery service. Orders can be placed online or by telephone.

WATTS, DA
THE BUNGALOW, SPRINGFIELD FARM, SAPCOTE LE9 4LD
Tel: 01455 272840 Contact: DA Watts
watts.donkeylane@btinternet.com
Soil Association G1251 P5631. Organic vegetable producer/own box scheme around Hinckley and surrounding area (50% own or local). Also fruit, eggs and bread. Small beef herd.

WHISSENDINE WINDMILL
MELTON ROAD, WHISSENDINE LE15 7EU
Tel: 01664 474172 Contact: Nigel Moon
OF&G P080027. Traditional windmill producing a range of stoneground meals: white, wholemeal flours, rye, spelt, oats, barley.

WOOD, MICHAEL F—FAMILY BUTCHER
51 HARTOPP RD., LEICESTER LE2 1WG
Tel: 0116 270 5194 Fax: 0116 270 5194 Contact: Richard Wood
www.mfwood.co.uk
Soil Association R1979. Retailing of beef, lamb, pork, chicken, turkey, cheese, eggs and butter from a traditional butcher's shop established in 1968.

Frizzled Brussels Sprouts
Here's a new sprout experience that should eradicate any memory of watery offerings forever. Cutting the sprouts lengthways allows you to cook them fast to retain their sweetness.

Cut 450g Brussels sprouts in half and cook in boiling water for 4 minutes till just tender. Drain. Heat 50g butter in a frying pan, add the sprouts and cook till they are golden brown. Season with sea salt and black pepper.

Frizzled sprouts are excellent with roasts or combine with chopped bacon and tagliatelle for a substantial supper dish.

From *Allotment Gardening: An Organic Guide for Beginners* by Susan Berger, Green Books, £9.95.

AGRIMARCHE LIMITED

2ND FLOOR, 2 ST MARY'S HILL, STAMFORD PE9 2DP
Tel: 01780 484640 Contact: Stephen Tutt
stephen.tutt@agrimarche.co.uk
Suppliers of organic soybeans for manufacturing and wholesale. All grades supplied from animal feed to tofu. Also suppliers of organic oil and expeller.

ALFORD FIVE SAILED WINDMILL

EAST STREET, ALFORD LN13 9EQ
Tel: 01507 462136 Contact: Geoff Dees
enquiries@fivesailed.co.uk www.fivesailed.co.uk
Working windmill producing stoneground flours from certified organic grain and cereals of high nutritional value and flavour. Mill, shop and tea room open all year. Open as follows:- Jan–Mar: Tues, Sat & Sun; Apr, May, June: Tues, Fri, Sat & Sun; July, Aug, Sep: Daily; Oct: Tues, Fri, Sat & Sun; Nov & Dec: Tues, Sat & Sun. Opening Times 10am–5pm (Sun 11am–5pm) Winter closing 4pm. Additional opening for school and bank holidays.

BARKSTON HEATH MUSHROOMS

HEATH LANE, BARKSTON HEATH, GRANTHAM NG32 2DE
Tel: 01400 230845 Fax: 01400 230901 Contact: Robert & Linda Ranshaw
barkstonheath@aol.com
Growing organic mushrooms.

BRIDGE FARM ORGANIC FOODS

BRIDGE FARM, SNITTERBY CARR, GAINSBOROUGH DN21 4UU
Tel: 01673 818272 Fax: 01673 818272 Contact: Patty Phillips
patty.bridgefarmconservat@virgin.net
Produce organic goats' milk and cheese, organic vegetables, free range eggs. Education resource centre. Rural skills workshops. Members join farm conservation group, receive newsletters, attend open days, undertake conservation tasks.

BROXHOLME FARM SHOP

GRANGE FARM, BROXHOLME, NR. SAXILBY LN1 2NG
Tel: 01522 704212 Contact: Carl Sutcliffe
Lincolnshire Organic Producers, Soil Association G4752. Soil Association eggs, potatoes and Christmas turkeys. Turkeys available mail order and collected from farm shop.

CHATEAU PAPILLON ESTATES

UNIT H, HOLMES COURT, BOSTON ROAD IND ESTATE, HORNCASTLE LN9 6AS
Tel: 0845 838 1790 Fax: 0870 131 3172 Contact: Simon Delow
simon@chateau-papillon.com www.chateau-papillon.com
UK importer, international distributor and UK wholesaler of organic & biodynamic wine, champagne and port. All wine is certified organic and/or biodynamic and comes from among the best producers in France and Portugal (port).

CHEERS NURSERIES

ELEVEN ACRE LANE, KIRTON, BOSTON PE20 1LS
Tel: 01205 724258 Fax: 01205 724259 Contact: Henry Cheer
henry@cheersnurseries.co.uk
Raise organic vegetable transplants.

ECO-TOM

46 PINCHBECK ROAD, SPALDING PE11 1QF
eco-tom@eco-tom.com www.eco-tom.com
ECO-TOM sells high quality 100% organic cotton tops (certified by SKAL). We offer comfortable, practical and durable clothes and clothing: T-shirts, women's tops, kids t-shirts, hoodies etc.. exclusively through our secure website. All products are Fairtrade (IRFT certified) and are produced by small scale farmers in northern India. Unique hand-painted designs available. Every aspect of our company is as eco-friendly as possible. Company run by committed and qualified ecologist/forester.

ECOLODGE

ROSE COTTAGE, STATION RD., OLD LEAKE, BOSTON PE22 9RF
Tel: 01205 871396 Contact: Geri Clarke
gclarke@internationalbusinessschool.net
www.internationalbusinessschool.net/ecolodge
Ecolodge built from Lincolnshire wood, powered by wood and wind. Filtered
rainwater for washing. Self-catering. Sleeps 4. Spacious, secluded in 8 acres
of wood/meadowland. Walking, cycling and birding. £150 short breaks £300 per
week. 10% discount for bookings 3 months or more in advance.

EDEN FARMS

OLD BOLINGBROKE, SPILSBY PE23 4EY
Tel: 01790 763582 Fax: 01790 763582 Contact: Marjorie Stein
info@edenfarms.co.uk www.edenfarms.co.uk
Soil Association S31M. Organic salads and vegetables. Eden Farms has been
growing organic vegetables for 23 years, and delivers to homes and shops in
Lincolnshire, Nottinghamshire and the East Midlands. Also farmers' markets in
these areas. Organic Food Awards 2004: Highly Commended Box Scheme.

ENTERPRISE SEEDS LTD

CLOVER HOUSE, BOSTON RD., SLEAFORD NG34 7HD
Tel: 01529 415555 Fax: 01529 413333 Contact: Dennis Pell
dennis.pell@entseeds.co.uk www.entseeds.co.uk
Soil Association P5679. Agricultural seed producers for cereals, peas, beans, grass
and forage crops for resale direct to farmers and grounds throughout England and
Wales.

GLEADELL AGRICULTURE LTD

LINDSEY HOUSE, HEMSWELL CLIFF, GAINSBOROUGH DN21 5TH
Tel: 01427 421223 Fax: 01427 421230 Contact: Brian Wilburn
brian.wilburn@gleadell.co.uk www.gleadell.co.uk
Organic grain marketing specialists. Soil Association no. P596. Organic marketing
company committed to serving and promoting organic farming since 1986. Market
specialists for all types and grades of certified organic cereals and pulses. See
display ad.

GOODACRE, JM & A

OLD MANOR FARM, SEWSTERN, GRANTHAM NG33 5RF
Tel: 01476 860228 Fax: 01476 860228 Contact: Andrew Goodacre
Soil Association G4146. Potato specialist business offering several different
varieties for sale and contract growing and grading services.

HOLBEACH WHOLEFOODS

32 HIGH ST., HOLBEACH, SPALDING PE12 7DY
Tel: 01406 422149 Contact: D R West
springsunshine@aol.com
Natural food store—loose wholefoods, vegetarian and vegan foods, natural
healthcare, organic bread, fruit and veg to order. Bulk discounts. Owners vegan,
ethical business. Local delivery service—not a box scheme.

JACK BUCK GROWERS

OAK HOUSE, HOLBEACH BANK, SPALDING PE12 8BL
Tel: 01406 422615 Fax: 01406 426173 Contact: Tony Ruigrok
www.jackbuck.co.uk
Soil Association P5546. Growers, packers and processors of speciality vegetables.

KEEP YOURSELF RIGHT 2

4 RAVENDALE STREET, SCUNTHORPE DN15 6NE
Tel: 01724 854236 Contact: Mary Moss
Health food shop selling a wide range of pre-packed organic foods.

LEECH'S DAIRY FARM

HALL FARM, BLANKNEY LN4 3BB
Tel: 01526 320797 Contact: David Leech
Soil Association G563. Supply of dried lucerne, hay, cereals, pulses, straight
from the farm.

LOUTH WHOLEFOOD CO-OP

7-9 EASTGATE, LOUTH LN11 9NB
Tel: 01507 602411 Contact: John Hough
Wholefood shop selling wide range of organic products including fresh fruit and vegetables, dried fruit, nuts, cereals, tea, coffee, wine, cheese, yoghurt, other chilled and frozen products, toiletries, essential oils, and much more.

MAUD FOSTER MILL

WILLOUGHBY RD., BOSTON PE21 9EG
Tel: 01205 352188 Contact: James Waterfield
The tallest working windmill in Britain producing stoneground organic flours to Organic Food Federation symbol standard for the wholesale and retail trade.

McARD (SEEDS), SM

39 WEST RD, POINTON, SLEAFORD NG34 0NA
Tel: 01529 240765 Fax: 01529 240765 Contact: Susan McArd (Manager)
seeds@smmcard.com www.smmcard.com
Organic seeds, vegetables, flowers and herbs. Unusual vegetables.

MELROW SALADS

GEEST LTD, WEST MARSH RD., SPALDING PE11 2BB
Tel: 01775 761111 Fax: 01775 763011 Contact: Niall Cameron
niall.cameron@geest.co.uk
We source and supply organic fresh produce (avocados, tomatoes, peppers, beetroot) to major multiple retailers.

MOUNT PLEASANT WINDMILL & TRUE LOAF BAKERY

NORTH CLIFF ROAD, KIRTON-IN-LINDSEY DN21 4NH
Tel: 01652 640177 Fax: 01652 640177 Contact: Mervin & Marie-Christine Austin
trueloafbakery@aol.com www.trueloafbakery.co.uk and www.mountpleasantwindmill.co.uk
Four sailed windmill, restored 1991, producing a range of 10 Soil Association (No. P1497) organic stoneground flours solely by windpower. Mill, flour sales, tea room, open Tuesday to Sunday all year. Organic bakery with traditional wood-fired oven producing good selection of organic breads. Open all year. School & Group visits welcome. Evening tours also available. Coaches must book prior to visit.

NATURAL REMEDY WAREHOUSE
4 BROADGATE HOUSE, WESTLODE ST., SPALDING PE11 2AF
Tel: 01775 724994 Fax: 01775 761104 Contact: H Girdlestone
nrw@enzymepro.com www.spalding.org.uk/nrw
We stock a variety of organic foods, e.g. bread, flour, honey, yoghurts. Special
requests taken. 10% discount on case orders.

NEWFARM ORGANICS
JF & J EDWARDS & SONS, SOULBY LANE, WRANGLE, BOSTON PE22 9BT
Tel: 01205 870500 Fax: 01205 871001 Contact: Jane Edwards
newfarmorganics@zoom.co.uk www.newfarmorganics.co.uk
Organic Farmers and Growers 31UKF120010. We produce food that is organic and
truly traceable. We specialise in growing potatoes, cauliflowers, cabbage, cereals
and beans. We also produce quality beef from our Lincoln Red x suckler herd.

NICELY NATURAL FARM SHOP
THE PIGGERY, GORSE LANE, GRANTHAM NG31 7UF
Tel: 01476 561657 Fax: 01476 561657 Contact: Diane Eggleston
info@nicelynaturalfarmshop.co.uk www.nicelynaturalfarmshop.co.uk
Farm shop selling certified organic produce, from Lincolnshire Farms when possible, also local garden produce. Organic milk and cream processed on a local farm,
local honey, Stilton cheese, jams and cordials. There is also local windmill-ground
flour, and bread made from it. A range of local craft items, knitwear and gift ideas.

NU-TREL PRODUCTS LTD
PARK FARM, KETTLETHORPE, LINCOLN LN1 2LD
Tel: 01522 704747 Fax: 01522 704748 Contact: Brian Aconley
www.nutrelgroup.co.uk
Soil Association I3022. Manufacturers of speciality fertilisers for use in organic
crop production.

OLIVER SEEDS

THE OLD WOOD, SKELLINGTHORPE, LINCOLN LN6 5UA
Tel: 0800 056 1122 Fax: 01522 507319 Contact: Francis Dunne
Soil Association P7038. Seed merchants. Grass mixtures, maize, fodder crops, green manure, amenity grass, wild flowers to farmers, and landscaping. Own production, mixing, warehousing, supported by technical team on phone and on-site.

OMEX AGRICULTURE

BARDNEY AIRFIELD, TUPHOLME, LINCOLN LN3 5TP
Tel: 01526 396011 Fax: 01526 396001 Contact: Andy Eccles
andye@omex.com www.omex.co.uk
Manufacture and application of tailor-made suspension fertilisers plus a range of foliar-applied crop health promoters and crop nutrients.

THE PINK PIG ORGANIC FARM SHOP, RESTAURANT AND FARM TRAIL

HOLME HALL, HOLME, SCUNTHORPE DN16 3RE
Tel: 01724 844466 Fax: 01724 866493 Contact: Sally Jackson
enquiries@pinkpigorganics.co.uk www.pinkpigorganics.co.uk
Fantastic wooden beamed farm shop and 80-seater restaurant. Home-grown pork, eggs, vegetables and chickens plus local beef and lamb. Home-made ready meals, quiches, cakes, pies and soups. Member of the Soil Association Organic Farms Network.

SADD, B M

BIRCHWOOD FARM, DRAWDYKE, SUTTON ST. JAMES, SPALDING PE12 0HP
Tel: 01945 440388 Contact: BM Sadd
Soil Association S34M. Field (potatoes, brassicas, etc.) and glasshouse salad crops. Not a box scheme, but boxes made up for collection.

SINCLAIR HORTICULTURE LTD, WILLIAM

FIRTH RD, LINCOLN LN6 7AH
Tel: 01522 537561 Fax: 01522 513609 Contact: The Manager
info@william-sinclair.co.uk www.william-sinclair.co.uk
Manufacturers of compost, lawn care, fertilisers, bark and mulches.

SPICE OF LIFE
4 BURGHLEY CENTRE, BOURNE PE10 9EG
Tel: 01778 394735 Contact: Ann West
drwnutrition@aol.com
Wholefood shop with emphasis on food/organics. Self-serve dispensers—dried
fruit, nuts, cereals, pulses, seeds. Fresh bread, all vegetarian takeaways.
Qualified nutritionist (MSc) and food intolerance testing available.

STRAWBERRY FIELDS
SCARBOROUGH BANK, STICKFORD, BOSTON PE22 8DR
Tel: 01205 480490 Fax: 01205 480490 Contact: Pam Bowers
pam@strawberryfields75.freeserve.co.uk
Soil Association B40M. Growing organically since 1975, we specialise in the higher
value, more exotic end of the market, inspirational and glowing with health! Our
reputation is built on quality, continuity, reliability and personal service.

SWEDEPONIC UK LTD
SPALDING RD., BOURNE PE10 0AT
Tel: 01778 424224 Fax: 01778 421200 Contact: Mark Powell
mark@swedeponic.co.uk
The UK's first certified organic potted herb specialist, supplying box schemes,
wholesalers and retailers.

UTOPIA UK
ENTERPRISE WAY, PINCHBECK, SPALDING PE11 3YR
Tel: 01775 716800 Fax: 01775 716808 Contact: Lucy Crawford
lcrawford@utopiauk.com www.utopiauk.com
Importation and supply of fresh exotic / tropical fruit and vegetables to the UK multiple retailers. Organic products include pineapple, papaya, mango, citrus, sweet
potato, asparagus and other exotics.

WATTS, PN

VINE HOUSE FARM, DEEPING ST. NICHOLAS, SPALDING PE11 3DG
Tel: 01775 630208 Fax: 01775 630244 Contact: Nicholas Watts
p.n.watts@farming.co.uk www.vinehousefarm.co.uk
Soil Association G2618. Organic farm that has won many conservation awards
including Silver Lapwing award, NFU Farming Excellence award, Waitrose Leaf
Marque award. Growing and selling potatoes, French beans, courgettes and
sweetcorn and producing other seasonal veg for the farm shop, which also sells
wild bird food.

WILSFORD ORGANICS

11 MAIN ST., WILSFORD, GRANTHAM NG32 3NS
Tel: 01400 230224 Contact: John Scott
Soil Association licensed G1708. Organic vegetables and free range eggs to public
and wholesale in village of Wilsford, between Sleaford and Grantham, Lincolnshire.

WOODLANDS

KIRTON HOUSE, KIRTON, NR. BOSTON PE20 1JD
Tel: 01205 722491 Fax: 01205 722905 Contact: Andrew Dennis
info@woodlandsfarm.co.uk www.woodlandsfarm.co.uk
Soil Association G2224, P5094. Mixed organic farm, producing vegetables, beef
and lamb for local, regional and multiple outlets. Organic bronze turkeys available
Christmas and Easter. Box scheme delivering to LN, PE, NN & LE postcodes.
Member of the Soil Association Organic Farms Network. Organic Food Awards
2004: Producer of the Year; Fresh Fruit and Veg Winner.

WORLDWIDE FRUIT LTD

WEST MARSH RD., SPALDING PE11 2BB
Tel: 01775 717000 Fax: 01775 717001 Contact: Mark Everett
mark.everett@worldwidefruit.co.uk www.worldwidefruit.co.uk
Major fruit importer and UK pip/soft fruit producer servicing all of the major
multiple retailers; specialists in fruit ripening. Year-round supply of apple, pear, kiwi,
avocado and dates.

CLEAN BEAN

170 BRICK LANE E1 6RU
Tel: 020 7247 1639 Fax: 020 7247 1639 Contact: Neil McLennan
cleanbean@ssba.info
Soil Association P2200. Clean Bean manufactures fresh organic tofu, which is supplied to restaurants and wholefood stores in the London area, and directly from our stalls at Borough Market every Saturday and Spitalfields Organic Market every Sunday.

THE CROWN

223 GROVE RD. E3 5SN
Tel: 020 8981 9998 Fax: 020 8983 2336 Contact: Jon Smart
crown@singhboulton.co.uk www.singhboulton.co.uk
Soil Association certified. Organic gastro-pub opposite Victoria Park. Beautiful listed building with balconies overlooking the park. Serving high quality food and drink, twice-daily changing menu, 40 wines, real ales. No-smoking restaurant area. Bookings in advance.

FRESH & WILD

194 OLD STREET, THE CITY EC1V 9FR
Tel: 020 7250 1708 Contact: Caroline Froud
Fresh & Wild are the leading specialist retailer of organic foods and natural remedies.

FUERST DAY LAWSON LTD

DEVON HOUSE, 58–60 ST. KATHERINE'S WAY E1 9LB
Tel: 020 7488 0777 Fax: 020 7702 3200 Contact: Frank Horan
seeds@fdl.co.uk
Seeds, pulses, honey, fruit juices, essential oils suppliers and processors of all dry commodities in a Soil Association approved facility.

NAPIER BROWN & CO LTD

1 ST. KATHARINE'S WAY E1W 1XB
Tel: 020 7335 2500 Fax: 020 7335 2502 Contact: C Sergeant
sales@napierbrown.co.uk www.napierbrown.co.uk
Napier Brown are the largest independent sugar distributor in the UK. We offer a wide range of organic sugars and syrups in both industrial and retail packs from factories approved by the Soil Association. Deliver nationally.

OLD SPITALFIELDS ORGANIC MARKET

65 BRUSHFIELD ST. E1 6AA
Tel: 01243 779716 Contact: Bart Ives
Every Sunday, covered market from 10am–5pm. Established 1993. The alternative to supermarkets and cheaper. Largest range of certified organic fresh fruit, veg, breads, dairy, meat, wine etc from producers and traders.

THE ORGANIC DELIVERY COMPANY

68 RIVINGTON ST., LONDON EC2A 3AY
Tel: 020 7739 8181 Fax: 020 7613 5656 Contact: John Barrow
info@organicdelivery.co.uk www.organicdelivery.co.uk
Large range of organic vegetarian and vegan groceries of the highest quality delivered to you, throughout London. Affordable and convenient. Order by telephone or securely online. Highly commended in the Soil Association awards, and registered with them. Licence number P8888. See display ad.

PIONEER CATERING SUPPLIERS LTD

UNIT 51/52 FAIRWAYS BUSINESS PARK, LAMMAS ROAD, LEYTON E10 7QB
Tel: 0800 085 1340 Fax: 020 8558 4674 Contact: Tony Hopkins & David Murphy
info@organicbutchers.net www.organicbutchers.net
Organic butchers—you can now enjoy the real taste of the countryside with our range of top quality organic meat fresh from the farm, which we will deliver to your door. Ranging from superb roasts for special occasions to a selection of great tasting organic cuts.

SECOND NATURE

78 WOOD ST., WALTHAMSTOW E17 3HX
Tel: 020 8520 7995 Fax: 020 8520 7995 Contact: Bob Clark
mail@econat.co.uk www.econat.co.uk
Second Nature is an organic and wholefood shop in east London. We deliver fruit
and veg locally—all of our stock is GMO-free.

TWIN TRADING LTD

THIRD FLOOR, 1 CURTAIN ROAD EC2A 3LT
Tel: 020 7375 1221 Fax: 020 7375 1337 Contact: Marc Monsarrat
info@twin.org.uk
Soil Association Licensed. Fairtrade importer of coffee, cocoa, nuts etc.

VERTUE GREEN CARPET CLEANING

60–64 UPPER CLAPTON RD, HACKNEY E5 9JP
Tel: 020 8806 7294 Contact: S Girardi
vertueltd@hotmail.com
Vertue have developed and supply the leading technology in cleaning products.
Liquids are kelp seaweed derived, non-toxic and not tested on animals.
Competitive range of 100% recycled paper products. Products extract toxic
chemicals whilst cleaning.

VINUM PERITUS LTD

VINUM PERITUS LTD, 19 COMBERTON ROAD, CLAPTON, LONDON E5 9PU
Tel: 020 8806 2385 Fax: 020 8806 2385 Contact: Richard Ossei
ro@vinumperitus.com www.vinumperitus.com
Official distributor of organic wine & spirits.

WAKEFIELD, DR & COMPANY LTD

MITRE HOUSE, 12–14 MITRE STREET EC3A 5BU
Tel: 020 7621 9345 Fax: 020 7621 9420 Contact: Simon Wakefield
coffee@drwakefield.com www.drwakefield.com
Importer of organic raw coffee from many producing countries, sourcing directly
from the farmer.

ALARA WHOLEFOODS

108–112 CAMLEY ST NW1 0PF
Tel: 020 7387 9303 Fax: 020 7388 6077 Contact: Alex Smith
alexsmith@alara.co.uk www.alara.co.uk
Alara are specialist manufacturers and packers of cereals, especially muesli, with over 40 different types of organic muesli currently produced in our BRC higher level accredited factory. Branded and own label available catering to over twenty-five international markets.

ALTERNATIVES HEALTH CENTRE

1369 HIGH ST., WHETSTONE N20 9LN
Tel: 020 8445 2675 Contact: D Thankey
www.naturesalternative.co.uk
Health food shop with clinic. Organic, tinned, packets, frozen and chilled products, supplements, homoeopathic and herbal remedies, tinctures, cosmetics, books and magazines.

BORN

168 STOKE NEWINGTON CHURCH ST STOKE NEWINGTON LONDON N16 0JL
Tel: 020 7249 5069 Fax: 020 7249 7225 Contact: Mrs Fernandes
info@borndirect.com www.borndirect.com
Retail and internet shop specialising in organic, natural and practical products for parents and their babies. We're the experts on washable cotton nappies! Organic range includes organic cotton and wool babywear (underwear, nightwear, outerwear and bedding), organic herbal teas for pregnancy and afterwards, toiletries made with organic ingredients (Weleda, Green People, Urtekram), organic massage oils. We are open Monday-Saturday 9.30-5.30.

BUMBLEBEE

30–33 BRECKNOCK RD. N7 0DD
Tel: 020 7607 1936 Fax: 020 7607 1936 Contact: Gillian Haslop
info@bumblebee.co.uk www.bumblebee.co.uk
A huge range of organic and vegetarian foods, specialising in organic fruit and
vegetables, cheeses, olive oils and mediterranean foods, organic wines and beers,
gluten- and wheat-free products, as well as Fairtraded and macrobiotic ranges.
Deliveries in London, Oxford and Greater London. Local box scheme. Carrier
deliveries cost £10 to anywhere in the UK mainland.

THE CELTIC BAKERS

42B WATERLOO RD., CRICKLEWOOD NW2 7UH
Tel: 020 8452 4390 Fax: 020 8452 8235 Contact: Syd Aston
info@thecelticbakers.co.uk www.thecelticbakers.co.uk
A dedicated organic vegetarian bakery specialising in most aspects of hand-made
bread production (including 100% ryes and sourdough methods), cakes, pastries
and savouries.

COMMUNITY FOODS LTD

BRENT TERRACE NW2 1LT
Tel: 020 8450 9419/9411 Fax: 020 8208 1551/1803 Contact: Dave Price
info@communityfoods.co.uk www.communityfoods.co.uk
Soil Association no. P1422. We are an importer and distributor of a large range
of natural products including several hundred organic lines. Bulk dried fruit,
nuts, pulses etc. plus brands like Sanchi, Crazy Jack, Nature's Path, Eunature,
Emile Noel, Monki, Shady Maple, Rebar and many more.

DAY PLUS ONE LTD

UNIT 11A&B, CRUSADER IND. ESTATE, 167 HERMITAGE RD., LONDON N4 1LZ
Tel: 020 8802 1088 Fax: 020 8802 3862 Contact: A Lauchlan
enquiries@dayplusoneltd.co.uk
Soil Association P1469. Packer of organic wholefoods under the Organic Day's
brand and customers own label. Supplier of a large range of organic pre-packs
in a wide variety of sizes. Product range includes amongst others: nuts, dried
fruit, rice, pulses, grains, cereals and snacks.

THE DUKE OF CAMBRIDGE

30 ST. PETER'S STREET, ISLINGTON N1 8JT
Tel: 020 7359 9450 Fax: 020 7359 1877 Contact: Geetie Singh
duke@singhboulton.demon.co.uk www.singhboulton.co.uk
Soil Association certified. Organic gastro-pub serving high quality organic
food and drink, twice daily changing menu, choice of 40 wines, real ales.
No-smoking restaurant area where bookings can be made in advance. Won Time
Out Gastro-Pub of the Year 2000. Organic Food Awards 2004: Restaurant of the
Year Highly Commended.

ECO-CUISINE.CO.UK

4 HEDGE LANE, PALMERS GREEN N13 5SH
Tel: 020 8882 0350 Contact: Sonya Meagor
enquiries@eco-cuisine.co.uk www.eco-cuisine.co.uk
Catering business. We use organic, free range products in our catering, using
the freshest produce available and supporting British farmers/producers.

FRESH & WILD

49 PARKWAY, CAMDEN, LONDON NW1 7PN
Tel: 020 7428 7575 Contact: Sha Bainbridge
Fresh & Wild are the leading specialist retailer of organic foods and natural remedies.

FRESH & WILD

32–40 STOKE NEWINGTON CHURCH STREET, STOKE NEWINGTON,
LONDON N16 0LU
Fresh & Wild are the leading specialist retailer of organic foods and natural remedies.

GREEN BABY CO LTD

345 UPPER STREET, ISLINGTON N1 0PD
Tel: 020 7226 4345 Fax: 020 7226 9244 Contact: Jill Barker
info@greenbaby.co.uk www.greenbaby.co.uk
A mail order and retail outlet for planet-friendly parents. Green Baby sells
washable nappies, organic cotton clothing, gel-free disposable nappies and
natural toiletries for mother and baby.

GROWING COMMUNITIES

THE OLD FIRE STATION, 61 LESWIN ROAD, LONDON N16 7NX
Tel: 020 7502 7588 Fax: 020 7502 0021 Contact: Kerry Rankine
grow.communities@btinternet.com www.growingcommunities.org
Growing Communities runs a weekly organic box scheme in Hackney, north London,
a weekly Farmers' Market in Stoke Newington where all the producers sell
organic, biodynamic or wild produce, and promotes organic food growing in the
city from its three sites in Hackney. See our website for more details and join
our box scheme online.

HAELAN CENTRE

41 THE BROADWAY, CROUCH END N8 8DT
Tel: 020 8340 4258 Fax: 020 8292 2232 Contact: John Krahn
www.haelan.co.uk
One of Britain's original wholefood and herbal stores, offering a complete range of
vegetarian and vegan organic food, organic skin care, also eco cleaning products, an
on-site complementary health clinic, herbal dispensary and homoeopathic pharmacy.

THE HAMPSTEAD TEA & COFFEE COMPANY

P.O. BOX 2448 NW11 7DR
Tel: 020 8731 9833 Fax: 020 8458 3947 Contact: Kiran Tawadey
info@hampsteadtea.com www.hampsteadtea.com
Organic Food Award winners 98 & 99 for our high quality range of bio-dynamic
and Fairtrade teas. Certified by BDAA. Products at health food stores and by
mail order.

HEALTHQUEST LTD

UNIT 7, WAVERLEY INDUSTRIAL PARK, HAILSHAM DRIVE, HARROW HA1 4TR
Tel: 020 8424 8844 Fax: 020 8424 8222 Contact: Ashwin Mehta
info@healthquest.co.uk www.healthquest.co.uk
HealthQuest supplies the stylish Organic Blue range of wellbeing products
(aromatherapy, bodycare and herbal supplement ranges), the award-winning Earth
Friendly Baby range (natural baby toiletries) and Natalia aromatherapy range
(pregnancy).

HONEY ROSE BAKERY
6 FORTUNE WAY NW10 6UF
Tel: 020 8960 5567 Fax: 020 8960 5598 Contact: Lise Madsen
cakes@honeyrosebakery.com www.honeyrosebakery.com
Dedicated organic operation handbaking award-winning muffins, brownies, cookies, and cakes. Beautifully packaged for retail and to go, or unwrapped for foodservice. We derive great satisfaction in preserving time-honoured baking crafts.

HUGO'S CAFÉ
23–25 LONSDALE ROAD NW6 6RA
Tel: 020 7372 1232 Fax: 020 7328 8097 Contact: Carol Jones
We serve organic vegetarian and meat dishes.

HUMAN NATURE
13 MALVERN RD. NW6 5PS
Tel: 020 7328 5452 Fax: 020 7328 5452 Contact: Nari Sadhuram
Shop with extensive vegetarian products, eco-products. Manufacturers of 'Energy Bomb and Massage', described in the press as 'the best in the world'.

ISLINGTON FARMERS' MARKET
ESSEX ROAD, OPPOSITE ISLINGTON GREEN, ISLINGTON N1
Tel: 020 7704 9659 Contact: London Farmers' Markets
info@lfm.org.uk www.lfm.org.uk
No details available.

JUST ORGANIC
113 WILBERFORCE RD. N4 2SP
Tel: 020 7704 2566 Fax: 020 7704 2566 Contact: Mike Adams
Mike_veg@hotmail.com
Soil Association P2042. Fresh organic fruit and vegetables, delivered to your door. £10 or £15 mixed boxes, free delivery.

LONDON FARMERS' MARKETS

PO BOX 37363, LONDON N1 7WB
Tel: 020 7704 9659 Fax: 020 7359 1968 Contact: Cheryl Cohen
info@lfm.org.uk www.lfm.org.uk
10 certified farmers' markets in London. No farmers' market is entirely organic, but each market has a range of organic farmers and producers. Saturday markets 9am–1pm: Ealing, Notting Hill, Twickenham, Pimlico & Wimbledon. Sunday markets 10am–2pm: Blackheath, Islington, Marylebone & Peckham. Wednesdays 10am–3pm: Swiss Cottage.

MARIGOLD HEALTH FOODS

102 CAMLEY ST. NW1 0PF
Tel: 020 7388 4515 Fax: 020 7388 4516 Contact: David Swinstead
sales@marigoldhealthfoods.com www.marigoldhealthfoods.com
Soil Association P2604, OF&G UK2 P0015. Wholesaler of vegetarian food, drinks, nutritional supplements and animal-free products particularly strong in organic and chilled. Distribute to South-East England; Marigold Bouillon Powder and Yogi Teas stocked by wholesalers throughout UK.

MOTHER EARTH HEALTH FOODS

5 ALBION PARADE, ALBION RD., STOKE NEWINGTON N16 9LD
Tel: 020 7275 9099 Fax: 020 7249 5965 Contact: Dominic Sutton
shop@motherearth-health.com www.motherearth-health.com
We've been here promoting healthy and organic food in the heart of our north London Community for more than 15 years.

NATURAL HEALTH

339 BALLARDS LANE, N. FINCHLEY N12 8LJ
Tel: 020 8445 4397 Fax: 020 8445 4397 Contact: D Thankey
www.naturesalternative.co.uk
Health food store with clinic for alternative therapies. Organic foods, supplements, tinctures, homoeopathic and herbal remedies, cosmetics, books, tapes and CDs.

NEAL'S YARD REMEDIES

68 CHALK FARM RD., CAMDEN NW1 8AN
Tel: 020 7284 2039 Fax: 020 7428 0390 Contact: A Rodriguez
mail@nealsyardremedies.com www.nealsyardremedies.com
Natural remedies: medicinal herbs and tinctures, homoeopathic remedies, flower
essences, essential oils, books.

ORGANIC LOGISTICS

ROSEBERY INDUSTRIAL PARK, PHASE ONE, UNITS 1–8, ROSEBERY AVENUE N17 9SR
Tel: 020 8886 0812 Fax: 0118 901 2702 Contact: Tony Mustafa
info@newburyphillips.co.uk www.newburyphillips.co.uk
We mainly supply wholesale/stockists and organisations involved in food
manufacturing with organic products and ingredients. Our product range includes
herbs and spices to dried fruits and products such as organic pitta bread
manufactured and packed under own label, Newbury Phillips.

PITFIELD BEER SHOP & BREWERY

14 PITFIELD ST. N1 6EY
Tel: 020 7739 3701 Fax: 020 7729 9636 Contact: Martin Kemp
sales@pitfieldbeershop.co.uk www.pitfieldbeershop.co.uk
Organic Farmers & Growers registered. Award-winning organic brewery and shop
offering over 600 beers and ciders, many organic. Self-brew wine and beer
supplies. Wholesale and mail order across UK.

PLOT 21 PERMACULTURE ALLOTMENTS

ALEXANDRA PALACE ALLOTMENTS, OFF ALEXANDRA PALACE WAY N17
Tel: 020 7916 7390 Contact: S Girardi
A loose non-profit making organisation running courses on permaculture and
producing home-grown crops using permaculture principles.

REVITAL HEALTHSHOP

35 HIGH RD, WILLESDEN GREEN NW10 2TE
Tel: 020 8459 3382 Fax: 020 8459 3722 Contact: Bakhat Khadka
enquire@revital.com www.revital.com
Health shop.

SAN AMVROSIA HEALTH FOODS

UNIT 8, THE STONEBRIDGE CENTRE, RANGEMOOR RD. N15 4LP
Tel: 020 8801 2180 Fax: 020 8801 8558 Contact: D Georgiou
Soil Association P4139. Manufacturers of fresh dips (vegetarian).

SIMPLY BREAD

BUILDING E, THE CHOCOLATE FACTORY, WESTERN ROAD N22 6UY
Tel: 020 8889 7159 Fax: 020 8889 2428 Contact: Jack Flatter
info@simply-bread.co.uk
Soil Association P2628. Wholesale bakery specialising in organic rye bread,
organic wholemeal, organic white and organic croissants.

SKOULIKAS, GEORGE LTD

UNIT 5, 998 NORTH CIRCULAR RD, COLES GREEN RD. NW2 7JR
Tel: 020 8452 8465 Fax: 020 8452 8273 Contact: Colin Morrison
gskoul1@aol.com
Imports and distribution of mediterranean organic foods including olives, olive
oil, tahini, halva, sesame bars, orange, lemon and lime juice, pesto and polenta.

SOUTH LONDON BAKERS & NATURAL RISE FOODS

21 BERNARD RD. N15 4NE
Tel: 020 8808 2007 Fax: 020 8808 2007 Contact: Mana/ Inder
inder333@aol.com
Organic craft bakers since 1981, specialising in hand-moulded organic yeasted
and sourdough breads produced without additives, flour improvers and
preservatives. Deliveries available throughout the Greater London area.

SPRING GREEN

21 PURLEY AVENUE NW2 1SH
Tel: 020 8208 0855 Fax: 020 8208 0855 Contact: Caroline Roberts
enquiries@spring-green.demon.co.uk
London home deliveries of fresh organic fruit and veg, plus a long list of other
organic foods and environment-friendly household products. Deliveries cover
Central, North, West and South-West London.

SWISS COTTAGE FARMERS' MARKET

02 CENTRE CAR PARK, FINCHLEY ROAD NW3
Tel: 020 7704 9659 Contact: London Farmers' Markets
info@lfm.org.uk www.lfm.org.uk
Wednesdays 10am–3pm. Here farmers sell home-grown foods grown or made within 100 miles of the M25, including fruit, veg, meat, dairy, eggs, honey, juice, bread, preserves and plants. NB: some, but not all, producers are organic. Run by London Farmers' Markets, PO Box 37363, London N1 7WB.

TEMPLE HEALTH FOODS

17 TEMPLE FORTUNE PARADE NW11 0QS
Tel: 020 8458 6087 Fax: 020 8905 0800 Contact: M Dadia
Complete range of wholefoods with many organic alternatives, books and information leaflets. Delivery service, free newsletter and samples.

TEXTURE

84 STOKE NEWINGTON CHURCH STREET N16 0AP
Tel: 020 7241 0990 Fax: 020 7241 1991 Contact: Jeff Gilbert
jag@textilesfromnature.com www.textilesfromnature.com
Eco Textiles, mail order, retail, wholesale and manufacturer of pillows, cushions, bed linen, curtains and fabric by the metre.

UK5 ORGANICS

60–64 UPPER CLAPTON RD., HACKNEY E5 9JP
Tel: 020 7237 7277 Fax: 020 7237 7277 Contact: Kevin Harrison
uk5organics@hotmail.com www.uk5.info
Enquiries line 07799 790279. Deliveries to East, South-East and North London of organic veg, fruit and groceries on Mondays, Tuesdays and Wednesdays, dependent on postcode.

ABEL & COLE

8–15 MGI ESTATE, MILKWOOD ROAD SE24 0JF
Tel: 08452 626262 Fax: 020 7737 7785 Contact: Matthew Harwood
organics@abel-cole.co.uk www.abel-cole.co.uk
Delivering organic food and drink across southern England including organic fruit and vegetables, British organic meats, sustainably caught fish, dairy goods, freshly baked bread and much more. Working with a network of over 50 British producers to bring delicious, local, seasonal and organic food fresh from the grower. With free home delivery and online ordering you can do your weekly shop in under 10 minutes! (Awarded Organic Retailer 2004 and Best Home Delivery Service 2004 by the Soil Association.) Organic Food Awards 2004: Local Food Initiative Highly Commended.

BALHAM WHOLEFOOD & HEALTH STORE

8 BEDFORD HILL, BALHAM SW12 9RG
Tel: 020 8673 4842 Contact: Robert Noakes
Wholefood shop selling a range of organic products and supplements. Open Monday, Wednesday, Friday and Saturday 9.30am–1.30pm and 2.30pm–6.00pm. Tuesday and Thursday 9.30am–1.30pm and 2.30pm–7.00pm.

BALDWIN, G, & CO

171–173 WALWORTH RD SE17 1RW
Tel: 020 7703 5550 Fax: 020 7252 6264 Contact: Stephen Dagnell
sales@baldwins.co.uk www.baldwins.co.uk
Herbalist and essential oils. Complementary and alternative product supplier.

BLACKHEATH FARMERS' MARKET

BLACKHEATH RAIL STATION CAR PARK, 2 BLACKHEATH VILLAGE SE3
Tel: 020 7704 9659 Contact: London Farmers' Markets
info@lfm.org.uk www.lfm.org.uk
No details available.

CAPRICORN ORGANICS
BROCKLEY SE24 2NL
Tel: 020 8306 2786 Contact: Alison Wise
alison@capricornorganics.co.uk www.capricornorganics.co.uk
A local service offering a wide range of fully certified fresh organic produce
delivered to your door. Place your own order or have a box from just £10.

DANDELION
120 NORTHCOTT ROAD SW11 6QU
Tel: 020 7350 0902 Contact: Hilel Friedman
Wide range of organic fresh and dried foods including take-away foods, vitamins,
supplements, etc.

FARMAROUND
OFFICES B143, NEW COVENT GARDEN MARKET, NINE ELMS LANE, LONDON SW8 5PA
Tel: 020 7627 8066 Fax: 01748 822007 Contact: Isobel Davies
info@farmaround.co.uk www.farmaround.co.uk
Organic Farmers and Growers UKP08009. Home delivery service of assorted bags
of fresh organic produce. Prices from £4 for a mini fruit box, also organic
grocery range. Delivery charge: £1 throughout Greater London and Berkshire.

FOOD BRANDS GROUP LTD
9–10 CALICO HOUSE, PLANTATION WHARF, BATTERSEA SW11 3TN
Tel: 020 7978 5300 Fax: 020 7924 2732 Contact: Edward Chapman
www.fbg.co.uk
Food Brands Group Ltd trades in teas and coffees (Percol), soft drinks (Santa
Cruz Organic) and wines. Organic Food Awards 2004: Coffee Winner.

THE FOOD FERRY COMPANY
UNIT B24–27, NEW COVENT GARDEN MARKET, NINE ELMS LANE SW8 5HH
Tel: 020 7498 0827 Fax: 020 7498 8009 Contact: Jonathan Hartnell-Beavis
e@foodferry.com www.foodferry.com
Grocery delivery to homes and businesses in central London. Full range of
organic fruit and vegetables (including boxes), meat, poultry, larder foods,
drinks and eco-friendly cleaning products.

FRESH & WILD

305–311 LAVENDER HILL, CLAPHAM JUNCTION, LONDON SW11 1LN
Fresh & Wild are the leading specialist retailer of organic foods and natural remedies.

FROM GREENWICH

17 ANCHORAGE POINT, ANCHOR & HOPE LANE SE7 7SQ
Tel: 020 8269 0409 Fax: 020 8269 0417 Contact: John Herbert
office@fromgreenwich.co.uk www.fromgreenwich.co.uk
Delicious cakes.

GREEN & BLACKS

2 VALENTINE PLACE SE1 8QH
Tel: 020 7633 5900 Fax: 020 7633 5901 Contact: Neil Turpin
enquiries@greenandblacks.com www.greenandblacks.com
Green & Black's make award-winning, quality organic chocolate combining the
highest environmental and ethical standards. Their delicious range of organic
chocolate products includes chocolate bars, hot chocolate, cocoa, ice creams,
chocolate covered almonds and chocolate hazelnut spread. Certified by the Soil
Association and available nationwide at supermarkets, good health food stores
and delicatessens. Now part of Cadbury Schweppes. Organic Food Awards 2004:
Chocolate Highly Commended.

GREENLEAVES HERBAL PHARMACY

46A STANGER RD., SOUTH NORWOOD SE25 5JZ
Tel: 020 8656 0754 Contact: Patricia Ferguson
herbalpatsy@aol.com www.greanleavesherbalpharmacy.co.uk
Qualified medical herbalist providing free advice, assistance and consultations
by telephone for your health problems. Tailor-made quality prescription herbal
medicines and first aid/basic healthcare kits by post.

HERE
CHELSEA FARMERS' MARKET, 125 SYDNEY ST, CHELSEA SW3 6NR
Tel: 020 7351 4321 Fax: 020 7351 2211 Contact: Michelle Smith
organicwarehouse@onetel.net.uk www.herestores.co.uk
The most comprehensive supermarket in the UK, stocking only 100% organic
foods & drink. Natural supplements and bodycare. Café area & take-out. Deliveries
in London. Mail Order.

LANGRIDGE ORGANIC PRODUCTS LTD
UNIT A55–57, NEW COVENT GARDEN MARKET, NINE ELMS LANE SW8 5EE
Tel: 020 7622 7440 Fax: 020 7622 7441 Contact: Alex Pearce
sales@langridgeorganic.com www.langridgeorganic.com
Soil Association P7570. Langridge specialise in the wholesale supply of organic
fruit, vegetables and dairy products to independent retailers, box schemes,
restaurants, schools and hospitals. Our produce is sourced from our network of
growers throughout the UK, Europe and the rest of the world. Langridge operates
a policy of buying the most locally available organic produce at all times.

MAISON PLASSE
32 HERBERT RD. SW19 3SH
Tel: 020 8544 1788 Contact: Sandrine Plasse Arnould
contact@maisonplasse.com www.maisonplasse.com
Online selection of organic dishes and deli items for francophiles craving a taste of
the holiday food bought from the local market and traiteur. Maison Plasse imports
organic French charcuterie, cheeses and ready-made dishes from the Auvergne,
delivering them within the M25. Certified in France by Ecocert SASF32600.

MATERIA AROMATICA
7 PENRHYN CRESCENT SW14 7PF
Tel: 020 8392 9868 Fax: 020 8255 7126 Contact: Isabelle Poignart
info@materia-aromatica.com www.materia-aromatica.com
Soil Association registered. Aromatherapy, essential oils and skin care products.
Certified organic essential oils and vegetable oils, 100% natural skin and body care
made with organic ingredients, free from chemicals and preservatives.

MIESSENCE & MIVITALITY
46A STANGER ROAD, SOUTH NORWOOD, LONDON SE25 5JZ
Tel: 020 8656 0754 Contact: Patricia Ferguson
herbalpatsy@aol.com www.onegrp.com/?herbalist
The world's first and internationally certified organic skincare range. Excellent for all
skin types, especially problem skin. Certified organic by authorities in the USA,
Japan and the International Federation of Organic Agricultural Movements (IFOAM).

MONMOUTH COFFEE COMPANY
2 PARK ST SE1 9AB
Tel: 020 7645 3561 Fax: 020 7645 3565 Contact: Sophie Deguillaume
beans@monmouthcoffee.co.uk www.monmouthcoffee.co.uk
Coffee roasters, wholesalers and retailers.

NATURISIMO.COM
UNIT 10, 28 OLD BROMPTON ROAD, LONDON SW7 3SS
Tel: 020 7584 7815 Contact: Cristina Manas
info@naturisimo.com www.naturisimo.com
Naturisimo.com—natural and organic skin care products from exceptional organic
brands including: Living Nature, The Organic Pharmacy, Weleda, Green People,
Spiezia Organics and Suki's Naturals.

NEAL'S YARD REMEDIES
32 BLACKHEALTH VILLAGE, BLACKHEATH SE3 9SY
Tel: 020 8318 6655 Contact: Alina Frymorgan
mail@nealsyardremedies.com www.nealsyardremedies.com
Retail shop selling Neal's Yard Remedies products.

NEAL'S YARD REMEDIES
6 NORTHCOTE ROAD, CLAPHAM JUNCTION SW11 1NT
Tel: 020 7223 7141 Fax: 020 7223 7174 Contact: Pamela Loch
mail@nealsyardremedies.com www.nealsyardremedies.com
Natural health shop with a therapy centre attached.

NEAL'S YARD REMEDIES
12–14 CHELSEA FARMERS MARKET, SYDNEY ST. SW3 6NR
Tel: 020 7351 6380 Contact: Bodhi Hunt
mail@nealsyardremedies.com www.nealsyardremedies.com
Neal's Yard Remedies manufactures and retails natural cosmetics in addition to stocking an extensive range of herbs, essential oils, homoeopathic remedies and reference material.

NEAL'S YARD REMEDIES (HEAD OFFICE)
8–10 INGATE PLACE, BATTERSEA SW8 3NS
Tel: 020 7498 1686 Fax: 020 7498 2505 Contact: The Manager
mail@nealsyardremedies.com www.nealsyardremedies.com
Neal's Yard Remedies manufactures and retails natural cosmetics in addition to stocking an extensive range of herbs, essential oils, homoeopathic remedies and reference material. Customer Services: 020 7627 1949, cservices@nealsyardremedies.com.

THE OLD POST OFFICE BAKERY
76 LANDOR RD., CLAPHAM SW9 9PH
Tel: 020 7326 4408 Fax: 020 7326 4408 Contact: John Dungavel
www.oldpostofficebakery.co.uk
Organic craft bakery, hand-made yeasted and sourdough bread including 100% rye sourdough. Soil Association Licence no. P5506.

ORGANIC EXPRESS LTD—CATERERS WHO CARE
17 ANSDELL RD, PECKHAM SE15 2DT
Tel: 020 7277 6147 Fax: 020 7277 6147 Contact: John Kavaliauskas
info@organic-express.co.uk www.organic-express.co.uk
Event Caterers. Organic Express—Caterers Who Care supply only accredited organic catering for conferences, events and special occasions. We support local producers and Fairtrade products whenever possible. Enjoy eating your ethics.

ORGANIC MAKEOVERS
16 BIRLEY ST., LONDON SW11 5XF
info@biancaparadis.com www.biancaparadis.com
Nutritionist & image consultant. Organic makeovers; hair, makeup, fashion, and body by Bianca Paradis CCN, nutritionist and image consultant. Become the best you can be naturally! For men and women.

THE ORGANIC TOWEL COMPANY LTD
TRB2 TROWBRAY HOUSE, 108 WESTON ST. SE1 3QB
Tel: 020 7378 7259 Fax: 0870 762 2371 Contact: Tamae Rykers
tamae@organictowel.co.uk www.organictowel.co.uk
The Organic Towel Company offers luxurious towels made of organic cotton (IMO certified) and natural bodycare products using organic ingredients.

ORGANIC TRADE LTD
PREMIER HOUSE, 325 STREATHAM HIGH ROAD, STREATHAM SW16 3NT
Tel: 020 8679 8226 Fax: 020 8679 8823 Contact: Raj Shah
rshah@organictrade.co.uk www.organictrade.co.uk
Import wholesalers of all organic edible nuts, dried fruits, pulses, seeds and cereals. Delivery to all of UK.

PECKHAM FARMERS' MARKET
PECKHAM SQUARE, PECKHAM HIGH STREET SE15
Tel: 020 7704 9659 Contact: London Farmers' Markets
info@lfm.org.uk www.lfm.org.uk
Sundays 9.30am–1.30pm. Here farmers sell home-grown foods grown or made within 100 miles of the M25, including fruit, veg, meat, dairy, eggs, honey, juice, bread, preserves, plants. NB: some, but not all, producers are organic. Run by London Farmers' Markets, PO Box 37363, London N1 7WB.

PIZZA ORGANIC LTD

75 GLOUCESTER RD. SW7 4SS
Tel: 020 7370 6575 Contact: Mike Traszko
info@pizzapiazza.co.uk www.pizza-organic.co.uk
A great menu packed full of organic options, featuring stonebaked pizza, sautéed pasta, gourmet burgers, grilled fish and fabulous desserts. Pizza Organic is certified by the Soil Association and was Highly Commended in the 2003 Organic Food Awards. All restaurants open 7 days a week but opening times may vary, call 020 8397 3330 for further details.

PIZZA ORGANIC LTD

20 OLD BROMPTON RD. SW7 3DL
Tel: 020 7589 9613 Contact: Mike Traszko
info@pizzapiazza.co.uk www.pizzaorganic.co.uk
A great menu packed full of organic options, featuring stonebaked pizza, sautéed pasta, gourmet burgers, grilled fish and fabulous desserts. Pizza Organic is certified by the Soil Association and was Highly Commended in the 2003 Organic Food Awards. All restaurants open 7 days a week but opening times may vary, call 020 8397 3330 for further details.

PLANET ORGANIC

25 EFFIE RD, FULHAM SW6
Tel: 020 7731 7222 Contact: Matt Goodhead
deliveries@planetorganic.com www.planetorganic.com
Planet Organic is about good food. We are the original one-stop organic and natural food supermarket with an in-house juice bar and freshly cooked organic food to go. We are the modern mecca for those seeking everything for a healthy lifestyle.

PROVENDER

103 DARTMOUTH ROAD, FOREST HILL SE23 3HT
Tel: 020 8699 4046 Fax: 020 8699 4046 Contact: Ali Megahead
Wholefoods, organic bakers, café, healthy food, organic croissants and pastries, quiches, organic meals.

RAVENSBOURNE WINE

UNIT 602, BELL HOUSE, 49 GREENWICH HIGH RD. SE10 8JL
Tel: 020 8692 9655 Fax: 020 8692 9655 Contact: Terry Short (Director)
sales@ravensbournewine.co.uk
Wine merchant. Retail/wholesale, delivery and mail order of select range of
organic wines and beers. Free delivery of mixed cases of wine and beers and
Decantae bottled mineral water to London addresses.

RDA ORGANIC

118 PUTNEY BRIDGE RD, LONDON SW15 2NQ
Tel: 020 8875 9740 Fax: 020 8875 0370 Contact: Patrick O'Flaherty
juice@rdaorganic.com www.rdaorganic.com
RDA Organic is an award-winning range of 100% fresh, pure, organic juices and
smoothies. The range consists of 5 delicious juices including 'The UK's Best Organic
Soft Drink' and the UK's only fresh, pure organic fruit smoothies. Each bottle provides you with your recommended daily allowance (RDA) of vitamin C and contains
the juice from your recommended daily intake of fruit. RDA Organic contains nothing
but organic fruit—no added sugar, no water, no flavourings—just premium organic
fruit. Organic Food Awards 2004: Non-Alcoholic Drinks Highly Commended.

REVITAL HEALTHPLACE

3A THE COLONADES, 123–151 BUCKINGHAM PALACE RD SW1W 9SH
Tel: 020 7976 6615 Contact: The Manager
enqire@revital.com www.revital.com
Health shop: over 80% organic foods and cosmetics.

RIVERFORD ORGANIC VEGETABLES—SOUTHWARK

6 PORTAL CLOSE, WEST NORWOOD SE27 0BN
Tel: 01803 762720 Fax: 01803 762718 Contact: Jake Webb
ged@riverfordhomedelivery.co.uk www.riverford
Veg box delivery scheme.

SCAN FOODS UK LTD

1A AMIES ST. SW11 2JL
Tel: 020 7228 4046 Fax: 020 7223 4534 Contact: Paul Aston
www.swedishkitchen.co.uk
Soil Association P6027. Supplier of Swedish organic meat and processed products
including organic Swedish meatballs.

SKINCARE CAFE LTD

RIVERBANK HOUSE, PUTNEY BRIDGE SW6 4JD
Tel: 0870 443 2744 Contact: Zoe Shields
customercomments@skincarecafe.com www.skincarecafe.com
Quality organic skincare range, certified by Ecocert, Vegan and Vegetarian Society
approved. 100% plant origin. Suitable for sensitive skin. Cleanser, moisturiser,
facemask, body lotion, anti-ageing treatment, bodywash, all-in-one shampoo and
conditioner.

SOORGANIC.COM

PO BOX 39380, LONDON SE13 7XL
Tel: 0800 169 2579 Fax: 020 8297 1802 Contact: Samantha Burlton
enquiries@soorganic.com www.soorganic.com
Online department store offering natural and organic cosmetics, skincare, body
care, toiletries, toothpaste, deodorant. Organic cotton baby, toddler, child and adult
clothing, towels, toys, feminine hygiene sanitary products, washable nappies and
environmentally friendly disposables. Silk duvets and remedies for sensitive skin,
eczema and allergy sufferers. Eco friendly household cleaning products and a wide
vegan range. Many certified organic brands including Spiezia, Mother Earth,
Essential Care and Natracare . . . because organic living is more than just a food
choice!

SPARKES, GG

24 OLD DOVER RD., BLACKHEATH SE3 7BT
Tel: 020 8355 8597 Fax: 020 8355 8597 Contact: Guy Sparkes
We are a family business established in 1952, and we have been selling organic
meat and cheeses for over 16 years. We deliver to London and the South-East.
Home deliveries, not a box scheme.

SPARKES, GG

MOBILE SHOP UNIT, NEW CROSS ROAD MARKET, EAST DULWICH SE22
Tel: 020 8355 8597 Contact: Guy Sparkes
Mobile shop unit. We are a family business established in 1952 and we have been selling organic meat and cheeses for over 16 years. We deliver to London and the South-East. Home deliveries, not a box scheme.

TODAY'S LIVING

92 CLAPHAM HIGH STREET SW4 7UL
Tel: 020 7622 1772 Fax: 020 7720 2851 Contact: H Soor
info@todaysliving.co.uk
Health food shop selling a wide range of supplements, foods, frozen goods and organic spices.

TODAY WAS FUN LTD

PO BOX 47072 SW18 1XU
Tel: 0870 240 0092 Contact: Sharyn Wortman
sharyn@todaywasfun.com www.todaywasfun.com
Producers of Tea & Philosophy—range of herbal infusions that come wrapped with a philosophy about life. All our products are made under licence by certified organic suppliers and manufacturers.

WELL BEAN

9 OLD DOVER ROAD, BLACKHEATH SE3 7BT
Tel: 020 8858 6854 Contact: Derek Rogers
Large range organic foods, wholefoods, gluten-free, diabetic, dairy-free. Nutritional advice, mail order, local deliveries. If we haven't got it, we'll get it!

WELL BEING

19 SYDENHAM ROAD SE26 5EX
Tel: 020 8659 2003 Contact: Melvyn Stevens (Proprietor)
Health Food Shop.

WESTFALIA MARKETING (UK) LTD
MARKET TOWERS, 1 NINE ELMS LANE SW8 5NQ
Tel: 020 7720 8544 Fax: 020 7720 4209 Contact: Simon Curry
simon@westfaliauk.co.uk www.westfaliauk.co.uk
Soil Association registered. Import of conventional and organic avocados and
mangos, primarily from parent company in South Africa, but also other sources.
Newly added Fairtrade ranges introduced.

WIMBLEDON PARK FARMERS' MARKET
WIMBLEDON PARK FIRST SCHOOL, HAVANA ROAD, WIMBLEDON SW19
Tel: 020 7704 9659 Contact: London Farmers' Markets
info@lfm.org.uk www.lfm.org.uk
No details available.

WINDMILL ORGANICS LTD
UNIT 4, ATLAS TRANSPORT ESTATE, BRIDGES COURT SW11 3QS
Tel: 020 7294 2300 Fax: 020 7223 8370 Contact: Noel McDonald
sales@windmillorganics.fsnet.co.uk
Organic Food Federation registered. Production and distribution of organic foods:
dairy products, tofu, margarine, bakery goods, pasta, canned pulses, juices etc.
Main brand: Biona.

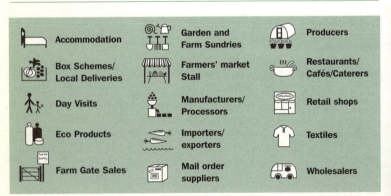

Accommodation	Garden and Farm Sundries	Producers
Box Schemes/ Local Deliveries	Farmers' market Stall	Restaurants/ Cafés/Caterers
Day Visits	Manufacturers/ Processors	Retail shops
Eco Products	Importers/ exporters	Textiles
Farm Gate Sales	Mail order suppliers	Wholesalers

AINSWORTHS HOMEOPATHIC PHARMACY

36 NEW CAVENDISH ST. W1G 8UF
Tel: 020 7935 5330 Fax: 01883 344602 Contact: Tony Pinkus
ainsworth01@btconnect.com www.ainsworths.com
Homoeopathic remedies for prevention and treatment of all your livestock. Books and courses on homoeopathy. All animals can be treated without residues. Help and advice in implementing homoeopathic regimes on the farm. Lectures and seminars by arrangement.

ALARA

58–60 MARCHMONT STREET WC1N 1AB
Tel: 020 7837 1172 Fax: 020 7833 8089 Contact: Xavier Kara
xavier@bio-terra.com
All organic products. Vitamins, beauty, fresh veg, fruit and dairy.

AS NATURE INTENDED

17–21 HIGH ST., EALING W5 5DB
Tel: 020 8840 1404 Fax: 020 8840 8278 Contact: Caroline Walker
caroline@asnatureintended.uk.com www.asnatureintended.uk.com
An organic food retailer stocking a wide range of organic and special dietary foods. Also stocks a large range of natural remedies.

AS NATURE INTENDED

201 CHISWICK HIGH RD., CHISWICK W4 2DA
Tel: 020 8742 8838 Fax: 020 8742 3131 Contact: Caroline Walker
caroline@asnatureintended.uk.com www.asnatureintended.uk.com
An organic food retailer stocking a wide range of organic and special dietary foods. Also stocks a large range of natural remedies.

AUSTRALIS DISTRIBUTION LTD
12 TOWNSEND HOUSE, 22 DEAN ST. W1D 3RY
Tel: 0845 456 0639 Fax: 020 7504 8099 Contact: Lara Smith
lara@australisdistribution.com www.australisdistribution.com
We import Australian personal care products that are naturally based, organic,
free from harmful additives and free from harmful by-products in manufacture.

BONTERRA VINEYARDS
BROWN-FORMAN WINES, REGENT ARCADE HOUSE, 19–25 ARGYLL ST. W1F 7TS
Tel: 020 7478 1300 Fax: 020 7287 4661 Contact: Kate Sweet
www.bonterra.com
Bonterra Vineyards are one of the world's leaders in organic viticulture, producing a
range of premium wines from organically grown grapes. Organic Food Awards
2004: Wines Commended.

BUSHWACKER WHOLEFOODS
132 KING STREET, HAMMERSMITH W6 0QU
Tel: 020 8748 2061 Fax: 020 8748 2061 Contact: Chris Shipton
Everything you would expect in a good wholefood shop, with the emphasis on
organically grown products including fresh fruit and vegetables, free range eggs and
baby foods. Lots of vegetarian takeaways, macrobiotic specialities, gluten-free
foods, natural remedies and bodycare. We veto genetically modified foods.

BUXTON FOODS LTD/STAMP COLLECTION/PETER RABBIT ORGANICS
12 HARLEY STREET W1G 9PG
Tel: 020 7637 5505 Fax: 020 7436 0979 Contact: Katie Towers
k.towers@buxtonfoods.com www.buxtonfoods.com
We also produce Peter Rabbit Organics, a range of children's foods with no added
salt or sugar and the Stamp Collection range of organic, wheat-free, dairy-free foods.

CAVIP UK LTD
2 SHERATON ST, SOHO W1F 8BH
Tel: 0870 366 6145 Fax: 0870 140 0377 Contact: Peter Catinis
cavipuk@cavipuk.co.uk www.cavipuk.co.uk
SKAL International Inspection & Certification.

CLEARSPRING LTD
19A ACTON PARK ESTATE W3 7QE
Tel: 020 8749 1781 Fax: 020 8746 2259 Contact: Christopher Dawson
info@clearspring.co.uk www.clearspring.co.uk
Soil Association P1474. Clearspring traditional and organic Japanese and
European foods regularly win awards for their great taste. They are produced to
vegan standards on a small scale and to the highest quality.

EALING FARMERS' MARKET
LEELAND RD, WEST EALING W13
Tel: 020 7704 9659 Contact: Cheryl Cohen
info@lfm.org.uk www.lfm.org.uk
Saturdays 9am to 1pm. Here farmers sell home-grown foods grown or made within
100 miles of the M25, including fruit, veg, meat, dairy, eggs, honey, juice,
bread, preserves, plants. NB: some, but not all, producers are organic. Run
by London Farmers' Markets, PO Box 37363, London N1 7WB.

ECO ALLIANCE LTD
DURHAM HOUSE, DURHAM HOUSE STREET WC2N 6HG
Tel: 020 7930 3538 Fax: 020 7839 3137 Contact: Bengt Saelensminde
www.eco-all.com
Soil Association P7377. Importer, broker and distributor of organic foods from
Chile. Eco owns and distributes Aimara organic oils and food products
(www.aimara.co.uk), and represents over 60 Chilean organic producers.

FARM W5

19 THE GREEN, EALING W5 5DA
Tel: 020 8566 1965 Fax: 020 8840 7600 Contact: Tom Beeston
shop@farmw5.com www.farmw5.com
Our organic and artisan food market supplies fresh, seasonal, locally sourced
food, produced properly and ethically. You will find organic and artisan breads,
cakes, vegetables, wines, meat and poultry, preserves, British cheeses,
hand-made chocolates and much more.

FRESH & WILD

210 WESTBOURNE GROVE, NOTTING HILL, LONDON W11 2RH
Tel: 020 7229 1063 Contact: Guini Short
Fresh & Wild are the leading specialist retailer of organic foods and natural remedies.

FRESH & WILD

69–75 BREWER STREET, SOHO, LONDON W1F 9US
Tel: 020 7434 3179 Contact: Mark Woollard
Fresh & Wild are the leading specialist retailer of organic foods and natural remedies.

THE FRESH FOOD CO

THE ORCHARD, 50 WORMHOLT RD. W12 0LS
Tel: 020 8749 8778 Fax: 020 8749 5936 Contact: Thoby Young
organics@freshfood.co.uk www.freshfood.co.uk
The Fresh Food Co along with Riverdale Farm and other certified organic producers
delivers fresh organic produce and meat, sustainably managed fish and game etc.
to retail, wholesale and customers nationwide.

FRESH! GOURMET ORGANICS

UNIT 3A, WESTWOOD BUSINESS CENTRE, 98 VICTORIA ROAD, LONDON NW10 6NB
Tel: 020 8838 0060 Fax: 020 8838 0056 Contact: Chantelle Ludski
chantelle@freshorganics.biz www.freshorganics.biz
Makers of damn fine sandwiches, wraps, salads, soups and cakes. Organic Food
Awards 2004: Food To Go Highly Commended.

JENKIM UK LTD

48 BOSTON RD., HANWELL W7 3TR
Tel: 020 8840 8687 Fax: 020 8840 8687 Contact: Ron Salim & Jennifer Quay
jenkim@onetel.com www.agrologistic.com
Distributor and supplier of Agroneem organic insecticide, emulsifiable concentrate
and Agroneem organic fertiliser. Product extracted from the neem tree. Organic
Material Review Institute (OMRI) listed and US EPA-approved.

LIDGATE, C

110 HOLLAND PARK AVENUE W11 4UA
Tel: 020 7727 8243 Fax: 020 7229 7160 Contact: David Lidgate
Organic beef and lamb from Highgrove, home of HRH Prince Charles. Deliveries to
City and West London daily. Eros award for Top Twenty London food shops,
National Pie Championships in 1993 & 1996, Utrecht European Championship
Gold Medal awards 1998, Tatler magazine Best UK Butchers 1998/99.

LUPPOLO LTD

42 WESTBOURNE TERRACE WC2 6QE
Tel: 020 7262 4562 Fax: 020 7262 9078 Contact: Claudio Bincoletto
luppolo@tiscali.co.uk
Importing products for the catering industry, day walks on organic farms, cookery
and dietetic courses. Teaching in Tuscany on local wild herbs, expert on ECC
2092/91.

MARYLEBONE FARMERS' MARKET

CRAMER ST. CAR PARK, CORNER MOXTON ST., OFF MARYLEBONE HIGH ST. W1
Tel: 020 7704 9659 Contact: Cheryl Cohen
info@lfm.org.uk www.lfm.org.uk
Sundays 10am to 2pm. Here farmers sell home-grown foods grown or made within
100 miles of the M25, including fruit, veg, meat, dairy, eggs, honey, juice,
bread, preserves, plants. NB: some, but not all, producers are organic. Run
by London Farmers' Markets, PO Box 37363, London N1 7WB.

MILLER OF KENSINGTON

14 STRATFORD ROAD, KENSINGTON W8 6QD
Tel: 020 7937 1777 Contact: Mohamed El Banna
Soil Association organic meat specialist; catering service up to 100 people.
Delicatessen and traiteur.

NEAL'S YARD REMEDIES

15 NEAL'S YARD, COVENT GARDEN WC2H 9DP
Tel: 020 7379 7222 Contact: Clare Madison
mail@nealsyardremedies.com www.nealsyardremedies.com
Soil Association certified products. Toiletries, herbs, aromatherapy products.

NEAL'S YARD REMEDIES

9 ELGIN CRESCENT W11 2JA
Tel: 020 7727 3998 Contact: The Manager
mail@nealsyardremedies.com www.nealsyardremedies.com
Neal's Yard Remedies manufactures and retails natural cosmetics in addition to
stocking an extensive range of herbs, essential oils, homoeopathic remedies and
reference material.

NOTTING HILL FARMERS' MARKET
CAR PARK BEHIND WATERSTONES, ACCESS VIA KENSINGTON PLACE W8
Tel: 020 7704 9659 Contact: London Farmers' Markets
info@lfm.org.uk www.lfm.org.uk
Saturdays 9am–1pm. Here farmers sell home-grown foods grown or made within
100 miles of the M25, including fruit, veg, meat, dairy, eggs, honey, juice, bread,
preserves, plants. NB: some, but not all, producers are organic. Run by
London Farmers' Markets, PO Box 37363, London N1 7WB.

PIZZA ORGANIC LTD
100 PITSHANGER LANE W5 1QX
Tel: 020 8998 6878 Contact: Mike Traszko
info@pizzapiazza.co.uk www.pizza-organic.co.uk
A great menu packed full of organic options, featuring stonebaked pizza, sautéed
pasta, gourmet burgers, grilled fish and fabulous desserts. Pizza Organic is certified
by the Soil Association and was Highly Commended in the 2003 Organic Food
Awards. All restaurants open 7 days a week but opening times may vary, call 020
8397 3330 for further details.

PLANET ORGANIC
42 WESTBOURNE GROVE W2 5SH
Tel: 020 7727 2227 Fax: 020 7221 1923 Contact: Neil Dugard
deliveries@planetorganic.com www.planetorganic.com
Planet Organic is about good food. We are the original one-stop organic and natural food supermarket with an in-house juice bar and freshly cooked organic food to
go. We are the modern mecca for those seeking everything for a healthy lifestyle.

PLANET ORGANIC
22 TORRINGTON PLACE WC1E 7HJ
Tel: 020 7436 1929 Fax: 020 7436 1992 Contact: Joe Duggan
deliveries@planetorganic.com www.planetorganic.com
Planet Organic is the original one-stop organic and natural food supermarket
with Juice Bar, Food to Go and café. We have 9,000 products in grocery, fruit &
veg, meat & fish, and health & bodycare. We are the modern mecca for those
seeking everything for a healthy lifestyle.

PORTOBELLO WHOLEFOODS
266 PORTOBELLO RD. W14 0EP
Tel: 020 8968 9133 Fax: 020 8960 1840 Contact: Kate Dafter
Portobello Wholefoods stocks an ever-increasing range of health food products, including natural remedies, vitamins and minerals, organic produce and gluten-free. Regular special offers and friendly service provides everything you need in a health food shop—and more. Open 7 days a week.

THE RITZ
150 PICCADILLY W1J 9BR
Tel: 020 7493 8181 Fax: 020 7493 2687 Contact: Trevor Burke
tburke@theritzlondon.com
Restaurant.

TASTE MATTERS LTD
IMPRESS HOUSE, MANSELL RD., LONDON W3 7QH
Tel: 020 8811 2555 Fax: 020 8811 2666 Contact: Alex Morritt
info@tastematters.co.uk www.tastematters.co.uk
Taste Matters Ltd. produces a premium range of chilled 'food to go' products sold under the Taste Matters brand through leading independent organic food retailers, health food stores, food halls and delicatessens. Winner of the 'Food To Go' category in Organic Food Awards 2004.

THE TEA & COFFEE PLANT
180 PORTOBELLO ROAD W11 2EB
Tel: 020 7221 8137 Contact: Ian Henshall
coffee@pro-net.co.uk www.coffee.uk.com
Coffee roaster; supplies coffee, cocoa, tea, herb tea for retail, retail mail order, caterers and own label packs for retailers. Coffee can be beans or ground, 100g packs upwards. Certified by the Fair Trade Foundation.

THOROGOODS OF EALING

113 NORTHFIELDS AVE, EALING W13 9QR
Tel: 020 8567 0339 Fax: 020 8566 3033 Contact: Paul Thorogood
Beef, lamb, pork, chicken, turkeys, bacon, cooked ham. Local delivery.

THE TROUBADOUR DELI

267 OLD BROMPTON ROAD, LONDON SW5 9JA
Tel: 020 7341 6341 Contact: Susie Thornhill
www.troubadour.co.uk
A delicatessen that sells organic, free range eggs from Chapell Farm amongst
other organic produce.

URBAN KITCHEN

63–65 GOLDNEY ROAD, LONDON W9 2AR
Tel: 020 7286 1700 Fax: 020 7286 1709 Contact: Matthew Turnbull
events@urban-productions.co.uk www.urban-productions.co.uk
Urban is a bespoke event-making company with full event production services and
a luscious kitchen in-house. We are accredited by the Soil Association to provide
organic menus for every occasion. Clients include BBC, MTV, Deutsche Bank,
Sony, M&C Saatchi, Armani and Marks & Spencer, along with a large number of
private clients.

 Accommodation

 Garden and Farm Sundries

 Producers

 Box Schemes/ Local Deliveries

 Farmers' market Stall

 Restaurants/ Cafés/Caterers

 Day Visits

 Manufacturers/ Processors

 Retail shops

 Eco Products

 Importers/ exporters

 Textiles

 Farm Gate Sales

 Mail order suppliers

 Wholesalers

Isle of Man

MANN SPECIALITY FOODS
KERE-VOLLEY, CORDEMAN SAINT MARKS, BALLASALLA IM9 3AJ
Tel: 01624 851971 Fax: 01624 852418 Contact: Robin Ratcliffe
raratcliffe.honey@manx.net
Import and distribution of organic honey.

Stress, Peace, Happiness and Satisfaction

Stress, it seems to me, is the disease of our times. And when we get stressed, we stress nature, too. In fact, I believe our stress is a primary cause of the stress in the environment today. For example, consider how my desire for cheap food affects the animals on the farm—the hens, pigs, calves and cows. I press the farmer for lower prices, the farmer presses the animals. I take the car instead of the bike, use the clothes dryer instead of the sun, eat frozen meals instead of home-cooked, all requiring extra energy and resulting in pollution—because I feel this thing called stress.

All of that changes in an instant when I recognize my power of choice, that I am in fact the boss in my own life. I learned that just as I could choose milder chemicals in place of stronger ones, so could I choose peaceful activities and thoughts in place of stressful ones, if I reflected a little, experimented and practised. I could almost always figure out a new way to do what was needed that was more harmonious, or fun. And even when I couldn't change the circumstances, I could always choose a different attitude, which made everything look different—and less stressful.

From *Ecology Begins at Home* by Archie Duncanson, Green Books, £4.95.

ANTONELLI BROTHERS LTD

THE BAKERY, WEYMOUTH RD., ECCLES M30 8FB
Tel: 0161 789 4485 Fax: 0161 789 5592 Contact: Mark Antonelli
info@antonelli.co.uk www.antonelli.co.uk
Soil Association P6011. The UK specialist maker of ice cream cones. Organic sugar
and Smoothy Waffle cones stocked. Other cones could be made to order with eight
week notice. Main stockists are Yeo Valley in Devon (home of Rocombe Ice Cream)
and September Dairy Ice Cream in Herefordshire. Direct deliveries can be arranged.

CHORLTON WHOLEFOODS

64 BEECH RD., CHORLTON-CUM-HARDY, MANCHESTER M21 9EG
Tel: 0161 881 6399 Fax: 0161 881 6399 Contact: Annie Lazenby
Established in 1982, we sell organic fruit and veg, dairy produce, dried goods,
herbal supplements etc. Home delivery within Greater Manchester. Practitioner
visits and consultations.

CORNMELL, R.M. ORGANIC BUTCHER & FOOD SPECIALIST

459 HALLIWELL RD., BOLTON BL1 8DE
Tel: 01204 846844 Contact: RM Cornmell
Our speciality organic foods: meats, bacon, ham, poultry, cheese, free range
organic eggs, honey, jam, butter, herbs, spices, juices, bread, cakes and many
more products, except vegetables, sold at the shop. Open Monday 9–5, Tuesday
9–5.30, Wednesday 9–2, Thursday at Altrincham farmers' market 9–4.
Friday 9–6, Saturday 9–5.

ECO-INTERIORS OF CHORLTON

9 HAZEL COURT, DUDLEY RD., WHALLEY RANGE, MANCHESTER M16 8DS
Tel: 0161 861 8219 Contact: Simon Corble
scorble@yahoo.co.uk
Painters, decorators and floor sanders. We provide a high quality painting and
decorating service using only organic, solvent-free products from recognised
sources. We also sand floors and varnish and treat garden fences/sheds.

EIGHTH DAY

111 OXFORD RD., MANCHESTER M1 7DU
Tel: 0161 273 4878 Fax: 0161 273 4869 Contact: Tim Gausden
mail@eighth-day.co.uk www.eighth-day.co.uk
Vegetarian health food shop, over 1,000 organic lines including foods and
complementary remedies, vegetarian café and catering with some organic food.

GLEBELANDS MARKET GARDEN LTD

C/O 24 ATHOL RD., WHALLEY RANGE M16 8QN
Tel: 0161 718 5328 Contact: Lesley Bryson
glebelands@ntlworld.com
Growers. Horticultural enterprise linked to Unicorn Grocery Ltd, local food
campaigning and educational work.

HEALTH & VEGETARIAN STORE

33 OLD CHURCH STREET, NEWTON HEATH, MANCHESTER M40 2JN
Tel: 0161 683 4456 Contact: Pamela Fynan
Health shop, all food vegetarian or vegan, special diets catered for. Herbal
and homoeopathic remedies, Hopi ear candles, chilled and frozen. Large selection
of organic foods, cereals, nuts, seeds, pulses and fruit and vegetables,
essential oils. Helpful friendly advice, local deliveries (not a box scheme).

LEES, JW & CO, (BREWERS) LTD

GREENGATE BREWERY, MIDDLETON JUNCTION M24 2AX
Tel: 0161 643 2487 Fax: 0161 655 3731 Contact: CG Dennis
giles.dennis@jwlees.co.uk www.jwlees.co.uk
Soil Association P7505. Brewers.

LIMITED RESOURCES

UNIT 3, BROOK ST, HIGHER HILLGATE, STOCKPORT SK1 3HS
Tel: 0161 477 2040 Fax: 0161 226 3777 Contact: Barbara Eadie
info@limited-resources.co.uk www.limited-resources.co.uk
Soil Association R1738. Free delivery service: organic fruit, veg, dairy, meat, fish,
wholefoods, beers, wines, gardening and pet supplies, toiletries and cleaning
products. Also mail order—ring for details.

MARBLE BEERS LTD

73 ROCHDALE RD., MANCHESTER M4 4HY
Tel: 0161 819 2694 Fax: 0161 819 2694 Contact: James Campell
www.marblebeer.co.uk
Organic and vegan brewery, situated within Marble Arch Inn, producing four regular
ales plus seasonals. Beer is available through Marble Arch and other free houses
around the country on request.

MOSSLEY ORGANIC AND FINE FOODS

11–13 ARUNDEL STREET, MOSSLEY OL5 0NY
Tel: 01457 837743 Fax: 01457 837542 Contact: Pauline Proctor
shop@mossleyorganicandfinefoods.co.uk www.mossleyorganicandfinefoods.co.uk
Huge range of natural food, many organic. Wide range of fresh, quality organic
fruit and vegetables available. Chilled, frozen, dairy produce, deli-counter.
Many organic wines and beers. Specialist, individual friendly service. Fair
Trade products supported. Soil Association member. Free delivery/box scheme.

NEAL'S YARD REMEDIES

29 JOHN DALTON ST., MANCHESTER M2 6DS
Tel: 0161 835 1713 Fax: 0161 835 9322 Contact: The Manager
mail@nealsyardremedies.com www.nealsyardremedies.com
Neal's Yard Remedies manufactures and retails natural cosmetics in addition to
stocking an extensive range of herbs, essential oils, homoeopathic remedies and
reference material.

ORGANIC 2000 LTD

UNIT B23, NEW SMITHFIELD MARKET, OPENSHAW M11 2WJ
Tel: 0161 223 4944 Fax: 0161 223 4955 Contact: Petra Dalton
02thousand@tiscali.co.uk
Umbrella co-operative. Largest and longest established organic fruit and
vegetable wholesaler in the North-West and beyond. We supply box schemes and
retail outlets, sourcing extensively from local producers. We offer an extensive list
of fruit, veg, dairy products and more, including imported goods. Fairtrade goods
are supported. Deliveries available.

ORIGINAL ORGANICS

A18 NEW SMITHFIELD MARKET, GORTON, MANCHESTER M11 2WJ
Tel: 0161 220 7788 Fax: 0161 220 9906 Contact: Nev Dunn or Stuart
originalorganics@hotmail.com www.original-organics.co.uk
We work with local producers of fresh organic food and import when necessary to
generate a comprehensive list of fruit, veg, milk, cheese, eggs, butter and
sprouted seeds offered to shops, box schemes and caterers. Delivery possible.

UNICORN GROCERY

89 ALBANY RD., CHORLTON, MANCHESTER M21 0BN
Tel: 0161 861 0010 Fax: 0161 861 7675 Contact: Kellie Bubble
office@unicorn-grocery.co.uk www.unicorn-grocery.co.uk
Soil Association GC5018, R2957. We are a large, friendly, wholesome foodstore
specialising in fresh and organic produce. Over 2,000 good value lines. We also
cater for people with more specialised dietary needs.

My Indoor Garden

My indoor garden graces the windowsills with greenery of many shapes and
hues, some grown by me from seeds. I use compost as fertilizer, and now and
then water them with washing-up water. If they get too many insects on them, I
put them under the shower or spray them with soapy water!

All of my gardens show a little bit of the wild in them. I tame them a bit, to
please my human sense of order, but deep down I know that it is Life itself that
rules and does the growing there, not me.

From *Ecology Begins at Home* by Archie Duncanson, Green Books, £4.95.

Merseyside

THE BILLINGTON FOOD GROUP LIMITED

CUNARD BUILDING, LIVERPOOL L3 1EL
Tel: 0151 243 9001 Fax: 0151 243 9011 Contact: Nick Eastwood (Industrial Sales), Keith Scarlett (Export Sales)
bfg@billingtons.co.uk www.billingtons.co.uk
Billington's supplies a range of organic cane sugars to retail and manufacturing sectors, both within UK and worldwide. All products are certified by the Soil Association.

CHURCH FARM ORGANICS

CHURCH FARM, CHURCH LANE, THURSTASTON, WIRRAL CH61 0HW
Tel: 0151 648 7838 Fax: 0151 648 9644 Contact: Steve & Brenda Ledsham
sales@churchfarm.org.uk www.churchfarm.org.uk
Soil Association G5381 & R2617. Picturesque farm with beautiful views, producing most vegetables for award-winning shop. 'Best Farm Shop', Organic Food Awards 2001 and second in the Radio 4 Food and Farming Awards 2004. Includes coffee bar. Bed and Breakfast Accommodation and holiday cottage. Wide range of seasons and events—see website for details.

FORSTER ORGANIC MEATS

SHOOTS DELPH FARM, BIRCHLEY VIEW, MOSS BANK, ST. HELENS WA11 7NU
Tel: 01942 831058 Fax: 01942 831867 Contact: Anne or Chris Forster
j&jforster@farmline.com www.forsterorganicmeats.co.uk
We produce our own beef and lamb. Sell and deliver locally fresh packs labelled and ready for eating or freezing. Farmers' Markets at Liverpool 1st and 3rd Saturdays every month and now Bootle. We have our own butchery on the farm. (Very close to Carr Mill off the East Lancs Road.) Customers are welcome to call by arrangement, or Thursdays when the butchery is open until 6.00pm. We prefer to sell directly the people who are going to enjoy our meat. We also make South African style 'Biltong', which is very popular with SA ex-pats. We are proud to say that no finished livestock has been sold through a market for over 5 years. Please call Anne or Chris for more details.

MOLYNEUX ORGANIC MEDICINAL AND AROMATIC PLANT FARM AND RESEARCH CENTRE

MILL HOUSE FARM, EAGER LANE, LYDIATE L31 4HS
Tel: 0151 526 0139 Fax: 0151 526 0139 Contact: David Molyneux
sales@phytobotanica.com www.phytobotanica.com
Producers of the first certified organic essential oils in th UK (lavender, peppermint, roman chamomile, german chamomile) and organic hydrosols. On-farm commercial hydrodistillation facilities, dispensary and conference centre for educational days (e.g. aromatherapy and holistic therapies).

ONLY NATURAL

48 WESTFIELD ST., ST. HELENS WA10 1QF
Tel: 01744 759797 Contact: B. Arrowsmith
Health food shop selling a wide range of vitamins, body building, food supplements, cosmetics, wholefoods including organic ranges. Allergy testing once a month. Friendly and helpful staff.

ORGANIC DIRECT

57 BLUNDELL ST., LIVERPOOL L1 0AJ
Tel: 0151 707 6949 Fax: 0151 707 6949 Contact: Ruth Weston
Fresh organic fruit and vegetables: weekly deliveries direct to your door from £6. Also vegan organic wholefood deliveries, many organic lines.

SEASONED PIONEERS LTD

UNIT 101, SUMMERS RD., BRUNSWICK BUSINESS PARK, LIVERPOOL L3 4BJ
Tel: 0151 709 9330 Fax: 0151 709 9330 Contact: Matthew Webster
info@seasonedpioneers.co.uk www.seasonedpioneers.co.uk
We supply authentic spice blends, herbs, chillies and peppercorns. Mail Order, retail, food service and manufacturing. Highly commended by many top UK food writers.

WINDMILL WHOLEFOODS CO-OP

337 SMITHDOWN ROAD, LIVERPOOL L15 3JJ
Tel: 0151 734 1919 Contact: Brian Rider
windmill@windmill.abelgratis.co.uk www.windmillorganic.co.uk
Grocery with a wide range of healthy, organic, vegan, vegetarian, and fair-trade whole-foods. We also stock vegan/organic delights, like wines and chocolate. Ethical body-care and cleaning products. Our veg box scheme delivers to the Liverpool area every Thursday.

The Importance of Biodiversity

There is another vitally important reason for creating as much biodiversity on a farm as possible—there is a direct correlation between the biodiversity of a system and its overall health. Ecologists were the first to recognize how important it is that any natural environment has as wide a range of plants and animals as possible. In fact they went further in realizing that they could measure the sustainability and stability of an ecosystem purely by the number of species recorded in a given area. When the species are reduced to only a few types, the system becomes fragile and unhealthy. On the other hand, an environment that is species rich, with a high genetic diversity, is very resilient. This strength and resilience comes from its diversity and flexibility. The same is true of the environment of a farm. Where there is a wide range of crops, animals, different varieties of grasses, clovers and other useful 'herbs' in a pasture, and a wide range of habitats and a healthy soil with a complicated mix of micro-organisms in it, the farm as a whole is a healthier and more productive place, with fewer pests and diseases.

From *Organic Futures: The Case for Organic Farming* by Adrian Myers, Green Books, £12.95.

BOMBAY HALWA LTD
23 MERRICK RD., SOUTHALL UB2 4AW
Tel: 020 8574 6275 Fax: 020 8813 8310 Contact: T Elyas
taibelyas@bombayhalwa.com www.
Soil Association P2936. Meat-free site for organic and conventional ready meals,
snacks, chutneys, desserts and speciality ethnic foods; Indian, Asian, Mexican, Italian.

BRENT COUNCIL PARKS SERVICE
660 HARROW ROAD, WEMBLEY HA0 2HB
Tel: 020 8937 5619 Fax: 020 8903 3799 Contact: Leslie Williams
leslie.williams@brent.gov.uk
Organic hay—approximately 60 hectares available for harvest.

CAPEL MANOR COLLEGE
BULLSMORE LANE, ENFIELD EN1 4RQ
Tel: 020 8366 4442 Contact: Andrea Brown
enquiries@capel.ac.uk www.capel.ac.uk
Soil Association G7651. An organic sheep flock with Lincoln Longwoods and
Suffolks. Sell organic hay, lamb and breeding stock. The farm is managed by
Capel Manor College, which specialises in horticulture and associated land-based
industry courses.

EVERYBODY ORGANIC LTD
110 EAST DUCK LEES LANE, ENFIELD EN3 7SR
Tel: 0845 345 5054 Fax: 020 8804 1657 Contact: George Harvey
enquiries@everybodyorganic.com www.everybodyorganic.com
Soil Association P7703. Supplying the finest organic fruits, vegetables and
groceries with delivery direct to your door. National coverage.

FIRST LEARNING DAY NURSERY
50 SHEEP WALK, SHEPPERTON TW17 0AJ
Tel: 01932 260600 Contact: Kimberley Foster
admin@firstlearning.co.uk
The first and only certified organic children's day nursery in the UK offering quality childcare for babies from 3 months to pre-school children aged 5 years. Part or full time places. Head office at 3 Union Court, Richmond, Surrey TW9 1AA, telephone: 020 8939 2288.

FRESH-COCONUT
145A WEMBLEY PARK DRIVE, WEMBLEY HA9 8HQ
directory@fresh-coconut.com www.fresh-coconut.com
IMO BIO—Siegel virgin coconut oil, hemp seed oil, flax oil, etc.

GAIA WHOLEFOODS
123 ST. MARGARET'S RD., TWICKENHAM TW1 2LH
Tel: 020 8892 2262 Contact: David Kennington
Soil Association R1562. Small, traditional, friendly, helpful wholefood shop. Wide organic range: fruit, vegetables, bread, eggs, chilled, macrobiotic, convenience, toiletries. Mon–Fri 9.30am–7pm, Sat 9.30am–5pm.

HORIZON FOOD LTD.
UNIT 21 & 25, REDBURN IND. ESTATE, WOODALL ROAD, ENFIELD EN3 4LE
Tel: 020 8443 3455 Fax: 020 8443 5040 Contact: Constantine Azar
cos@horizonfood.co.uk www.horizonfood.co.uk
Organic dried fruit including organic stuffed dried fruit. Packers for major distributors.

NEAL'S YARD BAKERY LIMITED
UNIT 1, SWAN ISLAND, STRAWBERRY VALE, TWICKENHAM TW1 4RP
Tel: 020 8744 1992 Fax: 020 8744 2992 Contact: John Loffler
info@nealsyardbakery.co.uk www.nealsyardbakery.co.uk
Neal's Yard Bakery was established in 1976 and bakes a wide range of tasty and healthy organic breads, cakes and pastries.

PIZZA ORGANIC LTD
3–5 HIGH ST., RUISLIP HA4 7AU
Tel: 01895 633567 Contact: Mike Traszko
info@pizzapiazza.co.uk www.pizza-organic.co.uk
A great menu packed full of organic options, featuring stonebaked pizza, sautéed pasta, gourmet burgers, grilled fish and fabulous desserts. Pizza Organic is certified by the Soil Association and was Highly Commended in the 2003 Organic Food Awards. All restaurants open 7 days a week but opening times may vary, call 020 8397 3330 for further details.

REVITAL HEALTH CENTRE (HEAD OFFICE)
78 HIGH ST, RUISLIP HA4 7AA
Tel: 01895 629950 Fax: 01895 630869 Contact: The Directors
enquire@revital.com www.revital.com
Revital has everything you need for optimum nutrition and health care. We are the largest independent health food retailer in the UK and offer a quick, efficient mail order service.

RIVERFORD HOME DELIVERY
FLAT 7, 4 WALDEGRAVE PARK, TWICKENHAM TW1 4TE
Tel: 020 8892 2204 Fax: 020 8892 2204 Contact: Simone McCue
simone@riverfordhomedelivery.co.uk www.riverford.co.uk
Organic vegetable box scheme operating in Richmond, Twickenham & West London. Various box sizes to suit different households. Can order online at www.riverford.co.uk.

TWICKENHAM FARMERS' MARKET
HOLLY ROAD CAR PARK, HOLLY ROAD, OFF KING STREET, TWICKENHAM TW1
Tel: 020 7704 9659 Contact: London Farmers' Markets
info@lfm.org.uk www.lfm.org.uk
Saturdays 9am–1pm. Here farmers sell home-grown foods grown or made within 100 miles of the M25, including fruit, veg, meat, dairy, eggs, honey, juice, bread, preserves, plants. NB: some, but not all, producers are organic. Run by London Farmers' Markets, PO Box 37363, London N1 7WB.

ABBEY FARM ORGANICS

ABBEY FARM, ABBEY RD, FLITCHAM, KINGS LYNN PE31 6BT
Tel: 01485 609094 Fax: 01485 609094 Contact: Edward Cross
xxflitcham@eidosnet.co.uk www.abbeyfarm.co.uk
No details available.

ARTHUR'S ORGANIC DELIVERIES

2 NEW BARN COTTAGES, OLD BUCKENHAM, ATTLEBOROUGH NR17 1PF
Tel: 01953 887582 Contact: Tony & Donna Park
arthurs@limpets.freeserve.co.uk www.eostreorganics.co.uk
A local box scheme for south central Norfolk in an area bounded by Watton,
Dereham, Hethersett, Diss, Thetford and including Wymondham and Attleborough.
Produce from local organic co-operative used wherever possible. Organic fruit
and veg, organic free range eggs, organic local apple juice, organic bread, monthly
wholefood delivery. Ecover refill service. 20 years experience selling organic goods.

ASH FARM ORGANICS

ASH FARM, STONE LANE, BINTREE, DEREHAM NR20 5NA
Tel: 01362 683228 Fax: 01362 683228 Contact: C and W van Beuningen
info@ashfarmorganics.co.uk www.ashfarmorganics.co.uk
In our farm shop we sell pork, beef, poultry and vegetables (when available),
all organically produced on our 370-acre family farm. We also sell lamb and
free range eggs, organically produced within Norfolk. We do make our own pork
sausages, including a gluten-free variety and cure and oak-smoke bacon and
gammon. Our farmshop is open Fridays 10.30am–3.00pm and Saturdays
9.30am–12.00noon; any other time by appointment (the first two weekends after
Christmas we'll be closed). You can also find us each 2nd Saturday of the month
on Dereham Farmers' Market. We organise occasional farm tours.

AU NATUREL

GROVE FARM, HOLT RD., AYLMERTON, NORWICH NR11 8QA
Tel: 01263 837255 Contact: Nick Amis
nicksherryamis@yahoo.co.uk
PYO or delivered strawberries, raspberries, blackberries, eating/cooking apples
and plums, plus soon to arrive, eggs.

THE AYLSHAM PANTRY

50 RED LION ST., AYLSHAM, NORWICH NR11 6HG
Tel: 01263 733530 Contact: Bonnie Dixon
bonniedixon@aylshampantry.co.uk www.aylshampantry.co.uk
The Aylsham Pantry is a retail shop that sells a wide range of organic products,
including organic coffee beans, chocolates, honey and wholefoods. We are constantly
expanding our range, and sell our organic goods online for nationwide UK delivery.

BARKER ORGANICS

THE WALLED GARDEN, WOLTERTON HALL, NORWICH NR11 7LY
Tel: 01263 768966 Contact: David Barker
Biodynamic Agricultural Association (Demeter) 370. Historic walled garden, a
real live working kitchen garden growing vegetables and fruit using biodynamic
methods. Selling all produce direct to the local community via a box scheme.

BARRIER ANIMAL HEALTHCARE

36–37 HAVESCROFT IND. ESTATE, NEW RD., ATTLEBOROUGH NR17 1YE
Tel: 01953 456363 Fax: 01953 455594 Contact: Sandy Morris
sales@barrier-biotech.com www.footrot.co.uk
Soil Association 12656. Manufacturer of animal health products and agricultural
healthcare products. Specialist manufacturers of high quality non-toxic, non-irritant
healthcare products. Our effective range of agricultural products are designed for
intensive farming and also Soil Association certified, and so suitable for organic
farming systems. Call 01953 456363 or visit www.ragwort.com.

THE BOOJA BOOJA COMPANY

HOWE PITS, NORWICH RD., BROOKE NR15 1HJ
Tel: 01508 558888 Fax: 01508 557844 Contact: Colin Mace
Soil Association P4181. Manufacturers of organic dairy-free, vegetarian, vegan, wheat- and gluten-free chocolates.

CASTLE ACRE ORGANIC

MANOR FARM, CASTLE ACRE, KING'S LYNN PE32 2BJ
Tel: 01760 755380 Fax: 01760 755548 Contact: Terry Bird
info@castleacreorganic.co.uk www.castleacreorganic.co.uk
Supplying the public, retail shops, restaurants and box delivery schemes with organic poultry, Aberdeen Angus beef, Poll Dorset and Lleyn lamb and mutton, pork, bacon, ham, sausages and burgers, eggs and vegetables.

CATTERMOLE QUALITY BUTCHERS, SIMON

KING ST., NEW BUCKENHAM, NR. NORWICH NR16 2AF
Tel: 01953 860264 Fax: 01953 860024 Contact: Sue Cattermole
simon@scatty.co.uk www.scatty.co.uk
Soil Association P6154. Butcher selling a large range of fresh organic meat and poultry products. Beef, pork, lamb, chicken, own sausages and bacon from our own smokehouse.

COURTYARD FARM

RINGSTEAD, HUNSTANTON PE36 5LQ
Tel: 01485 525251 Fax: 01485 525211
courtyard.organic@virgin.net
Organic cattle, sheep and pigs. Meat is sold direct from the farm, either pre-ordered or through the farm shop: open every Wednesday from 3pm to 5.30pm. Member of the Soil Association Organic Farms Network.

CRONE'S

FAIRVIEW, FERSFIELD RD., KENNINGHALL NR16 2DP
Tel: 01379 687687 Fax: 01379 688323 Contact: Robert Crone
info@crones.co.uk www.crones.co.uk
Soil Association P1587. Makers of a range of award-winning apple juices and
ciders. Also organic cider vinegar, apple cherry, pear and apple. Contact us
for our full range. Sales ex-gate by prior appointment.

DIANE'S PANTRY

8 MARKET PLACE, REEPHAM, NORWICH NR10 4JJ
Tel: 01603 871075 Contact: Diane Turner (Owner)
Wholefood, health foods, supplements and small bakery with coffee shop attached.
Organic bread baked to order.

DOMINI QUALITY FOODS

VILLAGE FARM, THE STREET, MARKET WESTON, DISS IP22 2NZ
Tel: 01359 221333 Fax: 01359 221835 Contact: Jane Capon
jcapon@dominifoods.fnset.co.uk
Small traditional farm selling top quality untreated milk, cream and butter from the
Domini Jerseys. Available from Wyken farmers' market, Stanton every Saturday or
telephone/email to order direct from the farm.

EOSTRE ORGANICS LTD

UNIT 2, NORTH SIDE HANGARS, OLD BUCKENHAM AIRFIELD, ATTLEBOROUGH
NR17 1PU
Tel: 01953 456294 Fax: 01953 456145 Contact: Dot Bane
office@eostreorganics.co.uk www.eostreorganics.co.uk
An organic grower co-operative, mainly wholesaling but also attend farmers'
markets and have stands at both Norwich Provisions Market (6 days) and Old
Spitalfields (Sundays), also pack boxes for distribution by others.

GARBOLDISHAM WINDMILL

DISS IP22 2RJ

Tel: 01953 681593 Contact: Adrian Colman

Soil Association P4546. Bread flours, oat products, gluten-free flours available from mill or through shops in Norfolk and Suffolk. Please telephone for details (may get answering machine).

GERMAIN'S TECHNOLOGY GROUP UK

HANSA RD., HARDWICK IND. ESTATE, KINGS LYNN PE30 4LG

Tel: 01553 774012 Fax: 01553 773145 Contact: Mark Butler

info@germains.com www.germains.com

Soil Association P7187. High performance seed technology products for organic use under the brand 'ProBio', including coatings, pellets, steeping, priming and non-chemical disinfection. Wide range of agricultural and horticultural seeds handled.

THE GREEN GROCERS

2 EARLHAM HOUSE, EARLHAM ROAD, NORWICH NR2 3PD

Tel: 01603 250000 Contact: Ben Binns

eat@thegreengrocers.co.uk www.thegreengrocers.co.uk

Organic supermarket offering local, organic and environmentally friendly groceries, the Green Grocers offers a new way of shopping: fruit and veg, meats, frozen pizzas, dried produce, milk etc., eco-products, 70% of fresh produce is locally sourced.

THE GREENHOUSE

42–46 BETHEL ST., NORWICH NR2 1NR

Tel: 01603 631007 Contact: Tigger

www.greenhousetrust.co.uk

The Greenhouse is an educational charity providing solutions to environmental problems. The building houses an organic, vegetarian/vegan licensed café and shop (open for Sunday lunch 12 to 3.30) plus meeting rooms and herb garden. The shop acts as a contact point for local veg box scheme and is stockist of a wide range of organic and GMO-free foods. A resource centre offering meeting space, offices and other facilities to local and regional voluntary groups.

HARVEYS PUREMEAT
63 GROVE RD., NORWICH NR1 3RL
Tel: 01603 621930 Fax: 01603 621908 Contact: Nigel Harvey
info@puremeat.org.uk www.puremeat.org.uk
Established 1924—Harveys is Norwich's only certified (O.F.F.) organic butcher
and game dealer. Retail shop, wholesale supplies to restaurants, hotels, etc.
by arrangement. Local game including venison. See website.

THE HERBARY
CHURCH FARM, MIDDLE RD., SHOULDHAM THORPE, KINGS LYNN PE32 1TF
Tel: 01366 348175 Fax: 01366 348176 Contact: K Vallance
theherbary@btconnect.com
Soil Association G6463. Salads, growers of organic leafy herb and speciality
salad crops.

HOUGHTON ORGANIC FARM
THE ESTATE OFFICE, HOUGHTON, KINGS LYNN PE31 6UE
Tel: 01485 528569 Fax: 01485 528167 Contact: Carwyn James
carwyn@houghtonhall.com www.houghtonhall.com
Soil Association G5603. Producers of organic beef and lamb from our herd of
Longhorn cattle and flocks of Southdown and Norfolk Horn sheep, supplying local
restaurants, box schemes and Fakenham farmers' market.

J & C FARMS
ESTATE OFFICE, GAYTON HALL, KINGS LYNN PE32 1PL
Tel: 01553 636292 Fax: 01553 636292 Contact: The Manager
marshamgaytonhall@farming.co.uk
Arable farm producing cereals, potatoes, sugar beet with organic pig enterprise
managed by others.

KENT, JR
CHURCH BARN FARM, ARMINGHALL NR14 8SG
Tel: 01508 495574 Contact: JR Kent
Soil Association G1819. Farm gate sales of top fruit, roots and squash. PYO
blackcurrants, broad beans and other (rabbits and pigeons permitting).

KETTLE FOODS LTD.
BARNARD RD, BOWTHORPE INDUSTRIAL ESTATE, NORWICH NR5 9JB
Tel: 01603 744788 Fax: 01603 740375 Contact: Nicola Hewlett
info@kettlefoods.co.uk www.kettlechips.co.uk
Kettle Foods supply Kettle® Organics, a range of organic hand-cooked potato
chips, available in two varieties: lightly salted and sea salt with crushed
black peppercorns; plus the perfect accompaniment, an organic salsa dip.

LETHERINGSETT WATER MILL
RIVERSIDE RD., LETHERINGSETT, HOLT NR25 7YD
Tel: Tel:01263 713153 Contact: Mike Thurlow
Water Mill (1798) restored to working order producing organic 100% wholewheat flour.
Demeter BDAA member (no. 262). Working demonstrations when we make flour (varies
between winter and summer). Mail order sales; deliveries to NR25 & all Norfolk.

MANGREEN TRUST
MANGREEN HALL, SWARDESTON, NORWICH NR14 8DD
Tel: 01508 570444 Fax: 01508 578899 Contact: Christopher Duffield
trust@mangreen.co.uk www.mangreen.co.uk
We farm one and a half acres of vegetables and fruit to Soil Association standards
(cert. no. D10E). Retail outlet supplies fresh produce, both local and imported,
complemented by general grocery items.

THE METFIELD ORGANIC BAKERY LTD

THE STORES, THE STREET, METFIELD, HARLESTON IP20 0LB
Tel: 01379 586798 Fax: 01379 586798 Contact: Phil Smith
Soil Association R1531. Bakery. Producers of hand-crafted organic bread, cakes and savouries.

MORTONS TRADITIONAL TASTE LTD

GROVE FARM, SWANTON ABBOTT, NORWICH NR10 5DL
Tel: 01692 538067 Fax: 01692 538478 Contact: Rob Morton
mortons@whitwellhall.co.uk www.mortonstraditionaltaste.co.uk
Specialist poultry producers supplying large processors.

NATIONWIDE FOOD PACKING LTD

13 NORWICH ROAD IND. ESTATE, WATTON, THETFORD IP25 6DR
Tel: 01953 885735 Contact: B Henderson
Soil Association P2619. Contract packers, bulk to retail. Mostly dry canning of bouillon gravy granules.

NATURAL FOODSTORE

NORFOLK HOUSE YARD, ST. NICHOLAS ST., DISS IP22 4LB
Tel: 01379 651832 Contact: M Meiracker
Soil Association R1547. Vegetarian wholefood shop stocking full range of dried and fresh organic wholefoods, Fairtrade and eco-products. Local organic dairy, fruit and vegetables, flour, fruit juices, speciality breads, cakes, savouries and chocolate.

NATURAL SURROUNDINGS

BAYFIELD ESTATE, HOLT NR25 7JN
Tel: 01263 711091 Fax: 01263 711091 Contact: Peter Loosley
loosley@farmersweekly.net www.naturalsurroundings.org.uk
Wildflower and countryside centre specialising in plants for the wildlife garden. Wildflower and herb nursery growing in peat-free, organic composts.

NEAL'S YARD REMEDIES
26 LOWER GOAT LANE, NORWICH NR2 1EL
Tel: 01603 766681 Contact: The Manager
mail@nealsyardremedies.com www.nealsyardremedies.com
Neal's Yard Remedies manufactures and retails natural cosmetics in addition to stocking an extensive range of herbs, essential oils, homoeopathic remedies and reference material.

THE ORGANIC FEED COMPANY
NORFOLK MILL, SHIPDHAM, THETFORD IP25 7SD
Tel: 01362 822903 Fax: 01362 822910 Contact: Sophie Edwards
sales@organicfeed.co.uk www.organicfeed.co.uk
Soil Association registered. Organic feed for layers, poultry, pigs, sheep, goats and cattle. Vegetarian Society Approved. Available nationally through retail outlets, in 20kg sacks.

ORGANICS-ON-LINE LTD
PARK HOUSE, GUNTHORPE HALL, MELTON CONSTABLE NR24 2PA
Tel: 0845 052 0777 Contact: Annette Ward (MD)
annette.ward@organics-on-line.com www.organics-on-line.com
Business to business internet trading site. Organics-on-line offers a large range of organic products. The site acts as a means of facilitating trade direct from the producer to the buyer, and is targeting business-to-business trade in organics.

PARADISE ORGANICS
64 GLENN RD., PORINGLAND, NORWICH NR14 7LU
Tel: 01508 494260 Contact: Debbie Paradise
deb@paradised.fsnet.co.uk www.paradiseorganics.co.uk
Member of Soil Association. Home delivery service of local (as much as possible) organic vegetables, fruit and wholefoods.

PEARCE LTD, ALFRED G

GARAGE LANE IND. ESTATE, COMMON LANE, SETCHEY, KINGS LYNN PE33 0BE
Tel: 01553 810456 Fax: 01553 811464 Contact: Simon Pearce
info@alfredgpearce.co.uk www.alfredgpearce.co.uk
Soil Association P5559. Suppliers of prepared and semi-prepared root vegetables, and a selection of IQF vegetables to the manufacturing and food service industry. We process products giving full traceability by using dedicated growers to ensure the continuity of supply.

PLACE UK (R & JM PLACE LTD)

CHURCH FARM, TUNSTEAD NR12 8RQ
Tel: 01692 536225 Fax: 01692 536928 Contact: SF Shaw
admin@placeuk.com www.placeuk.com
Soil Association P1734. Growers and processors of soft fruit, vegetables, beansprouts and carbohydrate products. Processing facility for IQF, bulk freezing, rehydrated, blanching, puréeing, cutting and slicing.

RAINBOW WHOLEFOODS

OLD FIRE STATION STABLES, LABOUR IN VAIN YARD, NORWICH NR2 1JD
Tel: 01603 630484 Fax: 01603 664066 Contact: Richard Austin
info@rainbowwholefoods.co.uk www.rainbowwholefoods.co.uk
A sensational traditional wholefood shop with fresh organic vegetables, fresh organic bread daily and 14 types of seaweed. All our goods are guaranteed GM-free.

SALLE MOOR HALL FARM

SALLE MOOR HALL FARM, SALLE, REEPHAM, NORWICH NR10 4SB
Tel: 01603 879046 Fax: 01603 879047 Contact: Douglas Whitelaw
douglas@salleorganics.com www.salleorganics.com
Soil Association G1883. Soil Association-registered organic farm selling lamb, beef, eggs and vegetables direct to the door, through vegetable box scheme and wholesale. Also self-catering cottage.

SAVORY EGGS, J

HIGHFIELD FARM, GREAT RYBURGH, FAKENHAM NR21 7AL
Tel: 01328 829249 Fax: 01328 829422 Contact: Elizabeth Savory
jegshighfield@onet.co.uk www.broadland.com/highfield
J. Savory Eggs laying flock, converting June 2000. Soil Association No G2947.
Speciality egg production. Mrs E. Savory, farmhouse B&B, member FHB, Four
Diamonds ETB.

STONEHOUSE ORGANIC FARM

STONEHOUSE FARM, WEST HARLING, NORWICH NR16 2SD
Tel: 01953 717258 Fax: 01953 717333 Contact: Richard Evans
stonehouse.farm@farming.co.uk
Organic farm producing cattle, sheep and pigs.

ST. BENEDICTS FOOD STORE

43 ST. BENEDICTS STREET, NORWICH NR2 4PG
Tel: 01603 623309 Contact: Tom Lamb
Retailer and wholesaler of some organic produce to the public and the catering trade.

TERROIR

WHALEBONE HOUSE, HIGH STREET, CLEY NEXT THE SEA NR25 7RN
Tel: 01263 740336 Contact: Kalba Meadows
terroir.restaurant@virgin.net www.terroir.org.uk
Award-winning, produce-led restaurant: dinner consists of just one fixed price, four
course menu, planned each afternoon to show off the best, freshest and most seasonal of ingredients. Specialise in the authentic vegetable cooking of the
Mediterranean regions of France and Italy, accompanied by fine organic wines.
Open for dinner from Tuesday to Sunday; booking essential. Weekend breaks start
at £280 per couple.

TRADITIONAL NORFOLK POULTRY
GARAGE FARM, HARGHAM ROAD, SHROPHAM NR17 1DS
Tel: 01953 498434 Fax: 01953 498962 Contact: Mark Gorton
enquiries@tnpltd.com
We are producers and processors of organic chicken and turkeys all year round.
We are members of Organic Farmers and Growers no. 31UKF120071.

THE TREEHOUSE
14–16 DOVE ST., NORWICH NR2 1DE
Tel: 01603 763258 Contact: Slogg
The Treehouse sells freshly made meals, salads and home-made cakes at
lunchtimes and Thurs–Sat evenings. We use a wide range of ingredients, from
local suppliers where possible.

ULULA—ORGANIC BABY FOOD
JORDAN HOUSE, WHITWELL, REEPHAM NR10 4RQ
Tel: 01362 688060 Contact: Sabine Gaszow
mail@ulula.co.uk www.ulula.co.uk
Certified organic and biodynamic baby food. Includes diet plan and allergy-aware
baby food. Our unique range of baby foods includes brands from Holle, Sunval and
ErdmannHAUSER, all producers truly devoted to healthy, natural and pure products
and with long traditions of producing biodynamic baby food for up to 70 years.

WEBSTER, TWC
EDGE GREEN FARM, KENNINGHALL, NORWICH NR16 2DR
Tel: 01953 887724 Contact: TWC Webster
Soil Association G7018. Farming mixed arable and livestock, beef cattle, all
cereals and pulses etc., sugar beet. All fully organic.

YETMAN'S
37 NORWICH RD., HOLT NR25 6SA
Tel: 01263 713320 Contact: The Manager
Restaurant using in-season local organic produce.

ALPRO UK

ALTENDIEZ WAY, LATIMER BUSINESS PARK, BURTON LATIMER NN15 5YT
Tel: 01536 720600 Fax: 01536 725793 Contact: Laura Colabuono
commercialuk@alpro.be www.alprosoya.co.uk
Europe's leading manufacturer of dairy-free alternatives to milk, cream, yoghurt and desserts.

ARCADIA ORGANICS

MOORFIELD COURTYARD, WARKTON, KETTERING NN16 9XJ
Tel: 01536 525298 Fax: 01536 373609 Contact: Wayne Davis
enquiries@arcadiaorganics.co.uk www.arcadiaorganics.co.uk
Retail farm shop—fresh fruit and veg, meats from Graig Farm Organics, box scheme delivery locally (10 miles). Also composts, grow bags, books, wines, beers etc. Opening times: Friday 10am–6pm, Saturday 9am–1pm.

DAILY BREAD CO-OPERATIVE LTD

THE OLD LAUNDRY, BEDFORD RD., NORTHAMPTON NN4 7AD
Tel: 01604 621531 Fax: 01604 603725 Contact: John Clarke
northampton@dailybread.co.uk www.dailybread.co.uk
Soil Association P1498. A drop-off point for Leafcycles organic box scheme, we retail wholefoods, with an increasing range of organic flours, grains, nuts, fruits, etc. Also organic soya milk, yoghurts and cheeses.

GOODNESS FOODS

SOUTH MARCH, DAVENTRY NN11 4PH
Tel: 01327 706611 Fax: 01327 300436 Contact: Lesley Cutts
lesley.cutts@goodness.co.uk www.goodness.co.uk
Soil Association P1636. We carry a fantastic range of organic foods: thousands of products incLuding frozen and chilled foods. We deliver throughout the the UK. Phone for details, or look at our websites—trade: www.goodness.co.uk or retail: www.GoodnessDirect.co.uk.

GOODNESSDIRECT

SOUTH MARCH, DAVENTRY NN11 4PH
Tel: 01327 704197 Fax: 01327 703179 Contact: Lesley Cutts
lesley.cutts@goodness.co.uk www.goodnessdirect.co.uk
Distributor of hundreds of organic products by wholesale and mail order. The one-stop organic supermarket delivered to your door.

GRANOVITA UK LTD

5 STANTON CLOSE, FINEDON RD. INDUSTRIAL ESTATE, WELLINGBOROUGH NN8 4HN
Tel: 01933 273717 Fax: 01933 273729 Contact: Kate Percival
kate.percival@granovita.co.uk www.granovita.co.uk
GranoVita UK manufactures a wide range of vegetarian products, many of which are organic. Our range includes the following organic products; breakfast cereals, sauces, soya drinks, patés, desserts—and a great deal more. Our organic certifying bodies are: QC&I, Organic Farmers & Growers (UK2), and the Soil Assn (UK5).

LEAFCYCLES

24 ST. MICHAELS AVE, NORTHAMPTON NN1 4JQ
Tel: 01604 628956 Contact: Laura Streamer
dig@blackcurrentcentre.org.uk blackcurrentcentre.org uk
We deliver organic fruit and vegetables from Eden Farms in Lincolnshire. Deliveries in Northampton, Daventry and Flore (but not outlying areas) can be made to your home or workplace. Collection from us possible up to 8pm. Evening deliveries also available in NN1.

MARTLET NATURAL FOODS

10–14 MEADOW CLOSE, ISE VALLEY, WELLINGBOROUGH NN8 4BH
Tel: 01933 442022 Fax: 01933 440815 Contact: The Manager
Producers and suppliers of retail and bulk organic products. Preserves, chutneys, cider and wine vinegars, honey, molasses, malt, sugar syrups, mincemeat, sauces. Also seaweed extract, biostimulants and fertilisers. Soil Association approved.

OLIVE ORGANIC
1 HIGHFIELD WAY, YARDLEY HASTINGS, NORTHAMPTON NN7 1HQ
Tel: 01604 696995 Contact: Pauline Savory
sales@oliveorganic.com www.oliveorganic.com
Natural organic skincare. Soil Association certified products. Essential Care,
Organic Blue, Mother Earth and more. Unbeatable customer service, great
products. Try us and see!

ONE (ORGANIC, NATURAL & ETHICAL) FOOD LTD
19 AUSTIN WAY, ROYAL OAK TRADING ESTATE, DAVENTRY NN11 5QY
Tel: 0870 871 1112 Fax: 0870 871 1113 Contact: Neil Stansfield
info@onefood.co.uk www.onefood.co.uk
One (organic, natural and ethical) produces, wholesales and markets the largest
range of fresh organic fruit, vegetables, meat and grocery to the UK. All of its range
including Seafresh (sustainable) Fish can be prepared for the restaurateur, retailer,
distributor, school, hospital or private home delivery—all from source to your door
in 48 hours.

ORGANIC TRAIL
18 DISWELL BROOKWAY, DEANSHANGER, MILTON KEYNES MK19 6GB
Tel: 01908 568952 Fax: 01908 568952 Contact: Jim Lawlor
jimlawlor@tiscali.co.uk www.organictrail.co.uk
Local delivery of English organic vegetables to your door (seasonal produce):
Milton Keynes, Towcester, Olney and surrounding villages.

PHOENIX FOODS
BRAKEY RD., CORBY NN17 5LU
Tel: 01536 200101 Fax: 01536 202218 Contact: C Wilding
sales@phoenixfoods.co.uk
Soil Association P3068. Manufacturer of dry powdered food stuffs: hot chocolate,
drinks, custard powder etc.

RIVER NENE HOME DELIVERY

22 TOWRISE, SULGRAVE, NORTHAMPTON OX17 2SB
Tel: 01295 760936 Fax: 01295 760936 Contact: Rob Smith
robandrachel@rivernene.co.uk www.rivernene.co.uk
Award-winning organic veg and fruit boxes delivered to your door.

RUSSELLS OF EVENLEY

23 THE GREEN, EVENLEY, BRACKLEY NN13 5SQ
Tel: 01280 702452 Fax: 01280 840274 Contact: Nick Russell
nicks40@v21.me.uk www.evenley.net
Village delicatessen offering some organic lines: organic bread daily, organic
produce occasionally. Other products available to order.

SAVE THE BACON

CASTLE ASHBY ROAD, YARDLEY HASTINGS NN7 1EL
Tel: 01604 696859 Fax: 01604 696859 Contact: Douglas Austin
doug@savethebacon.com www.savethebacon.com
We source British organic foods: meat, poultry, fish, cheese and farmhouse
cooking. We take orders over the telephone and internet. Deliveries locally
(Northants, Milton Keynes, Beds) and nationally.

THE SONORA FOOD COMPANY LTD

STEPHENSON CLOSE, DRAYTON FIELDS IND. ESTATE, DAVENTRY NN11 8RF
Tel: 01327 705733 Fax: 01327 703592 Contact: Janet Marnewick
janetm@sonora.co.uk www.discoveryfoods.co.uk
Manufacturers of flour tortillas and corn chips to major high street retailers.

BURNLAW CENTRE

BURNLAW WHITEFIELD, HEXHAM NE47 8HF

gvs38@hotmail.com

Smallholding. We also run retreats: course in dance painting and healing and mysticism and Baha'i wisdom. Good place for time out, come and stay, organic beef, (very scrumptious!) fabulous setting and lots of (natural) enlightenment on tap!!!

CROPPED UP

DILSTON COLLEGE, CORBRIDGE NE45 5RJ

Tel: 07947 856641 Fax: 01434 633721 Contact: Sue Hick

Soil Association G4553. Organic fruit and vet box scheme operating June 1st to Christmas only. All produce except potatoes grown on-site. Local deliveries to Hexham, Haydon Bridge and Allendale.

THE GOOD LIFE SHOP

50 HIGH ST., WOOLER NE71 6BG

Tel: 01668 281700 Contact: Liz Girdwood

goodlife_wooler@hotmail.com

Ours is a family-run business specialising in local and continental cheeses, wholefoods, organic ranges. Herbs and spices are weighed to order.

THE GREEN SHOP

30 BRIDGE ST., BERWICK UPON TWEED TD15 1AQ

Tel: 01289 305566 Fax: 01289 305566 Contact: Ross Boston

shop@thegreenshop.go-plus.net

Complete and only green shopping since 1993. Organic seeds, clothing, toiletries, alcohol. Nearly 2,000 organic pre-packed foods, plus breads, chilled, frozen, fruit, veg & meat. 30 mile delivery. Fairtrade. A very warm welcome.

HAVENS ORGANICS

THE HAVENS FARM, HEATHERWICK, OTTERBURN NE19 1LY
Tel: 01830 520806 Fax: 01830 520806 Contact: Andy Wilson
10-ha S.D.A. small farm. Own veg in-season box scheme, organic eggs, organic
pedigree Dexter beef, small bulk veg sales to shops and other box schemes.

THE MARKET SHOP

48 BRIDGE STREET, BERWICK-UPON-TWEED TD15 1AQ
Tel: 01289 307749 Fax: 01289 307749 Contact: Jill Spence
Health food shop, wholefoods, herbs and spices.

MATFEN HOME FARM

C/O CLUTTONS, BLACKETT HOWE, MATFEN NE20 0RP
Tel: 01661 886888 Fax: 01661 886777 Contact: Jonathan Shepherd
Soil Association registered. Production of quality finished lamb and beef.

NAFFERTON FARM

NAFFERTON FARM, STOCKSFIELD NE43 7XD
Tel: 01661 832246 Fax: 01661 832246 Contact: William Taylor
william.taylor@ncl.ac.uk www.naffertonorganicveg.co.uk
We supply organically grown vegetables, wholesale and in our box scheme, which
we are planning to expand to mail order via our secure website.

NOAH'S PLACE

31 MAIN ST, SPITTAL, BERWICK-UPON-TWEED TD15 1QY
Tel: 01289 332141 Contact: Humphrey & Nathalie Gudgeon
info@noahsplace.co.uk www.noahsplace.co.uk
Family-run B&B and tea room close to sandy beach, historic town of Berwick-upon-
Tweed, Holy Island, Scottish Borders. Organic food, natural bedclothes. English,
French, German spoken. Children welcome, bicycle storage.

*daylesford*organic

FARMSHOP

ORGANIC: THE BEST FOOD IS PRODUCED
WITH RESPECT FOR THE LAND

AT DAYLESFORD, WE OFFER THE FRESHEST SEASONAL FOOD
FROM OUR FULLY ORGANIC ESTATES, WITH A PASSIONATE
COMMITMENT TO QUALITY. WE PRACTICE COMPASSIONATE
FARMING AND SUSTAINABILITY: ORGANIC BEEF, LAMB, VENISON,
AND POULTRY; HERITAGE VARIETY VEGETABLES, AND FRUITS;
AWARD-WINNING HANDMADE ORGANIC CHEESES; ORGANIC
BREADS, PASTRIES…. OUR STORE OFFERS CUSTOMERS
AN EXCEPTIONAL RANGE OF FOOD. DISCOVER THE TASTE
OF DAYLESFORD AT OUR CAFÉ, RECENTLY VOTED ORGANIC
RESTAURANT OF THE YEAR. TO FIND OUT MORE, OR TO
SHOP ONLINE, VISIT WWW.DAYLESFORDORGANIC.COM

DAYLESFORD ORGANIC FARMSHOP DAYLESFORD NEAR KINGHAM
GLOUCESTERSHIRE GL56 0YG
TELEPHONE 01608 731 700 EMAIL enquiries@daylesfordfarmshop.com
PLEASE CALL TO CHECK SEASONAL OPENING HOURS

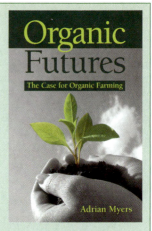

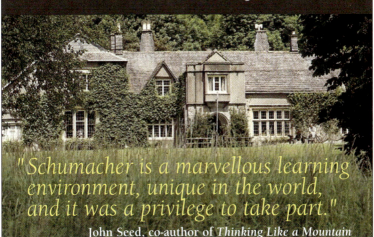

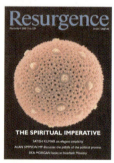

Centre for Alternative Technology
Mail Order

guilt-free
indulgence

Buy green by mail:

☎ **01654 705959**
mail.order@cat.org.uk

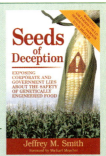

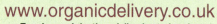

NORTH EAST ORGANIC GROWERS

EARTH BALANCE, WEST SLEEKBURN FARM, BOMARSUND, BEDLINGTON NE22 7AD
Tel: 01670 821070 Fax: 01670 821026 Contact: Cath Tyler
neog@care4free.net www.neog.co.uk
NEOG Ltd, a workers co-operative, has been running a box scheme since 1996 for
vegetables, fruit and eggs, serving Tyneside and Northumberland and more recently
County Durham. We grow a wide range of vegetables throughout the year including
salads and brassicas, and source also from the increasing number of local organic
growers. We were commended in the Organic Box Scheme of the Year Awards 2003.

NORTHUMBRIAN QUALITY MEATS

MONKRIDGE HILL FARM, WEST WOODBURN, HEXHAM NE48 2TU
Tel: 01434 270184 Fax: 01434 270320 Contact: Steve Ramshaw
enqs@northumbrian-organic-meat.co.uk www.northumbrian-organic-meat.co.uk
Distributor of organic beef, lamb and pork. Organic Food Awards 2004: Best
Beef/Sheep Farm; Fresh Meat Highly Commended.

ROCK MIDSTEAD ORGANIC FARM

ROCK MIDSTEAD, ROCK, ALNWICK NE66 2TH
Tel: 01665 579225 Contact: Beth Sutherland
ian@rockmidstead.freeserve.co.uk
No details available.

SMALES, LC & SON

THORNTON FARM, BERWICK-UPON-TWEED TD15 2LP
Tel: 01289 382223 Fax: 01289 382018 Contact: Jane Smales
janesmales@lcsmales-son.co.uk www.lcsmales-son.co.uk
Organic Farmers and Growers UKF040517. Produce, store and dry organic cereals.
Registered organic seed producer. Cater for all orders large and small.

STAKEFORD NURSERIES

EAST VIEW, STAKEFORD NE62 5TR
Tel: 01670 855130 Fax: 01670 855130 Contact: Derek Easton
Soil Association G2080. Producer of organic vegetables, herbs and tomatoes in modules and pots.

WHISTLEBARE

BOWSDEN, BERWICK-UPON-TWEED TD15 2TG
Tel: 01289 388777 Fax: 08700 941608 Contact: Alice & Dominic Elsworth
alice@whistlebare.co.uk www.whistlebare.co.uk
Artisan cured bacon, charcuterie and fresh pork from our pedigree Large Black pigs as well as beef from our grass-fed herd of pedigree Aberdeen Angus cattle. All meat is properly hung.

Watering the Fields

Every day, people in Britain excrete about 18 million gallons of urine. Most of it is flushed away. That day's urine contains an estimated 1.4 million pounds of nutrients in the form of nitrogen. By some estimates, that's enough nitrogen to fertilize up to 6,000 acres of maize in one year. And one year of UK urine could fertilize over two million acres of maize!

From *Liquid Gold: The Lore and Logic of Using Urine to Grow Plants* by Carol Steinfeld, Green Books. £4.95.

 Accommodation Garden and Farm Sundries Producers

 Box Schemes/ Local Deliveries Farmers' market Stall Restaurants/ Cafés/Caterers

Day Visits Manufacturers/ Processors Retail shops

Eco Products Importers/ exporters Textiles

 Farm Gate Sales Mail order suppliers Wholesalers

Nottinghamshire

FARMSHOP HOME DELIVERY

SHACKERDALE, FOSSE RD., CAR COLSTON, NR. BINGHAM NG13 8JB
Tel: 0800 169 7009 Fax: 01949 829124 Contact: David Rose
order@farmshop.net www.farmshop.net
Soil Association Licence applied for. The complete home delivery service for people living in the East Midlands.

HAYWOOD OAKS ORGANICS

HAYWOOD OAKS, BLIDWORTH, MANSFIELD NG21 0PE
Tel: 01623 795000 Fax: 01623 792268 Contact: Jamie Speed-Andrews
enquiries@haywoodoaks.com www.haywoodoaks.com
Soil Association G4551; P9058. Organic vegetable growers with nearly 500 acres of certified organic land. We aim to supply our produce locally where possible. Suppliers to wholesalers, retailers, box schemes, packers. Washing and packing facilities available. Delivery possible throughout the UK.

THE NATURAL FOOD CO

37 MANSFIELD ROAD, NOTTINGHAM NG1 3FB
Tel: 0115 955 9914 Fax: 0115 955 9914 Contact: Oren Harkavi
oren@naturalfoodcompany.net
We are a well stocked wholefoods shop. Organic lines expanding all the time: cereals, honeys, pulses, grains, condiments, teas, coffee, chocolate, baby foods, etc.

THE NATURAL FOOD CO

31 LONG ACRE, BINGHAM NG13 8AF
Tel: 01949 876483 Fax: 01949 876483 Contact: Oren Harkavi
oren@naturalfoodcompany.net
We are a well stocked wholefoods shop. Organic lines expanding all the time: cereals, honeys, pulses, grains, condiments, teas, coffee, chocolate, baby foods, etc.

NOTTINGHAM CITY COUNCIL

GREEN'S MILL & SCIENCE CENTRE, WINDMILL LANE, SNEINTON,
NOTTINGHAM NG2 4QB
Tel: 0115 915 6878 Fax: 0115 915 6875 Contact: David Bent
enquiries@greensmill.org.uk www.greensmill.org.uk
Soil Association P4518. Museum: a working tower windmill built in 1807, once
operated by the mathematician George Green (1793–1841) Now producing organic stoneground flours, including Organic Foods award-winning wholemeal and white
spelt flour. Organic Food Awards 2004: Flour Highly Commended.

ONIONS (FARMS), PJ

SHELTON LODGE, NR. NEWARK NG23 5JJ
Tel: 01949 850268 Fax: 01949 850714 Contact: Peter Onions
Organic cereal and pulse storage, drying and cleaning. TASCC-registered food
standards bagging line available to bag out of bulk storage.

OUT OF THIS WORLD

VILLA ST., BEESTON, NOTTINGHAM NG9 2NY
Tel: 0115 943 1311 Contact: Nigel Clifton
info@ootw.co.uk www.outofthisworld.coop
Small chain of ethical and organic supermarkets in Newcastle-upon-Tyne, Leeds
and Nottingham. Selling over 4,000 products, most food products certified
organic, plus fairly traded crafts, recycled paper and bodycare products etc.
Consumer co-op with over 17,500 members.

ROOTS NATURAL FOODS

526 MANSFIELD RD., SHERWOOD, NOTTINGHAM NG5 2FR
Tel: 0115 960 9014 Contact: Ken Dyke
Pure vegetarian, organic retailer, box scheme and delivery service.

ROSEMARY'S HEALTH FOODS
6 LINCOLN STREET, NOTTINGHAM NG1 3DJ
Tel: 0115 950 5072 Fax: 0115 950 5072 Contact: Tracey Marshall (Manageress)
enquiries@rosemaryshealthfoods.co.uk www.rosemaryshealthfoods.co.uk
We sell an extensive range of organic healthy, dried, fresh, chilled, frozen foods and
herbal remedies.

SHOULS, DI
BARN FARM COTTAGE, KNEETON ROAD, EAST BRIDGFORD NG13 8PJ
Tel: 01949 20196 Contact: Di Shouls
B&B £20 per person per night. A warm welcome awaits you here in this delightful
cottage overlooking the Trent Valley. Three large bedrooms, two sitting rooms, two
bathrooms, garden, good off-road parking. Soil Association member of long standing.

TRINITY FARM
AWSWORTH LANE, COSSALL NG16 2RZ
Tel: 0115 944 2545 Fax: 0115 944 2545 Contact: LR Winter
orders@trinityfarm.co.uk www.trinityfarm.co.uk
Meat, veg, salad, fruit. Farm shop with full range of dairy and dried goods
including nursery stock.

From 'Enclosure'

Ye fields, ye scenes so dear to Lubin's eye,
Ye meadow-blooms, ye pasture-flowers, farewell!
Ye banish'd trees, ye make me deeply sigh—
Inclosure came, and all your glories fell:
E'en the old oak that crown'd yon rifled dell,
Whose age had made it sacred to the view,
Not long was left his children's fate to tell;
Where ignorance and wealth their course pursue,
Each tree must tumble down—'old Lea-Close Oak',
adieu!

**by John Clare, in *Landscape into Literature*,
edited by Kay Dunbar, Green Books, £10.00.**

Oxfordshire

BARRINGTON PARK ESTATE
GREAT BARRINGTON, BURFORD OX18 4US
Tel: 01451 843015 Fax: 01451 844705 Contact: Adrian Dolby
adrian@barrington-park.co.uk
Situated in the Cotswold hills producing organic beef, lamb, eggs and arable crops.

BEANBAG NATURAL HEALTH
2 WESLEY WALK, WITNEY OX28 6ZJ
Tel: 01993 773922 Fax: 01993 708689 Contact: John Bright
john@beanbag-health.co.uk www.beanbag-health.co.uk
Vegetarian health food shop—over 250 organic products. Meat-free, dairy-free,
gluten-free, wheat-free. Pick-up point for Coleshill Organics box scheme.

BRITISH BAKELS
GRANVILLE WAY, OFF LAUNTON RD., BICESTER OX26 4JT
Tel: 01869 247098 Fax: 01869 242979 Contact: PJ Hemson
phemson@bakels.com www.bakels.com
Ingredient supplier. Manufacturers of organic cake mixes, scone mixes, muffin
mixes, bread improvers, crumb softeners and baking powders. National distribution.

CHIPPING NORTON ORGANICS
UNIT 11, ELMSFIELD INDUSTRIAL ESTATE, CHIPPING NORTON OX7 5XL
Tel: 01608 642973 Fax: 01608 642973 Contact: Serena Howard
sales@chippingnortonorganics.co.uk www.chippingnortonorganics.co.uk
Soil Association registered no. R1816. Wide range of local, UK and imported veg
and fruit. Boxes made up to suit individual requirements. Also bread, eggs, milk, all
organic. Weekly deliveries 15 mile radius of Chipping Norton.

COTSWOLD HONEY LTD

AVENUE 3, STATION LANE, WITNEY OX28 4HZ
Tel: 01993 703294 Fax: 01993 774227 Contact: N Dixon
neil@cotswoldhoney.co.uk www.cotswoldhoney.co.uk
Processor and bottler of organic honey for retail and industrial use.

ELLIOTT, R & S

BOW FARM, C/O 21–23 HIGH ST., STANFOLD IN THE VALE SN7 8LH
Tel: 01367 710595 Fax: 01367 710640 Contact: Robert Elliott
relliott@btconnect.com
Soil Association G4141. Old Gloucester (rare breed) herd; organic certification;
breeding and fattening/finishing stock available periodically. Please ring to discuss.

ELLIS ORGANICS

LITTLE BOTTOM FARM, COLLIERS LANE, READING RG9 5LT
Tel: 0118 972 2826 Fax: 0118 972 4187 Contact: Aidan Carlisle
ellis-organics@clara.net www.eatorganic.co.uk
Home delivery of a comprehensive range of organic foods to local people in and
around Reading and Henley-on-Thames. Established for over 18 years, the quality
and range of our fresh organic produce is legendary. Please visit our web site
for details. Eco goods available to order.

FELLER, SON & DAUGHTER M.

54/55 COVERED MARKET, OXFORD OX1 3DY
Tel: 01865 251164 Fax: 01865 200553 Contact: Mike or Mitzi Feller
Soil Association P4455. Family organic butcher shop. Local delivery service available.

FINE LADY BAKERIES LTD

SOUTHAM ROAD, BANBURY OX16 7RR
Tel: 01295 227600 Fax: 01295 271430 Contact: David Howlett
info@finelady.co.uk
Fine Lady Bakeries Ltd produce a range of organic bread and rolls for both the
retail and sandwich making industries. Soil Association Licence No P1543.

FRUGAL FOOD

17 WEST SAINT HELEN ST., ABINGDON OX14 5BL
Tel: 01235 522239 Contact: Val Stoner
Independent wholefood and organic grocery with friendly knowledgeable staff,
selling a wide range of food, drink, supplements, remedies, cleaning products,
bodycare and special diets.

GLUTTONS DELICATESSEN

110 WALTON STREET, OXFORD OX2 6AJ
Tel: 01865 553748 Contact: Adrian Tennissen
Friendly family-run delicatessen specialising in excellent home-cooked foods.
Comprehensive range of local and organic produce, large selection of organic wines.

IVY COTTAGE CAMPING

SULGRAVE ROAD, CULWORTH, BANBURY OX17 2AP
Tel: 01295 768131 Contact: J McKenzie (Proprietor)
Seasonal organic fruit and veg, free range eggs, geese, ducks, chickens, cats.
Many attractions nearby, easy distance to Oxford, Stratford and Warwick. Garden
flat for minimum of 6 monthly let. Camping field available £6 per tent per night
plus £1 per person.

MATTHEWS LTD, FWP—THE COTSWOLD FLOUR MILLERS

STATION RD., SHIPTON UNDER WYCHWOOD, CHIPPING NORTON OX7 6BH
Tel: 01993 830342 Fax: 01993 831615 Contact: Joy McCarthy
sales@fwpmatthews.co.uk www.fwpmatthews.co.uk
Soil Association P1521. Flour millers. An independent, family-owned flour mill
producing high quality organic flours, supplying all markets from the home
bread-maker to bakers' shops to large food production companies.

MUTCHMEATS LTD

NEWCLOSE LANE, WITNEY OX29 7GX
Tel: 01993 772972 Fax: 01993 776239 Contact: Andrew Mutch
Abattoir. Private kill facility.

NEAL'S YARD REMEDIES

56 HIGH ST., OXFORD OX1 4AS
Tel: 01865 245436 Fax: 01865 245436 Contact: Mark Higgins
mark.higgins@lineone.net www.nelsyardremedies.com
Supplier of organic natural medicines and natural cosmetics.

NEW SEASONS

THE OLD POST OFFICE, LOCKINGE, WANTAGE OX12 8QD
Tel: 01235 821110 Fax: 01235 834294 Contact: John Breakspear
jb@newseasons.co.uk www.newseasons.co.uk
Essential oils, vegetable oils, flower waters, massage oils, bath oils, bath milk, bath salts, face & body spritzers, room sprays, creams and lotions.

NORTH ASTON ORGANICS

3 SOMERTON RD., NORTH ASTON OX25 6HP
Tel: 01869 347702 Fax: 01869 347702 Contact: Mark Stay
We grow a wide range of vegetables and culinary herbs. We are committed to local delivery (20 mile radius) and freshness, with many items harvested on day of delivery.

PICKLES

8 UPPER HIGH ST., THAME OX9 3ER
Tel: 01844 212056 Contact: Heather Brown
www.picklesdeli.co.uk
Delicatessen specialising in fine food with café area and special diet products.

REAL FARM FOODS

BLANDYS FARMHOUSE, LETCOMBE REGIS, WANTAGE OX12 9LJ
Tel: 08080 067426 Fax: 01235 772526 Contact: Diane Glass
info@realfarmfoods.com www.realfarmfoods.com
Real Farm Foods delivers fresh organic meat, poultry, eggs, fruit, vegetables and groceries as well as fresh fish direct to your door with no delivery charge throughout the UK. Call Freephone 08080 067426 for a catalogue.

RED KITE FARMS

SOUTHEND FARM, TURVILLE HEATH, HENLEY ON THAMES RG9 6JR
Tel: 01491 638155 Fax: 01491 638633 Contact: Clare Pool
clare@redkitefarms.com www.redkitefarms.com
Mixed organic farm with 400 dairy cows and 1,650 acres. Small on-farm milk
processing unit.

RIVER NENE HOME DELIVERY (NORTHAMPTONSHIRE/OXON)

22 TOWRISE, SULGRAVE, BANBURY OX17 2SB
Tel: 01295 760936 Fax: 01295 760936 Contact: Rob Smith
robandrachel@rivernene.co.uk www.rivernene.co.uk
Award-winning organic vegetable box scheme delivering in Northamptonshire and
north Oxon, offering differing box sizes to suit all households, from single occupants
to a large family. A selection of fruit, dairy products, wine, fruit juices etc. also
available. Order weekly or whenever you like. Order online at www.rivernene.co.uk
or by telephone on 0845 078 6868.

ROWSE HONEY LTD

MORETON AVENUE, WALLINGFORD OX10 9DE
Tel: 01491 827400 Fax: 01491 827434 Contact: Stuart Bailey (MD)
rowse.honey@rowsehoney.co.uk www.rowsehoney.co.uk
Importer and processor of organic honey from Argentina, New Zealand, Australia,
Mexico, Turkey and Brazil. Also importer and processor of organic pure Canadian
maple syrup. Soil Association no. P2375.

SARSDEN ORGANICS

WALLED GARDEN, SARSDEN ESTATE, CHIPPING NORTON OX7 6PW
Tel: 01608 659670 Fax: 01608 659670 Contact: Rachel Siegfried
sarsdenorganics@btopenworld.com
Two-acre walled garden producing a variety of vegetables and fruit for sale
locally on regular farmers' market in Oxford. Veg box including fruit herbs and
flowers for collection from the walled garden one day a week (Friday) by
pre-arranged order form.

SAUNDERS, M

STEP FARM, LECHLADE ROAD, FARINGDON SN7 8BH
Tel: 01367 240558 Fax: 01367 244324 Contact: Miles Saunders
miles@stepfarm.fsnet.co.uk
Sell organic lamb and beef, jointed and frozen. Opening times by arrangement.
Member of the Soil Association Organic Farms Network.

TOLHURST ORGANIC PRODUCE

WEST LODGE, HARDWICK, WHITCHURCH-ON-THAMES, PANGBOURNE, READING
RG8 7RA
Tel: 0118 984 3428 Fax: 0118 984 3428 Contact: Iain Tolhurst
tolhurstorganic@yahoo.co.uk
Organic growers since 1976. Box scheme deliveries to Reading and Oxford
drop-off points. We produce over 90% of the vegetables that we sell. Organic
fruit also available. Alternative phone 01865 556151.

UHURU WHOLEFOODS

48 COWLEY RD., OXFORD OX4 1HZ
Tel: 01865 248249 Contact: Annette Mngxitama
Uhuru has 30 years experience in the organic and natural wholefoods trade. Our
stock ranges from organic dairy produce to organic fruits and vegetables, wines
and beers. Monthly local home deliveries.

WARRINER SCHOOL FARM

THE WARRINER SCHOOL, BLOXHAM, BANBURY OX15 4LJ
Tel: 01295 720777 Fax: 01297 721676 Contact: John Hirons
www.atschool.eduweb.co.uk/warriner
The Warriner School Farm is a mixed 16-hectare farm based at the Warriner
School, a secondary comprehensive at Bloxham in Oxfordshire. A further 24
hectares are rented nearby. The farm is a purpose-built educational resource.
It provides a practical, relevant and realistic experience of farming, the rural envi-
ronment and land use to students from Warriner and other schools. Visit to find out
more about this innovative and increasingly rare school farm. Member of the Soil
Association Organic Farms Network.

WILLOWBROOK FARM
HAMPTON GAY OX5 2QQ
Tel: 01865 849957 Fax: 01865 849957 Contact: Ruby Radwan
radwans@btinternet.com www.willow-brook-farm.co.uk
Family farm in Cherwell Valley ESA (Environmentally Sensitive Area) specialising in eggs, table birds, lamb and goat.

Here's what I did to reduce my rubbish
- Fewer throwaway bottles and aluminium cans, mostly returnables.
- No paper plates, cups, serviettes, towels—I used cotton serviettes and towels.
- No aluminium foil or clingfilm—I covered leftovers with a plate or put them in a container with a lid.
- Fewer tin cans and glass jars—lots of fresh food instead.
- Recycled the newspaper, or didn't buy it.
- Composted all vegetable scraps (beginning with tea leaves under the bushes in the garden!).
- Began measuring my rubbish and jotting down my actions in a checklist.

When I saw how much smaller it got, I knew I was on the right track!

From *Ecology Begins at Home* by Archie Duncanson, Green Books, £4.95.

Accommodation	Garden and Farm Sundries	Producers	
Box Schemes/ Local Deliveries	Farmers' market Stall	Restaurants/ Cafés/Caterers	
Day Visits	Manufacturers/ Processors	Retail shops	
Eco Products	Importers/ exporters	Textiles	
Farm Gate Sales	Mail order suppliers	Wholesalers	

Shropshire

BEAFRESH LTD
UNIT 2C, ARCHERS WAY, KNIGHTS WAY, BATTLEFIELD ENTERPRISE PARK,
SHREWSBURY SY1 3AB
Tel: 01743 233011 Fax: 01743 233011 Contact: L Beaman
Vegetable processors. Specialists in preparing vegetables for the catering trade.

BELTON CHEESE CO LTD
BELTON, WHITCHURCH SY13 1JD
Tel: 01948 662125 Fax: 01948 662125 Contact: Brian Gresty
briangresty@beltoncheese.co.uk www.beltoncheese.co.uk
Soil Association registered. Manufacturer of organic cheese, Cheddar and English
Territorials.

BOXFRESH ORGANICS
UNIT 5C, RODENHURST BUSINESS PARK, RODINGTON SY4 4QU
Tel: 01952 770006 Contact: Des Walker
box.fresh@virgin.net www.boxfreshorganics.co.uk
Delivery service of a wide range of organic fruit, veg, eggs, meat, dairy products
and honey. We deliver in Shropshire, Staffordshire, West Midlands and Cheshire.
Excellent, reliable customer service, easy on-line ordering, with the accent very
much on locally grown produce. Alternative telephone 07786 918322.

BROAD BEAN
60 BROAD STREET, LUDLOW SY8 1NH
Tel: 01584 874239 Contact: Maxwell Miller
Retailers of organic wines, dairy produce, meat, wholefoods and fine foods,
plus essential oils, vitamins, supplements, relaxation tapes, Brita water filters and
cartridges. Collection point for local vegetable box scheme.

THE CHICKEN CAME FIRST

LYNTON MEAD, OUTWOODS, NEWPORT TF10 9EB
Tel: 01952 691418 Contact: Clare Draper
clareword@btconnect.com
Soil Association G7745. Cruelty-free eggs from happy hens. Mixed colours
(chocolate brown, white green and blue shells). One-day workshops on keeping
chickens at home. As seen on Rick Stein's 'Food Heroes'.

CORVEDALE ORGANIC LAMB

CORVE HOUSE, ROWE LANE, STANTON LONG, MUCH WENLOCK TF13 6LR
Tel: 01746 712539 Fax: 01746 712539 Contact: Paul Mantle
mantlepaul@hotmail.com
Soil Association G4606. Organic lamb direct from farm to customer, traditional
English breeds, traditional taste, no order too small, free delivery in South
Shropshire area.

COW HALL ORGANIC PRODUCE

BETTWS Y CRWYN, CLUN, CRAVEN ARMS SY7 8PG
Tel: 01588 640307 Contact: The Manager
Soil Association producer no. G4116: organic Hereford beef, Clun Forest and
Kerry Hill lamb, and organic seed and eating potatoes. Outlet at Myriad Organics
(see below).

DOGGART, A

THE POPLARS, GWERN-Y-BRENIN, OSWESTRY SY10 8AR
Tel: 01691 652166 Fax: 01691 652166 Contact: A Doggart
Limited box scheme. I supply mainly to local wholefood shop, Honeysuckle in
Church Street, Oswestry, and also other fruit and vegetable outlets in the area,
including Llanfyllin.

EARTHWORM HOUSING CO-OP LTD
WHEATSTONE, LEINTWARDINE SY7 0LH
Tel: 01547 540461 Contact: Hil Mason
Suppliers of willow for basket-making, hurdles etc, venue for low cost hire for camps, courses, meetings. Demonstration wetland system and organic/veganic gardens. WWOOF host farm.

ELLESMERE ROAD ORGANIC NURSERY
ELLESMERE ROAD ORGANIC NURSERY, COCKSHUTT, ELLESMERE SY12 9AB
Tel: 01939 270270 Contact: RD Anderson
Soil Association G1447. All produce grown on our nursery. Vegetables, salads and fruit fresh-picked, also PYO fruit.

FOOD FOR THOUGHT
UNIT 3 HEATH HILL INDUSTRIAL ESTATE, DAWLEY, TELFORD TF4 2RH
Tel: 01952 630145 Fax: 01952 630145 Contact: Alastair Dargue
info@liveorganic.com www.liveorganic.com
Soil Association R2086. Organic food home delivery service covering Telford, Shrewsbury, Bridgnorth and Much Wenlock. Wide range of organic, Fairtraded and eco-friendly products. Long-established family business.

FORDHALL FARM
TERN HILL RD., MARKET DRAYTON TF9 3PS
Tel: 01630 638255 Contact: Charlotte Hollins
info@fordhallorganicfarm.co.uk www.fordhallorganicfarm.co.uk
We sell home-reared, grass-fed beef and lamb. Our pastures have been organic for 60+ years and livestock are organically reared. Not currently registered but working with the Soil Association and other environmental organisations to secure the farm's future. Farm shop and nature trail open Friday to Sunday. Visit our website for the full story of Fordhall Farm.

GET REAL (ORGANIC FOODS) LIMITED
SHOTTON FARM, SHOTTON LANE, HARMER HILL, SHREWSBURY SY4 3DN
Tel: 01939 210925 Fax: 01939 210925 Contact: Sue Gwilliam
info@get-real.co.uk www.get-real.co.uk
Manufacturers of organic meat-free pies and ready meals for major retailers,
independent health food stores and via mail order.

GREENVALE AP LTD
WARRANT RD., STOKE HEATH, MARKET DRAYTON TF9 2JJ
Tel: 01630 637444 Fax: 01630 638939 Contact: Craig Sankey
post@greenvale.co.uk www.greenvale.co.uk
Package and trade organic potatoes and make organic dehydrated potato flake,
sell organic potato seed.

GROCONTINENTAL LTD
WHITCHURCH BUSINESS PARK, SHAKESPEAR WAY, WHITCHURCH SY13 1JL
Tel: 01948 666600 Contact: Hugh Jones
hughjones@grocontinental.co.uk www.grocontinental.co.uk
Ingredients and fruit sorting. Multi-temperature storage and distribution with
associated added value services; ingredient sorting; blast freezing and re-packing.

GUNTON, JOHN & JACKIE
GREEN GORSE WOOD, WHITCHURCH RD, PREES SY13 3JZ
Tel: 01948 841376 Contact: John & Jackie Gunton
30 years on and we still grow organically and by hand, a wide range of
vegetables and some fruit which we pick fresh and sell exclusively from our own
stall on Whitchurch (Shropshire) traditional Friday Market throughout the year.

HARVEST WHOLEFOODS
LYDHAM, BISHOPS CASTLE SY9 5HB
Tel: 01588 638990 Fax: 01588 630298 Contact: Sue Jones
We stock a wide range of wholefoods, organically grown fruit and vegetables, herbs
and spices, natural remedies, environmental and biodegradable products, special
dietary foods etc.. Bulk discounts to order. Open Monday to Saturday 9am–5.30pm.

HONEYSUCKLE WHOLEFOOD CO-OPERATIVE LTD
53 CHURCH ST., OSWESTRY SY11 2SZ
Tel: 01691 653125 Contact: Barbara Farr
hwcl@madasafish.com
Soil Association P5639. Established in 1978, we sell a large range of organic
fresh vegetables and fruit, locally grown when available. Also a wide selection
of organic wholefoods and dairy products; also local bread, eggs and honey.

HOPE ORGANIC PRODUCE
HOPE HOUSE, SANDY LANE, STOKE HEATH, MARKET DRAYTON TF9 2LG
Tel: 01630 638348 Contact: Pete & Sue Bartram
pete@hopeorganicproduce.co.uk www.hopeorganicproduce.co.uk
Soil Association B42M. Herb plants, seasonal vegetables sold in local shops, garden
centres and farmers' markets.

HOPESAY GLEBE FARM
HOPESAY, CRAVEN ARMS SY7 8HD
Tel: 01588 660737 Contact: Nicky & Phil Moore
phil.moore@hopesay.freeserve.co.uk
Family-run organic smallholding selling at Birmingham and Moseley farmers'
markets and Shrewsbury indoor market every Saturday. We also offer self-catering
accommodation and B&B.

LONG MOUNTAIN DAIRY
THE HOLE FARM, ASTON PIGOTT, WESTBURY SY5 9HH
Tel: 01743 891231 Contact: Holly Middleton
holly@theholefarm.freeserve.co.uk
Organic dairy producer/processor. Main produce: milk, cheese, yoghurt, veal, beef,
locally available through market stall.

MASON, IAN AND RUTH

FIVE ACRES, FORD, SHREWSBURY SY5 9LL
Tel: 01743 850832 Contact: Ruth Mason
iangmason@btinternet.com www.organicapples.co.uk
Growers of over 80 varieties of apples, 15 varieties of plums, soft fruits in season
and free some vegetables. Soil Association no. G1457.

MYRIAD ORGANICS

22 CORVE STREET, LUDLOW SY8 1DA
Tel: 01584 872665 Fax: 01584 879356 Contact: Jane Straker
Soil Assn. R5414. One-stop organic food shop: all you need for a family shop plus
clothing, seeds, books. Nr. Ludlow Station, customer parking. Friendly, well informed staff.

ORGANIC BY ORDER

BENTLEY HOUSE, CLUNGUNFORD, CRAVEN ARMS SY7 0PN
Tel: 01588 660747 Fax: 01588 660126 Contact: G Lambert
enquiries@organicbyorder.co.uk www.organicbyorder.co.uk
Soil Association GCS012, G1915, P1916. Organic vegetables and fruit delivered
throughout Shropshire, north Herefordshire and west Staffordshire.

THE ORGANIC SMOKEHOUSE

CLUNBURY HALL, CLUNBURY, NR. CRAVEN ARMS SY7 0HG
Tel: 01588 660206 Fax: 01588 660206 Contact: Michael & Deborah Leviseur
info@organicsmokehouse.com www.organicsmokehouse.com
Multi award-winning artisan organic smokehouse, specialising in smoking salmon,
various types of cheese, butter and salt. Smoking is carried out using traditional
'draft' method. Soil Assn. no. P8263. Organic Food Awards 2004: Fish Winner.

PIMHILL FARM AND MILL

LEA HALL, HARMER HILL, SHREWSBURY SY4 3DY
Tel: 01939 290342 Fax: 01939 291156 Contact: Ginny Mayall
info@pimhillorganic.co.uk
Growers and millers of organic cereals, supplying wholemeal flour, porridge oats
and muesli.

RSPB LAKE VYRNWY

BRYN AWEL, LLANWDDYN SY10 0LZ
Tel: 01691 870278 Fax: 01691 870313 Contact: Jo Morris
jo.morris@rspb.org.uk www.rspb.org.uk
RSPB rears and produces organic lamb and beef. The lamb is sold locally through the RSPB shop at Lake Vyrnwy. The farm is part of a National Nature Reserve in the Berwyns. It is a viable business and farmed to be wildlife-friendly.

SHIBUMI

23 DOGPOLE, SHREWSBURY SY1 1ES
Tel: 01743 235822 Fax: 01691 682113 Contact: Lynda Adlington
Infor@shibumi-living.com www.shibumi-living.com
Our first store opened in Shrewsbury in August 2004, and the website offers the same services of information, advice and on-line shopping. Here you can find out the latest information on natural health supplements, natural bodycare products, healthy organic food, organic linen and yoga wear, Fairtrade items and much more.

THE SHROPSHIRE ORGANIC WINE COMPANY

GLEBELANDS, 25 KNIGHTON ROAD, CLUN SY7 8JH
Tel: 01588 640442 Fax: 01588 640442 Contact: John Adamson
info@organicwine-online.co.uk www.organicwine-online.co.uk
We import organic wine from personally selected vineyards in Beaujolais, Burgundy and Côte du Rhone. Nationwide deliveries to individuals and retail outlets. Emphasis on quality over quantity.

SHROPSHIRE SPICE COMPANY

UNIT 10 THE GREEN IND. ESTATE, CLUN, CRAVEN ARMS SY7 8LG
Tel: 01588 640100 Fax: 01588 640900 Contact: Jenny Jones
office@shropshire-spice.co.uk www.shropshire-spice.co.uk
Soil Association P4316. Manufacturers of dried stuffing mixes: sage & onion, parsley & thyme, celery & leek, garlic herb & mushroom which we supply to the multiples, wholesalers and retail outlets.

SWIFT, RICHARD C—BAKER & CONFECTIONER

CENTRAL BAKERY, HIGH ST., CLEE HILL, NR. LUDLOW SY8 3LZ
Tel: 01584 890003 Fax: 01584 891317 Contact: Robert Swift
www.bakery.co.uk/swifts
A traditional family craft bakery offering a range of five different organic breads, including organic white, brown, honey and sunflower, sunflower and soya and 100% rye. All hand-crafted.

WARD, DE & H

MANOR FARM, CRICKHEATH, OSWESTRY SY10 8BN
Tel: 01691 830262 Contact: David Ward
wardmanorfarm@btinternet.com
Fully organic dairy farm (we grow some organic corn).

WESTHOPE COLLEGE

WESTHOPE COLLEGE, CRAVEN ARMS SY7 9JL
Tel: 01584 861293 Contact: Anne Dyer www.westhope.org.uk
Soil Association No. G4886. Adult education weekend and weekly courses, C&G exams. Depth of the country, organic food.

WHEELER, S & SON

BRYNMAWR NEWCASTLE, CRAVEN ARMS SY7 8QU
Tel: 01588 640298 Fax: 01588 640298 Contact: Trev Wheeler
brynmawr@farmersweekly.net www.brynmawrorganics.co.uk
Soil Association G6570. Mixed hill farm with caravan accommodation, specialising in potatoes, carrots and daffodil bulbs.

WILD THYME WHOLEFOODS

1/2 CASTLE GATES, SHREWSBURY SY1 2AQ
Tel: 01743 364559 Contact: Jan Bridges
A wide range of organic and natural products including fresh fruit and vegetables, nuts, pulses, snacks, beverages, bodycare, household, local crafts and complementary medicines.

ALHAM WOOD CHEESES
HIGHER ALHAM FARM, WEST CRANMORE, SHEPTON MALLET BA4 6DD
Tel: 01749 880221 Contact: Frances Wood
www.buffalo-cheese.co.uk
Organic cheeses and dairy produce from our own herds of organic buffalo and cow.
A variety of soft and hard buffalo cheese made with buffalo milk from our own
organic herd, also buffalo meat and beef from same organic herds and buffalo
yoghurt in glass jars (therefore not by mail order).

ALVIS BROS LTD
LYE CROSS FARM, REDHILL, BRISTOL BS40 5RH
Tel: 01934 864600 Fax: 01934 862213 Contact: Mike O'Brien
abl.alvisbros@virgin.net www.lyecrosscheese.co.uk
Soil Association P1542. Organic farmhouse cheese-maker/packer of the renowned
Lye Cross Farm brand. Full range of organic cheddars, UK territorials and cheese
powder. All suitable for vegetarians. Nationwide distribution and farm shop.

ARCADIA ORGANICS
CLOVER NURSERY, STREAMCROSS, LOWER CLAVERHAM, NR. BRISTOL BS49 4QA
Tel: 01934 838634 Contact: Rosey Knifton
rosey@arcadiaorganics.com www.arcadiaorganics.com
Soil Association Symbol holder no. G1866. 20-acre organic market garden produc-
ing vegetables for our local box scheme delivering in North Somerset.

AVALON VINEYARD
THE DROVE, EAST PENNARD, SHEPTON MALLET BA4 6UA
Tel: 01749 860393 Contact: Hugh Tripp
pennardorganicwines@mail.com www.pennardorganicwines.co.uk
Soil Association P/T15W. Our organically grown grapes and other fruits we make into
table wine and a range of different fruit wines. We also make mead from organic
honey, also traditional Somerset cider, and we now produce bottled apple juice.

BATH ORGANIC COMMUNITY GARDEN

C/O 28 ASHLEY AVENUE, BATH BA1 3DS
Tel: 01225 312116 Contact: TJ Baines
tim@bathorganicgroup.org.uk
Community garden on inner city allotment site providing training, employment
and volunteering opportunities for the local community. Courses and workshops.
Open days. Plant sales. Open every Saturday 10am–1pm.

BATH ORGANIC FARMS

6 BROOKSIDE HOUSE, WESTON, BATH BA
Tel: 01225 421507 Contact: Paul Robinson
www.bathorganicfarms.co.uk
Soil Association R7796. Supply from our own farms. Beef, lamb, pork, poultry
and milk, cheese, eggs, fresh vegetables from local organic producers.
Restaurant/café. Organic Food Awards 2004: Fresh Meat Highly Commended.

BATH SOFT CHEESE/PARK FARM B&B

PARK FARM, KELSTON, BATH BA1 9AG
Tel: 01225 331601 Fax: 01225 331906 Contact: Graham Padfield
bathsoftcheese@hotmail.com www.bathsoftcheese.co.uk
Soil Association G6169. Handmade soft and blue cheese made from our own milk,
also Wife of Bath hard cheese. Mail order available, B&B in charming farmhouse.

BORN

134 WALCOT ST, ST. SWITHINS YARD, BATH BA1 5BG
Tel: 01225 311212 Fax: 01225 334434 Contact: Eva Fernandes
info@borndirect.com www.borndirect.com
Retail and internet shop specialising in organic, natural and practical products for
parents and their babies. We're the experts on washable cotton nappies! Organic
range includes organic cotton and wool babywear (underwear, nightwear, outerwear
and bedding), organic herbal teas for pregnancy and afterwards, toiletries made
with organic ingredients (Weleda, Green People, Urtekram), organic massage oils.
We are open Monday–Saturday 9.30–5.30.

BOWERINGS ANIMAL FEEDS LTD

THE DOCKS, BRIDGEWATER TA6 3EX
Tel: 01278 458191 Fax: 01278 445159 Contact: B Bowering
ben@boweringsfeeds.co.uk
Soil Association P2246. Manufacturers of organic compound feed for all stock.
Suppliers of blends, straights and seeds.

BRIDIE'S HEALTHY LIVING CENTRE AND ORGANIC FOOD CO-OP

UNIT 1A, NORTHOVER BUILDINGS, BECKERY OLD RD, GLASTONBURY BA6 9NU
Tel: 01458 830577 Contact: Simon Ganz
simonganz@hotmail.com
We are practising and promoting all forms of healthy sustainable living, recognising
raw organic food as being vital to sustain ourselves and our environment.

BROWN COW ORGANICS

PERRIDGE FARM, PILTON, SHEPTON MALLET BA4 4EW
Tel: 01749 890298 Contact: Judith Freane
organics@browncoworganics.co.uk
Soil Association G2130, P6108. Award-winning beef (Organic Food Awards
2001–2003) pork, poultry, vegetables, ready prepared meals and dairy products
delivered to your door. As featured on Rick Stein's 'Food Heroes' and BBC Radio
4's 'The Food Programme'. Member of the Soil Association Organic Farms Network.
Organic Food Awards 2004: Fresh Meat Winner.

BRYMORE SCHOOL FARM TRUST

BRYMORE SCHOOL, CANNINGTON, BRIDGWATER TA5 2NB
Tel: 01278 652428 Fax: 01278 653244 Contact: A Nurton
We are a secondary school of agriculture, horticulture and engineering with a
mixed farm enterprise. We sell beef and table birds through farmers' markets
and pork, lamb and free range eggs privately.

BURDGE, JC

FENSWOOD FARM, SAYS LANE, LANGFORD, NR. BRISTOL BS40 5DZ
Tel: 01934 852639 Contact: Jim Burdge
Soil Association G4489. We are producers of organic beef, pork and lamb using traditional breeds, i.e. Devon x Cattle, Hampshire Down sheep. Organic meat delivered locally at reasonable prices.

CASTLE FARM

MIDFORD, BATH BA2 7BU
Tel: 01225 344420 Fax: 01225 344420 Contact: Mark Edwards
markvedwards@blueyonder.co.uk
Established organic growers and producers. Organic beef, herbs, fruit and vegetables. Farm gate sales and local box delivery service.

CERES NATURAL FOODS LTD

9–11 PRINCES STREET, YEOVIL BA20 1EN
Tel: 01935 428791 Fax: 01935 426862 Contact: Peter Jenkins
info@ceresfoods,com www.ceresfoods.com
We are lacto-vegetarians and so do not sell meat or fish products, but supply foods from vegan through to those containing eggs, honey and dairy products. Our organic shop has own label organic and natural food ranges packed fresh in-house. Our food ranges include organic, gluten-free, dairy-free, sugar-free, ethnic, local produce and special diet needs. Non-food ranges include supplements, herbals, homoeopathics, aromatherapy, magnatherapy, flower remedies, ecological cleaning products, books, hardware and more. We recycle packaging materials.

COBBS WHOLEFOODS

NO. 7, BRUNEL PRECINCT, SOMERTON TA11 7PY
Tel: 01458 274066 Contact: Jane Close
Cobbs specialise in stocking locally sourced organic produce including fruit, veg and local organic free range eggs; organic specialist breads and gluten-free foods available daily. We also stock all-organic wholefoods.

COOMBE FARM
COOMBE FARM, ROUNDHAM, CREWKERNE TA18 8RR
Tel: 01460 279500 Fax: 01460 77349 Contact: Bob Pearce
info@coombefarm.com www.coombefarm.com
Producers and distributors of organic cheese, butter, cream, milk and also
bespoke fruit recipes for the food industry.

COUNTRY HARVEST
8 ST. JAMES COURTYARD, TAUNTON TA1 1JR
Tel: 01823 252843 Contact: Jill
Wholefoods, organic and gluten-free foods. Supplements, herbal and homoeopathic
remedies, pick-up point for box schemes, qualified staff. Local deliveries to post
code areas TA1, TA2, TA3, TA4, TA6.

COURT FARM
14 CHAPEL LANE, WINFORD, BRISTOL BS18 8EU
Tel: 01275 472335 Contact: JR Twine
Biodynamic farm for 30 years—products from our own milk production. Natural
and fruit yoghurt, unpasteurised milk, double cream, free range pork and beef.
Local deliveries into Bristol. Organic Food Awards 2004: Yoghurt Commended.

CRABTREE & EVELYN
TYLERS END, HIGHBRIDGE TA9 4JS
Tel: 01278 780913 Fax: 01278 795461 Contact: Toni Reed
Manufacturer of high quality organic preserves, marmalades and sauces. Soil
Association reg. no. P4419.

DAISY AND CO
TREE TOPS FARM, NORTH BREWHAM, BRUTON BA10 0JS
Tel: 01749 850254 Fax: 01749 850815 Contact: Richard Harbord
sales@daisyandco.co.uk www.daisyandco.co.uk
Dairy farm making soft and hard cheese from the milk produced by the Jersey
cows on our farm.

DEMUTHS VEGETARIAN RESTAURANT
2 NORTH PARADE PASSAGE, BATH BA1 1NX
Tel: 01225 446059 Contact: Rachel Demuth
us@demuths.co.uk www.demuths.co.uk
Demuths' food is exciting 'world' food with lots of choice for vegans and those on wheat-free diets. We source as many local vegetables as possible and all our wines, beers and coffees are 100% organic. Our *Green World Cookbook* is available to buy from the restaurant.

EDCOMBE FARM
RODNEY STOKE, CHEDDAR BS27 3UP
Tel: 01749 870073 Contact: Robert Mann
Grow a variety of mixed vegetables sold mainly through Bristol Farmers' Market.

THE ELMS ORGANIC DAIRY
FRIARS OVEN FARM, WEST COMPTON, SHEPTON MALLET BA4 4PD
Tel: 01749 890371 Fax: 01749 890371 Contact: Gillian Stone
elms.organic.dairy@care4free.net
OF&G-registered. Producers of organic sheep and cow dairy products.

THE FILLING STATION
THE OLD FILLING STATION, LOPEN HEAD, SOUTH PETHERTON TA13 5JH
Tel: 01460 241666 Fax: 01460 242471 Contact: Steve Friend
Started June 1999 as a wholefood shop with fresh organic fruit and vegetables, cut flowers and household/conservatory plants. We also specialize in Christmas trees, turkeys, logs and coal—a one-stop Christmas shop.

FLAXDRAYTON FARM
2 BROOMHILL LANE, LOPEN, SOUTH PETHERTON TA13 5LA
Tel: 01460 241427 Fax: 01460 241427 Contact: Peter Foster
peter@flaxdrayton.fsnet.co.uk www.somersetorganiclink.co.uk
Organic vegetable grower marketing all produce through Somerset Organic Link, a co-operative formed by organic growers in south Somerset.

GALINGALE

3 VICTORIA GARDENS, HENSTRIDGE BA8 0RE
Tel: 01963 362702 Contact: Susan Place
galingaleorganic@aol.com
Soil Association G4112. Vegetables, fruit, herbs and eggs: 2 acres with polytunnels, raised beds and small orchard.

GENTLE LENTIL

35 FORE ST., WELLINGTON TA21 8AG
Tel: 01823 400297 Fax: 01823 400297 Contact: Colin Stephenson
A totally organic wholefood shop promoting vegetarianism and vegan foods.
Advice on babies and children is on offer, as well as a huge range of products.

GODMINSTER

GODMINSTER FARM, BRUTON BA10 ONE
Tel: 01749 813733 Fax: 01749 812059 Contact: Zara d'Abo
sales@godminster.com www.godminster.com
Mixed organic farm with a dairy herd, free range organic chickens, apple orchards and fruit and vegetable gardens. Our milk goes into making the renowned Godminster Vintage organic cheddar and we also supply eggs, table birds, jams, chutneys and flavoured vodkas—made with organic produce from the farm. We supply shops, mail order and local farmers' markets. Visitors for farm gate sales ring in advance.

THE GOOD EARTH

4 PRIORY RD., WELLS BA5 1SY
Tel: 01749 678600 Contact: Andrea Harrington
We have a wholefood shop and restaurant established over 25 years ago. Organic products account for a substantial amount of our business today. We have over 1,000 natural and organic products on sale, from a combination of local suppliers and wholesalers.

THE GREEN GROCER

THE OLD DAIRY, POOLBRIDGE ROAD, BLACKFORD, WEDMORE BS28 4PA
Tel: 01934 713453 Contact: Quentin Isaac
greengrocer@madasafish.com
Soil Association G4668. Our own organic fruit and vegetables are supplied to local
shops and available to order from ourselves for collection.

GREENS OF GLASTONBURY

NEWTON FARM, REDLAKE DAIRY, PAGE LANE, WEST PENNARD,
NR. GLASTONBURY BA6 8NN
Tel: 01458 834414 Fax: 01458 835072 Contact: Lloyd Green
greensofglastonbury@ukonline.co.uk
Soil Association P5176, Organic Farmers & Growers UKF040548. Family business
since 1920 making hand-made cylindrical cloth-bound farmhouse Cheddar and
Double Gloucester cheese, available as whole round or in quarters.

HARDWICK BROTHERS

COBBS CROSS FARM, GOATHURST, BRIDGWATER TA5 2DN
Tel: 01278 671359 Fax: 01278 671359 Contact: John Hardwick
We produce organic beef, lamb, poultry, potatoes, and run a mountain board cen-
tre and a three-bedroom holiday cottage. Day visits—educational and activity.

HARVEST NATURAL FOODS

37 WALCOT STREET, BATH BA1 5BN
Tel: 01225 465519 Fax: 01225 401143 Contact: Laura Petherbridge
shop@harvest-bath.co.uk
We are a GM-free store selling a wide range of organic produce: wine and
champagne, grains and mueslis, veg (all kinds), dried fruits (all kinds), yoghurt, milk,
soya milk, tofu, tea, gluten-free, herbs etc. We also have a delicatessen selling fresh
vegetarian and vegan produce.

HEART OF DEVON ORGANICS

C/O CROXLEY SUTTON ROAD, SOMERTON TA11 6QL
Tel: 01647 24894 Fax: 01647 24894 Contact: Geoff Jones
The largest sole wholesaler of quality organic fresh fruit and vegetables in the
South-West. Working closely with local and near continent growers (visit website).
Deliveries from M4 to Lands End.

HEAVEN-SENT ORGANIC HERBS

7 QUEENWOOD AVENUE, FAIRFIELD PARK, BATH BA1 6EU
Tel: 01225 425362 Contact: Susan Shiner
herbsheavensent@yahoo.co.uk
New business producing organic herbs for garden market.

HIGH STREET ORGANICS

57A HIGH ST., BRUTON BA10 0AW
Tel: 01749 813191 Fax: 01749 813191 Contact: Camilla Robbins
Small, friendly shop offers full range of organic foods including fresh fruit and veg-
etables, frozen, chilled and dry goods, also 'eco' cleaning products and toiletries.

HIGHER RISCOMBE FARM

HIGHER RISCOMBE FARM, EXFORD, NR. MINEHEAD TA24 7JY
Tel: 01643 831184 Contact: Rona Amiss
intray@higherriscombefarm.co.uk www.higherriscombefarm.co.uk
Soil Association G4852. Organic farm bed and breakfast in the heart of Exmoor
National Park. Spacious rooms, home cooking, panoramic views. Specialist
producers of organic Christmas geese, ducks and lamb. Mail order available.

HINDON ORGANIC FARM

HINDON ORGANIC FARM, NR MINEHEAD, EXMOOR TA24 8SH
Tel: 01643 705244 Fax: 01643 705244 Contact: Penny & Roger Webber
info@hindonfarm.co.uk www.hindonfarm.co.uk
Soil Association G2707, P6655. Winners of The Organic Producer of the Year
Award 2003/4. Organic Exmoor hill farm: meat produce, accommodation and farm
shop. Only off our own farm: quality traditionally hung Aberdeen Angus beef,
hill lamb, Gloucester Old Spot pork, dry cured bacon, home-cured ham and real
sausages. B&B—s/c cottage (English Tourism Council 4 star); luxury organic
breakfasts. Member of the Soil Association Organic Farms Network. Organic Food
Awards 2004: Fresh Meat Commended.

HOUSE, DJ, MJ & PW

DYKES FARM, SLOUGH LANE, STOKE ST. GREGORY, TAUNTON TA3 6JH
Tel: 01823 490349 Fax: 01823 491360 Contact: PW House
peterhouse@farming.co.uk
Soil Association G6571. Pedigree Friesian dairy herd. Dairy replacements for
sale, all ages available. Farm gate sales of unpasteurised milk to the public.

HUEGLI INDUSTRIAL FOODS

PRIORYFIELD HOUSE, 20 CANON ST., TAUNTON TA1 1SW
Tel: 01823 350950 Fax: 01823 350953 Contact: Richard Bailey
huegli2@btconnect.com www.huegli.com
Soil Association P6844, OF&G UKP0092. HIF is the European market leader in the
organic bouillon sector. Products include organic bouillons, sauces, soups, generic
seasonings, mustards and desserts.

ILCHESTER CHEESE CO LTD

SOMERTON RD., ILCHESTER BA22 8JL
Tel: 01935 842800 Fax: 01935 842801 Contact: Melvin Glynn
sales@ilchester.co.uk www.ilchester.co.uk
Speciality and traditional cheese manufacturer producing traditional organic
cheeses for the UK and export markets.

IYB PARTNERSHIP
STOWEY ROCKS FARM, OVER STOWEY, BRIDGWATER TA5 1JB
Tel: 01278 733080 Fax: 01278 733080 Contact: Ian & Yta Batchelor
Family partnership farming 82 acres organically. Enterprises include soft fruit, vegetables, eggs and livestock. Sales via farm gate (PYO) and wholesale.

THE LARDER
22 WEST STREET, WIVELISCOMBE, TAUNTON TA4 2JP
Tel: 01984 623236 Fax: 01984 623236 Contact: Les Webber
We are a specialist food shop selling a range of organic products including vegetables, dairy products, beans, pulses, grains, jams, marmalades, pastas, beverages, pet food, and more.

LEIGH COURT FARM
ABBOTS LEIGH, BRISTOL BS8 3RA
Tel: 01275 375756 Fax: 01275 375756 Contact: Chris Loughlin
mail@leighcourtfarm.org.uk www.leighcourtfarm.org.uk
Veg box scheme, Bristol Farmers' Market (June–December), volunteers, practical training, working with communities, not for profit, promoting local food economy, Delivery to Southville, Hotwells, Easton, Cotham & offices with more than 20 customers.

LONDON ROAD FOOD CO-OP
RIVERSIDE COMMUNITY CENTRE, YORK PLACE, LONDON ROAD, BATH BA1 6AE
Tel: 07837 784715
We provide our members with foods from local organic and Fairtrade sources at the lowest possible prices, including wholefoods, locally produced veg boxes and bread. Annual membership costs £1–£10 on a sliding scale.

LUBBORN CHEESE LTD
MANOR FARM, CRICKET ST. THOMAS, CHARD TA20 4BZ
Tel: 01460 30736 Contact: Christina Baskerville
christina@lubborn.co.uk www.lubborn.co.uk
Sole makers of Somerset Brie, Somerset Camembert and Capricorn goats cheese, all traditionally ripened for full flavour and a creamy texture. Organic Food Awards 2004: Cheese Highly Commended.

LUCAS AND LUCAS ORGANICS

NORWOOD FARM COTTAGE, BATH RD., NORTON ST. PHILIP, BATH BA2 7LP
Tel: 01373 834022 Contact: Dide Lucas dide@lucasorganics.co.uk
Growers of seasonal veg including unusual heritage veg in our show garden, plants
and transplants for sale. Fruit coming soon. Other services include garden design
and planning through to maintenance, advice, tree planting, hedge laying etc.

LYNG COURT ORGANIC MEAT

LYNG COURT, WEST LYNG, TAUNTON TA3 5AP
Tel: 01823 490510 Contact: R Lloyd Jones
Quality beef and lamb grazed on the Somerset Levels. Farm Gate sales and local delivery. Beef in 10kg mixed packs of joints, steaks etc., lamb jointed and packed to order.

MAGDALEN FARM

MAGDALEN FARM, WINSHAM, CHARD TA20 4PA
Tel: 01460 30144 Fax: 01460 30177 Contact: Peter Foster
Soil Association Registered (G932) mixed farm, beef sucklers, pigs, field veg, polytunnels, and cereals, selling vegetables and meat via farmers markets, box scheme
and farm gate sales. Member of the Soil Association Organic Farms Network.

MARKUS PRODUCTS LTD

MURRAY WAY, WINCANTON BUSINESS PARK, WINCANTON BA9 9RX
Tel: 01963 435270 Fax: 01963 435271 Contact: Simon Clarke
simon@markusproducts.co.uk www.markusproducts.co.uk
Soil Association P4162. Manufacturer of flavoured butters, flavoured soft cheese
portions, crumb coatings, flavoured oils and stuffings in IQF format.

MERRICKS ORGANIC FARM

PARK LANE, LANGPORT TA10 0NF
Tel: 01458 252901 Fax: 01458 252901 Contact: Jane Brooke
simon@merricksorganicfarm.co.uk www.merricksorganicfarm.co.uk
22-acre market garden supplying farm-run box scheme with vegetables and fruit.
Also organic pork, poultry and eggs. Two holiday cottages on farm.

MILES, DJ & CO LTD
PORLOCK HOUSE, STEPHENSON RD., MINEHEAD TA24 5EB
Tel: 01643 703993 Fax: 01643 706303 Contact: John Halls
info@djmiles.co.uk www.djmiles.co.uk
Organic teabags packed in 40s and 80s, manufactured in Somerset.

MIMI HOLISTICA
5 GLOUCESTER ST., OFF RIVERS ST., BATH, SOMERSET, BA1 2SE
Tel: 01225 448432 Fax: 01225 442014 Contact: Claire Critchley
mail@mimiholistica.co.uk www.mimiholistica.co.uk
Soil Association Certification H9359. Holistic centre specialising in certified organic skin care, spa treatments and holistic therapies. Certified treatments include two different facials, a foot treatment, a hand treatment and a choice of massages.

MOLE VALLEY FARMERS LTD
HUNTWORTH MILL, MARSH LANE, BRIDGWATER TA6 6LQ
Tel: 01278 444829 Fax: 01278 446923 Contact: James Trebble
feeds@molevalleyfarmers.com www.molevalleyfarmers.com
Soil Association P2332, Organic Farmers & Growers UKP 030463. Manufacturers of organic feeds for dairy, beef, cattle, sheep, pigs and poultry, and suppliers of seeds, fertilisers and other inputs for organic farmers.

NATRACARE—BODYWISE (UK) LTD
UNIT 23, MARSH LANE INDUSTRIAL ESTATE, MARSH LANE, PORTBURY BS20 0NH
Tel: 01275 371764 Fax: 01275 371765 Contact: Susie Hewson
info@natracare.com www.natracare.com
Soil Association I303. Feminine hygiene products: Natracare organic cotton tampons and feminine pads made from natural and disposable materials, available from health stores and supermarkets nationwide.

NEAL'S YARD REMEDIES

7 NORTHUMBERLAND PLACE, BATH BA1 5AR
Tel: 01225 466944 Contact: The Manager
mail@nealsyardremedies.com www.nealsyardremedies.com
Neal's Yard Remedies manufactures and retails natural cosmetics in addition to
stocking an extensive range of herbs, essential oils, homoeopathic remedies and
reference material.

NORWOOD FARM

BATH ROAD, NORTON ST PHILIP, NR. BATH BA2 7LP
Tel: 01373 834856 Fax: 01373 834765 Contact: Catherine Le Grice-Mack
catemack@norwood.ndo.co.uk www.norwoodfarm.co.uk
Soil Association G814. Organic mixed farm, with rare and native breeds. Open to
visitors every day from March 28th–September 19th. Farm shop with organic meat
and local produce open all year. Fairtrade groceries. Member of the Soil
Association Organic Farms Network.

THE ORGANIC HERB TRADING COMPANY

COURT FARM, MILVERTON TA4 1NF
Tel: 01823 401205 Fax: 01823 401001 Contact: Amy Hampshire
info@organicherbtrading.com www.organicherbtrading.com
Soil Association P938. The leading UK supplier of organic raw materials including
herbs and spices, essential oils, tinctures, macerated oils and flower waters for use
in food, beverages, herbal medicines and cosmetics. Quantities from 1kilo/litre to
container. NOP certification for the American markets. Member of the Soil
Association Organic Farms Network.

ORGANIC MILK SUPPLIERS CO-OPERATIVE LTD

COURT FARM, LOXTON, NR. AXBRIDGE BS26 2XG
Tel: 01934 750244 Fax: 01934 750080 Contact: Sally Bagenal (C.E.)
enquiries@omsco.co.uk www.omsco.co.uk
UK-wide supplier of organic milk.

THE ORGANIC SHOP

20 MARKET ST., CREWKERNE TA18 7LA
Tel: 01460 74447 Fax: 01460 74447 Contact: Delilah Webb
We only sell organic produce, everything from fresh veg, meat, groceries, toiletries, baby products, dairy, yoghurt, eggs, ecover cleaning products, bodycare, baby clothes, nappies, frozen and chilled foods, tofu, pesto, a complete range of organic foods and environmentally friendly products. The shop has been completely refitted with environmentally friendly fittings, and we only use environmentally friendly products in the shop, including recycled paper till rolls and bags from the Soil Association. If we haven't got it in stock, we will do our best to obtain it for you.

ORGANICA

TWEENTOWN CORNER, CHEDDAR BS27 3JF
Tel: 01934 741644 Contact: Sue Gallacher
cheddarorganica@aol.com www.cheddarorganica.com
Organica is a retail outlet for organic wholefoods, fruit and vegetables from mainly local suppliers. A small range of supplements, boxes and gifts are also available. Specialist wholefoods available to order.

ORGARDEN PRODUCE

BORDER FARM, CLOSWORTH, YEOVIL BA22 9SZ
Tel: 01935 872483 Fax: 01935 873736 Contact: Jennifer Evans
Soil Association Licence no. E07W since 1985. Have eighteen 90-foot growing houses, and specialise in tomatoes, peppers, courgettes, aubergines, cucumbers and carrots in tunnels.

PITNEY FARM SHOP

GLEBE FARM, PITNEY, LANGPORT TA
Tel: 01458 253002 Fax: 01458 253002 Contact: Rob Walrond
Soil Association G4130. Mixed organic farm producing organic eggs, lamb, beef, pork, bacon and a range of organic sausages, also interesting seasonal vegetables. Mostly direct sales through our farm shop or local outlets.

PLOWRIGHT ORGANIC PRODUCE

29 HUNTSTILE, GOATHURST, BRIDGWATER TA5 2DQ
Tel: Fax: rplowright@tinyonline.co.uk Contact: Richard Plowright
Plowright Organic Produce is a small farm business in Somerset. POP grows a wide range of vegetables and fruit which it supplies to local homes and offices through a box scheme. Organic Food Awards 2004: Runner Up Box Scheme.

PROCKTERS FARM SHOP

PROCKTERS FARM, WEST MONKTON, TAUNTON TA2 8QN
Tel: 01823 413427 Fax: 01823 413390 Contact: Mark Besley & Lynn Norman
Farm shop in old stone buildings on working mixed organic farm. Full range of own organic beef, lamb and veg. Wide range of local cheeses, wine, bread, etc.

PROVENDER DELICATESSEN

3 MARKET SQUARE, SOUTH PETHERTON TA13 5BT
Tel: 01460 240681 Fax: 08701 694835 Contact: Roger Biddle
www.provender.net
Licensed delicatessen with large organic selection of groceries, cheeses, dairy and juices. Collection point for Merricks Organic Farm vegetable box scheme. Organic frozen vegetables and ice cream.

QUEENSWOOD NATURAL FOODS LTD

2 ROBINS DRIVE, APPLE BUSINESS PARK, BRIDGWATER TA6 4DL
Tel: 01278 423440 Fax: 01278 424084 Contact: Chris Claydon
sales@queenswoodfoods.co.uk www.queenswoodfoods.co.uk
Soil Association P1559. Supplies of bulk and pre-packed organic commodities, along with a wide range of branded, chilled and frozen products, with weekly deliveries throughout a large area. Organic ingredients also available.

RIVERFORD ORGANIC VEGETABLES—NORTH SOMERSET & BATH

46 WIMBLESTONE ROAD, WINSCOMBE BS25 1JP

Tel: 01934 844918 Fax: 01934 844918 Contact: Gilbert & Liz McPherson

gilbertandliz@riverfordhomedelivery.co.uk www.riverford.co.uk

Award-winning organic vegetable box scheme operating in north Somerset, Bath, Chippenham, Warminster and surrounding areas. Box sizes to suit all households from a single person to a large family. A selection of fruit, dairy products, wine, juices and chocolate are also available. Order weekly, fortnightly or whenever you like. Can order and pay online at www.riverford.co.uk or by phone: 0845 600 2311. BBC Radio 4 Farmer of the Year 2005.

ROBERT WILSON'S CEYLON TEAS

STONEHAVEN, NUTTREE, NORTH PERROTT, CREWKERNE TA18 7SX

Tel: 01460 77508 Fax: 01460 77508 Contact: Robert Wilson

info@wilstea.com www.wilstea.com

Organic Farmers & Growers UKP 030485. Packers and shippers. Our business in Sri Lanka works with single estates to have special dry season manufacture made to our specific requirements. We import for UK distribution or export internationally from Colombo. Retail shop on the web.

SEASONS WHOLEFOODS

10 GEORGE STREET, BATH BA1 2EH

Tel: 01225 469730 Contact: Peter & Anne Bassil

Take-away salads, savouries, soups etc. A large range of organic products available in the shop.

SOMERSET ORGANIC LINK

THE CIDER PRESS ROOM, FLAXDRAYTON FARM, DRAYTON, SOUTH PETHERTON TA13 5LR

Tel: 01460 241427 Fax: 01460 241427 Contact: Peter Foster & Steve Friend

peter@flaxdrayton.fsnet.co.uk www.somersetorganiclink.co.uk

A co-operative of organic farmers in Somerset, SOL supplies fresh organic produce to outlets in Somerset and beyond. SOL buys produce from outside the county when necessary to meet demand. Sales and marketing service for organic vegetable producers in Somerset, forum for crop planning, opportunities to share labour and equipment. Mobile: 07881 865709.

SOMERSET ORGANICS

GILCOMBE FARM SHOP, GILCOMBE FARM, BRUTON BA10 0QE
Tel: 01749 813710 Contact: Richard Stephens
info@somersetorganics.co.uk www.somersetorganics.co.uk
Mail order organic meat, farm shop, local and London farmers' markets, farmhouse
accommodation, e-commerce business of the year 2000. 300-acre organic farm.

SPENCERS GROCERY STORE

4 TUCKER STREET, WELLS BA5 2DZ
Tel: 01749 672357 Contact: J Spencer
shop@spencersofwells.co.uk www.spencersofwells.co.uk
Traditional family grocery store. Free local delivery. Personal counter service. Local
baked organic bread, cakes. Organic fruit juices, organic sugar. Local: cheeses,
cooked hams, honey, pickles. Brand-name goods.

SPRING GROVE MARKET GARDEN

SPRING GROVE, MILVERTON TA4 1NW
Tel: 07956 429531 Contact: Amanda Goddard
Box scheme delivering in Milverton, Wiveliscombe and Wellington.

STILLMANS (SOMERSET) LTD

55 STATION RD., TAUNTON TA1 1NZ
Tel: 01823 272661 Fax: 01823 332270 Contact: C Cook
peter@stillmansbutchers.co.uk www.stillmansbutchers.co.uk
Soil Association P3014. Stillmans is a small welfare-friendly farm abattoir
providing a service to local farmers.

STILLPOINT

OLD OAK FARM, CHAPEL ALLERTON, AXBRIDGE BS26 2PD
Tel: 01934 712726 Contact: Carol Harper
carol@stillpoint.uk.com www.stillpoint.uk.com
Holistic stress management, McTimoney therapy, life coaching, Hawaiian massage.
We provide practical on-site stress management and well-being clinics. Chair
massage, organic aromatherapy products, nutritious organic snacks and fruit.
Clients include OMSCo, Lakewood Conference Centre and local organic farmers.
Member of HDRA and Soil Association.

STONEAGE ORGANICS

STONEAGE FARM, COTHELSTONE, TAUNTON TA4 3ED
Tel: 01823 432488 Fax: 01823 432488 Contact: Keith Martin
keith@stoneageorganics.co.uk www.stoneageorganics.co.uk
Soil Association M49W. Organic vegetables, box scheme deliveries from Taunton
to Bristol to Shepton Mallet and en route. Organic lamb also available.

SUNSEED

12 SOUTH STREET, WELLINGTON TA21 8NS
Tel: 01823 662313 Contact: Tony Bourne
info@sunseed.co.uk www.sunseed.co.uk
Health and wholefood retailer specialising in all things as natural as possible. Wide
variety of usual things and unusual things: organic vegetables, fruit, food, drinks,
chilled, frozen etc. Complementary therapies.

SWADDLES ORGANIC

SWADDLES GREEN FARM, HARE LANE, BUCKLAND ST. MARY, CHARD TA20 3JR
Tel: 01460 234387 Fax: 01460 234591 Contact: Sue Alexander
info@swaddles.co.uk www.swaddles.co.uk
Soil Association P1904. Producers of many award-winning meats, pies, bacon,
hams, sausages, ready meals. Mail order service of own produce throughout UK,
plus full range of organic dairy, grocery, fruit and veg.

TOUCAN WHOLEFOODS

3 THE PARADE, MINEHEAD TA24 5NL
Tel: 01643 706101 Fax: 01643 708624 Contact: Jane Hart
mail@toucan.wholefoods@virgin.net
Independent wholefood shop with a wide range of organic produce, including fresh fruit and veg, specialist breads, dairy and organic wines and beers. Also quality vitamin supplements with free information.

TRUUULY SCRUMPTIOUS ORGANIC BABY FOOD

UNIT 2, CHARMBOROUGH FARM, CHARLTON RD, HOLCOMBE, RADSTOCK BA3 5EX
Tel: 01761 239300 Fax: 01761 239300 Contact: Topsy Fogg
sales@bathorganicbabyfood.co.uk www.bathorganicbabyfood.co.uk
Award-winning frozen organic baby and toddler food. Entire range Soil Association certified. Winners of the Soil Association Organic Food Awards in 2002 and 2004. Our range includes such delights as salmon and broccoli pie, sweetcorn chowder and apple & mango. Organic Food Awards 2004: Baby Food Winner.

TUCKMARSH FARM LTD

MARSTON BIGOT, FROME BA11 5BY
Tel: 01373 836325 Contact: RB Christie
rbonhamchr@aol.com
Soil Association G4078. Suckler herd of Hereford x heifers and stores.

WESTAR & WEEDMACHINE

MANOR FARM, HEWISH, NR. CREWKERNE TA18 8QT
Tel: 07977 206530 Fax: 01460 75317 Contact: George van den Berg
george@weedmachine.co.uk www.weedmachine.co.uk
Soil Association G6756. Producer of organic eggs.

THE WHOLEFOOD STORE
29 HIGH STREET, GLASTONBURY BA6 9DR
Tel: 01458 831004 Contact: Henry Cox
One of Somerset's biggest and best organic, natural food stores. Our comprehensive range includes fresh bread from five different bakeries, a vibrant fresh fruit and vegetable section, and chilled and frozen products. We also stock bulk medicinal herbs, herbal and homoeopathic remedies plus nutritional supplements. You can refill your bottles at the eco-refill station: ten different shampoos, conditioners and liquid soap, as well as Ecover cleaning products.

WINCANTON GROUP LTD
CALE HOUSE, STATION RD., WINCANTON BA9 9AD
Tel: 01963 828282 Fax: 01963 31850 Contact: Stuart James
stuart.james@wincanton.co.uk www.wincanton.co.uk
Soil Association P6716. Wincanton Group are specialists in warehousing and distribution activities including organic milk collected for numerous customers.

THE YEO VALLEY ORGANIC CO LTD
CANNINGTON CREAMERY, CANNINGTON TA5 2ND
Tel: 01761 462798 Fax: 01761 462181 Contact: Mike Pollak
enquiries@yeo-organic.co.uk www.yeo-organic.co.uk
Soil Association P2168. This family-owned independent business won The Queen's Award for Enterprise for Sustainable Development in 2001. Now the UK's biggest organic dairy brand, products include yoghurts, desserts, butter and ice cream. Organic Food Awards 2004: Cheese Commended; Whole Milk Winner; Semi Skimmed Highly Commended; Yoghurt Commended.

ZUMO ZEST
HAYESWOOD RD., TIMSBURY, BATH BA2 0FQ
Tel: 01761 470523 Fax: 01761 471018 Contact: Mary Young
A family-run business in the heart of the West Country making 'to order' organic citrus zest and juice, for use as an ingredient to enhance quality of puddings, cakes etc., by the trade.

Staffordshire

BELLA HERBS

BROCTON LEYS, BROCTON, STAFFORD ST17 0TX
Tel: 01785 663868 Contact: Beverley Squire
beverleysquire@aol.com
We are a two-acre organic garden licensed by the Soil Association, where we run leisure courses in organic gardening. We are also producers of vegetables, fruit and herbs.

BESTFOODS UK LTD—FOOD INGREDIENTS

WELLINGTON ROAD, BURTON-ON-TRENT DE14 2AB
Tel: 01283 511111 Fax: 01283 510194 Contact: Jean Cattanach
jean.cattenach@unilever.com www.unilever.com
Bestfoods Ingredients specialise in the production of stocks and bouillons for manufacturers of prepared savoury foods. Licensed products include organic vegetable bouillon and organic light bouillon.

BETTER TASTING SNACK FOODS PLC

UNITS 3–12, BRIDGE STREET IND. ESTATE, TRINITY RD., UTTOXETER ST14 8ST
Tel: 01889 567338 Fax: 01889 562701 Contact: Andy Baldwin
andy@bettertastingsnackfoods.co.uk www.bettertastingsnackfoods.co.uk
Soil Association P2184. Snack manufacturer specialising in batch-fried potato crisps, vegetable crisps (parsnip, beetroot, carrot and sweet potato), croutons, crackers and tortillas.

BIOBABY

Tel: 01384 877155 Contact: Hester Lyons
hester@bio-baby.co.uk www.bio-baby.co.uk
A small company providing a range of beautiful organic baby clothes by Cut4Cloth, Disana and other manufacturers. We sell both locally in the Stourbridge and Bridgnorth area, and worldwide through our Internet site. We aim to provide excellent quality organic clothes, manufactured through ethical means, at a reasonable price. We are always looking out for ranges that are baby-proof (we have our own little one to test them on), beautiful, practical, and fun to wear.

BOOTS HERBAL STORES LTD
5 CASTLE WALK, NEWCASTLE ST5 1AN
Tel: 01782 617463 Fax: 01782 636098 Contact: Keith Woolley
keith.woolley@btinternet.com
Family business, established 1939. Stock organic vegetarian foods wherever
possible. Organic herbal tinctures available.

COPE, TH & SON
HUDDLESFORD HOUSE FARM, NR. LICHFIELD WS13 8PY
Tel: 01543 432255 Fax: 01543 433447 Contact: Tom Cope
huddlesford.holsteins@virgin.net
Soil Association G2538. Dairy farmer, milking 260 organic cows and processing
own milk into organic cheese.

EARTHOIL PLANTATIONS LTD
UNIT 3, SHIRES INDUSTRIAL ESTATE, ESSINGTON CLOSE, LICHFIELD WS13 7AU
Tel: 01543 264268 Fax: 01543 410885 Contact: Campbell Walter
campbell.walter@earthoil.com www.earthoil.com
Earthoil Plantations is a grower based production and marketing organisation
specialising in the sourcing and supplying of certified organic essential and
vegetable oils.

GROVE FARM
THE GROVE FARM, WELLS LANE, BRADLEY, STAFFORD ST18 9EE
Tel: 01785 780252 Contact: Graham Holt
graham@grahamholt.wanadoo.co.uk
Staffordshire beef. Top quality farm produced organic beef. Each piece is
labelled with the weight and price and all meat is vacuum-packed. Quality and
freshness is guaranteed. Free local doorstep delivery, not a box scheme.

HOLGRAN LTD

GRANARY HOUSE, WETMORE ROAD, BURTON-ON-TRENT DE14 1TE
Tel: 01283 511255 Fax: 01283 511220 Contact: Alan Marson
bits4bread@holgran.co.uk www.holgran.co.uk
Industrial bakery ingredients: malt, cereal, seed ingredients for the bakery industry.
Supplier of ingredients, mixes. Soil Association membership. Delivery: UK, Europe,
N. America.

THE KERRYGOLD COMPANY LTD

BARNFIELDS IND. ESTATE, SUNNYHILLS RD., LEEK ST13 5SP
Tel: 01538 399111 Fax: 01538 399918 Contact: Chris Proctor
sales@kerrygold.co.uk www.kerrygold.com
Soil Association P5200. Pre-packed natural cheese and grated cheese for retail
and industrial applications.

MOORLAND WASTE RECYCLING

CRESFORD FARM, CAVERSWALL LANE, DILHORNE ST10 2PH
Tel: 01782 397907 Fax: 01782 392928 Contact: Anne Wagstaff
anne@moorlands35.freeserve.co.uk
Producers of organic compost, mulches, soil improver, top soil.

PHYTONE LTD

THIRD AVENUE, CENTRUM 100, BURTON ON TRENT DE14 2WD
Tel: 01283 543300 Fax: 01283 543322 Contact: Richard Perry
info@phytone.co.uk www.phytone.co.uk
Soil Association P5468. Supplier of a range of organic products including dried
herbs and spices, vegetables and fruit juice concentrates and powders, caramel
syrup and powder, malt extract, molasses and vanilla.

THE REAL FOOD COMPANY
50 SANDBACH ROAD SOUTH, ALSAGER, STOKE-ON-TRENT ST7 2LP
Tel: 01270 873322 Contact: Carol Dines
realfood.co@ntlworld.com
Organic wholefoods, vegetables and fruit (including box scheme, frozen and chilled), herbal, homoeopathic, supplements etc. Large choice to be found in helpful shop with knowledgeable staff. Local deliveries.

REGENCY MOWBRAY CO LTD
HIXON INDUSTRIAL ESTATE, HIXON ST18 0PY
Tel: 01889 270554 Fax: 01889 270927 Contact: CH Malbon
sales@regencymowbray.co.uk www.regencymowbray.demon.co.uk
Soil Association P4570. Manufacturer of organic food ingredients. Organic fruit preparations for yoghurt and ice cream. Organic flavourings. Organic purées and sauces. Natural flavourings for use in organic products. Also manufacturers of standard flavourings, colours, fruit preparations, chocolate products, emulsifiers and stabilisers.

STAFFORDSHIRE ORGANIC CHEESE
NEW HOUSE FARM, ACTON, NEWCASTLE UNDER LYME ST5 4EE
Tel: 01782 680366 Fax: 01782 680366 Contact: David Deaville
d.deaville@virgin.net
Makers of traditional hand-made, hand-pressed cheeses from organic cows milk. Also makers of Whitmore organic sheeps milk cheese.

WOOTTON ORGANIC
RAMSHORN, FARLEY, OAKAMOOR ST10 3BZ
Tel: 01538 703228 Fax: 01538 709900 Contact: Denise Flanagan
wholesale@woottonorganic.co.uk www.woottonorganic.com
Specialists in the finest organic meats: beef, lamb, venison, pork and poultry. In our organically certified on-site abattoir our Master Butcher prepares cuts fresh to order, and will happily discuss specific requirements.

Suffolk

ASPALL
THE CYDER HOUSE, ASPALL HALL, STOWMARKET IP14 6PD
Tel: 01728 860510 Fax: 01728 861031 Contact: Barry Chevallier Guild
info@aspall.co.uk www.aspall.co.uk
Founder members of the Soil Association and organic producers of apple juice, cyder and cyder vinegar for over 57 years. Our products are widely available through good retail food outlets.

ASTON ORGANIC ORCHARDS
THE ORCHARD, WELHAM LANE, RISBY, BURY ST EDMUNDS IP28 6QS
Tel: 01284 811668 Fax: 01284 700011 Contact: Tony Fuller
tonyfuller@btinternet.com
Soil Association-registered organic apple orchard. The following varieties are grown (mainly for the wholesale market). Dessert apples: Spartan & Lord Lambourne. Cooking apples: Bramley & Grenadier.

BARENBRUG UK LTD
33 PERKINS RD., ROUGHAM IND. ESTATE, BURY ST. EDMUNDS IP30 9ND
Tel: 01359 272000 Fax: 01359 272001 Contact: James Ingles
info@baruk.co.uk www.barenbrug.co.uk
Soil Association P6199. Barenbrug are specialist grass and forage seed producers who produce organic grass seed mixtures, specifically designed for organic farmers. These include the new white clover Barblanca, which is extremely productive.

BRYDEN ORGANICS
BRYDEN, MINSMERE ROAD, DUNWICH IP17 3DF
Tel: 01728 648960 Contact: Debra Hyatt
debra.hyatt@btinternet.co.uk
Soil Association G9119. Currently in conversion. 10-acre smallholding in Suffolk Sandlings. We are returning 8 acres to acid grassland in order to create habitats for woodlark, adder and a range of invertebrates. Our major enterprise is growing oriental salad leaves—available from the farm gate.

BUSHY LEY FARM SHOP

ELMSETT, IPSWICH IP7 6PQ

Tel: 01473 658671 Contact: C Thoroughgood

Soil Association T12E. Wide range of vegetables and fruit when in season. Open July to October, 8am–8pm seven days a week. All produce sold is grown on this farm.

CAPEL ORGANIC MUSHROOMS

CAPEL ST. MARY, IPSWICH IP9 2LA

Tel: 01473 311245 Fax: 01473 310380 Contact: Patrick Hearne

patrick@capelmushrooms.co.uk

Growers and packers of organic white button, cups, flats and brown button, cups and Portobello mushrooms. Also organic mushroom compost.

CARLEY AND WEBB

52 THOROUGHFARE, WOODBRIDGE IP12 1AL

Tel: 01394 385650 Fax: 01394 388984 Contact: Mark Balaam

www.carleyandwebb.com

We are a natural food store specialising in organic vegetables, bread and macrobiotic products. Large delicatessen, fresh fish.

CARLEY AND WEBB

29 MARKET HILL, FRAMLINGHAM IP13 9AN

Tel: 01728 723503 Fax: 01728 724153 Contact: Steve Bax

www.carleyandwebb.com

Specialist delicatessen and natural food store specialising in organic vegetables, bread, and macrobiotic products.

CHURCH (BURES) LTD, WA

HIGH ST., BURES CO8 5JQ

Tel: 01787 227654 Fax: 01787 228325 Contact: Tim Church

organicseed@churchofbures.co.uk www.churchofbures.co.uk

Soil Association P7482. All organic grass mixtures available; vetch, mustard, red clover, white clover and all organic seed mixtures.

CLARKES LANE ORCHARD

CLARKES LANE, ILKETSHALL ST. ANDREW, BECCLES NR34 8HR
Tel: 07786 663351 Contact: Jim Cooper
One and a half-acre orchard/smallholding with old fruit tree varieties plus 400
dwarf trees, mostly apple, with pear, plum and cherry. Some fruit and vegetables
available from the gate.

DAGANYA FARM

NUTTERY VALE, HOXNE, EYE IP21 5BB
Tel: 01379 668060 Contact: Michael Knights
Soil Association G2108. Organic fruit and vegetables in season. Founder member
of EOSTRE organics.

DESMOND DUNCAN'S ORGANIC VEGETABLE BOX SCHEME

TYES HILL COTTAGE, BLACKSMITH GREEN, WETHERINGSETT, STOWMARKET IP14 5PY
Tel: 01728 860883 Fax: 01728 860883 Contact: Desmond Duncan
daduncan1962@aol.com www.organicsforall.co.uk
Organic fruit and vegetable box scheme, home delivery and wholesale.

DJ PRODUCE LTD

UNIT 1, GRIFFITHS YARD, GAZELEY RD., MOULTON, NEWMARKET CB8 8SR
Tel: 01638 552709 Fax: 01638 552709 Contact: Derek Mason
djproduce2005@yahoo.co.uk www.djproduce.co.uk
Organic Farmers & Growers 11UKP110089. Wide range of fruit and vegetable
boxes delivered weekly to Cambridge and the surrounding area. Personal orders
welcomed. Long-established reputation for personal service, quality and value for
money.

EDEN ORGANICS AND WHOLEFOODS

SOUTHVIEW, 165, YARMOUTH ROAD, BROOME, BUNGAY NR35 2NZ
Tel: 07789 965904 Fax: 01986 896378 Contact: David Hirst
david.hirst@edenorganics.co.uk www.edenorganics.co.uk
We provide an organic fruit and vegetable box scheme together with a range of
wholefoods and eco-friendly products. We deliver on Thursday and Fridays to
Bungay, Beccles, Lowestoft, Halesworth and surrounding villages.

ESSENTIAL CARE

C/O LONGWOOD FARM, TUDDENHAM, BURY ST EDMUNDS IP28 6TB
Tel: 0870 345 9569 Contact: Margaret Weeds
info@essential-care.co.uk www.essential-care.co.uk
From the purest plant oils, herbs and floral waters we create organic skin & body
care and the only Soil Association-certified shampoo. Hand-made and formulated
without unnecessary synthetics, especially for sensitive and eczema-prone skin. We
are a caring & friendly, family-run company.

FOCUS ORGANIC LTD

14 THE THOROUGHFARE, HALESWORTH IP19 8AH
Tel: 01986 872899 Fax: 01986 872995 Contact: Juan Suarez
info@focusorganic.co.uk www.focusorganic.co.uk
Our wholefood shop sells as much organic produce as possible including cereals,
nuts, fruits, flour, seeds, jams, sauces, spreads, juices, pasta and vegetables.
Organic clothes and bed linen, Ecover products, aromatherapy candles, essential
oils, recycled jewellery.

FOCUS ORGANIC LTD

76 HIGH ST, SOUTHWOLD IP18 6DN
Tel: 01502 725299 Contact: Samantha Frost
info@focusorganic.co.uk www.focusorganic.co.uk
Cereals, nuts, fruits, flour, seeds, jams, sauces, spreads, juices, pasta, essential
oils, cosmetics, cleaning materials etc.

GOBBLIN WHOLEFOODS LTD

STATION RD. IND. ESTATE, ELMSWELL, BURY ST. EDMUNDS IP30 9HR
Tel: 01359 241841 Fax: 01359 241841 Contact: Peter Dow
Soil Association P5476. Manufacturer of vegetarian wholefoods, including
organic sweet and savoury lines, for delivery within the M25 and throughout the
east of England, to retail, catering and licensed outlets.

HILLSIDE NURSERIES

HINTLESHAM, IPSWICH IP8 3NJ
Tel: 01473 652682 Fax: 01473 652624 Contact: Roberta Simpson
Soil Association G594. Box scheme (vegetables, fruit, eggs) using local and own
produce wherever possible. Delivery Ipswich, Woodbridge, Felixstowe and
surrounding areas.

HOME FARM NACTON

ORWELL PARK ESTATE OFFICE, NACTON, IPSWICH IP10 0EG
Tel: 01473 659209 Contact: Andrew Williams
Soil Association G4705. Specialising in organic vegetables i.e. broccoli, cauliflower,
carrots, leeks, potatoes and also organic cereals.

HORIZON SEEDS

UNIT 3, AIRFIELD INDUSTRIAL PARK, LANGTON GREEN, EYE IP23 7HN
Tel: 01379 873377 Fax: 01379 873373 Contact: Martin Keats
info@horizonseeds.com www.horizonseeds.com
Retailers of organic seed: grass leys, forage maize, cereals, pulses and fodder
crops. We supply to farms throughout the country.

HUNGATE HEALTH STORE

4 HUNGATE, BECCLES NR34 9TL
Tel: 01502 715009 Contact: Theresa Hale
Retailers of a wide range of organic foods including fresh bread, biscuits, dried fruit
and nuts, beans and lentils, chocolate, drinks. Also essential oils, bath and hair
products.

JAMES WHITE DRINKS LTD

WHITES FRUIT FARM, ASHBOCKING, IPSWICH IP6 9JS
Tel: 01473 890111 Fax: 01473 890001 Contact: Lawrence Mallinson
info@jameswhite.co.uk www.jameswhite.co.uk
James White press and bottle a range of organic and non-organic apple and pear
juices at their site in Suffolk. These include apple & crushed ginger, carrot &
apple, cranberry & apple and raspberry & pear. They are available from specialist
retailers and caterers throughout the UK and also can be ordered by phone or via
the website for home delivery.

KOPPERT UK LTD

HOMEFIELD BUSINESS PARK, HOMEFIELD ROAD, HAVERHILL CB9 8QP
Tel: 01440 704488 Fax: 01440 704487 Contact: Matthew Cook
info@koppert.co.uk www.koppert.co.uk
Europe's largest producer of natural enemies. Supplier of organic pesticides such
as DIPEL WP for caterpillars and SAVONA, a wide spectrum organic pesticide. Also
large range of pest monitoring traps. Delivery to UK & Ireland.

LONGWOOD FARM

TUDDENHAM ST. MARY, BURY ST. EDMUNDS IP28 6TB
Tel: 01638 717120 Fax: 01638 717120 Contact: Matthew Unwin
Soil Association no. G669. Specialist organic meat producers, retailers of fine
organic foods—meat, dairy, cheese and provisions. Huge range of over 2,000
items. Delivery nationwide plus local deliveries to postcode areas IP, NR, CB.

MAPLE FARM

BY THE CROSSWAYS, KELSALE, SAXMUNDHAM IP17 2PL
Tel: 01728 652000 Fax: 01728 652001 Contact: Tim Lewis
info@bythecrossways.co.uk
Small organic farm and market garden which produces and sells a wide range of
vegetables, home-milled flour, eggs and honey.

MICROCIDE
SHEPHERDS GROVE, STANTON, BURY ST. EDMUNDS IP31 2AR
Tel: 01359 251077 Fax: 01359 251545 Contact: N Balfour
microcide@microcide.co.uk www.microcide.co.uk
Soil Association I1616. Manufacturers of vegetable oil adjuvants which maximise
the performance of plant protection products and increase droplet deposition, spread
and uptake. Reduces drift and improves rain fastness. They are biodegradable.

NORTON ORGANIC GRAIN LTD
CASTLINGS HEATH COTTAGE, GROTON, SUDBURY CO10 5ES
Tel: 01787 210899 Fax: 01787 211737 Contact: John Norton
john.norton@nortonorganic.co.uk www.nortonorganic.co.uk
Organic grain/pulse supplier, sourcing organic grains and pulses from UK farms
and European/third country sourced soya, oilseeds, grains etc. Soil Association
licence no. P1674, OFF no. SAL/97. International coverage.

NOSYMBOLREQUIRED
31 GARLAND ST., BURY ST.EDMUNDS IP331HB
Tel: 07739 897616 Contact: Levi Wallace
levistone@nosymbolrequired.co.uk www.nosymbolrequired.co.uk
Organic cotton t-shirt design for skateboarders, snowboarders, wakeboarders and
mountainbikers.

OMEGA INGREDIENTS LIMITED
THE TECHNOLOGY CENTRE, STATION RD., FRAMLINGHAM IP13 9EZ
Tel: 01728 726626 Fax: 01728 726533 Contact: Steve Pearce
sales@omegaingredients.co.uk www.omegaingredients.co.uk
Essential oils, natural extracts, flower and herb waters, fruit juices, flavours and fragrances, ingredients for flavours & fragrances, aloe vera, dried aloe flowers.

OREGANO
169/171 LONDON ROAD NORTH, LOWESTOFT NR32 1HG
Tel: 01502 582907 Contact: Dawn Fellows
Health foods, vits, supplements; organic foods are featured in a large section in the store.

QUEEN'S HEAD
THE STREET, BRAMFIELD, HALESWORTH IP19 9HT
Tel: 01986 784214 Fax: 01986 784797 Contact: Mark Corcoran
qhbfield@aol.com www.queensheadbramfield.co.uk
Award-winning dining pub, serving food daily. Many ingredients collected direct from small local organic farms. Close to Southwold and the rest of Suffolk's Heritage Coast.

RED POLL MEATS
CHERRY TREE HOUSE, HACHESTON, WOODBRIDGE IP13 0DR
Tel: 01728 748444 Fax: 07050 600079 Contact: Sebastian Hall
info@redpollmeats.co.uk www.redpollmeats.co.uk
Red Poll Meats supply organic Norfolk Black & Bronze turkeys, organic lamb, organic beef, organic pork, free-range venison and organic fruit & vegetables nationwide. We try where possible to use unusual or rare breeds.

ST. PETER'S BREWERY
ST. PETER'S BREWERY CO LTD, ST. PETER'S HALL, ST. PETER SOUTH ELMHAM, BUNGAY NR35 1NQ
Tel: 01986 782322 Fax: 01986 782505 Contact: Colin Cordy
colin@stpetersbrewery.co.uk www.stpetersbrewery.co.uk
Soil Association P5891. Organic brewery. Production of organic beers and ales using organic barley and organic hops, presented in cask or bottle for shipment around the world.

SUFFOLK ORGANIC GARLIC

WHITE HOUSE FARM, UBBESTON, HALESWORTH IP19 0HA
Tel: 01986 798227 Fax: 01986 798179 Contact: Allan Pike
allanpike@farmersweekly.net
Soil Association G6065. Veg production: 2.5 acres of garlic in 2004. Arable: 15
acres of wheat in 2004.

SWALLOW ORGANICS

HIGH MARCH, DARSHAM, SAXMUNDHAM IP17 3RN
Tel: 01728 668201 Fax: 01728 668201 Contact: Malcolm Pinder
Naturally grown fruit and vegetables, herbs and pot plants. Farm gate sales and
vegetable boxes supplied to order, for collection only. Self-catering holiday
accommodation available.

THOMPSON & MORGAN

POPLAR LANE, IPSWICH IP8 3BU
Tel: 01473 695224 Fax: 01473 680199 Contact: Vicky Ager
www.thompson-morgan.co.uk
Experts in the garden since 1855. Suppliers of seeds.

WAKELYNS AGROFORESTRY

METFIELD LANE, FRESSINGFIELD IP21 5SD
wolfe@wakelyns.demon.co.uk
Soil Association G2249. Organic arable and agroforestry research undertaken
largely as part of the Elm Farm Research Centre programme. Vegetables, potatoes
and other produce are sold locally, principally through the Eostre organic
co-operative.

BIG OZ ORGANIC

126 ACRE ROAD, KINGSTON-UPON-THAMES KT2 6EN
Tel: 020 8541 3636 Fax: 020 8541 5850 Contact: Anne Lotter
bigozorganic@btconnect.com www.bigoz.co.uk
Big Oz Organic is a specialist puffing company, making a range of whole grain
puffed cereals for packaging in our own brand, Morning Puffs, and for selling in
bulk to other producers.

BODY AND SOUL ORGANICS

REAR OF 1 PARADE COURT, OCKHAM ROAD SOUTH, EAST HORSLEY KT24 6QR
Tel: 01483 282868 Fax: 01483 282060 Contact: Sarah Webber
bodyandsoul@organic-gmfree.co.uk www.organic-gmfree.co.uk
Colect and delivery service, wide range of fruit and veg, wholefoods, dairy, wines,
beers, meat, poultry, etc., gluten-free, dairy-free, special diets, over 2,000 organic
lines. Home delivery in Surrey, phone for details.

BROADWAY HEALTH CENTRE

60 THE BROADWAY, CHEAM, SUTTON SM3 8BD
Tel: 020 8643 5132 Contact: R Franeta
Stockists of organic cereals, nuts and dried fruits, drinks, teas, chocolate, etc. No
fresh fruit or vegetables.

CHASE ORGANICS/THE ORGANIC GARDENING CATALOGUE

RIVERDENE BUSINESS PARK, MOLESEY RD., HERSHAM KT12 4RG
Tel: 01932 253666 Fax: 01932 252707 Contact: Mike Hedges
enquiries@chaseorganics.co.uk www.organiccatalogue.co.uk
The Organic Gardening Catalogue contains mail order seeds and gardening
products suitable for organic gardening and allotments. Catalogue produced in
association with the HDRA.

CONFOCO (UK) LTD

DUNCAN HOUSE, HIGH STREET, RIPLEY GU23 6AY
Tel: 01483 211288 Fax: 01483 211388 Contact: Christina Wood
confocouk@confocouk.com www.confocouk.com
Supplier of organic food ingredients to the baking, confectionery and breakfast
cereal industries.

CRANLEIGH ORGANIC FARM SHOP

LOWER BARRIHURST FARM, DUNSFORD ROAD, CRANLEIGH GU6 8LG
Tel: 01483 272896 Fax: 01483 273486 Contact: Ray Parker
organicfarmshop@btopenworld.com
Mixed farm producing: vegetables, herbs, meat and poultry. Our farm shop also
sells produce from other local organic farms.

DRYDOWN FARM

HOUND HOUSE RD., SHERE GU5 9JG
Tel: 01483 203821 Fax: 01483 205419 Contact: Peter Bond
profound-pursuits@yahoo.co.uk
Local deliveries of organic and free range meat. Lamb, beef and pork from traditional &
rare breeds, reared for outstanding flavour and texture. Turkeys and hams at Christmas.

DUCHY ORIGINALS

THE OLD RYDE HOUSE, 393 RICHMOND ROAD, EAST TWICKENHAM TW1 2EF
Tel: 020 8831 6800 Fax: 020 8538 9991 Contact: Petra Mihaljevich
office@duchyoriginals.com www.duchyoriginals.com

GORDON'S FINE FOODS

GORDON HOUSE, LITTLEMEAD IND. ESTATE, CRANLEIGH GU6 8ND
Tel: 01483 267707 Fax: 01483 267783 Contact: Adam Gordon
info@gordonsfinefoods.com www.gordonsfinefoods.com
Soil Association P2386. Organic mustard, chutney and sauces available under
brand or own label. A private independent family business producing products to
the highest standard.

GROVE FRESH LIMITED

SAXLEY COURT, 121–129 VICTORIA RD, HORLEY RH6 7AS
Tel: 01293 820832 Fax: 01293 822741 Contact: Trica Smith
trica.smith@grovefresh.co.uk www.grovefresh.co.uk
Soil Association P1814. Manufacturer of organic fruit juices.

HEHLIS HOLISTICS

17 LANSDOWNE COURT, BRIGHTON RD., PURLEY CR8 2BD
Tel: 020 8660 7954 Fax: 020 8660 7954 Contact: Andrea Hehlmann & Tim Gunner
info@hehlis-holistics.com
Mail order shop for organic baby sleeping bags, organic teas, organic spices and
organic sheepskin yoga mats.

HORTI HALCYON

HEATH MILL HOUSE, HEATH MILL LANE, FOX CORNER, WORPLESDON GU3 3PR
Tel: 01483 232095 Contact: Miranda Broadwood
enquiries@hortihalcyon-organic.co.uk www.hortihalcyon-organic.co.uk
Over 50 varieties of organic vegetables and herbs are grown by us. Boxes range
from £9.50 upwards and contents can be varied to suit customer needs, delivery
within 15-mile radius. Farmers' markets in Wimbledon and Chiswick. Visitors by
appointment.

KALLO FOODS LTD

COOPERS PLACE, COMBE LANE, WORMLEY GU8 5SZ
Tel: 01428 685100 Fax: 01428 685800 Contact: David Wilkinson
marketing@kallofoods.com www.kallofoods.com
Kallo Foods is the UK's leading supplier of organic breadsticks, organic crackers
and biscuits and organic stocks and gravies, as well as organic chocolate and
gluten-free products.

LATIN AMERICAN PRODUCE LTD
30 WESTMEADS, ONSLOW VILLAGE, GUILFORD GU2 7ST
Tel: 01483 561719 Fax: 01483 571035 Contact: MSS Namor
lap@mssn.freeserve.co.uk
LAP Ltd is an import house with many contacts in Latin America. We aim to help Latin American producers to sell organic fresh produce (fruit and vegetables) in the UK (supermarkets) and the European marketplace.

NEAL'S YARD REMEDIES
NEAL'S YARD REMEDIES, 15 KING STREET, RICHMOND TW9 1ND
Tel: 020 8948 9248 Contact: Heather Richards
mail@nealsyardremedies.com www.nealsyardremedies.com
Natural health and beauty shop with two therapy rooms.

NEAL'S YARD REMEDIES
2 MARKET ST., GUILDFORD GU1 4LB
Tel: 01483 450434 Contact: The Manager
mail@nealsyardremedies.com www.nealsyardremedies.com
Neal's Yard Remedies manufactures and retails natural cosmetics in addition to stocking an extensive range of herbs, essential oils, homoeopathic remedies and reference material.

OLIVERS WHOLEFOOD STORE
5 STATION APPROACH, KEW GARDENS, RICHMOND TW9 3QB
Tel: 020 8948 3990 Fax: 020 8948 3991 Contact: Sara Novakovic
sara@oliverswholefoods.co.uk
"This shop is an inspiration. Effortless, curved displays are plumped with Rococco chocolate, Richmond Park Honey, organic cooking oils and alcohol. The fridges have a wide selection of tofu and tempeh and there's river trout and organic meat in the freezers. At Christmas organic poultry and hams, and free game are available. . . . [there are] regular bakery deliveries from Cranks and the Authentic Bakery . . . the entire Dr Hauschka range is stocked including the make-up. Education is the key theme— as well as selling books galore, Oliver's runs weekly lectures from health experts like John Briffa."—*Time Out Shopping Guide 2004*. Soil Association Award: Organic Community Shop of the Year 1999.

PIZZA ORGANIC LTD

BARWELL BUSINESS PARK, LEATHERHEAD RD., CHESSINGTON KT9 2NY
Tel: 020 8397 3330 Fax: 020 8974 1298 Contact: Mike Traszko
info@pizzapiazza.co.uk www.pizza-organic.co.uk
Head office for expanding range of Soil Association accredited restaurants. A
great menu packed full of organic options, featuring stonebaked pizza, sautéed
pasta, gourmet burgers, grilled fish and fabulous desserts. Pizza Organic is
certified by the Soil Association and was Highly Commended in the 2003 Organic
Food Awards. All restaurants open 7 days a week but opening times may vary,
call 020 8397 3330 for further details.

PIZZA ORGANIC LTD

42–46 HIGH ST., KINGSTON KT1 1HN
Tel: 020 8541 5186 Contact: Mike Traszko
info@pizzapiazza.co.uk www.pizza-organic.co.uk
A great menu packed full of organic options, featuring stonebaked pizza, sautéed
pasta, gourmet burgers, grilled fish and fabulous desserts. Pizza Organic is certified
by the Soil Association and was Highly Commended in the 2003 Organic Food
Awards. All restaurants open 7 days a week but opening times may vary, call 020
8397 3330 for further details.

PIZZA ORGANIC LTD

3 LINKFIELD ST., REDHILL RH1 1HQ
Tel: 01737 766154 Contact: Mike Traszko
info@pizzapiazza.co.uk www.pizza-organic.co.uk
A great menu packed full of organic options, featuring stonebaked pizza, sautéed
pasta, gourmet burgers, grilled fish and fabulous desserts. Pizza Organic is certified
by the Soil Association and was Highly Commended in the 2003 Organic Food
Awards. All restaurants open 7 days a week but opening times may vary, call 020
8397 3330 for further details.

THE PUMPKIN PATCH

10 HIGH STREET, BANSTEAD SM7 2LJ
Tel: 01737 371007 Contact: Jane Willis & Susan Conlay
Natural health shop and vegetarian deli. Therapy centre. Organic foods.

RIVERFORD HOME DELIVERY GUILDFORD

HOLLY HEIGHTS, FARNHAM LANE, HASLEMERE GU27 1HE
Tel: 0845 600 2311 Contact: Annie Jermain
annie@riverfordhomedelivery.co.uk www.riverford.co.uk
Home delivery of organic vegetable boxes.

ROUNDHURST FARM LTD

TENNYSONS LANE, HASLEMERE GU27 3BN
Tel: 01428 656445 Fax: 01428 656380 Contact: Paul Kerry
roundhurstfarm@virgin.net www.roundhurstfarm.com
Producing organic beef from pedigree pure bred Sussex herd. Beef is well hung
and sold at farmers' markets or at the farm or by mail order.

SUNSHINE ORGANICS

Tel: 01483 268014 Contact: Amanda Porter
amanda@sunshine-organics.co.uk www.sunshine-organics.co.uk
Sunshine organics is a home delivery service for the Surrey and West Sussex borders, delivering fresh organics produce on a weekly basis. Set boxes including
local seasonal produce. Very good selection of organic fruit, vegetables and eco-
products. Individual orders tailored to your own requirements.

Superfact

20% of the earth's land surface is too dry for agriculture. About 20% is too cold,
20% is too mountainous and 20% is forested or too marshy. That leaves only
20% suitable for growing food.

**From *SuperKids: Over 200 incredible ways for kids to save the planet* by
Sasha Norris and Rupert Davies, Think Books, £5.99.**

WHOLE EARTH FOODS LTD

KALLO FOODS, COOPERS PLACE, COMBE LANE, WORMLEY, GODALMING GU8 5SZ
Tel: 01428 685100 Fax: 01428 685800 Contact: David Wilkinson
enquiries@wholeearthfoods.co.uk www.wholeearthfoods.co.uk
Since 1976 Whole Earth Foods have led and guided the movement to organic
food. We offer a wide range of organic products: peanut butters, spreads, breakfast
cereals, canned goods, and soft drinks. Available nationally in major supermarkets
and good health food stores.

WILSON & MANSFIELD

HADDON HOUSE, HINDHEAD RD., HASLEMERE GU27 1LH
Tel: 01428 651331 Fax: 01428 641552 Contact: Shirley Humphrey
sales@wmjuice.co.uk www.wmjuice.co.uk
Fruit juices & purées. Wilson & Mansfield are recognised as leaders in the import of
organic fruit juices and purées. Serving the UK and other continental European
markets.

WINTERBOTHAM DARBY & CO LTD

5–7 NEWMAN RD., PURLEY WAY, CROYDON CR9 3SN
Tel: 020 8664 3000 Fax: 020 8664 3001 Contact: Michelle Watson
www.windar.co.uk
Soil Association P4319. Importing and distributing meat products, charcuterie,
confectionery, snacks and other grocery items to retailers, wholesalers and
food processors.

WINTERSHALL PARTNERSHIP

BRAMLEY GU5 0LR
Tel: 01483 892167 Fax: 01483 898709 Contact: Paul Huntley
susan@huntleygroup.com www.wintershall-estate.com
We are producers of Aberdeen Angus beef and lamb, available retail through our
box scheme, delivered to the door. We also sell wholesale and produce several
arable crops.

AGRIPAL ENTERPRISES 'WICKHAM MANOR FARM'

WICKHAM MANOR FARM, PANNEL LANE, WINCHELSEA TN36 4AG
Tel: 01797 226216 Fax: 01797 226216 Contact: Mason Palmer
mason@wickhammanor.co.uk www.wickhammanor.co.uk
Soil Association G4537. Specialists in quality organic beef, lamb, and mutton.
Suckler herd of Simmental x Cows producing prime finished cattle from extensive
grazing marshes. Hampshire Down x Lleyn lambs producing top quality meat with
characteristic tender juicy texture and unique flavour. Breeders of pedigree Lleyn
stock. Also growers and retailers of organic potatoes, cereals, and pulses.

ASHURST ORGANICS

THE ORCHARD, ASHURST FARM, ASHURST LANE, PLUMPTON, LEWES BN7 3AP
Tel: 01273 891219 Fax: 01273 891943 Contact: Peter Haynes & Collette Pavledis
ashurstveg@tiscali.co.uk
Soil Association G1796, P1796. Local organic vegetable box scheme supplying
fresh vegetables to Brighton, Lewes, Haywards Heath, Eastbourne, and Worthing.

BABY-O

KINGSWAY HOUSE, 134–140 CHURCH RD., HOVE BN3 2DL
Tel: 0870 760 7552 Contact: David Maden
dave@baby-o.co.uk www.baby-o.co.uk
Organic cotton baby clothes, blankets, bedding and babycare products.

BARCOMBE NURSERIES

MILL LANE, BARCOMBE, LEWES BN8 5TH
Tel: 01273 400011 Contact: Adrian Halstead
Vegetable growers throughout the year with our own local box scheme delivered to
your door, weekly or fortnightly. We grow a wide range of vegetable varieties and
offer some choice.

BATTLE HEALTH STORE
83 HIGH ST., BATTLE TN33 0AQ
Tel: 01424 772435 Contact: N Crawshaw
sussexhealth@hotmail.com
A family-run, local health store selling wholefoods, vegetarian and special diet foods, herbal remedies and supplements. We aim to provide as many organic lines as possible.

BEANS AND THINGS
HARVEST HOME, CHUCK HATCH, HARTFIELD TN7 4EN
Tel: 01273 477774 Fax: 01273 477774 Contact: Dave Flintan
Door to door deliveries of organic fruit, veg, dairy and wholefoods to Brighton, Newhaven, Seaford, Hove etc.

BOATHOUSE ORGANIC FARM SHOP
THE ORCHARD, UCKFIELD RD., RINGMER, LEWES BN8 5RX
Tel: 01273 814188 Fax: 01273 814188 Contact: Martin Tebbutt
Shop providing full range of organic meats, veg, groceries and dairy, some sourced from our own farm. Prize winning sausages, home-cured and smoked bacon. Meat cut to order. Farm address: Boathouse Organic Farm, Isfield, Uckfield TN22 5TY. Tel: 01825 750641.

CORIANDER RESTAURANT & DELI
5 HOVE MANOR, HOVE STREET, HOVE BN3 2DF
Tel: 01273 730850 Fax: 01273 774555 Contact: Katrin Smale
info@corianderbrighton.com www.corianderbrighton.com
Innovative restaurant serving simple yet exotic food from around the world—absolutely delicious and 90% organic. We promote sustainable living in all aspects of our business. Delicatessen selling prepared foods, cooked meats, dried goods etc..

DAVENPORT VINEYARDS

LIMNEY FARM, CASTLE HILL, ROTHERFIELD, CROWBOROUGH TN6 3RR
Tel: 01892 852380 Contact: Will Davenport
info@davenportvineyards.co.uk www.davenportvineyards.co.uk
Producer of organic English wine, sold under the Limney label. Specialities include a
dry white 'Horsmonden' single vineyard wine and Limney Estate bottled-fermented
sparkling wine.

DEAN, K & E

COURT LODGE FARM, UDIMORE, RYE TN31 6BB
Tel: 01424 882206 Fax: 01424 882206 Contact: Keith Dean
clfarm@onetel.com
Soil Association G5591. Romney sheep and pedigree Sussex cattle breeding stock
for sale. Organic beef and lamb in packs or cuts from the farm and from local
farm shops. Organic wheat, barley and peas available.

EMERSON COLLEGE

HARTFIELD ROAD, FOREST ROW RH18 5JX
Tel: 01342 822238 Fax: 01342 826055 Contact: Alysoun Barrett
mail@emerson.org.uk www.emerson.org.uk
Soil Association & Demeter registered. Emerson College runs a three year, full-time
training in Biodynamic Organic Agriculture, as well as short courses in biodynamics.
Students at the college run a commercial biodynamic market garden through spring
and summer.

FESTIVAL WINES

P.O. BOX 5088, BRIGHTON & HOVE BN52 9BZ
Tel: 01273 325307 Fax: 01273 325307 Contact: Ben Walgate
ben@festivalwines.co.uk www.festivalwines.co.uk
Importer of biodynamic and organic wines from around the world, our website has
an extensive database of vegan and vegetarian wines from our small producers.
Next day delivery within the UK.

FOOD FORE THOUGHT

WICKHAM MANOR FARM, PANNEL LANE, WINCHELSEA TN36 4AG
Tel: 01797 225575 Fax: 01797 225575 Contact: Todd Cameron-Clarke
grant.culwick@btconnect.com
Grower and processor of all our own livestock: lamb, beef and pork, catering for
for local farmers' markets in London and wholesale to both London and local
restaurants.

FRANCHISE MANOR FARM

SPRING LANE, BURWASH, Nr ROBERTSBRIDGE TN32 5BL
Tel: 01435 883151 Fax: 01435 883151 Contact: Simon Bishop
simon@thenetherfieldcentre.co.uk
Organic mixed farm: arable, beef, sheep, pigs, laying hens. Has on-site meat
chiller store and butchery room with Soil Association licence

FULL OF BEANS

96 HIGH STREET, LEWES BN7 1XH
Tel: 01273 472627 Fax: 01273 472627 Contact: Sara Gosling
tempeh@globalnet.co.uk
We manufacture organic tofu, tempeh, wholegrain mustard, miso. Shop has
home-made vegetarian/vegan snacks, cakes, pulses, dried fruit, nuts, herbs,
spices and many more delights.

GOSSYPIUM

GOSSYPIUM HOUSE, ABINGER PLACE, LEWES BN7 2QA
Tel: 01273 488221 Fax: 01273 488721 Contact: Thomas Petit
info@gossypium.co.uk www.gossypium.co.uk
Gossypium is about understanding the real value of clothing. All Gossypium products
are made with organic and fairly traded cotton. The collection includes yogawear,
casual wear, nightwear, underwear and babywear.

HANKAM ORGANICS

HANKHAM HALL RD., HANKHAM, PEVENSEY BN24 5BE
Tel: 01323 741000 Fax: 01323 741000 Contact: Miles Denyer
One and a half acres of organic crops under glass, lots of leafy crops including spinach, lettuce and herbs. Local box scheme with doorstep deliveries. Also supply wholesale.

HARVEST SUPPLIES

HARVEST HOME, CHUCK HATCH, HARTFIELD TN7 4EN
Tel: 01342 823392 Fax: 01342 825594 Contact: Dave Flintan
Distribute for local growers. Retail business at home, door to door deliveries, wholesale deliveries to shops, restaurants etc. Full selection of veg, fruit, herbs and wholefoods in Sussex and Kent.

HEN ON THE GATE FARM SHOP

CLAYTON FARM, NEWICK LANE, MAYFIELD TN20 6RE
Tel: 01435 874852 Fax: 01435 873930 Contact: Cathy Swingland
claytonfarm@btinternet.com
Organic farm shop selling home-produced beef, lamb, pork and chicken, vegetables and ready meals as well as a wide selection of groceries. Art gallery, café and farm walks.

HENLEY BRIDGE INGREDIENTS LTD

UNIT 1 FOORDS FARM, VINES CROSS, HEATHFIELD TN21 9EX
Tel: 0870 350 8808 Fax: 0870 350 7808 Contact: Tony Mycock
sales@hbingredients.co.uk www.hbingredients.co.uk
Suppliers of organic & conventional ingredients to food processors: sugar, sugar syrups, chocolate, cereal syrups, cocoa powder, cocoa butter, dextrose, praline paste, marzipan, fondant, milk powders, etc..

HERONS FOLLY GARDEN

HERONS FOLLY, FLETCHING STREET, MAYFIELD TN20 6TE
Tel: 01435 873608 Contact: Patrick Treherne
Organic vegetable and fruit crops in season. We sell mainly wholesale and for schools, restaurants etc..

HIDDEN SPRING VINEYARD & ORGANIC ORCHARDS

VINES CROSS ROAD, HORAM TN21 OHF
Tel: 01435 812640 Fax: 01435 813542 Contact: Sue Mosey
info@hiddenspring.co.uk www.info@
Soil Association G1459. Hidden Spring Vineyard and Organic Orchards are set in gentle Sussex countryside. Visitors can sample the wine and seasonal fruit—ten apple varieties and three pear varieties. Phone first.

HIGHLANDS ORGANIC FARM

HORAM, HEATHFIELD TN21 OLG
Tel: 01435 812461 Contact: Peter Mason
petermason_uk@yahoo.co.uk
We produce very traditional Sussex beef, Jacob and Texel lamb, really high quality farmyard organic free range chicken and pond-reared ducks. We are Soil Association registered and we farm in conjunction with conservation principles.

HODSON, JHW & SE

HIGHAM FARM, BELLS YEW GREEN, TUNBRIDGE WELLS TN3 9AU
Tel: 01892 750363 Fax: 01892 752179 Contact: Sarah Hodson
Soil Association G4555. Organic beef from our own pedigree Sussex herd and organic lamb from our pedigree Poll Dorset flock. Self-catering granary accommodation in High Weald area of outstanding natural beauty.

HOLLYPARK ORGANICS

HOLLYPARK NORTH LANE, GUESTLING TN35 4LX
Tel: 01424 812229 Fax: 01424 812025 Contact: Linda Beaney
hollyparkorg@yahoo.co.uk
Certified Biodynamic farm (BDAA 303 UK6). Home produced goat's milk, cheeses and yoghurts a speciality. Vegetables and salads all year through. Culinary/medicinal herbs. Welsh lamb and Christmas turkeys.

INFINITY FOODS CO-OPERATIVE LTD
25 NORTH RD., BRIGHTON BN1 2AA
Tel: 01273 603563 Fax: 01273 675384 Contact: Grahame Mayo
www.infinityfoods.co.uk
Organic and wholefoods, cruelty-free cosmetics, fresh fruit and vegetables, organic
bread baked on the premises.

INFINITY FOODS CO-OPERATIVE LTD
FRANKLIN RD, PORTSLADE, BRIGHTON BN41 1AF
Tel: 01273 424060 Fax: 01273 417739 Contact: Charlie Booth
sales@infinityfoods.co.uk www.infinityfoods.co.uk
Leading UK wholesaler of organic foods. Soil Association no. P1465. Over 3,500
organic lines in stock offering the most comprehensive range of organic products
available anywhere. Delivery to the trade throughout the UK. See display ad.

IZZARD, MRS MARGARET
GIFFORD FARM COTTAGE, BATTLE RD., DALLINGTON TN21 9LH
Tel: 01424 838210 Fax: 01424 838210 Contact: M Izzard
I have poultry, eggs, single cows and calves, do B&B, plus gardening.

KAI ORGANIC CAFE
52 GARDNER ST., BRIGHTON BN1 1UN
Tel: 01273 684921 Fax: 01273 604021 Contact: Simon & Carol Thompson
kaiorganic@btinternet.com www.kaiorganic.com
Fast moving café using only organic ingredients. Fresh salad bar, sandwiches,
including wheat-free selection, seasonal soups and daily specials. Superb cakes
including unique wheat and gluten-free range. Organic Food Awards 2004: Cakes,
Pastries, Biscuits Highly Commended.

LADYWELL ORGANIC

COURT LODGE FARM, UDIMORE, RYE TN31 6BB
Tel: 01424 882206 Fax: 01424 882206 Contact: Mr or Mrs K Dean
clfarm@onetel.com
Packs of fresh or frozen farm-born and reared pedigree Sussex beef and Romney
lamb. Packs from 4 to 11 kg, ready cut or cut to your requirements. Other packs
available to order.

LANSDOWN HEALTH FOODS

44 CLIFFE HIGH ST., LEWES BN7 2AN
Tel: 01273 474681 Contact: Cindy Holmes
Retail health food shop selling a wide range of organic goods, takeaway, bread,
dairy, bodycare, herbal remedies, household and baby products.

LITTLE WARREN FARM

FLETCHING COMMON, NEWICK BN8 4JJ
Tel: 01825 722545 Fax: 01825 722545 Contact: Jim & Diana Murray
littlewarrenfarm@fletchingcommon.fsbusiness.co.uk
Specialist farm producing continuous supply of high quality organic veal.

MARIPOSA ALTERNATIVE BODYCARE

15A SHELLDALE RD., PORTSLADE BN41 1LE
Tel: 01273 242925 Fax: 01273 242925 Contact: Steve Brown
enquiries@mariposa.co.uk www.mariposa-alternative-bodycare.co.uk
Organic and natural skin care as well as baby care, feminine hygiene, organic
cotton wool and Fairtrade products. Order online or phone 01273 242925.

MONTEZUMA'S CHOCOLATES

15 DUKE ST., BRIGHTON BN1 1AH
Tel: 0845 450 6304 Fax: 0845 450 6305 Contact: Claire Beech
claire.beech@montezumas.co.uk www.montezumas.co.uk
Soil Association P6067. Manufacturer and retailer of award-winning British
organic chocolate. Highly acclaimed innovative and exciting products.

THE NATURAL STORE

57 SILLWOOD ST., BRIGHTON BN1 2PS
Tel: 01273 746781 Contact: Rachel Rogers
info@thenaturalstore.co.uk www.thenaturalstore.co.uk
Natural and organic luxury department store. Organic cotton clothes, bedlinen
and towels, organic food and drink, natural and organic toiletries, products
for babies, little ones, pets, travel and the garden.

NEAL'S YARD REMEDIES

2A KENSINGTON GARDENS, BRIGHTON BN1 4AL
Tel: 01273 601464 Contact: The Manager
mail@nealsyardremedies.com www.nealsyardremedies.com
Neal's Yard Remedies manufactures and retails natural cosmetics in addition to
stocking an extensive range of herbs, essential oils, homoeopathic remedies and
reference material.

THE NETHERFIELD CENTRE

NETHERFIELD PLACE FARM, NETHERFIELD, NR. BATTLE TN3 9PY
Tel: 01424 775615 Fax: 01424 775616 Contact: Topsy Jewell
simon@thenetherfieldcentre.co.uk
The Netherfield Centre for Sustainable Food and Farming runs education courses,
training and networking for those interested in sustainable agriculture. The
Netherfield Centre is located on an organic farm and linked to a network of
farms sharing a cutting room and marketing meat locally.

NHR ORGANIC OILS

5 COLLEGE TERRACE, BRIGHTON BN2 0EE
Tel: 0845 310 8066 Fax: 0845 310 8068 Contact: Kolinka Zinovieff
r@nhrorganicoils.com www.nhrorganicoils.com
The purest organic essential oils at affordable prices, beautifully presented
in clear glass bottles within elegant metal tubes. The largest Soil Association
certified range of the finest aromatherapy oils—over 80 types available.

THE NICE NAPPY COMPANY

61 NEW MOORSITE, WESTFIELD TN35 4QP
Tel: 08453 457193 Fax: 0870 0560165 Contact: Helen Armfield
info@nicenappy.co.uk www.nicenappy.co.uk
WAHM business selling washable nappies and covers, organic and Fairtrade
children's clothes, washable sanitary products, slings and the Bravado! range.
Products in cotton and hemp, organically produced wherever possible.

NOANAHS ORGANICS

NOLANDS FARM, STATION RD., PLUMPTON GREEN BN7 3BT
Tel: 01273 890295 Contact: Noanah Hall
Lone worker who grows seasonal mixed organic vegetables. Need help from any
WWOOFERs out there! Small, very peaceful place to work and collect your
thoughts. Sell mostly at farmers' markets and to a few restaurants.

OAKWOOD FARM

POPPINGHOLE LANE, ROBERTSBRIDGE TN32 5BL
Tel: 01580 830893 Fax: 01580 830201 Contact: Matthew Wilson
Soil Association G2575 & P6079. Top fruit, soft fruit, apple juice, pear juice,
cider and potatoes. Also attend Lewes Farmers' Market.

OLIVER, EM & RJH

BLACKLANDS, CROWHURST, BATTLE TN33 9AB
Tel: 01424 830360 Fax: 01424 830360 Contact: Robb & Marianne Oliver
architects@mnroliver.fsbusiness.co.uk
HDRA 55251, Soil Association (personal membership) 8718. An organic smallholding
producing vegetables and goats milk for family, any surplus for sale to B&B, campers
and holiday guests. Architects (RIBA) to environment-conscious designs. Camping.

ORCHIDWOOD MUSHROOMS LTD
HOBBS LANE, BECKLEY TN31 6TS
Tel: 01797 260411 Fax: 01797 260603 Contact: Nathan Goodsell
nathan.goodsell@orchidwood.co.uk www.orchidwood.co.uk
Soil Association P4568. Processing of IQF sliced, diced, whole mushrooms for
supply to food manufacturers.

ORGANIC BOTANICS
PO BOX 2140, HOVE BN3 5BX
Tel: 01273 773182 Fax: 01273 773182 Contact: Celsi Richfield
richfield@cwctv.net www.organicbotanics.com
Manufacturer/supplier of organic skin care. Superb organic skin care made with
organic, cold-pressed plant oils and extracts. Organic essential oils, natural
vitamins, natural UV filter. Telephone for further information and free sample.

THE ORGANIC CAKE COMPANY
3 FACER COTTAGES, HIGHGATE ROAD, FOREST ROW RH18 5AZ
Tel: 01342 823564 Contact: Paul Kirby
paul@theorganiccakecompany.co.uk www.theorganiccakecompany.co.uk
Delicious organic cakes, freshly baked with local and Fairtrade ingredients. Supremely
tangy lemon sponge; very chocolatey chocolate sponge; luscious carrot cake with
local cheese topping; a rare fruit cake made with porter that tastes like fruit cake
ought, and lasts 3 months. Available at farmers' markets, retailers and online.

PASKINS HOTEL
18/19 CHARLOTTE ST., BRIGHTON BN2 1AG
Tel: 01273 601203 Fax: 01273 621973 Contact: R Marlowe (Director)
welcome@paskins.co.uk www.paskins.co.uk
Most of our food is organic and we are justly proud of our varied vegetarian breakfasts. Our tasteful rooms are individually designed and we have a welcoming bar.

PILE, JOHN S (FARMS) LTD

MIDDLE FARM, WEST FIRLE, LEWES BN8 6LJ

Tel: 01323 811411 Fax: 01323 811622 Contact: Helen Marsh

info@middlefarm.com www.middlefarm.com

Soil Association P6214 (shop), G5831 (beef). Open family farm with own butchery, bakery, specialist food and cheese sections, restaurant and The National Collection of Cider and Perry, producing and selling raw milk from pedigree Jersey herd and organic beef.

REAL FOOD DIRECT

UNIT 4, LEVEL 3, NEW ENGLAND HOUSE, NEW ENGLAND STREET, BRIGHTON BN1 4GH

Tel: 01273 621222 Fax: 01273 626226 Contact: Kate Baker

info@realfood-direct.com www.realfood-direct.com

Organic food home delivery for Brighton and Hove: fruit and vegetables, fresh bread, meat and fish, dairy, wholefoods, baby food, green cleaning products and lots more.

RYE HEALTH STORE

90 HIGH ST, RYE TN31 7JN

Tel: 01797 223495 Contact: NC Crawshaw

sussexhealth@hotmail.com

A busy local shop selling a full range of wholefoods, special diet foods, supplements and natural remedies. Many organic wines are stocked.

SCHMIDT NATURAL CLOTHING

CORBIERE, NURSERY LANE, NUTLEY TN22 3NS

Tel: 0845 3450498 Fax: 01825 714676 Contact: Glenn Kositzki-Metzner

glenn@naturalclothing.co.uk www.naturalclothing.co.uk

Catalogue of organic clothing, nappies, bedsheets, duvets, toys and toiletries for babies, children and adults by mail order. Eczema, sensitive skin, chemical allergy specialists. Excellent range of underwear, socks, slippers, nightwear, including specialised sleepsuit for eczema and biodynamic lambskins. Emphasis is placed on hygiene and comfort of products, Fairtrade practice, and attentive personal service. Products certified by International Natural Textile Association, BDAA (Demeter), Real Nappy Association.

SEASONS FOREST ROW LTD

10–11 HARTFIELD ROAD, FOREST ROW RH18 5DN
Tel: 01342 824673 Fax: 01342 826119 Contact: John Walden
seasonsforestrow@btinternet.com www.seasons-forest-row.co.uk
Two shops. Large range of wholefoods and fresh produce, most organic, many
biodynamic. Also natural cosmetics, wooden toys, large range of books on
biodynamics and anthroposophy. Separate shop for organic fruit and vegetables.
Wholesale to shops, restaurants and institutions in Sussex. Business owned by
charitable trust.

SEASONS OF LEWES

199 HIGH STREET, LEWES BN7 2NS
Tel: 01273 473968 Contact: Carol Mercer
Vegetarian/Vegan restaurant, 75% ingredients organic. GM-free. Outside catering
available. Weddings, buffets etc. Food from the freezer (vegetarian meals, soups,
pies). Family business. Open Tues–Sat, 10am–5pm.

SEDLESCOMBE ORGANIC VINEYARD

HAWKHURST RD., CRIPP'S CORNER, NR. ROBERTSBRIDGE TN32 5SA
Tel: 01580 830715 Fax: 01580 830122 Contact: Irma Cook
sales@englishorganicwine.co.uk www.englishorganicwine.co.uk
England's oldest organic vineyard (est. 1979) producing a range of award-winning
English red, white and sparkling wines, as well as fruit juices, fruit wines, liqueurs
and cider, all to Soil Association organic standards. Member of the Soil Association
Organic Farms Network.

SIMPLY WILD FOOD COMPANY

SCRAGOAK FARM SHOP, BRIGHTLING RD., ROBERTSBRIDGE TN32 5EY
Tel: 01424 838454 Fax: 01424 838800 Contact: Howard Lee
enquiries@simplywildorganics.co.uk www.simplywild.biz
Simply Wild at Scragoak Farm is a retail outlet for organic fruit, vegetables, eggs,
home-produced meat and freshly baked bread. A large selection of other organic
products is also available. Member of the Soil Association Organic Farms Network.

STONELINK FARM

STONELINK FARM, STUBB LANE, BREDE, RYE TN31 6BL
Tel: 01424 882747 Fax: 01424 882584 Contact: Siân Griffiths
sian@stonelinkfarm.co.uk www.stonelinkfarm.co.uk
Organic sloe gin.

ST. MARY'S RETREAT HOUSE

CHURCH STREET, HARTFIELD TN7 4AG
Tel: 01892 770305 Contact: Rose Moore
Restore body, soul and spirit in a peaceful setting near the Ashdown Forest.
Vegetarian home cooking with organic produce. Not a B&B!

THE SUSSEX WINE COMPANY

47 SOUTH STREET, LITTLE CHELSEA, EASTBOURNE BN21 4UT
Tel: 01323 431143 Fax: 01323 431143 Contact: Ben Furst
sales@thesussexwinecompany.co.uk www.thesussexwinecompany.co.uk
Specialist independent wine merchant with great organic wines from around the
world, including Australia, Chile, Spain, New Zealand & France.

TABLEHURST FARM

LONDON RD., FOREST ROW RH18 5BJ
Tel: 01342 823173 Fax: 01324 824873 Contact: Peter Brown
tablehurst_farm@talk21.com
Mixed biodynamic community farm producing and selling excellent award-winning
home-grown biodynamic and organic meat, some seasonal fruit, vegetables and
eggs. Shop open Thursday–Saturday only, 9–5. Organic Food Awards 2004:
Fresh Meat Highly Commended; Sausages Winner.

TRINITY WHOLEFOODS CO-OPERATIVE LTD
3 TRINITY STREET, HASTINGS TN34 1HG
Tel: 01424 430473 Contact: Rhian Thomas
Soil Association R1595. Trinity Wholefoods is a co-operative founded in 1985 by local residents. We sell a range of products including fresh bread, bagged nuts, seeds, pulses, grains, frozen goods, chilled products, fresh organic veg and we have a takeaway counter. All welcome. Mon–Sat 9am–5.30pm.

WEALDEN WHOLEFOODS
PILGRIMS, HIGH ST., WADHURST TN5 6AA
Tel: 01892 783065 Fax: 01892 783351 Contact: Barbara Godsalve
barbara@wealdenwholefoods.co.uk www.wealdenwholefoods.co.uk
Wholefood shop and café selling mostly organic products. We also stock fair traded and environmentally friendly products. In the process of expanding both the shop and café, and the range of goods carried.

WOODEN WONDERS
FARLEY FARM HOUSE, CHIDDINGLY BN8 6HW
Tel: 01825 872856 Fax: 01825 872733 Contact: Kerry Negahban
info@woodenwonders.co.uk www.woodenwonders.co.uk
Wooden Wonders was the first wooden craft gift manufacturer in the UK with Forest Stewardship Council accreditation, making practical and ornamental gifts—all suitable for customisation with our in-house laser engravers.

WWW.BABY-O.CO.UK
KINGSWAY HOUSE, 134–140 CHURCH RD., HOVE BN3 2DL
Tel: 0870 760 7552 Contact: David Maden
dave@baby-o.co.uk www.baby-o.co.uk
Organic cotton baby clothes, blankets, bedding and babycare products.

THE ACORN CENTRE

TODHURST SITE, NORTH HEATH, PULBOROUGH RH20 1DL
Tel: 01798 873533 Fax: 01798 873533 Contact: Rachel Smither
michellewykes@aldingbournetrust.co.uk
Training centre for adults with learning disabilities, we grow our own organic
vegetables which are sold through our farm shop. Other organic produce also
available. Coffee shop. Soil Association G2586, P5118.

ALDINGBOURNE COUNTRY CENTRE

BLACKMILL LANE, NORTON, CHICHESTER PO18 0JP
Tel: 01243 542075 Fax: 01243 544807 Contact: Lucinda Healey
acc@aldingbournetrust.co.uk www.aldingbournetrust.co.uk
A sheltered training centre for adults with learning difficulties. A wide range of organic
products are produced on the 1.7 hectare site and these are available on the menu
in the café, from the site shop and at local farmers' markets. Conference facilities for
hire, a woodland walk and conservation area and also specialises in horticulture (bed-
ding/herbaceous plants, hanging baskets), furniture restoration and hand-made art
and craft products. For further details contact Linda Thompson or Matt Swanson.

BARFOOTS OF BOTLEY LTD

SEFTER FARM, PAGHAM ROAD, BOGNOR REGIS PO21 3PX
Tel: 01243 268811 Fax: 01243 262842 Contact: Peter Gimbel
peterg@barfoots.co.uk www.barfoots.com
Barfoots are growers and suppliers of quality fresh produce including sweetcorn,
courgettes, legumes, pumpkins, rhubarb and squash.

BEAUTY IN A BOX

11 PARSONAGE ROAD, HENFIELD BN5 9JG
Tel: 01273 491475 Contact: Debora Villa
sales@beautyinabox.co.uk www.beautyinabox.co.uk
Organic skincare products for all the family delivered to your door! From body lotions to
shampoos, from shaving cream to baby nappy cream! Luxury products at great prices.

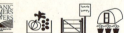

BERRY, N

GREAT WATER FARM, ASHURSTWOOD RH9 3PQ
Tel: 01342 826752 Contact: Nick Berry
Organic lamb in freezer ready packs available all year round. Free local delivery, whole lamb £85, half lamb £45, also delicious garlic-flavoured lamb burgers, the healthy alternative for children.

BIOWISE

HOYLE DEPOT, GRAFFHAM, PETWORTH GU28 0LR
Tel: 01798 867574 Fax: 01798 867574 Contact: Sue Cooper
post@biowise-biocontrol.co.uk www.biowise-biocontrol.co.uk
Soil Association-approved biological controls for gardeners and growers.

COCOA LOCO

1 MAPLE COTTAGE, HIGH STREET, PARTRIDGE GREEN, WEST SUSSEX RH13 8EW
Tel: 01403 713130 Contact: Sarah Payne
Sarah@Cocoaloco.co.uk www.cocoaloco.co.uk
Scrumptious organic chocolate brownies and truffles. Perfect as a gift for any occasion. From a single brownies in a box, right up to a party box of 24! Free UK delivery.

CORNERWEIGHS

ELM LODGE, CAUDLE STREET, HENFIELD BN5 9DQ
Tel: 01273 492794 Contact: Judie Johnson cornerweighs@aol.com
An Aladdin's cave for natural and organic foods specialising in dietetic needs, with a state of the art computer enquiry system for health concerns, putting you in control of your purchases.

COTTON BOTTOMS LTD

UNITS 7-9, WATER LANE IND. ESTATE, WATER LANE, STORRINGTON RH20 3XX
Tel: 08707 778899 Fax: 08707 778700 Contact: Joanne Freer
sales@cottonbottoms.co.uk www.cottonbottoms.co.uk
Exciting and innovative modern cotton nappies and accessories. Leading the way in environmental systems, helping parents care for their baby and its future.

DOWN TO EARTH
2–3 GOLDRINGS, WEST STREET, MIDHURST GU29 9NQ
Tel: 01730 815133 Fax: 01730 815133 Contact: Carol Granger
down_to_earth@btinternet.com
Local organic foods including dairy, greengrocery, meat and gourmet prepared foods.
Wholefoods and special dietary needs. Veg-boxes for delivery or collection, refill service for eco-detergents, organic toiletries and food supplements, real nappies.

FARGRO LTD
TODDINGTON LANE, LITTLEHAMPTON BN17 7PP
Tel: 01903 721591 Fax: 01903 730737 Contact: J McAlpine
promos@fargro.co.uk www.fargro.co.uk
Horticultural wholesaler providing organic fertiliser and a full range of biological and
organic pest control products.

GREEN PEOPLE
PONDTAIL FARM, WEST GRINSTEAD RH13 8LN
Tel: 08702 401444 Fax: 01403 741810 Contact: Sue Losson
organic@greenpeople.co.uk www.greenpeople.co.uk
Manufacturer of handmade organic health and beauty products for all the family.
Sun care, dental care, body care, baby care, skin care, hair care and home care
products. No petrochemicals, sodium lauryl sulphate or parabens. Approved by
the Vegan Society. Call for a free catalogue and trial sachet. See display ad.

G&G FOOD SUPPLIES LTD
VITALITY HOUSE, 2–3 IMBERHORNE WAY, EAST GRINSTEAD RH19 1RL
Tel: 01342 311401 Fax: 01342 301904 Contact: Jeremy Stephens
jstephens@gandgvitamins.com www.gandgvitamins.com
Soil Association approved contract encapsulator of herbal and vitamin capsules. Own
label product range created. Visit www.gandgcontract.com. EssentialFood, a certified
organic superfood, excellent for boosting energy levels: visit www.essentialfood.co.uk.
For mail order, internet and distributors, visit gandgvitamins.com.

THE GOODWOOD ESTATE CO LTD

HOME FARM, GOODWOOD, CHICHESTER PO18 0QF
Tel: 01243 755150 Fax: 01243 755155 Contact: Karl Barton
farm@goodwood.co.uk www.goodwood.co.uk
Producers of beef, lamb, pork, milk and cream for retail or wholesale. Native breeds finished to a high standard.

HIGH WEALD DAIRY

TREMAINS FARM, HORSTED KEYNES, HAYWARDS HEATH RH17 7EA
Tel: 01825 791636 Fax: 01825 791641 Contact: Mark Hardy
info@highwealddairy.co.uk www.highwealddairy.co.uk
Soil Association P1772. High Weald make a wide range of cheeses from organic sheep milk and organic cows milk, and supply outlets throughout the UK. Telephone for your nearest stockist.

KPS COMPOSTING SERVICES LTD

AWBROOK PARK FARM, HAM LANE RH17 7PR
Tel: 01444 831010 Fax: 01444 831340 Contact: Edward Watson
ed@kps.uk.com www.kpscomposting.com
Contract hire of green waste processing machinery. Organic compost also supplied.

LAINES ORGANIC FARM

47 NEWBURY LANE, CUCKFIELD RH17 5AA
Tel: 01444 452480 Fax: 01444 452480 Contact: Toos Jeuken
Soil Association J04S. Producer of organic outdoor traditional and seasonal field vegetables. Family business, self-service farm shop.

LANGMEADS OF FLANSHAM LTD—ROOKERY FARM EGGS

ROOKERY FARM, FLANSHAM, BOGNOR REGIS PO22 8NN
Tel: 01243 583583 Fax: 01243 585354 Contact: Rupert Langmead
Soil Association G7241, OF&G 11UK F02075. Our organic eggs are available wholesale from the farm or via our delivery rounds, and retail from the farm or via farmers' markets.

LEE HOUSE FARM

PLAISTOW RH14 0PB
Tel: 01403 753311 Fax: 01403 751534 Contact: Grant Roffey
grant@leehousefarm.co.uk www.leehousefarm.co.uk
Soil Association G2181. Small but perfectly formed mixed organic farm on Surrey borders producing traditional, free range, organic eggs, pork, sausages, bacon, vegetables, beef, lamb, bronze turkeys and sawn oak, all raised on our farm.

MONTEZUMA'S CHOCOLATES

BIRDHAM BUSINESS PARK, BIRDHAM PO20 7BT
Tel: 0845 450 6304 Fax: 0845 450 6305 Contact: Claire Beech
claire.beech@montezumas.co.uk www.montezumas.co.uk
Soil Association P6067. Manufacturer and retailer of award-winning British organic chocolate. Highly acclaimed, innovative and exciting products.

MONTEZUMA'S CHOCOLATES

29 EAST ST., CHICHESTER PO19 1HS
Tel: 0845 450 6304 Fax: 0845 450 6305 Contact: Claire Beech
claire.beech@montezumas.co.uk www.montezumas.co.uk
Soil Association P6067. Manufacturer and retailer of award-winning British organic chocolate. Highly acclaimed, innovative and exciting products.

MYRTLEGROVE LTD

MYRTLEGROVE FARM, PATCHING, NR. WORTHING BN13 3XL
Tel: 01903 871334 Fax: 01903 772747 Contact: Jill Angell
jillmangell@aol.com
Soil Association G7054—Organic. Producers of pedigree Sussex Cattle from single suckler herd on downland farm; also participating in the South Downs Environmentally Sensitive Area scheme. Cattle reared on grass and silage and outwintered. Store cattle and replacement heifers available all year round.

NATURAL WAY
33A CARFAX, HORSHAM RH12 1EE
Tel: 01403 262228 Fax: 01403 262228 Contact: Jean Earl
Offer wide range of prepacked wholefoods and produce sold by well known names in the wholefood industry. Not vegetables or eggs.

NORDTANG® THE SEAWEED COMPANY
WARREN VIRGATE, PLUMMERS PLAIN RH13 6PD
Tel: 01444 400403 Fax: 01444 400493 Contact: Simon Ranger
seaweed@seagreens.com
Products: wild seaweed harvesting business, supplying bulk bags of dried granules, powders and liquid forms. Outstanding arctic wild wrack seaweeds. Customers: manufacturers of food/animal feed/horticultural products, merchants & wholesalers of bulk ingredients, farmers for animals/plants and soil. Special offer: organic farms entitled to 15% off our trade price.

OCEANS OF GOODNESS
WARREN VIRGATE, PLUMMERS PLAIN RH13 6PD
Tel: 084506 400403 Fax: 01444 400493 Contact: The Manager
post@oceansofgoodness.com www.oceansofgoodness.com
Products: internet retailer of Seagreens® wild seaweed food products.
Customers: consumers, healthcare practitioners and patients, caterers.

OLD PLAW HATCH FARM LTD
SHARPTHORNE, EAST GRINSTEAD RH19 4UL
Tel: 01342 810652/810201 Fax: 01342 811478 Contact: Michael Duveen
161-acre biodynamic farm producing upasteurised milk, cream, cheese (winner in the 1999 Soil Association's Organic Food Awards), quark, eggs, beef, pork sausages and smoked bacon, soft fruit, vegetables and salads. All available through its own farm shop which opens seven days a week.

PASTA REALE
FLEMING WAY, CRAWLEY RH10 9JW
Tel: 01293 649700 Fax: 01293 649741 Contact: Michelle Jeffrey/ Chris Redman
michelle.jeffrey@pastareale.com www.pastareale.com
Soil Association P5554. Pasta Reale specialise in the manufacture of fresh pasta
and fresh sauce to the retail sector. All products are made using natural ingredients.

RIVERFORD HOME DELIVERY WORTHING
Tel: 0845 600 8311 Contact: Michelle Smith
Local licensed distributor for Riverford Organic Vegetables.

SEAGREENS®
WARREN VIRGATE, PLUMMERS PLAIN RH13 6PD
Tel: 084506 400403 Fax: 01444 400493 Contact: The Manager
post@seagreens.com www.seagreens.com
Products: natural consumer products and remedies from seaweeds sustainably wild
harvested and produced to Demeter (Biodynamic Agricultural Association) and
Soil Association standards, for use in organic foods. Complete nutritional profile
and balance. Customers: retailers & wholesalers, healthcare practitioners, catering,
manufacturers (ingredients), biodynamic and organic farms. Contacts: for local high
street stockists or mail order contact Seagreens Information Service on 084506
400403.

STEEPWOOD FARM
BROADFORD BRIDGE RD., ADVERSANE, BILLINGSHURST RH14 9EG
Tel: 01403 785434 Fax: 01403 784730 Contact: AJ Challis
val@steepwoodfarm.fsnet.co.uk
Soil Association G7049. Producer, wholesaler and retailer of the finest quality
meat and game.

ST. MARTIN'S TEA ROOMS

3 ST. MARTIN'S ST., CHICHESTER PO19 1NP
Tel: 01243 786715 Fax: 01243 786715 Contact: Keith Nelson
info@organictearooms.co.uk www.organictearooms.co.uk
Medieval tea room in centre of Chichester, sensitively restored in 1979 by
Keith Nelson (present proprietor). No smoking throughout. No convenience or
tinned foods. Three cosy log fires and walled garden.

WAYSIDE ORGANICS

WAYSIDE, WOODHORN CORNER, OVING, CHICHESTER PO20 2BT
Tel: 01243 779716 Fax: 01243 779716 Contact: Bart Ives
bart.ives@talk21.com
Soil Association G1510; P5555. Local deliveries, farm gate sales, stall at old
Spitalfields market on Sundays. Growers of salads, vegetables, herbs and top and
soft fruits to Soil Association standards.

THE WHOLE FOOD SHOP

12 THE HORNET, CHICHESTER PO19 7JG
Tel: 01243 790901 Contact: Jackie Manners
We sell a wide range of loose and pre-packed organic food including wheat-free
and dairy-free. We are also the collection point for a local box scheme.

WILLOW NURSERY

44 HILL LANE, BARNHAM PO22 0BL
Tel: 01243 552852 Fax: 01243 552852 Contact: David & Michele Wheeler
Soil Association W31S & PW31S. Grow a wide range of vegetables and salad crops
sold through a year round box scheme. Also supply fruit boxes. Deliveries
within West Sussex and East Hampshire.

BLENDEX FOOD INGREDIENTS LTD

HETTON LYONS INDUSTRIAL ESTATE, HETTON LE HOLE DH5 0RG
Tel: 0191 517 0944 Fax: 0191 526 9546 Contact: NJ Robinson
blendex@blendex.co.uk www.blendex.co.uk
Blenders of organic herbs and spices for the food industry, specifically meat, poultry
and bakery. Soil Association certified no. P1654.

BRITISH ECO

NORTHGATE HOUSE, ST. MARYS PLACE, NEWCASTLE UPON TYNE NE1 7PN
Tel: 0191 209 4161 Contact: Nick Pringle
britisheco@hotmail.com www.britisheco.com
Online shop selling solar powered lights, panels, water features and rechargers.
Wildlife products, organic fertiliser, mulch and lawn feed, wind-up radios,
composters, garden furniture, plus loads more.

F.M. (FOODS) LTD (TROPICAL WHOLEFOODS)

50 SOUTHWICK IND. ESTATE, SUNDERLAND SR5 3TX
Tel: 0191 548 0050 Fax: 0191 516 9946 Contact: The Manager
info@fmfoods.co.uk www.fmfoods.co.uk
Soil Association P4707. Import of Fairtrade and organic dried fruit and vegetables.
Packing of imported products into retail display packs. Processing of imported prod-
ucts into snack bars, for own and private label.

NEAL'S YARD REMEDIES

19 CENTRAL ARCADE, NEWCASTLE UPON TYNE NE1 5BQ
Tel: 0191 232 2525 Contact: Lynda Airey
mail@nealsyardremedies.com www.nealsyardremedies.com
Neal's Yard Remedies manufactures and retails natural cosmetics in addition to
stocking an extensive range of herbs, essential oils, homoeopathic remedies and
reference material.

OUT OF THIS WORLD

106 HIGH ST., GOSFORTH, NEWCASTLE UPON TYNE NE3 1HB
Tel: 0191 213 5377 Fax: 0191 213 5378 Contact: Jon Walker
info@ootw.co.uk www.outofthisworld.coop
Head office of small chain of ethical and organic supermarkets in Newcastle upon
Tyne, Nottingham and Leeds. Selling over 5,000 products, most food products
certified organic plus fairly traded crafts, recycled paper and bodycare products etc.
Delivery scheme from Newcastle shop. Consumer co-op with over 16,500 members.

OUT OF THIS WORLD

GOSFORTH SHOPPING CENTRE, HIGH ST., GOSFORTH,
NEWCASTLE UPON TYNE NE3 1JZ
Tel: 0191 213 0421 Fax: 0191 213 0429 Contact: Simon Critchley
info@ootw.co.uk www.outofthisworld.coop
Small chain of ethical and organic supermarkets in Newcastle upon Tyne, Leeds
and Nottingham. Selling over 5,000 products, mostly certified organic food plus
fairly traded crafts, recycled paper and bodycare products etc. Consumer co-op
with over 16,500 members.

PUMPHREYS COFFEE LTD

BRIDGE ST., BLAYDON NE21 4JH
Tel: 0191 414 4510 Fax: 0191 499 0526 Contact: M Archer
www.pumphreys-coffee.co.uk
Soil Association P4547. Roasters and blenders of the finest quality coffees and
teas to the wholesale, retail and catering sectors, established 1750.

RISING SUN FARM

KINGS RD. NORTH, WALLSEND NE28 9JL
Tel: 0191 234 0114 Contact: D Shanks
organics@risingsunfarm.freeserve.co.uk
Soil Association producer no. P1490. Cereals, horticultural, pigs, cattle. Urban
fringe farm providing education, day service for special needs. Open farm for
community. Livery yard for DIY liveries.

SCOTSWOOD NATURAL COMMUNITY GARDEN
JOHN MARLEY CENTRE, WHICKHAM VIEW, SCOTSWOOD,
NEWCASTLE-UPON-TYNE NE15 6TT
Tel: 0845 4581653 Fax: 0845 4581654 Contact: William Mortada
office@sncg.org.uk www.sncg.org.uk
Award-winning urban permaculture garden with woodlands, ponds, meadows,
orchards and vegetable plots. The two-acre site is a haven for local wildlife and an
example of sustainable food production in an urban environment. We organise
public open days in the summer and host visiting school and community groups
throughout the year. Please see our website for more details.

TRAIDCRAFT PLC
KINGSWAY, GATESHEAD NE11 0NE
Tel: 0191 491 0591 Fax: 0191 482 2690 Contact: Joe Osman
joeo@traidcraft.co.uk www.traidcraft.co.uk
Importer and distributor of organic honey, tea, chocolate. Soil Association no. P2321.

TWINING, R & CO LTD
EARL GREY WAY, NORTH SHIELDS NE29 6AR
Tel: 0191 296 0000 Contact: Hector Galley
www.twinings.com
Soil Association P4121. 295-year-old tea manufacturer. Offers a wide variety of
organic tea and infusions.

> ### Casual Agricultural Workers
> Their ancestors created what you see.
> The earth tamed, ordered, nurtured.
> Pushing up daisies
> They could not even afford
> Stones to mark their graves,
> Only a slight hummock in the evening light.
> **By James Crowden, from *Landscape into Literature***
> **edited by Kay Dunbar, Green Books, £10.00.**

CHARLECOTE MILL
HAMPTON LUCY, WARWICK CV35 8BB
Tel: 01789 842072 Contact: John Bedlington
john@charlcotemill.co.uk www.charlecotemill.co.uk
Soil Association P1555. Watermill producing wholemeal flour, including organic.

CITADEL PRODUCTS
32 ST. ANDREWS CRESCENT, STRATFORD-UPON-AVON CV37 9QL
Tel: 01789 297456 Fax: 01789 297456 Contact: K Heming
info@citadelpolytunnels.com www.citadelpolytunnels.com
Manufacturers of polytunnel greenhouses for over 30 years. Suitable for
horticulture, livestock housing, storage etc.

ELMHURST ORGANIC FARM
BOW LANE, WITHYBROOK, COVENTRY CV7 9LQ
Tel: 01788 832233 Fax: 01788 832690 Contact: Ann Pattison
Soil Association G761. Organic meat producer and retailer. Beef, sheep, pigs
and poultry and eggs. Shop retails only own produce, open Monday, Tuesday,
Friday and Saturday, 9am–4pm. Member of the Soil Association Organic Farms
Network.

FELDON FOREST FARM
FELDON FOREST FARM, FRANKTON, RUGBY CV23 9PD
Tel: 01926 632246 Contact: George Browning
georgebrowning@farmersweekly.net www.feldon-forest-farm.co.uk
Soil Association G2209. Organic mixed farm with rare breeds. Produce includes
beef, eggs, flour, fruit, herbs, vegetables, lamb, wheat, wool, sheepskins and
wood. Local delivery possible. We only sell our own produce. Educational
visits by arrangement. Universities, colleges and groups all catered for.

GAIA

7 REGENT PLACE, LEAMINGTON SPA CV31 1EH
Tel: 01926 338805 Contact: Joanna
shop@gaia.coop www.gaia.coop
Soil Association P5739. Vegetarian workers co-op selling organic vegetables and wholefoods, locally produced where possible, Fairtrade foods (mainly organic), and eco-friendly household products. Box scheme three days a week, delivered by bicycle.

HDRA, HENRY DOUBLEDAY RESEARCH ASSOCIATION, RYTON ORGANIC GARDENS

RYTON-ON-DUNSMORE, COVENTRY CV8 3LG
Tel: 024 7630 3517 Fax: 024 7663 9229 Contact: Angela Bull
enquiry@hdra.org.uk www.hdra.org.uk
Soil Association T9217. Standards for organic products for amenity horticulture. HDRA is Europe's largest organic gardening organisation. It is dedicated to researching and promoting organic gardening, farming and food. Ryton Organic Gardens, ten acres displaying all aspects of organic horticulture for gardens, plus The Vegetable Kingdom, an interactive exhibition for all ages on the history and role of vegetables. Organic restaurant and shop open daily.

HEALTHY LIFESTYLE ORGANICS LTD

KINGS LANE, SNITTERFIELD, STRATFORD-UPON-AVON CV37 0QA
Tel: 01789 730055 Fax: 01789 730056 Contact: Helen & Adrian Ross
info@hlorganics.co.uk www.hlorganics.co.uk
We are an organic and earth-friendly shopping delivery company. We deliver in our own temperature-controlled vehicles direct to your door.

IMPLEMENTATIONS

P.O. BOX 2568, NUNEATON CV10 9YR
Tel: 0845 330 3148 Contact: Jane Cobbald
enq@implementations.co.uk www.implementations.co.uk
Beautiful hand-crafted copper garden tools. Hard-wearing, kind to the soil, hand-made in Austria by craftsmen coppersmiths, with shafts of European hardwoods and bronze blades, hand-beaten for added durability. Alternative telephone: 024 7639 2497.

KITCHEN GARDEN

WAVERLY CENTRE, COVENTRY RD., CUBBINGTON CV32 7UJ
Tel: 01926 851415 Fax: 01926 851997 Contact: Mike Jack
manager@kitchen-garden.co.uk www.kitchen-garden.co.uk
OF&G registered. Range of organic condiments, herbs, spices, nut butters, herbal
teas, essential oils. Established 10 years.

MYTHE FARM ORGANIC PRODUCE

MYTHE FARM, PINWALL LANE, SHEEPY MAGNA, ATHERSTONE CV9 3PF
Tel: 01827 712367 Fax: 01827 715738 Contact: Joe & David Garland
garland_joseph@hotmail.com
Premium organic beef and lamb for sale. Organic feed barley, feed wheat, malting
barley produced. Organic wheat and barley straw available. Organic ware/baking
potatoes delivered to wholesalers. B&B, organic produce used occasionally.

NORTHLEIGH HOUSE

NORTHLEIGH HOUSE, FIVE WAYS ROAD, HATTON, WARWICK CV35 7HZ
Tel: 01926 484203 Fax: 0121 707 4780 Contact: Viv Morgan
viv@northleigh.co.uk www.northleigh.co.uk
Northleigh House is a bed and breakfast and family evening meals with nine
rooms, and we use almost entirely organic food. It is comfortable and quiet with
nice gardens in the countryside and with a nice friendly atmosphere. It has four
shields from The Tourist Board.

PIZZA ORGANIC LTD

33 JURY ST., WARWICK CV34 4EH
Tel: 01926 491641 Contact: Mike Traszko
info@pizzapiazza.co.uk www.pizza-organic.co.uk
A great menu packed full of organic options, featuring stonebaked pizza, sautéed
pasta, gourmet burgers, grilled fish and fabulous desserts. Pizza Organic is certified
by the Soil Association and was Highly Commended in the 2003 Organic Food
Awards. All restaurants open 7 days a week but opening times may vary, call 020
8397 3330 for further details.

REALITY BITES ORGANIC MARKET GARDENS
38 OLD ROAD, BISHOPS ITCHINGTON, SOUTHAM CV47 2RX
Tel: 01926 614968 Contact: Tristan Luke Coverdale
trist1@phreaker.net
We are a small family business growing a large variety of herbs, salads and
vegetables with a passion. Home deliveries around L/Spa, Stratford, Warwick and
Kenilworth. Expect very fresh produce, often picked on the day of delivery.
Farmers' markets: Warwick, Stratford, L/Spa, Oxford, Kenilworth and Rugby.
April-Xmas. Wide variety of organically raised veg plants available in spring.
We look forward to seeing you there.

REVITAL HEALTHFOOD
UNIT 1, GREENHILL ST, STRATFORD UPON AVON CV37 6LF
Tel: 01789 292353 Contact: The Manager
www.revital.com
Health shop.

RIVER NENE ORGANIC VEGETABLES—HOME DELIVERY (WARWICK)
7 VILLEBON WAY, WHITNASH, LEAMINGTON SPA CV31 2RD
Tel: 01926 338668 Contact: Melanie Cheung
melanie@rivernene.co.uk www.rivernene.co.uk
Award-winning organic vegetable box scheme delivering in south Warwickshire.
Offering differing box sizes to suit all households, from a single occupant to a
large family. A selection of fruit, dairy products, wine, fruit juices etc. also
available. Order weekly, fortnightly or whenever you like. Can order online at
www.rivernene.co.uk or by telephone on 0845 078 6868.

SHAKESPEARE BIRTHPLACE TRUST
MARY ARDEN'S HOUSE & THE SHAKESPEAR COUNTRYSIDE MUSEUM,
STRATFORD-UPON-AVON CV37 9XL
Tel: 01289 293455 Fax: 01789 415404 Contact: Joe Moore
joemoore@farmersweekly.net www.shakespeare.org
Soil Association registered. We are an organic farm surrounding the childhood
home of William Shakespeare's mother, displaying rare breeds and open
throughout the year to visitors.

WARWICK HEALTH FOODS
40A BROOK ST, WARWICK CV34 4BL
Tel: 01926 494311 Contact: PR Gooding
Family-run business for 25 years, stockists of all kinds of organic foods, fresh
fruit and vegetables always in stock, yeast-free bread and other speciality organic
breads available.

WELLESBOURNE WATERMILL
KINETON ROAD, WELLESBOURNE CV35 9HG
Tel: 01789 470237 Contact: Andrew Hamilton
hamilton.a@btconnect.com
Traditional water powered mill that produces organic and non-organic wholemeal
stoneground flour, and organic and non-organic plain white flour, semolina and bran.

THE WHOLEFOOD SHOP
C/O ST ANDREWS CHURCH HOUSE, CHURCH STREET, RUGBY CV21 3PT
Tel: 01788 567757 Contact: Dave Kerruish
d.kerruish@ntlworld.co.uk
Retailing organic wholefoods, veg, fruit, bread, cakes, savouries—all organic;
eco-products, box scheme, local deliveries. Focal point for environmental groups.
Open Thursday and Friday.

WILD & FREE
2 CENTRAL BUILDINGS, RAILWAY TERRACE, RUGBY CV21 3EL
Tel: 01788 570400 Contact: Steve Prime
info@wildandfree.net
Retail shop offering full range of organic fresh fruit and vegetables together with a
box scheme, fresh breads, milk and dairy products, meat and poultry from local
farms, wide range of organic packaged groceries, full range of Ecover cleaning
products, natural hair and body care products, free deliveries to surrounding area.

BIRMINGHAM FARMERS' MARKET

NEW STREET, NEAR VICTORIA SQUARE, BIRMINGHAM B1
Tel: 0121 303 3004 Contact: Sam Ghera
citycentre@birmingham.gov.uk www.birmingham.gov.uk/farmers
1st and 3rd Wednesday of the month, 10am–4pm.

DOWN TO EARTH

96A EARLSDON STREET, EARLSDON, COVENTRY CV5 6EJ
Tel: 024 7667 7500 Contact: Suzanne Bristow
downtoearthorganic@compuserve.com www.downtoearthorganic.co.uk
Soil Association P6189. Small, friendly retail shop and café packed top to bottom
with fruit, vegetables (local wherever possible), groceries, dairy, eggs, meat and
fish, wholefoods, nuts, seeds, rice and pulses, eco household products, skincare,
bodycare. Home delivery and box scheme.

DROP IN THE OCEAN

17 CITY ARCADE, COVENTRY CV1 3HX
Tel: 024 7622 5273 Fax: 024 7622 5273 Contact: Paula Harris
We specialise in wholefoods, herbal remedies, vitamins and vegetarian foods. We
stock a large range of organic produce including nuts, fruit, cereals, and grains.

RYAN EVANS ORGANICS

Tel: 01902 762785 Contact: Susan Ryan Evans
Organic meat and fish. Very competitive prices.

FINN BUTCHERS, M

19 STANTON ROAD, GREAT BARR, BIRMINGHAM B43 5QT
Tel: 0121 357 5780 Contact: Vaughan Meers
Organic, chemical and hormone-free meat and poultry specialists. Maynards dry
cure bacon and ham. Mail order available: phone for price list.

GREENSCENE
UNIT 7, GIBB TERRACE, THE CUSTARD FACTORY, BIRMINGHAM B9 4AA
Tel: 0121 224 7362 Contact: Jane Cummins
info@greensceneonline.co.uk www.greensceneonline.co.uk
A natural lifestyle shop with the lower floor retailing organic cotton children's and adults' yoga clothes, baby clothes and towels. We also have organic skincare and haircare for babies and adults, organic sanitary products, chemical-free cleaning, and organic Auro paints.

GROUNDWORK BLACK COUNTRY
WOLVERHAMPTON ENVIRONMENT CENTRE, WEST ACRE CRESCENT, FINCHFIELD, WOLVERHAMPTON WV3 9AY
Tel: 01902 766199 Fax: 01902 574600 Contact: Terry Bird
terry_bird@groundwork.org.uk www.groundwork-bc.org.uk
Soil Association G5900. Enterprises in organic food production including protected salads, environment considered decorative/native horticultural products, recycled timber/green wood products, training, education and community links, open days.

HEALTH FOOD CENTRE
146–148 HIGH ST., SOLIHULL B91 3SX
Tel: 0121 705 0134 Fax: 0121 705 0134 Contact: H Hards
barbara@healthfoodcentre.com www.healthfoodcentre.com
Dairy, meat, poultry, vegetables, bread, cakes, eggs, chocolates, dried fruit. Retail organic vegetables, pulses, etc.; also bread and supplements.

HOPWOOD ORGANIC FARM
BICKENHILL LANE, CATHERINE-DE-BARNES, SOLIHULL B92 ODE
Tel: 0121 711 7787 Fax: 0121 704 4033 Contact: John Cattell
sales@hopwoodorganic.co.uk www.hopwoodorganic.co.uk
Soil Association P5539 & G5540. Farm shop and home delivery of our own produce plus meat, poultry, cheeses, wholefoods, juices, jam and cereals.

THE KNOBBLY CARROT

210 WALSALL WOOD ROAD, ALDRIDGE, WALSALL WS9 8HW
Small retail shop selling fresh organic fruit and vegetables, organic wholefoods and convenience foods. We also carry a range of eco-friendly household products and toiletries.

LEVERTON & HALLS

218 MARY VALE RD., BOURNVILLE, BIRMINGHAM B30 1PJ
Tel: 0121 451 1246 Contact: Dee Leverton
deniseleverton@aol.com
Organic greengrocer selling fruit and veg, cheeses, breads, dried products, frozen products, Ecover and refills. A Fairtraded coffee shop and light snacks. Delivery service available.

THE MANIC ORGANIC CAFE

46 POPLAR RD., KINGS HEATH, BIRMINGHAM B14 7AG
Organic and local foods café with home-baked cakes and Fairtrade coffees and teas.

MOODY LTD., JACK

HOLLY BUSH FARM, WARSTONE RD., SHARESHILL, WOLVERHAMPTON WV10 7LX
Tel: 01922 417648 Fax: 01922 413420 Contact: Mark Beasley
markbeasley@jackmoodylimited.co.uk www.jackmoodylimited.co.uk
Soil Association 14369. Producer of soil conditioners/compost. Centralised composting of green materials for the production of compost, soil conditioner, mulch and top dressing, supplied nationwide. All products accredited to BSI PAS 100.

MOSELEY FARMERS' MARKET

VILLAGE GREEN, JUNCTION AT ALCESTER RD. TRAFFIC LIGHTS, MOSELEY, BIRMINGHAM B13
Tel: 0121 449 3156 Contact: David Isgrove
david@isgrove.co.uk
4th Saturday of the month (except December, when it's the Saturday before Christmas). Organic produce includes, meat, ice cream, cheese, butter, yoghurt, salmon, fruit, vegetables and soft fruit in season.

NATURAL WORLD

596 BEARWOOD RD., SMETHWICK B66 4BW
Tel: 0121 420 2145 Contact: The Manager
naturalworld@healthfoodshop.co.uk www.healthfoodshop.co.uk
We have the largest range of organic food and drink products in the Midlands, plus bodycare products.

NATURAL WORLD

26 GREAT WESTERN ARCADE, BIRMINGHAM B2 5HU
Tel: 0121 233 9931 Contact: The Manager
naturalworld@healthfoodshop.co.uk www.healthfoodshop.co.uk
We have the largest range of organic food and drink products in the Midlands, plus bodycare products.

ONE EARTH SHOP

54 ALLISON STREET, DIGBETH, BIRMINGHAM B5 5TH
Tel: 0121 632 6909 Contact: Tina Rickards
Vegan shop with large range of organic and Fairtrade products; wholefoods, chilled, confectionery etc. Local delivery (not a box scheme).

ORGANIC ROOTS

CRABTREE FARM, DARK LANE, KINGS NORTON, BIRMINGHAM B38 0BS
Tel: 01564 822294 Fax: 01564 829212 Contact: Bill Dinenage
info@organicroots.co.uk www.organicroots.co.uk
Soil Association G1880. Organic Roots is the only organic shop in the West Midlands wholly dedicated to supplying organic food of all types. Home delivery service based on our 500 lines of organic produce.

A.R. PARKIN LTD

UNIT 8, CLETON STREET BUSINESS PARK, CLETON STREET, TIPTON DY4 7TR
Tel: 0121 557 1150 Fax: 0121 522 4086 Contact: Peter Gregory
enquiries@arparkin.co.uk www.arparkin.co.uk
Soil Association licence number P2508. Manufacturer and supplier of organic seasoning blends, ingredients, herbs, spices, peppers and crumbs.

RIVER NENE ORGANIC VEGETABLES HOME DELIVERY (SOLIHULL)

35 ULLENHALL RD, KNOWLE, SOLIHULL B93 9JD
Tel: 0845 078 6868 Fax: 0845 466 0060 Contact: Colin Atkins
colin@rivernene.co.uk www.rivernene.co.uk
Independent local licensed distributor from Riverford Organic Vegetables. Award winning organic vegetable box scheme delivered to homes in Solihull and surrounding areas. Box sizes to suit single person up to large families. Wide range of other organic produce including fruit, dairy, alcohol and fruit juices. For more information or to place an order go to our website www.rivernene.co.uk or alternatively call 0845 078 6868.

ROSEMARY'S HEALTH FOODS

2/3 MANDER SQUARE, MANDER CENTRE, WOLVERHAMPTON WV1 3NN
Tel: 01902 427520 Fax: 01902 426147 Contact: Duncan Gillan
enquiries@rosemaryshealthfoods.co.uk www.rosemaryshealthfoods.co.uk
We sell an extensive range of organic healthy, dried, fresh, chilled, frozen foods and herbal remedies.

ROSSITER, S & A—TRADITIONAL FAMILY BUTCHERS

247 MARYVALE ROAD, BOURNVILLE, BIRMINGHAM B30 1PN
Tel: 0121 458 1598 Fax: 0121 458 1598 Contact: Stephen Rossiter
Soil Association R2037, NFMT. Meat and poultry, bread, cheeses, eggs, cooked meats, pickles, preserves, trout and salmon. Small friendly family-run business with emphasis on customer satisfaction and confidence.

SAGE WHOLEFOODS

148 ALCESTER RD., MOSELEY, BIRMINGHAM B13 8HS
Tel: 0121 449 6909 Fax: 0121 449 6909 Contact: George Howell
sagewholefoods@talk21.com www.sagewholefoods.com
A not-for-profit workers co-operative retailing a wide range of organic foods including fruit and vegetables, Fairtrade goods, specialist dietary food, supplements and remedies. Mon–Sat, 9.30am–6.30pm.

SIBILA'S AT BODY AND BEING
THE WATERMARQUE, 100 BROWNING STREET, BIRMINGHAM B16 8EH
Tel: 0121 456 7633 Contact: Shruti Whittington
welcome@bodyandbeing.co.uk www.bodyandbeing.co.uk
Organic vegetarian restaurant awaiting certification.

WOODBROOKE QUAKER STUDY CENTRE
1046 BRISTOL RD., SELLY OAK, BIRMINGHAM B29 6LJ
Tel: 0121 472 5171 Fax: 0121 472 5173 Contact: Kathleen Russell
kathleen@woodbrooke.org.uk www.woodbrooke.org.uk
Set in ten acres of organically managed gardens, Woodbrooke is a residential
Quaker education centre, also offering conference facilities and general
accommodation. Guests enjoy organic food grown on the premises.

 Accommodation

 Garden and Farm Sundries

 Producers

 Box Schemes/ Local Deliveries

 Farmers' market Stall

 Restaurants/ Cafés/Caterers

 Day Visits

 Manufacturers/ Processors

 Retail shops

 Eco Products

 Importers/ exporters

 Textiles

 Farm Gate Sales

 Mail order suppliers

 Wholesalers

AGRALAN GARDEN PRODUCTS

THE OLD BRICKYARD, ASHTON KEYNES, SWINDON SN6 6QR
Tel: 01285 860015 Fax: 01285 860056 Contact: Alan Frost
sales@agralan.co.uk www.agralan.co.uk
Agralan offer a range of non-poisonous and effective treatments for many pest problems: vegetables can be grown without pesticides. New products allow control of slugs, ants and flies. Distribute Biobest biological controls and bumble bees.

BEANS AND HERBS

THE HERBARY, 161 CHAPEL STREET, HORNINGSHAM, WARMINSTER BA12 7LU
Tel: 01985 844442 Contact: Pippa Rosen
info@beansandherbs.co.uk www.beansandherbs.co.uk
Organic seed—specialising in herbs and vegetables. Very large number of unusual varieties of French bean seed, both climbing and dwarf. Also many herbs. All seeds suitable for the home-grower or allotment holder. Mail order all year. Visit our website, or send A5 first class SAE for current catalogue.

BERKELEY FARM DAIRY

BERKELEY FARM, SWINDON RD., WROUGHTON, SWINDON SN4 9AQ
Tel: 01793 812228 Fax: 01793 845949 Contact: N Gosling
berkeleyfarmdairy@fwi.co.uk
Soil Association G4670, P4891. Organic dairy and arable farm, organic Guernsey milk processed on-farm for Abel & Cole. Contract processing of organic milk.

CLOTHWORKS

P.O. BOX 3233 BA15 2WB
Tel: 01225 309 218 Contact: Linda Row
clothworks.info@virgin.net www.clothworks.co.uk
Clothworks offers Organic Essentials, a range of organic clothing for women and babies including cardigans, vests and polo necks for day wear. The Unique range is a craft-based designer collection made from hemp and silk.

COLESHILL ORGANICS

59 COLESHILL, SWINDON SN6 7PT
Tel: 01793 861070 Fax: 01793 861070 Contact: Sonia Oliver
coleshillorganics@msn.com www.coleshillorganics.co.uk
Home-grown organic vegetables, fruit and eggs: boxes of seasonal produce delivered
weekly within radius of 25 miles. Also farm shop within the walled garden selling
wide range of fresh organic fruit and vegetables. Shop closed Sun, Mon, Tues and
Wed am. Member of the Soil Association Organic Farms Network. Organic Food
Awards 2004: Best Horticulture, Winner Best Box Scheme.

DIBBLE, G & E

EASTROP FARM, HIGHWORTH SN6 7PP
Tel: 01793 762196 Contact: Guy Dibble
guy@dibble18.freeserve.co.uk
Organic beef sold direct, freezer ready, vacuum-packed, handy box sizes £100 &
£200 per box. School visits by arrangements.

EASTBROOK FARMS ORGANIC MEAT

EASTBROOK FARM, THE CALF HOUSE, CUES LANE, BISHOPSTONE,
SWINDON SN6 8PL
Tel: 01793 790460 Fax: 01793 791239 Contact: Barbara Rayner
orders@helenbrowningorganics.co.uk www.helenbrowningorganics.co.uk
Soil Association PH53S. Nationwide home delivery service of organic meat.
Supplier to the major supermarkets. The Helen Browning's organic range of organic
products is sold through Sainsbury's and the Co-op. Helen Browning's Flying Pig
will answer your catering needs, be it major outside event or private party. Member
of the Soil Association Organic Farms Network. Organic Food Awards 2004:
Charcuterie Highly Commended; Fresh Meat Winner.

GREEN CUISINE

PILLAR HOUSE, THE STREET, CHARLTON SN16 9DL
Tel: 01666 824584 Contact: Anna Ross
anna@greencuisine.org.uk
Delivery service. Local fresh organic veg delivered weekly to your door.

THE GREEN HOUSE

120 FISHERTON ST., SALISBURY SP2 7QT
Tel: 01722 325515 Contact: Sana Stephens
sanastephens@yahoo.co.uk www.loveorganic.com
Organic clothing from well established organic companies such as People Tree, Bishopston trading and many more. All the companies we use have their own certified cotton. We also sell Green Baby clothing and other organic products such as bedding.

HAMBLEDEN HERBS

PO BOX 2711, MARLBROUGH SN8 4ZR
Tel: 01672 811145 Fax: 01672 811863 Contact: Lyn Seymour
lyn@organicmanufacture.com www.hambledenherbs.co.uk
The Hambleden Herbs range of over 135 organic herbal products includes teas, culinary herbs and spices, infusions, tinctures and Christmas products. The range has won over 30 trade and consumer awards in the last nine years. High quality, unadulterated herbal products, ethically produced and traded, using only essential processing and minimal recycled packaging. Hambleden Herbs are produced on a working organic farm in Somerset and can be purchased from health food stores, organic farm shops and delicatessens.

HARVEY, M & A

GOULTERS MILL, NETTLETON, NR. CHIPPENHAM SN14 7LL
Tel: 01249 782555 Fax: 01249 782555 Contact: A Harvey
We produce Lleyn sheep for breeding and for meat. Eggs for sale from the farm gate. Light Sussex chicks also available from farm gate. We also have paying guests to stay. Soil Association no. G2641. Deliveries made all over UK.

HAZELBURY PARTNERS

HAZELBURY MANOR, BOX, CORSHAM SN13 8HX
Tel: 01225 812088 Fax: 01225 810875 Contact: The Manager
Soil Association G1825. Delicious organic lamb, pork, and beef, hens and duck eggs, produced on family-run farm using rare breed lambs and pigs.

THE HERBARY

THE HERBARY, 161 CHAPEL STREET, HORNINGSHAM, WARMINSTER BA12 7LU
Tel: 01985 844442 Contact: Pippa Rosen
info@beansandherbs.co.uk www.beansandherbs.co.uk
Organic seed—specialising in herbs and vegetables. Very large number of unusual
varieties of French bean seed, climbing and dwarf. Suitable for the home-grower or
allotment holder. Mail order all year. Visit our website, or send A4 first class SAE for
catalogue.

HIGGINS, R & S

CHURCH FARM, MAIDEN BRADLEY, WARMINSTER BA12 7HN
Tel: 01985 844221 Fax: 01985 844221 Contact: Sally Higgins
Milk for OMSCo and a local dairy, farm gate sales of lamb to order.

KENSONS FARM

SUTTON MANDEVILLE, SALISBURY SP3 5NG
Tel: 01722 714815 Fax: 01722 714815 Contact: Hugh Collins & Liz Barrah
Soil Association G5971. Intensive and field scale organic vegetables, including
asparagus.

KIT FARM

SOUTHVIEW, LITTLE CHEVERELL, DEVIZES SN10 4JJ
Tel: 01380 818591 Fax: 01380 818591 Contact: Lynn Rooke & Peter Edwards
lynnrooke6@aol.com
We produce top quality beef animals. They are sired by Sussex bulls, single suckled
and finished on grass. They yield tender, succulent, marbled meat. Soil Association
symbol no. G1941.

LAKESIDE EGGS

LAKESIDE STABLES, STEEPLE LANGFORD, SALISBURY SP3 4NH
Tel: 01722 790786 Contact: John Delaney
Soil Association G2215. We have free ranging laying hens.

LANGLEY CHASE ORGANIC FARM

KINGTON LANGLEY, CHIPPENHAM SN15 5PW
Tel: 01249 750095 Fax: 01249 750095 Contact: Jane Kallaway
post@langleychase.co.uk www.langleychase.co.uk
Soil Association G4302. Pedigree flock of rare breed Manx Loghtan sheep carefully
reared to produce organic whole, half lambs or joints. Nationwide delivery. Award
winner Organic Food Awards 2001, 2002, Winner of Best Lamb Organic Food
Awards 2003. Please phone to discuss requirements. Farm visits welcome. Organic
Food Awards 2004: Fresh Meat Winner.

LOTMEAD FARM

WANBOROUGH, NR. SWINDON SN4 0SN
Tel: 01793 790260 Contact: Norman Parry
200-acre organic dairy farm specialising in milk from grass. Pick your own fruit and
vegetables. Business village on farm.

LOWER SHAW FARM

OLD SHAW LANE, SHAW, SWINDON SN5 9PJ
Tel: 01793 771080 Contact: Andrea Hirsch
enquiries@lowershawfarm.co.uk www.lowershawfarm.co.uk
Courses and gatherings. Permaculture, fungus forays, crafts, yoga, circus skills,
singing, cooking, herbs, families. Friendly atmosphere, home-grown and local food.
Organic gardens and animals. Ask us for a programme.

MANOR FARM PARTNERSHIP

MANOR FARM, EAST GRAFTON, MARLBOROUGH SN8 3DB
Tel: 01672 810735 Fax: 01672 810749 Contact: Pip Browning
pip.james@btopenworld.com
Organic beef and cereals.

NEAL'S YARD REMEDIES
27 MARKET PLACE, SALISBURY SP1 1TL
Tel: 01722 340736 Contact: The Manager
mail@nealsyardremedies.com www.nealsyardremedies.com
Neal's Yard Remedies manufactures and retails natural cosmetics in addition to stocking an extensive range of herbs, essential oils, homoeopathic remedies and reference material.

THE ORGANIC EXPERIENCE
7 THE BRIDGE, CHIPPENHAM SN15 1HA
Tel: 01249 720274 Contact: Steve Cronin
We sell an extensive range of food, drink, ecological cleaning and body care products including our own and others' fresh fruit and vegetables, fresh meat, dairy, frozen, ice cream, and a full range of groceries including cereals, pulses etc. Home delivery available.

ORGANIC PRINCESS
6 AYLESWADE ROAD, SALISBURY SP2 8DR
tanya@organicprincess.com www.organicprincess.com
Australia Certified Organic (ACO). Following a United States Department of Agriculture (USDA) ruling, we have the only skin care range that meets the USDA requirements for organic food production.

PERTWOOD ORGANIC CEREAL CO LTD
LORD'S HILL BARN, LONGBRIDGE DEVERILL, WARMINSTER BA12 7DY
Tel: 01747 820499 Fax: 01985 841919 Contact: Mark Houghton Brown
www.pertwood.co.uk
Range of organic breakfast cereals processed from own produce: oat-based, wheat-free, GMO-free muesli with delicious fruits, porage oats, crunchy with raisins and almonds, crunchy with mixed nuts. UK coverage. Large quantities available. Member of the Soil Association Organic Farms Network.

PURE ORGANICS LTD
STOCKPORT FARM, STOCKPORT RD., AMESBURY SP4 7LN
Tel: 01980 626263 Fax: 01980 626264 Contact: Pauline Stiles
pauline@pureorganics.co.uk www.pureorganics.co.uk
Soil Association P2269. We specialise in the production of organic, additive-free foods for children, providing popular alternatives to mass-produced convenience foods: we produce chicken nuggets, burgers, sausages and vegetarian products. We specialise in addressing dietary intolerances. We produce under our own brand 'For Georgia's Sake', own label products for two of the major multiples, and food for school meal services.

PURELY ORGANIC
DEVERILL TROUT FARM, LONGBRIDGE DEVERILL, WARMINSTER BA12 7DZ
Tel: 01985 841093 Fax: 01985 841268 Contact: Tony Free
trout@purelyorganic.fsnet.co.uk www.purelyorganic.co.uk
Trout farm and shop selling a full range or organic produce, smoked trout, paté, watercress, etc.

PURTON HOUSE
PURTON HOUSE, CHURCH END, PURTON, SWINDON SN5 4EB
Tel: 01793 772287 Fax: 01793 772750 Contact: Rowie Meers
rowie@purton-house.co.uk www.purton-house.co.uk
Organic vegetable, fruit, egg & meat box scheme. Local door deliveries or collection points. Farmers' markets. We grow over 90 types of vegetables and fruit and many different varieties of each. Our boxes are excellent value for money and always have a good variety of fresh produce.

RIVERFORD HOME DELIVERY—SWINDON
130 PARK LANE, FRAMPTON COTTERELL BS36 2ER
Tel: 01454 777404 Fax: 01454 777404 Contact: Richard Prosser
richardandjo@riverfordhomedelivery.co.uk www.riverford.co.uk
Home and workplace delivery of Riverford Organic Vegetables via box scheme for Swindon and Wiltshire. Products delivered include vegetables, fruit, eggs, milk, wine and other Organic foods. See www.riverford.co.uk for full details.

RUSHALL FARM
DEVIZES RD., RUSHALL, PEWSEY SN9 6ET
Tel: 01980 630361 Fax: 01980 630095 Contact: Lesley Walford
info@rushallorganics.co.uk www.rushallorganics.co.uk
Grain and organic pigs. Soil Association no. W09S.

SAGE ORGANIC LTD
CLENCH LODGE, WOOTTON RIVERS, MARLBOROUGH SN8 4NT
Tel: 01672 811777 Fax: 01672 811888 Contact: Jayne Baker
info@sageorganic.com www.sageorganic.com
We produce a high quality range of food supplements with the inclusion of
organic ingredients. The right combination of organic herbs, vitamins, minerals
and other nutrients are available in our easy-to-use Dual Pack range.

STONEGATE LTD
CORSHAM RD., LACOCK SN15 2LZ
Tel: 01249 730700 Fax: 01249 732200 Contact: John Sayer
enquiries@stonegate.co.uk www.stonegate.co.uk
Soil Association P6229, Organic Farmers & Growers 12UKCP030028. Stonegate
Ltd currently produce, pack and deliver organic eggs to the UK. We supply all large
retailers and specialise in special breed organic eggs such as Columbian Blacktail
and Speckledy.

SUMMERLEAZE GALLERY
EAST KNOYLE, SALISBURY SP3 6BY
Tel: 01747 830790 Fax: 01747 830790 Contact: Trish Scott Bolton
trish@summerleazegallery.co.uk
Soil Association G4877. Art gallery holding three exhibitions a year, four-day
painting courses and lectures in converted farm buildings on organic farm.
Dinner, bed and breakfast in nearby farmhouse.

SWINDON PULSE WHOLEFOOD CO-OP

27 CURTIS ST., SWINDON SN1 5JU
Tel: 01793 692016 Contact: Steph Robbshaw
www.swindonpulse.co.uk
Thirty year old co-op selling organic fruit and vegetables, wide range of groceries,
cruelty-free cosmetics, frozen and chilled goods, all vegetarian, many vegan and
gluten-free products, all GM-free.

TALLYWACKER FARM

50 THE RIDINGS, KINGTON ST. MICHAEL, CHIPPENHAM SN14 6JG
Tel: 01249 750035 Contact: Steve O'Connor
sales@tallywackerfarm.co.uk www.tallywackerfarm.co.uk
Soil Association registered producer/processor. Producers of organic fruit and veg.
Home delivery box scheme to Corsham, Chippenham, Devizes, Malmesbury,
Tetbury, Wooton Bassett, west Swindon, Calne, Melksham, Neston, Somerfords,
Trowbridge, surrounding villages and all areas in between. Commended for veg in
Organic Food Awards 2004.

THOMAS FAMILY BUTCHERS, MICHAEL

51 THE TRIANGLE, MALMESBURY SN16 0AH
Tel: 01666 823981 Fax: 01666 823981 Contact: Steve Cox
www.michaelthomasbutchers.co.uk
Fruit/veg, organic nuts, pulses, dried fruit, dairy products, whole foods, eco
cleaning products, vitamins, minerals.

THROOPE MANOR FARM

BISHOPSTONE, SALISBURY SP5 4BA
Tel: 01722 718318 Fax: 01722 718544 Contact: M Head
vishead@aol.com
Soil Association G5089. Flock of 500 Mule ewes producing organic texel x fat
lambs on ESA chalk downland, lambing out of doors in May. Also from 2005, 60
hectares of spring sown cereals/pulses.

THE TRACKLEMENT COMPANY LTD
THE DAIRY FARM, PINKNEY PARK, SHERSTON SN16 0NX
Tel: 01666 840851 Fax: 01666 840022 Contact: Guy Tullberg
info@tracklements.co.uk www.tracklements.co.uk
Soil Association P4261. Manufacturers of high quality chutneys, sauces, jellies,
mustards and dressings (accompaniments to meat, fish and cheese). Organic Food
Awards 2004: Condiments Winner.

TRAFALGAR FISHERIES
BARFORD FISH FARM, DOWNTON SP5 3QF
Tel: 01725 510448 Fax: 01725 511165 Contact: John Williams
info@trafish.com www.trafish.com
Soil Association G4381, P5061. Fish farm/processors. Producers and processors
of organic rainbow and brown trout for the table.

UPPER BURYTOWN FARM PARTNERS
UPPER BURYTOWN FARM, BLUNSDON, SWINDON SN26 7DQ
Tel: 01793 700595 Contact: Arend Von Freeden
Soil Association G7025. Beef, cereal, sheep, small amount of direct sale meat.

VITACRESS SALADS LTD
MULLENS FARM, MANNINGFORD, BOHUNE COMMON, NR. PEWSEY SN9 6LY
Tel: 01672 851711 Fax: 01672 851774 Contact: Rob Corlett
rob.corlett@vitacress.co.uk www.vitacress.com
Soil Association G7887. We are producers of baby leaf salads with land in
conversion at present.

WARMINSTER MALTINGS LTD
39 POUND ST., WARMINSTER BA12 8NN
Tel: 01985 212014 Fax: 01985 212015 Contact: Chris Garratt
info@warminster-malt.co.uk www.warm inster-malt.co.uk
Soil Association P5961. Manufacture of malt from cereal (barley/wheat) using
traditional floor malting process. For use in brewing and food.

WESTWOOD FARM

RODE HILL, COLERNE, NR. CHIPPENHAM SN14 8AR
Tel: 01225 742854 Contact: J Trotman
Organic farm growing delicious seasonal vegetables, fruit and herbs. The fruit is used for the hand-crafted preserves (jams, jellies, marmalades, chutneys). Hand-made Dundee and rich celebration cakes are another speciality available by order and direct sales.

WILTSHIRE ORGANIC MILK

HOUSECROFT FARM, EDINGTON, NR. WESTBURY BA13 4NN
Tel: 01380 870985 Fax: 01380 870985 Contact: Julie Osborne
pf.josborne@tinyworld.co.uk
Produce and sell wholesale pasteurised organic milk, whole and semi-skimmed, also organic cream; ideally to shops, boxes, milkmen, restaurants, cafés, hotels etc in Wiltshire.

YATESBURY ORGANICS

GR GANTLETT & SON, YATESBURY HOUSE FARM, YATESBURY, CALNE SN11 8YF
Tel: 01672 539191 Fax: 01672 539039 Contact: Richard Gantlett
yatesbury@farming.co.uk www.easisite.co.uk/yatesburyorganicfarm
Soil Association G2931. Vegetables, pedigree Aberdeen Angus beef, lamb. All home-grown. Box deliveries. Please come and see us.

Go Native!

The loss of valuable wildlife habitats has been severe owing to changes in agricultural practice, new housing and industrial development. If you buy and plant native trees, shrubs, wildflowers and bulbs you'll be helping to recreate some of these lost habitats and wildlife havens, and you'll also be safeguarding a significant part of our cultural and landscape heritage. For a wide selection of native trees, plants and wildflowers contact BTCV (British Trust for Conservation Volunteers) on 01302 572 300 or visit www.btcv.org.

From *Go MAD! Go Make A Difference 2: Over 500 daily ways to save the planet* by The Ecologist, Think Books, £6.99.

BEEWELL

4 ROYAL ARCADE, PERSHORE WR10 1AG
Tel: 01386 556577 Contact: Jen Creese
beewellhealth@hotmail.com
Health food shop, established 1986, specialising in organic wholefoods, fresh organic vegetables and fruit, organic meats and poultry. Small café/coffee shop.

THE COTTAGE HERBERY

MILL HOUSE, BORASTON, NR. TENBURY WELLS WR15 8LZ
Tel: 01584 781575 Fax: 01584 781483 Contact: Kim & Rob Hurst
www.thecottageherbary.co.uk
Organic peat-free herbs, cottage garden plants and native plants. All plants grow in a permitted certified growing medium, Fertile Fibre. Talks given to groups. Catalogue: send 6 first class stamps. In 2006 we celebrate 30 years of organic and peat-free growing.

CRIDLAN & WALKER

23 ABBEY ROAD, MALVERN WR14 3ES
Tel: 01684 573008 Fax: 01684 566017 Contact: The Manager
Organic Farmers & Growers no. UKP100013. Organic meat, vegetables, milk, cheese and groceries.

DINGLEY, WL & CO

BUCKLE ST., HONEYBOURNE, EVESHAM WR11 7QE
Tel: 01386 830242 Fax: 01386 833541 Contact: Alan Bown
dingley1921@hotmail.com www.wldingley.com
Soil Association I656. Manufacturer of organic fertilisers to the Soil Association certification scheme.

THE DOMESTIC FOWL TRUST

HONEYBOURNE PASTURES, HONEYBOURNE, EVESHAM WR11 5QG
Tel: 01386 833083 Contact: C Landshoff
domestic-fowl-trust@mywebpage.net mywebpage.net/domestic-fowl-trust
Suppliers of high quality poultry housing and equipment. Traditional and hybrid
poultry, ducks and geese. Mail order service. Countrywide delivery. Open to the
public.

ELYSIA NATURAL SKIN CARE

27 STOCKWOOD BUSINESS PARK, STOCKWOOD, NR. REDDITCH B96 6SX
Tel: 01386 792622 Fax: 01386 792623 Contact: Joanne Gould
enquiries@drhauschka.co.uk www.drhauschka.co.uk
Elysia distributes the Dr Hauschka skin care range, holistic products using
organically grown herbs and plants from certified bio-dynamic farms. The products
and ingredients are not tested on animals.

FERTILE FIBRE

TENBURY WELLS WR15 8LT
Tel: 01584 781575 Fax: 01584 781483 Contact: Rob Hurst
sales@fertilefibre.fsnet.co.uk www.fertilefibre.com
Soil Association I1408. Organic coir compost. We supply seed, multi-purpose and
potting composts, plus coir blocks, and fertilisers. Trade and mail order services
available.

GREENLINK ORGANIC FOODS

11 GRAHAM RD., GREAT MALVERN WR14 2HR
Tel: 01684 576266 Fax: 01684 576266 Contact: Mike Gatiss
greenlinkorganics@tiscali.co.uk
Retail outlet specialising in organic foods, fresh fruit and veg, meat, fish, poultry, a
wide range of wholefoods and body care products. Small café/snack bar selling
fresh daily prepared vegetarian food, teas and coffees.

JOHNSON, AP

WORDLEY FARM, DUNLEY, STOURPORT-ON-SEVERN DY13 0UT
Tel: 01299 896344 Contact: Louise Johnson
Beef cattle, sheep, laying hens.

LIFE CHANGES LTD

2ND FLOOR, 28–30 BELLE VUE TERRACE, GREAT MALVERN WR14 4PZ
Tel: 0800 043 6309 Contact: Dawn Salter
dawn@lifechanges.co.uk www.saferwithorganics.net
Products of unrivalled purity for skin, hair, body, oral care & cosmetics. International organic certification to food grade standards: USDA, IFOAM, ACO, JAS. No synthetic chemicals, just cold processed, nutrient-rich high quality ingredients. New to UK since Feb 05. Available mail order and online. Distributors required across UK & Eire.

OAKFIELD FARM PRODUCTS LIMITED

NEWTOWN, OFFENHAM, EVESHAM WR11 8RZ
Tel: 01386 425222 Fax: 01386 49835 Contact: Hugh Owens
oakfieldoffice@aol.com
Soil Association Licence nos: P2110, P2253 (UK5) Mushroom grower—all organic grades of chestnut mushrooms and various exotic varieties of mushrooms, also organic. Delivery nationwide.

OXTON ORGANICS

BROADWAY LANE, FLADBURY, PERSHORE WR10 2QF
Tel: 01386 860477 Fax: 01386 860477 Contact: Jayne Arnold
boxes@oxtonorganics.co.uk www.oxtonorganics.co.uk
Soil Association E17M. Fruit, vegetables and eggs delivered locally via our box scheme. Also on-line ordering via our website.

PHOENIX ORGANICS LTD

PULLEN'S FARM, BROMYARD RD., CRADLEY, NR. MALVERN WR13 5JN
Tel: 01886 880713 Fax: 01886 880743 Contact: Geoff Mutton
phoenixorganics@btconnect.com www.phoenixorganics.ltd.uk
We are wholesalers of organic fruits and vegetables, specialising in sales to box
schemes, independent retail outlets, farm shops, caterers, processors and other
non-supermarket outlets. See display ad.

PRICHARD, STEPHEN

WOODCOTE FARM, DODFORD, BROMSGROVE B61 9EA
Tel: 01562 777795 Fax: 01562 777024 Contact: SJ Prichard
woodcotefarm@btinternet.com www.woodcotefarm.com
Soil Association G4109. Woodcote Farm produces organic fat lamb and Aberdeen
Angus beef. We also provide bed and breakfast and self-contained apartments for
holidays or long lets.

PRIMAFRUIT LTD

ENTERPRISE WAY, VALE BUSINESS PARK, EVESHAM WR11 1TG
Tel: 01386 425000 Fax: 01386 425001 Contact: The Manager
www.primafruit.co.uk
Importer of fresh organic fruit including grapes, stone fruit, berries, top fruit and
citrus supplies to the industries. Committed to the organic market, growers,
customers and consumers.

RED DEER HERBS LTD

EARL'S CROOME, WORCESTER WR8 9DF
Tel: 01386 750734 Contact: Margaret Herbert
enquiries@reddeerherbs.co.uk www.reddeerherbs.co.uk
RDH import and grow herbs for the food manufacturing industry. We will supply
from 1kg to 1tonne. M&S, Sainsbury, Waitrose, Asda, Tesco sell products with our
herbs. Deliveries nationally and throughout Europe.

THE RETREAT

THE RETREAT, STOKE BLISS, TENBURY WELLS WR15 8RY
Tel: 01885 410431 Contact: Maggie Kingston
maggie@retreatstokebliss.freeserve.co.uk www.uk.geocities.com/peastwing
Space to be! Self-catering accommodation, sleeps 2–4 people. Hereford/
Worcestershire borders, wildflower meadow, walks and peace. Pets and children
welcome, local food available to order.

ROSEMARY'S HEALTH FOODS

10 THE SHAMBLES, WORCESTER WR1 2RF
Tel: 01905 612190 Fax: 01905 612190 Contact: Marie Cockill
enquiries@rosemaryshealthfoods.co.uk www.rosemaryshealthfoods.co.uk
We sell an extensive range of organic healthy, dried, fresh, chilled, frozen foods and
herbal remedies.

SONG OF THE EARTH

2 CONISTON CLOSE, POOLBROOK, MALVERN WR14 3SN
Tel: 01684 892533 Fax: 01684 892533 Contact: Fiona Hopes
fiona@song-of-the-earth.com www.song-of-the-earth.com
Garden designer. Individual and special gardens created by a qualified and
experienced designer, working with the subtle energies of the land to create
sustainable landscapes that are ecologically sound, practical, productive and
beautiful. Co-principal of The Earth School.

STEELE, WO & SONS

CHAPEL FARM, NETHERTON, NR. PERSHORE WR10 3JG
Tel: 01386 710379 Fax: 01386 710379 Contact: Adrian Steele
adrian@wosteele.fsnet.co.uk
Soil Association S37M; Organic Arable Marketing Group; Organic Seed Producers
Ltd, Graig Farm. Mixed lowland organic farm specialising in wheat, oats, beans,
potatoes, beef and lamb since 1986. Farm gate sales and sales to mills, butchers
and box schemes. Please phone first.

UPPER WICK FARM

UPPER WICK FARM, RUSHWICK WR2 5SU
Tel: 01905 422243 Contact: Will Edmonds
www.rootsrushwick.com
Upper Wick Farm is a 100 hectare farm lying in the beautiful Teme valley in
Worcestershire, minutes from Worcester city itself. The farm has beef cattle
and sheep together with a farm shop, traditional orchards, cereals and potatoes.
Visit the farm to discover more. A small, self-contained holiday cottage is available
with views across the orchard. Home-grown prepared meals are available using
organic ingredients. Member of the Soil Association Organic Farms Network.

WALCOT ORGANIC NURSERY

LOWER WALCOT FARM, WALCOT LANE, DRAKES BROUGHTON, PERSHORE WR10 2AL
Tel: 01386 553697 Fax: 01905 841587 Contact: Kevin O'Neill
enquiries@walcotnursery.co.uk
Soil Association G5594. Producers of organically grown fruit trees. Available
bare-root November to March, and in containers. Mail order anywhere in mainland
UK. Visitors welcome by appointment. Catalogue available.

The Fertilizer Value of Urine

Two Swedish university studies report that one northern European adult (who
consumes plant and animal proteins) produces enough fertilizer in urine to grow
50 to 100 percent of the food requirement for another adult. We excrete these
nitrogen-containing compounds as urea, creatine, ammonia and a small
amount of uric acid. These nutrients could feed a hungry and growing popula-
tion at a lower cost than producing more expensive chemical fertilizer.
(Sundberg, 1995; Drangert, 1997)

The world needs all the nutrients we are flushing away each day in our urine.
Given the far-reaching costs of using manufactured fertilizers, utilizing this valuable
and usually sterile resource deserves more consideration. Urine costs nothing to
produce (unless you count the plant and animal protein we eat), but it does have
storage and transportation costs, as does commercial chemical fertilizer.
**From *Liquid Gold: The Lore and Logic of Using Urine to Grow Plants* by
Carol Steinfeld, Green Books. £4.95.**

East Yorkshire

AARHUS UNITED UK LIMITED

KING GEORGE DOCK, HULL HU9 5PX
Tel: 01482 701271 Fax: 01482 709447 Contact: Steve Tate
steve.tate@aarhusunited.com
Importing, processing and packaging, organic extra virgin olive, safflower, sesame and sunflower oils, palm oil (and fractions) certified by the Soil Association, licence no. P966.

ARTHUR STREET TRADING COMPANY LTD

UNIT 2, 23 ARTHUR STREET, HULL HU3 6BH
Tel: 01482 576374 Fax: 0870 132 3035 Contact: Graham Brooks
brooksy@arthursorganics.karoo.co.uk www.arthursorganics.com
A workers co-operative that make home deliveries in a solar powered veg-float, supplying comprehensive range of organic fruit & vegetables, eco-cleaning products, wholefoods, beers, wines and own brand range of organic hummus.

BARMSTON ORGANICS

ALLISON LANE END FARM, LISSETT, DRIFFIELD YO25 8PS
Tel: 01262 468128 Fax: 01262 468128 Contact: Tony & Colleen Hunt
barmstontone@aol.com
Soil Association P5571 & G1855. 273-acre mixed farm selling vegetables, flour from our own wheat and lamb & beef. Box scheme and local farmers' markets.

COLEMAN, WG & PARTNERS

WESTFIELD FARM, BURTON FLEMING, NR. DRIFFIELD YO25 3PZ
Tel: 01262 470850 Contact: Jim Coleman
Mixed farm including organic pigs and crops. Half pigs sometimes available for your freezer.

CRANSWICK COUNTRY FOODS

INGLEMIRE LANE, COTTINGHAM, HULL HU16 4PJ
Tel: 01482 848180 Fax: 01482 876146 Contact: J Brisby
jim.brisby@cranswick.co. uk
Producers of fresh pork, sausage, cooked meats.

DENSHOLME FARM

GREAT HATFIELD, HULL HU11 4UR
Tel: 01964 535315 Contact: Denys Fell
denys_fell@wcg.org.uk
Member of the Soil Association Organic Farms Network.

FOSTON NURSERIES

FOSTON ON THE WOLDS, DRIFFIELD YO25 8BJ
Tel: 01262 488382 Contact: Jenny Webb
Soil Association W28N. Grower of organic produce. Gate sales—supplying three
box scheme outlets, also sales at Driffield Farmers' Market. Self-contained
holiday flat, sleeps two.

GREEN GROWERS

1 STATION COTTAGES, WANSFORD RD., NAFFERTON, DRIFFIELD YO25 8NJ
Tel: 01377 255362 Contact: GM Egginton
mail@greengrowers.fsnet.co.uk
Soil Association G2175. Green Growers is an organic nursery, retailing a wide variety
of organic vegetables, fruit and wholefoods, specialising in fresh salads and herbs,
and herb plants.

HEJHOG

FREEPOST RLSB-GZKT-CUGG, HEJHOG, GOOLE DN14 8HY
Tel: 01724 798747 Fax: 01724 798785 Contact: Shaun Mudge
info@hejhog.co.uk www.hejhog.co.uk
Natural and organic babywear, sleeping bags, soft toys, baby slings . . . products by
Engel, Lana and Didymos, all highly regarded throughout Europe for their outstanding quality and ecological standards. For a free colour catalogue call 0845 606
6487 or visit our website. Open Monday–Friday 10am–7pm.

HNP DIRECT.COM

EVERTHORPE GRANGE, COMMON LANE, NORTH CAVE HU15 2PE
Tel: 01430 425531 Fax: 01430 423196 Contact: Tony Roach
info@hnpdirect.com www.hnpdirect.com
Internet company supplying Coia coir composts, fertilisers, magna therapy.

HUMBER VHB

COMMON LANE, WELTON, BROUGH HU15 1UT
Tel: 01482 661600 Fax: 01482 665095 Contact: Ian Ball
sales@humbervhb.com www.humbervhb.com
Humber VHB are growers and packers of glasshouse grown tomatoes (including
speciality), cucumbers, peppers and herbs for the retail market and local box schemes.

HUMDINGER LTD

GOTHANBURG WAY, SUTTON FIELDS INDUSTRIAL ESTATE, HULL HU7 0YG
Tel: 01482 625790 Fax: 01482 625791 Contact: Paul Sangwin
paul.sangwin@humdinger-foods.co.uk
Packaging company packing for major brands within the wholefoods industry.

HURRELL AND McLEAN (HURRELL'S)

BEVERLEY ROAD, CRANSWICK, DRIFFIELD YO25 9PF
Tel: 01377 271400 Fax: 01377 271500 Contact: Nick Gladstone
nick@hurrells.fsbusiness.co.uk www.hmseeds.co.uk
Specialise in supply of organic farm seeds, forage/grass and combinable crops.

MOTHERHEMP LTD.

SPRINGDALE FARM, RUDSTON, DRIFFIELD YO25 4DJ
Tel: 01262 421100 Contact: Ria Spencer
www.motherhemp.com
MotherHemp produces a quality range of organic hemp food products. Hemp's claim as a superfood lies in its balance of essential fatty acids and high quality protein. The range includes hemp pasta and pesto, Hemp Ice—a dairy-free ice cream, hemp oil and seeds. MotherHemp products will be of interest to anyone on a lactose-free, dairy-free, vegan, low sugar and low gluten diet.

SLATER ORGANICS

16 CROSS ST., ALDBROUGH, HULL HU11 4RW
Tel: 01964 527519 Contact: Bob Slater
slaterorganics@yahoo.co.uk
Soil Association G1917. Family business growing wide range of organic vegetables in walled garden at Rise Village. Working with other local growers, we supply box schemes in Hull, Beverley and local villages.

SPRINGDALE CROP SYNERGIES LTD

SPRINGDALE FARM, RUDSTON, DRIFFIELD YO25 4DJ
Tel: 01262 421100 Fax: 01262 421101 Contact: Simon Meakin
info@springdale-group.com www.springdale-group.com
Soil Association P7844. Seed merchant/advisor. Agronomy-based crop development business offering buy-back contracts and advice on organic crops. Supplier and trader of organic seeds and the only UK registered specialist organic oilseed supplier.

AGGLOMERATION TECHNOLOGY LTD
UNIT 7, MONKSWELL PARK, MANSE LANE, KNARESBOROUGH HG5 8NQ
Tel: 01423 868411 Fax: 01423 868410 Contact: Enid Rispin
enid.rispin@aggtech.co.uk
Agglomeration (granulation) of sweet and savoury powdered ingredients and
products (soups, gravy, chocolate drinks etc.) and spray crystallisation of real
chocolate.

ALLIGATOR
104 FISHERGATE, YORK YO10 4BB
Tel: 01904 654525 Contact: Steve Heyman
Tel & Fax: 01904 654525 Contact:
Independent vegetarian & wholefood grocers and greengrocers offering a wide
range of organic fruit, veg and groceries. Speciality diets catered for. Home
delivery service within the York area.

ASPIN ORGANICS
LOW ST., SPROXTON, HELMSLEY, YORK YO
Tel: 01439 771848 Contact: JD Farrar
Soil Association G6005. Organic horticultural enterprise growing organic vegetables
for veg box scheme, farm shop, farm gate sales and local sales.

BLUEBELL ORGANICS
FORCETT HALL WALLED GARDEN, FORCETT, RICHMOND DL11 7SB
Tel: 01325 718841 Contact: Katrina Palmer
katrina@bluebell30.fsbusiness.co.uk www.bluebellorganics.co.uk
Run a year-round box scheme with quality local vegetables predominantly grown by
themselves on 8 acres of land and in a growing partnership with S.J. Ward. Part of
that land will be registered under the new 'stock-free' regulations so it is suitable
for vegetarians and vegans. Also sell at local farmers' markets a range of home-
made produce including organic apple juice, marmalade, pickles and preserves.

BRUNSWICK ORGANIC NURSERY

APPLETON RD., BISHOPTHORPE, YORK YO23 2RF

Tel: 01904 701869 Fax: 01904 701869 Contact: Jennifer Aitken

jennifer@brunswickyork.org.uk

Soil Association G1903, HDRA member. Charity working with adults who have learning difficulties. Produce includes bedding plants, cottage garden plants, perennials, herbs, organic fruit and vegetables. All to Soil Association standards. Farm shop open weekdays in winter, seven days a week in summer. Organic Food Awards 2004: Fresh Fruit and Veg Highly Commended.

CAMPHILL VILLAGE TRUST—BOTTON VILLAGE

DANBY, WHITBY YO21 2NJ

Tel: 01287 660871 Contact: Erwin Wennekes

botton@camphill.org.uk www.camphill.org.uk

Botton Village is a Camphill Village Trust community for adults with special needs. It has five mixed farms which are run on biodynamic principles, several craft and food processing workshops. Day visits are possible, and there is a coffee bar (not a restaurant) on site.

CAMPHILL VILLAGE TRUST—LARCHFIELD COMMUNITY

STOKESLEY RD., HEMLINGTON, MIDDLESBROUGH TS8 9DY

Tel: 01642 593688 Fax: 01642 595778 Contact: Pink, Smith, Fish, Hodkinson

Producers of real organic meat, vegetables, seasonal fruit, bread, etc. Also hand-crafts—weaving and wooden toys.

CASTLE HOWARD ESTATE LTD

THE ESTATE OFFICE, CASTLE HOWARD, YORK YO60 7DA

Tel: 01653 648444 Contact: Helen Orchison

horchison@castlehoward.co.uk www.castlehoward.co.uk

Soil Association registered. Organic farmers. Producers of organic meats and arable crops. Day visits by appointment only.

CORNMILL LODGE VEGETARIAN GUEST HOUSE

120 HAXBY RD., YORK YO31 8JP
Tel: 01904 620566 Fax: 01904 620566 Contact: Jen Williams
cornmillyork@aol.com www.vegetarianyork.net
Vegetarian/vegan guest house using organic and Fairtrade produce where possible (80% organic), 15 minutes walk from York Minster, completely smoke-free, animal-free toiletries used.

COUNTRY PRODUCTS LIMITED

UNIT 11A & B CENTRE PARK, MARSTON BUSINESS PARK, TOCKWITH, YORK YO26 7QF
Tel: 01423 358858 Fax: 01423 359858 Contact: Liz Blacker
mail@countryproducts.co.uk www.countryproducts.co.uk
Soil Association P1987. Contract packer. Wholesaler and contract packer of high quality food products, especially wholefoods and organic products.

DEMETER SEEDS STORMY HALL

STORMY HALL FARM, BOTTON VILLAGE, DANBY, WHITBY YO21 2NJ
Tel: 01287 661368 Fax: 01287 661369 Contact: Hans Steenbergen
stormy.hall.botton@camphill.org.uk
Producer, processor, and retailer of biodynamic and organic vegetable, herb and flower seeds.

EL PIANO

15–17 GRAPE LANE, YORK YO1 7HU
Tel: 01904 610676 Fax: 01904 643049 Contact: Maggie or Sally
info@elpiano.co.uk www.elpiano.co.uk
Open 10am–midnight Mon–Sat, Sundays midday–5pm. licensed Hispanic informal vegetarian restaurant. Function rooms, event-catering inside or out. Children welcome all hours. Organic staples used in restaurant, Spanish foods. Wheat-free, gluten-free, vegan catered for. Hand to Mouth, no ordinary cookbook published.

FARMAROUND

THE OLD BAKERY, MERCURY RD., RICHMOND DL10 4TQ
Tel: 01748 821116 Fax: 01748 822007 Contact: Isobel Davies
info@farmaround.co.uk www.farmaroundnorth.co.uk
Organic Farmers and Growers UKP08009. From their base in Richmond, Farmaround delivers organic fruit and vegetables boxes to North and South Yorkshire, Tyne and Wear, County Durham and Cleveland. Also a fully organic vegetarian grocery range. Wholesale enquiries welcome.

FARNDALE FREE RANGE LTD

HILL HOUSES, FARNDALE, KIRKBYMOORSIDE YO62 7LH
Tel: 01751 430323 Fax: 01751 430323 Contact: Barry Sunley
barry@farndale.com www.farndale.com
We produce SA organic eggs to the highest standard, which we deliver to discerning local shops in North Yorkshire, Cleveland and Teeside. We also design websites and provide computer services.

FIFE, AM

BRAMPER FARM, THRINTOFT, NORTHALLERTON DL7 0PS
Tel: 01609 770151 Fax: 01609 777436 Contact: Andy Fife
andy@bramper.demon.co.uk
Soil Association G6867. Producer of organic cereals, vegetables and meat.

FIRST SEASON

1 ST. ANN'S LANE, WHITBY YO21 3PF
Tel: 01947 601608 Fax: 01947 601608 Contact: Keith Mollison
Wholefood shop with a wide range of organic products including fresh fruit and vegetables, Botton Village bread and jams, and local eggs. Organic vegetable boxes can be ordered and collected from the shop.

GIBSON, JR & E

PRIEST GARTH FARM, GILLAMOOR, YORK YO62 7HX
Tel: 01751 431872 Fax: 01751 431872 Contact: John & Eileen Gibson
gillamoorganics@yahoo.co.uk
Soil Association G3083. Fully organic mixed farm with Ayrshire dairy herd. Potatoes
and field vegetables for sale, all home-grown.

GOOSEMOORGANICS

WARFIELD LANE, COWTHORPE, NR. WETHERBY LS22 5EU
Tel: 01423 358887 Fax: 01423 358887 Contact: Alex Marsh
vegebox@goosemoor.info www.goosemoor.info
Soil Association G802, P802. Goosemoor grows and distributes organic fruit,
vegetables and vegetarian groceries to shops and restaurants throughout the
north of England, as well as home deliveries via our veg box scheme.

THE GREEN HOUSE

5 STATION PARADE, HARROGATE HG1 1UF
Tel: 01423 502580 Fax: 01423 505439 Contact: Bob Fisher
Shop selling arguably the best organic food and drink selection in North Yorkshire.
Also vegetarian and special diet foods. Delivery within 5 miles of shop.

GREENVALE FARMS LTD

LEEMING, NORTHALLERRTON DL7 9LY
Tel: 01677 422953 Fax: 01677 425358 Contact: David Stonebank
Marketing@rooster.uk.com
Soil Association I809. Organic fertilisers. Greenvale produce organic pellets and
fertilisers for garden centres, horticulture and agriculture.

GROWING WITH GRACE

CLAPHAM NURSERIES, CLAPHAM, NR. LANCASTER LA2 8ER
Tel: 01524 251723 Fax: 01524 251548 Contact: N Marshall
info@growingwithgrace.co.uk www.growingwithgrace.co.uk
Soil Association G4295, P5562. We are a Quaker co-operative seeking to provide local people with home/locally produced vegetables and Fairtrade dried goods, through our bag scheme and farm shop. We cover north and east Lancashire, south-east Cumbria and the southern Yorkshire dales.

HAZELBROW VISITOR CENTRE

LOW ROW, RICHMOND DL11 6NE
Tel: 01748 886224 Contact: Catherine Calvert
hazelbrowfarm@aol.com www.hazelbrow.co.uk
Organic working farm in Yorkshire Dales National Park producing lamb and milk, with visitor centre, shop and café open 11am–5pm five days a week, March to September (closed Mondays & Fridays). Member of the Soil Association Organic Farms Network.

HOLLINGWORTH, DJ

ADAMSON HILL, CHOP GATE, MIDDLESBOROUGH TS9 7HY
Tel: 01642 778284 Fax: 01642 778366 Contact: David Hollingworth
djholl@hotmail.com
Soil Association G5624. Pedigree beef Shorthorn cattle, pedigree North Country Cheviot sheep, and eggs. Farm gate sales for eggs only.

HOOK HOUSE FARM

HOOK HOUSE FARM, KIRKBY FLEETHAM, NORTHALLERTON DL7 0SS
Tel: 01609 748977 Contact: Steven Peirson
hookhousefarm@hotmail.co.uk
Small mixed farm in the Vale of York producing lamb, beef, Christmas turkeys and honey. Contact us to go on our mailing list.

HUNTERS OF HELMSLEY
13 MARKET PLACE, HELMSLEY YO62 5BL
Tel: 01439 771307 Fax: 01439 771307 Contact: Tony Cowley
info@huntersofhelmsley.com www.huntersofhelmsley.com
High class food specialist stocking cooked meats, bacon, port and game pies, fish, cheeses, many varieties of jams, chutneys, teas, coffees, Belgian chocolates. We also offer mail order and specialist hampers.

THE KERFOOT GROUP LTD
MAWSON HOUSE, THE BRIDGE, ASKEW, BEDALE DL8 1AW
Tel: 01677 424881 Fax: 01677 422560 Contact: Robin Frost
packed@kerfootgroup.co.uk www.kerfootgroup.co.uk
Soil Association P5494. Blending, packaging and distribution of vegetable oils to the food, pharmaceutical, technical and pet food industries.

KIRK, GA & SON
THE ABATTOIR, NUNNINGTON, YORK YO62 5UU
Tel: 01439 748242 Fax: 01439 788546 Contact: Richard Kirk (Director)
ashberrygrangefarm@hotmail.com
We are a small country abattoir able to slaughter any animals, and will deliver (if a volume) by arrangement.

LARBERRY FARM SHOP
LARBERRY PASTURES, LONGNEWTON, STOCKTON ON TEES TS21 1BN
Tel: 01642 583823 Fax: 01642 582249 Contact: Eileen & Merilyn Wade
larberry@farmersweekly.net
Farm shop selling our own home-reared beef, lamb and organic free range eggs. Pork from Houghall Agricultural College, fruit and veg, groceries including flour, dairy, spreads, jams, herbs, spices—you name it, we do it. Also cater for special diets, gluten-free, dairy-free, wheat-free and diabetic products.

LAZY DOG TOOL COMPANY LTD
HILL TOP FARM, SPAUNTON, KIRKBYMOORSIDE YO62 6TR
Tel: 01751 417351 Fax: 01751 417351 Contact: Philip Trevelyan
philip@lazydogtoolco.co.uk www.lazydogtoolco.co.uk
Specialist hand-tools for removing individual plants (weeds).

LENG'S GROCERS
36 COLD BATH RD, HARROGATE HG2 0NA
Tel: 01423 503815 Fax: 01423 503815 Contact: Peter Schofield
lengsgrocers@btconnect.com
Traditional family-run grocers near the heart of Harrogate offering an ever-expanding range of organic, locally produced, Fairtrade & wholefood goods. Free local delivery & organic box scheme.

THE LITTLE DELICATESSEN
3 HIGH STREET, TADCASTER LS24 9AP
Tel: 01937 833244 Contact: Wendy Preston
High class delicatessen with a wide range of wholefoods, organic beer and lager.

LOW GILL BECK FARM
LOW GILL BECK FARM, GLAISDALE YO21 2QA
Tel: 01947 897363 Contact: R&P Drew
Home-grown parsnips, carrots, turnips, brassicas, runner beans, dwarf beans, peas, potatoes. Strawberries & raspberries in conversion.

LOW LEASES ORGANIC FARM
LOW ST., NR. LEEMING BAR, NORTHALLERTON DL7 9LU
Tel: 01609 748177 Fax: 01609 748177 Contact: Elaine McGregor
rjm96@tutor.open.ac.uk www.lowleasesorganicfarm.co.uk
Soil Association G4475. A local family business committed to delivering quality produce. Our own and partners' fresh local veg, fruit, eggs, rare breed meat, groceries to your door in North Yorkshire, Darlington, Durham and Teeside. Meat available by mail order.

MERCER, HARVEY
UNIT 15 CLARO COURT BUSINESS CENTRE, CLARO ROAD, HARROGATE HG1 4BA
Tel: 01423 528822 Fax: 01423 529977 Contact: Paul Mercer
enquiries@harveymercer.com www.harveymercer.com
Soil Association P7691. Producers of Hearty's brand of soy-based foods and
snacks. These are healthy, vegetarian and often organic and gluten-free.

NATURE'S WORLD
LADGATE LANE, ACKLAM, MIDDLESBOROUGH TS5 7YN
Tel: 01642 594895 Fax: 01642 591224 Contact: Stuart Goldie
stuart@naturesworld.org.uk www.naturesworld.org.uk
The north of England's pioneering environmental centre with over 25 acres of organic demonstration gardens and wildlife areas. Open daily to the public, school groups
and tours. Also farm shop, tea rooms and play areas. Monthly farmers' market.

NEWFIELDS ORGANIC PRODUCE
THE GREEN, FADMOOR, KIRKBY MOORSIDE YO62 7HY
Tel: 01751 431558 Fax: 01751 432061 Contact: Howard Wass
Farm producing winter vegetables, potatoes, carrots, parsnips, onions, cabbages,
swedes, beetroot, parsley, leeks, sprouts, broccoli, cauliflower, celeriac and lettuce.
Organic Food Awards 2004: Fresh Fruit and Veg Commended.

THE ORGANIC FARM SHOP
STANDFIELD HALL FARM, WESTGATE CARR RD., PICKERING YO18 8LX
Tel: 01751 472249 Fax: 01751 472249 Contact: Mike Sellers
mike@theorganicfarmshop.com www.theorganicfarmshop.com
Soil Association PS21N. Specialist retailer or organic goods since 1984. Home-
produced vegetables and beef, plus one of the biggest ranges of organic products
in Yorkshire. Scarborough/Ryedale free delivery.

THE ORGANIC PANTRY (NATURAL DELIVERY WHOLEFOODS)

ST.HELENS FARM, NEWTON KYME, TADCASTER LS24 9LY
Tel: 01937 531693 Fax: 01937 834062 Contact: Fanny Watson
organic.pantry@virgin.net www.organicpantry.co.uk
Family-run farm. Complete organic shop selling fruit, vegetables, meat, dairy,
bread, wholefoods etc. box scheme, farm shop and website. Individual diets/special
requirements and requests welcome. Deliveries throughout Yorkshire and
Derbyshire. Farmers' markets.

PADMORE, CF & ET

BANK HOUSE FARM, GLAISDALE, WHITBY YO21 2QA
Tel: 01947 897297 Fax: 01947 897297 Contact: Chris & Emma Padmore
em-chris-padmore@onetel.net
Soil Association G1135. Organic beef and lamb and woodland-reared pork. All
meat home-produced, butchered, bagged and labelled. Please phone regarding
availability.

PASTURE COTTAGE ORGANICS

PASTURE COTTAGE, BOG HOUSE FARM, MICKLEBY, WHITBY TS13 5NA
Tel: 01947 840075 Contact: Jenny Summerson
jenny@yorkshireorganics.freeserve.co.uk
Soil Association G5723. On our small family farm we produce a wide range of
seasonal vegetables and eggs for retail sale at our farm shop, through our box
scheme and at local shops.

R & R TOFU

5 RYE CLOSE, YORK ROAD IND. PARK, MALTON YO17 6YD
Tel: 01653 690235 Fax: 01653 699091 Contact: Bruce McKenzie Malarkey
Soil Association P1516. Manufacturers of 'Clear Spot' organic tofu and tofu products.

ROBINSON, DS

FIR TREE FARM, NORTHALLERTON DL6 2RW
Tel: 01609 772032 Contact: DS Robinson
mail@britishbeef.org www.britishbeef.org
Soil Association G4193. We are a specialist producer delivering organic beef from
our pedigree herd of British White Cattle direct to your home. We also produce
organic pork and lamb.

SMITHY FARM SHOP

BALDERSBY, THIRSK YO7 4BN
Tel: 01765 640676 Fax: 01765 640898 Contact: Susan Brown
Meat, poultry, dairy, vegetables, bread and pasta. Large range of pulses, cereals,
sauces, wines beers.

STAMFREY FARM ORGANIC PRODUCE

STAMFREY FARM, WEST ROUNTON, NORTHALLERTON DL6 2LJ
Tel: 01609 882297 Fax: 01609 882297 Contact: Sue Gaudie
info@clottedcream.org
Traditionally made clotted cream using milk from our own dairy herd. Low fat
organic yoghurt production to start soon.

STEENBERGS ORGANIC ENGLISH TEA

PO BOX 48, BOROUGHBRIDGE YO51 9ZW
Tel: 01765 640088 Fax: 01765 640101 Contact: Sophie Steenberg
enquiries@steenbergs-tea.com www.steenbergs-tea.com
Organic and Fairtrade single estate loose leaf teas in kraft or aluminium canisters.
Great for food halls, delis and tea connoisseurs everywhere. Assam, Darjeeling,
Green and Earl Grey. Guest organic teas starting shortly including Chinese green tea.

STEENBERGS ORGANIC PEPPER & SPICE

THE SPICE FACTORY, BARKER BUSINESS PARK, MELMERBY, NR. RIPON HG4 5NE
Tel: 01765 640088 Fax: 01765 640101 Contact: Sophie Steenberg
sophie@steenbergs.co.uk www.steenbergs.co.uk
Organic Barbeque ribs. Full range of organic pepper, spice and herbs packed in
glass, stainless steel, gift boxes and bulk (including seasonings) for food producers.
Blends hand-produced in North Yorkshire to our own recipes—from curry powders
through to sausage and bacon seasonings. Many of our products are sourced direct
from farmers all around the world to ensure freshness and provenance. Wholesale
available packed for retail (including retail support) or bulk for food producers.
Traditional Portuguese sea salt also available.

SUNFLOURS

THE HUTTS MILL, GREWELTHORPE, RIPON HG4 3DA
Tel: 01765 658534 Fax: 01765 658903 Contact: Mark Exelby
info@sunflours.com www.sunflours.com
Soil Association P1495. We are organic and specialist flour producers and
retailers. We mill, blend and supply many types of flour including a large range
of gluten-free flour.

TAYLORS OF HARROGATE

PAGODA HOUSE, PROSPECT RD., HARROGATE HG2 7LD
Tel: 01423 814000 Fax: 01423 814001 Contact: John Thompson
www.bettysandtaylors.co.uk
Tea blenders and coffee roasters.

TREVELYAN, PE

HILL TOP FARM, SPAUNTON, KIRKBYMOORSIDE YO62 6TR
Tel: 01751 417351/417799 Fax: 01751 417351 Contact: Philip Trevelyan
philip@lazydogtoolco.co.uk
Sheep and cereals.

TWEDDLE, BP&M

FAIRHOLME, MORTON ON SWALE, NORTHALLERTON DL7 9RW
Tel: 01609 774539 Fax: 01609 774539 Contact: Barry Tweddle
Produce potatoes, cereals, pulses.

UK JUICERS LTD

UNIT 3 WATERLINE ESTATE, ACASTER MALBIS, YORK YO23 2UY
Tel: 01904 704705 Fax: 01904 771007 Contact: Nick Ledger
enquiries@ukjuicers.com www.ukjuicers.com
UK Juicers are stockists of high quality juice extractors, blenders, water purifiers,
food dehydrators and other healthy products perfect for making good use of organic
produce.

UNITRITION

OLYMPIA MILLS, BARLBY RD, SELBY YO8 5AF
Tel: 01757 244111 Fax: 01757 244088 Contact: AC Dickins
www.unitrition.co.uk
Soil Association registered. Oilseed crusher. Unitrition are specialist oilseed
crushers and raw material upgraders, supplying crude oils and expeller cakes to
food and agricultural industries.

WARD, SJ

MANOR HOUSE FARM, MORTON ON SWALE, NORTHALLERTON DL7 9RJ
Tel: 01609 773538 Fax: 01609 773538 Contact: Steve Ward
Field-scale grower of wide variety of vegetables—potatoes, carrots, parsnips, onions,
celeriac, beetroot, leeks and a variety of brassicas. Organic meat also available.

WENSLEYDALE DAIRY PRODUCTS LTD

WENSLEYDALE DAIRY PRODUCTS LTD, GAYLE LANE, HAWES DL8 3RN
Tel: 01969 667664 Fax: 01969 667638 Contact: Phil Jones
creamery@wensleydale.co.uk www.wensleydale.co.uk
Producers of Organic Wensleydale Cheese.
Originators & producers of Organic Wensleydale Cheese with Cranberries.

WESTLER FOODS LTD
AMOTHERBY, MALTON YO17 6TQ
Tel: 01653 693971 Fax: 01653 600187 Contact: Trevor Newbert
trevor.newbert@westler.com www.westlerfoods.com
We manufacture the Chesswood range of organic meals in easy open cans:
vegetable curry and vegetable hot pot.

WILD GINGER VEGETARIAN BISTRO
BEHIND THE GREEN HOUSE, 5 STATION PARADE, HARROGATE HG1 1UF
Tel: 01423 566122 Contact: Rachel Melton
www.wild-ginger.co.uk
100% vegetarian foods, freshly prepared and home-made. Large choice for vegans,
also gluten/dairy/wheat/sugar-free and other exclusion diets catered for. Licensed,
selling organic wines and beer. Regular gourmet evenings and special events.

YORK BEER & WINE SHOP
28 SANDRINGHAM STREET, FISHERGATE, YORK YO1 4BA
Tel: 01904 647136 Fax: 01904 647136 Contact: Eric Boyd
ybws@york10.freeserve.co.uk www.yorkbeerandwineshop.co.uk
We are a specialist off-licence selling beer, wine, cider and cheese. We sell
organic lines of all our categories.

YORKSHIRE FARMHOUSE EGGS LTD.
VILLAGE FARM, CATTON, THIRSK YO7 4SQ
Tel: 01845 578376 Fax: 01845 578660 Contact: Adrian Potter
enquiries@yorkshirefarmhouse.co.uk www.yorkshirefarmhouse.co.uk
We produce and pack organic eggs ro the highest standards, under the Soil
Association and Organic Farmers and Growers accreditation schemes. Eggs sold in
most multiples and local catering and wholesale businesses.

BEANIES

205–207 CROOKES VALLEY ROAD, SHEFFIELD S10 1BA
Tel: 0114 268 1662 Fax: 0114 268 1555 Contact: H Adams
sheffield.wholefoods@virgin.net
Soil Association No R1731, Award-winning workers' co-operative. Shop open seven days a week. Box scheme delivery service within Sheffield, also Doncaster, Barnsley, Chesterfield, Rotherham. Organic greengrocery, wholefoods, bread, chilled and frozen produce, vegan and vegetarian produce and speciality foods.

DOWN TO EARTH

406 SHARROWVALE RD, HUNTERS BAR, SHEFFIELD S11 8ZP
Tel: 0114 268 5220 Contact: John Leeson
dte@blueyonder.co.uk
Wholefood retailer with wide range of organic produce including dairy, spreads, nuts, beans, pulses, rice, grains, cereals, etc.—not fresh fruit and veg.

THE DRAM SHOP

21 COMMONSIDE, SHEFFIELD S10 1GA
Tel: 0114 268 3117 Contact: Linda Taylor
Specialist off licence wines, beers, ciders and spirits.

FISHACE

sbc@fishace.demon.co.uk www.fishace.demon.co.uk
International site promoting sustainable organic aquaculture on the internet for the past ten years. Organic aquaculture directory, news & events.

FIVE A DAY

5 LISTERDALE SHOPPING CENTRE, ROTHERHAM S64 3JA
Tel: 01709 532007 Contact: Michael Mavrakis
Fresh fruit & veg, vegetarian salads and meals, freshly juiced organic fruit, olive oils, sauces, etc., all organic.

HEELEY CITY FARM

RICHARDS RD, SHEFFIELD S2 3DT
Tel: 0114 258 0482 Fax: 0114 255 1400 Contact: The Manager
farm@heeleyfarm.org.uk www.heeleyfarm.org.uk
A community environmental and horticultural project based on an inner city educational farm and environmental visitor attraction. Food produced using organic methods available in our farm café and from our garden centre during times of surplus. Local crafts, compost bins and gifts in farm shop.

POLLYBELL FARMS

HOLMES FARM, WROOT RD., EPWORTH, DONCASTER DN9 1EA
Tel: 01427 872461 Fax: 01427 874427 Contact: The Manager
pollybell@farmline.com
Producer of large range of organic vegetables.

POTTS BAKERS

STANLEY ROAD, STAIRFOOT, BARNSLEY S70 3PG
Tel: 01226 249175 Fax: 01226 249175 Contact: Andrew Potts
potts.bakers@care4free.net www.pottsbakers.co.uk
Soil Association P4477. Bakers of organic bread, cakes and puddings for independent and multiple retailers.

THE REAL BREAD BAKEHOUSE LTD
REAR OF 36 CAT LANE, SHEFFIELD S2 3AY
Tel: 0114 249 5459 Fax: 0114 281 7965 Contact: John Coatman
jcoatman@blueyonder.co.uk
Soil Association P4265. Hand-made organic bread for wholesale to retail outlets
(or individuals who order above a minimum quantity and can collect). Deliveries
to Sheffield, Nottingham, Leicester, Leeds, Manchester and London.

YORKSHIRE ORGANIC EARTH
33 DEVONSHIRE DRIVE, HALLBALK, BARNSLEY S75 1EE
Tel: 07785 901215 Contact: Stuart Allen
stuartallen@yorkshireorganicearth.fsnet.co.uk
Soil Association G2238. Organic Food Awards: Highly Commended 1998 (vegetables), Highly Commended 1999 (eggs). Summer seasonal vegetables. Some farm
gate sales.

Superfact
Cars spend an average of 44 days a year stuck in traffic. In Bangkok there are
long periods every day when the traffic moves at only 3km an hour. You can walk
faster than that!
**From *SuperKids: Over 200 incredible ways for kids to save the planet* by
Sasha Norris and Rupert Davies, Think Books, £5.99.**

	Accommodation		**Garden and Farm Sundries**		**Producers**
	Box Schemes/ Local Deliveries		**Farmers' market Stall**		**Restaurants/ Cafés/Caterers**
	Day Visits		**Manufacturers/ Processors**		**Retail shops**
	Eco Products		**Importers/ exporters**		**Textiles**
	Farm Gate Sales		**Mail order suppliers**		**Wholesalers**

BEANO WHOLEFOODS

36 NEW BRIGGATE, LEEDS LS1 6NU
Tel: 0113 243 5737 Fax: 0113 243 5737 Contact: Simone Ivatts Nash
info@beanowholefoods.co.uk www.beanowholefoods.co.uk
Vegetarian and vegan wholefood shop, with specialism in organic products.
Organic fruit and vegetables delivered Monday, Tuesday and Thursday. Fair-trade
products stocked. Special diets catered for.

BEANSTALK ORGANIX

UNIT 9, TOWNHEAD TRADING CENTRE, MAIN STREET, ADDINGHAM LS29 OPD
Tel: 01943 831103 Fax: 01943 839199 Contact: Helen Roberts
info@beanstalkorganix.co.uk www.beanstalkorganix.co.uk
Soil Association P4995. Yorkshire's leading organic home delivery service and
one-stop organic shop of fresh produce, Groceries, meat & poultry, bread &
cakes, eco-baby, personal care & household products. We accept all major credit
and debit cards.

BRADFORD WHOLEFOODS

THE CELLAR PROJECT, THE OLD SCHOOL, FARFIELD RD., SHIPLEY BD18 4QP
Tel: 01422 202648 Contact: Jack First
jackfirstgrove@aol.com
Specialist organic food retailer selling fresh vegetables and fruit, some locally grown
in season, groceries, eco-friendly toiletries and cleaning products.

BRICKYARD ORGANICS

BRICKYARD ORGANIC FARM, BADSWORTH, PONTEFRACT WF9 1AX
Tel: 01977 617327 Contact: John Brook
Soil Association G598. Organic farm growing cereals, legumes, sheep, plants,
vegetables.

ELYSIUM NATURAL PRODUCTS LTD
UNIT 12, MODERNA BUSINESS PARK, MYTHOLMROYD, HALIFAX HX7 5QQ
Tel: Fax: 01422 884629 Contact: G Carroll
elysiumproducts@aol.com
Distribute organic foods: veg in jars, seeds, pulses, cakes, honey, biscuits, tortilla chips, juices, pet food, sweets, chocolate, health bars, gluten-free goods across the whole organic range.

FOOD THERAPY
11 NORTHGATE, HALIFAX HX1 1UR
Tel: 01422 350826 Fax: 01422 362106 Contact: K Benson
An award-winning store and restaurant with a huge range of organic wholefoods.

FYFFES GROUP LTD
WAKEFIELD 41 IND. PARK, KENMORE RD., WAKEFIELD WF2 0XE
Tel: 01924 826446 Fax: 01924 820109 Contact: Andrew Joyce
dellam@fyffes.com www.fyffes.com
Ripening bananas, preparing and packing bananas. Distributing bananas to wholesalers and retailers.

HALF MOON HEALTHFOODS
6 HALF MOON ST., HUDDERSFIELD HD1 2JJ
Tel: 01484 456392 Fax: 01484 310161 Contact: Judith Beresford & Adrian Midgley
adrian@halfmoonhealthfoods.co.uk www.halfmoonhealthfoods.co.uk
We are a wholefood store specialising in organic lines, vegetables, breads, dairy products, eggs, beers and wines. Our organic box scheme has been established 15 years.

KERSHAW'S GARDEN SHOPPING CENTRE
THE NURSERIES, HALIFAX RD., BRIGHOUSE HD6 2QD
Tel: 01484 713435 Contact: Mark Yates
Garden centre stocking a range of organic composts, feeds, pest controls and seeds.

LOVE ORGANIC!

4 REGENT ST., CHAPEL ALLERTON, LEEDS LS7 4PE
Tel: 0113 266 3030 Contact: Helen Roberts
A new organic/healthy food shop in the heart of Chapel Allerton. We stock all the organic essentials, with a fabulous range of groceries, fresh produce, meat, poultry and fish, baby, personal care and eco-products. We accept all major credit cards.

MEANWOOD VALLEY URBAN FARM

SUGARWELL RD., MEANWOOD, LEEDS LS7 2QG
Tel: 0113 262 9759 Fax: 0113 239 2551 Contact: Susan Reddington
info@mvuf.org.uk www.wwf-leeds.org.uk
Soil Association R27N. City farm, combining organic market garden, environmental education services to schools. Farm animals, including rare breeds. Purpose-built environment centre, interactive displays. Shop café and play area. Registered charity, open every day to visitors. Member of the Soil Association Organic Farms Network.

NATURAL CHOICE

72 WESTBOURNE RD., MARSH, HUDDERSFIELD HD1 4LE
Tel: 01484 513162 Fax: 01484 687466 Contact: Graham Rushworth
graham.trudy@rush2001.freeserve.co.uk
Top quality organic fresh produce, also non-organic fresh produce. All the usual Suma-related products. Local deliveries.

NEAL'S YARD REMEDIES

20 COUNTY ARCADE, VICTORIA QUARTER, LEEDS LS1 6BN
Tel: 0113 243 8924 Contact: The Manager
mail@nealsyardremedies.com www.nealsyardremedies.com
Neal's Yard Remedies manufactures and retails natural cosmetics in addition to stocking an extensive range of herbs, essential oils, homoeopathic remedies and reference material.

ORG

79 GREAT GEORGE ST., LEEDS LS1 3BR
Tel: 0113 234 7000 Fax: 0113 242 7201 Contact: Novita Williamson
novita@org-organics.org.uk www.org-organics.org.uk
Soil Association R6296. Treatment centre. Local fruit and vegetables, deliveries,
hot/cold food, eat in/takeaway, dairy & dairy alternatives, meat and fish, juice bar,
tea, coffees, groceries, cosmetics, frozen foods, household, alcohol, books, bulk
grains, catering.

ORGANIC HOLIDAYS

TRANFIELD HOUSE, 4 TRANFIELD GARDENS, GUISELEY, LEEDS LS20 8PZ
Tel: 01943 870791 Contact: Linda Moss
lindamoss@organicholidays.com www.organicholidays.com
Guide to holiday accommodation on organic farms/smallholdings and to B&Bs,
guest houses and small hotels where organic produce is used according to
availability.

ORGANIC HOUSE

2 MARKET ST, HEBDEN BRIDGE HX7 6AA
Tel: 01422 843429 Contact: Ellie
enquiries@organic-house.co.uk www.organic-house.co.uk
Organic retail and refreshment, fresh fruit, veg, bread, dairy, dried goods, pulses,
grains, nuts, cereals, coffees, teas, wines, beers, Fairtrade products, wide range of
vegan, gluten-free and wheat-free produce. Also bodycare and organic clothing.
Vegetarian café with wheat, gluten-free and vegan options always available.

OUT OF THIS WORLD

20 NEWMARKET ST., LEEDS LS1 6DG
Tel: 0113 244 1881 Fax: 0113 234 1808 Contact: Damian Tapper
info@ootw.co.uk www.outofthisworld.coop
Small chain of ethical and organic supermarkets in Newcastle-upon-Tyne, Leeds
and Nottingham. Selling over 5,000 products, mostly certified organic food plus
fairly traded crafts, recycled paper and bodycare products etc. Consumer co-op
with over 15,000 members.

SALTAIRE WINES & WHOLEFOODS

32 BINGLEY RD, SALTAIRE, SHIPLEY BD 18 4RU
Tel: 01274 583629 Fax: 01274 583629 Contact: Sally Wolfe
len@thewolfes.freeserve.co.uk
Fine foods, luxury chocolates, wines, regional beers, whisky, liqueurs.

SNOWDEN, PA & SJ

HAWTHORNE HOUSE FARM, DUNKESWICK, HAREWOOD, LEEDS LS17 9LP
Tel: 0113 288 6637 Fax: 0113 288 6754 Contact: P.A. & S.J. Snowden
Soil Association G1630. Organic arable farm growing milling wheat, field beans
and fattening lambs. Selling potatoes, carrots, parsnips, leeks and other
vegetables from the farm.

SUMA WHOLEFOODS

LACY WAY, LOWFIELDS BUSINESS PARK, ELLAND HX5 9DB
Tel: 0845 458 2290 Fax: 0845 458 2295 Contact: Chris Sadler
info@suma.co.uk www.suma.co.uk
Soil Association P968. The UK's largest independent wholesaler, of organic,
Fairtrade & natural foods. We also have extensive ranges of special diet and envi-
ronmentally friendly products. Suppliers of RSPB wildlife-friendly foods. Please con-
tact us for more information & our catalogue. Organic Food Awards 2004 Store
Cupboard Staples Winner.

SWILLINGTON ORGANIC FARM

GARDEN COTTAGE, SWILLINGTON ORGANIC FARM, COACH RD.,
SWILLINGTON LS26 8QA
Tel: 0113 286 9129 Fax: 0113 286 9129 Contact: Jo Cartwright
jo.cartwright@farming.me.uk www.swillingtonorganicfarm.co.uk
Soil Association G5062. Mixed organic farm producing organic pork, lamb, beef,
chicken, eggs, and vegetables. Sold through farmers' markets and farm shop open
Fridays 3pm–6pm and Saturdays 10am–4pm. Phone first at other times. Mob:
07974 826876. Organic Food Awards 2004: Fresh Meat Commended.

VALLEY GARDEN ORGANICS

31 MARKET ST, HEBDEN BRIDGE HX7 6EU
Tel: 01422 846651 Contact: Mary-Ann Reed
Wide range of fresh organic fruit and veg, priority given to local produce, wide range of other organic products including vegan, vegetarian, gluten-free. Organic meat, Fairtrade products, household and bodycare products.

VINCEREMOS WINES AND SPIRITS LTD

74 KIRKGATE, LEEDS LS2 7DJ
Tel: 0113 244 0002 Fax: 0113 288 4566 Contact: Jem Gardener
info@vinceremos.co.uk www.vinceremos.co.uk
The UK's longest established organic wine specialists. We also supply organic beers, ciders, juices and spirits. Free catalogue, friendly service and nationwide delivery. Trade enquiries welcome. We also run the HDRA Organic Wine Club. Organic Food Awards 2004: Wines Winner, Commended. See display ad.

WEST RIDING ORGANICS

UNIT 3 NEAR BANK, SHELLEY, HUDDERSFIELD HD8 8LS
Tel: 01484 609171 Fax: 01484 609166 Contact: Julian Chambers
julian@wrorganics.co.uk www.organics.uk.co.uk
Manufacturers of Nature's Own and Bio-Pak organic composts (Soil Association registered). Module, blocking, potting and grow bags all supplied. Volcanic rock dust. Trade enquiries welcome.

WOODVIEW FARM

MANOR RD., FARNLEY TYAS, HUDDERSFIELD HD4 6UL
Tel: 01484 665434 Contact: G Chambers
sales@biogro.co.uk
Soil Association G2468. Aberdeen Angus beef.

ARKHILL FARM

25 DRUMCROONE ROAD, GARVACH, CO. LONDONDERRY BT51 4EB
Tel: 028 2955 7920 Contact: Paul Craig
Irish Organic Farmers and Growers licence no. 1003. Box delivery service. Organic hen and duck eggs, pork, including bacon, sausages, ham, chops, fillets and roasts, lamb, chickens and turkeys. Open to groups e.g. schools etc..

BALLYLAGAN ORGANIC FARM

12 BALLYLAGAN RD., STRAID, BALLYCLARE, CO. ANTRIM BT39 9NF
Tel: 028 9332 2867 Fax: 028 9332 2129 Contact: Tom Gilbert
ballylagan@aol.com www.ballylagan.com
Soil Association G1513. Farm shop selling home-produced meat and poultry products, fruit and vegetables, plus full range of organic groceries. Shop opens Thursday 2.00–6.30, Friday 9.30–6.30, Saturday 9.30–5.00.

BARRYS-TEA.COM

232 FROCESS RD., CLOUGHMILLS, CO. ANTRIM BT44 9PX
Tel: 028 2763 8314 Contact: Andrew Boyd
info@barrys-tea.com www.barrys-tea.com
Offer a range of organic teas including organic camomile and organic green tea. Worldwide delivery.

BULRUSH HORTICULTURE

NEWFERRY RD., BELLAGHY, MAGHERAFELT, CO. LONDONDERRY BT45 8ND
Tel: 028 7938 6555 Fax: 028 7938 6741 Contact: Ann McCann
bulrush@dial.pipex.com www.bulrush.co.uk
Soil Association I2467. Suppliers and manufacturers of organic substrates for use in the horticulture industry.

CAMPHILL COMMUNITY—CLANABOGAN

CAMPHILL COMMUNITY CLANABOGAN, OMAGH BT78 1TJ
Tel: 028 8225 6111 Fax: 028 8225 6114 Contact: Martin Sturm
martinsturm@firenet.uk.net www.camphillclanabogan.com
Mixed biodynamic farm & renewables demonstration farm, with 320kw biomass
district heating system 20kw wind turbine, geothermal heating for polytunnel,
solar pannels, photovoltaic array, domestic wood pellet boiler.

CAMPHILL COMMUNITY—HOLYWOOD

8 SHORE ROAD, HOLYWOOD, CO. DOWN BT18 9HX
Tel: 028 9042 3203 Fax: 028 9089 7818 Contact: Rob van Duin
camphillholywood@btconnect.com www.camphillholywood.co.uk
Organic retail dry goods and bakery, café serving all organic teas, coffees, soups
and sandwiches.

GILPINS FARM

72 DRUMILLY RD., LOUGHGALL, CO. ARMAGH BT61 8JJ
Tel: 028 3889 1528 Contact: Drew Gilpin
drewgilpin@hotmail.com
Soil Association G5833. Farmer, fruit grower. Finisher of organic beef cattle and
grower of organic apples, pears, plums.

HELEN'S BAY ORGANIC GARDENS

COASTGUARD AVE, HELEN'S BAY BT18 9DT
Tel: 028 91853122 Fax: 028 90423063 Contact: John McCormick
johneimar.mccormick@btinternet.com www.helensbayorganicgardens.com
Weekly deliveries of fresh organic vegetables from our fields in Helen's Bay. Our
delivery area covers greater Belfast and North Down. We supply large, medium and
small bags to cater for different needs.

LIFE TREE
37 SPENCER ROAD, DERRY, CO. LONDONDERRY BT47 6AA
Tel: 028 7134 2865 Fax: 028 7134 7880 Contact: A Munro
lifetreeshop@hotmail.com
Health food shop run by qualified therapist with medical background, specialising in
foods for special diets.

LITTLE EARTHLINGS
RIVERTON HOUSE, 151 DRUMAGARNER RD., KILREA, CO. DERRY BT51 5TW
Tel: 028 2954 1214 Fax: 028 2954 1498 Contact: Shauna Newman
info@littleearthlings.com www.littleearthlings.com
Specialising in the very best quality of organic cotton clothing, nappies and
educational toys for babies up to four. We also have a range of toiletries
especially designed for pregnant mums.

McARDLE ORGANIC MUSHROOMS
KNOCKACONEY, ALLISTRAGH, CO. ARMAGH BT61 8DT
Tel: 028 3889 1506 Fax: 028 3889 1529 Contact: John McArdle
info@mcardle-mushrooms.com www.mcardle-mushrooms.com
We cater for every type of customer of organic mushrooms, from the individual
to multinational multiples.

McGEARY MUSHROOM GROUP
53–58 ARMASH RD., MOY, DUNGANNON, CO.TYRONE BT71 7HR
Tel: 028 3754 8292 Fax: 028 3754 8779 Contact: Thomas & Linda
info@compost-ireland.com www.compost-ireland.com
Soil Association registered. We manufacture organic mushroom compost, grow
organic mushrooms and deliver with a fleet of refrigerated lorries throughout
the UK daily, with farms throughout Ireland and Scotland.

MULLEN FARM/PASTURE POULTRY
84 RINGSEND RD., LIMAVADY BT49 0QJ
Tel: 028 7776 4157 Contact: Michael Mullen
jandm@andycameron.com www.pasturepoultry.com
A family business located in Co. Derry, north-west Ireland. Fully organic, specialising in poultry products, offering free range eggs, bronze turkeys, geese and chickens. Member of Soil Association and NWO Co-op.

NORTH WEST ORGANIC CO-OPERATIVE SOCIETY LTD
2 FOREGLEN RD., KILLALOO BT47 4HY
Tel: 028 7133 7950 Fax: 028 7133 7146
Contact: George Macdonald (Development Manager) george@nworganic.com
The purpose of North West Organic is to co-ordinate the sale of locally produced organic food. At the moment we are seeking a buyer for large quantity organically produced lamb and organically produced heifers and bullocks. All the farmers in North West Organic are registered with either the Soil Association or Irish Organic Farmers and Growers Association.

OAKDENE DAIRY/ORGANIC DOORSTEP
125 STRABANE RD., CASTLEDERG, CO. TYRONE BT81 7JD
Tel: 028 8167 1257 Fax: 028 8167 9820 Contact: Glenn Huey
glenn@oakdenedairy.co.uk www.organicdoorstep.co.uk
We specialise in the production, processing and retailing of organic milk, from the farm to the doorstep.

ULSTER WILDLIFE TRUST
JOHN McSPARRAN MEMORIAL HILL FARM, GLENDUN, CUSHENDEN, CO. ANTRIM BT44 0PZ
Tel: 028 2176 1403 Fax: 028 2176 1403 Contact: Barrie Elkin
ulsterwt@glendunfarm.fsnet.co.uk
Soil Association G6697. Farming together with wildlife in a progressive and sustainable manner, producing lamb and beef from traditional and native breeds. Native trees are also produced in our nursery.

BIODYNAMIC SUPPLIES

LORIENEEN, BRIDGE OF MUCHALLS, STONEHAVEN, ABERDEEN AB39 3RU
Tel: 01569 731746 Fax: 01569 731746/739137 Contact: Paul Van Midden
Specialist supplies to biodynamic farmers, gardeners and Demeter symbol holders.

BRIDGEFOOT ORGANICS

BRIDGEFOOT, NEWMACHAR AB21 7PE
Tel: 01651 862041 Contact: Colin Ward
bridgefoot.organics@btopenworld.com www.bridgefootorganics.co.uk
Soil Association nos. SG1071, SP5286. Producing vegetables, soft fruit and eggs.
Home delivery service for organic fruit, vegetables, eggs and mushrooms in the
Aberdeen area.

CROFT ORGANICS

SKELLARTS CROFT, DAVIOT, INVERURIE AB51 0JL
Tel: 01467 681717 Contact: Vic Hunter
croftorganics@hotmail.com www.croft-organics.co.uk
Soil Association SP6495, HDRA. Soil Association box scheme; vegetables and soft
fruit grown on SA-registered land. Farm shop sales, also organic wines, coffee
and tea. Free range eggs.

FEARNS

REDFORD FARM, GARVOCK, LAURENCEKIRK AB30 1HS
Tel: 01561378861 Contact: Allan Fearn
allan@fearns.uk.com www.fearns.uk.com
Swedes grown, washed and packed for various outlets.

FRASER, J & M
BURNORRACHIE, BRIDGE OF MUCHALLS, STONEHAVEN AB39 3RU
Tel: 01569 730195 Contact: John & Maggie Fraser
Biodynamic Agricultural Association (Demeter). A 40-acre farm growing field veg
for the wholesale market and local deliveries, specialising in supplying other
box schemes. We also have 'meat days' when meat is available. Organic Food
Awards 2004: Fresh Fruit and Veg Commended.

GOSPEL, TWB
AUCHMACLEDDIE, STRICHEN, FRASERBURGH AB43 6SP
Tel: 01771 637533 Fax: 01771 637533 Contact: Trevor Gospel
Soil Association G1867. North-east Scotland organic farm selling beef; large and
small orders.

GRAMPIAN COUNTRY FOOD (BANFF) LTD
TANNERY ST., BANFF AB45 1FR
Tel: 01261 815881 Fax: 01261 818387 Contact: C Barrie
cbarrie@gcfg.com www.gcfg.com
Soil Association P7487, CMI organic standards. Processors of whole chickens.

GREENESS ORGANICS
ROSEBRAE, GREENESS, CUMINESTOWN, TURRIFF AB53 8HY
Tel: 01888 544877 Contact: Victoria Doran
Soil Association G2381. Weekly box delivery of locally grown vegetables and
occasionally fruit around Turriff, Banff, Aberchirder and their environs.

HAY, M&M
EDINGLASSIE, HUNTLY AB54 4YD
Tel: 01466 700274 Fax: 01466700374 Contact: Malcolm Hay
malcolm.hay@btinternet.com
Soil Association SG7519. Quality Angus cross beef store cattle and Shetland
Cheviot/Texel cross lambs.

HOWEGARDEN, A DIVISION OF TRUXPLUS LTD
AUCHTURLESS, TURRIFF, ABERDEEN AB53 8EN
Tel: 01888 511808 Fax: 01888 511841 Contact: Adrian Walker
Packing organic produce to major supermarket chains. Specialise in locally grown produce.

JOHNS, DH & SON
MAINS OF KINNAIRDY, BRIDGE OF MARNOCH, HUNTLY AB54 7RX
Tel: 01466 780856 Fax: 01466 780856 Contact: Malcolm Johns
johns@kinnairdyorganics.freeserve.co.uk
Producers of organic cereals and pulses, manufacturer of organic animal feeds.

LEMBAS
LORIENEEN, BRIDGE OF MUCHALLS, STONEHAVEN, ABERDEEN AB39 3RU
Tel: 01569 731746 Fax: 01569 739137 Contact: Paul Van Midden
Biodynamic Agricultural Association (Demeter) 307; Soil Association SP6660.
Growers and distributors of Demeter and organically grown foods. We stock fresh fruit and vegetables, mushrooms, eggs, preserves, cheese and meat. Wholesale and retail service.

REID G & G
CANTERLAND, MARYKIRK AB30 1XJ
Tel: 01674 840316 Fax: 01674 840316 Contact: Gabriela Reid
Organic Aberdeen Angus beef, sold fresh at farmers' market, sold vacuum-packed and frozen from farm gate.

SALMAC SALES LTD
4 ALBYN TERRACE, ABERDEEN AB10 1YP
Tel: 01224 626261 Fax: 01224 626206 Contact: Debbie Benzie
debbie@salmac.co.uk www.salmac.co.uk
Salmac is the only supplier of Shetland organic salmon approved by the main organic certifying authority in the UK, the Soil Association. The salmon is also certified by Ecocert Sas for French customers.

SCOTTISH AGRICULTURAL COLLEGE

CRAIBSTONE ESTATE, BUCKSBURN, ABERDEEN AB21 9YA
Tel: 01224 711072 Fax: 01224 711293 Contact: David Younie
d.younie@ab.sac.ac.uk www.sac.ac.uk/organic-farming
Licensed producer of organic crops, beef and sheep. Advice, Research, Education:
SAC provides advice on organic farming (including telephone helpline: 01224
711072) to Scottish farmers, education and vocational training, and multi-disciplinary
research across most aspects of organic farming.

TERRAMAR ORGANICS

MIGNON HOUSE, MURTLE ESTATE, BIELDSIDE, ABERDEEN AB15 9EN
Tel: 07929 371684 Contact: Peter Marx
peter@terramar.co.uk www.terramar.co.uk
Ethical fairly traded organic clothing. Online shop with limited edition printed t-shirts
and classic basics. We specialise in customising clothing for business with printing
and embroidery—stylish clothing that doesn't cost the earth.

UNITED FISH PRODUCTS

GREENWELL PLACE, ABERDEEN AB12 3AY
Tel: 01224 854444 Fax: 01224 854333 Contact: Alison Chree
chreea@ufp.co.uk
Soil Association P3007. UFP manufactures organic fish meal to Soil Association
standards from local fish trimmings. The company is accredited to the Femas
standard and can assure safe, pure and traceable fish meal.

VITAL VEG

NORTH TILLYDAFF FARM, MIDMAR, INVERURIE AB51 7LS
Tel: 01330 833823 Fax: 01330 833823 Contact: Wendy Seel
info@vitalveg.co.uk www.vitalveg.co.uk
Vital Veg grow and supply mouthwatering organic vegetables, fruit and eggs, with
the emphasis on flavour and freshness. We deliver boxes of veg and fruit to homes
and offices in the Aberdeen area. We also grow and supply vegetable starter plants
grown from organic seed in certified organic compost, so you can grow your own!
We design vegetable gardens and potagers, and give advice and seminars on
organic growing. Vital Veg is the complete organic vegetable service!

Angus

AIRLIE ORGANICS

AIRLIE ESTATE OFFICE, CORTACHY, KIRRIEMUIR DD8 4LY
Tel: 01575 540294 Fax: 01575 540400 Contact: Susan Dyce
office@airlieestates.com www.airlieestates.com
We are retail and wholesale suppliers of home-produced Aberdeen Angus organic beef.

ANGUS FARMERS' MARKET

WESTBY, 64 WEST HIGH ST., FORFAR DD8 1BJ
Tel: 01307 465454 Contact: Veronica Baillie
jbrewster@ntlworld.com
Angus Farmers' Market held 2nd Saturday March to December. Local farmers interested in selling contact Veronica Baillie on 01307 850207 (tel/fax) or email veronica.baillie@btinternet.com.

ANGUS ORGANICS LTD

AIRLIE ESTATE OFFICE, CORTACHY, KIRRIEMUIR DD8 4LY
Tel: 01575 540294 Fax: 01575 540400 Contact: Susan Dyce
info@angusorganics.com www.angusorganics.com
Scottish organic certified Aberdeen Angus beef and Scottish organic lamb from our own farms. Nationwide deliveries, mail order, retail and wholesale. Traditionally produced, traditionally butchered.

BEE-ORGANIC

THE FENS, DRONLEY RD., BIRKHILL DD2 5QD
Tel: 01382 581186 Contact: Roger Beecroft
roger@bee-organic.co.uk www.bee-organic.co.uk
Locally produced organic veg boxes delivered weekly to the Tayside, Dundee and north Fife areas of Scotland.

SKEA ORGANICS

EAST MAINS OF AUCHTERHOUSE, DUNDEE DD3 0QN
Tel: 01382 320453 Fax: 01382 320454 Contact: Andrew Skea
andrew@skea.sol.co.uk www.skeaorganics.co.uk
Soil Association SP7982. We are specialist growers and wholesalers of organic
seed potatoes. Our range of 25 varieties is especially selected for taste and
suitability for organic and low input farming.

Argyll & Bute

ARGYLL HOTEL

ARGYLL HOTEL, ISLE OF IONA PA76 6SJ
Tel: 01681 700334 Fax: 01681 700510 Contact: Claire Bachellerie
reservations@argyllhoteliona.co.uk www.argyllhoteliona.co.uk
Small, friendly hotel on the sea shore of Iona with great views, open fires and
celebrated restaurant serving home-grown organic vegetables and herbs, local
seafood and organic meats. Garden certified by the Soil Association SG9023.

HODGE, C & C

ACHALIC FARM, LERAGS, BY OBAN PA34 4SE
Tel: 01631 566100 Fax: 01631 571202 Contact: Colin Hodge
achalic@hotmail.com
SOPA Membership No. 430 Certificate No. 1101/02/2101. Approved producer of
organic grass and pure Blackface lambs. Require organic finisher for lambs
Aug/Sept onwards.

INVERAWE SMOKEHOUSES

TAYNUILT PA35 1HU
Tel: 01866 822058 Fax: 01866 822744 Contact: Lucy MacLean
info@inverawe.co.uk www.smokedsalmon.co.uk
Inverawe Smokehouses is a leading company supplying traditionally smoked seafoods and Scottish fine foods. The organic range currently comprises organic smoked salmon certified by the Soil Association.

KILDALLOIG FARM

KILDALLOIG, CAMPBELLTOWN PA28 6RE
Tel: 01586 553192 Fax: 01586 553192 Contact: Mary Turner
maryturner1@btopenworld.com
Self-catering holiday cottages on organic farm. Organic beef and lamb to order. Organic breeding stock—Aberdeen Angus heifers, pedigree registered Blueface Leicester, Blackface and North Ronaldsay rams or ewe lambs.

MILLSTONE WHOLEFOODS

15 HIGH STREET, OBAN PA34 4BG
Tel: 01631 562704 Fax: 01631 562704 Contact: Ray & Linda Grant
Fresh local organic vegetables and bread on Wednesdays to Fridays, wholefoods, herbal remedies, nutritional supplements, aromatherapy etc.

STONEFIELD FARM—TA GROVES

GLENMASSAN, DUNOON PA23 8RA
Tel: 01369 706640 Contact: TA Groves
Soil Association G2325. Organic: Blackface sheep, Highland mules, Highlander cattle-meat, hay, soft fruit.

VERNON, R & H

RASHFIELD FARM, BY KILMUN PA23 8QT
Tel: 01369 840237 Contact: H Vernon
Soil Association G768. Organically registered since 1985, specialising in the breeding of the original Black Highland cattle of the Western Highlands, reared in the traditional manner. Alternative Therapies.

BARWINNOCK HERBS

BARWINNOCK HERBS, BARRHILL KA26 0RB
Tel: 01465 821338 Contact: Dave Holton
herbs@barwinnock.com www.barwinnock.com
Garden and nursery with hardy plants from a cool climate, propagated and grown without any chemical fertilisers or pesticides. Culinary and medicinal herbs available by mail order.

BUTTERWORTHS ORGANIC NURSERY

GARDEN COTTAGE, AUCHINLECK ESTATE, CUMNOCK KA18 2LR
Tel: 01290 551088 Contact: John Butterworth
butties@webage.co.uk www.butterworthsorganicnursery.co.uk
Scottish Organic Producers Association 625G. Fruit tree nursery specialising in northern conditions. 70 apple varieties plus some pears, plums and cherries. Mail order, visitors by arrangement, internet catalogue or 2 x 1st class stamps please. Mobile 07732 254300.

DRUMSKEOCH FARM B&B

DRUMSKEOCH FARM, PINWHERRY, GIRVAN KA26 0QB
Tel: 01465 841172 Contact: Romana Holloway
drumskeoch@wildmail.com www.drumskeoch.co.uk
Organic, exclusively vegetarian/vegan B&B in beautiful hilly countryside, panoramic views, excellent local walks. Home cooked dinner/packed lunch available using some home-grown produce, water from own underground source.

GLENDRISSAIG HOUSE

GLENDRISSAIG BY GIRVAN KA26 0HJ
Tel: 01465 714631 Fax: 01465 714631 Contact: Kate McIntosh
Modern farmhouse with wonderful views. Peaceful location in Gulf Stream climate. Spacious en-suite rooms with one on ground floor. Home cooking with vegetarian option. Organic produce and spring water. Secure parking.

STAIR ORGANIC GROWERS
11 THE YETTS, TARBOLTON KA5 5NT
Tel: 01292 541369 Contact: Steve Hilbourne
sales @organicgrowing.com www.organicgrowing.com
Box scheme and fruit and veg to order. Home delivery service. On line ordering, no credit cards needed. Locally produced in season.

WILDLY ORGANIC
25 SEAFIELD COURT, ARDROSSAN KA22 8NS
Tel: 01294 472075 Fax: 01294 472075 Contact: Gillian Scott
info@wildlyorganic.co.uk www.wildlyorganic.co.uk
Suppliers of fresh organic fruit, vegetables and groceries. Local box scheme delivering between Largs and Troon. Mail and internet order of organic deodorants, natural soaps and personal care goods, and organic Active Manuka honey. Our retail outlet within Stanley Plant Nurseries, Ardrossan, is open every Friday, Saturday and Sunday.

Borders

ACME ORGANICS
KIRKURD GARDENS, BLYTH BRIDGE, WEST LINTON EH46 7DH
Tel: 01721 752633 Contact: Seb Rose
organicdirectory@acmeorganics.co.uk www.acmeorganics.co.uk
We deliver a huge range of organic, Fairtrade and eco-friendly products to households in the Borders and south Lanarkshire. We grow much of our own produce and source as much as possible from our network of local producers. Delivery is free (subject to minimum order).

BORELAND FARM

DUNSCORE, DUMFRIES DG2 0XA
Tel: 01387 820287 Contact: Simon Barnes
barnes@borelandfarm.co.uk www.borelandfarm.co.uk
Soil Association SG7881. Bed and breakfast accommodation and farm holidays on an organic sheep farm, set in the rolling hills of Dumfries & Galloway, south-west Scotland. Pets welcome.

CREAM O'GALLOWAY DAIRY CO LTD

RAINTON, GATEHOUSE OF FLEET, CASTLE DOUGLAS DG7 2DR
Tel: 01557 814040 Fax: 01557 814040 Contact: Wilma Finlay
info@creamogalloway.co.uk www.creamogalloway.co.uk
Soil Association P2928. Farm-based manufacturer of organic ice cream and frozen yoghurt. Open to public with nature trails, tea room and adventure playground. Member of the Soil Association Organic Farms Network.

FARM FUTURE—JM & PM ANDERSON

NETHERFIELD FARM, BEESWING, DUMFRIES DG2 8JE
Tel: 01387 730217 Contact: JM Anderson
www.netherfieldguesthouse.co.uk
BDAA/Demeter certification 325. Small farm guest house in Galloway Hills, offering own biodynamic and organic vegetarian based catering. Hauschka massage with rest and care. Self-catering cottages available.

LOCH ARTHUR CREAMERY

CAMPHILL VILLAGE TRUST, BEESWING, DUMFRIES DG2 8JQ
Tel: 01387 760296 Fax: 01387 760296 Contact: Barry Graham
creamery@locharthur.org.uk www.locharthur.org.uk
Biodynamic Agricultural Association (Demeter). Produce of Demeter certified cheeses and yoghurt. Organic farm shop selling our own cheeses, meat, bread and vegetables and much more. Open Monday–Saturday. Also trade enquiries and mail order.

LOW CRAIGLEMINE FARM HOLIDAYS

LOW CRAIGLEMINE, WHITHORN, NEWTON STEWART, WIGTOWNSHIRE DG8 8NE
Tel: 01988 500730 Fax: 01988 500730 Contact: Kirsty Hurst
enquiries@www.lowcraiglemine-farm-holidays.co.uk
www.lowcraiglemine-farm-holidays.co.uk
BDAA Certificate No 354. Self-catering accommodation: organic family farm, cosy,
comfortable cottage and bothy sleeping 6, 3. Warm welcome and peace await you.
Biodynamic beef available. Bowen technique available.

THE ROSSAN

THE ROSSAN, AUCHENCAIRN, CASTLE DOUGLAS DG7 1QR
Tel: 01556 640269 Fax: 01556 640278 Contact: Elizabeth Bardsley
bardsley@rossan.freeserve.co.uk www.the-rossan.co.uk
Small guest house in North Solway Shore. Large garden over 20 years organic.
All home cooking, mostly organic. Plus vegetarian, vegan, gluten-free, med diets.
Well behaved dogs welcome free. Stairlift to bedroom floor. J.P.C.Golden
Achievement Award of Excellence for Quality and Service 2004.

SUNRISE WHOLEFOODS

49 KING ST., CASTLE DOUGLAS DG7 1AE
Tel: 01556 504455 Contact: Pauline Tilbury
Wholefood shop, specialising in organic dried and fresh foods; organic meat,
fruit and veg, cheese, wine, bread, books. Fresh veg from smallholding in summer.

Roasted Root Vegetables

Pre-heat the oven to 2000C. Chop into 4 cm chunks, 6 each of carrots, parsnips
and medium-size red onions. Place in a large bowl and drizzle on 50g of olive oil,
sea salt and black pepper. Spread in a single layer in a roasting tin and roast until
fully cooked about 30 mins. Be vigilant: they should be caramelized, not burnt.
Serve sprinkled with chopped thyme, parsley or rosemary.
**From *Allotment Gardening: An Organic Guide for Beginners* by Susan
Berger, Green Books, £9.95.**

BELLFIELD ORGANIC NURSERY

STRATHMIGO, CUPAR KY14 7RH
Tel: 01337 860764 Fax: 01337 860764 Contact: Irene Alexander
order@bellfield-organics.com www.bellfield-organics.com
Grower of organic vegetables. Home delivery service.

CRAIGENCALT ECOLOGY CENTRE

CRAIGENCALT FARM, KINGHORN KY3 9YG
Tel: 01592 891567 Fax: 01592 891567 Contact: Ronnie Mackie
cfec@free.uk.com www.cfec.org.uk
The Craigencalt Farm Ecology Centre is used by schools and adult groups for
ecological studies, by weekend study groups and various craft/arts persons. Visitors
are welcome to take part, walk, bird watch, chat to members, even pitch in with
the various projects underway.

ELMWOOD COLLEGE FARM

CUPAR MUIR, CUPAR KY15 5RN
Tel: 01334 658900 Fax: 01334 658888 Contact: Peter McKinnon
pmkinnon@elmwood.ac.uk www.elmwood.ac.uk
Soil Association G4447. College of Further Education. Courses in organic agriculture.
Producer of beef, lamb and cereals. Member of the Soil Association Organic Farms
Network.

ORGANIC MEAT & PRODUCTS (SCOTLAND) LTD

JAMESFIELD FARM, ABERNETHY KY14 6EW
Tel: 01738 850498 Fax: 01738 850741 Contact: Alan Dickson
jamesfieldfarm@btconnect.com www.jamesfieldfarm.co.uk
Soil Association. Producers of organic beef, lamb, sausages, pies, ready-made
meals, soups, hampers etc. for mail order and the farm shop.

PILLARS OF HERCULES FARM

PILLARS OF HERCULES, STRATHMIGLO ROAD, FALKLAND KY15 7AD

Tel: 01337 857749 Contact: Bruce Bennett

bruce@pillars.co.uk www.pillars.co.uk

Soil Association SB26C. Organic farm with on-site shop and café. Selling wide range of fruit, vegetables, salads, herbs, eggs and Christmas turkeys from own farm plus meat, dairy products and wholefoods. Open daily 10am–6pm. Member of the Soil Association Organic Farms Network.

SCOTMED HERBS

GARDEN BY THE LOCH, CRAIGENCALT FARM, KINGHORN KY3 3YG

Tel: 01592 872689 Contact: Alan Steedmann

alan@scotmedherbs.co.uk www.scotmedherbs.co.uk

Soil Association G910. Grower and retailer (see shop entry) of medicinal and culinary herbs (plants and cut herbs), retailer of herbs, spices and other organic products, aromatherapy products, cosmetics, soaps, crystals, CDs, herbal medicines and gift-ware.

SCOTMED HERBS

113/115 HIGH STREET, BURNTISLAND KY3 9AA

Tel: 01592 872689 Contact: Alan Steedman

alan@scotmedherbs.co.uk www.scotmedherbs.co.uk

Grower and retailer of medicinal and culinary herbs (plants and cut herbs), retailer of herbs, spices,organic herbal teas, organic teas and cordials, aromatherapy products, cosmetics, soaps, crystals, CDs, herbal medicines (including Hambleden Herb Organic Tinctures) and giftware. We also now sell online at www.scotmedherbs.co.uk.

Go Bare

Nowadays almost everything we buy comes swathed in layers of excess packaging. Indeed, 90% of the material used in the production of, or contained within consumer goods, becomes waste within just six weeks of sale. Shop with a critical eye, and avoid buying over-packaged goods. Also, reduce the amount of disposable products you buy, and always look for alternatives that will last.

From *Go MAD! Go Make A Difference 2: Over 500 daily ways to save the planet* by The Ecologist, Think Books, £6.99.

AQUASCOT GROUP LTD

FYRISH WAY, ALNESS IV17 0PJ
Tel: 01349 880711 Fax: 01349 884162 Contact: Gail Evans
gail.evans@aquascot.com www.aquascot.uk.com
A Highland-based manufacturer of fresh and frozen fish products. Scottish organic salmon is a key raw material from which the company continues to base its new product development.

BLACK ISLE BREWERY

BLACK ISLE BREWERY, OLD ALLANGRANGE, MUNLOCHY IV8 8NZ
Tel: 01463 811871 Fax: 01463 811875 Contact: David Gladwin / Jay Jay Gladwin
greatbeers@blackislebrewery.com www.blackislebrewery.com
Soil Association registered. Black Isle Brewery is a small, intensely independent brewery in the heart of the Scottish Highlands producing a range of outstanding organic beers.

DANDELION PARTNERSHIP

WALLED GARDEN, BRAHAN, DINGWALL IV7 8EE
Tel: 01349 861982 Contact: J Henderson & S Barclay
Soil Association G5162. Community-supported agriculture (no deliveries). Growing a complete range of organic vegetables for committed customers and restaurants. Also organic eggs and organic cut flowers. We only sell what we grow ourselves. Experienced teacher/speaker on organic horticulture.

DONALDSON, MARJ

13 NEWTON KINKELL, MUIR OF ORD IV6 7RB
Tel: 01349 861956 Contact: Marj Donaldson
Sides of lamb from organic farm, butchered to your requirements, for your freezer.

EDINBURGH SMOKED SALMON CO LTD
1 STRATHVIEW, DINGWALL BUSINESS PARK, DINGWALL IV15 9XD
Tel: 01349 860600 Fax: 01389 860606 Contact: J Prentice
essco@btconnect.com
Soil Association P6793. Smoked salmon company specialising in high quality consistent products with a degree of innovation.

THE HEALTH SHOP
20 BARON TAYLOR'S STREET, INVERNESS IV1 1QG
Tel: 01463 233104 Fax: 01463 718144 Contact: Martin Sellar
healthshopinvern@aol.com
We are delighted to offer you a large range of organic products—just get in contact and we'll do the rest! Look forward to hearing from you.

HIDDENGLEN HOLIDAYS
LAIKENBUIE, GRANTOWN ROAD, NAIRN IV12 5QN
Tel: 01667 454630 Contact: Peter & Therese Muskus
muskus@bigfoot.com www.hiddenglen.co.uk
Watch roe deer and woodpeckers from top quality holiday homes with beautiful outlook over loch amid birch woods. Fun for children. Photos on website. Eggs, freezer-ready lamb and weaned calves sold.

HIGHLAND WHOLEFOODS
UNIT 6, 13 HARBOUR ROAD, INVERNESS IV1 1SY
Tel: 01463 712393 Contact: The Manager
halina@highlandfoods.co.uk
Free delivery service throughout Northern Scotland. Cash and carry warehouse in Inverness. Over 800 organic lines stocked, including chilled and frozen. Soil Association reg. no. P2113.

MACLEOD ORGANICS

KYLERONA FARM, ARDERSIER, INVERNESS IV2 7QZ
Tel: 01667 462555 Fax: 01667 461138 Contact: Donnie Macleod
macleod.organics@virgin.net www.macleodorganics.com
Soil Association SP6506, SG8730. Main distributors for organic produce to and
from the Highlands. Organic farm centre including fully certified café, shop, box
scheme and tourist accommodation.

MARCASSIE FARM

MARCASSIE FARM, RAFFORD, FORRES IV362RH
Tel: 01309 676865 Fax: 01309 676865 Contact: Betsy van der Lee
marcassie@marcassie.fsnet.co.uk
Based in Scotland (nr. Findhorn). Association for Environmentally Conscious
Builders, Association of Scottish Hardwood Sawmillers. Sawmill & joinery shop
(building components, bespoke joinery, lamp posts, street furniture & specialist
commissions, all in Scottish grown timber), organic farm (grains, wheatgrass, eggs,
hay), commercial kitchen (being established), esoteric healing, self-catering accommodation (for 4–6 people), educational courses (being established).

MILLERS OF SPEYSIDE

STRATHSPEY IND. ESTATE, GRANTOWN ON SPEY PH26 3NB
Tel: 01479 872520 Fax: 01479 872892 Contact: A Milne
info@millersofspeyside.co.uk www.millersofspeyside.co.uk
Millers of Speyside are a small private abattoir situated in the Highlands of
Scotland. Suppliers of quality beef, lamb and pork to the catering and retail trade.

PHOENIX COMMUNITY STORES LTD

THE PARK, FINDHORN BAY, MORAY IV36 3TZ
Tel: 01309 690110 Fax: 01309 692124 Contact: David Hoyle
info@phoenixshop.org www.findhorn.org/store/
Full service award-winning food shop plus café and organic bakery. The Phoenix
also offers a wide range of complementary products including apothecary, books,
crafts, household, music and gifts.

POYNTZFIELD HERB NURSERY
BLACK ISLE, BY DINGWALL IV7 8LX
Tel: 01381 610352 Fax: 01381 610352 Contact: Duncan Ross
info@poyntzfieldherbs.co.uk www.poyntzfieldherbs.co.uk
Biodynamic Agricultural Association (Demeter) 326. We are biodynamic growers of over 400 varieties of herbal plants and seeds, especially medicinals. Not importers, we export mainly to EU countries.

RAASAY WALLED GARDEN
ISLE OF RAASAY, BY KYLE OF LOCHALSH IV40 8PB
Tel: 01378 660345 Contact: Sadie McLeod raasaywalledgarden@btinternet.com
Skye & Lochalsh Horticultural Development Association, Highlands & Islands Organic Association. An organic garden growing a wide variety of fruits, vegetables, salads, herbs, cut and dried flowers for sale in season, plus hardy plants, climbers and shrubs.

RHANICH FARM
RHANICH RD., EDDERTON, TAIN IV19 1LG
Tel: 01862 821265 Contact: Pam Shaw
Fairly isolated hill farm offering camping in summer, farm gate sales (eggs, fruit, veg) in season. Mail order organic coloured fleece for spinning or sheepskins.

TIO LTD (THIS IS ORGANICS)
13 GRESHOP ROAD, FORRES IV36 2GU
Tel: 01309 696040 Fax: 01309 696060 Contact: Kirstine Dinnes
mail@tio.co.uk www.tio.co.uk
Growers, packers and importers of organic root vegetables. Supply wholesale and multiple markets.

WESTER LAWRENCETON
WESTER LAWRENCETON, FORAY IV36 2RH
Tel: 01309 676566 Fax: 01309 676162 Contact: Pam & Nick Rodway
Wester Lawrenceton is a 24 hectare (ha) mixed organic farm, with a further 12 ha in conversion, overlooking the Moray Firth to the mountains of Sutherland beyond. Member of the Soil Association Organic Farms Network.

Lanarkshire

BLACK MOUNT FOODS

8 THE WYND, BIGGAR ML12 6BU
Tel: 01899 221747 Fax: 01899 221518 Contact: John Bryan
orgmeat@aol.com www.scottishorganicmeats.com
Biodynamic Agricultural Association (Demeter) 275. Family-run business dedicated
to the supply of finest Scottish produced organic and biodynamic beef, lamb, pork
and poultry. Sausages and bacon also available. Wholesale and mail order.

BROUGHTON ALES

BROUGHTON, BIGGAR ML12 6HQ
Tel: 01899 830345 Contact: Alastair Mouat
beer@broughtonales.co.uk www.broughtonales.co.uk
Soil Association P4734. Brewers of Border Gold organic ale, Angel organic lager,
Waitrose Organic Ale and Marks & Spencers Organic Ale and Lager. All products
available in 500ml bottles.

CLYDE ORGANICS

MUIRHOUSE FARM, LIBBERTON, CARNWATH ML11 8LX
Tel: 01555 840271 Fax: 01555 841294 Contact: Murray Brown
muirhouse@clydeorganics.co.uk www.clydeorganics.co.uk
We are a family-run, organic dairy farm that supplies wholesale and direct to the
public. Our farm is in the Clyde Valley between Lanark and Biggar, and all of our
milk is produced on our own farm from clover-rich pastures. Our milk is available in
non-standardised full cream and semi-skimmed. Cream can be supplied as single
cream or double cream. We supply to the retailing and wholesaling sectors and our
milk and cream are available in a comprehensive range of packaging. We also
grow a wide selection of vegetables and potatoes, which we sell at the farm.

CRAIGTON PACKAGING

43–45 SCOTT'S ROAD, PAISLEY PA2 7AN
Tel: 0141 887 0244 Fax: 0141 887 5462 Contact: Kevan Jones
info@craigton.com www.craigton.com
Specialist contract bottling and packing company. Three expert business areas.
Bottling fine alcohol. Packing, assembly and QA services to print and publishing
industry, and wrapping bagging and filling operations. Services the UK and international customers.

THE NATURAL FRUIT & BEVERAGE COMPANY LIMITED

VIEWFIELD PARK, VIEWFIELD ROAD, COATBRIDGE ML5 5QS
Tel: 01236 429042 Fax: 01236 424234 Contact: Gerry Dunn
gerry@nfbc.biz
Manufacturer of organic fruit juices.

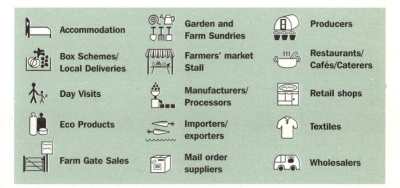

Lothian

THE CALEDONIAN BREWING CO LTD

42 SLATEFORD ROAD, EDINBURGH EH11 1PH
Tel: 0131 337 1286 Fax: 0131 313 2370 Contact: Robert Burton
www.caledonian-brewery.co.uk
Soil Association P903. Britain's first licensed organic brewer. Caledonian brews the world renowned Golden Promise organic beer, available in most UK supermarkets.

CAMPBELL, ALLAN

47 BOSWALD PARKWAY, EDINBURGH EH5 2BR
Tel: 0131 552 3486 Fax: 0131 552 3486 Contact: Dennis Flynn Manager
This is a high street shop selling organic meat and poultry, eggs and cheeses.

DAMHEAD ORGANIC FOODS

32A DAMHEAD, OLD PENTLAND RD., LOTHIANBURN, EDINBURGH EH10 7EA
Tel: 0131 448 2091 Fax: 0131 448 2504 Contact: Susan Gerard
enquiries@damhead.co.uk www.damhead.co.uk
Biodynamic Agricultural Association (Demeter) 238. Scotland's organic food specialists: award-winning home delivery service (Soil Association highly commended 2002), farm shop and wholesale division. Vast range of organic products available to order online.

DODS OF HADDINGTON

BACKBURN, LETHAM RD., HADDINGTON EH41 4NN
Tel: 01620 823305 Fax: 01620 824406 Contact: Gordon Bonnington
Soil Association SP6841. Dods of Haddington Limited, established 1782, are growers and producers of agricultural seeds for the organic farmer and grower.

EAST COAST ORGANIC BOXES

24 BOGGS HOLDINGS, PENCAITLAND EH34 5BD
Tel: 01875 340227 Fax: 01875 340227 Contact: Mike Callender
ecobox@eastcoastorganics.freeserve.co.uk www.eastcoastorganics.co.uk
East Coast Organics operate a highly successful & productive biodynamic farm.
Various sizes of boxes are available & can include fruit, eggs, bread, etc. Free
home delivery to Edinburgh /Lothians. Edinburgh Farmers' Market now every
Saturday. Organic Food Awards 2004: Commended Box Scheme.

THE ENGINE SHED

19 ST. LEONARD'S LANE, EDINBURGH EH8 9SD
Tel: 0131 662 0040 Fax: 0131 667 5319 Contact: M MacDonald
engineshed@aol.com www.engineshed.org.uk
Training centre for adults with learning disabilities. Training in catering setting
towards employment. Five production workshops: café, bakery, outside catering,
food processing and wholefood shop.

THE ENGINE SHED SHOP

123 BRUNTISFIELD PLACE, EDINBURGH EH
Tel: 0131 229 6494 Contact: Heather Wilson
engineshed@aol.com www.engineshed.org.uk
Small health food shop selling a range of organic dry products, organic fruit and
veg, bread and cakes, etc., incorporating a healthy, light snacks, take away service.

GLENORA HOTEL

14 ROSEBERY CRESCENT, EDINBURGH EH12 5JY
Tel: 0131 337 1186 Fax: 0131 337 1119 Contact: Morag & Georges Thomas
glenorahotel@aol.com glenorahotel.co.uk
A beautifully refurbished Victorian town house hotel in the centre of Edinburgh
serving entirely organic continental buffet, full cooked breakfast and offering
complimentary organic & Fairtrade tea and coffee in our 11 bedrooms. All
rooms have en suite shower & wc, and we have a non-smoking policy.

GROW WILD

UNIT 8, BLOCK3, WHITESIDE INDUSTRIAL ESTATE, BATHGATE EH48 2RX
Tel: 0845 2263393 Fax: 01506 656543 Contact: Chris Purser
sales@growwild.co.uk www.growwild.co.uk
Established in 1998, we are a company committed to supplying quality fresh
organic produce at reasonable prices. To make it easier for the customer we deliver
directly to your door—either at home or work; alternatively, we can leave it with a
friend or neighbour. Freshness is key—so all produce is chilled throughout the supply chain. We believe strongly in providing a good service and have a customer-
focused approach with a personal touch. Please see our website for full details.

HELIOS FOUNTAIN

7 GRASSMARKET, EDINBURGH EH1 2HY
Tel: 0131 229 7884 Fax: 0131 622 7173 Contact: Jos Bastiaensen
info@helios-fountain.co.uk www.helios-fountain.co.uk
A shop selling gifts, crafts, toys and beads. Our book selection includes most
works by or about Rudolf Steiner.

HERBARIA PRODUCTS LTD

51BC BRUNSWICK ROAD, EDINBURGH EH7 5PD
Tel: 0131 656 9000 Contact: Monica Wilde
enquiries@herbaria.co.uk www.hedgerowherbals.com
Herbaria makes organic and natural herbal hand-made soaps and other bath &
body products. For trade customers can supply own range or make to order under
your own label. Shoppers can purchase directly from our website.

MACRAE HOLDINGS

MACRAE EDINBURGH, 50A WEST HARBOUR ROAD, GRANTON, EDINBURGH EH5 1PP
Tel: 0131 552 5215 Fax: 0131 552 7521 Contact: Katrina Durward
katrina@macrae.co.uk www.macrae.co.uk
A processor of ready to eat seafood products, including organic Scottish smoked
salmon, organic salmon paté, organic trout paté, organic hot smoked trout
fillets and organic Scottish salmon gravelax. Licence P5868. Deliveries to UK
and EEC.

NAIRN'S OAT CAKES

90 PEFFERMILL ROAD, EDINBURGH EH16 5UU
Tel: 0131 620 7000 Fax: 0131 620 7750 Contact: John Holroyd
info@nairns-oatcakes.com www.nairns-oatcakes.com
Nairn's produce a range of oat cakes and oat biscuits. All of the Nairn's products are wheat-free and contain no hydrogenated fat, no artificial colourings, flavourings or preservatives and no GM ingredients. They are suitable for vegetarians and vegans, and for anyone with an allergy to nuts.

NATURE'S GATE

83 CLERK STREET, EDINBURGH EH8 9JG
Tel: 0131 668 2067 Contact: Bahram Ajodani
Soil Association R1827. Wholefood shop with large organic range including bread, cereals, dried fruit, nuts, herbs, spices, coffees, teas, chilled and frozen, fresh fruit and vegetables, wines, toiletries, vitamin supplements and herbal remedies.

NEAL'S YARD REMEDIES

102 HANNOVER ST., EDINBURGH EH2 2LE
Tel: 0131 226 3223 Fax: 0131 225 9947 Contact: Gill Hames
mail@nealsyardremedies.com www.nealsyardremedies.com
Retailer of organic essential oils and cosmetics and therapy room offering herbalist, homoeopath, massage and aromatherapy.

THE NEW LEAF

20 ARGYLE PLACE, MARCHMONT, EDINBURGH EH9 1JJ
Tel: 0131 228 8840 Contact: Linda Goodman
Soil Association R3002. Vegetarian and organic wholefood shop dedicated to ethical trading. Fine selection of wholefoods including gluten and dairy-free. Local fresh organic produce, eco-friendly, cruelty-free products and much more.

ORGANIC WORLD (SCOTLAND) LTD
BLOCK 3, UNIT 8, WHITESIDE INDUSTRIAL ESTATE, BATHGATE EH48 2RX
Tel: 01506 632911 Fax: 01506 652444 Contact: Robert Kingdon
trading@organic-world.co.uk www.organic-world.co.uk
We are primary wholesalers of organically grown fruit and vegetables, supplying throughout Scotland and northern England. We also have a retail shop on our premises where the public can buy fruit and vegetables, chilled, dairy and grocery products, all from organic production. Open Monday–Friday, 8.30am–5.00pm.

PATERSON ARRAN LTD
THE ROYAL BURGH BAKERY, LIVINGSTON EH54 5DN
Tel: 01506 431031 Fax: 01506 432800 Contact: The Manager
enquiries@paterson-arran.com www.paterson-arran.com
Producers of organic shortbread, oatcakes and biscuits, marmalades, preserves and chutneys.

PET ORGANIC
PO BOX 23625, 4/11 CONSTITUTION STREET, EDINBURGH EH6 7YY
Tel: 0131 555 6366 Fax: 0131 555 6366 Contact: Merredith Hutton
sales@petorganic.com www.petorganic.com
Make the organic choice for your pet. We offer a range of organic pet food and products for dogs, cats, small animals, horses and birds. Quality organic and natural grooming supplies, toys and bedding also available. Pet care advice and product information available. Secure online purchase with delivery throughout the UK.

PHANTASSIE FOOD
PHANTASSIE, EAST LINTON EH40 3DF
Tel: 01620 860285 Fax: 01620 861531 Contact: Patricia Stephen
veg@phantassie.co.uk www.phantassie.co.uk
Veg and egg producer operating local box scheme in Lothian and Borders, local farmers' markets, wholesale to shops and caterers in Edinburgh and the Lothians.

SEAVEG

55 WALLACE CRESCENT, ROSLIN EH25 9LN
Tel: 0131 440 4104 Contact: Maire Devlin
maire@seaveg.co.uk www.seaveg.co.uk
We supply a range of quality Seaveg including dulse, wakame, kombu, carragheen
& mixed sea salad. Our Seaveg is wild (non-farmed), hand-harvested and all locally
sourced from the unspoilt Atlantic shores of West Donegal. We supply retail and
wholesale customers and aim to keep our prices as low as possible and our product
as natural and unprocessed as possible.

SIMMERS OF EDINBURGH LTD

90 PEFFERMILL ROAD, EDINBURGH EH16 5UU
Tel: 0131 620 7000 Fax: 0131 620 7750 Contact: John Holroyd
john@simmersofedinburgh.co.uk www.nairns-oatcakes.com
Producer of organic oat cakes and biscuits.

SIMPLY ORGANIC

19/21 DRYDEN VALE, BILSTON GLEN EH20 9HN
Tel: 0131 448 0440 Contact: Belinda Mitchell
belinda@simplyorganic.co.uk www.simplyorganic.co.uk
Simply Organic are an award-winning, all-organic company. We produce fresh
organic convenience products including soups, pasta sauces and ready meals all
of which are suitable for vegetarians, under the Simply Organic brand.

THE WHOLE SHEBAG

SOUTH COBBINSHAW, WEST CALDER EH55 8LQ
Tel: 01501 785436 Fax: 01501 785436 Contact: David Murray
baga@thewholeshebag.com www.thewholeshebag.com
Fresh local produce delivered to your door. Family-run farm-based organic produce
delivery service to Edinburgh, Glasgow, West Lothian, Lanarkshire, Inverclyde and
Ayrshire. Products include fruit, vegetables, milk, eggs, wholefoods and meat.
Minimum order £10. Self-catering accommodation also available.

ZONKER ORGANICS
66 CUMBERLAND STREET, EDINBURGH EH3 6RE
Tel: 0131 558 1136 Contact: Hilary Mason
hilary@zonker.freeserve.co.uk www.zonker.co.uk
Small food shop located in New Town area of Edinburgh selling 100% organic food and drink. Items include fresh meat, prepacked cold meats and charcuterie, some fresh vegetables, groceries and chocolates. Also espresso-based coffee to go and sandwiches. Selection of wine and soft drinks. Nationwide sales via internet.

Isle of Mull

ARDALANISH ORGANIC FARM & ISLE OF MULL WEAVERS
BUNESSAN PA67 6DR
Tel: 01681 700265 Fax: 01681 700674 Contact: Aeneas & Minty MacKay
info@ardalanishfarm.co.uk www.ardalanishfarm.co.uk
info@isleofmullweavers.co.uk and www.isleofmullweavers.co.uk.
Traditional organic farm and tannery selling native Highland beef and Hebridean mutton. Weaving mill selling Hebridean tweed, throws, rugs, scarves, etc. woven on the farm. Sheepskins and cattle hides organically tanned on the farm. Local delivery—not a box scheme. Member of the Soil Association Organic Farms Network.

FINDHORN FOUNDATION
ISLE OF ERRAID, FIONPHORT PA66 6BN
Tel: 01681 700384 Contact: Paul Johnson
paul@erraid.fslife.co.uk www.erraid.com
Spiritual community living lightly on a tiny Hebridean island.

ISLAND BAKERY ORGANICS
TOBERMORY PA65 6PY
Tel: 01688 302223 Fax: 01688 302378 Contact: Joseph Reade
organics@islandbakery.co.uk www.islandbakery.co.uk
Soil Association P6294. Producers of award-winning organic biscuits, first
launched in September 2001. Available in delicatessens, organic stores, food
halls and farm shops across the UK. See our website for more information.

Orkney Islands

ORCA HOTEL
76 VICTORIA ST., STROMNESS KW16 3BS
Tel: 01856 850447 Contact: D Fischler
info@orcahotel.com www.orcahotel.com
Two star guesthouse, six rooms (single, twins, doubles, family), all en-suite; situated
in historic harbour village of Stromness, Orkney.

ORKNEY ORGANIC MEAT
NEW HOLLAND FARM, HOLM, ORKNEY KW17 2SA
Tel: 01856 781345 Fax: 01856 781345 Contact: Tony & Elizabeth BOWN
info@orkneyorganicmeat.co.uk www.orkneyorganicmeat.co.uk
Organic farm producing Aberdeen Angus beef and lamb with emphasis on health for
both animal and customer. Meat processed here on the farm by our own butcher.
Mail order sales of beef, lamb, speciality sausages and ready meals, delivered
throughout UK. Farm gate sales. Self-catering holiday cottage.

THE ORKNEY SALMON COMPANY LTD

CROWNESS CRESCENT, HATSTON, KIRKWALL, ORKNEY KW15 1RG
Tel: 01856 876101 Fax: 01856 873846 Contact: The Manager
www.orkneysalmon.co.uk
Soil Association SP2924. The pure waters off the coast of Orkney, where the
North Sea and the Atlantic Ocean collide, are the ideal natural environment for
raising organic salmon. Soil Association approved. See also www.aquascot.com.

TODS OF ORKNEY

25 NORTH END ROAD, STROMNESS KW16 3AG
Tel: 01856 850873 Fax: 01856 850213 Contact: Eddie Wight
info@stockan-and-gardens.co.uk www.stockan-and-gardens.co.uk
Soil Association P1905. Manufacturer of traditional oatcakes.

WHEEMS ORGANIC PRODUCE

WHEEMS EASTSIDE, SOUTH RONALDSAY, ORKNEY KW17 2TJ
Tel: 01856 831537 Fax: 01856 831537 Contact: Michael Roberts
Small mixed family farm concentrating on vegetable production for the local
market. Hostel accommodation for WWOOF helpers and other visitors: site half
mile above sandy bays and cliffs on northern Scottish island.

The Nest

How curious is the nest no other bird
Uses such loose materials or weaves
Their dwellings in such spots—dead oaken leaves
Are placed without and velvet moss within
And little scraps of grass—and scant and spare
Of what seems scarce materials down and hair
Far from man's haunts she seemeth naught to win
Yet nature is the builder and contrives
Homes for her children's comfort . . .

**From The Nightingale's Nest by John Clare, in *Landscape into Literature*
edited by Kay Dunbar, Green Books, £10.00.**

ATHOLL GLENS ORGANIC MEAT

MAINS OF KILLIECHANGIE, PITLOCHRY PH16 5NB
Tel: 07771 714951 Fax: 01796 482297 Contact: Elizabeth Stewart
info@athollglens.co.uk www.athollglens.co.uk
The highest quality organic beef and lamb direct from the Atholl region in Highland
Perthshire, one of the largest Special Protection Areas in the United Kingdom.
Atholl Glens' objective is to produce the highest quality organic beef and lamb
available, giving our customers absolute peace of mind that they are purchasing a
product which is not just wholesome, but full of taste and tender to perfection.

THE BEAN SHOP

THE BEAN SHOP, 67 GEORGE ST., PERTH PH1 5LB
Tel: 01738 449955 Fax: 01738 632693 Contact: John Bruce
sales@thebeanshop.com www.thebeanshop.com
The Bean Shop is an independent coffee roaster and tea specialist with a large
range of gourmet organic coffees. We roast all our coffee by hand on the premises
for optimum flavour and freshness.

BORLAND FARM

BLACKLUNANS, BLAIRGOWRIE PH10 7LA
Tel: 07789 301751 Fax: 01250 882214 Contact: Kenneth Headspeath
kenneth@highlanddrovers.co.uk www.borlandfold.co.uk
Soil Association SG5245. Organic Highland beef, Hebridean lamb, pedigree
highland cattle and Hebridean sheep. National Delivery.

GAME CONSERVATION CONSULTANCY

BLACKLUNANS, BLAIRGOWRIE PH10 7LA
Tel: 07789 301751 Contact: Kenneth Headspeath
www.borlandfold.co.uk
Organic farm specialising in Highland cattle and belted Galloway beef, pedigree
stock sales and Hebridean sheep for meat. Sale of registered lambs.

HIGHLAND HEALTH STORE

7 ST. JOHN ST., PERTH PH1 5SP
Tel: 01738 628102 Fax: 01738 447541 Contact: Kate Hood
email@highlandhealth.fsnet.co.uk www.perthcitydirectory.com/healthstore/
Vegetarian and health food shop.

HIGHLAND SPRING LTD

STIRLING ST., BLACKFORD, AUCHTERARDER PH4 1QA
Tel: 01764 660500 Fax: 01764 660501 Contact: Lisa Campbell
lisa@highland-spring.com www.highland-spring.com
Soil Association G5068. Highland Spring is the UK's leading producer of natural mineral water. In 2001 Highland Spring became the first British brand of natural mineral water to achieve organic status for its catchment area, granted by the Soil Association.

HUGH GRIERSON

NEWMILN FARM, TIBBERMORE, PERTH PH1 1QN
Tel: 01738 730201 Fax: 01738 730201 Contact: Hugh Grierson
hgrierson@freeuk.com www.the-organic-farm.co.uk
Finest Aberdeen Angus beef, lamb and pork from your local farm. All our food is grass fed and properly hung for maximum tenderness and flavour. We deliver nationwide or locally to your home in the evenings. Traditional local produce safeguards local jobs.

LURGAN FARM SHOP

LURGAN FARM, DRUMDEWAN, BY ABERFELDY PH15 2JQ
Tel: 01887 829303 Fax: 01887 829303 Contact: Sally Murray
sally@lurganfarm.demon.co.uk www.lurganfarmshop.co.uk
Soil Association SP6485. We sell our home-produced organic lamb and Aberdeen Angus beef. We make ready meals in our shop kitchen with our meats and bought in organic vegetables. We have a huge range of organic wholefoods and dairy produce.

WONDERMESH LTD

SOUTH INCH BUSINESS CENTRE, SHORE ROAD, PERTH PH2 8BW
Tel: 01738 444170 Contact: Dominic Martinez
sales@wondermesh.co.uk www.wondermesh.co.uk
Wondermesh is recognised in the UK as the leading supplier of quality insect
netting for the agricultural and horticultural industries.

Isle of Skye

ACHNACLOICH ORGANIC VEGETABLES

2 & 3 ACHNACLOICH, TARSKAVAIG IV49 8SB
Tel: 01471 855315 Contact: Chris Marsh
chris_marsh@madasafish.com
Soil Association GCS025/G2605. Established 1998, AOV supplies 50 households
in South Skye with weekly vegetables (June–October). All produce grown by us on
our 3-acre croft.

GLENDALE SALADS

19 UPPER FASACH, GLENDALE IV55 8WP
Tel: 01470 511349 Fax: 01470 511349 Contact: K&B Hagmann
Salads, herbs, veg and soft fruit to hotels, restaurants and through a box scheme.
Varieties selected for flavour and attractiveness. Delivered chilled on regular runs
several times a week. SA certificate G2263. Mail order throughout the UK. Organic
Food Awards 2004: Fresh Fruit and Vegetables Winner.

RUBHA PHOIL FOREST GARDEN/ SKYE PERMACULTURE

RUBHA PHOIL, ARMADALE PIER IV45 8RS
Tel: 01471 844700 Contact: Sandy Masson
sandyru@tiscali.co.uk www.skye-permaculture.org.uk
Soil Association GCS025/G4609, HDRA, Permaculture Association, Centre for Alternative Technology Ecosite. Herbs, vegetables, displays and demonstration of alternative systems, holiday accommodation, woodland walk, otter/bird hide, solitude in wilderness.

Stirlingshire

GLENSIDE ORGANICS

2/4 BANDEATH IND. ESTATE, THROSK, STIRLING FK7 7XY
Tel: 01786 816655 Fax: 01786 816100 Contact: Matt Thomson
enquiries@glensideorganics.co.uk www.glensidefarming.co.uk
Glenside's fertility farming system uses the Albrecht soil analysis, natural soil conditioning fertilisers and seaweed products optimising farm resources in the profitable production of quality crops and healthy livestock.

Superfact

Every Christmas we throw away enough rubbish to fill 400,000 double decker buses. That's enough to stretch all the way from London to New York!
From *SuperKids: Over 200 incredible ways for kids to save the planet* by Sasha Norris and Rupert Davies, Think Books, £5.99.

EPO GROWERS

KENNELS COTTAGE, HARDGATE, GLASGOW G81 5QR
Tel: 01389 875337 Contact: Echo Mackenzie
info@epogrowers.co.uk
We grow and sell organic vegetables, herbs and soft fruit under a Community
Supported Agriculture subscription system. Deliveries to households in Glasgow
and NW area; we use compost, manure and rock dust for fertility.

GRASSROOTS

20–22 WOODLANDS ROAD, CHARING CROSS, GLASGOW G3 6UR
Tel: 0141 353 3278 Fax: 0141 353 3078 Contact: Sarah Duncan
sarah@grassrootsorganic.com www.grassrootsorganic.com
Vegetarian wholefood shop retailing organic produce and groceries. All your shopping
needs, organic where possible, Fairtrade if we can get it. Licensed, and stocking a
range of organic wines and beers.

GRASSROOTS CAFE

97 ST. GEORGES ROAD, CHARING CROSS, GLASGOW G3 6JA
Tel: 0141 333 0534 Fax: 0141 332 9227 Contact: Lesley McNeil
www.grassrootsorganic.com
Grassroots café offers an informal atmosphere in which to enjoy a wide variety
of vegetarian cuisine with plenty of choice for vegans and those with special
dietary requirements.

GREENCITY WHOLEFOODS

23 FLEMING ST., GLASGOW G31 1PQ
Tel: 0141 554 7633 Contact: Lorna Donaldson
sales@greencity.co.uk www.greencity.co.uk
Soil Association P2370. Wholesaler/distributor of wide range of vegetarian
wholefoods, including many organic, Fairtrade and vegan products. Also stock
organic wines and beers and eco-friendly cleaning products.

INGRAM BROTHERS LTD
12 LAWWMOOR PLACE, DIXONS BLAZES IND. ESTATE, GLASGOW G5 0YE
Tel: 0141 429 2224 Fax: 0141 429 2227 Contact: Simon Young
sales.ingrambros@btinternet.com www.ingrambrothers.co.uk
Soil Association P3006. Manufacturers of bakery ingredients including organic icings, toppings, marzipan and icing sugar. Wholesaler of organic sugar and cocoa powder.

NEAL'S YARD REMEDIES
11 ROYAL EXCHANGE SQUARE, GLASGOW G1 3AJ
Tel: 0141 248 4230 Contact: Laurie Heaps
mail@nealsyardremedies.com www.nealsyardremedies.com
Neal's Yard Remedies manufactures and retails natural cosmetics in addition to stocking an extensive range of herbs, essential oils, homoeopathic remedies and reference material.

ROOTS & FRUITS, WHOLEFOODS & ORGANICS
455 GREAT WESTERN ROAD, GLASGOW G12 8HH
Tel: 0141 339 3097 Fax: 0141 334 3530 Contact: Wendy Inglis
Stockists of over 1,000 organic products including fruit and vegetables, fresh meats and breads, dairy and general provisions. A comprehensive range of baby foods and child care products. Box scheme and delivery service throughout the Glasgow area.

TAPA COFFEE & BAKEHOUSE
21 WHITEHILL ST, DENNISTOUN, GLASGOW G31 2LH
Tel: 0141 554 9981 Contact: Robert Winters
tapa-ltd@tiscali.co.uk www.tapacoffeeandbakehouse.co.uk
Tapa Coffee and Bakehouse produces great breads and cakes from fine organic ingredients. We have a range of delicious wheat-free bread and cakes. We make fresh sandwiches, soups and salads daily for sale in our café and shop, and stock an ever-increasing range of organic groceries. We also roast rare and organic coffees from around the world for superior freshness and flavour.

WEST MINCH SALMON LTD
GRAMSDALE FACTORY, GRAMSDALE, BENBECULA HS7 5LZ
Tel: 01870 602081 Fax: 01870 602083 Contact: Hector Macleod
wmsltd@zetnet.co.uk
Soil Association SG6059 (production), SP5504 (processing). Producers of organic
farmed Atlantic Salmon.

Garden Waste
RE-USE Clippings can be sawn up for firewood or stacked as wildlife habitat
areas—a fallen tree is a wildlife refuge, as is a pile of woody prunings—so if you
have space, leave a corner with a wildlife pile. Amphibians, especially newts and
toads, love a pile of slowly rotting wood, as do scores of beetles, some of which
are becoming very scarce because of our over-tidy gardening habits.
From *Reduce, Reuse, Recycle* by Nicky Scott, Green Books, £3.95.

 Accommodation

 Box Schemes/
Local Deliveries

  Day Visits

 Eco Products

Farm Gate Sales

 Garden and
Farm Sundries

 Farmers' market
Stall

 Manufacturers/
Processors

 Importers/
exporters

 Mail order
suppliers

 Producers

 Restaurants/
Cafés/Caterers

 Retail shops

 Textiles

 Wholesalers

ABACA LTD

UNIT 1, TYCROES BUSINESS PARK, AMMANFORD SA18 3RD
Tel: 01269 598491 Fax: 01269 598492 Contact: Rhiannon Rowley
info@abacaorganic.co.uk www.abacaorganic.co.uk
Handmade organic mattresses and hardwood beds. Abaca produces both luxury
pocket sprung and metal-free mattresses, as well as cot mattresses and mattress
pads. All standard sizes as well as a bespoke service.

BLACK MOUNTAIN FOODS

CWMCOCHIED, CWMDU, LLANDEILO SA19 7EE
Tel: 01558 685018 Fax: 01558 685185 Contact: Peter Mitchell
mynydddu@aol.com www.blackmountainfoods.co.uk
Soil Association G1802. Specialise in the distribution of organic meat to
retailers in London and south of England. We are now expanding our operation to
include the distribution of organic cheese, vegetables and other products.

CALON WEN ORGANIC FOODS

UNIT 4, WHITLAND INDUSTRIAL ESTATE, SPRING GARDENS, WHITLAND SA34 0HZ
Tel: 01994 241368 Fax: 01994 241063 Contact: Roger Kerr
orderline@calonwen-cymru.com
Calon Wen is a farmer owned and run co-operative. Our aim is to deliver the highest quality, fresh, local organic produce to you while ensuring a long term sustainable living to our staff and farmer members. We deliver a selection of fresh organic
fruit and vegetables in a box to your door each week. You either just choose from
one of our range of boxes or you can top up a box with extra items if you like. Extra
items include meat, milk, cheese, butter, yoghurt, soup, juices, bread and cakes,
wholefoods, baby foods, household cleaners, beauty products—in fact, if it's organic, we sell it. If you are interested, give us a ring or email us. We can tell you when
we are delivering in your area and we can take your order.

EADON, RH & EI
ESGAIRWEN ISAF, CWMANN, LAMPETER SA48 8HH
Tel: 01570 423285 Contact: Richard Eadon
eadon1@onetel.com
Soil Association G4623. Livestock farm producing lamb and beef supplied to the doorstep.

FORDHAM, ANG & MDA
DOLGOCH, BREGEST, NEWCASTLE EMLYN SA38 9EU
Tel: 01239 851466 Contact: A & M Fordham
Soil Association G2082. Dairy and vegetable farmer. Organic Farm Network farm. Tir Goval trail open to the public. Member of the Soil Association Organic Farms Network.

FRANKLANDS FARM FEEDS
UNIT 23 ANTHONY'S WAY, CILLEFWR IND. ESTATE, JOHNSTOWN, CARMARTHEN SA31 3RB
Tel: 01267 222422 Fax: 01267 237479 Contact: Andrew Morrey
amorrey@countrywidefarmers.co.uk www.countrywidefarmers.co.uk
Producers of approved non-organic ruminants coarse mixtures. SA 16, 18 and 20 are non-mineralised mixes designed for a variety of ruminant feeding situations. Bags or bulk throughout south and mid-Wales.

FRONTLINE ORGANICS
UNIT 4, WHITLAND INDUSTRIAL ESTATE, WHITLAND SA34 0HR
Tel: 01994 241368 Fax: 01994 241063 Contact: Dai Miles
frontline.organics@ukgateway.net www.frontlineorganics.co.uk
Soil Association P16WW. Deliveries direct to individuals, shops, restaurants and box schemes of fresh vegetables and fruit, dairy products, bread and wholefoods. Locally produced where possible, but we import to satisfy year-round demand.

GLO 4LIFE LTD

GLASFRYN STUDIOS, 83 LLANDEILO RD., UPPER BRYNAMMAN,
AMMANFORD SA18 1BE
Tel: 01269 824695 Contact: Mr Jones (Director)
info@glo4life.com www.glo4life.com
Glo 4life wholesale and retail high-quality certified 100% organic cotton T-shirts,
made to their own designs, printed with cool urban graphic designs. glo 4life care
about what they do.

IECHYD DA

11 BROAD ST., LLANDOVERY SA20 0AR
Tel: 01550 720703 Contact: J Nisbett
General health foods etc., organic fresh veg, dried fruit, yoghurts, coffee,
cider vinegar, tofu, bread, tea, soya milk, rice, pasta, flour, oats and bran.

JONES, ORIEL & SON LTD

TEIFY PARK, LLANBYDDER SA40 9QE
Tel: 01570 480284 Fax: 01570 480260 Contact: Meinir Thomas
ojonline@hotmail.co.uk www.oriel-jones.co.uk
Abattoir. Lamb slaughtering and processing. Beef slaughtering only.

KITE WHOLEFOODS

Y CADW, 38 FFORD ANEURIN, PONTYBEREM SA15 5DF
Tel: 01269 871035 Fax: 01269 871035 Contact: Paul Hartland
sales@kitewholefoods.co.uk www.kitewholefoods.co.uk
Soil Association P5857. Producing award-winning and highly acclaimed organic
mayonnaise in retail and catering packs.

LLANBOIDY CHEESEMAKERS

CILOWEN UCHAF, LOGIN, WHITLAND SA34 0TJ
Tel: 01994 448303 Fax: 01994 448303 Contact: Sue Jones
sue@llanboidycheese.co.uk
Soil Association P7158. Award-winning Cilowen Organic Cheese made by Llanboidy
Cheesemakers on their farm in West Wales using local organic milk. Milk is
pasteurised on farm and cheese hand-made in traditional way, hard-pressed
slowly and matured in its own natural rind to produce a distinctly different
truckle cheese. 'Best New Organic Cheese' & Gold Medal, British Cheese Awards
2001. 'Best New Cheese Marketed in UK', World Cheese Awards 2001. Suitable
for vegetarians. Organic Food Awards 2004: Cheese Commended.

MANSE ORGANICS

THE MANSE, CAPEL ISAAC, LLANDEILO SA
Tel: 01558 669043 Contact: Pete & Gary Wignall
info@graftedwalnuts.co.uk www.graftedwalnuts.co.uk
Soil Association G7180. Organic Scheme for Wales member. Specialists in fruiting
and ornamental walnut trees. Native, European and American (black walnut) varieties
and hybrids are grafted on to sturdy walnut rootstocks selected for UK conditions.
Range of sizes available.

THE MAY ORGANIC FARMS

PANTEG, CELLAN, LAMPETER SA48 8HN
Tel: 01570 423080 Fax: 01570 423080 Contact: Geoff Spawton
geoff@themay.co.uk www.themay.co.uk
All the organic Highland beef, lamb and mutton that we produce comes exclusively
from our small farms. You do your bit for conservation when you buy from us, as
our animals graze some 80ha of conservation land in Wales. We produce only five
times a year, so visit our website and put yourself on the mailing list to receive an
order form.

PEN PYNFARCH

PEN PYNFARCH, LLANDYSUL SA44 4RU
Tel: 01559 384948 Contact: Eeva-Maria Mutka
enquiries@penpynfarch.co.uk www.penpynfarch.co.uk
Simple, cosy holiday cottage with woodburner, sleeps 4/6. Organic veggie breaks
offered. Retreat/course centre with studio, accommodation and catering. Wooded
valley with stream and lake, 30 mins to the sea.

PENCAE MAWR TRADITIONAL FARM FOODS

PENCAEMAWR, LLANFYNYDD, CARMARTHEN SA32 7TR
Tel: 01558 668613 Contact: Peter Burgess
organic.chutney@ntlworld.com
As a diversification from our organic farm, we produce certified organic chutneys
and preserves using locally produced ingredients wherever possible. Small batches
and long cooking times give our chutneys a depth of flavour not possible with mass
produced products.

PENRALLT HOME FARM

PENTRECWRT, LANDYSUL SA44 5DW
Tel: 01559 370341 Contact: David & Jinsy Robinson
djwj@penrallt.freeserve.co.uk
Converted barns for self-catering holidaymakers. Mixed livestock. Member of the
Soil Association Organic Farms Network.

POULSON, JS

BLAENHIRAETH FARM, LLANGENNECH, LLANELLI SA14 8PX
Tel: 01554 773779 Contact: Stuart Poulson
Dairy farm usually with surplus dairy replacements and male store cattle for sale.

RILEY, JH & TJ

CAEPONTBREN FARM, PONTHENRI, LLANELLI SA15 5PB
Tel: 01269 860930 Contact: Tim Riley
Soil Association G5983. We have an organic beef suckler herd and are able to sell
calves from 10 months onwards to producers wishing to fatten organic beef cattle.

S & J ORGANICS

LLWYNCRYCHYDDOD, LLANPUMSAINT, CARMARTHEN SA33 6JS
Tel: 01267 253570 Fax: 01267 253562 Contact: Juliet Fay
info@sjorganics.co.uk www.sjorganics.co.uk
Soil Association certified poultry specialists. Producers of organic chickens, Muscovy
ducks, Pekin ducks, geese, turkeys & guinea fowl. Whole birds & portions available.
Supplying both retail & trade. Our poultry is processed through our low throughput,
DEFRA registered, on-farm, Soil Association licensed abattoir. Organic Food Awards
2004: Poultry Highly Commended.

SANDS, D & PJ

BLOSSOM FARM, NEW INN, PENCADER SA
Tel: 01559 384621 Contact: D Sands
Soil Association G6750. Welsh Black beef and Suffolk lambs delivered nationwide.
Mutton available seasonally.

WEALE, MRS S

WAUNGRON, LLANBYDDER SA40 9SB
Tel: 01570 481378 Contact: Sally Weale
Soil Association G6331. A small farm business producing organic beef and lamb.
Organic point of lay completely free range bantam-type hens.

CAMBRIAN ORGANICS

HOREB, LLANDYSUL SA44 4JG
Tel: 01559 363151 Fax: 01545 581071 Contact: Mick Shaw
info@cambrianorganics.com www.cambrianorganics.com
Soil Association P7702. Co-operative of organic livestock farmers from Wales selling beef, pork and lamb by mail order. Native breed specialities include Welsh mountain lamb and Welsh Black beef. Organic Food Awards 2004: Prepared Dishes Winner.

CARPENTER, MBP & TWYFORD, CA

TY GWYN, LLWYN RHYDOWEN, RHYDOWEN, LLANDYSUL SA44 4PX
Tel: 01545 590687 Contact: M Carpenter & C Twyford
peasants@care4free.net
Soil Association G4267. Small registered flock Lleyn sheep, meat and breeding females available. All season mixed vegetables available at home or group stall at Ceredigion Farmers' markets.

CAWS CENARTH

FFERM GLYNEITHINOG, ABERCYCH SA37 0LH
Tel: 01239 710432 Contact: Thelma Adams
thelmaadams@virgin.net www.cawscenarth.co.uk
Soil Association G2093. Hand-made organic farmhouse cheese made on our Soil Association certified organic farm. Available in many varieties including gold award winners, suitable for vegetarians. Visitors welcome to watch the cheese-making.

CERI ORGANICS

LLWYN YR EOS, RHYDLEWIS, LLANDYSUL SA44 5QU
Tel: 01239 851850 Contact: Ian Sumpter
Soil Association G5980. Fresh organic vegetables and year round fruit and veg box scheme.

GARTHENOR ORGANIC PURE WOOL

GARTHENOR, LLANIO ROAD, NR. TREGARON SY25 6UR
Tel & Fax: 01570 493347 or 0845 408 2437 Contact: Chris and Sally King
garthenor@organicpurewool.co.uk www.organicpurewool.co.uk
Soil Association G4388 & X8787. A small mixed farm producing eggs, lambs and
wool from many traditional and rare breeds of sheep from our own and other certified
organic flocks. Fleece: raw; washed; washed & carded. Beautiful knitting yarns in natural colours, now including the first Soil Association certified yarns—undyed and
unbleached: 4Ply; DK; Aran; Chunky and Super chunky. Others spun to your specification (for weaving etc.) subject to minimum order. Hand-knitted garments and babywear. Hand-woven floor rugs, hand-knitted & hand-woven cushions. Ex- stock or made
to order. Commissions welcome. Visitors by appointment. See display ad.

THE HIVE ON THE QUAY

CADWGAN PLACE, ABERAERON SA46 0BU
Tel: 01545 570445 Contact: Sarah Holgate
hiveon.thequay@btinternet.com www.hiveonthequay.co.uk
Member of the Soil Association. A busy seasonal café/restaurant on the harbour
specialising in regional dishes, local seafood from our own boat and honey ice
creams.

HOLDEN, PH & RM

BWLCHWERNEN FAWR, LLANGYBI, LAMPETER SA48 8PS
Tel: 01570 493244/493427 Contact: Patrick or Becky Holden
pholden@soilassociation.org
Soil Association symbol no. H09WW. Established 1973. Ayrshire dairy herd of 60,
6 x beef cross Welsh Black, 12 acres of oats, 12 acres of carrots. Farmed at
720 feet.

INSTITUTE OF RURAL SCIENCES
INSTITUTE OF RURAL SCIENCES, UNIVERSITY OF WALES, ABERYSTWYTH SY23 3AL
Tel: 01970 624471 Fax: 01970 622238 Contact: Nic Lampkin
organic@aber.ac.uk www.organic.aber.ac.uk
Soil Association certified. Research/demonstration farm. BSc, PgCert and PgDipl
in organic agriculture with student bursary support available, sponsored by
Waitrose and Horizon Organic Dairy. Extensive DEFRA and EU-funded organic
research programme.

JACOBS, CAROLE & ALLEN
BRONIWAN, RHYDLEWIS, LLANDYSUL SA44 5PF
Tel: 01239 851261 Fax: 01239 851261 Contact: Allen Jacobs
broniwan@beeb.net
A 45-acre (19 ha) grassland Aberdeen Angus suckler beef herd with 'tack' sheep.
Small vegetables and soft fruit. A Tir Gofal Conservation Farm. Developing
educational services. Farm guesthouse. Visits by appointment.

THE KNOBBLY CARROT FOOD COMPANY
UNIT 18, LLANBED BUSINESS PARK, TREGARON RD., LAMPETER SA48 8LT
Tel: 01570 422064 Fax: 01570 422064 Contact: Julian Evans
sales@theknobblycarrot.co.uk www.theknobblycarrot.co.uk
Manufacturers of fresh organic soups, ready to eat salads and sandwich fillings
available to retailers and foodservice. Our real food products are healthy, convenient
and delicious. Soil Association certified.

LLUEST GROWERS
LLUEST Y CONSCIENCE, TREFENTER, ABERYSTWYTH SY23 4HE
Tel: 01974 272218 Contact: John Crocker
Soil Association G2225. We produce organic eggs and seasonal organic vegetables
and salads which are sold at the farm gate, through local shops and farmers'
markets.

MAETH Y MEYSYDD
16 CHALYBEATE ST., ABERYSTWYTH SY23 1HX
Tel: 01970 612946 Fax: 01970 612946 Contact: Yvonne Crocker
Retail shop selling in season organic produce, eggs, bread, cheese and much more.
Everything for vegetarian, vegan and special diets. Unique herb and spice room.

MENTRO LLUEST
LLANBADORN FAWR, ABERYSTWYTH SY23 3AU
Tel: 01970 612114 Fax: 01970 612114 Contact: R Allen
mentro.lluest@talk21.com
Soil Association G3081. Mentro Lluest teaches skills to people with special needs
within a framework of organic growing, environmental sustainability and social
cohesion. We specialise in producing salad, seasonal vegetables and herbs.

MULBERRY BUSH
2 BRIDGE STREET, LAMPETER SA48 7HG
Tel: 01570 423317 Fax: 01570 423317 Contact: Stella Smith
Friendly wholefood vegetarian store, established 1974. Large range of organic
cereals, grains, pulses, fruit, nuts and convenience foods, plus natural remedies,
books and excellent health advice.

NANTCLYD FARM PRODUCE
NANTCLYD, LLANILAR, ABERYSTWYTH SY23 4SL
Tel: 01974 241543 Contact: Liz Findlay
liz.findlay@clara.co.uk
A small farm producing eggs, seasonal fruit and veg e.g. strawberries, carrots,
potatoes, cabbage, etc. and lemon curd. Produce available in Treehouse shop,
Aberystwyth, and also from the farm. Visitors welcome—phone for details. Local
delivery. Organic Food Awards 2004: Fresh Fruit and Veg Commended.

NANTGWYNFAEN ORGANIC FARM

CROESLAN, LLANDYSUL SA44 4SR
Tel: 01239 851914 Fax: 01239 851914 Contact: Amanda Edwards
nantgwynfaen@hotmail.co.uk
We are a 62-acre mixed family farm. We sell our own poultry, eggs, beef and pork direct from the farm including sausages and burgers. Call first to make sure we are in. Local delivery, not a box scheme.

ORGANIC FARM FOODS

LLAMBED ENTERPRISE PARK, TREGARON RD., LAMPETER SA48 8LT
Tel: 01570 423099 Fax: 01570 423280 Contact: The Manager
www.organicfarmfoods.co.uk
Widest range of fresh fruit and vegetables available for supermarkets, wholesalers, retailers and processors.

PENBRYN ORGANIC CHEESE

TY-HEN, SARNAU, LLANDYSUL SA44 6RD
Tel: 01239 810347 Fax: 01239 810347 Contact: A. Degen
penbryn.cheese@talk21.com
Soil Association no. G528, Specialist Cheesemakers Assoc. (S.C.A.). Family business producing organic cheese since 1989 using a unpasteurised milk from our own Friesian/MRI herd.

RACHEL'S ORGANIC DAIRY

UNIT 63, GLANYRAFON INDUSTRIAL ESTATE, ABERYSTWYTH SY23 2AE
Tel: 01970 625805 Fax: 01970 626591 Contact: Margaret Oakley
enqs@rachelsdairy.co.uk www.rachelsdairy.co.uk
Rachel's Dairy Organic dairy products, made solely from fresh liquid milk, organic fruit, organic sugar and live cultures. No flavours, colours, preservatives or stabilisers used. Soil Association member. Nationwide coverage.

RIVERSIDE HEALTH
ADPAR, NEWCASTLE EMLYN SA38 9EE
Tel: 01239 711440 Contact: Gary & Julie Newman
Wholefood shop, largely organic. Good stock of herbal supplements and essential oils. Therapy rooms upstairs. Fairtrade products as much as possible.

STRANG DESIGN & BUILD
CORGAM BWLCHLLAN, LAMPETER SA48 8QR
Tel: 01974 821624 Fax: 01974 821624 Contact: Tim Strang
tstrang@btinternet.com www.strangbuild.co.uk
Soil Association. Mid-Wales based eco-builder, also selling a range of eco-friendly building materials, including liners/paints.

THE TREEHOUSE
14 BAKER ST., ABERYSTWYTH SY23 2BJ
Tel: 01970 615791 Contact: Jane Burnham
jane@aber-treehouse.com www.aber-treehouse.com
We have a ten-acre market garden growing vegetables and fruit which are retailed in our organic food shop and made into delicious meals in our restaurant.

TROPICAL FOREST PRODUCTS
P.O. BOX 92, ABERYSTWYTH SY23 1AA
Tel: 01970 832511 Fax: 01970 832511 Contact: David Wainwright (M.D.)
mail@tropical forest.com
Soil Association no. P923. Importers, packers and sellers of exotic honey. We have a particular interest in promoting the produce of traditional regional artisans. Our Zambian and Tanzanian honey and wax carry Soil Association approval.

Clwyd

WILLIS LTD, JH
GRESFORD BANK, GRESFORD, WREXHAM LL12 8UT
Tel: 01978 852220 Fax: 01978 853737 Contact: RH Willis
j.h.willisltd@roadtransport.net www.j.h.willis.co.uk
Transport. We carry ex-farm organic milk for OMSCO, Calon Wen, South
Caernarvon, Dairy Farmers of Britain.

Conwy

COUNTRY KITCHEN
10 SEAVIEW ROAD, COLWYN BAY LL29 8DG
Tel: 01492 533329 Contact: David or Sally Frith
General independent natural food store in business 18 years: vitamin supplements,
organic products. Willing to order individual requirements. Free delivery possible
within 5 mile radius of shop on orders of £25 minimum.

TY NEWYDD UCHAF
TY NEWYDD UCHAF, PENMACHNO, BETWS Y COED LL24 0AJ
Tel: 01690 760350 Contact: Claire Barnard
doctordennis@hotmail.com
Organic chicken, duck and goose eggs. Organic ducks (pairs only) for sale.

BRYN COCYN ORGANIC BEEF & LAMB

BRYN COCYN, LLANNEFYDD, DENBIGH LL16 5DH
Tel: 01745 540207 Contact: Patrick Noble
noblep243@aol.com www.bryncocynorganic.co.uk
Organic beef and lamb produced on the oldest registered organic farm in north
Wales. Visit us in Denbigh market on Wednesdays or the last Friday of every
month in the Denbigh People's Market. Alternatively call at the farm or phone us.
Soil Association licence no. G727, P6478.

DAVIES, ARWEL REES & LLINOS JONES

BLAENGWNODL UCHAF, CYNWYD, CORWEN LL21 0ET
Tel: 01490 413110 Fax: 01490 413110 Contact: Arwel Rees Davies
davies@peniel.fsnet.co.uk
The production of beef and sheep to organic status.

HAFOD ELWY HALL

BYLCHAU, DENBIGH LL16 5SP
Tel: 01690 770345 Fax: 01690 770180 Contact: Andrea Lee
andrea@hafodelwyhall.co.uk www.hafodelwyhall.co.uk
Soil Association G6524. Peace and tranquillity among lakes and mountains in
former shooting lodge on the edge of Snowdonia. Exclusive 4 Star WTB accommodation, with breakfast and evening meals using produce from our organic farm.

HOUSE OF RHUG

RHUG ESTATE OFFICE, CORWEN LL21 0EH
Tel: 01490 413000 Fax: 01490 413300 Contact: Peta Baxter & Philip Hughes
petabaxter@rhugorganicfarm.co.uk www.rhugorganic.com
Organic café, farm butchery and shop on the A5, 2 miles west of Corwen on Lord
Newborough's estate, centred around the estate's award-winning home-reared meat.
Alternative email: philiphughes@rhugorganicfarm.co.uk. Member of the Soil
Association Organic Farms Network. Organic Food Awards 2004: Highly Commended.

THE ORGANIC STORES

7 MWROG ST., RUTHIN LL15 1LR
Tel: 01824 705796 Contact: Allan Hughes
We are a one-stop organic shop. We only sell organic goods. Fruit, veg, meat, fish,
poultry and much more at sensible prices. We offer discounts for those on special
diets such as the Gerson. You will always be welcomed by a friendly, helpful team
whose ambition is to help. Ample car parking space and carry out service to your car,
if it's too heavy we don't expect you to lift a finger. Home delivery, not a box scheme.
Established in 1996, please feel free to give us a call, if we can help, we will.

Accommodation

Box Schemes/
Local Deliveries

Day Visits

Eco Products

Farm Gate Sales

Garden and
Farm Sundries

Farmers' market
Stall

Manufacturers/
Processors

Importers/
exporters

Mail order
suppliers

Producers

Restaurants/
Cafés/Caterers

Retail shops

Textiles

Wholesalers

ALEMBIC PRODUCTS LTD

RIVER LANE, SALTNEY, NR. CHESTER CH4 8RQ
Tel: 01244 680147 Fax: 01244 680155 Contact: The Manager
alembic@alembicproducts.co.uk www.alembicproducts.co.uk
Manufacturer of variety of organic mayonnaises and dressings.

THE ORGANIC STORES

BROOKLYN FARM, SEALAND ROAD, DEESIDE CH5 2LQ
Tel: 01244 881209 Contact: Allan Hughes
We are a one-stop organic shop. We only sell organic goods. Fruit, veg, meat, fish, poultry and much more at sensible prices. We offer discounts for those on special diets such as the Gerson. You will always be welcomed by a friendly, helpful team whose ambition is to help. Ample car parking space and carry out service to your car, if it's too heavy we don't expect you to lift a finger. Home delivery, not a box scheme. Established in 1996, please feel free to give us a call, if we can help, we will.

Packaging

RECYCLE or compost as much as you can of the cardboard and paper packaging. DONATE If there is a mail order business locally, they may well want your polystyrene chips.

Because packaging has become such a large part of our waste, various new (and some old) ideas are around to lessen the wastage.

• One Dutch group of designers is experimenting with growing gourds into specific shapes, using plywood moulds, to produce natural packaging.

• Polystyrene chips can now be made with foamed starch polymer, using steam instead of harmful CFC gas. The end product can then be composted after use.

• Another idea is the air box. Goods can be posted inside their own bubble of air inside a reusable plastic bag. Apparently IBM invited people to the launch of the product with an egg enclosed!

From *Reduce, Reuse, Recycle* by Nicky Scott, Green Books, £3.95.

BEANFREAKS LTD

3 ST. MARY ST., CARDIFF CF10 1AT

Tel: 029 2025 1671 Contact: Alison James

kevin@swissherbalremedies.com www.swissherbalremedies.com

Fully stocked health food stores specialising in herbal medicine; advice line and mail order enquiries on 029 2041 7803. Website sales plus stores at Cardiff, Newport, Cwmbran and Bridgend.

THE CREATIVE COOKING CO LTD

UNIT 4 BRYNMENYN BUSINESS CENTRE, ST. THEODORE'S WAY, BRYNMENYN INDUSTRIAL ESTATE, BRYNMENYN, BRIDGEND CF32 9TZ

Tel: 01656 722555 Fax: 01656 729977 Contact: Carole Evans

info@creativeorganics.co.uk

Soil Association P7672. Manufacturing a range of organic mustards, relishes, preserves and dressings combining traditional flavours with innovative modern twists. All our products are hand-crafted by a Masterchef of Great Britain, Carole Evans.

GREEN CUISINE

Tel: 029 2039 4321 Fax: 029 2039 4321 Contact: A&M Robinson

info@greencuisineorganics.co.uk www.greencuisineorganics.co.uk

A customer choice home delivery service (no visitors) from twelve-page price list: meat, poultry, fish, eggs, dairy, frozen, chilled, deli, groceries, fruit, veg, baked goods, chocolates, body care, cleaning products.

JADE GATE ORGANIC PRODUCE

16 HOLTS FIELD, MURTON, SWANSEA SA3 3AQ

Tel: 01792 232643 Contact: Edward Revill

Soil Association G2504 & P4667. Organic vegetable box scheme grown using horses and delivered using a horse and cart in Swansea and Mumbles. Local produce only and reusable packaging. Aiming toward a carbon neutral service.

JUST ORGANIC/CLYNGWYN ORGANIC FARM

CLYNGWYN ORGANIC FARM, YSTRADFELLTE RD, PONTNEATHVAUGHAN,
NEATH SA11 5US
Tel: 01639 722930 Fax: 01639 722930 Contact: Alan & Jayne Clements
sales@just-organic.com www.just-organic.com
Organic produce at Clyngwyn Farm: vegetables, fruit, herbs, eggs through our
farm shop and via our market stall in Crickhowell on Saturdays throughout the
year. Bunkhouse accommodation set in glorious scenery in 'waterfall country';
sleeps up to 15. Complementary clinic, specialising in osteomyology, acupuncture,
meridian therapies, pain control, help with phobias and emotional problems.

MULTIPLE ORGANICS

LAKE FARM BARNS, ST. ATHAN RD, COWBRIDGE CF71 7HY
Tel: 01446 772964 Fax: 01446 772964 Contact: Leighton Maurice
multipleorganics@btinternet.com
Soil Association G6003. Organic herb and wild flower nursery, supplying plants,
feed, composts; all organically registered. We have a catalogue, weekly 'looking
good' list, and are open to the general public.

NEAL'S YARD REMEDIES

23–25 MORGAN ARCADE, CARDIFF CF1 2AF
Tel: 029 2023 5721 Contact: The Manager
mail@nealsyardremedies.com www.nealsyardremedies.com
Neal's Yard Remedies manufactures and retails natural cosmetics in addition to
stocking an extensive range of herbs, essential oils, homoeopathic remedies and
reference material.

PENRHIW FARM ORGANIC MEATS

PENRHIW FARM, TRELEWIS, TREHARRIS CF46 6TA
Tel: 01443 412949 Contact: John & Celia Thomas
penrhiw.farm@virgin.net
Soil Association G4720. Producers of quality Aberdeen Angus beef and Welsh
mountain lamb. Meat is sold at local farmers' markets. A local home delivery
service is operated.

PULSE WHOLEFOODS LTD
171 KINGS ROAD, CANTON, CARDIFF CF1 9DE
Tel: 029 2022 5873 Fax: 029 2023 1694 Contact: Michaela Rosa
pulse@pulsewholefood.co.uk www.pulsewholefood.co.uk
We offer a wide range of organic fruit, vegetables, wines, beers, wholefoods and
environmentally offering a friendly and helpful service.

PUR NATURAL SKINCARE
UNIT 4 HUBERT JOHN YARD, PANT IND. EST., DOWLAIS, MERTHYR TYDFIL CF48 2SR
Tel: 029 2055 2691 Contact: Linda Jones
linda@purskincare.co.uk www.purskincare.co.uk
Gentle spa and skincare products brimming with natural and organic extracts,
minerals, and herbal compounds.

THE SOURCE
26, CARDIFF ROAD, CAERPHILLY CF83 1JP
Tel: 029 2088 3236 Fax: 029 2088 3236 Contact: Leigh & Helen Shattock
hebenlee@btopenworld.com www.healthstore24.co.uk
Retail store offering fresh organic fruit and veg box scheme with delivery service.
Health foods, wholefoods, organic ranges, dairy and meat alternatives.
Wheat/gluten-free ranges, organic food supplements.

SPICE OF LIFE
1 INVERNESS PLACE, ROATH, CARDIFF CF2 4RU
Tel: 029 2048 7146 Contact: Gareth Cooksley
www.spiceoflife.co.uk
Wholefood shop established 1980.

SUNSCOOP PRODUCTS LTD
UNITS K1/K3 COEDCAE LANE IND.ESTATE, PONTYCLUN CF72 9HG
Tel: 01443 229229 Fax: 01443 228883 Contact: John Llewellyn
nuts@sunscoop.co.uk
Manufacturers of natural and processed nut products for retail outlets and the industrial sector.

SWISS HERBAL REMEDIES
18 NOLTON ST., BRIDGEND CF31 1DU
Tel: 01656 661441 Contact: Sally Robinson
kevin@swissherbalremedies.com www.swissherbalremedies.com
Fully stocked health food stores specialising in herbal medicine; advice line and mail order enquiries on 029 2041 7803. Website sales plus stores at Cardiff, Newport, Cwmbran and Bridgend.

UNITED WORLD COLLEGE OF THE ATLANTIC
ST. DONATS CASTLE, LLANTWIT MAJOR, VALE OF GLAMORGAN CF61 1WF
Tel: 01446 799012 Fax: 01446 799013 Contact: AE Davies
estate@uwcac.uwc.org
Soil Association G5656. An international 6th Form College with a 20 hectare farm unit producing organic lamb and beef.

Pea Soup
This is a simply delicious summer treat. If you have a bumper crop of peas you can freeze the soup and add the cream when re-heating. Boil 450g peas, 1 small chopped onion and 1 medium chopped potato in a litre of stock until soft. Scoop out the cooked vegetables and blend in a mixer then return to the stock. Heat gently stirring in 125ml of cream and 1 tbsp chopped mint. Season with sea salt and black pepper.
From *Allotment Gardening: An Organic Guide for Beginners* by Susan Berger, Green Books, £9.95.

AVEA ORGANIC

MOPLA HOUSE, PWYLLMEYRIC, CHEPSTOW NP16 6LA
Tel: 0870 199 9220 Fax: 0709 202 1615 Contact: Rick Havemann
organic@avea.co.uk www.avea.co.uk
Avea sells organic cosmetics and skin care products online. All the products are
paraben-free and do not contain petrochemicals, synthetic preservatives or
colourants, phthalates or sodium laureth sulphate. We stock six different ranges
and cater for every skin type.

BEANFREAKS LTD

5 CHARTIST TOWERS, UP DOCK ST., NEWPORT NP1
Tel: 01633 666150 Contact: Teresa Llewellyn
kevin@swissherbalremedies.com www.swissherbalremedies.com
Fully stocked health food stores specialising in herbal medicine; advice line and
mail order enquiries on 029 2041 7803. Website sales plus stores at Cardiff,
Newport, Cwmbran and Bridgend.

BEANFREAKS LTD

7 CARADOC RD., CWMBRAN NP44 1PP
Tel: 01633 482507 Contact: Pauline Price
kevin@swissherbalremedies.com www.swissherbalremedies.com
Fully stocked health food stores specialising in herbal medicine; advice line and
mail order enquiries on 029 2041 7803. Website sales plus stores at Cardiff,
Newport, Cwmbran and Bridgend.

BROOKLANDS FARM

CHEPSTOW RD., RAGLAN NP15 2EN
Tel: 01291 690782 Fax: 01291 690782 Contact: Rachel Price
brooklands-farm@raglan.fsbusiness.co.uk
Family-run organic farm 200 metres from Raglan village. Home-cooked breakfast
and evening meal. Children welcome. Pets by appointment. Spacious garden and
ample parking.

CARROB GROWERS

LLANGUNVILLE, LLANROTHAL, MONMOUTH NP25 5QL
Tel: 01600 712451 Contact: Caroline & Robert Boyle
Soil Association G1803. Specialist fruit growers, some vegetables. Produce picked to order. Local deliveries to Monmouthshire & south Herefordshire.

HOLT-WILSON, AD & CM

CEFN MAEN FARM, USK RD, RAGLAN NP15 2HR
Tel: 01291 690428 Contact: M Holt-Wilson
holtw@cmfm.freeserve.co.uk
Soil Association G5270. Producers of bronze turkeys reared and processed on the farm, dry plucked and hung for improved flavour and texture.

IRMA FINGAL-ROCK

64 MONNOW ST., MONMOUTH NP25 3EN
Tel: 01600 712372 Fax: 01600 712372 Contact: Tom Innes
tom@pinotnoir.co.uk www.pinotnoir.co.uk
Shop-wines our speciality. Also olive oil, eggs. Mail order and wholesale for wines.

JANES, MH & BM

THE WAUN, PENRHOS, RAGLAN, USK NP15 2LE
Tel: 01600 780356 Fax: 01600 780356 Contact: Bronwen Janes
mj@farm80.fsnet.co.uk
Soil Association G6540. Meat producers of beef & lamb, specialising in South Devon beef.

KEDDIE SAUCEMASTERS LTD
PRINCE OF WALES INDUSTRIAL ESTATE, ABERCARN NP11 5AR
Tel: 01495 244721 Fax: 01495 244626 Contact: Lisa Holman
www.gcosta.co.uk
Manufacturer of an extensive range of quality sauces for the retail, industrial and catering sector. We can offer an array of pack formats, from sachets, bottles, jars, catering to bulk formats. We are Soil Association approved.

LITTLE MILL FARM
LLANFAENOR, NEWCASTLE, MONMOUTH NP25 5NF
Tel: 01600 780449 Contact: Ann Eggleton
Soil Association G661. Small, ancient organic farm offers friendly comfort in beautiful Welsh Marches. Chill out in complete peace. B&B £20-£26; Weekend breaks including evening meal £70-£82.

PEN-Y-LAN FARM & GOLDEN LAMB RUGS
DINGESTOW, MONMOUTH NP25 4DX
Tel: 01600 740252 Fax: 01600 740252 Contact: James & Mary Yule
jyulefarm@btopenworld.com
Local delivery by arrangement (not a box scheme) of freezer packs of organic Angus beef, lamb and organic eggs. Organic sheepskins.

RIVERFORD ORGANIC VEGETABLES
12 LAMB LANE, PONTHIR, NEWPORT NP18 1HA
Tel: 01633 431104 Fax: 01633 431105 Contact: Anne Hampson
anne@riverfordhomedelivery.co.uk www.riverford.co.uk
Home delivery of organic vegetables. Award-winning organic vegetable box scheme operating under license in the Newport and Cardiff areas. Various boxes for all households from single occupant to a large family. A selection of fruit, dairy products, eggs, fruit juices, wine etc. also available. Order weekly, fortnightly or whenever you like. Can order online at www.riverford.co.uk or telephone 0845 600 2311. BBC Radio 4 Farmer of the Year 2005.

UPPER RED HOUSE FARM

LLANVIHANGEL, MONMOUTH NP25 5HL
Tel: 01600 780501 Fax: 01600 780572 Contact: Teona Dorrien-Smith
Soil Association G4969. Tir Gofal. The farm is mainly pasture with some arable,
producing forage and spring cereals with emphasis on conservation and educational
visits to study environment and wildlife. Educational visits, all ages welcome, but
booking essential.

WARMAN, SG & SE

NANT-Y-GOLLEN FARM, FOLLY LANE, TREVITHIN, PONTYPOOL, TORFAEN NP4 8TS
Tel: 01495 763780 Contact: S Warman
Soil Association G4651. Aberdeen Angus beef, big bale hay/silage.

WYE VALLEY PLANTS

THE NURTONS, TINTERN NP16 7NX
Tel: 01291 689253 Fax: 01291 689253 Contact: Elsa or Adrian Wood
info@thenurtons.fsnet.co.uk www.thenurtons.co.uk
Soil Association G1215. Sale of herbaceous/amenity perennials and herbs. Plant
list available for details. Organic B&B available. Garden open for visitors March to
October except on Tuesdays.

WYEDEAN WHOLEFOODS

113 MONNOW STREET, MONMOUTH NP25 3EG
Tel: 01600 715429 Contact: Barry Cocker
Hundreds of organic lines. Wholefoods, gluten and dairy-free, cruelty-free cosmetics;
SLS-free toiletries. Excellent range of vitamins, minerals and herbals. Wide range of
chilled and frozen products.

ANGLESEY SEA SALT CO

BRYNSIGNCYN, ANGLESEY LL61 6TQ
Tel: 01248 430871 Fax: 01248 430213 Contact: Tanya Geldard
enq@seasalt.co.uk www.seasalt.co.uk
Pure, white, organically certified (by Soil Association) sea salt, produced from the fresh waters around Anglesey. Also sea salt with organic spices. Range of eclectic salt bowls. Carriage at cost for small orders, UK-wide. Free delivery for larger orders.

CWM BYCHAN FARM

LLANBEDR, NR. HARLECH LL45 2PH
Tel: 01630 657001 Contact: S Walkden
Soil Association G7384. Sweet mountain lamb and Dexter beef raised slowly in the Harlech Dome on SSST land.

DIMENSIONS HEALTH STORE

15 HOLYHEAD RD., BANGOR LL57 2EG
Tel: 01248 351562 Fax: 01248 351562 Contact: Christine Volney
info@dimensionshealthstore.com www.dimensionshealthstore.com
Soil Association no. P1857. Dimensions is an ethical retail store and online business dedicated to providing foods, supplements, remedies and other goods necessary to create health and well being.

FOREMAN, HELEN

YSGUBOR BACH, FFORDD CERRIG MAWR, CAERGEILIOG, HOLYHEAD, ANGLESEY LL65 3LU
Tel: 01407 742293 Contact: Helen & Roger Foreman
Soil Association GCS068, G5882. Seasonal Organic Box scheme, soft and top fruit, farmers' market stall.

GIBBONS, E & M
PEN-YR-ORSEDD, TREFOR, HOLYHEAD, ANGLESEY LL65 3YY
Tel: 01407 720227 Fax: 01407 720227 Contact: E Gibbons
Soil Association G4333. Organic beef producer with pedigree Limousin herd also offering organic bulls, heifers and cows/calves for breeding purposes, and store stock for finishing. Unique wooden coffee/occasional tables.

HUGHES, JL & CO
LLWYN, DOLGELLAU LL40 2YF
Tel: 01341 423575 Contact: The Manager
Soil Association G4317. Producing beef and lamb sympathetically with conservation.

LLANGYBI ORGANICS
MUR CRUSTO, LLANGYBI, PWLLHELI LL53 6LX
Tel: 01766 819109 Contact: Val Lynas
info@llangybi-organics.co.uk www.llangybi-organics.co.uk
HDRA, Soil Association G7096. Aims to be model of sustainable development with vegetables (polytunnel and field) and seasonal fruit. Works in partnership with neighbouring organic farm Ty'n Lon Ychaf. Vegetable box scheme. Educational farm visits by arrangement.

THE NATIONAL TRUST WALES
HAFAD Y LLAN, NANT GWYNANT, BEDDGELERT, CAERNARFON LL
Tel: 01766 890473 Fax: 01766 890473 Contact: John Till
Soil Association G7325. This is an upland holding extending to the summit of Snowdonia. Formed by the Trust, we are putting into practice the organic aims of our extensive beef and sheep enterprise. Member of the Soil Association Organic Farms Network.

PENTRE BACH HOLIDAY COTTAGES

PENTRE BACH, LLWYNGWRIL, NR. DOLGELLAU LL37 2JU
Tel: 01341 250294 Fax: 01341 250885 Contact: Margaret Smyth
smyth@pentrebach.com www.pentrebach.com
Holiday cottages (two with log fires) in Southern Snowdonia. Organic produce,
free range eggs. Central heating, scenic Land Rover tours, train station nearby.
Secluded, not isolated, between mountains and sea. Magnificent views. Winner,
Wales Environment Award for Sustainable Tourism 2003. Special offers available
October to May, outside school holidays, 4 nights midweek for the price of 3, or 3
nights midweek for the price of 2.

PLAS LLANFAIR ORGANICS

PLAS LLANFAIR, TYN-Y-GONGL, YNYS MON LL74 8NU
Tel: 01248 852316 Contact: Mike Parker
mike@plasllanfair.freeserve.co.uk
Anglesey smallholding specialising in soft and top fruit and the processing thereof,
jams, preserves and chutneys. Wide range of vegetable production on a small
scale. Supply direct and local outlets.

RHOSFAWR CARAVAN PARK

RHOSFAWR, PWLLHELI LL53 6YA
Tel: 01766 810545 Contact: Janet Kidd
Small-scale home-produced organic produce. Also touring caravan and camping
park.

ROBERTS, MO & JS

BRON HEULOG FARM, LLANDDEUSANT, HOLYHEAD, ANGLESEY LL65 4AU
Tel: 01407 730292 Contact: Martin Roberts
Soil Association G7296. Producing organic beef calves, Blonde x to sell as
weaned calves and stores, possibility to finish some. Mobile: 07884 213217.

THOMAS, GO

BLAEN Y NANT, NANT FFRANCON, BETHESDA LL
Tel: 01248 600400 Fax: 01248 600400 Contact: Gwyn Thomas
Soil Association G4482. Traditional Welsh upland farm specialising in Welsh
black beef/Welsh mountain lamb. Educational visits for organic and conservation
information. Bed and breakfast. Located in panoramic views, mountains and lakes.
Member of the Soil Association Organic Farms Network.

TILL, RICHARD LLOYD

LLWYNGWANADL UCHAF, CLYNNOGFAWR, CAERNARFON LL54 5DF
Tel: 01286 660275 Contact: Richard Till
mefusmelys@hotmail.com
Soil Association G7393. Meat: Cig oen organic Cymreig, wyn stôr a gwartheg
stôr. Organic welsh lamb, store lambs and store cattle.

TY'N LON UCHAF

TY'N LON UCHAF, LLANGYBI, PWLLHELI LL53 6TB
Tel: 01766 810915 Contact: Jill Jackson
mike.langley@ntlworld.com
Soil Association G6139. Smallholding producing a wide range of fresh, seasonal,
organic vegetables. Together with Mur Crusto, Llangybi, we sell through our own
box scheme 'Llangybi Organics'—collection from Llangybi only (no deliveries).
Also produce organic eggs.

WELSH LADY PRESERVES

Y FFOR, PWLLHELI LL53 6RL
Tel: 01766 810496 Fax: 01766 810067 Contact: John Jones
info@welshladypreserves.com www.welshladypreserves.com
Soil Association P5669. A family business producing a premium quality range of
organic jams, marmalades and meal accompaniments designed for the grocery,
delicatessen and gift markets. We offer bespoke private-label production services.

BLACKMOOR FARM

LUDCHURCH, NARBERTH SA67 8JH
Tel: 01834 831242 Fax: 01834 831242 Contact: LT Cornthwaite
ltecornth@aol.com www.infozone.com.hk/blackmoorfarm
Farm-backed tourism, grazing cattle and tack sheep.

BUMPYLANE RARE BREEDS

SHORTLANDS FARM, DRUIDSTON, BROAD HAVEN, HAVERFORDWEST SA62 3NE
Tel: 01437 781234 Contact: Pam and David Williams
davidandpam@btconnect.com www.bumpylane.co.uk
Soil Association G4793. Rare breed meat. Recapture the real taste of lamb and
beef from the traditional British breeds born and reared on our organic coastal
farm overlooking St. Bride's Bay, Pembrokeshire. Holiday caravan to let.

CAERHYS ORGANIC FARM

BEREA, ST. DAVIDS SA62 6DX
Tel: 01348 831244 Fax: 01348 831244 Contact: Gerald Miles
gm@stdavids.co.uk www.organicfarmholidays.co.uk
Soil Association G4085. Farm organic holidays, participating in the everyday
chores in an organic environment, eating organic produce—milk, cheese, pork,
potatoes, beef, cheese and vegetables.

CALON WEN ORGANIC MILK CO-OPERATIVE LTD

3 ARCH OFFICES, STABLEYARD, LAWRENNY, KILGETTY SA68 0PW
Tel: 01994 241368 Fax: 01994 241063 Contact: Lee Griffiths
orderline@calonwen-cymru.com
A farmers' co-operative established in 2000 by four Welsh organic farmers and
now has over twenty farmer members across Wales. We sell fresh organic milk
(non-homogenised), butter and cheese across Wales and the borders. We have
rules at Calon Wen—not only must our cows eat healthily and exercise regularly,
but there is no late night partying or petting behind the barn. This may seem harsh
but it ensures our milk is always full of natural goodness and nothing else. To find
out where you can buy our produce, please contact Ashley or Lee.

THE CELTIC HERBAL CO LTD

BALDWINS MOOR, MANORBIER, TENBY SA70 7TY
Tel: 01834 870128 Fax: 01834 870128 Contact: Nicola Dent
info@celticherbs.co.uk www.celticherbs.co.uk
Soil Association G5767/P7499. We grow a wide selection of herbs organically, and incorporate these in a range of beautiful handmade herbal soaps and other bath products.

CLYNFYW COUNTRYSIDE CENTRE

CLYNFYW, ABERCYCH, BONCATH SA37 0HF
Tel: 01239 841236 Fax: 01239 841236 Contact: Jim Bowen
jim.clynfyw@virgin.net www.clynfyw.co.uk
Soil Association G4192. Clynfyw is a residential, all-access countryside activity, education, arts and respite care holiday centre set on a working organic farm. Animals include Welsh Black cattle and Saddleback pigs. With excellent Tourist Board approved cottages, Clynfyw makes the perfect holiday destination. Walk in the woods, help make charcoal, explore the decrepit wall garden or watch the badgers! There are few places more appealing! Member of the Soil Association Organic Farms Network.

DOVE COTTAGE, DYFFRYN ISAF

DYFFRYN ISAF, LLANDISSILIO SA66 7QD
Tel: 01437 563657 Contact: Bettina Becker & Stephen Jennings
bettina@dyffrynisaf.fsnet.co.uk www.pembrokeshire-organic-holidays.co.uk
Small organic farm with self-catering holiday cottage. Shetland sheep, wool and crafts. Goats, chickens and honey. Quiet location close to Pembrokeshire coast and Preseli Hills.

EGGLETON, SIMON

LEDGERLAND FARM, LLANTEG, NARBERTH SA67 8PX
Tel: 01834 831634 Contact: Simon Eggleton
Organic beef store cattle, Limousin and Hereford available in Spring/early summer, dependent on natural weaning.

EVANS, DW & CM

CAERFAI FARM, ST. DAVIDS, HAVERFORDWEST SA62 6QT
Tel: 01437 720548 Fax: 01437 720548 Contact: Wyn Evans
chrismevans69@hotmail.com www.caerfai.co.uk
In the Pembrokeshire coast National Park, 140-acre organic dairy farm producing unpasteurised milk and home-made cheeses, early potatoes. Sales from farm shop and box schemes. Camping and self-catering cottages.

FFYNNON SAMSON

LLANGOLMAN, CLUNDERWEN SA66 7QL
Tel: 01437 532570 Contact: Wendy Lane
Soil Association G7339. Production of organic vegetables, fruit and eggs. Local box scheme. Please phone for all orders.

FFYNNONSTON ORGANICS

FFYNNONSTON, DWRBACH, FISHGUARD SA65 9QT
Tel: 01348 873004 Contact: Ann Hicks
annhicks@waitrose.com
Soil Association G5836. Small-scale organic producers located one mile from Pembrokeshire coast. Salads, herbs, vegetables and soft fruit. Also organically grown cut flowers. Self-catering units available.

GROWING HEART WORKERS CO-OPERATIVE LTD

HENPARCAU FARM, BONCATH SA37 0JY
Tel: 01239 841675 Contact: Willow
growingheart2@hotmail.com
Soil Association G6287. We grow fruit and vegetables on 7.5 acres, wholesaling and retailing locally. We have a fruit tree and bush nursery and specialise in planting edible forests. Vegetables delivered to cafés, festivals and events.

HOME FARM BOARDING CENTRE

HOME FARM, EGLWYSWRW, CRYMYCH SA41 3PP
Tel: 01239 891449 Contact: B Rees
Soil Association G5406. Dog and cat boarding centre. Boarding centre offering
best possible care for dogs, cats and other domestic pets. Breeders of pedigree
Aberdeen Angus beef cattle and pure Poll Dorset sheep, stock sometimes
available for sale, also producers of free range organic eggs.

JENKINS, RHGE & TR

MAESYRHEDYDD & PORTIS FARMS, LLANDISSILIO, CLYNDERWEN SA66 7TX
Tel: 01437 563283 Contact: M Jenkins
6 months short tenancy lets. Pembs border, main A476 Cardigan to Tenby road on
farm. At Llandissilio, Clynderwen Organic Farm. Dairy farm.

KNOCK FARM ORGANICS

CLARBESTON ROAD SA63 4SL
Tel: 01437 731342 Contact: Christine Jones & Peter Trevelyan-Jones
Deliver between Clarbeston Road and Cheltenham. Day visits by appointment.
Produce: x Charolet suckler cow herd and Llanwennog sheep.

LATTER, TRE & AT

PENRHIW, GOODWICK SA64 0HS
Tel: 01348 873315 Fax: 01348 873315 Contact: Tom Latter
tom.latter@btopenworld.com
Beef, sheep, potatoes, eggs, and cereals. Self-catering visitor accommodation.

THE OLD RECTORY

THE OLD RECTORY, CASTLEMARTIN SA71 5HW
Tel: 01646 661677 Fax: 01646 661677 Contact: Emma Younghusband
www.theoldrectoryweb.com
Comfortable old rectory, organic B&B, in wild Pembrokeshire. Sandy beaches and
fabulous walking. Two charming stone cottages also available for holidays.

THE RESPONSIVE EARTH TRUST

PLASDWBL BIODYNAMIC FARM, MYNACHLOG DDU, CLYNDERWEN SA66 7SE
Tel: 01994 419352 Contact: A Kleinjans

Plasdwbl Biodynamic Farm is a charitable trust run for the benefit of students wishing to gain practical experience in biodynamic farming and gardening. We have a Welsh Black herd and two Jersey milkers. The farm is 40ha, and on 4ha we grow vegetables and forage. We make our own butter, cheese and bread. Demeter cert. no. 111.

SARRA, MR & T

PEEPOUT FARM, PORTFIELD GATE, HAVERFORDWEST SA62 3LS
Tel: 01437 762323 Fax: 01437 762323 Contact: Romeo Sarra
romeo@fwi.co.uk

150 acres specialising in a wide range of vegetables. Pembrokeshire new potatoes from May and all year round. Delivered direct to box schemes, wholesalers. Retail shop, groceries, wines, fruit and veg.

WELLS, WC

PENBACK, LLANDISSILIO SA66 7UP
Tel: 01437 563364 Fax: 01437 563364 Contact: WC Wells
wells.penback@btinternet.com

Soil Association G6198. Pedigree Welsh Black cattle producer, in-calf cows and heifers available for sale.

WELSH HOOK MEAT CENTRE LTD

WOODFIELD, WITHYBUSH ROAD, HAVERFORDWEST SA62 4BW
Tel: 01437 768876 Fax: 01437 768877 Contact: Emrys Davies
welshhookmeat@talk21.com www.welsh-organic-meat.co.uk

Wholesale and retail butchers specialising in organic pork, beef, lamb, veal, poultry, bacon and home-made sausages. Deliveries local and M4 corridor to London. Mail order to anywhere in the UK. Organic Food Awards 2004: Fresh Meat Highly Commended.

WHOLEFOODS OF NEWPORT
BWYDYDD CYFLAWN, EAST ST., NEWPORT SA42 0SY
Tel: 01239 820773 Fax: 01239 820773 Contact: Lorna & Ian Hipkins
alinor@dial.pipiex.com
Lively general wholefood grocer, largely organic, healthy snacks, special diets, dairy-free, gluten-free, wheat-free catered for. Welsh cheeses, cakes, confectionery, wines, beers, teas, coffees, Pembrokeshire honey, conserves. Large selection of fresh fruit and vegetables. Complementary remedies. Bodycare. Bike Hire.

How to Watch Wildlife
Watching any wild animal is a battle of wits – yours against a creature's natural instinct to survive. To enjoy seeing hares boxing, deer rutting or the courting ceremony of great-crested grebe, you do not need to get too close; but it is thrilling to watch a wild animal from just a few paces away, not just on TV. To get close, you may need to use some of our now less used senses. Instinct is a powerful ally: if you are not sure what to do, just follow your natural feelings. Keeping still and quiet is the simplest way to watch wildlife successfully. Many birds and insects are quite easy to approach if you do so slowly and with care. Except for owls, most birds react more to movement than sound. Mammals are more difficult: most have amazingly keen senses of smell and hearing. Deer also have acute eyesight, and bats can 'see' you in pitch dark. Even insects have remarkably good sight – try getting close to a butterfly. It can be done if you approach very slowly, especially when the air temperature is cool in early morning. Just think and move like a chameleon! At first, to increase your chances of success, try visiting places where wildlife is already accustomed to the presence of people – country parks and popular nature reserves. Stay on the paths, and wild creatures will often ignore you. Step off a regular track, and they will be gone.
From *Secret Nature of Devon* by Andrew Cooper, Green Books, £12.95.

BACHELDRE WATERMILL

CHURCHSTOKE, MONTGOMERY SY15 6TE
Tel: 01588 620489 Fax: 01588 620105 Contact: Matt & Anne Scott
bacheldre@onetel.net.uk www.bacheldremill.co.uk
17th-century watermill, camping site and holiday apartments. Produce award-winning 'Bacheldre' stoneground organic flour. Organic Food Awards 2004: Flour Winner.

BHC (HONEY SUPPLIERS) LTD

UNIT 3, FFRWDGRECH INDUSTRIAL ESTATE, BRECON LD3 8LA
Tel: 01874 622335 Fax: 01874 623141 Contact: Anne Preece
bhchoney@aol.com www.bhchoneysuppliers.co.uk
Soil Association P1059. The packing of organic honey into either retail packs or buckets for industrial customers.

BICYCLE BEANO VEGGIE CYCLING HOLIDAYS

BICYCLE BEANO, ERWOOD, BUILTH WELLS LD2 3PQ
www.bicycle-beano.co.uk
Sociable cycling holidays on the idyllic lanes of Wales and the Welsh Borders of England. Delicious vegetarian cuisine, using home-grown organic fruit and vegetables whenever available. Relaxed atmosphere. All ages welcome.

Away with Waste!

Reducing waste is the best option. It is staggering how much of what we throw away is perfectly good. A classic example of this is the increasing number of computers that are thrown out by large offices: when a whole system gets upgraded, often all the old ones are thrown into a skip. Yet old office computers can be wiped with approved software and sold on to people on low incomes, community groups etc.

From *Reduce, Reuse, Recycle* by Nicky Scott, Green Books, £3.95.

CANNON FARM

LLANERFYL, WELSHPOOL SY21 0JJ
Tel: 01938 820251 Fax: 01938 820136 Contact: Nigel Elgar
nigel@cannonfarm.co.uk www.cannonfarm.co.uk
Soil Association registered. Organic beef and sheep farm in Mid-Wales. Joint
Organic Producer of the Year Award Winner 2001, Director of Graig Farm Producers
Group Ltd.

CEFN GOLEU ORGANIC TURKEYS

CEFN GOLEU, PONT ROBERT, MEIFOD SY22 6JN
Tel: 01938 500128 Contact: MB Moorhouse
cefngoleuturkeys@btclick.com
Soil Association G2967. Registered packing station, eggs supplied to retail shops
and direct farm gate sales. Oven-ready fresh Christmas turkeys, farm gate sales.
Frozen turkeys, chickens throughout year. Lamb, pork when available.

CENTRE FOR ALTERNATIVE TECHNOLOGY

MACHYNLLETH SY20 9AZ
Tel: 01654 705950 Fax: 01654 702782 Contact: Information Officer
info@cat.org.uk www.cat.org.uk
Soil Association L09WW. Established in 1974, the Centre for Alternative Technology
is Europe's leading eco-centre, with information on renewable energy, environmental
building, energy efficiency, organic growing and alternative sewage systems. Services
include a visitor centre open 7 days a week, practical and informative publications, a
mailorder service of 'green' books and products, educational services for schools,
consultancy for individuals and businesses, residential courses, membership and a
free information service. See display ad.

THE CILIAU

THE CILIAU, ERWOOD, BUILTH WELLS LD2 3TZ
Tel: 07887 656887 Contact: Roger Capps
Organic breeding stock, pure breed beef and lamb. Private sales and deliveries.
All feed stuff produced on farm for pedigree North Devons, Shropshire and Lleyn
sheep.

THE CILIAU

LOWER PORTHAMEL, TALGARTH, BRECON LD3 0DL
Tel: 07752 236773 Fax: 01874 711224 Contact: Joel Durrell
joeldurrell@yahoo.com
We encourage members of the public to our 400-acre farm and shop to enjoy the unique taste and environment of the upper Wye valley.

CLYRO HILL FARM

CLYRO HILL FARM, CLYRO HR3 6JU
Tel: 01497 820520 Fax: 01497 820520 Contact: Sally Herdman
info@clyrohillfarm.co.uk www.clyrohillfarm.co.uk
Organic Farmers and Growers UKF 001475. Organic poultry, Hereford Beef, Welsh lamb and pork raised on our farm. Free range chickens, turkeys, goose, duck, guinea fowl, pork, lamb and beef mail order. Eggs and vegetable boxes delivered locally.

COMPOST TECHNOLOGY LTD

TREWERN, WELSHPOOL SY21 8EA
Tel: 01938 570678 Fax: 01938 570678 Contact: Edwin Kentfield
www.compost-technology.co.uk
Manufacturers of Cluck! The 100% organic fertiliser. Delivery to UK except N. Ireland and offshore.

DYFIGUEST ORGANIC B&B

DYFIGUEST, 20 FFORDD MYNYDD GRIFFITHS, MACHYNLLETH SY20 8DD
Tel: 01654 702562 Contact: Carol Handcock
dyfiguest@yahoo.co.uk www.dyfiguest.co.uk
B&B: luxurious WTB four-star bungalow situated in the town of Machynlleth with spectacular views of the Dyfi valley and Snowdonia National Park, yet within 4 minutes walk of Machynlleth market town for evening meals. We serve organic breakfasts with most of the ingredients grown & produced in the Dyfi valley, a varied breakfast menu with home-made breads is available. We serve traditional Welsh breakfasts, also vegetarian & vegan.

GEORGE & SON, S

DOLL-LLUGAN, BLEDDFA, KNIGHTON LD7 1NY
Tel: 01547 550208 Fax: 01544 230604 Contact: E Gorst
Soil Association G5456. A farm producing quality beef and lamb where extensive
farming practices have always been exercised. Root vegetables are also grown.

GOOD FOOD DISTRIBUTORS

35 DDOLE ROAD INDUSTRIAL ESTATE, LLANDRINDOD WELLS LD1 6DF
Tel: 01597 824728 Fax: 01597 824760 Contact: Tracy
gfd.wholesale@btinternet.com www.goodfooddistributors.co.uk
Soil Association P5894. Free delivery service, wholefoods in bulk and pre-packs,
free own-name labelling service and contract mixing. 100% vegetarian and GMO-
free products. Vast range of products listed in our free price list.

GRAIG FARM ORGANICS

DOLAU, LLANDRINDOD WELLS LD1 5TL
Tel: 01597 851655 Fax: 01597 851991 Contact: Bob or Carolyn Kennard
sales@graigfarm.co.uk www.graigfarm.co.uk
Award-winning organic meats, fish and other organic foods available by mail order,
internet, retail outlets. Organic Retailer of the Year 2001/2. Winner Soil Association
Home Delivery/Internet Service Award 2004; Organic Food Awards 1993–2004.
Livestock supplies through producer group of 200 farmers across Wales and the
borders. Organic Food Awards 2004: Charcuterie Winner. See display ad.

GREAT OAK FOODS

12 GREAT OAK ST., LLANIDLOES SY18 6BU
Tel: 01686 413222 Contact: Gareth Davies
gareth@perpetualearth.com
Retail certified organic fruit and veg and non-certified locally grown produce using
organic principles. We stock organic cheese, wine and spirits. Local production and
low food miles are encouraged.

GWALIA FARM
GWALIA, CEMMAES, MACHYNLLETH SY20 9PZ
Tel: 01650 511377 Contact: Olivia Chandler
www.gwaliafarm.co.uk
Peaceful, remote small farm with goats, hens, sheep and large vegetable and fruit gardens. Vegetarian bed and breakfast. Beautiful views, spring water, tranquil lake, woods, birds and silence. Camping and self-catering caravan. Centre for Alternative Technology nearby.

MATTHEWS, RG & PARTNERS
ABERHYDDNANT, CRAI, BRECON LD3 8YS
Tel: 01874 636797 Fax: 01874 636797 Contact: Liz Matthews
liz@abercottages.co.uk www.abercottages.com
Two comfortable cottages sleeping 2 to 12 making an ideal location for short breaks and family holidays. Situated on 92 hectare, family-run organic beef and sheep farm in Brecon Beacons National Park. Also member of Tir Gofal environmental scheme. Educational farm visits welcome by arrangement. Colour brochure. Member of the Soil Association Organic Farms Network. Organic Food Awards 2004: Commended.

NATURAL FOODS LLANIDLOES LTD
17 GREAT OAK ST., LLANIDLOES SY18 6BU
Tel: 01686 412306 Contact: Martine Frost
We are retailers of organic health foods, dietary supplements, herbal remedies and other quality foods including a wide range of chilled and frozen foods. We also do bulk and special orders.

PENPONT
PENPONT ESTATE, BRECON LD3 8EU
Tel: 01874 636202 Contact: Gavin Hogg
penpont@clara.co.uk www.penpont.com
Soil Association G4529. We offer bed and breakfast and self-catering accommodation in a historic listed mansion. We are restoring two Victorian walled gardens where we grow registered organic vegetables. We are now an Organic Demonstration farm, and will host a number of day courses in Horticulture organised jointly by OCW and Farming Connect.

PENTWYN HERBS

C/O 1 CAERLLAN, LLANWRTHWL, LLANDRINDOD WELLS LD1 6NS
Tel: 01597 810113 Contact: Susy Pegrum
susypeg@btopenworld.com
Grow herbs organically as crops (culinary and medicinal) and herbs in pots; herb collection of over 100 different herbs. Herb garden open to the public.

PRESTEIGNE TROUT

THE OLD LEAT, BOULTIBROOKE, PRESTEIGNE LD8 2EU
Tel: 01544 267085 Fax: 01544 267085 Contact: IH Bennett
Soil Association G4310. Producer of organic rainbow trout.

PRIMROSE ORGANIC & SACRED EARTH CENTRE

FELINDRE, BRECON LD3 0ST
Tel: 01497 847636 Contact: Paul Benham
paul.benham@ukonline.co.uk www.organic-sacred-earth.co.uk
A well established and thriving organic permaculture fruit and vegetable business offering a host of inspiring opportunities including volunteering and paid support work, education, accommodation, spiritual and sound healing workshops/retreats. Member of the Soil Association Organic Farms Network.

THE QUARRY SHOP & CAFE

13 & 27 MAENGWYN ST., MACHYNLLETH SY20 8EB
Tel: 01654 702624/702339 Fax: 01654 702624
Contact: Annie Lowmass & Amanda Green quarry.cafe@cat.org.uk www.cat.org.uk
A vegetarian café and shop including some organic products. We are 25 years old this year and are part of the Centre for Alternative Technology.

RAIKES, D

TREBERFYDD, BWLCH, BRECON LD3 7PX
Tel: 01874 730205 Contact: The Manager
Soil Association G964. Small organic Welsh Black suckler herd.

SUPER DUG EXTRA

TREWERN, WELSHPOOL SY21 8EA
Tel: 01938 570678 Fax: 01938 570678 Contact: Edwin Kentfield
superdugextra@aol.com www.super-dig.co.uk
Unique organic fertiliser. Leading mail order supplier since 1959. High analysis, easy to apply, 25kg sacks (75 litres), home delivery.

THOMAS, KP & CS

GYFFOG, LLANFIHANGEL, NANT BRAN, BRECON LD3 9LY
Tel: 01874 638925 Contact: Kate Thomas
Small family farm on the edge of Brecon Beacons. The farm has pedigree Welsh Black cattle and Beulah Speckleface sheep. Finished store and breeding stock available.

Warm Salad with Goats Cheese

Pick a selection of lettuce, salad leaves, radicchio, rocket and flat leaf parsley. Wash and dry the leaves, tearing the larger ones into bite-size pieces. Make a dressing: combine 2 tbsps each of walnut oil, olive oil, white wine vinegar, a dash of French mustard, sea salt and black pepper. Slice a fresh goat's cheese weighing 225g into 8 and sit on top of 8 slices of toasted French bread. Put under a hot grill until soft and golden then place on top of the lightly dressed leaves.

From *Allotment Gardening: An Organic Guide for Beginners* by Susan Berger, Green Books, £9.95.

Many of the entries below are farms and other organic producers that offer education opportunities. For fuller details, please use the main index to find their entry in the first part of the Directory.

ABERDEEN BIODYNAMIC LAND TRUST
BEANNACHAR, BANCHORY-DEVENICK, ABERDEEN AB12 5YL
Tel: 01224 861200 Contact: Richard Phethean
Community Land Trusts. Purchase of agricultural land to hold in trust for bio-dynamic or organic food production, and support businesses renting that land.

THE ACORN CENTRE
TODHURST SITE, NORTH HEATH, PULBOROUGH RH20 1DL
Tel: 01798 873533 Fax: 01798 873533 Contact: Rachel Smither
michellewykes@aldingbournetrust.co.uk
Training centre for adults with learning disabilities.

AGROFORESTRY RESEARCH TRUST
46 HUNTERS MOON, DARTINGTON, TOTNES TQ9 6JT
Tel: 01803 840776 Contact: M Crawford
mail@agroforestry.co.uk www.agroforestry.co.uk
Research charity producing books and information on fruits, nuts and agroforestry; also plants, seeds and rootrainers.

AINSWORTHS HOMOEOPATHIC PHARMACY
36 NEW CAVENDISH ST., LONDON W1G 8UF
Tel: 020 7935 5330 Fax: 01883 344602 Contact: Tony Pinkus
ainsworth01@btconnect.com www.ainsworths.com
Homoeopathic remedies for prevention and treatment of all your livestock. Books and courses on homoeopathy. All animals can be treated without residues. Help and advice in implementing homoeopathic regimes on the farm. Lectures and seminars by arrangement.

ALDINGBOURNE COUNTRY CENTRE
BLACKMILL LANE, NORTON, CHICHESTER PO18 0JP
Tel: 01243 542075 Fax: 01243 544807 Contact: Lucinda Healey
acc@aldingbournetrust.co.uk www.aldingbournetrust.co.uk
A sheltered training centre for adults with learning difficulties. The centre has conference facilities for hire, a woodland walk and conservation area and also specialises in horticulture (bedding/herbaceous plants, hanging baskets), furniture restoration and hand-made art and craft products. For further details contact Linda Thompson or Matt Swanson.

THE ANIMAL HEALING CENTRE
HEGGERSCALES COTT, KABER, KIRKBY STEPHEN CA17 4HZ
Tel: 01768 372691 Contact: Joy Barrett
joy@animalhealing.org.uk www.animalhealing.org.uk
We educate about natural healing methods for pets, equines and farm animals.

APPLIED RURAL ALTERNATIVES
10 HIGHFIELD CLOSE, WOKINGHAM RG40 1DG
Tel: 0118 962 7797 Contact: DS Stafford
Education of the general public in organic farming and growing issues by visits,
meetings and publication of papers. Send SAE for details and programmes.

ASHLYNS ORGANIC FARM
HIGH LAVER HALL, HIGH LAVER, ONGAR CM5 0DU
Tel: 01277 890188/9 Fax: 01277 890188 Contact: Jim Collins
info@ashlyns.co.uk www.ashlyns.co.uk
Visitors welcome to see progress, walk farm trails and enjoy special open days.
School and group visits are welcome by appointment. Member of the Soil
Association Organic Farms Network.

AVON ORGANIC GROUP
C/O 3 DUBBERS LANE, BRISTOL BS5 7EL
Tel: 0117 935 4261 Contact: Rachel Hudson
aogbristol@yahoo.co.uk www.beehive.thisisbristol.com/avonorganics
Monthly meetings on organic gardening, local food and environmental themes.
Visits to members' allotments. Run organic orchard on Horfield Allotment site.

BATH ORGANIC COMMUNITY GARDEN
C/O 28 ASHLEY AVENUE, BATH BA1 3DS
Tel: 01225 312116 Contact: TJ Baines
tim@bathorganicgroup.org.uk
Community garden on inner city allotment site providing training, employment and
volunteering opportunities for the local community. Courses and workshops. Open
days. Open every Saturday 10am to 1pm.

BELLA HERBS
BROCTON LEYS, BROCTON, STAFFORD ST17 0TX
Tel: 01785 663868 Contact: Beverley Squire
beverleysquire@aol.com
We are a two-acre organic garden licensed by the Soil Association, where we run
leisure courses in organic gardening.

BIODYNAMIC AGRICULTURAL ASSOCIATION (BDAA)
PAINSWICK INN PROJECT, GLOUCESTER STREET, STROUD GL5 1QG
Tel: 01453 759501 Contact: Bernard Jarman
office@biodynamic.org.uk www.biodynamic.org.uk
With links across the world, BDAA promotes the unique biodynamic approach to
organic agriculture, operates the Demeter Symbol (UK6), publishes a journal, sells
books and offers training courses and workshops.

BLACKLAKE FARM
EAST HILL, OTTERY ST. MARY EX11 1QA
Tel: 01404 812122 Contact: Catherine & Nick Broomfield
catherine@blacklakefarm.com www.blacklakefarm.com
Educational visits. Member of the Soil Association Organic Farms Network.

BRIDGE FARM ORGANIC FOODS
BRIDGE FARM, SNITTERBY CARR, GAINSBOROUGH DN21 4UU
Tel: 01673 818272 Fax: 01673 818272 Contact: Patty Phillips
patty.bridgefarmconservat@virgin.net
Education resource centre. Rural skills workshops. Members join farm conservation
group, receive newsletters, attend open days, undertake conservation tasks.

BRYMORE SCHOOL FARM TRUST
BRYMORE SCHOOL, CANNINGTON, BRIDGWATER TA5 2NB
Tel: 01278 652428 Fax: 01278 653244 Contact: A Nurton
We are a secondary school of agriculture, horticulture and engineering with a mixed
farm enterprise.

CAMPHILL COMMUNITY—CLANABOGAN
CAMPHILL COMMUNITY CLANABOGAN, OMAGH BT78 1TJ
Tel: 028 8225 6111 Fax: 028 8225 6114 Contact: Martin Sturm
martinsturm@firenet.uk.net www.camphillclanabogan.com
Mixed biodynamic farm & renewables demonstration farm, with 320kw biomass
district heating system 20kw wind turbine, geothermal heating for polytunnel, solar
pannels, photovoltaic array, domestic wood pellet boiler.

CAMPHILL OAKLANDS PARK
HORTICULTURE, OAKLANDS PARK, NEWNHAM ON SEVERN GL14 1EF
Tel: 01594 516550 Fax: 01594 516550 Contact: Kai Lange
kaigarden@onetel.com www.oaklandspark.org.uk
Biodynamic Agricultural Association (Demeter) registered. Working community with
people with special needs. Involved with regional biodynamic land training (2 years).

CAMPHILL VILLAGE TRUST—BOTTON VILLAGE
DANBY, WHITBY YO21 2NJ
Tel: 01287 660871 Contact: Erwin Wennekes
botton@camphill.org.uk www.camphill.org.uk
Botton Village is a Camphill Village Trust community for adults with special needs.
It has five mixed farms which are run on biodynamic principles, several craft and
food processing workshops. Day visits are possible.

CANON FROME COURT
CANON FROME COURT, CANON FROME, LEDBURY HR8 2TD
Tel: 0870 765 0711 Contact: Membership Secretary
membership@canonfromecourt.org.uk www.canonfromecourt.org.uk
Organic (uncertified) farming community comprising 18 households living in
Georgian house and stable block set in 40 acres of park and farmland. Cows,
goats, sheep, chickens, bees, arable fields, orchard and 2-acre walled garden.
WWOOFers and potential community members welcome.

CAPEL MANOR COLLEGE
BULLSMORE LANE, ENFIELD EN1 4RQ
Tel: 020 8366 4442 Contact: Andrea Brown
enquiries@capel.ac.uk www.capel.ac.uk
Soil Association G7651. An organic sheep flock with Lincoln Longwoods and Suffolks.
The farm is managed by Capel Manor College, which specialises in horticulture and
associated land-based industry courses.

CENTRE FOR ALTERNATIVE TECHNOLOGY
MACHYNLLETH SY20 9AZ
Tel: 01654 705950 Fax: 01654 702782 Contact: Information Officer
info@cat.org.uk www.cat.org.uk
Soil Association LO9WW. Established in 1974, the Centre for Alternative Technology
is Europe's leading eco-centre, with information on renewable energy, environmental building, energy efficiency, organic growing and alternative sewage systems.
Services include a visitor centre open 7 days a week, practical and informative
publications, a mail order service of 'green' books and products, educational services for schools, consultancy for individuals and businesses, residential courses,
membership and a free information service. See display ad.

THE CHICKEN CAME FIRST
LYNTON MEAD, OUTWOODS, NEWPORT TF10 9EB
Tel: 01952 691418 Contact: Clare Draper
clareword@btconnect.com
One-day workshops on keeping chickens at home.

CHURCH FARM ORGANICS

CHURCH FARM, CHURCH LANE, THURSTASTON, WIRRAL CH61 0HW
Tel: 0151 648 7838 Fax: 0151 648 9644 Contact: Steve & Brenda Ledsham
sales@churchfarm.org.uk www.churchfarm.org.uk
School visits by arrangement—see website for details.

CLYNFYW COUNTRYSIDE CENTRE

CLYNFYW, ABERCYCH, BONCATH SA37 0HF
Tel: 01239 841236 Fax: 01239 841236 Contact: Jim Bowen
jim.clynfyw@virgin.net www.clynfyw.co.uk
Soil Association G4192. Clynfyw is a residential, all access countryside activity,
education, arts and respite care holiday centre set on a working organic farm.
Animals include Welsh Black cattle and Saddleback pigs. Member of the Soil
Association Organic Farms Network.

COMMONWORK

BORE PLACE, CHIDDINGSTONE, EDENBRIDGE TN8 7AR
Tel: 01732 463255 Fax: 01732 740264 Contact: Lyn Kelly
info@commonwork.org www.commonwork.org
Conference and study centre with organic, wildlife and permaculture gardens on
commercial organic farm. Residential accommodation for groups undertaking their
own training and development work. Environmental/arts education programme and
organic farm/food study days offered to schools and community groups by
Commonwork. Plus, hands-on vocational training in organic farming for people of
all abilities, and seasonal open days for the public. Commonwork also runs a development education centre (global education) from Maidstone, going out to schools,
youth and community groups.

COMMUNITY COMPOSTING NETWORK

67 ALEXANDRA ROAD, SHEFFIELD S2 3EE
Tel: 0114 258 0483 Fax: 0114 258 0483 Contact: Nick McAlister
ccn@gn.apc.org www.communitycompost.org
We are the national network providing support and representation for community
groups that are in some way involved in the sustainable management of organic
waste resources and community composting.

COMPASSION IN WORLD FARMING

CHARLES HOUSE, 5A CHARLES STREET, PETERSFIELD GU32 3EH
Tel: 01730 264208 Fax: 01730 260791 Contact: Sarah Sanderson
sarah@ciwf.co.uk www.ciwf.co.uk
Compassion In World Farming is an international farm animal welfare organisation
that has campaigned since 1967 to bring about the abolition of all factory farming
systems, live animal exports and the cruelty suffered by farm animals as a result of
intensive farming. CIWF works to achieve its aims through legal routes, hard hitting
campaigning, public education and vigorous political lobbying.

COSWINASAWSIN

THE DUCHY COLLEGE, ROSEWARNE, CAMBOURNE TR14 0AB
Tel: 01209 722100 Fax: 01209 722159 Contact: Steve Roderick
Farm trail, educational visits, open days and farm walks are all available by
arrangement with the office. Coswinsawsin Farm is an important resource for the
newly created Organic Studies Centre at the Duchy College, Rosewarne, and is the
most westerly of the Elm Farm Research Centre demonstration farms network.
Member of the Soil Association Organic Farms Network.

CRAIGENCALT ECOLOGY CENTRE

CRAIGENCALT FARM, KINGHORN KY3 9YG
Tel: 01592 891567 Fax: 01592 891567 Contact: Ronnie Mackie
cfec@free.uk.com www.cfec.org.uk
The Craigencalt Farm Ecology Centre is used by schools and adult groups for
ecological studies, weekend study groups and various craft/arts persons. Visitors
are welcome to take part, walk, bird watch, chat to members, even pitch in with
the various projects underway.

CREAM O'GALLOWAY DAIRY CO LTD

RAINTON, GATEHOUSE OF FLEET, CASTLE DOUGLAS DG7 2DR
Tel: 01557 814040 Fax: 01557 814040 Contact: Wilma Finlay
info@creamogalloway.co.uk www.creamogalloway.co.uk
Open to public with nature trails, tea room and adventure playground. Member of
the Soil Association Organic Farms Network.

DEMETER COMMITTEE OF THE BDAA

17 INVERLEITH PLACE, EDINBURGH EH3 5QE
Tel: 0131 624 3921 Contact: Fiona Mackie
fionajmackie@hotmail.com www.biodynamic.org.uk
Inspection, certification, and information service for biodynamic production.

DEPARTMENT FOR ENVIRONMENT, FOOD AND RURAL AFFAIRS (DEFRA)

NOBEL HOUSE, 17 SMITH SQUARE SW1P 3JR
Tel: 020 7238 6000 Fax: 020 7238 6609 Contact: The Help Desk
organic.standards@defra.gsi.gov.uk www.defra.gov.uk
Defra has taken over responsibility for UK organic standards, previously monitored
by UKROFS.

DERBY COLLEGE

BROOMFIELD HALL, MORLEY, ILKESTON DE7 6DN
Tel: 01332 836607 Fax: 01332 836601 Contact: Ian Baldwin
eileen.swann@derby-college.ac.uk www.derby-college.ac.uk
Soil Association registered. Full-time and part-time courses in organic horticulture.
Contact 'Course Student Services'.

DORSET WILDLIFE TRUST
45 HIGH ST., TOLLER PORCORUM, DORCHESTER DT2 0DN
Tel: 01300 320573 Contact: Paul Comer
paul@paulcomer1.f9.co.uk
We run as a farmed nature reserve.

EARTHWORM HOUSING CO-OP LTD
WHEATSTONE, LEINTWARDINE SY7 0LH
Tel: 01547 540461 Contact: Hil Mason
Suppliers of willow for basket making, hurdles etc, venue for low cost hire for camps, courses, meetings. Demonstration wetland system and organic/veganic gardens. WWOOF host farm.

EAST MALLING RESEARCH
NEW RD, EAST, MALLING ME19 6BJ
Tel: 01732 843833 Fax: 01732 849067 Contact: Jean Fitzgerald
jean.fitzgerald@emr.ac.uk www.eastmallingresearch.com
We carry out research projects on organic apples and strawberries, and plan to include more top and soft fruits in our organic demonstration area.

ELM FARM RESEARCH CENTRE
HAMSTEAD MARSHALL, NEWBURY RG20 0HR
Tel: 01488 658298 Fax: 01488 658503 Contact: Pat Walters
elmfarm@efrc.com www.efrc.com
EFRC provides agricultural and policy research, education and training courses, a farm trail, organic, OCIS and in-conversion advisory service, organic demonstration farm network, soil analysis, publications, consultancy and producer groups. Member of the Soil Association Organic Farms Network.

ELMWOOD COLLEGE FARM
CUPAR MUIR, CUPAR KY15 5RN
Tel: 01334 658900 Fax: 01334 658888 Contact: Peter McKinnon
pmkinnon@elmwood.ac.uk www.elmwood.ac.uk
Soil Association G4447. College of Further Education. Courses in organic agriculture. Member of the Soil Association Organic Farms Network.

EMERSON COLLEGE
HARTFIELD ROAD, FOREST ROW RH18 5JX
Tel: 01342 822238 Fax: 01342 826055 Contact: Alysoun Barrett
mail@emerson.org.uk www.emerson.org.uk
Soil Association & Demeter registered. Emerson College runs a three year, full-time training in Biodynamic Organic Agriculture, as well as short courses in biodynamics. Students at the college run a commercial biodynamic market garden through spring and summer.

FARMS FOR CITY CHILDREN
NETHERCOTT HOUSE, IDDESLEIGH, WINKLEIGH EX19 8BG
Tel: 01837 810573 Contact: Jane Feaver
ffcc@nethercott-house.freeserve.co.uk www.farmsforciytchildren.org
Educational Charity. Farms For City Children runs three organic farms where urban
children come to stay and help the farmers. They learn to work together for the
common good and gain a sense of achievement.

FEDERATION OF CITY FARMS AND COMMUNITY GARDENS
THE GREENHOUSE, HEREFORD STREET BS3 4NA
Tel: 0117 923 1800 Fax: 0117 923 1900 Contact: Anna Nicholls
admin@farmgarden.org.uk www.farmgarden.org.uk
FCFCG supports and represents city farms, community gardens and similar
community-led growing initiatives in the UK. We provide advice on a wide range of
topics including funding and budgeting, community involvement, animal husbandry,
horticulture, land management and legal issues. We arrange training and networking events for our members and represent the movement at a national level.

FELDON FOREST FARM
FELDON FOREST FARM, FRANKTON, RUGBY CV23 9PD
Tel: 01926 632246 Contact: George Browning
georgebrowning@farmersweekly.net www.feldon-forest-farm.co.uk
Educational visits by arrangement. Universities, colleges and groups all catered for.

FIRST LEARNING DAY NURSERY
50 SHEEP WALK, SHEPPERTON TW17 0AJ
Tel: 01932 260600 Contact: Kimberley Foster
admin@firstlearning.co.uk
Situated in Shepperton, Middlesex, this is the first and only certified organic children's day nursery in the UK offering quality childcare for babies from 3 months to
pre-school children aged 5 years. Part or full time places. Head office at 3 Union
Court, Richmond, Surrey TW9 1AA, telephone: 020 8939 2288.

FISHACE
Contact: Stephen Clark
sbc@fishace.demon.co.uk www.fishace.demon.co.uk
International site promoting sustainable organic aquaculture on the internet for the
past ten years. Organic aquaculture directory, news & events.

FLAXDRAYTON FARM
2 BROOMHILL LANE, LOPEN, SOUTH PETHERTON TA13 5LA
Tel: 01460 241427 Fax: 01460 241427 Contact: Peter Foster
peter@flaxdrayton.fsnet.co.uk www.somersetorganiclink.co.uk
Organic vegetable grower marketing all produce through Somerset Organic Link, a
co-operative formed by organic growers in south Somerset.

THE FOOD COMMISSION
94 WHITE LION STREET N1 9PF
Tel: 020 7837 2250 Contact: Ian Tokelove
enquiries@foodcomm.org.uk www.foodcomm.org.uk
The UK's leading independent food watchdog, campaigning for healthier, safer food.
Publishes the award-winning *Food Magazine*. Call or write for a free copy.

FORDHALL FARM
TERN HILL RD., MARKET DRAYTON TF9 3PS
Tel: 01630 638255 Contact: Charlotte Hollins
info@fordhallorganicfarm.co.uk www.fordhallorganicfarm.co.uk
Farm shop and nature trail open Friday to Sunday.

THE FRESH NETWORK
THE FRESH NETWORK LTD., PO BOX 71, ELY CB6 3ZQ
Tel: 0870 800 7070 Fax: 0870 800 7071 Contact: Karen Knowler
info@fresh-network.com www.fresh-network.com
We specialise in promoting and supplying organic raw and living foods and publish
Get Fresh! magazine, hold an annual Fresh Festival featuring many of the world's
leading authorities on natural healthy living, and offer an extensive range of specialist books, foods and kitchen equipment by mail order, including juicers, sprouting equipment, dehydrators and much more.

FRIENDS OF THE EARTH
26–28 UNDERWOOD ST, LONDON N1 7JQ
Tel: 0808 800 1111 Fax: 020 7490 0881 Contact: Information Service
info@foe.co.uk www.foe.co.uk
Environmental pressure group. Friends of the Earth's 'Real Food' campaign asks the
government to reform farming and food production to enable farmers to manage the
countryside sustainably and provide high quality food for a fair income.

GENEWATCH UK
THE MILL HOUSE, MANCHESTER ROAD, TIDESWELL, BUXTON SK17 8LN
Tel: 01298 871898 Fax: 01298 872531 Contact: Sue Mayer
mail@genewatch.org www.genewatch.org
Policy research group. Research and analysis on GM crops and foods. Up-to-date
information on latest developments and their implications.

GREEN CUISINE LTD
PENRHOS COURT, KINGTON HR5 3LH
Tel: 01544 230720 Fax: 01544 230754 Contact: Daphne Lambert
info@greencuisine.org www.greencuisine.org
Soil Association E2051. Green Cuisine runs courses on food and health and offers
consultations and natural therapies. The company also produce books and
educational material. See also Penrhos Ltd and The Penrhos Trust.

THE GREENHOUSE
42–46 BETHEL ST., NORWICH NR2 1NR
Tel: 01603 631007 Contact: Tigger
www.greenhousetrust.co.uk
The Greenhouse is an educational charity providing solutions to environmental problems. The building houses an organic, vegetarian/vegan licensed café and shop (open for Sunday lunch 12 to 3.30) plus meeting rooms and herb garden. A resource centre offering meeting space, offices and other facilities to local and regional voluntary groups.

GREENPEACE UK
CANONBURY VILLAS N1 2PN
Tel: 020 7865 8100 Fax: 020 7865 8200 Contact: Charlotte Duggett
info@uk.greenpeace.org www.greenpeace.org.uk
International environmental organisation which fights abuse to the natural world.

GROUNDWORK BLACK COUNTRY
WOLVERHAMPTON ENVIRONMENT CENTRE, WEST ACRE CRESCENT, FINCHFIELD, WOLVERHAMPTON WV3 9AY
Tel: 01902 766199 Fax: 01902 574600 Contact: Terry Bird
terry_bird@groundwork.org.uk www.groundwork-bc.org.uk
Training, education and community links, open days.

GUILDEN GATE SMALLHOLDING
86 NORTH END, BASSINGBOURN, ROYSTON SG8 5PD
Tel: 01763 243960 Contact: Simon Saggers
simon.saggers@home.pipex.com www.guildengate.co.uk
Soil Association G5970. Mixed organic smallholding offering guided tours. Wildflower meadow, veg & herb fields, woodland, pond and orchards. Interesting on-site water and energy resource cycles. A practical design for living and working in a more ecologically sound and sustainable way. Member of the Soil Association Organic Farms Network.

HAZELBROW VISITOR CENTRE
LOW ROW, RICHMOND DL11 6NE
Tel: 01748 886224 Contact: Catherine Calvert
hazelbrowfarm@aol.com www.hazelbrow.co.uk
Organic working farm in Yorkshire Dales National Park with Visitor Centre, shop and café open 11am to 5pm five days a week, March to September (closed Mondays & Fridays). Member of the Soil Association Organic Farms Network.

HDRA, HENRY DOUBLEDAY RESEARCH ASSOCIATION, RYTON ORGANIC GARDENS

RYTON ON DUNSMORE, COVENTRY CV8 3LG
Tel: 024 7630 3517 Fax: 024 7663 9229 Contact: Angela Bull
enquiry@hdra.org.uk www.hdra.org.uk
Soil Association T9217. Standards for organic products for amenity horticulture. HDRA is Europe's largest organic gardening organisation. It is dedicated to researching and promoting organic gardening, farming and food. Ryton Organic Gardens, ten acres displaying all aspects of organic horticulture for gardens, plus The Vegetable Kingdom, an interactive exhibition for all ages on the history and role of vegetables. Organic restaurant and shop open daily.

HDRA, HENRY DOUBLEDAY RESEARCH ASSOCIATION, THE ORGANIC KITCHEN GARDEN

AUDLEY END HOUSE, SAFFRON WALDEN CB11 4JF
Tel: 024 7630 3517 Fax: 024 7663 9229 Contact: Susan Kay-Williams
enquiry@hdra.org.uk www.hdra.org.uk
HDRA, the organic organisation, runs the walled kitchen garden at Audley End House, an English Heritage property. The 2-acre walled gardens include heritage vegetables, vinery and fruit house. For opening hours, please contact English Heritage: 01799 522399.

HDRA, HENRY DOUBLEDAY RESEARCH ASSOCIATION, YALDING ORGANIC GARDENS

BENOVER RD., YALDING, NR. MAIDSTONE ME18 6EX
Tel: 01622 814650 Fax: 01622 814650 Contact: Tania Neumann
enquiry@hdra.org.uk www.hdra.org.uk
Yalding Organic Gardens trace the course of garden history through 16 landscaped displays, illustrating the organic techniques used to maintain them.

HEELEY CITY FARM

RICHARDS RD, SHEFFIELD S2 3DT
Tel: 0114 258 0482 Fax: 0114 255 1400 Contact: The Manager
farm@heeleyfarm.org.uk www.heeleyfarm.org.uk
A community environmental and horticultural project based on an inner city educational farm and environmental visitor attraction.

HERTFORDSHIRE ORGANIC GARDENERS

C/O 15 BISHOPS RD., WELWYN AL6 0NR
Tel: 01438 798593 Contact: Dagmar Brook
hogs@btinternet.com
Members of HDRA. Gardening group.

HOLME LACY COLLEGE

HOLME LACY HR2 6LL
Tel: 01432 870316 Fax: 01432 870566 Contact: Peter Savidge
holmelacy@pershore.ac.uk www.pershore.ac.uk
Holme Lacy College is host to 'Project Carrot', which aims to create a leading
European centre for sustainable agriculture and land management on its 600-acre
farm and woodland estate. Member of the Soil Association Organic Farms Network.

THE HORTICULTURAL CORRESPONDENCE COLLEGE

LITTLE NOTTON FARMHOUSE, 16 NOTTON, LACOCK, CHIPPENHAM SN15 2NF
Tel: 01249 730326 Fax: 01249 730326 Contact: Kay Pidgeon
info@hccollege.co.uk www.hccollege.co.uk
Tel & Contact: Kay Pidgeon
Home study courses in garden and horticulture-related subjects, including a Soil
Association approved organic gardening course. Also organic arable farming.

INSTITUTE OF RURAL SCIENCES

INSTITUTE OF RURAL SCIENCES, UNIVERSITY OF WALES, ABERYSTWYTH SY23 3AL
Tel: 01970 624471 Fax: 01970 622238 Contact: Nic Lampkin
organic@aber.ac.uk www.organic.aber.ac.uk
Soil Association certified. Research/demonstration farm. BSc, PgCert and PgDipl
in organic agriculture with student bursary support available, sponsored by
Waitrose and Horizon Organic Dairy. Extensive DEFRA and EU-funded organic
research programme.

INTERNATIONAL FEDERATION OF ORGANIC AGRICULTURAL MOVEMENTS (IFOAM)

CHARLES-DE-GAULLE-STR. 5, 53113, BONN, GERMANY
Tel: +49 (0) 228 926 5010 Fax: +49 (0) 228 926 5099
headoffice@ifoam.org www.ifoam.org
IFOAM is the world umbrella organisation of the organic agriculture movement with
750 members. It offers publications, such as the directory *Organic Agriculture
Worldwide* and the magazine *Ecology and Farming*, and organises international
conferences and workshops.

INTERNATIONAL SOCIETY FOR ECOLOGY AND CULTURE

FOXHOLE, DARTINGTON, TOTNES TQ9 6EB
Tel: 01803 868650 Fax: 01803 868651 Contact: Carole Powell
info@isec.org.uk www.isec.org.uk
ISEC is a non-profit organisation concerned with the protection of both biological
and cultural diversity. Our emphasis is on education for action: moving beyond
single issues to look at the more fundamental influences that shape our lives.

IPSWICH ORGANIC GARDENERS GROUP
BABOUSHKA, 223 MERSEA ROAD, COLCHESTER CO2 8PN
Tel: 01206 570859 Contact: Jill Carter
tetley@macunlimited.net www.irene.org.uk
Gardening group affiliated to the HDRA, meeting once a month September to May, with a speaker each month. Bi-monthly newsletter, discount seeds and bulk purchasing scheme. Also attend local events to promote organic gardening.

IRISH ORGANIC FARMERS AND GROWERS ASSOCIATION (IOFGA)
MAIN ST., NEWTOWNFORBES, CO. LONGFORD, IRELAND
Tel: (+353) 043 42495 Fax: (+353) 043 42496 Contact: Pascal Gillard
iofga@eircom.net www.irishorganic.ie
IOFGA is a company limited by guarantee, open to farmers, growers, consumers and others interested in the production of healthy food and the protection of the environment. IOFGA operates an inspection and certification scheme, publishes a magazine, *Organic Matters*, and other practical information for organic farmers and growers. Producers and processors registered with IOFGA may display the IOFGA symbol on their products and produce. Details of IOFGA registered producers, processors, wholesalers and those offering box delivery and market stalls are available directly from IOFGA.

JIGSAW ENVIRONMENTAL
MAIN STREET, GISBURN, CLITHEROE BB7 4HN
Tel: 01200 415979 Contact: Ellen Pope
gisburnproject@hotmail.com
We aim to support the long term development of people with disabilities and those disadvantaged through economic or social exclusion. Organic horticulture is the platform from which we deliver accredited horticultural training. Best environmental practice is also a key component of the site and the project as a whole.

THE KINDERSLEY CENTRE AT SHEEPDROVE ORGANIC FARM
THE KINDERSLEY CENTRE, SHEEPDROVE ORGANIC FARM, WARREN FARM, LAMBOURN RG17 7UU
Tel: 01488 674737 Fax: 01488 72285 Contact: Pippa Regan
pippa.regan@thekindersleycentre.com www.thekindersleycentre.com
Sustainable, organic and environmentally sound, The Kindersley Centre combines exceptional surroundings with the most advanced technology and attentive service. Set at the heart of award-winning Sheepdrove Organic Farm, the centre is housed within a beautiful, eco-friendly building, surrounded by fields and woodlands. A range of meeting places and adaptable seating for up to 200 people.

THE KINGCOMBE CENTRE

LOWER KINGCOMBE, TOLLER PORCORUM, DORCHESTER DT2 0EQ
Tel: 01300 320684 Fax: 01300 321409 Contact: Nigel Spring
nspring@kingcombe-centre.demon.co.uk www.kingcombe-centre.demon.co.uk
Residential study centre in converted farm buildings beside the River Hooke; offers courses and holidays in a wide range of subjects for adults and children, fit and disabled. Day visits for schools and guided walks.

KITTOW, JD & SE

ELBURY FARM, BROADCLYST, EXETER EX5 3BH
Tel: 01392 462817 Fax: 01392 462817 Contact: Jon Kittow
Soil Association G7302. Traditional Devon mixed farm farm trail and the opportunity to see how the dairy, beef, sheep and arable enterprises integrate into a sustainable farming system. Visitors by appointment, occasional open days.

LACKHAM COLLEGE

LACOCK, CHIPPENHAM SN15 2NY
Tel: 01249 443111 Fax: 01249 444474 Contact: Trevor Arnes
A range of qualifications both part time and full time: City & Guilds Organic Gardening, Certificate in Organic Horticulture, National Certificate in Organic Horticulture, HND & HNC in organic crop production.

LAKEWOOD CONFERENCE CENTRE

RHODYATE, BLAGDON, BRISTOL BS40 7YE
Tel: 01761 463366 Fax: 01761 463377 Contact: Angela Cary-Brown
info@lakewoodcentre.co.uk www.lakewoodcentre.co.uk
A new contemporary conference centre with stunning views over lakes close to Bristol, Bath and the M5. Purpose-designed with state of the art audio visual equipment. Local, fresh and organic food.

LAND HERITAGE

SUMMERHILL FARM, HITTISLEIGH, EXETER EX6 6LP
Tel: 01647 24511 Fax: 01647 24588 Contact: Robert Brighton
landheritage@hotmail.com www.landheritage.org
Land-based charitable trust. Seeks to protect and preserve small family farms, creating organic tenancies; promotes community supported agriculture schemes; supplies educational packs raising awareness of organic farming; publishes material and provides conversion advice.

THE LAND OF ROOTS LTD

17 KINGSTON AVENUE, BEARPARK, DURHAM DH7 7DJ
Tel: 0191 373 5109 Contact: Wilf Richards
15-acre permaculture smallholding, 2 miles from Durham City. Run work camp weekends—volunteers welcome.

LEAFCYCLE

COOMBE FARM, COVE, TIVERTON EX16 7RU
Tel: 01398 331808 Fax: 01398 331808 Contact: Michael Cole
www.leafcycle.co.uk
Leafcycle camps—a green space for green camps.

LONG CRICHEL ORGANIC GARDEN

LONG CRICHEL GARDEN, (OPPOSITE LONG CRICHEL BAKERY), LONG CRICHEL,
WIMBORNE BH21 5LF
Tel: 01258 830295 Contact: Anni Sax
longcrichelgarden@cooptel.net
Registered for WWOOFers.

LOWER SHAW FARM

OLD SHAW LANE, SHAW, SWINDON SN5 9PJ
Tel: 01793 771080 Contact: Andrea Hirsch
enquiries@lowershawfarm.co.uk www.lowershawfarm.co.uk
Courses and gatherings. Permaculture, fungus forays, crafts, yoga, circus skills,
singing, cooking, herbs, families. Friendly atmosphere, home-grown and local food.
Organic gardens and animals. Ask us for a programme.

LUPPOLO LTD

42 WESTBOURNE TERRACE WC2 6QE
Tel: 020 7262 4562 Fax: 020 7262 9078 Contact: Claudio Bincoletto
luppolo@tiscali.co.uk
Importing products for the catering industry, organising day walks on organic farms,
cookery and dietetic courses. Teaching in Tuscany on local wild herbs, expert on
ECC 2092/91.

MARCASSIE FARM

MARCASSIE FARM, RAFFORD, FORRES IV362RH
Tel: 01309 676865 Fax: 01309 676865 Contact: Betsy van der Lee
marcassie@marcassie.fsnet.co.uk
Offers educational courses (being established).

MENTRO LLUEST

LLANBADORN FAWR, ABERYSTWYTH SY23 3AU
Tel: 01970 612114 Fax: 01970 612114 Contact: R Allen
mentro.lluest@talk21.com
Soil Association G3081. Mentro Lluest teaches skills to people with special needs
within a framework of organic growing, environmental sustainability and social
cohesion.

MOLYNEUX ORGANIC MEDICINAL AND AROMATIC PLANT FARM AND RESEARCH CENTRE

MILL HOUSE FARM, EAGER LANE, LYDIATE L31 4HS
Tel: 0151 526 0139 Fax: 0151 526 0139 Contact: David Molyneux
sales@phytobotanica.com www.phytobotanica.com
Conference centre for educational days (e.g. aromatherapy and holistic therapies).

NATIONAL FARMERS' RETAIL AND MARKETS ASSOCIATION

PO BOX 575, SOUTHAMPTON SO15 7BZ
Tel: 0845 230 2150 Contact: The Secretary
justask@farma.org.uk www.farmersmarkets.net
A farmers' market is one in which farmers, growers or producers from a defined
local area are present in person to sell their own produce direct to the public. All
products sold should have been grown, reared, caught, pickled, baked, smoked or
processed by the stallholder.

THE NATIONAL INSTITUTE OF MEDICAL HERBALISTS

56 LONGBROOK STREET, EXETER EX1 6AH
Tel: 01392 426022 Fax: 01392 498963 Contact: The Secretary
nimh@ukexeter.freeserve.co.uk www.nimh.org.uk
Professional body of practising medical herbalists. Offers details/information on all
aspects of western herbal medicine and how to source a qualified practitioner.
Details on education and research available. All members have undergone a
rigorous four year training.

NATURE'S WORLD

LADGATE LANE, ACKLAM, MIDDLESBOROUGH TS5 7YN
Tel: 01642 594895 Fax: 01642 591224 Contact: Stuart Goldie
stuart@naturesworld.org.uk www.naturesworld.org.uk
The north of England's pioneering environmental centre, with over 25 acres of organic
demonstration gardens and wildlife areas. Open daily to the public, school groups and
tours. Also farm shop, tea rooms and play areas. Monthly farmers' market.

NEAL'S YARD REMEDIES (HEAD OFFICE)

8–10 INGATE PLACE, BATTERSEA SW8 3NS
Tel: 020 7498 1686 Fax: 020 7498 2505 Contact: The Manager
mail@nealsyardremedies.com www.nealsyardremedies.com
Neal's Yard Remedies runs courses on Natural Medicine, Organic Nutrition,
Aromatherapy, Herbalism, Flower Remedies and Homoeopathy. Contact Emma
Thomson on 020 7574 0031 for further information.

THE NETHERFIELD CENTRE

NETHERFIELD PLACE FARM, NETHERFIELD, NR. BATTLE TN3 9PY
Tel: 01424 775615 Fax: 01424 775616 Contact: Topsy Jewell
simon@thenetherfieldcentre.co.uk
The Netherfield Centre for Sustainable Food and Farming runs education courses,
training and networking for those interested in sustainable agriculture.

NIXORGANIX

CRYSTAL SPRINGS FARM, BRAILSFORD, ASHBOURNE DE6 3BG
Tel: 01335 360996 Contact: Nick Adams
nick@adams4.wanadoo.co.uk www.nixorganix.org
Educational visits and informal circular walks to view farm and conservation activities.

NORFOLK ORGANIC GROUP

25 ST MILDRED'S ROAD, NORWICH NR5 8RS
Tel: Contact: Jan Hunt
contact@norfolkorganic.org.uk www.norfolkorganic.org.uk
Local group of Soil Association and HDRA. We aim to promote the organic
movement in Norfolk by increasing public awareness of organic methods of farming
and gardening.

THE NORTH WALES ORGANIC GROWERS AND PERMACULTURE GROUP

PEN-Y-BRYN, TALWRN, LLANGEFNI, YNYS MON LL77 7SP
Tel: 01248 750029 Contact: Kath Turner
Group of members who put newcomers to the area in touch with existing organic
growers and permaculturists.

NORTH WEST ORGANIC CO-OPERATIVE SOCIETY LTD

2 FOREGLEN RD., KILLALOO BT47 4HY
Tel: 028 7133 7950 Fax: 028 7133 7146
Contact: George Macdonald (Development Manager) george@nworganic.com
The purpose of North West Organic is to co-ordinate the sale of locally produced
organic food. At the moment we are seeking a buyer for large quantity organically
produced lamb and organically produced heifers and bullocks. All the farmers in
North West Organic are registered with either the Soil Association or Irish Organic
Farmers and Growers Association.

NORWOOD FARM

BATH ROAD, NORTON ST PHILIP, NR. BATH BA2 7LP
Tel: 01373 834856 Fax: 01373 834765 Contact: Catherine Le Grice-Mack
catemack@norwood.ndo.co.uk www.norwoodfarm.co.uk
Soil Association G814. Organic mixed farm, with rare and native breeds. Open to
visitors every day from March 28th–September 19th. Member of the Soil
Association Organic Farms Network.

NOTTINGHAM CITY COUNCIL

GREEN'S MILL & SCIENCE CENTRE, WINDMILL LANE, SNEINTON,
NOTTINGHAM NG2 4QB
Tel: 0115 915 6878 Fax: 0115 915 6875 Contact: David Bent
enquiries@greensmill.org.uk www.greensmill.org.uk
Soil Association P4518. Museum: a working tower windmill built in 1807, once
operated by the mathematician George Green (1793–1841) Now producing organic stoneground flours.

ORGANIC CENTRE WALES

UNIVERSITY OF WALES, ABERYSTWYTH SY23 3AL
Tel: 01970 622248 Fax: 01970 622238 Contact: Neil Pearson
organic@aber.ac.uk www.organic.aber.ac.uk
Operated in partnership with Soil Association, Elm Farm Research Centre, IGER,
UWA and ADAS. Advice and demonstration. Dissemination of information on organic
farming at all levels from producers, to consumers, through training courses, advice,
demonstration farms, discussion groups, publications and website.

THE ORGANIC FARM SHOP

ABBEY HOME FARM, BURFORD ROAD, CIRENCESTER GL7 5HF
Tel: 01285 640441 Fax: 01285 644827 Contact: Hilary Chester-Master
info@theorganicfarmshop.co.uk www.theorganicfarmshop.co.uk
Cookery courses, educational visits, woodland walk. Large meeting room, yurt and
hut for hire, greenfield camping. Member of the Soil Association Organic Farms
Network.

ORGANIC FARMERS AND GROWERS LTD (OF&G)

ELIM CENTRE, LANCASTER RD., SHREWSBURY SY1 3LE
Tel: 0845 330 5122 Fax: 0845 330 5123 Contact: Richard Jacobs
info@organicfarmers.org.uk www.organicfarmers.org.uk
We carry out inspection and certification of organic production, processing and a
wide range of other organic enterprises. For more information, please contact us.

ORGANIC FOOD FEDERATION (OFF)

31 TURBINE WAY, ECO TECH BUSINESS PARK, SWAFFHAM PE37 7XD
Tel: 01760 720444 Fax: 01760 720790 Contact: Julian Wade
info@orgfoodfed.com www.orgfoodfed.com
EC listed certification body for the organic food industry certifying producers, processors, caterers and importers. UKAS-accredited for producing and processing. Also
able to offer certification against our private standards for cosmetics and acquacul-
ture. Authorised by DEFRA under the member state code UK4. Representation and
lobbying at Government, EU and Non-Government level. Personal service offered at
all times with telephones answered between 9.00–5.30 each weekday.

ORGANIC STUDIES CENTRE
DUCHY COLLEGE, ROSEWARNE, CAMBOURNE TR14 0AB
Tel: 01209 722155 Fax: 01209 722159 Contact: Jean Burke
j.burke@cornwall.ac.uk
Soil Association G4694. Organic agricultural research and demonstration and training. Arable/field vegetables demonstration farm, farm walks, trials and demos. R&D including farmers' participatory studies in all sectors of organic agricultural production.

ORGANIC TRUST LTD
VERNON HOUSE, 2 VERNON AVENUE, CLONTARF, DUBLIN 3, IRELAND
Tel: 00 353 1 8530271 Fax: 00 353 1 8530271 Contact: Helen Scully
organic@iol.ie www.organic-trust.org.
Organic inspection and certification service. Publication of quarterly professional journal, educational services and information.

PEN PYNFARCH
PEN PYNFARCH, LLANDYSUL SA44 4RU
Tel: 01559 384948 Contact: Eeva-Maria Mutka
enquiries@penpynfarch.co.uk www.penpynfarch.co.uk
Retreat/course centre with studio, accommodation and catering.

THE PENRHOS TRUST
PENRHOS COURT, KINGTON HR5 3LH
Tel: 01544 230720 Fax: 01544 230754 Contact: Martin Griffiths
martin@penrhos.co.uk www.penrhostrust.org
Charity for the restoration of historic farm buildings regenerated with organic and ecological small businesses. Education: conservation, food heritage, organic food production. See also Penrhos Ltd and Green Cuisine Ltd.

THE PINK PIG ORGANIC FARM SHOP, RESTAURANT AND FARM TRAIL
HOLME HALL, HOLME, SCUNTHORPE DN16 3RE
Tel: 01724 844466 Fax: 01724 866493 Contact: Sally Jackson
enquiries@pinkpigorganics.co.uk www.pinkpigorganics.co.uk
Children's play area, sandpit & farm trail. School visits welcome. Member of the Soil Association Organic Farms Network.

PLANTS FOR A FUTURE
THE FIELD, HIGHER PENPOL, ST. VEEP, LOSTWITHIEL PL22 0NG
Tel: 01208 873554
www.pfaf.org
A registered charity researching and demonstrating ecologically sustainable vegan organic horticulture in the form of woodland gardening and other permacultural practices. Day visits and tours, courses on woodland gardening, permaculture, nutrition, research, information, demonstration and supply of edible and otherwise useful plants.

PLOT 21 PERMACULTURE ALLOTMENTS
ALEXANDRA PALACE ALLOTMENTS, OFF ALEXANDRA PALACE WAY N17
Tel: 020 7916 7390 Contact: S Girardi
A loose non-profit-making organisation running courses on permaculture and producing home-grown crops using permaculture principles.

POLEMONIUM PLANTERY
POLEMONIUM PLANTERY, 28, SUNNYSIDE, TRIMDON GRANGE,
TRIMDON STATION TS29 6HF
Tel: 01429 881529 Contact: David Nichol-Brown
organic@polemonium.co.uk www.polemonium.co.uk
Offers garden visits, talks and garden plans. See website for full details.

PRIMROSE ORGANIC & SACRED EARTH CENTRE
FELINDRE, BRECON LD3 0ST
Tel: 01497 847636 Contact: Paul Benham
paul.benham@ukonline.co.uk www.organic-sacred-earth.co.uk
An organic permaculture fruit and vegetable business offering a host of inspiring
opportunities including volunteering and paid support work, education, accommodation, spiritual and sound healing workshops/retreats. Member of the Soil
Association Organic Farms Network.

PROPER JOB
CRANNAFORDS IND PARK, CHAGFORD TQ13 8DJ
Tel: 01647 432985 Fax: 01647 432985 Contact: Jo Hodges
compost@properjob.eclipse.co.uk www.properjob.ik.com
Holistic co-op working on waste and resource issues, especially composting, collecting
compostables, education/consciousness raising. Setting up training in related issues.

PROSPECTS TRUST
SNAKEHILL FARM, REACH, CAMBRIDGE CB5 0HZ
Tel: 01638 741551 Fax: 01638 741873 Contact: Phil Creme
prospect@farming.co.uk www.prospectstrust.org.uk
Soil Association registered. Charitable trust, working together with people with
learning disabilities. Provision of training, work experience and work opportunities in
organic market gardening and horticulture for people with learning disabilities.

RARE BREEDS SURVIVAL TRUST
NATIONAL AGRICULTURAL CENTRE, STONELEIGH PARK, KENILWORTH CV8 2LG
Tel: 024 7669 6551 Fax: 024 7669 6706 Contact: Robert Terry
enquiries@rbst.org.uk www.rbst.org.uk
Registered charity for the conservation of rare and endangered livestock breeds.

REDFIELD COMMUNITY
BUCKINGHAM RD., WINSLOW MK18 3LZ
Tel: 01296 713661 Fax: 01296 714983 Contact: Chrissy Schmidt
info@redfieldcommunity.org.uk www.redfieldcommunity.org.uk
Redfield is an intentional community. We grow and raise our own organic produce
as well as run courses and offer accommodation for groups.

REGIONAL CENTRE FOR ORGANIC HORTICULTRE
RCOH, SCHOOL FARM, DARTINGTON, NR. TOTNES TQ9 6EB
Tel: 01803 400999 Fax: 01803 408168 Contact: Mike Blakeley
mblakeley@dartingtontech.co.uk www.dartingtontech.co.uk
The Regional Centre for Organic Horticulture is based on the Dartington Hall Estate
near Totnes in South Devon. Established as a training centre under the guide of its
parent company Dartington Tech, to promote horticultural training throughout South
Devon. Training enquiries welcome.

THE RESPONSIVE EARTH TRUST
PLASDWBL BIODYNAMIC FARM, MYNACHLOG DDU, CLYNDERWEN SA66 7SE
Tel: 01994 419352 Contact: A Kleinjans
A charitable trust run for the benefit of students wishing to gain practical experience
in biodynamic farming and gardening. Demeter cert. no. 111.

RISING SUN FARM
KINGS RD. NORTH, WALLSEND NE28 9JL
Tel: 0191 234 0114 Contact: D Shanks
organics@risingsunfarm.freeserve.co.uk
Urban fringe farm providing education, day service for special needs. Open farm for
community.

ROBERT OWEN COMMUNITIES
LOWER SHARPHAM BARTON FARM, ASHPRINGTON, TOTNES TQ9 7DX
Tel: 01803 732502 Fax: 01803 732502 Contact: B Roodenburg-Vermaat
sharphamfarm@roc-uk.org
Day centre for people with learning disabilities. Dairy, beef, sheep, laying birds and
vegetables.

RSPB LAKE VYRNWY
BRYN AWEL, LLANWDDYN SY10 0LZ
Tel: 01691 870278 Fax: 01691 870313 Contact: Jo Morris
jo.morris@rspb.org.uk www.rspb.org.uk
The farm is part of a National Nature Reserve in the Berwyns. It is farmed to be
wildlife-friendly.

RUBHA PHOIL FOREST GARDEN/ SKYE PERMACULTURE

RUBHA PHOIL, ARMADALE PIER IV45 8RS
Tel: 01471 844700 Contact: Sandy Masson
sandyru@tiscali.co.uk www.skye-permaculture.org.uk
Soil Association GCS025/G4609, HDRA, Permaculture Association, Centre for
Alternative Technology Ecosite. Herbs, vegetables, displays and demonstration of
alternative systems, holiday accommodation, woodland walk, otter/bird hide, solitude
in wilderness.

RUSHALL FARM

SCRATCHFACE LANE, BRADFIELD RG7 6DL
Tel: 0118 974 4547 Contact: The Manager
jst@rushallfarm.org.uk www.rushallfarm.org.uk
Rushall Farm is a mixed organic farm and also home to the John Simonds Trust, an
educational charity that promotes a love and understanding of farming and the
countryside.

RUSKIN MILL COLLEGE

THE FISHERIES, HORSLEY GL6 1PL
Tel: 01453 837500 Fax: 01453 837506 Contact: Julian Pyzer
www.ruskin-mill.org.uk
Biodynamic Agricultural Association 245. Part of special needs further education
college with biodynamic market garden and mixed farm, and fish farm. Café and
shop; crafts, exhibitions, workshops, concerts, storytelling and talks.

SCOTSWOOD NATURAL COMMUNITY GARDEN

JOHN MARLEY CENTRE, WHICKHAM VIEW, SCOTSWOOD,
NEWCASTLE-UPON-TYNE NE15 6TT
Tel: 0845 4581653 Fax: 0845 4581654 Contact: William Mortada
office@sncg.org.uk www.sncg.org.uk
Award-winning urban permaculture garden with woodlands, ponds, meadows,
orchards and vegetable plots. The two-acre site is a haven for local wildlife and an
example of sustainable food production in an urban environment. We organise
public open days in the summer and host visiting school and community groups
throughout the year. Please see our website for more details.

SCOTTISH AGRICULTURAL COLLEGE

CRAIBSTONE ESTATE, BUCKSBURN, ABERDEEN AB21 9YA
Tel: 01224 711072 Fax: 01224 711293 Contact: David Younie
d.younie@ab.sac.ac.uk www.sac.ac.uk/organic-farming
SAC provides advice on organic farming (including telephone helpline: 01224
711072) to Scottish farmers, education and vocational training, and multi-disciplinary
research across most aspects of organic farming.

SCOTTISH ORGANIC PRODUCERS ASSOCIATION (SOPA)
SCOTTISH ORGANIC CENTRE, 10TH AVENUE, ROYAL HIGHLAND CENTRE,
INGLISTEN, EDINBURGH EH28 8NF
Tel: 0131 333 0940 Fax: 0131 333 2290 Contact: Christine Robb
info@sopa.org.uk www.sopa.org.uk
SOPA primarily offer an organic certification service to farmer producers. SOPA is
the leading Scottish organic sector body.

SOIL ASSOCIATION
BRISTOL HOUSE, 40–56 VICTORIA STREET BS1 6BY
Tel: 0117 929 0661 Fax: 0117 925 2504 Contact: Martin Trowell
info@soilassociation.org www.soilassociation.org
The Soil Association is a membership organisation with charitable status, founded in
1946. It encourages an ecological approach to agriculture and offers organic cultiva-
tion as the sustainable long-term option above chemical farming. Mail order book
catalogue, bookshop, information packs, publications and magazine *Living Earth*. Its
subsidiary the Soil Association Symbol Scheme is an EC-approved certification body
which inspects and licenses commercial food producers, processors and other manufacturers to the highest organic standards and acts as the consumer's guarantee
of organic quality.

SOIL ASSOCIATION CERTIFICATION LTD. (SA CERT)
40–56 VICTORIA STREET BS1 6BY
Tel: 0117 914 2405 Fax: 0117 925 2504 Contact: Information Officer
info@soilassociation.org www.soilassociation.org
Soil Association Certification Limited is the largest of the UK certification bodies
and currently inspects and certifies over 70% of UK licensed organic producers and
processors. We certify to the Soil Association Standards for Organic Food and
Farming which are well respected worldwide. The well known Soil Association
Organic Symbol, featured in this book and displayed on much organic food and
packaging, is widely recognised and trusted by consumers.

SOMERSET ORGANIC LINK
THE CIDER PRESS ROOM, FLAXDRAYTON FARM, DRAYTON,
SOUTH PETHERTON TA13 5LR
Tel: 01460 241427 Fax: 01460 241427 Contact: Peter Foster & Steve Friend
peter@flaxdrayton.fsnet.co.uk www.somersetorganiclink.co.uk
A co-operative of organic farmers in Somerset offering sales and marketing service
for organic vegetable producers in Somerset, forum for crop planning, opportunities
to share labour and equipment. Mobile: 07881 865709.

SOUTH DEVON ORGANIC PRODUCERS LTD

C/O WASH BARN, BUCKFASTLEIGH TQ11 0LD
Tel: 01803 762100 Fax: 01803 762100 Contact: Ian Noble
sdop@farmersweekly.net www.sdopltd.co.uk
Co-operative of growers producing organic vegetables.

SOUTH PENQUITE FARM

SOUTH PENQUITE, BLISLAND, BODMIN PL30 4LH
Tel: 01208 850491 Fax: 0870 136 7926 Contact: Dominic & Cathy Fairman
thefarm@bodminmoor.co.uk www.southpenquite.co.uk
Soil Association G4771. Camping and field studies on a working organic hill farm
high on Bodmin Moor. Interesting farm walk including diverse wildlife habitats, a
bronze age hut settlement, a mile of beautiful riverbank and an imposing standing
stone. Mongolian Yurt available for that 'back to nature' holiday! Member of the
Soil Association Organic Farms Network.

STOCKLEY FARM ORGANICS

SMITHY FARMHOUSE, ARLEY, NORTHWICH CW9 6LZ
Tel: 01565 777492 Fax: 01565 777501 Contact: John Walton
organics@stockleyfarm.co.uk www.stockleyfarm.co.uk
Stockley Farm is open to the public and schools from March to October.

STROUD COMMUNITY AGRICULTURE LTD

48C HIGH ST., STROUD GL5 1AN
Tel: 0845 458 0814 Contact: Carole Vaughan
info@stroudcommunityagriculture.org www.stroudcommunityagriculture.org
A community co-operative which runs a farm business. The farm grows vegetables
and has pigs and cattle. Anyone can become a member and a weekly veg bag with
an option to buy meat also. Membership: 01453 840037.

ST. AUGUSTINES FARM

ARLINGHAM, GLOUCESTER GL2 7JN
Tel: 01452 740277 Fax: 01452 740277 Contact: Rob & Elaine Jewell
staugustines@btconnect.com
Visit a friendly family working organic dairy farm in the beautiful Severn Vale. Feed
the many different farm animals, watch the milking, discover the wildlife and enjoy
the real countryside. Member of the Soil Association Organic Farms Network.

SUGARBROOK FARM

MOBBERLEY RD., ASHLEY, NR. ALTRINCHAM WA14 3QB
Tel: 0161 928 0879 Contact: JF Erlam
mail@sugarbrookfarm.co.uk www.sugarbrookfarm.co.uk
Soil Association G4603. Sheep and arable farm welcoming educational access
under Countryside Stewardship, i.e. free visits.

SUSTAIN

94 WHITE LION ST. N1 9PF
Tel: 020 7837 1228 Fax: 020 7837 1141 Contact: The Secretary
sustain@sustainweb.org www.sustainweb.org
Sustain—the alliance for better food and farming—advocates food and agriculture
policies and practices that enhance the health and welfare of people and animals,
improve the working and living environment, promote equity and enrich society and
culture.

THE SUSTAINABLE LIFESTYLES RESEARCH CO-OP LTD

THE OFFICE, POND COTTAGE EAST, CUDDINGTON RD., DINTON,
AYLESBURY HP18 0AD
Tel: 01296 747737 Contact: Mike George
mikegeorge.lara@btinternet.com
Organic Food Federation 0071/01/981. Full public access to 70 acres. Farm Walks
through woodland to the riverside. Run by volunteers.

ULSTER WILDLIFE TRUST

JOHN MCSPARRAN MEMORIAL HILL FARM, GLENDUN, CUSHENDEN,
CO. ANTRIM BT44 0PZ
Tel: 028 2176 1403 Fax: 028 2176 1403 Contact: Barrie Elkin
ulsterwt@glendunfarm.fsnet.co.uk
Soil Association G6697. Farming together with wildlife in a progressive and sustain-
able manner.

UNITED WORLD COLLEGE OF THE ATLANTIC

ST. DONATS CASTLE, LLANTWIT MAJOR, VALE OF GLAMORGAN CF61 1WF
Tel: 01446 799012 Fax: 01446 799013 Contact: AE Davies
estate@uwcac.uwc.org
Soil Association G5656. An international 6th Form College with a 20 hectare farm
unit producing organic lamb and beef.

UNSTONE GRANGE ORGANIC GARDENING FOR HEALTH

CROW LANE, UNSTONE, NR. CHESTERFIELD S18 4AL
Tel: 01246 411666 Fax: 01246 412344 Contact: Jennie Street
garden@unstonegrange.co.uk www.unstonegrange.co.uk
We provide gardening opportunities for volunteers from all over Derbyshire: people
with learning disabilities, mental health issues, single parents, retired, people
changing careers or down-shifting. Others are well and want to stay well, or want to
learn about organic horticulture. We run an OCN-approved organic horticulture
course.

UPPER RED HOUSE FARM

LLANVIHANGEL, MONMOUTH NP25 5HL
Tel: 01600 780501 Fax: 01600 780572 Contact: Teona Dorrien-Smith
Soil Association G4969. Tir Gofal. The farm is mainly pasture with some arable, producing forage and spring cereals with emphasis on conservation and educational visits to study environment and wildlife. Educational visits, all ages welcome, but booking essential.

THE VILLAGE BAKERY

MELMERBY, PENRITH CA10 1HE
Tel: 01768 881811 Fax: 01768 881848 Contact: Chris Curry
info@village-bakery.com www.village-bakery.com
Baking courses offered.

WALTHAM PLACE FARM

WALTHAM PLACE FARM, CHURCH HILL, WHITE WALTHAM, MAIDENHEAD SL6 3JH
Tel: 01628 825517 Fax: 01628 825045 Contact: Steve Castle
estateoffice@walthamplace.com www.walthamplace.com
Soil Association No G557 since 1989. Mixed organic farm and gardens open to the public Wed (NGS) and Fri only (bookings please) 10am–4pm to September. Member of the Soil Association Organic Farms Network. See display ad.

THE WATERMILL

LITTLE SALKELD, PENRITH CA10 1NN
Tel: 01768 881523 Fax: 01768 881047 Contact: Ana Jones
organicflour@aol.com www.organicmill.co.uk
Soil Association (P632) and Biodynamic Agriculture Association registered. Water powered 18th-century watermill: mill shop, tea room, mill tours and baking courses.

THE WESSEX ORGANIC MOVEMENT (WORM)

LINDEN COTTAGE, DUCK STREET, HILTON, BLANDFORD DT11 0DQ
Tel: 0845 330 3953 Fax: 0845 330 3953 Contact: Philip Clive
sec@wessexorganic.org.uk www.wessexorganic.org.uk
Soil Association, HDRA, BTCV. We hold a series of talks and visits to promote and educate farmers, producers or consumers about organic methods and to network information, set up projects to meet their needs.

WEST HILL FARM

WEST HILL FARM, WEST DOWN, ILFRACOMBE EX34 8NF
Tel: 01271 815477 Fax: 01271 813316 Contact: Susi Batstone
info@westhillfarm.org www.westhillfarm.org
We welcome school visits and are a demonstration farm for the Soil Association. Member of the Soil Association Organic Farms Network.

WESTHOPE COLLEGE
WESTHOPE COLLEGE, CRAVEN ARMS SY7 9JL
Tel: 01584 861293 Contact: Anne Dyer
www.westhope.org.uk
Soil Association No. G4886. Adult education weekend and weekly courses, C&G exams.

WHITEHOLME FARM
WHITEHOLME, ROWELTOWN, CARLISLE CA6 6LJ
Tel: 016977 48058 Contact: Jon and Lynne Perkin
whiteholmefarm@hotmail.com www.whiteholmefarm.co.uk
Whiteholme Farm is an organic livestock farm situated in the north-east of Cumbria. Accommodation, education and farm walks are all available. Member of the Soil Association Organic Farms Network.

WHOLESOME FOOD ASSOCIATION
1 BARTON COTTAGES, DARTINGTON HALL, TOTNES TQ9 6ED
Tel: 01237 441118 Contact: Philip Chandler
info@wholesomefood.org www.wholesomefood.org
The Wholesome Food Association provides a low cost alternative to organic certification for the small scale grower and small farmer. We operate a unique 'peer review' verification system backed by our 'open gate' growing policy, which enables customers to visit growers' premises by appointment. We welcome producers, processors, suppliers, distributors and supporters who support local, chemical-free food production.

WILTSHIRE COLLEGE—LACKHAM
LACKHAM PARK, LACOCK, CHIPPENHAM SN15 2NY
Tel: 01249 466800 Fax: 01249 444474 Contact: Trevor Armes
wiltscoll@ac.uk www.wiltscoll.ac.uk
We offer a range of FE & HE courses in organic horticulture at National Certificate/Diploma and National Award in Organic Horticulture. For further details visit the website or telephone 01249 466873.

WOMEN'S ENVIRONMENTAL NETWORK
PO BOX 30626 E1 1TZ
Tel: 020 7481 9004 Fax: 020 7481 9144 Contact: Caroline Fernandez
info@wen.org.uk www.wen.org.uk
Educational environmental charity. Educating women and men who care about the environment from a women's perspective. Projects include local food, women's food growing groups, health, real nappies and waste prevention.

WOODBROOKE QUAKER STUDY CENTRE
1046 BRISTOL RD., SELLY OAK, BIRMINGHAM B29 6LJ
Tel: 0121 472 5171 Fax: 0121 472 5173 Contact: Kathleen Russell
kathleen@woodbrooke.org.uk www.woodbrooke.org.uk
Set in ten acres of organically managed gardens, Woodbrooke is a residential
Quaker education centre, also offering conference facilities and general accommodation. Guests enjoy organic food grown on the premises.

THE WORLD LAND TRUST
BLYTH HOUSE, BRIDGE ST., HALESWORTH IP19 8AB
Tel: 01986 874422 Fax: 01986 874425 Contact: Vivien Burton
info@worldlandtrust.org www.worldlandtrust.org
The World Land Trust is a UK based, international conservation organisation (charity
reg. no. 1001291) working to preserve the world's most biologically important and
threatened lands. The Trust has helped purchase and protect more than 300,000
acres of habitats rich in wildlife, in Belize, Costa Rica, the Philippines, South
America and the UK. For a unique, eco-friendly gift, save an acre of rainforest for
£25. Donations can be made on our website or by calling the office.

WWF (WORLDWIDE FUND FOR NATURE)
PANDA HOUSE, WEYSIDE PARK, GODALMING, SURREY GU7 1XR
Tel: 01483 426444 Fax: 01483 426409
The WWF works on both global and local environmental issues. Much of our work is
in areas where the most critically endangered wildlife and the least protected habitats
are found. However, the origins of many environmental problems lie in developed
countries, including the UK, and in our attitudes and behaviour—for example our
consumption of natural resources.

WWOOF (WORLD WIDE OPPORTUNITIES ON ORGANIC FARMS)
PO BOX 2675, LEWES BN7 1RB
Tel: 01273 476286 Fax: 01273 476286 Contact: Fran Whittle
hello@wwoof.org www.wwoof.org.uk
WWOOF helps volunteers find host farms worldwide to be able to experience organic growing, meet like-minded people, exchange skills and get into rural areas. Help
in exchange for bed and board.

YORKSHIRE ORGANICS
BOG HOUSE FARM, MICKLEBY, SALTBURN TS13 5NA
Tel: 01947 840075 Contact: Jenny Summerson
jenny@yorkshireorganics.freeserve.co.uk
A producer group aiming to promote organic awareness in Yorkshire. We hold
quarterly meetings which are farm walks, talks and socials, and publish a quarterly
newsletter.

Many of the organisations in the previous sections also produce their own publications.

CENTRE FOR ALTERNATIVE TECHNOLOGY
MACHYNLLETH SY20 9AZ
Tel: 01654 705950 Fax: 01654 702782 Contact: Information Officer
info@cat.org.uk www.cat.org.uk
Soil Association LO9WW. Established in 1974, the Centre for Alternative Technology
CAT publish practical and informative publications, run a mail order service of
'green' books and products, and provide educational services for schools. See main
entry under Associations and display ad.

COUNTRY SMALLHOLDING MAGAZINE
FAIR OAK CLOSE, EXETER AIRPORT BUSINESS PARK, CLYST HONITON EX5 2UL
Tel: 01392 888481 Contact: Diane Cowgill
editorial.csh@archant.co.uk www.countrysmallholding.com
Monthly magazine for smallholders, small farmers and anyone interested in small
scale livestock, poultry keeping, growing crops, food and all matters relating to self-
sufficiency.

ECO-LOGIC BOOKS
MULBERRY HOUSE, 19 MAPLE GROVE, BATH BA2 3AF
Tel: 01225 484472 Fax: 0117 942 0164 Contact: Peter Andrews
info@eco-logicbooks.com www.eco-logicbooks.com
Publish and sell mail order books that promote practical solutions to environmental
problems, organic gardening, permaculture and sustainability.

THE ECOLOGIST
UNIT 18, CHELSEA WHARF, 15 LOTS RD. SW10 0QJ
Tel: 020 7351 3578 Fax: 020 7351 3617 Contact: The Editor
editorial@theecologist.org www.theecologist.org
The dangers of globalisation, the real reasons behind climate change, the threat of
corporate power, the risks of GM food, the truth about global cancer—just some of
the issues covered regularly by *The Ecologist*.

ETHICAL CONSUMER

UNIT 21, 41 OLD BIRLEY ST., MANCHESTER, GREATER MANCHESTER, M15 5RF
Tel: 0161 226 2929 Fax: 0161 226 6277 Contact: Lindsay Whalen
mail@ethicalconsumer.org www.ethicalconsumer.org
Ethical Consumer is the leading consumer organisation for those concerned about
the environment, animal welfare, buying organic and fair trade. Ethical Consumer
magazine and www.ethiscore.org help you buy the most ethical products available.
Also www.corporatecritic.org.

THE FOOD MAGAZINE

94 WHITE LION ST. N1 9PF
Tel: 020 7837 2250 Contact: Ian Tokelove
info@foodcomm.org.uk www.foodcomm.org.uk
The Food Magazine is essential reading for anyone who cares about the food they
eat. Hard-hitting research, news and articles from award-winning journalists. Call or
write for a free copy.

GREEN BOOKS LTD

FOXHOLE, DARTINGTON, TOTNES TQ9 6EB
Tel: 01803 863260 Fax: 01803 863843 Contact: John Elford
john@greenbooks.co.uk www.greenbooks.co.uk
Besides publishing *The Organic Directory*, we have a wide range of other books on
organic living, including *The Organic Baby Book*, *Green Living in the Urban Jungle*
and *Gaia's Kitchen: Vegetarian Recipes for Family and Community*. Also books on
eco-building, organic gardening, green politics and economics, etc. Mail order and
trade catalogues available on request.

HDRA, HENRY DOUBLEDAY RESEARCH ASSOCIATION, RYTON ORGANIC GARDENS

RYTON ON DUNSMORE, COVENTRY CV8 3LG
Tel: 024 7630 3517 Fax: 024 7663 9229 Contact: Angela Bull
enquiry@hdra.org.uk www.hdra.org.uk
Soil Association T9217. Standards for organic products for amenity horticulture.
HDRA is Europe's largest organic gardening organisation, and produces many publi-
cations. See main entry under Associations.

HEALTH FOOD BUSINESS MAGAZINE

THE OLD DAIRY, HUDSONS FARM, FIELD GATE LANE, UGLEY GREEN CM22 6HJ
Tel: 01279 816300 Fax: 01279 816496 Contact: Alistair Forrest
info@targetpublishing.com www.targetpublishing.com
'Health Food Business' trade magazine is sent free of charge to all registered,
named buyers of natural organic foods, drinks, toiletries, herbals and dietary supplements. Serve UK and Eire.

IMPACT PUBLISHING LTD
12 PIERREPONT STREET, BATH BA2 5SJ
Tel: 01225 446666 Fax: 01225 339494 Contact: Sophie Newman
info@impactpublishing.co.uk www.impactpublishing.co.uk
Green Essentials, a series of practical organic gardening guides produced in association with the Soil Association and the HDRA. Just £2.99 each. Current titles: Banish Slugs, Grow Vegetables, Create Compost, Grow Fruit, Attract Wildlife, Healthy Plants, Successful Allotments, Control Pests, Garden Birds, Create Ponds, Perfect Roses, Perfect Lawns.

J & J PUBLISHING
MAINS OF STRUTHERS FARM, KINLOSS, FORRES IV36 2UD
Tel: 01309 672001 Contact: Jacqui Jones
jj@theboxingclevercookbook.co.uk www.theboxingclevercookbook.co.uk
Publish The Box Scheme cookbook.

NATURAL COLLECTION
PO BOX 135, SOUTHAMPTON SO14 0AF
Tel: 0870 331 3333 Fax: 0870 331 3334
info@naturalcollection.com www.naturalcollection.com
Natural Collection is a large showcase of unusual and beautiful lifestyle products chosen with a fairer planet in mind, including certified organic, natural, eco, fairly traded and hand-crafted products.

ORGANIC & NATURAL BUSINESS MAGAZINE
THE OLD DAIRY, HUDSONS FARM, FIELDGATE LANE, UGLEY GREEN CM22 6HJ
Tel: 01279 816300 Fax: 01279 816496
Contact: Target Publishing Ltd, Carlota Hudgell
kathryn@targetpublishing.com www.organic-business.com
Organic & Natural Business magazine is the UK's premier platform for showcasing organic and natural products. Reporting authoritatively on developments within the organic and wider natural food, healthy eating and Fairtrade markets. No other magazine is as committed to servicing the needs of multiple retail buyers, farm shops, convenience and grocery stores, delis and other food service retailers. To subscribe email info@targetpublishing.com

ORGANIC GARDENING
PO BOX 29, MINEHEAD TA24 6YY
Tel: 01643 707339 Fax: 01643 707339 Contact: Gaby Bartai Bevan
jeanarmin@orgardening.fsnet.co.uk
The UK's only all organic monthly gardening magazine. Practical hands on advice on every aspect of the garden—vegetables, fruit, herbs. Ornamentals, wildlife. Call for details of our £10 trial subscription offer.

ORGANIC HOLIDAYS
TRANFIELD HOUSE, 4 TRANFIELD GARDENS, GUISELEY, LEEDS LS20 8PZ
Tel: 01943 870791 Contact: Linda Moss
lindamoss@organicholidays.com www.organicholidays.com
Guide to holiday accommodation on organic farms/smallholdings and to B&Bs, guest houses and small hotels where organic produce is used according to availability.

ORGANIC TRADE SERVICES
NORTHORPE HOUSE, NORTHORPE, DONINGTON PE11 4XY
Tel: 07974 103109 Contact: Neil Butler
info@organicts.com www.organicts.com
The organic industry portal on the internet. Marketplace, news, newsfeeds, directory, discussion information and more. News and trade offers via e-mail.

PERMACULTURE MAGAZINE
PERMANENT PUBLICATIONS, THE SUSTAINABILITY CENTRE, EAST MEON, PETERS-FIELD GU32 1HR
Tel: 01730 823311 Fax: 01730 823322 Contact: Maddy Harland
info@permaculture.co.uk www.permaculture.co.uk
Permaculture Magazine—solutions for sustainable living, published quarterly. Earth Repair Catalogue of over 500 books, videos, tools and products available free and online at www.permaculture.co.uk

POSITIVE NEWS
5 BICTON ENTERPRISE CENTRE, CLUN SY7 8NF
Tel: 01588 640022 Fax: 01588 640033 Contact: Carole Hudson
office@positivenews.org.uk www.positivenews.org.uk
Quarterly newspaper covering organics and organic farming, green energy and green building, health, peace, recycling, new economics, national and international news—including book reviews. Magazine, Living Lightly on the Earth, free to subscribers.

RESURGENCE MAGAZINE
FORD HOUSE, HARTLAND, BIDEFORD EX39 6EE
Tel: 01237 441293 Fax: 01237 441203 Contact: Satish Kumar
satish@resurgence.org www.resurgence.org
Resurgence Magazine brings together leading writers and educationalists to present topics of vital importance to our world including: ecology, climate change, sustainable development, organic living, human scale education and conflict resolution. See display ad.

SAWDAY PUBLISHING, ALASTAIR

THE HOME FARM STABLES, BARROW GURNEY, BRISTOL BS48 3RW
Tel: 01275 464891 Fax: 01275 464887 Contact: Andreea Petre-Goncalves
andreea@sawdays.co.uk www.sawdays.co.uk
Publisher producing and selling guides to Special Places to Stay across Europe and in India and Morocco. Developing and piloting a 'Fine Breakfast Scheme' to celebrate the exceptional quality of breakfasts served in B&Bs listed in their British B&B guide. Most owners use home-grown, local or organic produce. Also produces the Fragile Earth Book series, sets of mini-essays on environmental and social themes. See also: www.specialplacestostay.com and www.fragile-earth.com.

SEA SPRING PHOTOS

LYME VIEW, WEST BEXINGTON, DORCHESTER DT2 9DD
Tel: 01308 897766 Fax: 01308 897735 Contact: Joy Michaud
sales@seaspringphotos.com
The slide library contains many images of certified organic products and scenes on organic, agricultural and horticultural holdings.

SMALLHOLDER BOOKSHOP

STOKE FERRY, KINGS LYNN PE33 9SF
Tel: 01366 500466 Contact: V Charlesworth
bookshop@lodgecottage1.freeserve.co.uk www.smallholder.co.uk
Mail order publisher. Books and videos on smallholding, livestock, poultry, organics, growing, environment and general rural interests.

SMALLHOLDER MAGAZINE

3 FALMOUTH BUSINESS PARK, BLICKLAND WATER RD., FALMOUTH TR11 4SZ
Tel: 01326 213333 Fax: 01326 318749 Contact: Liz Wright / Wendy Symons
liz.wright@btconnect.com www.smallholder.co.uk
Smallholder Magazine covers all aspects of livestock and crops plus up to date news for both organic and non-organic but has an organic sympathy—targeted at the small farmer and those exploring niche markets.

SOIL ASSOCIATION

BRISTOL HOUSE, 40–56 VICTORIA STREET BS1 6BY
Tel: 0117 929 0661 Fax: 0117 925 2504 Contact: Martin Trowell
info@soilassociation.org www.soilassociation.org
The Soil Association produces many publications. See above under Associations.

WORLDLY GOODS

10–12 PICTON ST. BS6 5QA
Tel: 0117 942 0165 Fax: 0117 942 0164 Contact: Peter Andrews
wg@eco-logicbooks.com www.eco-logicbooks.com
Specialise in wholesale/trade sales of books that provide practical solutions to environmental problems, permaculture, organic gardening etc. Contact us for free catalogue.

Other Services

BRAMLEY WOOD & BUCKLAND FILLEIGH ORGANIC
BRAMLEY WOOD, BUCKLAND FILLEIGH, BEAWORTHY EX21 5JD
Tel: 01409 281693 Contact: Jane & Peter Bartlett
Sustainable planning permission advice, alternative energy.

COMMUNITY COMPOSTING NETWORK
67 ALEXANDRA ROAD, SHEFFIELD S2 3EE
Tel: 0114 258 0483 Fax: 0114 258 0483 Contact: Nick McAlister
ccn@gn.apc.org www.communitycompost.org
We are the national network providing support and representation for community groups that are in some way involved in the sustainable management of organic waste resources and community composting.

DANDELION PARTNERSHIP
WALLED GARDEN, BRAHAN, DINGWALL IV7 8EE
Tel: 01349 861982 Contact: J Henderson & S Barclay
Experienced teacher/speaker on organic horticulture.

DE FACTO SOFTWARE
THE RUTHERFORD CENTRE, 8 DUNLOP ROAD, IPSWICH IP2 0UG
Tel: 01473 417200 Fax: 01473 417201 Contact: Ian Tiley-Nunn
enquiries@defactosoftware.com www.defactosoftware.com
Provides fully integrated accounting, ERP, MRP and CRM solutions to mid-sized food enterprises (SMEs). Our customer base covers produce, wine and drinks trade, food, packaging, building and construction, electronics and components, engineering and more.

ECLIPSE SCIENTIFIC GROUP LTD
MEDCALFE WAY, BRIDGE STREET, CHATTERIS PE16 6QZ
Tel: 01354 695858 Fax: 01354 692215 Contact: S Leavey
sales@esglabs.co.uk www.esglabs.co.uk
A comprehensive technical support service, providing expert consultancy through to high quality chemical, microbiological and analytical research and testing services.

ECOLOGY BUILDING SOCIETY
7 BELTON RD., SILSDEN, NR. KEIGHLEY BD20 0EE
Tel: 0845 674 5566 (local rate) Fax: 01535 650780 Contact: Jenny Barton
info@ecology.co.uk www.ecology.co.uk
A mutual building society providing ethical savings accounts and green mortgages for run-down properties in need of renovation or conversion and ecological self-build projects.

ECOTRICITY

AXIOM HOUSE, STATION ROAD, STROUD GL5 3AP
Tel: 01453 756111 Fax: 01453 756222 Contact: Customer Services
info@ecotricity.co.uk www.ecotricity.co.uk
Green electricity supplier. Dedicated to building clean new energy sources that won't contribute to global warming. Ecotricity matches the standard price of your local electricity supplier so it shouldn't cost you more than 'normal' polluting electricity.

ENGLISH ORGANIC FOODS PLC

THE OLD VICARAGE, 226 ASHBOURNE RD., TURNDITCH DE56 2LH
Tel: 01773 550173 Fax: 01773 550855 Contact: Brian Ashby
Organic matching agency.

THE ETHICAL INVESTMENT CO-OPERATIVE LTD

12 ST NICOLAS DRIVE, RICHMOND DL10 7DY
Tel: 0845 458 3127 Contact: Ian Harland
ian@ethicalmoney.org www.ethicalmoney.org
The Ethical Investment Co-operative is a firm of independent financial advisers dedicated to ethical and socially responsible investment. Established as a co-operative, we are a democratically run organisation which draws advisers from across the country to share experience, skills and resources to help promote ethical investment in the UK. Our clients range from concerned individuals to charities, trade unions, small businesses and NGOs. We pride ourselves on providing clients with quality ethical, financial planning advice.

EVA'S ORGANICS

EVA BOTANICALS LTD., MEDBURN, MILTON, BRAMPTON CA8 1HS
Tel: 01697 741906 Fax: 01697 741205 Contact: Debbie Simpson
debbie.simpson@evabotanicals.co.uk www.evabotanicals.co.uk
Scientific consultancy on botanicals in foods and nutritional products.

GOULD, JOAN & ALAN

WOODRISING, THORN LANE, GOXHILL DN19 7LU
Tel: 01469 530356 Contact: Joan & Alan Gould
alan@agolincs.demon.co.uk
Always willing to help with advice after a lifetime of organic producing.

GREEN ISP

LEE MILL RD, HEBDEN BRIDGE HX7 8LJ
Tel: 01422 847691 Fax: 01422 847691 Contact: Paul Palmer
info@greenisp.net www.greenisp.net
Green Isp provide environmentally guided internet services, providing broadband, unmetered dial-up, 0845, email and web space, solar powered office, advanced solar web hosting. Features and links on green issues.

GREENACRES ORGANIC PRODUCE
COOMBE BANK, TIPTON ST. JOHN, SIDMOUTH EX10 0AX
Tel: 01404 815829 Fax: 01404 815829 Contact: Roger Cozens
roger@greenacres-consultancy.co.uk
Consultancy in arable and horticulture, overseas aid and relief consultancy.

GREENLEAVES HERBAL PHARMACY
46A STANGER RD., SOUTH NORWOOD SE25 5JZ
Tel: 020 8656 0754 Contact: Patricia Ferguson
herbalpatsy@aol.com www.greanleavesherbalpharmacy.co.uk
Qualified medical herbalist providing free advice, assistance and consultations by
telephone for your health problems. Tailor-made quality prescription herbal medicines and first aid/basic healthcare kits by post.

LUCAS AND LUCAS ORGANICS
NORWOOD FARM COTTAGE, BATH RD., NORTON ST. PHILIP, BATH BA2 7LP
Tel: 01373 834022 Contact: Dide Lucas
dide@lucasorganics.co.uk
Garden design and planning through to maintenance, advice, tree planting, hedge
laying etc.

MILK LINK LTD
PLYM HOUSE, 3 LONGBRIDGE RD, PLYMOUTH PL6 8LT
Tel: 01752 331805 Fax: 01752 331812 Contact: Lee Richards
lee.richards@milklink.com www.milklink.co.uk
Milk Link is the UK's third largest integrated dairy business with the capacity to
process and add value to up to 80 per cent of our members' milk; allowing them
to benefit from a long-term secure outlet for their milk, together with the additional
margins available from processing it into added-value products.

O&F CONSULTING
THE OLD BAKERY, 8A REPLINGHAM RD. SW18 5LS
Tel: 020 8870 5383 Fax: 020 8870 8140 Contact: Simon Wright
simon@organicandfair.com www.organicandfair.com
Simon Wright is founder of O&F Consulting. Since 1986 Simon has specialised in
the manufacturing, retailing, legislation and marketing of organic and Fairtrade food
and drink, working with companies throughout Europe and in the USA. Clients
range from small manufacturers of natural foods through to one of the UK's largest
multiple retailers. For more information please visit www.organicandfair.com

ORGANIC MAKEOVERS
16 BIRLEY ST., LONDON SW11 5XF
Tel: Contact: Bianca Paradis
info@biancaparadis.com www.biancaparadis.com
Nutritionist/Image Consultant. Organic Makeovers; hair, makeup, fashion, and body by Bianca Paradis CCN, nutritionist and image consultant. Become the best you can be naturally! For men and women.

ORGANIC MONITOR LTD
79 WESTERN RD W5 5DT
Tel: 020 8567 0788 Fax: 020 8567 7164 Contact: Tina Gill
postmaster@organicmonitor.com www.organicmonitor.com
Organic Monitor provides business research and consulting on the international organic and natural products industry.

ORGANIC POULTRY EQUIPMENT LTD
PETERHALES HOUSE, TRINITY, CULLOMPTON EX15 1PE
Tel: 07974 353073 Fax: 01884 35004 Contact: Peter Crowe
organicpoultryequipment@yahoo.co.uk www.organicpoultryequipment.co.uk
Suppliers of well insulated, low cost, modular poultry housing, developed by organic table bird producers. Features include a highly efficient feeding system, excellent welfare standards and a very durable structure. Secondary telephone number: 0188433218.

ORGANICA LP
NERINE HOUSE, P.O. BOX 434, ST. GEORGE'S ESPLANADE, ST. PETER PORT, GUERNSEY GY1 3ZG
Tel: +44 1481 739584 Fax: +44 1481 701619 Contact: Peter R. Geiser
info@organica-guernsey.com www.organica-guernsey.com
Worldwide consultants in marketing of organic farm produce.

PRODEK LIMITED
26 WHITE HART LANE, HAWKWELL, HOCKLEY SS5 4DQ
Tel: 01702 202123 Fax: 01702 202932 Contact: Lindsey Thompson
linbjo1@aol.com
Supply eco-friendly slurry tank, water containment, capping for slurry waste, liners for fish farms, bund lining using EPDM heat welded lining.

SINGLE MARKETING LTD
HIPLEY HOUSE, HIPLEY STREET, WOKING GU22 9LQ
Tel: 01483 771152 Fax: 01483 766808 Contact: Jeff Bayley
singlemktg@aol.com
Complete sales and marketing service to regional and national retail chains.

SOMERSET FOOD LINKS

THE OLD TOWN HALL, BOW ST., LANGPORT TA10 9PR
Tel: 01458 259485 Fax: 08700 527256 Contact: Vivien Grammer
enquiries@foodlinks.org.uk www.somerset.foodlinks.org.uk
County food links project established in 1999 to encourage thriving local food economy by supporting Somerset businesses (producers, processors, retailers, caterers, accommodation providers), schools and community groups. Advice to local food businesses (including direct marketing, co-operation, public procurement), advice to community food growing projects, social enterprise development, advocacy, lobbying and awareness raising.

SONG OF THE EARTH

2 CONISTON CLOSE, POOLBROOK, MALVERN WR14 3SN
Tel: 01684 892533 Fax: 01684 892533 Contact: Fiona Hopes
fiona@song-of-the-earth.com www.song-of-the-earth.com
Garden designer. Individual and special gardens created by a qualified and experienced designer, working with the subtle energies of the land to create sustainable landscapes that are ecologically sound, practical, productive and beautiful. Co-principal of The Earth School.

SPRINGDALE CROP SYNERGIES LTD

SPRINGDALE FARM, RUDSTON, DRIFFIELD YO25 4DJ
Tel: 01262 421100 Fax: 01262 421101 Contact: Simon Meakin
info@springdale-group.com www.springdale-group.com
Soil Association P7844. Seed merchant/advisor. Agronomy-based crop development business offering buy-back contracts and advice on organic crops. Supplier and trader of organic seeds and the only UK registered specialist organic oilseed supplier.

SUMMERLEAZE GALLERY

EAST KNOYLE, SALISBURY SP3 6BY
Tel: 01747 830790 Fax: 01747 830790 Contact: Trish Scott Bolton
trish@summerleazegallery.co.uk
Soil Association G4877. Art gallery holding three exhibitions a year, four-day painting courses and lectures in converted farm buildings on organic farm. Dinner, bed and breakfast in nearby farmhouse.

TEACRATE

151 SCRUBS LANE NW10 6RH
Tel: 020 8282 0000 Fax: 020 8282 0061 Contact: Kate Barrett
kateb@teacrate.com www.teacrate.com
Tray rental, purchase and washing company. We offer food tray washing services to Soil Association organic standard, tray rental and purchase as well as full logistic and financial packages for anyone in the food industry. Diverse range of crates and also plastic pallets.

TRIODOS BANK

BRUNEL HOUSE, 11 THE PROMENADE, BRISTOL BS8 3NN
Tel: 0800 328 2181 Fax: 0117 973 9303
mail@triodos.co.uk www.triodos.co.uk
Tel: 0800 328 2181 for free information on banking services for organisations. Tel: 0500 008720 for personal savings details. Triodos Bank's unique Organic Saver Account offered in partnership with the Soil Association, gives you a secure and rewarding way to target your savings to organic enterprises. We provide full banking services for organic food and farming enterprises, including current and investment accounts, overdrafts and loan facilities. As Europe's leading ethical bank we have financed a wide range of organic businesses over many years and understand the needs and dynamics of the sector. "The growing support we receive from this account is making a huge difference to the Soil Association," explains Martin Cottingham, marketing director of the Soil Association. "As our largest single corporate supporter, Triodos Bank is not only giving our work a huge boost but also empowering savers who want to support healthy, sustainable food production." Contact us for more details.

VITAL VEG

NORTH TILLYDAFF FARM, MIDMAR, INVERURIE AB51 7LS
Tel: 01330 833823 Fax: 01330 833823 Contact: Wendy Seel
info@vitalveg.co.uk www.vitalveg.co.uk
We design vegetable gardens and potagers, and give advice and seminars on organic growing.

WINCANTON GROUP LTD

CALE HOUSE, STATION RD., WINCANTON BA9 9AD
Tel: 01963 828282 Fax: 01963 31850 Contact: Stuart James
stuart.james@wincanton.co.uk www.wincanton.co.uk
Soil Association P6716. Wincanton Group are specialists in warehousing and distribution activities including organic milk collected for numerous customers.

Main Index

Accommodation Index

Baby Care Index

Cosmetics & Toiletries Index

Household Products Index

This includes cleaning products, paints, pet care etc.

National Box Schemes Index

Restaurants, Cafés & Caterers Index

Textiles Index

Future editions & online version

Future editions of *The Organic Directory*

Please contact us if:

- You think your company or organisation should be included in *The Organic Directory*
- You want the details of your entry to be amended
- You know of a company or organisation that you think should be included in *The Organic Directory*
- You have suggestions as to how we can improve *The Organic Directory*

In all cases, please email Clive Litchfield at:

organiceco@aol.com

or write to him c/o Green Books Ltd, Foxhole, Dartington, Totnes TQ9 6EB.

There is no charge for inclusion in *The Organic Directory*, although we have a section of paid advertising in the printed version.

The Organic Directory online

You can find *The Organic Directory* online at the Soil Association's website:

www.whyorganic.org